BUDO

PERSPECTIVES

Edited by
Alexander Bennett

First Edition: © 2005 by Kendo World Publications Ltd.
Auckland, New Zealand

This Edition: © 2014 by Bunkasha International Corp.

ISBN 978-4-907009-11-3

For further information on this and other martial arts books please visit us at:
www.kendo-world.com

Contents

Introduction 1
Editorial Note 7
Symposium Participants 9

Budo Ideals

Twentieth Century *Budō* and Mystic Experience 15
Suzuki Sadami
Research of Miyamoto Musashi's *Gorin no sho*:
From the Perspective of Japanese Intellectual History 45
Takashi Uozumi
Zen and Japanese Swordsmanship Reconsidered 69
William H. Bodiford
Ken-Zen-Sho: An Analysis of Swordsmanship, Zen, and
Calligraphy and their Relevance Today 105
Terayama Tanchū

Budo Concepts

Cultural Friction in *Budō* 125
Abe Tetsushi
From "*Jutsu*" to "*Dō*"
The Birth of Kōdōkan Judo 141
Murata Naoki
Budō as a Concept: An Analysis of *Budō*'s Characteristics .. 155
Irie Kōhei
Confusion in the Concept of *Budō* in South Korean Society ... 171
Na Young-il
The Culture of '*Bu*' 185
Sakudō Masao

Budo and Education

What Should be Taught Through *Budō*? 195
Sogawa Tsuneo
Central Issues in the Instruction of Kendo: With Focus on the
Inter-connectedness of *Waza* and Mind 203
Oya Minoru
The Promotion of *Budō* for the Disabled 221
Matsui Kantarō
Budō in the Physical Education Curriculum of Japanese Schools .. 233
Motomura Kiyoto
Budō & Education 239
Duncan Robert Mark

Budo Perspectives

Off the Warpath: Military Science & *Budō* in the Evolution of
Ryūha Bugei... 249
Karl Friday

Internationalization of Budo

The Influence of the Japanese Martial Disciplines on the Development
of the United States Marine Corps Martial Arts Program............ 269
Richard Schmidt and George R. Bristol
Thinking Differently about the Teaching of Judo in Japan........... 287
David Matsumoto
Folk Martial Arts and Ritual: Continuity through Economic Change... 305
Raymond P. Ambrosi
Kendo or Kumdo: The Internationalization of Kendo and the
Olympic Problem... 327
Alexander Bennett
Tilting at Windmills: Observations on the Complexities in
Transmission of the *Koryū Bujutsu* in Japan and the United States..... 351
Meik Skoss
Budō's Potential for Peace: Breaking Down Barriers in the
Israeli/Palestinian Conflict 361
Danny Hakim

Public Lectures

The Paradox of "Judo as an Olympic Sport" and "Judo as Tradition".... 379
Anton Geesink
The Role of Judo in an Age of Internationalization................. 403
Yamashita Yasuhiro

Introduction

In an attempt to clarify the characteristics that make *budō* special, The Japanese Budo Association formulated the *Budō Charter* in six articles in 1987. The English translation was recently revised, and I was fortunate to have been included on the committee to oversee this revision. It was a positive attempt to put *budō* in perspective, and I include the entire translation here for reference as it lies at the core of the issues discussed in this book:

The Budō Charter
(*Budō Kenshō*)

Budō, the Japanese martial ways, have their origins in the age-old martial spirit of Japan. Through centuries of historical and social change, these forms of traditional culture evolved from combat techniques (*jutsu*) into ways of self-development (*dō*).

Seeking the perfect unity of mind and technique, *budō* has been refined and cultivated into ways of physical training and spiritual development. The study of *budō* encourages courteous behaviour, advances technical proficiency, strengthens the body, and perfects the mind. Modern Japanese have inherited traditional values through *budō* which continue to play a significant role in the formation of the Japanese personality, serving as sources of boundless energy and rejuvenation. As such, *budō* has attracted strong interest internationally, and is studied around the world.

However, a recent trend towards infatuation just with technical ability compounded by an excessive concern with winning is a severe threat to the essence of *budō*. To prevent any possible misrepresentation, practitioners of *budō* must continually engage in self-examination and endeavour to perfect and preserve this traditional culture.

It is with this hope that we, the member organisations of the Japanese Budō Association, established *The Budō Charter* in order to uphold the fundamental principles of *budō*.

Article 1: Objective of Budō
Through physical and mental training in the Japanese martial ways, *budō* exponents seek to build their character, enhance their sense of judgement, and become disciplined individuals capable of making contributions to society at large.

Article 2: Keiko (training)
When training in *budō*, practitioners must always act with respect and courtesy, adhere to the prescribed fundamentals of the art, and resist the temptation to pursue

mere technical skill rather than strive towards the perfect unity of mind, body, and technique.

Article 3: Shiai (competition)

Whether competing in a match or doing set forms (*kata*), exponents must externalise the spirit underlying *budō*. They must do their best at all times, winning with modesty, accepting defeat gracefully, and constantly exhibiting self-control.

Article 4: Dōjō (training hall)

The *dōjō* is a special place for training the mind and body. In the *dōjō*, *budō* practitioners must maintain discipline, and show proper courtesies and respect. The *dōjō* should be a quiet, clean, safe, and solemn environment.

Article 5: Teaching

Teachers of *budō* should always encourage others to also strive to better themselves and diligently train their minds and bodies, while continuing to further their understanding of the technical principles of *budō*. Teachers should not allow focus to be put on winning or losing in competition, or on technical ability alone. Above all, teachers have a responsibility to set an example as role models.

Article 6: Promoting Budō

Persons promoting *budō* must maintain an open-minded and international perspective as they uphold traditional values. They should make efforts to contribute to research and teaching, and do their utmost to advance *budō* in every way.[1]

Budō is one of Japan's most significant contributions to the world's athletic heritage. In fact, I consider *budō* to be Japan's most successful cultural export. Wherever you go in the world, even in the remotest towns of the farthest countries, there is a high probability that there will be a '*dōjō*' of some sort in the community. In that *dōjō* you will find the local people barefooted, dressed in Japanese *dō-gi*, obeying commands in the Japanese language, bowing the Japanese way, and more often than not, there will be a Japanese flag or a picture of some great Japanese master from the past occupying a prominent part of the *dōjō*. Interestingly, probably not one of the members will have ever been to Japan, and contact with Japanese people will be limited. There will always be some idiosyncrasies in the way training is conducted stemming from the fact that it is not actually Japan, and there are many aspects which have to be adapted to suit that particular social milieu. Nevertheless, much of *budō's* "Japanese-ness" will be retained, and the locals attracted for a number of possible reasons:

- Cultural reasons: in the case of *Nikkeijin* (descendants of Japanese heritage) or newly settled immigrant Japanese families, in an attempt to keep contact with their Japanese heritage. Also, Japanese exchange students or businessmen

Introduction

wanting contact in the community, or general interest in Japan by local people.
- Combat reasons: to learn how to fight, self defence skills, armed forces, police etc.
- Physical fitness.
- Mental well-being: some people start martial arts training in the hope that they will increase in self-confidence and discipline. This also corresponds with parents who encourage their children to study the martial arts for the same benefits.
- As a competitive sport.
- Pursuit of spiritual development and enlightenment: there is a significant attraction to the perceived 'mysterious' metaphysical attributes of the Eastern martial arts.
- Strategy: although by no means a driving force now, in the days of Japan's bubble economy, there were widespread opinions that Japan's economic and business success was based around management practices stemming from 'samurai strategy', prompting small numbers of businessmen to take up martial arts training.
- Forced participation by Japanese government or military in WW II and before: Koreans and Taiwanese as annexed Japanese states. Also a very small number of POWs who inadvertently learned the arts though being practiced upon by Japanese guards or soldiers. Although an extreme minority, there are a number of *jūjutsu* schools in the West whose founders claim to have learned the art through such means.

Thus, there are many characteristics of Japanese *budō* that are recognized and attract large numbers of people from around the world for a variety of different reasons. Although I am not Japanese, many years training in *budō* in Japan has exposed me to Japanese pride attached to this aspect of their culture. I have been praised countless times for my diligence in studying the "Japanese spirit" through *budō*. More often than not, those who bestow such praise are not actually practitioners themselves, but *budō* seems to be accepted universally in Japan as representing what is most noble, honourable, and unique in Japanese culture. Therefore, it is a great source of pride and surprise for many to see the extent with which *budō* has proliferated throughout the world. For some, however, this fact has become a point of urgency and concern for reasons which will become apparent by reading this volume.

It was Kanō Jigorō, the founder of judo—who retains a prominent position within the pages of this volume—who suggested over a century ago that *budō* (judo) would be Japan's greatest contribution to the international community, and would enable Japan to hold its head up high alongside the other great cultures of the world. Indeed, in many ways his prophecy has come true. At the grass roots level, Japanese *budō* has afforded Japan more respect than the most ardent and skilled diplomats could ever hope to achieve.

Nevertheless the *budō* world is fraught with contradictions. Although claiming its roots in the battlefields of old—where warriors excelled in the martial arts to stay alive—modern *budō* is just that, modern. Many of the so-called traditional *budō* arts practiced so widely around the world are, to use Hobsbawm's term a "reinvention" of tradition. For the most part, *bujutsu* was refashioned to suit the social, political, and educational needs of Japan, rapidly trying to modernize during the Meiji period. Maybe "reinvention" is too strong a term. More appropriately, perhaps, it was this period in history that encouraged *budō* to take a great leap forward in its evolutionary course. If this had not happened, the traditional Japanese *bugei* (martial arts) were doomed to extinction. *Budō*'s survival was in no small part due to the efforts of innovators and educators such as Kanō Jigorō. *Bujutsu/bugei* was able to redefine itself, and take a new role in Japanese society, this time for the masses rather than the privileged *bushi* class.

Once the educational potential was fully realized, the government became actively involved in promoting the adaptation and utilization of *budō* as an indigenous form of physical education along with recently imported Western sports and gymnastics. Gradually it became considered more than a useful educational tool in the conventional sense, and was elevated to a special position superior to any imported sport. *Budō* was actively promoted as uniquely Japanese—stemming directly from *bushi* culture—and was thus was a manifestation of the very essence that made Japanese the way they were, and set them apart from the rest of the world. To learn *budō* was to learn to be Japanese. This mentality had obvious uses especially in the 1930s as Japan prepared for war, when nationalistic fervour, self-sacrifice, and fighting spirit were qualities most needed by the militaristic regime.

Upon Japan's defeat in WWII, recognizing the role which *budō* played in Japan's wartime aggression, the General Headquarters of the Allied Occupation Forces (GHQ) banned participation in schools and in the community. When *budō* was finally reinstated in the early 1950s, it was promoted as "sport" suitable to a new "democratic" society. In other words, overtly spiritual, religious, and nationalistic connotations were consciously removed, serving as yet another leap in *budō*'s evolution into a form of modern sport. Still, there always remained a strong undercurrent of subconscious thought that *budō* was unique, and in its true unadulterated form was different to 'sport'.

Undoubtedly, the most significant event for *budō* in the post-war period was judo's appearance in the 1964 Tokyo Olympic Games. The Games were Japan's chance to showcase to the world their startling economic, technological, and social recovery from the ashes of war less than two decades before. This was also the time when the Nippon Budokan was built, and has since served as the umbrella organization for the modern *budō* arts. Since judo's introduction into the Olympics, *budō* in general has seen spectacular growth around the world. Indeed, it was actively encouraged by Japanese who saw the potential of *budō* in helping Japan regain trust and respect in the international community, just as Kanō predicted.

For many years after, Japan was recognized as the leader country for *budō*. After

Introduction

all, it did come from Japan. However, it seems that the honeymoon maybe coming to an end for a number of reasons, and Japan's position at the top of the *budō* world is increasingly becoming jeopardized. This is not only due to the drastically improved overall technical ability of non-Japanese *budō* practitioners, or how *budō* has proved able to take root and prosper in a diverse range of communities regardless of race, colour, and creed. The main problem seems to lie within Japan.

Many would agree that the Japanese *budō* world is rife with contradictions, and in many has failed to continue adapt with the times. Conversely, continued evolution has been negated and consciously blocked. For example, the age-old debate still rages of whether *budō* is a sport or not, but there is little attention given as to what sport actually is. There is a desperate clinging to perceived "tradition", and longing for recognition that the value of *budō* is as a "Way of life", a value that far exceeds the momentary glee of winning a championship. However, the ideal and the reality of *budō* seems to be growing wider apart, and although few would doubt the potential of *budō* to aid in character development and serve as a barometer for life, those entrusted with the overseeing of the various *budō* continue to flog the dead horse of yesteryear, rather than care for the newly born foal. *Budō*'s value is as a living form of culture, but is becoming increasingly antiquated as many of the concepts are vague—hidden by shrouds of "tradition"—and for the most part becoming seemingly irrelevant to the needs of youth in the twenty-first century. Judging by the declining popularity of *budō* in Japan of recent years, this is a great cause for concern. The general consensus (amongst *budō* practitioners) is that *budō* is a wonderful thing, people who do *budō* are wonderful human beings, and the fact that younger people are more interested in baseball or soccer shows that the youth of today have no appreciation for tradition. This common attitude among *budō* practitioners is arrogant, simplistic, and merely passing the blame.

Indeed, if *budō* is to continue to prosper, there is a dire need for all concerned to sit down and put their cards on the table. There is a need to question all that we hold dear in *budō* and honestly assess whether or not we strayed into a quagmire of irrelevance, rather than sit comfortably on the laurels of our predecessors. What is lacking in the *budō* world is meaningful inter-disciplinary heart-to-heart dialogue. It may come as a surprise that very few judo experts enter discussion with experts of kendo, karatedo, or sumo. Hardly any dialogue exists between practitioners of aikido and *jūkendō*, *kyūdō*, or *shōrinji kempō*. Each year, the Budō Gakkai (Japanese Academy of Budō) convenes at a designated university, and members present their research findings in front of their colleagues. All of this research is valuable as it contributes to our understanding of various aspects of *budō*. However, most is in the field of bio-mechanics or sports science, and comparatively little is presented in the field of social sciences. Furthermore, researchers take note only of their preferred *budō*, and a judo expert rarely ventures into the next classroom to hear what research is being done in the world of kendo. Thus, inter-*budō* interaction is minimal, as is communication with experts in other fields such as anthropology or other sports, and even less exchange with experts in various fields outside Japan. It is all too apparent that this has created a recipe for shortsightedness.

It was with these problems in mind that we decided to hold an international symposium at the International Research Centre for Japanese Studies from November 18-22, 2003, headed by an Associate Professor at the centre, Yamada Shōji. The title of the symposium was "The Direction of Japanese Budō in the 21st Century: Past, Present, Future". With the intention of discussing the essence of *budō* from as broad a range of perspectives as possible we invited experts in the various *budō* arts, both well known scholars and practitioners, as well as authorities from other fields such as literature and art history, as well as scholars from around the world. The resulting presentations and discussions were stimulating and contentious. The gathering was one of the first ever large-scale cross disciplinary international symposiums concerning *budō* in Japan, with a cast of presenters, commentators, and observers who constitute the who's who of the *budō* world. This volume is the result of that symposium.

The content is comprised only of the papers that were presented, and although there are hours of transcribed comments and discussions which would surely be of great interest to the *budō* aficionado, we were unable to include them in this book. Indeed, these will be edited and collated into another volume in the future. Nevertheless, the content of this book should be a source of great interest to the *budō* reader. Due to the variation in presenter background and subjects some chapters maybe difficult to follow. Similarly, the reader may disagree with the insights presented by any given author. If that is the case, then the symposium and this book will have served its original purpose. During the symposium there were many occasions where the participants had to agree to disagree. Every time this happened, we moved a little closer to understanding the various perspectives surrounding *budō*. There is no one perspective, but there are common threads. The symposium was a great success in demonstrating how tangled these threads are, and considerably more questions arose than were answered. This is a positive outcome, and it is hoped that this work will stimulate the reader to also think about the complexities and significance surrounding *budō* in the twenty-first century.

A.C. Bennett
Kyoto, February 2005

---

[1] Member Organisations of the Japanese Budo Association:
All Japan Judo Federation, All Japan Kendo Federation, All Nippon Kyudo Federation, Japan Sumo Federation, Japan Karatedo Federation, Aikikai Foundation, Shorinji Kempo Federation, All Japan Naginata Federation, Japan Jukendo Federation, Nippon Budokan Foundation. Established on 23 April, 1987 by the Japanese Budo Association (Nippon Budō Kyōgikai) English translation revised 16 September, 2004.

Editorial Note

All Japanese words are italicised with appropriate macrons. However, common words in Japanese studies such as era names (Taisho, Showa etc) are not italicised and macrons are not used. The *budō* arts of kendo, aikido, judo, sumo, and karate are listed in the *Concise Oxford Dictionary*, and are treated as Anglicised words. All other *budō* arts are italicised with macrons except in cases where official English organization names do not do so. Japanese personal names are referred to with surname first, followed by given name.

Budo Perspectives

Symposium Participants
(* indicates a presenter).

*Abe Tetsushi
Lecturer- The Gate of Dharma Buddhist College (Hungary)

*Alexander Bennett
Research Associate- International Research Centre for Japanese Studies

*Anton Geesink
IOC Member

*Danny Hakim
Wingate Institute

*David Matsumoto
Professor- San Francisco State University

*Duncan Robert Mark
Shorinji Kempo Headquarters

Edo Kōkichi
Professor- Kanazawa University

Enomoto Shōji
Professor- Nanzan University

Frederik Cryns
Research Associate- International Research Centre for Japanese Studies

Funakoshi Masayasu
Professor- Osaka Kyoiku University

Hamada Hatsuyuki
Professor- National Institute of Fitness and Sports in Kanoya

Hasegawa Kōichi
Associate Professor- Aizu University

Heiko Bittmann
Associate Professor- Kanazawa University

Budo Perspectives

Inaga Shigemi
Professor- International Research Centre for Japanese Studies

Inoue Shun
Professor- Konan Women's University

*Irie Kōhei
Professor Emeritus- Tsukuba University

*Karl Friday
Professor- Georgia University

Kashiwazaki Katsuhiko
Professor- International Budo University

Kimura Masahiko
Associate Professor- Yokohama National University

Maebayashi Kiyokazu
Professor- Kobe Gakuin University

*Matsui Kantarō
Associate Professor- International Budo University

Matsuo Makinori
Lecturer- International Budo University

*Meik Skoss
Associate Editor- Koryu Books

Mimura Yuki
Research Associate- National Defence Academy in Japan

*Motomura Kiyoto
Professor- Japan Women's College of Physical Education

*Murata Naoki
Kōdōkan Museum Curator

Murayama Kinji
Professor- Shiga University

Participants

*Na, Young-Il
Professor- Seoul National University

Nakajima Takeshi
Professor- Kokushikan University

Nakiri Fuminori
Professor- Tokyo University of Agriculture and Technology

Ōboki Teruo
Professor- Saitama University

Ōta Yoriyasu
Associate Professor- Osaka Kyoiku University

*Ōya Minoru
Professor- International Budo University

*Raymond Ambrosi
PhD candidate- University of Alberta

*Richard Schmidt
Professor- Nebraska University

Sakai Toshinobu
Lecturer- Tsukuba University

*Sakudō Masao
Professor- Osaka University of Health and Sport Sciences

*Sogawa Tsuneo
Professor- Waseda University

*Suzuki Sadami
Professor- International Research Centre for Japanese Studies

Takeda Ryūichi
Associate Professor- Yamagata University

Tanaka Mamoru
Professor- International Budo University

*Terayama Tanchū
Professor- Nishōgakusha University

Tōdō Yoshiaki
Associate Professor- Tsukuba University

Toyoshima Tatehiro
Professor- Reitaku University

*Uozumi Takashi
Professor- International Budo University

Wang Cheng
Associate Professor- Capital Normal University (China)

*William Bodiford
Associate Professor- UCLA

Yamada Shōji
Associate Professor- International Research Centre for Japanese Studies

*Yamashita Yasuhiro
Professor- Tokai University

Editorial Staff

Editor
　　Alexander Bennett

Associate Editors
　　Lachlan Jackson
　　Michael Komoto
　　Sean O'Connell

SECTION 1

BUDO IDEALS

Chapter 1

Twentieth Century *Budō* and Mystic Experience

Suzuki Sadami
International Research Centre for Japanese Studies

Internationalization of *Budō*, the Martial Ways

Japanese martial Ways (*budō*) have gained international popularity through a diverse range of channels. Together with "traditional" Japanese *bushidō* (the Way of the warrior), *budō* has flourished as forms of physical and spiritual training, self-defence, combative exercises for armies around the world, and also on the silver screen as a form of entertainment.

Japanese martial arts eventually came to be thought of as ineffective by the Tokugawa shogunate and the various *han* (clans or domains) during the *bakumatsu* period. Except for *kenjutsu* (swordsmanship), most of the traditional martial arts (*bujutsu*) had fallen out of fashion. *Jūjutsu* embarked on the road to modernization with a name change to judo. Eventually, *bujutsu* in general became known as "martial Ways" (*budō*) throughout the Taisho period (1912-1926), but the historical development of the various *budō* arts was by no means uniform. For example, aikido and its concepts, now popular around the world, were actually fashioned in the 1920s.

Perhaps the first time that people of influence from outside Japan witnessed Japanese martial arts of sorts was in July 1879. Shibusawa Ei'ichi (1840-1931), a wealthy entrepreneur and business leader who played a central role in establishing industry in Japan, and who was also a lifelong patron of culture, displayed before the visiting General Grant[1] the arts of *jūjutsu* and *kenjutsu*. One of the students of the Imperial University (*Teikoku Daigaku*) who participated in the demonstration at the time was the then twenty-year-old Kanō Jigorō (1868-1938), who three years later in 1882 established the Kōdōkan judo school in Tokyo.

By combining techniques from various different schools of *jūjutsu*, and incorporating physiology and other sciences, he reformed *jūjutsu* into the modern martial art of judo (lit. gentle way). Modern judo gained rapid popularity as a form of physical training, and soon gained overwhelming membership compared to other more traditional styles. Known for his mediation of the peace settlement after the Russo-Japanese War (1904-05), the 26th President of the United States, Theodore Roosevelt (1858-1919, president 1901-1909), learned judo from Chiba Heizō. This was an early example of the internationalization of a modern *budō* art. However, the process of modernization leading to internationalization demonstrated by judo at the time was the exception rather than the rule.

After Japan's victory in the Sino-Japanese War of 1894-1895, esteem for militarism and things martial gathered momentum. In 1895, the *Dai Nihon Butoku Kai* (Great Japan Martial Virtue Society - hereafter referred to as Butokukai), was established as an organization focusing on nurturing martial artists and propagating Japan's traditional *bujutsu* culture. They made efforts to uphold the perceived "traditional" aspects of *budō* and made a clear distinction between *budō* and modern sports. At this time many soldiers also applied themselves to the study of *budō*.

Bashford Dean (1867-1928), a professor of zoology at Columbia University in New York, was a visiting fellow at Tokyo Imperial University from 1900 to 1905, during which time he applied his past interest in European arms to an interest in those of Japan. Collecting voraciously, the body of weapons he amassed became the largest of its kind overseas, and it eventually became the basis for the establishment of the oriental weapons section of the Metropolitan Museum of Art. After serving some time as an honorary curator, Bashford Dean was appointed curator in 1912.[2] With growing interest in the Eastern martial Ways in the West, there was also fascination with the artistic worth of arms such as swords, helmets, and armour.

In 1945, GHQ forced the defeated Japan to dissolve the Butokukai, and not only issued publications criticising Japan's traditional sword arts, but direct participation was also prohibited for some years. Judo, however, was treated with more leniency being merely removed from the school curriculum, and it was not long before this ban was lifted. Europe served as the basis for judo's rapid international popularity, culminating with inclusion as an official Olympic event during the Tokyo Olympics in 1964. Women's judo was also eventually included as an official event in 1982. In 1997, the number of countries that were members of the International Judo Federation reportedly stood at 178.

While judo and karate have enjoyed international popularity, other *budō* such as kendo have not seen the same scale of international dissemination.[3] According to Alexander Bennett, a research assistant at the International Research Centre for Japanese Studies, the number of countries and regions affiliated to the International Kendo Federation has reached forty-four (as of 2003).

International interest in Eastern martial arts has changed in a variety of different ways. While interest in judo as a sporting event has waned to a large extent, we cannot ignore the interest in the spirituality expressed in perceptions of *bushidō*, which has been a factor in the internationalization of *budō*; more specifically, it is difficult to ignore the adoration for the perceived mystery of the East by many Westerners.

Japanese archery (*kyūjutsu, kyūdō*) had been marked for abolition by the Tokugawa shogunate and the *han* during the *bakumatsu* period due to the increasing prevalence of guns and cannons. However, in the Taisho period it was revitalised in great part through the efforts of Awa Kenzō (1880-1939) of Sendai, who enhanced and promoted the spiritual qualities of *kyūjutsu* by incorporating Zen ideals. A German professor of philosophy, Eugen Herrigel (1885-1955), who learned the art from Awa Kenzō, gave a lecture in 1936 at the German-Japan Society in Berlin entitled *Die ritterliche Kunst des Bogenschiessens* (The martial art of archery). He conveyed the art to Europe as a concept accompanied by Eastern mystic thought. Later on it was also translated into Japanese as *Nihon no kyūjutsu* (The archery of Japan) by Shibata Jisaburō, and published by Iwanami Shoten in March 1941. Herrigel rewrote the content and published it in 1948 as the well-known book *Zen in der Kunst des Bogenschiessens* (Zen in the Art of Archery), and has since been translated into a number of languages. A recent Japanese translation of the book was published by Fukumura Shuppan in 1959, entitled *Yumi to Zen* (Zen and the bow).

Herrigel came to Japan in 1924 and worked as a professor at Tohoku Imperial University until 1929. Lecturing on philosophy of the southwest German school of neo-Kantian thought, he transferred his interest in Eckhart's mysticism (Johannes Eckhart, c1260-1327/8). Eckhart explored the relationship between the individual soul and God. Herrigel's fascination in mysticism led him to take up an interest in Japanese Zen. It was through this connection that he became a pupil of the man who came to be known as the "god of *kyūdō*"–Sendai's Awa Kenzō. While he struggled to understand Awa's teachings, he supposedly attained a considerable level of technical expertise, and combined his experiences and philosophical knowledge as the basis for the two books mentioned above. Following a process that differed from the modernization and international propagation of judo, a German philosopher with an interest in mysticism encountered a "spiritually enhanced" reinterpretation of *kyūdō*, and conveyed this "spirit" of Eastern martial arts to Europe as the culmination of his studies in the art.

Curiosity in the "mysteries of the East" that Herrigel introduced continued to grow in the West together with interest in practical physical application. Peter Payne's *Martial Arts: the Spiritual Dimension* is an introductory guide to *budō* containing a number of old photographs and diagrams. The book describes the martial arts as ways to overcome the failings of modern Western thought, and seeks a view of physicality that is contained in the Eastern martial arts. *Budō* is described as a path to access the traditional thinking of the East. It takes the concepts of "graceful movement" over "taut muscle", "unity of mind and body" over "mental and physical separation", and furthermore "union with the universe", as its core esoteric teachings. The author, Peter Payne, was born in London in 1945 and majored in psychology at Harvard University. Since boyhood he engaged training in a diverse range of Eastern martial arts including judo, karate, aikido, and tai-chi, and has also studied acupuncture.

On page 47, the author quotes a passage of Ueshiba Morihei (1883-1969), the so-called founder of aikido in the 1920s:

"Then, how can you straighten your warped mind, purify your heart, and be harmonized with the activities of all things in Nature? You should first make God's heart yours. It is a Great Love, Omnipresent in all quarters and in all times of the universe. 'There is no discord in love. There is no enemy of love'. A mind of discord, thinking of the existence of an enemy, is no more consistent with the will of God."

Recollections of the founder of aikido are also introduced. Experiencing a sense of "unity with the universe" in the spring of 1925, the founder recollected that he had experienced a revelation that within the source of *budō* there exists a "divine love" (*kami no ai*) that was the "Creator of the universe", namely a "spirit of loving protection for all beings".

The present paper will focus on the *kyūdō* of Awa Kenzō that Herrigel encountered, and by comparing his experiences with Ueshiba Morihei, I will pursue an outline of the history of the *budō* within the purview of contemporary and modern Japanese thought and cultural history. I urge the reader to bear in mind that I am very much a lay person in regards to not only *kyūdō*, but also other *budō* and to Zen. With regard to Awa Kenzō, rather than focusing on the secret teachings of his *kyūdō*, I will confine myself to outlining the developmental process of his *kyūdō* ideals which first become fathomable by retracing modern Japanese thought and cultural history. I should add that the impression regarding modern Japanese thinking and cultural history presented here, particularly during the period from 1910 to 1929 when *kyūdō* was reinterpreted with heightened spirituality, urge a fundamental change in the image of cultural history that has constituted the orthodoxy until the present day. This is especially true in the history of mind-body perspectives and views and attitudes on "life". The key term here is Taisho life-centrism (*Taishō seimei-shugi*). Furthermore, this paper will investigate the source of Japanese cultural perspectives and the views on "life" held by Sakurai Yasunosuke, whose commentaries on the *kyūdō* ideals developed by Awa Kenzō greatly facilitates our understanding today.

The Modernization of Judo

Throughout the Tokugawa period, the various Japanese martial arts gradually became more regulated. With the Kansei Reforms (1787-93) of Matsudaira Sadanobu, *han* schools (*hankō*) were established all over Japan but were initially restricted to educating the children of the samurai elite. Martial arts training areas and halls were included in the schools, and organized training regimes were conducted as ways to instil discipline. At the beginning of the nineteenth century, emphasis shifted to practical considerations such as military science and ballistics. At this time, *kenjutsu* in particular witnessed rapid growth in numbers of practitioners originating from the ranks of country samurai, or from farming backgrounds, who studied at the many newly formed fencing schools. This essentially spelled the end of the warrior class

Twentieth Century Budo and Mystic Experience

monopoly on the martial arts. From the latter days of the Tokugawa period until the Meiji Restoration (1868), the shogunate, *han*, and then the newly formed Meiji government still encouraged *kenjutsu* training, but most other traditional arts were all but abolished. Despite a little rekindled interest in the traditional martial arts through conflicts such as the Battle of Aizu (1867) and the Satsuma Rebellion (1877), the stark reality was that martial arts were discarded as ineffective relics of a bygone era, and of no use to a nation desperately trying to catch up with the West.

With its origins in the hand-to-hand fighting techniques of warriors on the battlefield, *jūjutsu*, which had gained popularity in the Tokugawa period as the generic term for the art of fighting with one's bare hands or with short weapons, was also facing extinction. Kanō Jigorō reorganized this into a modern system for use as a form of education. Utilizing the characteristics of the various schools, he systematized throwing and grappling techniques, regulated forms of practice including free sparring (*randori*), and created match rules, among many other innovations. While formulating judo as a competitive sport through these changes, Kanō also strongly advocated the effectiveness of the art as a form of physical education, which would aid both mental and physical training of young people through the application of physiology and other modern sciences. Even now, there is a scroll hanging at the front of the main Kōdōkan *dōjō* (training hall) that gives instructions passed down by Kanō emphasizing judo as a means of character building:

> "Judo is the way of the highest or most efficient use of both physical and mental energy. Through training in the attack and defence techniques of judo, the practitioner nurtures their physical and mental strength, and gradually embodies the essence of the way. Thus, the ultimate objective of judo discipline is to be utilised as a means to self-perfection, and to make a positive contribution to society." (1915)

The maxims "most efficient use of energy (*seiryoku-zenyō*); mutual prosperity for the self and others (*jita-kyōei*)" became the basis for judo ideology, and it was argued by Kanō that this was to be for the benefit not only for the self, but ultimately for society at large. (*Kōdōkan Bunkakai Kōryō*, 1922).

The stance taken by the Ministry of Education at the beginning and middle of the Meiji period (1868-1912) was to include Western gymnastics in the school curriculum for physical education, while the traditional Japanese martial arts were completely excluded from use in this context. However, with the rise of nationalism and spirit of militarism around the Sino-Japanese and Russo-Japanese Wars, as well as "the spirit of indomitable perseverance" (Middle School Decree Enforcement Regulation, 1901), physical education called for methods that would emphasize "training the mind and body". There were increasingly passionate calls stemming from the late Meiji period through to the Taisho period for "cultivation" and "character building". The philosophy behind judo played an important role in this process. We can also surmise that the use of catch-phrases such as Kanō's "mutual prosperity" is a reflection of the times which saw the humanitarianism of the Taisho period and the formation of the League of Nations (1920).

Added to this we see that judo widely gained popularity as a tool for educating the younger generation. In 1911, the martial arts were introduced into teachers' colleges (either combined study or as separate electives of *kenjutsu* and *jūjutsu*). These electives became available to boys in middle schools (introduction of martial arts through partial revision of the Middle School Decree) as regular lessons in physical education, becoming compulsory regular physical education classes in 1931 (under a Ministry of Education decree for judo and kendo). The subject was subsequently set for boys in the fifth year or above in primary schools.

The result of these developments also meant there was an increasing need for qualified martial arts instructors. In 1902, Kanō Jigorō changed the course in gymnastics at Tokyo Teachers College to a special course combining ethics and gymnastics. He subsequently made this into a four-year course that combined liberal arts and gymnastics. He sought to educate physical education instructors not just in sports or gymnastics, but in liberal arts as well, and it is clear that his attitude was to promote physical education as an integral part of the school system. In 1916, this became a special physical education course (*tokka*), and the regular course (*honka*) at the college in 1921.

On the other hand, the Butokukai was established around the time of Japan's victory in the Sino-Japanese War. It created a training school for martial arts instructors in 1905, and inaugurated a more established technical school for the martial arts in 1911 (*Bujutsu Senmon Gakkō*). After receiving approval from the Ministry of Education two years later, the name of the school was changed to the *Budō Senmon Gakkō* (Technical School for Martial Ways).[4] Thus, through the Taisho era the word *budō* (martial Ways) became increasingly used to replace the term *bujutsu* (lit. martial techniques).

If we consider the creation of judo ideology as an educational tool, and the systematic organization of training and matches as being a mode of modernization, we can also state that *kyūjutsu* was modernized too. The introduction of the latest in Western weaponry dictated that *kyūjutsu* as a combat art had no place on the modern battlefield. Accordingly, the only means by which the art could survive was for it to be transformed into a recreational pursuit. In the Tokugawa period, archers competed for the honour of greatest technical competency in the *tōshiya* contests by firing arrows through the Sanjūsangendō hall in Kyoto. However, with time, archery naturally progressed into a competitive sport concerned with hitting targets. From ancient times in China, practitioners of archery had considered form and etiquette to be of great importance, and the fact that this trait was inherited in Japan as well is clearly seen in the expanded aspect of etiquette that exists in the original Japanese school of the art, the Ogasawara-ryū tradition. The transformation into competitive sport where the main objective was to hit the target or recreational pastime was seen by many as a regression of the true form of archery.

With the victories in the Sino-Japanese and Russo-Japanese Wars, however, there was a gradual increase in the enthusiasm of people advocating concepts of a "glorious warrior past" and *bushidō*. This started to escalate around the time of the publication of Mikami Reiji's *Nihon bushidō* (1899), Inoue Tetsujirō's *Bushidō sōsho* (1905), Nitobe Inazō's *Bushidō* (Japanese translation by Sakurai Ōson in 1908), and Shigeno Yasutsugu's *Nihon bushidō* (1909). These two works are said to be the most influential works on the subject in their day. *Gendai taika bushidō sōron* (1905), edited by Akiyama Goan, and *Zen to bushidō* (1907) by Shaku Goan were also published to much acclaim. Rather than just outlining a revival of *bushidō* as a culture unique to Japan, many of these discourses sought to encourage Japanese readers of a desirable disposition in the new international era. That era was one of imperialist expansion and war, and the *bushidō* espoused by these authors outlined ethical ideals of being both distinguished scholars and loyal soldiers, dedicated to bettering Japan's lot in the world.

At this time, Honda Toshizane (1836-1917), a former shogun vassal who had sought to preserve *kyūjutsu* for some time, indicated his disgust at the transformation of *kyūjutsu* into a recreational pastime, and actively set about popularizing "*kyūdō*" as serious pursuit possessing highly esteemed traditional values. Venerating the old ways stemming back to Hiokidanjō Masatsugu (active during the Muromachi Period 1333-1568), Honda argued that there was only one origin to the plethora of archery schools in existence. Appealing to technical rationality, mind-body training, and elegance in form, a reinterpretation of "*kyūdō*" thus took shape under his guidance. Three schools emerged after the death of Honda Toshizane, including the Tokyo Imperial University's *kyūdō* club.

It is thought that Awa Kenzō became a pupil of Honda around 1909. Awa honed his archery skills, achieving positive results at prestigious tournaments such as those held by the Butokukai. With his increasing fame in the world of *kyūdō*, he later became an instructor at the Second Higher School (*Dai Ni Kōtō Gakkō*) in Sendai, and applied himself to mastering the way of *kyūdō*. In the 1917 Butokukai tournament in Kyoto, Awa won a special award for his skills, and two years later one of his students became the Japan champion.

Awa Kenzō's *Kyūdō* Ideology

In the afterword of his book, *Awa Kenzō – Ōinaru sha no michi no oshie*, Sakurai Yasunosuke, who came into contact with Awa at the Second Higher School, understands the framework of Awa's ideology to be firstly the "building of personality" (*jinkaku no kenzō*) through martial practice, and mastery through experience.[5] In a radio lecture given in 1936, Awa actually starts with the reasons why Confucius' archery was described as being "holy shooting", and states that "the bow is a tool for building one's personality".[6] From this we can see a resemblance to the judo ideology of Kanō Jigorō.

The outline of Awa's ideology given in Sakurai Yasunosuke's afterword continues as follows:

"The bow and arrow are not for piercing the evil of others, but are a direct means of piercing the evil within oneself. With the very existence of *kōsha* (conduct-shooting), the stubborn ego barrier that separates inward and outward aspects is shattered to bits, and the self becomes one with the universe. This is *kan'nagara no michi* (the divine way)."

Awa Kenzō (1931)

Sakurai Yasunosuke emphasizes, however, that the *kan'nagara no michi* explicated by Awa Kenzō was not the same as the divine [imperial] way which was often referred to during the extremely militaristic period after 1937.

Awa incorporated the breathing techniques and the philosophy of Zen into his *kyūdō*, and is said to have experienced "unity with the universe" on an autumn evening in 1920- the precise date eludes me. Based on this experience he expounded *shari kensei* (world-perception lying behind shooting- *kensei* referring to expression of the true nature of the world) as the fundamental principle of *kyūdō*. The concept eventually took the name *daisha dōkyō* (meaning "the unison of shooting (arrows), the Way, and the teachings"). The state of mind described here encapsulated the concepts of "the universe and the self as one" (*uchū to ware to ichimai*) and "lunging into a state of complete selflessness" (*zettai muga no kyōchi e no tosshin*). The *budō* ideology that strengthened this spiritual concept is very different to that of Kanō Jigorō's judo. He added spiritual concepts to the modern rationality of Honda Toshizane, although the result was far removed from the path to the preservation of *kyūdō* that Honda originally advocated.

While there were some who thought Awa Kenzō insane for his words and actions, he resolved to bring about a "*budō* revolution" that would revive the ideal of "martial virtue" (*butoku*), and pushed forward with his self-appointed task.[7] Awa became known throughout Japan, and in 1927, *Kingu*, the most popular magazine produced by the publishers Dai Nippon Yūben Kai (Greater Japan Oratorical Society Kodansha) ran a special feature on "the masterful champion of Japan" (*Nihon ichi meijin*), where he was praised as being the Nasu no Yoichi of the times.[8] Nasu no Yoichi is famous for shooting down an enemy's fan that was tied to a mast as a challenge when the Heike punitive force led by Minamoto no Yoshitsune were engaged in the Battle of Yashima in the province of Sanuki in 1185. Here the name of Nasu no Yoichi is, of course, synonymous with "a master of the bow".

Before experiencing "unity with the universe", Awa was already skilled enough to never miss the target, but this is why he disliked being involved in shooting matches. After his experience of "unity" he became intensely set against competition shooting of just trying to hit the target. The intensity of this feeling could be seen when the Second Higher School entered the national tournament held at Tohoku Imperial University in 1922, in which they participated only in the *shadō* (shooting form) division, not in the target shooting events.[9]

As we have seen, the German philosopher Herrigel had also taken up an interest in Zen which derived from his interest in Christian mystic thought. He admired the mystic experience-based ideology of *kyūdō* and the techniques that attained a mystic realm that seemed, as it were, to substantiate that experience. It appears that Awa became acutely aware of the differences in Eastern and Western styles of thinking through his association with Eugen Herrigel.

Awa Kenzō was born the eldest son of the Satō family–malted rice producers with village-head status in Yokokawa, a landing place close to the mouth of the Kitakami river. After experiencing a mischievous and unmanageable childhood, he most probably graduated from elementary school. He subsequently learned the Chinese classics from the chief priest of the Daininji temple (Tendai sect), which was also the Satō family's place of worship. It is said that at one time he opened a private tutoring school and taught the Chinese classics. Unfortunately, the family home was razed in a large fire. He later married the daughter of, and was adopted into, the Awa family, who were malted rice producers in Ishinomaki. Besides the family business, he also learned *kyūjutsu*, *kenjutsu*, *jūjutsu*, and other arts, and three years later opened a martial arts training hall that catered to dock workers. Losing his estate in another extensive fire, Awa travelled to Sendai and there opened a *kyūdō* training hall in 1909. He lived with his wife and two young daughters in a dilapidated house beside rice fields, almost completely exposed to the elements. To quote from notes that he made about his life, "unity with heaven, earth, and the natural world – this is divine wisdom or reason (*tenri*)."[10]

Here, we can see an almost defiant sense of humour as he equates his poverty-stricken lifestyle as if he was living at one with nature. With these words we can also see a faint glimmer of the scope of his teaching up to this point. One normally equated Taoist thinking such as Laozi and Zhuangzi with the concept of "unity with heaven, earth, and the natural world", and orthodox neo-Confucianism typified by Zhu Xi with the concept of "*tenri*". Confucian concepts from well known books such as *Daigaku*, *Chūyō*, and other works can also be readily detected in Awa's ideals. In writing

Daishadōkyō, Sakurai Yasunosuke carefully reviewed the manuscripts that remained unpublished in Awa's lifetime. Although Awa's thinking was not systematic, he states that "the terminology of Mahayana (Great Vehicle) Buddhism, particularly that in Zen thinking, and the terminology of Confucian thought, especially in the philosophy of Wang Yangming, are inseparably linked. Furthermore, in the background we can see native thought relating to "natural law".[11] Sakurai was most of the opinion that Awa possessed a sense of "unity with the natural world" since his childhood.

In 1904, before Awa became an instructor, a student bemoaned the popularity of tennis as recreational exercise among students in an article entitled *Kyūjutsu ni tsuite* (In regards to *kyūjutsu*- authored anonymously), a work by the *kyūjutsu* committee published in *Shōshikai zasshi*, a magazine of the Second Higher School in Sendai. He criticized the sport's popularity as a form of imitating Westerners, and in loudly praising the "sense of the aesthetic" found in *kyūjutsu*, stated the following:

> "[*Kyūjutsu*] develops physical and mental efficiency, and moreover, many great people have trained in the art [in the past]. Through such historical association, a certain martial temperament (*shōbu*) is displayed, and physiological agency induces activity in the mind and body (*shinshin*). All of the various movements and forms executed in *kyūjutsu* stimulate the digestive functions, and thus increase overall vitality (*seikatsuryoku*). However, you should all know that no exercise will be efficacious unless it is enjoyable."[12]

At a time when the Russo-Japanese War was at its height, cultivation of a "martial temperament" was in vogue, and the wording used to explain its physiological implementation was not thought to be irrational. The terms *shinshin* (神身 - duality of psychospiritual and physical attributes), and *seikatsuryoku* (vitality in life and activities), were both common terms of the Meiji period.

Awa Kenzō endeavoured to maintain "rationality" in his thinking up to around 1919. There are seventeen instances in his notebook where he raises the "important aspects of shooting practice".[13] Firstly he asserts the idea of "building up a completely rational physique", and in the tenth instance aims to, "inform people of rational breathing techniques". The sixth instance states, "make students concentrate mentally on the abdominal region", the seventh, "is a way of developing the *tanden* (centre of abdominal region)", and in the eighth he advocates "discipline and perseverance to avoid changes after development", making it conceivable that these were linked to Zen. Instance eleven, "endeavour to improve expressions of insight", twelve, "train physical and spiritual powers, involve oneself in pain", thirteen "have a cheerful prospect about the self", fourteen "exude solemnity and an earnest nature", fifteen, "fight the ego with all one's might", sixteen, "endeavour to improve expressions of vitality", and seventeen, "make them develop unity". These are not unique to *kyūdō* itself, but we can see clearly his educationalist attributes showing. Expressions such as those of *seimeiryoku* (vitality), and its unity (*tōitsu*) – that being a phrase to describe the essential nature of unity between the flesh and the spirit – were expressions widely advocated during this period. We could interpret the sense of "fight the ego with all one's might" to be something akin to controlling self-interests or egocentricity.

Experiencing "Unity with the Universe"

Furthermore, in a *kyūdō* club report published in December 1919 in the *Shōshikai zasshi*, the words "*muchi sokushin*" (no-knowledge, mind-attainment) appear.[14] This is where Awa began to use Zen and its terminology in teaching his students. In the notebooks thought to have been written by Awa around the year 1920, the words "*kyūzen ichimi*" (the bow and Zen are of the same nature) also appear, which further clarifies the connection between Zen and his ideology.[15]

The famous Zen priest Takuan Sōhō (1573-1645) showed clearly the relationship between the martial arts and Zen. Improvement of technical skill, and particularly training that seeks to keep the mind calm have been essential in the martial arts since the beginning. When the *bushi* came to political power, being both a distinguished scholar and skilled warrior became a prerequisite in the latter part of the middle-ages, just as was the case with the elite bureaucrats (*shidaifu*) of Song dynasty China. This is when the martial arts link to Zen became unshakeable.

Yamaoka Tesshū (1836-88) was the founder of the Mutō-ryū tradition of swordsmanship. He was originally a vassal of the shogun and later a lord-in-waiting to the Emperor Meiji from the end of the Tokugawa period and into the early Meiji period. He is well-known for his adherence to the ideal of the "sword and Zen being of the same nature" (*kenzen ichimi*). Earlier I made mention of Shaku Goan's *Zen to bushidō*. As we have seen, this book was published in an era of increasing nationalism and military success in the wars with China and Russia, a period when *bushidō* was reaching a peak in renewed popularity. It was also a time when Zen gained widespread popularity amongst the general populace. 'Nervous depression' was considered a disease of civilization, and observance of Zen as a method for mental concentration was popular with "therapies" such as dry-towel and cold wet-towel rubdowns, and other treatments which were used to train the mind and body. Morita Masatake (1874-1938) developed treatment for neuroses, *shinkeishitsu*. His therapy stems from a hypochondriacal temperament characterized by excessive introversion, self-consciousness, and hypersensitivity to one's physical or mental condition. Morita advocated that patients "accept things as they are" (*aru ga mama ni*), and abandon their compulsive desire for self-control and instead concentrate on immediate and concrete experience rather than verbal exchange, speculation, and conjecture. These trends indicate how the use of such Zen terminology as "*musho jūshin*" (*lit.* no-place dwelling mind) were recognised as methods for attaining an unfettered [healthy] mental state.

With Awa becoming an instructor at the Second Higher School in Sendai, the strengthening of his attitude in learning Zen linked to the martial arts as a form of self-development accompanied his increase in social status and responsibility to his students. Also, Awa learned the Chinese classics from the head priest of the Daininji temple which had close links to Zen. Taking these points into consideration, we could well say that *kyūdō*, a martial art that used a weapon now wholly useless in modern warfare, was in many ways forced to seek a higher sense of spirituality and a significance-of-being than was required in other *budō* such as kendo, or judo.

Furthermore, in the *kyūdō* club's report published in December 1920 in *Shōshikai zasshi*, a passage reads, "The bow is at one with the macrocosmic universe and the self. It is a means of breaking into the world of absolute selflessness; the bow is religion, and ought to be called *kyūkyō* (religion of the bow)."[16] Sakurai Yasunosuke surmises that Awa possibly had his experience of "unity with the universe" in the autumn of that year.

After this experience, Awa's notebooks from 1921 to around 1926 are peppered with phrases referring to the unification of the self with nature and the universe. For example, "the mind is all things in the universe", "the aim of the Way of the bow is to sever the delusions of worldly desires permeating the mind and body. The mind and body must be an imbued in the universe, be serene, free of all obstacles: that is the Way of the bow". Also, "when the self is forgotten, all things come from the universe identify with us. From the origin of the universe, all manifestations of the self are expressed without beginning and without end. The universe and the self are of the same origin. Unity between all things and the self." Again, "Do not look as the arrow hits the target. The momentary, mystical divine-reverberation of the self and the sound of hitting the target is the echo of universal nature."[17]

Buddhist terminology is prominent in the quotations given above. The phrases, "the universe and the self are of the same origin. Unity between all things and the self", are the words of the monk, Zhao (J: *Chō*; c 374-414), said to be the foremost authority on Buddhist philosophy during the Six Dynasties period in China. He used these phrases in his discussion of nirvanic anonymity, *Zhao-lun*, and were well-known at the time. Did Awa learn this from the head priest of Daininji temple, or possibly from reading an expository guide or similar such text? Either way it is fair to surmise that he obtained support for his "mystic experience", took conviction in the meaning of the words, and integrated them into his own beliefs. What is more, the "divine region" (*shinkyō*), mentioned in the final "mystically divine region" (*shinpiteki no shinkyō*), has the meaning of a spiritual state of mind and was a usage still common at the time.

Awa copied a poem of Wang Yangming's into his notebook at around this time.[18] Slightly further along, he wrote the words *"mihatsu senchū"* (hitting the target before launching).[19] This probably means the experience of unity with the target before the arrow is even shot. However, Sakurai Yasunosuke views this as an application of words taken from Wang Yangming's *Zhuan xi lu* (J: *Denshūroku*; Record of conveyed learning). From the beginning we can see the words *"mihatchū"* (as yet un-launched) in the Confucian work entitled *Chūyō*. The *"chū"* in *"mihatsu senchū"* refers to the still un-released state of varied emotions. Zhu Xi, the great philosopher of orthodox neo-

Twentieth Century Budo and Mystic Experience

Confucianism, argued that this meant mental imperturbability generally inherent in the hearts of people. Wang Yangming, however, advocated that this was the throwing off of desire and the experiential learning of natural law. When one reads the words *"mihatsu senchū"* being used by Awa, they seem to be reverberating this meaning. Later on, in September 1936, Awa also gave a commentary on *"Wang Yangming: The accounts of Kantokutei"* at the Tokyo Army Cadet School. There is no doubt that Awa's ideology had a close connection with the philosophy of Wang Yangming.

Wang Yangming's philosophy was revived among the *bushi* class along with the Zhu Xi school of neo-Confucianism in the latter days of the Tokugawa period. In the first decade of the Meiji period there was a revival in the study of Chinese classics, with many of the Meiji intelligentsia, in particular those who opposed the shogunate system, becoming devoted readers of Wang Yangming's writings. Inoue Tetsujirō, a professor of philosophy at Tokyo Imperial University who promoted research into Eastern thinking, also arranged the work *Nihon Yōmeigaku* (Philosophy of Wang Yangming in Japan) in the 1890s. The philosophy's popularity is evident if one peruses the following and other similar works: Uchimura Kanzō's *Daihyōteki Nihonjin* (*Representative Men of Japan*, 1894, 1908), the diaries of Nishida Kitarō, an outstanding Japanese philosopher, and the famous writer Kunikida Doppo's *Azamukazaru no ki*.

During his youth, Wang Yangming became absorbed in the study of archery, and it seems plausible that Awa drew closer to Wang Yangming's philosophy while studying historical events relating to archery. This, however, is probably not the entire story. Wang's philosophy placed importance on "mastering the mind" and was sometimes called the Zen of Confucianism. In regard to the dualism of *ri* (C: *li*) as the basic principle (or reason) of the universe and *ki* as the spirit or energy of all things, adhered to by Zhu Xi, the aspect of unification with heaven (J: *ten*) is similar in a way to the unification with "the Absolute" referred to in Zen. After his mystic experience, Awa probably felt that the philosophy of unification with the divine advocated in Wang's philosophy was applicable to his own experience. In this sense, Awa's education in the Chinese classics deeply linked to Zen and the philosophy of Wang Yangming became increasingly relevant. The passages written in his notebooks impart a strong nuance of identifying these as part of his own mystic experience.

If we exclude direct mention of physical techniques of *kyūdō* in the writings of Awa, we are more likely to find in his books fragments pertaining to Mahayana Buddhism and Confucianism, with prominent references to Zen and Wang Yangming's school of thought. Furthermore, Sakurai was perfectly right when he stated that Awa's philosophy did not follow a systematic logic. Lying at the heart of his *kyūdō* was the mental state of "unity with the universe" or "unification with nature and the universe", and acquisition of this through experience. Treating these as the central rivet in a folding fan, the passages in the notebooks are scattered throughout, and the arguments and other aspects of lectures appear to have been conceived and developed as occasion required.

What exactly was this mystic experience? Probably the experience was something that overcame him while undertaking *kyūdō* training one fateful autumn day in 1920, as surmised by Sakurai. The precise moment he shot a particular arrow, his "self" suddenly crumbled and scattered into the surrounds, and he was overcome by a reeling giddiness. Awa recorded this experience as, "when the shooting self becomes the focus and great ripples fill nature and the universe" and "The great ripples of the shooting self that fill nature and the universe".[20] He named this *daishūen* (great-encompassing-circle). The phrase "great ripples fill[ing] nature and the universe" is close to a realization, and I believe it appropriate for us to take the meaning of the word *daishūen* as being akin to the state where the shape of the world, as expounded by the Lotus Sutra, passes and dissolves in all directions in *enyū* (a form of perfect harmony or melting together).

This can be explained in physiological terms as a phenomenon occurring during multiple abdominal breathing, with intense mental concentration, where the brain undergoes ecstatic hallucination due to a shortage of oxygen. That is to say there would be no direct relationship to one's ability in *kyūdō*. In ascetic yoga these hallucinations are often said to be accompanied by blue, red, and other visions of light. It appears that Awa did not see a vision of light. Nevertheless, the giddiness that accompanied his mystic experience led to his realization that he had experienced something quite extraordinary.

Awa did not consider this experience to be the *satori* (enlightenment) as seen in Zen. Alternatively, he may have thought that perhaps *satori* was something similar to what he had experienced, but was critical of the fact that Zen did not entail physical training.[21] It is certain that at the time Zen tended to emphasize spirituality over such physical training. Accordingly, the term "*daishūen*" was selected by him as a word that would not, as it were, smack of religion. Awa was furthermore aided by knowledge of such philosophies as that of Wang Yangming's and considered that he had experienced that very "unity with the universe". Before long, though, he would use the term "*shinjin gōitsu*" (divine entity and humanity as one) in reference to this experience.

Earlier I mentioned an article where Awa's pupils argued for the aesthetics of *kyūjutsu* along lines of rationalism at the height of the Russo-Japanese war. In the same year that that article appeared, Waseda University lecturer, Tsunashima Ryōsen, had a realization that he was a "*child of god*"", and published a text entitled *Kenshin no jikken* (Real experience of god) that advocated his conviction of the spiritual personality of god and "eternal life". This surprised many people. Six years later Hiratsuka Raichō's introduction to the first issue of the literary magazine *Seitō* was entitled "*Genshi josei wa taiyō de atta*" (In the beginning a woman was the sun), and the fact that it was written with religious inspiration is mentioned in the text. Eight years later in about 1919, Awa considered the rationality of *kyūdō*'s physical technique and was ready to apply Zen breathing techniques. However, before that the intelligentsia had already spoken of their own mystic experiences, and rumours of these abounded, thus he was by no means unique in this sense.

Phrases such as "harmony between one's mind and the macrocosmic universe", "the absolute mental state", "the world of selflessness", and "the bow is religion", appeared in the *kyūdō* committee's magazine published in December 1920. In the report of July

1923, however, we see the words "*muga*" (no-self) and "*mushin*" (no-mind) appearing along side "die with this single arrow. Dying everyday you will gain a new life each day" and "be like a new-born baby", as a record of the instructor's teachings.[22]

One can well see how the teachings of Awa spread through his students at the Second Higher School in Sendai. These teachings are relatively unfamiliar in the present age, and while emanating from the mouth of their respected *kyūdō* instructor were most probably accepted as something new and fresh by his students. However, at that time they were not necessarily considered something overly strange and fantastic. Nishida Kitarō's *Zen no kenkyū* (translated as *A Study of Good*) advocated that the very unity of humanitarianism for all humankind was good, and furthermore, on a higher plain, the existence of a religious desire that advocated unity with all life in the universe based on the model of Zen enlightenment was the essence of religion. If one considers that the "life of the universe" (*uchū no seimei*) will manifest itself in the depths of the body when consciousness of the self has disappeared, then the "universe" and the "self" will be directly linked. If we consider the life of the universe to be a divine entity (*kami*), then we can explain such experiences as *kenshin* (experiencing God) through that. By positing such a concept of "life of the universe" as the principle behind the world, Nishida attempted to overcome the limitations of modern logic. After its publication in 1911, *Zen no kenkyū* was only known in philosophical circles, but upon republication by Iwanami Shoten in 1921, the book became essential reading for higher school and university students. Its positive acceptance by young people was due to the fact that people during that period were enthusiastically investigating the idea of overcoming modern rationality.

The idea of "gain[ing] a new life everyday" is similar to the words used by Hiratsuka Raichō in the introduction to her 1913 collection of essays, *Marumado yori* (From the circular window), "Always together with the new sun, I wish renewal everyday, and from the new birth I wish to be a flame of life that burns on endlessly." Contemplating the self as something existing in the flow of all life in the universe, these words readily issue forth if one just invokes the words "*hibi aratamari*" (day to day renewal) used in the well-known Confucian textbook *Daigaku*.

Furthermore, the phrase, "be like a new-born baby", was often spoken by people as a symbol of a pure and innocent life. Nishida Tenkō, who opened the Ittōen, a training group in Kyoto, was greatly influenced by Tolstoy's *What I Believe* in 1903, and entered a religious life of abstinence, voluntary service, and introspection. A widely known episode in his life came when he was struck by the sound of an infant crying: The fasting Nishida was awakened to the fact that the ideal in life is to attain a state of mental nothingness, like that of a baby.

The thinkers, Nishida Kitarō, Nishida Tenkō, and Hiratsuka Raichō, were all adherents to philosophies centring around "life" that made all things manifestations of "great life in the universe" (*uchū daiseimei*). Extending also into the field of natural science, this mode of thinking found particular popularity in the world of literary and fine arts. This was eloquently expressed in *tanka* (traditional 5-line Japanese verse

Ueshiba Morihei (year unknown)

Twentieth Century Budo and Mystic Experience

of 5, 7, 5, 7 and 7 syllables) by Saitō Mokichi in his *Tanka ni okeru shasei no setsu*: "Depict life of the unity of nature and self by truly understanding real aspects with the mind's eye".

I do not think that Awa was very familiar with the works of these scholars when he instructed the *kyūdō* club of the Second Higher School. While we cannot rule out the possibility that he may have seen or heard such ideas among his contemporaries, his understanding was gleaned through the context of having learned Zen, his experience of "unity with the universe", and through his own practice of *kyūdō*. While there were those who treated him as being insane, people who accepted Awa's thought were flooded in a vague stream of Taisho life-centrism prevalent at the time.

Ueshiba Morihei: The Mystic Experience of Aikido

Awa Kenzō formed a religious society in 1925 with the name *Daishadōkyō*. Such examples as the following can be found in the teaching syllabus with motives such as correcting improper words and deeds caused by rashness: "Forever grateful for the shooting-life, and living a religious life as a great enterprise in personality building", and "[with] self-awareness of the duty of *Daishadōkyō*, one therefore desires a clear manifestation of the spirit of national founding in an enlightened age."[23] It is said the students at the Second Higher School *kyūdō* club and alumni who continued their studies at Tohoku Imperial University objected to this *en masse*, and distanced themselves from the idea. Similarities to the Ōmoto-kyō, a new religious sect suppressed by the government in 1921, are given as reasons for this.[24]

The Ōmoto-kyō movement was founded in 1892 by Deguchi Nao (1837-1918), the daughter of a carpenter in Ayabe, Kyoto prefecture, after she claimed to have religious visions. The religion advocated a "day of judgment", and relief through belief in Maitreya. Nao's son-in-law, Deguchi Onisaburō (1871-1948), eventually became the movement's leader, and widely incorporated aspects of Buddhism, theories of *yin-yang* and the five elements, and other beliefs into the Shinto-based core, with the ideology of *reishu taijū* (spirit-main body-subordinate- the spirit as principle entity and the body as a secondary one) and *bankyō dōkon* (all teachings coming from the same origin). As a form of mysticism that posits a union of God and humanity, Onisaburō publicized and expanded a communal living group, appealed for social reform, and attained phenomenal growth attracting a large number of both intellectuals and soldiers alike. Apart from the Ōmoto-kyō there were numerous other "self-cultivation groups" that sprung up between the Taisho period (1912-26) and the early Showa period (1926-1989) that were rather similar in character even if the points they emphasized were different. Most of them incorporated positive aspects of various religions and advocated spiritual training.

Whatever Awa's reasons were for starting his new society, it was really just a sign of the times. However, the university students were concerned about Awa's society transmogrifying into an organization of the same nature as other "religious study groups". The influence and severe repression of the Ōmoto movement by the police was well known and probably a cause for concern.[25]

Ueshiba Morihei, who announced himself as the founder of aikido, continued to teach *bujutsu* in cooperation with the Ōmoto-kyō. While experiencing the trials and tribulations of life in Manchuria and inner-Mongolia, where he had ventured with Deguchi Onisaburō in his search for a mental state encapsulating a "unity of *ki*, mind, and body", he became able to see "a projection of white light flying momentarily before bullets" fired by opposition soldiers (1924). After returning to Japan, it is reported that he repeatedly experienced various religious visions. Then one spring day in 1925, immediately after facing the wooden swords of naval officers who were master kendo instructors, Ueshiba recollects "while cleansing myself beside a well, suddenly my whole body became clear and at the same time I was surrounded by a golden life energy (*ki*) that poured from the heavens and gushed forth from the ground; without my realizing it, I felt a response that was as if I and my physical form had transformed into a golden body",[26] this "golden body swelled out in an instant and looked as if it would expand to fill the whole universe."[27] This is the experience to which Ueshiba attributed the title "*gasoku uchū - ware sunawachi uchū*" (the self meaning the universe) and "*kenshin*" (experience of the divine.) He described this state of mind as transforming into "the very love of *musubi* (the procreative spirit) that is the unity of self and other, the unity of the divine and humankind, and the universe being the self." The very attainment of "the absolute victory of the deity of *Takemusu* (the procreative martial spirit)" meant that one was able to express the quintessence of *budō* (the martial Way).[28]

Ueshiba considered his experience of mental and physical transformation into a golden light to be "*kenshin*" and he described this by linking it to the concept of *musubi*. This act is strongly related to the fact that Ueshiba was within the scope of Deguchi Onisaburō's ideology. The nucleus of Deguchi's worldview is expressed in such passages found in the movement's tenets, "The source of the universe is vital energy, and that is God. All things are a manifestation of the vital force, and these are fragments of God", and "God is the universal spirit of all things, and humankind the main body in the governing of the universe. Here, with God and humankind in unity, we display boundless authority." We can obtain this structural system by replacing the concept of "*ki*" with "the vital energy of the universe" in the former passage, and replacing the ideas from the *Chinese Book of Mundane Mutations* (J: *Ekikyō*) in which the vital force is "*kami*" and all things achieve form through the congealing of "*ki*" (the true spirit of the universe) with "the manifestation of vital energy" and its products. Of the latter passages, "humankind [is] the main body in the governing of the universe" has almost the same meaning as the "humankind participates in the [affairs of the] universe" passage in the text *Daigaku*. While the passage, "Here, with God and humankind in unity, we display boundless authority", may perhaps appear to be predicated on the concept of a "saintly being" (*seijin*), it is an idea unique to Deguchi.

The 70-year History of Ōmoto explicates Deguchi's new spiritual canon, the *Reikai*

Twentieth Century Budo and Mystic Experience

monogatari (Accounts of the spiritual world). It states that "in Ōmoto [cosmology] the great originating spirit (*Daigenrei*) is named *Ōkunihitachi no ōkami* (*Ame no minaka nushi no kami*- Lord Deity of Heaven's Centre), the activity of fire (the spirit) is called *Takami musubi no kami* (High Procreative Deity), and the activity of water (the body) called *Kami musubi no kami* (Divine Procreative Deity). Through the interaction of fire and water all things in the universe were created." "The principle vital energy of the universe" is likened to the three creation deities of the *Kojiki* (Record of Ancient Matters, from Japanese mythology).

Deguchi Onisaburō reorganized the logic behind the concept of *ki* (C: *qi*) in Chinese philosophy through Taisho life-centrism, and here it is clear that he attempted to reconfigure the pantheon of ancient Japanese mythology, receiving much influence from the thought of Hirata Atsutane, an Shintoist of the late Tokugawa period. The *Reikai monogatari* assumes the existence of a divine, spiritual atom (*shinrei genshi*), in a world that mostly ought to be described as a cartoon-like one with the spiritual element equated to the fire element and the bodily element to the element of water.[29] But this aside, the phrases surrounding Ueshiba Morihei's mystic experience clearly rely on the view of *musubi* (the procreative spirit) held by Deguchi Onisaburō and therefore are posited within the scope of Taishō life-centrism.

In contrast to this we do not see such concepts as "*uchū daiseimei*" (great life of the universe) or "*shizen no daiseimei*" (great life of nature) in the words of Awa in describing his experience of "unity with the universe". The word "*seimei*" (life) appears only occasionally in Awa's notebooks, and while phrases such as "concentrate all life-force" are seen in his lectures,[30] their application was extremely ordinary. There is no evidence that would allow one to emphatically state that a concept similar to that of "*uchū daiseimei*" lay at the centre of his philosophy. The nearest thing would be where Awa stated casually in some notes that he considered the Way of shooting [arrows] from the standpoint of his experience of "unity with the universe", that "*shu no myōkyō*" (the rapture of archery) is the same as "*the state of heaven and earth as one*". This level becomes "*daichisha*" (great-knowledge-archery), "*daijisha*" (great-love-archery), and "that being nirvanic, living archery, that is called *shasei* (shooting life) and is a life that makes its way on forever". He stated that archery was the same as undergoing ascetic training (*shugyō*) without intention of doing so, and that is what makes it more than a religion. He also mentions that an "everlasting life can be attained" through archery, "that is, what are we without the great teaching of human redemption?"[31]

The "*mushō shō*" (nirvanic living) of Jōdo (Pure Land) Buddhism has the sense of an endless life separated from this life, and the mental state that attains this is the same as union with the "*uchū daiseimei*" (great life of the universe) spoken about by Nishida Kitarō. In Awa's case, however, "*mushō shō*" is something that should be acquired through experience, or it is the ideal state of mind that he experienced. Even if this was "a life that makes its way on endlessly", he did not consider this to be "a life that passes through all living things". That is, he did not consider it to be the source of all things or the principle for uniting the world. In other words, while Awa's thinking came extremely close to Taisho life-centrism, it did not fall completely within its scope.

Kan'nagara no Michi (The Way of the Gods)

As explained by Sakurai Yasunosuke, the *kan'nagara no michi* (the divine way) expounded by Awa was not something that took advantage of, or that was spoken in the same breath as *"shinkoku Nihon"* (divine Japan) under the heightened trend of militarism from around 1937 onwards. In approximately 1921, Awa mentioned the following (in a Chinese poem), "Continuous Imperial line– Forever revered - Brilliance of Emperor Jimmu's martial virtue - Japanese people embody the spirit of Japan."[32]

The originator of modern *kyūdō*, Honda Toshizane, stated in the 1889 draft of his *Kyūdō hozon kyōju oyobi enzetsu shui- ichimei yumiya no tebiki"* (Principle ideas of instruction and oration in the preservation of *kyūdō*- An individual guide to archery) that the Way of archery had "existed since the age of the gods", and that the classical traditions were hereditary to generations of emperors.[33] Honda, originally a shogunate retainer, was also at one stage employed as the head priest of the Shiba Hachimangū shrine. Hachiman was a popular Shinto deity who protects warriors. The Chinese poem quoted from Awa's notebook could be described as concurring with this traditional thought. Although Awa used much of the lexicon of Zen and Wang Yangming philosophy, it is difficult to say that *kan'nagara no michi* was self-evident for him, a practitioner of *kyūdō*. Such writings by Honda, however, were made before the "revival" of *bushidō*, and the contemporaneous thought surrounding the Emperor system was rather different to when Awa wrote the poem in his journal.

Kōtō renmen (Emperor ruling in a continuous line- mentioned in the above poem) formed the continuous historical perspective of Japanese from ancient times until the medieval period. While it also, in such texts as the *Jinnō shōtō ki* (Chronicle of direct descent of divine sovereigns- 1339, 1343), expressed Japanese superiority over the system of good imperial lines replacing bad ones in revolutions in China. This mode of thought persisted during the Meiji Restoration. It became a mainstay for national edification (*kokumin kyōka*) as the imperial-way thought of *bansei ikkei* (lit: the unbroken eternal line) clearly stated in the 1880 Imperial Rescript on Education (*kyōiku chokugo*). However this was insufficient as an ethical standard in itself. Another mainstay that was advocated in earnest was Japanese-style Confucian morality with its emphasis on loyalty to the monarch, in this case shifting allegiance from the respective *daimyō* from each *han* to the emperor.

While the idea of Japan as a "divine land" can be seen in such texts as the *Jinnō shōtō ki*, the popularity of this mode of thought soared when combined with the Shinto theory of Hirata Atsutane (1776-1843) and the philosophy of the Mito *han* of the late Tokugawa era, and gave birth to the divinely entangled notion of national polity (*kokutairon*). There had been a compromise with constitutionalism in the establishment of the Meiji Constitution. Subsequent to this, however, constitutionalism gained popularity in the press, and at the time of the Russo-Japanese War the ideology of *shinshū* (divine land) only fleetingly appeared. After the Russo-Japanese War, there was an escalation in the popularity of the theory of the state as family (*kazoku kokkaron*) that rearranged the Confucian ideology of "the people as the children of the Emperor" into a Japanese-styled "children of the Tennō". Representing a German-styled theory of an organic state, Minobe Tatsukichi's (1873-1948) theory of the Emperor as [merely] an organ of state was advocated in 1911, and until it was criticised by the *Kokutai meichō undō* (Movement for the clarification of the national polity), it was officially recognized rather than disapproved.

"Harmony between the East and West" was repeatedly advocated by opinion leaders after the Russo-Japanese War. The League of Nations was established after the European conflict of World War I, and when Japan became a permanent member of the League there was a popular trend towards opening the way for a peaceful, cultural coexistence of mutual prosperity where countries respected each other's cultures namely from the standpoint of cultural relativism. From this point in time, Japan's own uniqueness was emphasized and there was an ever-growing tendency to reinterpret traditional culture. At this time the ideology of shrine-Shinto once more began to show heightened popularity.

While the phrase *kōtō [no] renmen* (Emperor ruling in an unbroken line) and the term *shinshū* (divine land) is used by Awa, in actuality the phrase *kan'nagara no michi* (the divine way) rarely appear in Awa's journals until around the year 1921. Awa first became active in presenting lectures like the *"seishin bunka kōenkai"* (spiritual and cultural lecture meetings), in such places as Miyagi prefecture in 1934. Even in a radio lecture given in Sapporo in February 1936 entitled *"Shadō ni tsuite"* (With regards to the Way of archery) he stresses the relationship between archery and improving character and morals. Moreover, "Eastern morals" such as those of Confucius are emphasized.[34]

Phrases such as, "a unity of the divine and humankind, training to preach the truth and combat error" and "because it is an expression of preaching the truth and combating error, the bow became the symbol of the heavenly god Amaterasu (the sun goddess) and of the Imperial grandchild (Susano O)"[35] were directed at students of the *Shinshokukai* (Shinto priest society), in a collection of lectures entitled *Waga kokutai to kyūdō seishin* (National polity and the spirit of *kyūdō*). This being the case, one would estimate this to be the year 1930, around the time that construction had begun on the *Daishadōkyō* training hall within the precincts of the Miyagi prefecture Shinto priest training school.

Furthermore, phrases such as, "I am acutely aware that the divine inspiration of this arrow and the effort for unity between the divine and that which is human is the most blessed thing, along with nature, the training of the personality, and self-improvement"[36] appear in the notebook, *Shadō zappitsu* (Miscellaneous writings on the Way of the bow), that is thought to date from around 1936 or 1937. Among the written reflections of individuals who attended a lecture meeting for primary school principal instructors held in September 1937, we see a unanimous use of the term *"the mental state of unity between the divine and humanity"*[37] in relation to archery, and therefore it is safe to assume that Awa used the term himself during the lecture.

In actuality the phrase "the place of unity between heaven and earth is the pure-hearted place of unity between the divine and humankind"[38] and the term "unity between the divine and humankind" appear even as early as the first half of 1923 in the kendo club's report published in Sendai's Second Higher School magazine *Shōshikai zasshi*. These are the words of a school pupil, however, and we do not know whether they were uttered by Awa himself. Nishida Kitarō's *Zen no kenkyū* uses this phrase with respect to Christian mysticism. Herrigel may have explained that the "unity with endless life" that Awa spoke of, was the "unity between god and humankind" in Christian mysticism. Moreover, as seen earlier, Ueshiba Morihei, who was influenced by the thought of Deguchi Onisaburō, used the term "unity between God and humankind" in describing his experience of "oneness / unity with the universe". Both Ueshiba and Awa enjoyed a heightened level of popularity around this time from *budō* exponents in the military. It would not be at all strange if both were aware of each other's thoughts.

Furthermore, we see the phrase "*kan'nagara no michi*" (the divine way) appearing in the text of a judge's report that Awa wrote for the national technical college *kyūdō* tournament held in July 1937 by Tohoku Imperial University. Descriptions in his notebook such as *shadō seihō* (correct method in the Way of shooting), designated as being "the divine path", and "virtuous individuals perform the venerable work of nature, they being the divine, great spirit of our country", can of course be considered penned at around this time.[39]

The term "*kan'nagara*" appears in the description of "the third year of the reign of Emperor Kōtoku (1454)" in the *Nihon Shoki* (Chronicle of Japan). The inserted notes give this as "*kan'nagara [no] michi* (the divine way)" or "*jiyū shintō* (self-existing way of the gods)". This means "being as the gods are" or "being the way of the gods". Of course, it possessed no ethical structure in itself. That can only be affected by the words introduced from China, whether it is *seimeishin* ("the clear, bright heart") or *shisei* ("single-minded devotion"). Awa Kenzō's imparting of ethics to the imperial way (*kōdō*) was through the term *haja kensei* (preaching the truth and combating error) that shows a Buddhist ethical view rather than Shintoistic.

Kan'nagara was used in the opening of both the Emperor Meiji's *Senkyō no mikotonori* (missionary statement of the Emperor) and the Showa Emperor's (Hirohito) Imperial Rescript on the Coronation (*gosokui shiki no chokugo*). However, apart from amongst Shintoists, it did not gain popularity in the Meiji and Taisho eras, or in the early years of the Showa period. We can see in a lecture by Kakei Katsuhiko, a professor of Constitutional studies at Tokyo Imperial University to the next Emperor in the fall of 1925, that his thoughts were based on the view that the Japanese Emperor is the direct and real appearance of the "great life of the universe". There are visible signs of a popular trend emerging from around 1935, when Inoue Tetsujirō published *Nihon seishin no honshitsu* (The essence of the Japanese spirit). In its explanation, the book draws on the Confucian texts *Daigaku* and *Chūyō*, and calls upon Taoism and the philosophy of Wang Yangming, also referring to Mahayana Buddhism as well as to Western philosophies. These are used to explain that "unity between the divine and humankind" is adherence to the universe and nature, that it is mostly fair and impartial, and that it is a universal concept. However, he asserted that this was a spirit unique to Japan as it was the only country that had actually experienced it. Nevertheless, this was different from the ideals of militarism.

The fact that this "universal reason" was manifestly unique to Japan, and the fact that a martial philosophy is not advocated, among other factors, shows clear differences to the philosophy of Awa. He most probably deepened the shades of Shintoistic thinking in his own philosophy through acquaintances with Shinto priests, deriving from the fact that he now had the *Daishadōkyō* main training hall in the precincts of Miyagi Prefecture Shinto priest training school.

Awa stated that "*jita yūgō gōitsu*"[40] (melting of the self and the other) was an innermost secret of *kyūdō*. In a radio lecture given in 1936, he describes the historical episode in which two sword masters from the Meiji Restoration, Yamada Jirōkichi and Yamaoka Tesshū, faced off against one another with their swords held in an overhead stance (*jōdan*). After a forty-minute battle of wills they both ended up groaning the word "*maitta*" (I concede defeat), and retreated. Awa relayed this story to emphasize that the martial Ways were not just about technical skill.[41] Furthermore, his pupil Sakurai Yasunosuke also, in *Shasei Awa Kenzō*, describes and reviews the concept of *ainuke* (where if two enlightened individuals met in battle, recognizing each other's skill, both withdraw without recourse to fighting) as the ultimate state of mind in *budō*, as propounded by Harigaya Sekiun (?-1662) in *Sekiun-ryū kenjutsu sho* (Book on the swordsmanship of the Sekiun-ryū).[42]

This could furthermore be said to have a base in common with the words of Ueshiba Morihei, quoted in Peter Payne's *Martial Arts*, which I introduced earlier, representing harmony in the universe as a spiritual attitude that tenderly attempts to protect all life. It is also clear that its foundation is a re-rendering of the "*benevolence or love of all things united*" that was explicated by *Cheng Hao* (J: Tei Kei) during the formative years of orthodox neo-Confucianism. The individual who stated that "benevolence" (*jin*) had the same meaning as "love" (*ai*) was the early Tokugawa era Confucianist, Itō Jinsai.

While Ueshiba Morihei stated that God (*kami*) was the "Creator of the universe", this was probably not because he had been influenced by or was cognizant of the creationist theories of Christianity. Maybe it was just a loose translation by Peter Payne. The wording used by Ueshiba in describing his experience of "unity with the universe" centred on an event that occurred during a walk in a garden, which disagrees slightly with the version given in his biography. Perhaps, as these were recollections after the war, the wording had been adapted to suit post-war society. In the *Zhou mu zhuan* of Liezi we see the phrase "*zōbutsusha*" (the creator) used. It is not strange for *tentei* (God; lit. heavenly emperor) to be considered as being similar in meaning. Furthermore, in Shinto there existed the concept of *musubi*, the begetter of all things. Ueshiba never ceased to be a Shinto follower.

Peter Payne posits aikido as having the highest rationality among Eastern martial arts. He also quotes Ueshiba, "aikido is non-resistance. Because one offers no resistance one will always win", and compares this with the teachings of Jesus Christ in the Gospel according to St. Matthew, "if someone strikes you on the right cheek, turn the other cheek".[43] The understanding to not treat one's enemy as an enemy and to accept this into the universe of one's own heart is something special to aikido, and becomes quite convincing when one actually sees Ueshiba Morihei's *kami-waza* (super-human techniques). That is why we can state that true *budō* entails a love of peace. Furthermore, this represented to them *"kan'nagara no michi"* and *"Yamato-damashi"* (the Japanese spirit).

Despite this, Taisho life-centrism with its "great life of the universe" posited as the origin of the world, was reconstituted as *daijō seishin* (the spirit of the "greater vehicle"= Mahayana Buddhism), and when the people were called upon to sacrifice their lives in the war effort, it gave birth to the idea of *sange no shisō* ("scattering of flowers" philosophy [of death in battle]). Life-centrism, and the ideology of twentieth century Japanese *budō* exponents which drew close to this, was in itself *kan'nagara no michi* and was able to act in accord with it without compromising its principles. It is obvious under these circumstances that *budō* was able to act as a strong spiritual mainstay for *budō* exponents in the military.

But it was not only life-centrism, reinterpreted as *Yamato-damashii* that was able to blend in with militarism. In Yoshikawa Eiji's *Miyamoto Musashi* (1934) we can also see a reforming of the sword from a lethal weapon for troubled times to a tool for protecting peace with the pursuit of *kenzen itchi* (the sword and Zen as one). Furthermore, as war was publicized as something needed to "protect the Eastern peace" from the time of the Sino-Japanese War until World War II, it is plainly obvious that the "Eastern spirit" of questing for truth (*gudō seishin*) was "distributed" to a large readership as an emotional or spiritual prop for living in tumultuous times of time of war.[44]

Still, this was not limited to *budō* philosophy. During the war, praise for the non-violent principles of Mahatma Gandhi was unceasing. This is not at all strange as the very longing for a realized "Eastern peace" to counter the dominance of Western imperialism was strongly felt in Japan, and constituted the ideological basis to support militarism. Although some fault both Awa and Ueshiba for their ideological inclinations I think such scrutiny should be avoided, with the larger realization that these men were nurturing their ideologies in the context of their own personal development, based on the uniquely Japanese thought that had proceeded them.

Life-views of the Pre-war Generation

As I introduced earlier in this paper, Sakurai Yasunosuke saw "a native thought relating to natural law"[45] in the background of Awa's "unity with the universe" and "unity with nature". Illustrated with examples such as the explanations of Date Masamune (1567-1636) regarding adherence to the heavenly Way (*Tendō*) each passing day, he argued for worshipping the sun as the source of life, and believed that "*natural law in a pantheistic universe*"[46] constituted a unique Japanese spiritual grounding. He also saw this theoretical expression in the popular moral teachings of Ishida Baigan (*Sekimon Shingaku*).

A tradition of nature worship continued on, even up until the 1970s among mountain, farming, and fishing villages, as well as among the older generations of Japanese in urban cities. Even today in Japan we can see the remnants of these beliefs. However, holding on to these beliefs to explain the life-view of contemporary-modern Japan would be to make the same mistake of reducing contemporary-modern European and American views of life down only to [the precepts of] Christianity.

Stating that there was one root origin to Shinto, Confucianism, and Buddhism, and furthermore advocating the use of the mind in accordance with the "true nature" of all things in the universe, and advocating the existence of a "merchant ethic" that sought actual benefit, the practical branch of Ishida Baigan's ideology spread throughout Japan from the latter half of the eighteenth century with backing from the shogunate and the *han*. Baigan's doctrines were called *Shingaku* ("Heart Learning"). He preached in terms of "heart" and "knowing the nature." The purpose of devotion was to overcome one's "selfish heart", thereby learning the "true heart". This meant realizing that standard Confucian morality was completely natural and in accord with the laws of the universe. I believe the Japanese acceptance of the equal philosophy of the natural rights of man was partly due to Ishida Baigan's popular moral teachings acting as a receptor. Perhaps these teachings were conveyed through to Awa's place of birth. Of course, the establishment of Ishida Baigan's brand of popular moral teachings could not have occurred without orthodox neo-Confucianism or Wang Yangming thought.

Moreover, Confucianism, Taoism, Taoist thought, Shintoism, and Buddhism take universal nature worship in primitive beliefs as their direct foundation, and generally speaking assert the concept of humankind being at one with the universe and nature. Accordingly, to this extent we cannot say that this is an "indigenous philosophy" of Japan. Furthermore, these philosophies and religions take the concept of "natural life" (*shizen no seimei*) as their major premise. This, however, first comes into existence when we project upon others the concept of *seimei* that we ourselves use.

If we line up the philosophies that worship the life-force of the universe and nature, such as in the "great life of the universe" and the "life of nature", and those that worship based on these conceptual assumptions, and call these life-centrism, then the Jōdo (Pure Land) Buddhist philosophy recorded in Awa's journals would perhaps also fall within this category. However, to consider the subject in this way would also mean applying the same descriptive title to all such ideologies as animism, spiritualism, the theory of vitalism in European biologies (*seikiron*), the concept of *ki*, pantheism, and to the mental attitude that senses "nature to be living". In the same way that the European word "vitalism" had multiple ambiguous meanings such as the "theory of ether" that continued to hold sway in European scientific history until the early twentieth century, the ideological trend of placing emphasis on "vital energy", or the principle of prolonging life in medicine and similar trends are not sufficient to categorize as ideological or spiritual histories.

The biological view of life, that being the commonality of having cells, and the idea of describing both plant forms and animals as *"organisms"* (*seibutsu*) established itself in the 1830s. Subsequently, Darwin's theory of evolution for living organisms spread together with the "social evolutionism" of Herbert Spencer in the latter half of the nineteenth century. At the turn of the century, the unfolding of modern philosophy based on the awareness of sensation and perception beginning with Ernst Mach, a famous Austrian physicist, and further expanded by William James in America, Henri Bergson in France, Edmund Hussert in Germany, and others, along with concepts of "life" (*seimei*) became popular. This was brought about by such factors as the institution of Dorish's neo-vitalism in biology and the universal life theory of Ernst Heckel in Germany. In brief, at the turn of the century, there was a stream of thought where the notion of "life" was considered equally with "absolute God" in theism, and matter in Natural Sciences. These were regarded in the same light as the principle behind the world, assuming this as something that permeates all things. In other words, specifying the period and form of thinking that I refer to as *life-centrism* (*seimei-shugi*).

During the Meiji period, the word *seimei*, which rarely appears in literature before, became widely referred to through such debate as that over the natural rights of man. This, coupled with the fact that the theory of evolution in living organisms was still a vague concept, encouraged debate more in Japan than the West or in Islamic countries. The idea that humankind was one form of life, and that humankind's instinct was the same as that of other animals, took hold in Japan. Into this flowed the West's fundamental unsettling of world understanding prevalent at the turn of the century. By combining this with Buddhist thinking such as Zen and Jōdo, and philosophies such as that of Wang Yangming, I believe that Japan's unique *life-centrism* became a great influential current, replacing the idea of *ki* or *tenri* as the reason of the universe with *seimei*.

Sakurai Yasunosuke considered that *"unity with the great life of nature"* was part of Awa's ideal, and while he uses the concept of *"principle life activities"*[47] in the interpretation of Zen and yoga, the term *"seimei"* used by Awa was not a mystical form of life assumed as the source of *"the great life of the universe"*, that being the source of all life. Nor did it have conceptual nuances to it; Buddhism aimed to interpret this from the outset as deriving from the reincarnation of life. These interpretations could only have derived from Sakurai Yasunosuke himself who held the belief of a *"life permeating all things"*.

Furthermore, Origuchi Shinobu, for example, argued in *Kokubungaku no hassei* that the basis of Japanese folk customs was an indigenous "felicitation in life"; Watsuji Tetsurō— who attempted to perceive expressions of the joy of life that lay at the base of Japanese culture in the trends of Buddhist art from ancient times until the medieval period— argued in *Nihon bunka no jūsōsei* (The multi-tiered nature of Japanese culture) (*Zoku nihon seishinshi kenkyū*) that Shinto had shaped "an important opportunity for Japanese ethnic life". Furthermore the book *Bukkyō tokuhon* by Okamoto Kanoko, with the 2500th anniversary of the birth of the Buddha in 1934 in the background,

Twentieth Century Budo and Mystic Experience

argued Mahayana Buddhism was the "great life of the universe". Okamoto was active in interpreting Mahayana Buddhism for a general audience. Origuchi, Watsuji, and Okamoto were all within the sphere of Taisho life-centrism. In this way, the concept of "nature" and more precisely "life" worship continuing as the uninterrupted base of the Japanese mind since ancient times, as well as the idea that a concept of "the great life of the universe" existed in the basis of Buddhism, were concepts that had been formed in Sakurai Yasunosuke's youth. The views of the world and of life that had been formed through these discourses were used by him to explain the philosophy of Awa.

While the debates regarding this kind of "life" worship were argued affirmatively as being mostly Asian or characteristically Japanese in nature, after defeat in World War II the "mind and spirit" of the Japanese purportedly extending back to the Tokugawa period was associated with overtones of backwardness and as being animistic. Whether you agree or not, these concepts are variations of what Sakurai terms "a native philosophy relating to natural law". Furthermore, this is not peculiar to Sakurai alone. While a vague concept, it is appropriate to view such thought as being widely held by Japanese born before the war.

Concepts of worshipping natural life represented by Shinto became established firmly in the 1930s, and exists in the under-layer of Japanese culture. It was continued after the war, and took firm hold through the popularity of cultural structuralism from around the 1970s. Indeed, through the views of life and Japanese culture commonly held by people from the pre-war generations, Sakurai's *Ōinaru sha no michi no oshie* was interpreted as consenting to the legitimacy of Awa's ideology, and his mystic experience was seen as confirming the principle life (*seimei*) of the universe.

However, in *Shasei*, the concept of the principle life does not appear in the interpretation of Confucianism, Wang Yangming's philosophy, or Zen. While there may have been some different interpretations in his book, it emphasized the unique nature of a Japanese "native philosophy relating to natural law". One reason for this was he probably tried to explain Awa's idea unification of the principle life restricting the confines of his his explanation to Awa's "*kan'nagara no michi*". Furthermore, *Shasei* attempts to depict him and his ideology "as [constituting an] advocate for protection of nature and the universe" anticipating the enthusiasm for preservation of the natural environment evidenced today. Or, rather than viewing this as a diagram of East versus West, we may perhaps be able to describe it as reflecting a shift to an era where Japan's identity and uniqueness is once more being called into question.

Endnotes

[1] Ulysses S. Grant (1822-1885) 18th President of the United States (1869-1877).

[2] Dean K. Boorman, *"A Personal Reminiscence of Bashford Dean"* (The American Society of Arms Collectors, Bulletin of Metropolitan Museum of Art, No.70, Spring 1994, pp.18-19). The author gratefully received the assistance of Metropolitan Museum curator Donald LaRocca in researching this information.

[3] For examples of this see Deguchi Hiromitsu, *Mishima Yukio: Shōwa no meikyū*, p. 77.

[4] Imamura Yoshio, *Nihon tai'ikushi*, in *Sengo tai'iku kihon shiryōshū dai 15 kan*.

[5] Sakurai Yasunosuke, *Ōinaru sha no michi no oshie* (hereinafter abbreviated to *Daishadōkyō*). *Atogaki* (Afterword), p. 486.

[6] *Ibid.*, p. 389.

[7] *Ibid.*, p. 369.

[8] Sakurai Yasunosuke, *Shasei Awa Kenzō: Tenchi daishizen no daigensha* (hereinafter abbreviated to *Shasei*), p. 59.

[9] As per chronological histories given at the end of *Daishadōkyō* and *Shasei*.

[10] *Daishadōkyō*, p. 105.

[11] *Ibid.*, p. 6.

[12] *Ibid.*, p. 116.

[13] *Ibid.*, p. 156.

[14] *Ibid.*, p. 210.

[15] *Ibid.*, p. 182.

[16] *Shasei*, p. 135.

[17] *Daishadōkyō*, pp. 181-84.

[18] *Ibid.* p173-174; *"Shasei"*, p. 164.

[19] *Ibid.*, p. 181.

[20] *Ibid.*, pp. 193-94.

[21] *Ibid.*, p. 232.

[22] *Ibid.*, p. 211.

[23] *Ibid.*, p. 216-17.

[24] *Shasei*, p. 209.

[25] Awa Kenzō's notebooks from 1921 until around 1925, however, make mention of the words, *"Taishō ishin"* [the Taisho [era] Restoration] (*Daishadōkyō*, p. 184). The passage, *"Youth of today, proceed with the determination of the youth of the time of the restoration"*, appears, and while this does not directly suggest a connection with Ōmoto, the concept of a "Taisho Restoration" was widely known as the assertions of firstly Deguchi Onisaburō at around the end of World War I. This was after the death of Deguchi Nao, and advocated the repealing of taxes and the abolition of the gold and silver exchange system. Furthermore, Kimura Tsugimori's compilation, *"Deguchi Onisaburō gyokugonshū shingetsu no kage"* p. 47, states that towards the end of the Meiji period, Onisaburō was also known as a "master of the bow" who would never miss the target. Alternatively, he may well have been a person who weighed on the mind of Awa Kenzō.

[26] *Aikidō kaiso Ueshiba Morihei den-"Nenpu"* (Chronological history), p. 305.

[27] *Ibid.*, p. 172.

[28] *Ibid.*,

[29] *Ibid.*, pp. 136-41.

[30] *Daishadōkyō*, p. 346.

[31] *Ibid.*, p. 194.
[32] *Ibid.*, p. 181.
[33] *Ibid.*, p. 108.
[34] *Ibid.*, pp. 388-92.
[35] *Ibid.*, p. 384.
[36] *Ibid.*, p. 384.
[37] *Ibid.*, p. 353.
[38] *Ibid.*, p. 422.
[39] *Ibid.*, p. 422.
[40] *Daishadōkyō*, p. 392.
[41] *Ibid.*, pp. 390-391.
[42] *Ibid.*, pp. 489-493.
[43] Payne, op. cit., pp. 34-35.
[44] Suzuki Sadami, "Yoshikawa Eiji no rekishikan" in *Kokubungaku kaishaku to kanshō*. Refer to the special feature on Yoshikawa Eiji.
[45] *Ibid.*, p. 7.
[46] *Ibid.*, p. 30.
[47] *Ibid.*, p. 155.

Bibliography

Akiyama Goan. (ed.). *Gendai taika bushidō sōron* (Assorted discussions on contemporary *bushidō* masters). Hakubunkan, 1905.

Deguchi Hiromitsu. *Mishima Yukio: Shōwa no meikyū* (Mishima Yukio: The labyrinth of the Showa period). Shinchōsha, 2002.

Herrigel, Eugen. (Translated by Inatomi Eijirō and Ueda Takeshi). *Yumi to Zen*. Fukumura Shuppan, 1959.

Imamura Yoshio. *Nihon tai'iku shi* (History of Japanese physical education). Kaneko Shobō, 1951. In *Sengo tai'iku kihon shiryōshū Dai 15 Kan* (Collection of basic materials on post-war physical education, Vol. 15). Taikūsha, 1995.

Inoue Tetsujirō and Arima Sukemasa. *Bushidō sōsho* (*Bushidō* series). Hakubunkan, 1905.

Kayaoka Tomiei and Kayaoka Yūko, (trans.). *Māsharu-ātsu: Bujutsu no reiteki jigen* (Translation of *Martial Arts: the Spiritual Dimension*). Heibonsha, 1992.

Kimura Tsugimori. *Deguchi Onisaburō gyokugonshū shingetsu no kage* (Collection of Deguchi Onisaburō's words of wisdom: the light of the new moon). Nihon Taniha Kenkyūjo, 1988.

Kunikida Doppo. *Azamukazaru no ki* (Undeceiving record). Ryūbunkan, 1908.

Mikami Reiji and Naitō Chiyō. *Nihon bushidō* (Japanese *bushidō*). Mikami Iemitsu, 1899.

Nishida Kitarō. *Zen no kenkyū* (*A Study of Good*). Iwanami Shoten, 1950.

Nitobe Inazō. (Translated by Sakurai Ōson). *Bushidō*. Teibi Shuppansha, 1908.

Okamoto Kanoko. *Bukkyō tokuhon* (Reader in Buddhism). Daitō Shuppansha, 1934.

Origuchi Shinobu. *Kokubungaku no hassei* (The origin of Japanese literature, vol. 1). Chūō Kōronshinsha, 2003.

Payne, Peter. *Martial Arts: the Spiritual Dimension*. London: Thames & Hudson, 1981.

Saitō Mokichi. *Tanka ni okeru shasei no setsu* (Theory on sketches in *tanka*). Iwanami Shoten, 1981.

Sakurai Yasunosuke. *Awa Kenzō – Ōinaru sha no michi no oshie* (Great teachings on the way of Archery). *Awa Kenzō Sensei seitan hyakunensai jikkō i'inkai* (Executive committee for the centennial anniversary of the birth of Awa Kenzō), Sendai: 1981.

Shasei Awa Kenzō: Tenchi daishizen no daigensha (Shooting Saint: Awa Kenzō as advocate for nature and the universe) *Awa Kenzō seitan hyakunijūnen kinen jigyō jikkō i'inkai* (Executive committee for the 120th anniversary of the birth of Awa Kenzō), Sendai: 1999.

Shaku Goan. *Zen to bushidō* (Zen and *bushidō*). Kōyūkan, 1907.

Shibata Jisaburō. *Nihon no kyūjutsu*. (Japanese archery). Iwanami Shoten, 1941.

Shigeno Yasutsugu and Kusaka Hiroshi. *Nihon bushidō*. (Japanese *bushidō*). Taishūdō, 1909.

Suzuki Sadami, (ed.). "Yoshikawa Eiji no rekishikan" (The historical perspectives of Yoshikawa Eiji). In *Kokubungaku kaishaku to kanshō* (Japanese literature: Interpretation and appreciation). Shibundō, 2001.

Seimei de yomu Nihon kindai: Taishō seimei-shugi no tanjō to tenkai (Reading modern Japan from the viewpoint of "life": The birth and development of Taisho life-centrism). NHK Books, 1998.

Uchimura Kanzō. *Daihyōteki Nihonjin* (Representative men of Japan). Ichihachi, 1894.

Ueshiba Kisshōmaru. (Revised edition by Ueshiba Moriteru). *Aikidō kaiso Ueshiba Morihei den* (Biography of Ueshiba Morihei: Founder of aikido). Shuppan Geijutsusha, 1999.

Watsuji Tetsurō. *Nihon seishinshi no kenkyū (zoku)* (A study of Japanese spiritual history). Iwanami Shoten, 1940.

Yoshikawa Eiji. *Miyamoto Musashi*. Dai Nihon Yūbenkai Kōdansha, 1934.

Chapter 2

Research of Miyamoto Musashi's *Gorin no sho*— From the Perspective of Japanese Intellectual History

Uozumi Takashi
International Budo University

Introduction

Very little research has been conducted into *budō* from an intellectual history or other academic perspective. As *bujutsu* fundamentally concerns technical aspects, it is often difficult to express the content in words. Furthermore, it is difficult to interpret the texts describing budō that were actually written by *budō* exponents. Also, in texts concerning *budō* or *budō* exponents, often sections are added or changed in the process of transmission, and fictional untruths are sometimes proliferated as fact. Taking these characteristics problems with *budō* research into consideration, research methodology should be clarified first and it is necessary to establish the position of *budō* within the realm of Japanese intellectual history.

In this paper, I will outline the standard methodology for research into *budō* and examine the representative case of Miyamoto Musashi's *Gorin no sho* from the perspective of intellectual history. Firstly, I will outline the following points in regards to research methodology of *budō* study, and then I will discuss the study of Musashi's *Gorin no sho*.

I. Investigation of the Life of the Author—Musashi's Life History
II. Philological Research—Confirmed Works and Texts
III. Philosophical Research—The Philosophy of *Gorin no sho*
IV. Positioning in Japanese Intellectual History—The Meaning of *Gorin no sho*

I. Investigation of the Life of the Author—Musashi's Life History

At the outset of research into historical thought, it is necessary to clarify how the person in question lived, the period they lived in, as well as how they formed their particular mode of thought. Great exponents of *budō* are often elevated to legendary status, and fictional dramatizations such as those seen in novels are commonly accepted as fact. For this reason, the researcher must avoid accepting common assumptions as fact, and endeavour to conduct research based on reliable historical records. The following points should be taken into consideration when conducting such research.

(1) Critical analysis of historical records
Ascertain reliability and authenticity of a particular historical record by considering the period in which it was written, the nature of the text, its sources, background leading to transmission, and its compatibility with other historical records. In Musashi's case there are a large number of stories that claim to be factual but appear approximately seventy years after his death. From the mid-Tokugawa period these became coloured by various other fictional events, making it necessary for the criticism of historical records, in particular, to be thorough.[1]

(2) Discovering new historical records
An investigation is required not only of published records but also related geographical regions and locations where historical records may exist. Even for an individual as well known as Musashi, there are a great many historical records that have remained unknown until recently. For example, among the works authored by Musashi himself, three new texts have been confirmed in recent years.

(3) Determination of historical fact
While paying attention to the degree of historical accuracy in the records based on historical setting, thorough research should combine any number of sources to try and determine facts. Creative folklore, oral traditions, and other forms of fiction should be excluded. Points of query will be marked for future investigation.

(4) Interpretation of literary works and secret or transmitted texts (densho)
These must be accurately interpreted while paying attention to the nature of the document. Secret or transmitted writings on *budō* differ greatly depending on what depth the technical skills can be interpreted.

(5) Research of [martial] techniques
Current *budō* research requires scrutinizing surviving techniques from the *ryūha* (martial tradition) in question that have been transmitted through the generations to present-day successors. It must be ascertained that they do indeed represent transmission of the old forms.

The Life of Miyamoto Musashi

Constant awareness of the above factors in researching Musashi has revealed a widely disparate factual figure to that of the image often depicted up until now. As detailed demonstration is given in my work *Miyamoto Musashi—Nihonjin no michi* (2002), here I will give a simplified report focusing on the philosophical history pertaining to Miyamoto Musashi.

(1) Musashi's birth and youth
Musashi gives himself the title *Shōkoku harima no bushi* (warrior born in Harima) in *Gorin no sho*. He was born into the Tahara family near Himeji in Harima (present day

Miyamoto Musashi's Gorin no sho

Hyogo prefecture) in 1582. By age nine, he is thought to have become the adopted child of Miyamoto Munisai, who was in the vassalage of the Shinmen family of Mimasaka (present day Okayama prefecture).[2] It seems that Musashi's home was destroyed in a battle just prior to his birth, and he was adopted in order to remain in the warrior class, as warrior-farmer separation policies (*heinō bunri*) were being enforced at the time. His adoptive father, Miyamoto Munisai, distinguished himself in battle with the cross-shaped spear (*jūmonji yari*) in the late 1570s. In the text *Tōri-ryū mokuroku* (1598) he takes the names *Kaizan* (founder of the school) and *Tenkamusō* (matchless under the sun), and had already created the two-sword school (Nitō-ryū) by this time.[3] Given the fact that several terms of the Shinkage-ryū tradition can be seen in the *mokuroku* (inventory of techniques and teachings), it appears he had organized a system of his own style of techniques whilst being influenced by this school. From this we can assume that Musashi had not independently created the two-sword school (for which he is famous), but that his adoptive father, Munisai, was in fact the founder of the school. Evidently, his father was a first-class martial artist with a number of students, and Musashi, who demonstrated great talent undoubtedly received special education from his adoptive father from a young age.

(2) Musashi's days of musha shugyō

In the year 1600, Japanese feudal ascendancy was split by the battle of Sekigahara, with Tokugawa Ieyasu gaining supremacy after his victory in the battle. At this time, Munisai was with the Kuroda domain from Kyushu. This suggests that at the time of the battle of Sekigahara he must have participated in a considerable portion of the battle under the Kuroda banner. They fought on the side of the Tokugawa in Kyushu, and also participated in two attacks on opposition castles. It is thought that Musashi also participated in these battles.[4] Two years subsequent to this at the age of twenty-one, Musashi travelled north to Kyoto and began his itinerant warrior training (*musha shugyō*). Two years later he challenged the celebrated Yoshioka swordsmen of Kyoto, who were employed as martial arts instructors to the Muromachi shogunate. He fought three contests against the head of the school, his younger brother, offspring, and the school's pupils, winning them all and claimed to be unrivalled. He then decided to author a book on the "rationale" of technique, taking until the next year to complete *Heidōkyō* (1605). In the process of writing his first book, he also established his own style, the Enmei-ryū.[5] Grounded on the inventory of his adoptive father, *Heidōkyō* combined technical innovations based on his own practical experience in combat. He gave detailed descriptions of the rationale and principles for some twenty-eight techniques. Musashi then went on to tour the various provinces of Japan, accepting challenges from martial artists of other traditions, finally ending his itinerant warrior training with his famous victory over Kojirō at the age of twenty-nine.[6]

(3) Musashi in his prime

After reaching the age of thirty, Musashi looked back over his sixty-odd contests, and despite having won them all believed that his victories were "not [due to] great tactics". He states in *Gorin no sho* that he then pursued "a more profound philosophy". In the summer siege of Osaka castle in 1615, Musashi participated as a mounted samurai for Mizuno Katsunari, *fudai daimyō* to the Tokugawa (*Mizuno* domain campaign list). With the conclusion of the siege at Osaka, the Tokugawa shogunate proclaimed regulations such as decrees limiting each province to one castle and promulgated the *Buke shohatto* (Laws for military houses) to restrict the financial power and freedom of the *daimyō*, thus making Tokugawa dominance unshakeable.

After the campaign it appears that Musashi returned to Himeji near his birth place, and was entertained by the Honda domain, vassals to the shogun that had moved to Himeji. There he adopted Mikinosuke from the Mizuno domain, and subsequently brought into the service of the son of the lord. In 1623, Musashi adopted Iori, his nephew, after Mikinosuke followed his lord to the grave (*junshi*). He was brought into the service of the Ogasawara domain in neighbouring Akashi. Five years later, Iori rose to the position of senior retainer (*karō*) of the domain.

In the prime of his life, Musashi possessed the relatively strong social position of being guest to *fudai daimyō* of the Tokugawa shogun, and was free to practice *zazen* and enjoy various artistic pursuits such as the tea ceremony and painting. Of course, he also trained in swordsmanship through most of the day, and is said to have become enlightened to the true nature of the "Way" at around the age of fifty. It appears that in the following year, the Ogasawara were moved to Kokura, a strategic position in Kyushu, with Iori as senior retainer and Musashi in tow.

The various *daimyō* in Kyushu were called into service in 1638 to suppress the Shimabara uprising that had broken out a year earlier. Musashi participated in the campaign together with Iori who had by then become overall magistrate (*sōgun bugyō*) of the 8,113 man force supplied by the Ogasawara domain. Musashi was sent as a messenger from the head *karō* (senior retainer) of the Kumamoto domain at the time of the campaign, and also wrote a letter to the Miyazaki *daimyō* proving his meritorious service in battle. Musashi was in a position close enough to know what the lords were doing. After the battle, he wrote *Heihō kakitsuke* (1638) which provides explanations on the technical principles of swordsmanship, and argues for all-inclusive consideration of various situations where one might meet an opponent, as well as habitual training to hone one's own skills. This was probably an extension of the content of *Heidōkyō* which describes separate methods of attack for different opponents.[7]

(4) Musashi's later years and Gorin no sho

In 1640 Musashi became a guest of the Kumamoto domain. One year later he presented the *daimyō*, Hosokawa Tadatoshi, a pupil of Yagyū Munenori, with the *Heihō sanjūgokajō* (1641). After his lord's death two years later, Musashi began to write *Gorin no sho* in an attempt to describe the "Way of strategy" centred on the art of the sword for the benefit of future generations. Musashi spent the next year and a half writing vigorously to complete the treatise before finally dying.

What becomes clear from the above prosopographical investigation is that Musashi did not form his *kenjutsu* ideals unaided. He was taught from a young age by his adoptive father, a leading martial artist himself, finally arriving at the reasoning recorded

Miyamoto Musashi's Gorin no sho

in *Gorin no sho* after progressing through many levels of expertise. From a young age he attempted to master the "Way of strategy" (*heihō no michi*). He formulated his concepts on actual combat experience, adding to the basic inventory of techniques he learned from his father. He had already created a basic document of technical principles by the age of twenty-five. While reflecting on these preliminary principles and those of other martial traditions, Japan finally settled down to a period of relative peace in the Tokugawa period. Here, Musashi continued to pursue a universal reasoning integrating the essence of the way of arts as well, and then advocated the summation of his discoveries as a philosophy or Way of life for the warrior. *Gorin no sho* is the culmination of Musashi's lifelong search.

II. Philological Research—Confirmed Works and Texts

When studying classical texts the most important overriding factor is the need for accurate, error-free interpretation of the literature.

(1) Determining documents
With Tokugawa period literature pertaining to *budō*, copied manuscripts (*shahon*) are often the only information available to us. However, we must first determine whether a particular text is the work of the claimed author or not. There is no extant original manuscript in Musashi's hand of *Gorin no sho*, and as the oldest known copied manuscript was made twenty-two years after his death, there are theories questioning whether Musashi really did in fact author the work. Confronted with such problems, there is a need to investigate the various copies and circumstances regarding their transmission.

The results of my own extensive investigation leads me to believe that *Gorin no sho* was truly authored by Musashi.[8] Of Musashi's works, *Heihō sanjūgokajō* (1641) and *Dokkōdō* (1645) are most certainly authored by him. The existence of three other works by him have also been identified. Of these, *Heidōkyō* (1610) gives the name *Miyamoto Musashi no Kami Fujiwara Gikei*, not *Genshin* as given in *Gorin no sho*. With six copied manuscripts and four related texts, there are three textual systems extant that attest to the fact that it is indeed the work of the young Musashi.[9] *Heihō kakitsuke* (1638) has survived from copied manuscripts from the mid-Tokugawa period and printed copies from the Meiji period. Certain sections correspond with the posthumous writings of Musashi in the *Heihō sanjūkyūkajō* (enlarged edition of *Heihō sanjūkyūkajō* transmitted in Kumamoto).[10] I was able to prove that the introductory Chinese writing, *Gohō no tachi no michi*, that was rumoured to be directly written by him, was indeed Musashi's own work.[11] Please refer to the documentation compiled in my book, *Miyamoto Musashi – Nihonjin no michi*, for evidence regarding the three publications and reprints of the texts.

(2) Determining the text

When only copied manuscripts exist, the most accurate copy must be ascertained by comparison with other extant copies. The original text found in present publications of *Gorin no sho* relies on a single copied manuscript (of the Hosokawa domain). Proofreading of the ten extant manuscript copies reveals 115 characters omitted in five locations and fifty-four instances of what appear to be errors in the copying. Refer to *Teihon Gorin no sho* (revised and annotated by Uozumi, 2005), for the revised original text. At present there are a large number of foreign language translations of *Gorin no sho* that reflect, of course, the omissions and erroneous copying of the Hosokawa text without alteration, and upon perusal of the English translations I have spotted a number of points that ought to be described as mistranslations.[12] As the translation of the literature in the international communication of culture plays a large role, it goes without saying that it is preferable to have accurate translations based upon omission- and error-free original texts.

(3) Interpreting the literature

The author's motivation for writing a text, the envisioned readership, and the actual nature of the literature must also be taken into consideration. There are various examples of literature pertaining to *budō*, such as those that impart technical methodology of a particular school (*ryūha*), those that record the traditions of the school and its founder, and there are also texts written in order to clarify the style's perspectives. There are also examples of general *budō* texts without adherence to any particular tradition. The content and style of writing found within each text will differ depending on all of these factors. The researcher must also consider the text's relationship to the techniques, and in what way it has been transmitted down over the generations to the present day.

In Musashi's case, *Heihō sanjūgokajō* and *Gorin no sho* were written in his later years with the information related to *kenjutsu* techniques mostly overlapping. The *Heihō sanjūgokajō* was a document presented to a *daimyō* as an initiation into the intricacies of Musashi's *kenjutsu*, and much secretive metaphor is used to describe an array of techniques. *Gorin no sho*, on the other hand, was written as a record pertaining to the ideal lifestyle of the warrior for the benefit of later generations, and nebulous figurative speech has mostly been omitted.[13] Consequently, a more accurate understanding can be obtained concerning the swordsmanship of Miyamoto Musashi by reading *Gorin no sho* in combination with *Heihō sanjūgokajō*.

(4) Positing the literature

Perusal of the texts appearing before and after the literature in question is vital when trying to ascertain the position of that text. In regards to literature pertaining to a particular *ryūha* it is necessary to discern which texts have been directly transmitted (within the *ryūha*) and which have been influenced by outside sources. If the author has produced other texts as well, the researcher should consider the overall process of their development. I also refer to later interpretations and annotations if these exist.

With Musashi's works we must consider his first work *Heidōkyō* in combination with his adoptive father's inventory. From there it is necessary to pursue the development

Miyamoto Musashi's Gorin no sho

of techniques contained in *Heidōkyō*, *Heihō kakitsuke*, through to the publication of *Heihō sanjūgokajō*, and up until the writing of *Gorin no sho*. The numerous secret or transmitted texts that interpret or explain the literary works and teachings of Musashi in the Niten Ichi-ryū tradition all serve as useful references here. An accurate interpretation of the Chinese writing, *Gohō no tachi no michi*, which is thought to be the original introduction to *Gorin no sho*, requires analysis of the annotated documents transmitted within the Niten Ichi-ryū style first. In turn, this poem enables a clearer understanding of Musashi's intentions and awareness while writing *Gorin no sho*.

III. Philosophical Research—The Philosophy of *Gorin no sho*

Upon completion of the two above sections, research can be conducted to ascertain the philosophy contained within the text. The content is analyzed and interpreted while paying attention to the overall structure of the text. However, research into *budō* poses several special problems.

(1) Necessity for experiential understanding of the techniques
As *budō* documents of the Tokugawa period were based on the techniques of a particular *ryūha*, experiential understanding of the techniques through actually training in them is especially important. Musashi himself warns readers in the beginning of the 'Water' scroll of *Gorin no sho* that as the techniques are difficult to express in words, the readers should themselves attempt the techniques described and try being creative in their application.

(2) Understanding of the movements of classical martial arts (koryū)
There is a strong need to be aware of the differences in movement seen in the older styles of martial arts and present-day *budō*. The method of striking and the points aimed for differ between *kenjutsu*, which uses a wooden Japanese swords, and kendo, which uses the bamboo practice sword (*shinai*). Therefore, their methods of making an attack and avoiding attack are completely different. The use of the *shinai* in *kenjutsu* occurs widely after the nineteenth century. Nevertheless, it is necessary to seek out how the movements of the classical martial arts differ from the sports-like movements of the present day, while giving practical test to various postulations.

(3) Handling of transmitted techniques
There are aspects of *ryūha* that are handed down generations imbued in the techniques, but may not be given any particular mention in the literature. Often perceptual facets that are particularly difficult to express, such as interaction with the opponent, distancing and rhythm in movement, and so on, were transmitted to the adept orally and meant to be acquired through actual experience and training. While we can say that the techniques of a tradition are the expression of its own ideology, there are often circumstances where one cannot possibly understand the finer points without knowing them even with access to the transmitted writings. Also, we must

somehow try to confirm to what extent the transmitted techniques have been accurately conveyed in comparison with the original forms. In the process of transmission, the techniques may change, and new techniques may also be added. If traditional and older documents detailing the oral transmission of techniques exist, then these need to be used to try and ascertain accuracy.

The Philosophy of *Gorin no sho*

As Musashi states, the content of *Gorin no sho* was based on his own combat experience and was arranged in a particular order. He clarifies the points not reached in *ryūha*, and also seeks "principles" that correspond with the various arts writing with strong conviction of the concept of universal "reason" (*dōri*). Amongst much literature pertaining to *budō*—in which the main emphasis is on conveying details of the *ryūha*'s techniques—in *Gorin no sho* Musashi puts forth the rationale behind his own school, as well as the fundaments of techniques found in other *ryūha*.

Gorin no sho is divided into five scrolls—Earth (地), Water (水), Fire (火), Wind (風), and Void (空). The Earth scroll describes general outlines of strategy and how to grasp military tactics, and methods for learning the "Way"; the Water scroll describes the technical theory of *kenjutsu* that is at the heart of strategy; the Fire scroll, describing methods of fighting, shows how the principles of *kenjutsu*, only one part of *heihō*, were applicable to the "greater *heihō*" of great numbers of warriors in a large battle.[14] The Wind scroll specifies the errors found in the tactics of other styles and espouses a direct path to correct technique; the Void scroll states the need for incessant training and the state of the "void" that is reached as the culminating pinnacle of training. Based on this overall structure, the present study will assess the information contained within *Heihō sanjūgokajō*, the basis for *Gorin no sho*, and will attempt to consider how this book theorizes the martial Ways with regard to technical principles in *kenjutsu*.

(a) Basics of techniques—training of mind and body

The Water scroll analyzes the fundamentals of combat in great detail. Firstly, in *Heihō kokoromochi* (state of mind required in *heihō*), Musashi states that when practicing military tactics there should be no excessive tension or carelessness. He states, "make your mind broad and straight, do not overstretch it, but allow no slack...place the mind in your centre, fluctuate your mind quietly, never let it stop." Such advice is not so much a theory on the training of the mind that relies on Zen or other ideologies, but is clearly a practical instruction for how to deal with a true combat situation. In the latter half, he writes that the adept should cast off any misunderstandings, keep the mind pure, and be determined in everyday life to unceasingly hone one's wisdom and sharpen the mind.

He then describes in great detail, from head to foot, how the body should be when holding a sword in readiness for combat. He states that the body should be mostly erect, both shoulders lowered and relaxed, assuming a posture where the hips lead, directing energy into the knees and down into the toes, maintaining stability no matter what the surface, whether it be sand dunes, swamp, or other terrain. The phrase "*kusabi o shimuru*" means tightening the stomach via the scabbard held at one's waist, which indicates a physical position where the *tanden* (lower abdominal region) is substantiated. As one never knows when or where one will be attacked, Musashi advocates special attention to the whole body leaving nothing off guard, and urges a stance (*kamae*) paying "attention from the head to the soles of the feet, with no imbalance" (*Heihō sanjūgokajō*). He also writes that the thumbs should rise slightly when holding a sword and that the ring and little fingers should be where strength is concentrated. What Musashi desired was a "gradual readiness of encounter between the hands and the sword, without stiffness, and ease for proper cutting technique", enabled by a "living body" that can move immediately whenever and however required.

Musashi promotes habitually moving the feet left and right when striking with a single sword, and striking with total concentration and unification of the whole body. He negates the use of jumping, as the upward motion and the landing lead to an over settling in one spot. He looked for no deviation in the line of the hips, and a style of movement consisting of stable sliding in the direction the adept was attempting to move.

In regards of where to fix one's gaze, Musashi states that one's "observational sight should be strong, and [one's] looking eye weak." He advocates wrinkling one's brows, viewing that which is distant as near, and the near as distant. Do not move the eyeballs, or look both to the left and right sides, and "know your opponents sword, but do not look at it one bit."

As we can see, Musashi writes in detail on how the fundamentals of combative movement should be integrated into natural body movement, and clarifies the method of preparation for this. Thus, one can glean an image of how movement ought to have been done originally in the martial arts. Moreover, he asserts that one should be careful in everyday life with regard to one's state of mind, appearance, and sight, and clearly expresses the need to always be training in the basics of the art be it combat oriented or otherwise.

(b) Rationale of sword use—principles and methods of training

Musashi states that the stances (*kamae*) of the sword are the "stances of the five-directions": upper, middle, lower, left side, and right side. In actual combat, stances are varied as the easiest stance for attacking the enemy depends entirely on the situation. However, viewed from the direction of the sword, the stances can be put into five categories. The various *kamae* are considered variations that combine the five directions, and in actuality, his theoretical principles derive from the idea that there are an infinite number of stances.

The technical principles of sword-use centre on the "way of the sword" (*tachi no michi*). The sword has weight, curvature, and it cuts through pulling or with an upward sliding motion. The sword is not to be swung with brute strength or quickly with reckless abandon; it must be wielded with just the right strength and speed making use of the sword's curvature and weight. From the assumed *kamae*, the sword should be guided effortlessly, unconsciously, and naturally. Use of the sword in accordance to *tachi no michi* infers that the wielder is paying attention to how the body feels when one strikes, which must be natural and smooth. By sharpening one's senses and skills through unremitting training, the adept will begin to have an exquisite understanding of *tachi no michi*

The training method for mastering this *tachi no michi* is through pre-defined forms (*kata*) called *itsutsu no omote* (the five fundamental techniques). In other *ryūha*, typically several dozen *kata* were ordered into stages such as *shoden* (first transmissions), *chūden* (middle transmissions), *okuden* (esoteric transmissions), and *gokui* (innermost secrets), with techniques of the next stage only being taught once a licence of mastery had been obtained for the respective preceding levels. It is usual for the method of performing *kata* to be written in great detail, as they constitute a pivotal role in the teachings of any tradition. Musashi, however, believed that one could learn all the ways of application afterwards if one first mastered the *tachi no michi* or way of using the sword from the five *kamae*. The various stances were summarized in the five directions, and constituted a mere five *kata*. The *itsutsu no omote* was a model for movements adapted to the *tachi no michi* from the five-directional stances, and Musashi emphasizes by simplifying the explanation of their performance and by repeated training in these *kata*, the adept would be able to grasp via their own senses the most rational and effective way to use the sword. When one comes to this understanding, Musashi states, the adept will be able to distinguish just how skilled their opponent is merely by looking at the movement of their sword.

Musashi cautions readers that one should use *ukō mukō*, that is, while there are stances (for each particular enemy) there is no "predetermined stance". He is speaking of not being overly caught up in a stance when engaging in actual combat, and of how one ought to be creative in finding the most appropriate stance at that point in time. That is, a stance that allows for the best possible attack on the opponent, and also facilitates defence if necessary. Writing this cautionary note after the description of the five *kata* is to encourage creative thinking in finding the easiest swing of the sword. He emphasizes that the adept should not become attached to predetermined forms.

Along with extracting principles from actual techniques, Musashi also indicates training methods for their acquirement. Musashi does not go into detail regarding the actual performance of the *itsutsu no omote kata*, but insists that it is important to know the *tachi no michi* through their practice.

While it is important that *Gorin no sho* clearly describes the meaning of *kata* training in *budō*, we must be careful not to be complacent with his idea of *kata*. In the Water scroll, which delves into the use of the sword, it does not touch at all upon the points of attack and defence with one's opponent. However, it does explain that in *kata* training where blows are exchanged with a training partner, it is important to perform technique in accordance with their rhythm (*hyōshi*), distancing, and other idiosyncrasies of that opponent. It is necessary to interpret this in combination with another of Musashi's posthumous writings that describes points regarding attack.[15]

(c) Methods of combat—practical devising

At the beginning of the Fire scroll that explains the way of combat, Musashi describes how to choose the position for battle. No matter where one fights, whether it is on a narrow mountain path, river bank, muddy rice field, indoors, or some other location, one should choose a spot with firm footing with even the slightest elevation over your opponent, forcing them into a position of uneven footing where obstacles impede their way. He advocates taking a position with the sun at your back, as the opponent will be dazzled but your view will be unimpeded. In this way he is stating that one ought to first "win the best position" for fighting. This well indicates the principle of combat where one needs to be creative in devising ways to remain in an even a slightly more advantageous situation than the enemy.

Musashi then goes on to describe the three *"sen"* (advantage) through an analysis of various fighting situations. These are *ken no sen*, where one attacks one's opponent; *tai no sen*, where one entices the opponent to attack first; and *taitai no sen*, where both sides attack at the same time. With *ken no sen* one seems calm and then suddenly unleashes an attack whether the opponent approaches or not. In *tai no sen* one displays weakness and strikes forward forcefully when the opponent makes a careless attack. In *taitai no sen* one attacks strongly and calmly if the opponent attacks quickly, and one attacks lightly and vigorously when the opponent attacks calmly. Either way, Musashi is stating that one must control *sen*, that being the initiative in combat.

The latter half of the Water scroll mentions tricks for gaining the initiative by turning the opponent's methods back on them by immediately striking with one rhythm (*ichi byōshi*), feinting a strike and then attacking (*ni no koshi*), free from all distracting thoughts and without showing intention to strike, or by striking with a "delayed rhythm". He also states that if the opponent is unguarded, one should triumphantly move into their space.

In a competitive environment the warrior must calmly predict the enemy's skill and mindset in light of the "principles of *tachi no michi*". If the opponent's movements are unpredictable, try to sound out their defences. Predicting the opponent's movements in this way, sensing the beginnings of their technique and intention to attack, making preparation in order to answer any possible mode of attack, and clearly demonstrating that if attacked one would immediately return the attack, the opponent will be unable to launch any techniques (*makura no osae*). Musashi also says that if the enemy strikes once, trample them with your sword, body, and mind, so that they will not attack a second time (*ken o fumu*).

As described above, when trading blows with an opponent, take a "living body" stance that can immediately change to suit any situation, and prepare to execute techniques with effortless movement in accordance to the natural way of using the sword that will cause the enemy to contravene the "principles of the way of the sword". In the Water scroll, Musashi advocates causing the opponent to bend backwards by incessantly pointing the tip of the sword at their face, neck, and chest. Furthermore, he encourages creativity in psychological aspects of dealing with each situation. His tactics include unsettling the opponent by taking them by surprise, making them angry, startling them, and injuring them anywhere on the body. Musashi's method of attack was to destroy the opponent's stance in this way, make them stationary, and then when they attempted a forced unnatural move, to then go completely on the attack without giving them time to recover.

Musashi also touches on the mental attitude required in combat. One should be unrelenting until the enemy utterly believes they have lost. Musashi suggests that the warrior should look upon their opponent in combat as a soldier who moves according to your commands. He also stresses the importance of fighting at one's own pace, and being daring whilst paying careful attention to what is going on in the broader picture.

When simultaneously engaging in combat against a number of opponents, he suggests fighting with a broad stance with a sword in each hand, distinguishing which will attack first, and then cutting the opponent who approaches from the front first, followed by the opponent approaching from the side with the returning blade.[16] Restrict and direct the enemy's movement, and by cutting through where they are bunching together, Musashi says, "even ten or twenty opponents will not pose a concern." One can infer Musashi's self-confidence garnered from actual experience.

While Musashi states "don't think too hard about the details of my Way, and you will attain the knowledge of *hyōhō* which will result in victory in any situation", his technical and tactical theories were rational, and he calculated various forms and creative methods that would lead to victory in combat.

(d) Indicating the errors in other ryūha, and confirming the "correct way"

Musashi indicates the errors in the various methods of fencing of other schools in the Wind scroll of *Gorin no sho*, without making specific reference to their names. His concern is that later generations will lose sight of the "Way", and he specifies errors that are easily fallen into and attempts to show the "correct way". His arguments are based on whether the respective techniques would actually be useful in the various arenas of actual combat.

While there are advantages in being particular about using a longer sword or a shorter one, or using a particular way of looking, or of footwork, these things can also turn out to be a disadvantage in some situations. According to Musashi, relying on predetermined stances, pre-defined *kata*, and so on, actually constitutes a wavering mind. A stance enabling effortless and stable attack and defence is obviously good, but as there is an infinite number of ways by which to cut down enemies, to needlessly hark on about the advantages of one sword over another, or to emphasize speed or other individual elements, is to go against the most natural *tachi no michi*. This leads to forced actions and improper cutting, both in technique and in opportunity. Warning against "concentrating on the fine details and forgetting the larger issues", the warrior must continually correct techniques while looking at their overall application.

There is no "innermost secret sword [technique]" that will ensure victory. Musashi negated the practise of swearing students to secrecy when imparting to them the techniques and philosophy of his *ryūha*, as was usually the case with other schools. He also negated the idea common among other schools of secretly transmitting knowledge, from initial teachings through to inner secrets in stages, as no such distinctions would be made in a practical combat situation. "In the same field, why are there many different ways?" (*Gohō no tachi no michi*). Musashi was confident that if anybody pursued the way of military tactics thoroughly, they would arrive at the same point that he did.

Musashi's philosophy was to watch the student, and teach them aspects that they found easiest to perform, and then gradually make the content more complete. Teaching the "correct way" mentioned in the Water and Fire scrolls, the student would then be encouraged to dispel erroneous impressions and habits so that they naturally enter the "true way" of the warrior. This was ultimately Musashi's method of teaching.

(e) The way of mastery and the opened world

Musashi mentions the necessity of "thoroughly" training in the art. "A journey of one thousand leagues is accomplished by taking one step at a time." One ought to "think that today we will defeat the self of yesterday, tomorrow we will defeat ineptitude, and later we will defeat skilfulness", "one thousand days of training to forge, and ten thousand days to temper." He advocated that the warrior must build up a stock of training over many long months and years.

Moreover, as we have seen so far, the adept must always be prepared in training to expel all habits and leave no unguarded moments in their daily posture and movements. They must constantly use their accrued wisdom to ensure comfortable victory while continually refining the mind. Accordingly, training in the way of strategy ought to be carried out as a part of daily life, while training in the techniques of the sword. As Musashi writes at the end of the Earth scroll under the topic of "method for practicing the Way", one should learn from the various arts and occupations, develop intuitive judgement and understanding for everything, distinguish between gain and loss in worldly matters, and selectively choose that which one needs, and incorporate that knowledge into one's being.

A warrior should not only aim to excel in *kenjutsu*, but should strive to succeed over others in all physical and psychological posturing. Moreover, Musashi also states in the Earth scroll that the warrior must excel in such situations as a general using his men advantageously, or in ruling a province, fostering a nation's people, and in all other possible paths and occupations, great or small. The tactical training that Musashi spoke of permeated all facets and levels of the warrior's life in this way, not just combat.

In order to thoroughly master this way, Musashi suggests thinking of "the large place", "the void". The "void" that Musashi spoke of is the concept of a "non-existential place" contrasted with the "existential place" of specific actions. As the warrior becomes caught up in "mental partiality for each respective posture, and distortions of each respective view" while they are still ignorant of the "sincere way" (*makoto no michi*), and even if they think themselves to be acting appropriately, they must fix their minds on the void and constantly improve themselves, persistently re-capturing the self. It is through this way alone that one can thoroughly practice the way of strategy and not be caught up in other matters or be contented in one place.

"Once reason (*dōri*) is understood, free yourself from it"—if one can experientially acquire intuitive reason then one may move in accordance with reason without being conscious of it any longer. The warrior will then be able to "strike naturally, and one will hit the opponent". While moving in conjunction with reason, drive the opponent back, and then strike them when they move against reason. In *heihō*, if the warrior can become "oneself and free" in this way, then the respective *dōri* will become clear in other Ways (arts), and an appropriate method will make itself apparent.

Musashi states that after the warrior has "worked hard in the martial arts" and also after having refined the self daily "without neglecting training for a minute" in "applying oneself in the Way practiced by the warrior", the "sincere void" then reveals itself to be "a place of no gloom where the clouds of delusion are cleared away." The state attained at the end of thorough training in *heihō* involving all aspects of life, is a way of living without illusion, and is spiritually lucid. In this way, one will be able to naturally achieve actions that are suited to the Way in all things, not just in military strategy. One "enters the sincere way naturally."

As can be seen from (a) to (e), *Gorin no sho* establishes martial arts training as something that ought to be pursued in daily life and throughout one's lifetime.

IV. Positioning in Japanese Intellectual History— The Meaning of *Gorin no sho*

When one attempts to posit *budō* and its thought in the greater realm of philosophical history, problems may appear from the following perspectives.

(1) Positioning within budō history

With the history of the *budō* up until the present time, many problems appear such as defining the way in which the topic is posited, the historical and social context, relations with contemporary *budō* exponents, generational influences, and relevance to the modern-day.

(2) Placement within Japanese cultural delineations

The meaning of the topic within Japanese philosophy or thought overall, and culture outside the framework of *budō* itself requires scrutiny. The martial Ways were established under the influence of other traditional arts, and also in an ideological sense greatly influenced by Zen. Some interpretations of *budō* were influenced not only by Zen, but also more broadly by Buddhism, Shinto, and philosophies of Confucianism and the Chinese philosopher Zhuangzi (Wade-Giles: Chuang-tzu). Furthermore, there are various issues concerning the position of *budō* within warrior society in the Tokugawa period, the relationship to and influence of Western sports in the modern period, and the various social strata that had access to *budō*, what they discovered, and so on. These all need to investigated.

(3) Contemporary meanings

As *budō* continues to grow in popularity internationally, what meaning does it hold from an ideological perspective, and what sort of contribution can it make to the development of world culture in the future? The conceptualizing of the present-day meaning of the various *budō* arts is a growing area of investigation.

Bearing these issues in mind, I would like to put forth in simple terms what can be gleaned from research into the meaning of Miyamoto Musashi's *Gorin no sho*.

(1) Positioning within budō history

The period in which Musashi lived, the end of the sixteenth century until the first half of the seventeenth century, saw the establishment of systemized *ryūha* based *kenjutsu* which took on great significance in warrior society. In the mid-sixteenth century, figures such as Tsukahara Bokuden, Kamiizumi Ise no Kami Nobutsuna, and Itō Ittōsai made many innovations which contributed greatly to the formation of the three major schools of fencing which became the basis for a plethora of future traditions, the Shintō-ryū, Shinkage-ryū, and Ittō-ryū. In the latter part of the sixteenth century, which saw the gradual unification of Japan after a tumultuous period of civil war, the students of these master swordsmen, the second generation of students in the schools, found employment as martial arts instructors for the various *daimyō*, including Japan's eventual unifier Tokugawa Ieyasu. Musashi's adoptive father also formed the Tōri-ryū which was greatly influenced by the Shinkage-ryū, and he also found employment as an instructor to a *daimyō* in his latter years.

As these new systematized schools of *kenjutsu* gained sway in society, the third generation was subjected to comprehensive training regimes in the various styles from a young age. At the beginning of the seventeenth century, society was still unstable with the Tokugawa shogunate only just being established, and individuals with special martial ability were given preferential treatment, especially when looking for employment. *Musha shugyō* became popular during this period and warriors competed for position and privilege. Musashi, who is said to have won over sixty fights in his twenties, survived living in a world where such rivalry was at its most intensive.

When the Tokugawa wiped out the Toyotomi in the siege of Osaka castle in 1615, they strengthened their control by issuing various edicts directed at the *daimyō*, the imperial court, and temples and shrines. Japan was thus ushered into a 250-year period of peace. Within these great societal changes, the meaning and role of swordsmanship was questioned once more.

In *Heihō kadensho* (1632) Yagyū Munenori (1571-1646), a martial arts instructor to the shogun's family, stated that the "killing sword" (*setsunin-tō*) of "a world of war" must be a "life-giving sword" (*katsujin-ken*) to bring prosperity and peace in a peaceful world. While basing the actual techniques on the inventory of his father Yagyū Sekishūsai Munetoshi, he incorporated the teachings of the Zen monk Takuan Sōhō, emphasized the importance of the spiritual aspect of *heihō* and the "void", and advocated the practice of sword technique in a state of "no mind".[17] The concept of the "sword and Zen as one" (*kenzen-itchi*) suited an age in which war had become a thing of the past. Through his capacity of being martial arts instructor to the shogun, his ideals grew in popularity, and exerted great influence on martial arts theories overall, and are still often referred to in modern times.

At the same time, however, Yagyū Hyōgonosuke (1579-1650), an instructor to the Owari-based Tokugawa family had succeeded the third generation of the Shinkage-ryū from his grandfather Munetoshi, wrote critically of the emphasis on "spirituality" in his book *Shijū fujasho* (1620; 1649). Instead, he placed emphasis on technical fundamentals, and negated unnatural techniques without ease of movement, even those taught by school-founder Kamiizumi, or the teachings of Munetoshi. He wrote comments that had more in common with Musashi's theories rather than those of Munenori, whose he had inherited.[18] It is thought that Hyōgonosuke's analysis of these issues was greatly influenced by his study of other schools during his *musha shugyō* experience. Hyōgonosuke's theories, however, were mostly limited to technical application in combat, and he did not write as Munenori and Musashi did of the deeper psychological meaning or applications of *kenjutsu*.

Seen from the perspective of *budō* history, Munenori, Hyōgonosuke, Musashi, and other prominent figures, belonged to the third generation of *kenjutsu*, and lived during a period of constant change. Thus, rationalizing swordsmanship and the establishment of organized styles was an important issue for them. Their efforts and influence on those in power brought about a reinterpretation of *budō* from actual combat martial arts to martial Ways linked to personal development.

Musashi, a third generational figure who had much success in combat against students of other schools, was a warrior who pursued universal principles for utilization in actual battle. He emphasized mastery of technical fundamentals, extracted and clarified important principles, gave much consideration to training methodology, and eventually set forth one of the most thorough and influential ways for training.

The subsequent fourth generation of swordsmen saw the disappearance of actual combat opportunity. Inter-*ryūha* contests and *musha shugyō* were banned, *ryūha* succession became hereditary, and spiritual interpretations for the martial arts were greatly developed.[19] *Ryūha kenjutsu* centred on repetitive *kata* practice, and became increasingly ostentatious and impractical, and "stagnated" (*kahōka*) from the latter part of the seventeenth century. *Shinai kenjutsu,* in which adepts put on protective equipment and struck each other with bamboo swords, was developed to allow freedom in actual striking, and from the early nineteenth century onwards *gekken* (or *gekiken*), a form of *shinai kenjutsu* became widely practiced. While *ryūha kenjutsu* continued *kata* practice with wooden swords as it had done in the past, the *shinai kenjutsu* form of the art allowed contests between different schools, which in turn promoted more enthusiastic training. *Shinai kenjutsu* had gained immense popularity by the end of the Tokugawa period, and became the matrix for the birth of modern kendo.

In the Tokugawa period, Musashi's school was continued as Niten Ichi-ryū and

Miyamoto Musashi's Gorin no sho

Enmei-ryū in such areas as Kumamoto, Fukuoka, and Nagoya. Despite the fact that *Gorin no sho* negated that the writings were the "secret transmissions" by Musashi himself, the book and its content became exclusive to the Niten Ichi-ryū from the third generation onwards. Thus, its content was for the most part unknown to those outside the school during the Tokugawa period.

The point at which people were able to freely gain access to the teachings contained within *Gorin no sho* was with the publication of the 1909 book *Miyamoto Musashi*, edited by *Kenshōkai*. Takano Sasaburō's *Kendō* (1915) described a new rationalization of modern kendo and gave methods for its teaching, of which the influence of Musashi's teachings is obvious. *Kendō* quotes from *Gorin no sho* in various places, and in the appendix the entire text is reproduced. Much of the subsequent kendo literature is a reworking of Takano's book. This, however, provides only technical knowledge necessary for *shinai*-based kendo, and I do not believe that the philosophy behind *Gorin no sho* has been truly interpreted and applied.

Now that we have obtained a clear image of Musashi, we can begin to understand the works he authored from a young age. In the future, there is a need to promote an accurate understanding of *Gorin no sho*, and to consider its position in the history of *budō*, and in the development of *budō* from now.

(2) Placement within Japanese intellectual history

Gorin no sho emphasizes the phrase, the "Way of strategy". From his thirties, Musashi pursued a "more profound principle" for the martial arts, and attempted to theorize combat while learning Zen and the ways of other arts.

Before *budō*, the ways of the arts (*geidō*) were established with the emergence of so-called *ryūha* from the medieval period onwards. Theoretical texts were written for such arts at noh theatre and the tea ceremony. Theory on performing arts by Zeami (1363-1443) is the first theoretical text on the arts that appeared in the early fifteenth century. Zeami understood art as a "way" toward human perfection. His ideal actor achieved flawless responsiveness to audiences and expressive freedom. His writings displayed arguments that struck a common accord with those of Musashi in analysis of the arts based on actual knowledge, and one's own physical senses. It gave a theory to the importance of life-long training and learning, in order to excel in the intense contests seen in *sarugaku* and *dengaku* performances.[20] The tea ceremony, which developed in the sixteenth century, took the austere refinement of *wabi* as its base for aesthetic feeling and spoke of "Tea and Zen as one" from the influence it received from Zen, and also carried on the ideology of lifelong training. Zen philosophy asserted that if one achieved a state of "no-mind" (*mushin*) in training, then truth would manifest everywhere. From this, performing arts and martial arts aimed for "no-mind techniques", and it is thought that the philosophy of the "Way" was established in trying to attain the ultimate truth through training and physical experience of that state.[21]

Gorin no sho gives examples from Confucianists, Buddhists, *sukisha* (practitioners of the way of tea), and *rambusha* (noh performers), and speaks that "one knows the Way in a wide sense, one comes into contact with all things." It attempts to show in all places that the reasoning behind *heihō* can be comprehended in the various performing arts. The nine articles given as the "methods for performing the Way" in the Earth scroll can be described as knowledge that is comprehended not only in *budō*, but also in the various arts. The phrase "if one performs the ways of the various arts with reliance upon the logic of military tactics, one will never have need of a teacher" is also proven by Musashi's superb ink paintings. If one knows one way thoroughly and perfectly, then that will hold true in all things.[22]

Musashi attempted to show the way a warrior should live by explaining the Way of strategy. Influenced by the fact that he came from a family that lost their status as warriors, Musashi's thinking on the concept of the warrior was intense, and he believed that a warrior was one who "made it a principle to outdo people in all areas", win in all things, "gain fame and make a career for oneself", and to become a superior leader. He represented the consciousness of an experienced and ambitious Sengoku period warrior who strove to advance in every aspect of life. Later in his career, he lived within the framework of a stable domain in which the possibility of war had been almost removed. Still, he was clearly different to many of his contemporaries who came to place importance on unwavering loyalty to their lord, and upon the formalities of social status instead of combat readiness.[23]

Viewed in this light, *Gorin no sho* is an expression of the philosophy of a warrior who stood up as an individual and possessed a spirit of independence and self-respect. He created a unique but universal philosophy of the Way from his relentless training and experience in the martial arts .

(3) Contemporary meanings of Gorin no sho

What meaning does Musashi's *Gorin no sho* hold in the modern world? Without being caught up in a particular tradition or specific ideology, Musashi excelled in the Way of strategy. With a broad view of the other styles to deepen his overall understanding, he carefully considered physical sensations, and developed an extremely rational theory based on and certified through his own combat experience. While *Gorin no sho* is definitely a volume born from Japanese tradition, it most certainly has a universal aspect to it that transcends this limited framework. One intuitively feels that *Gorin no sho* is a superb text of universal application, especially when considering its current international popularity, despite the oversights in the translations, lack of sufficient research, and many misunderstandings.

In a society in which computer technology has advanced, and we are inundated by massive volumes of information, we must reconsider the role and enormous potential that physical culture and *budō* has as a means towards restoring a more humanistic lifestyle. Such motives are advocated, for example, in the official "*Concept of Kendo*" (All Japan Kendo Federation), formulated to reinstall consciousness of kendo as a Way of life. *Gorin no sho* truly evokes a powerful image of the potential of a Way that is not seen in contemporary sports literature. I believe that for the rapidly transforming contemporary *budō* arts which are increasingly placing emphasis on competition results, *Gorin no sho* provides a tremendous source of information on the original form of *budō*, the martial Ways.

Miyamoto Musashi's Gorin no sho

Endnotes

[1] The appearance of folkloric documentation begins with the publication of Hinatsu Shigetaka's *Honchō bugei shōden* (Brief biographies of Japanese martial art heroes, 1716). This book gives the Musashi Memorial Monument (*Kokura hibun*) (1654) established by Musashi's adopted son, Miyamoto Iori. Musashi's name gained fame after the acclaimed 1737 *kabuki* and puppet show narrative production of *Katakiuchi Ganryūjima* (Duel at Ganryūjima island), the themes of which were subsequently taken up in theatres, storytelling, textbooks, and in other media. In 1776 Toyoda Kagehide's biography, *Niten ki*, appeared. While this text is the basis for popular contemporary biographies, it contains much that was changed or added if compared to *Bukōden* written by his grandfather.

[2] Refer to the dedication board (1653) at Tomari shrine where Musashi's adopted son, Iori, was born, and the *Miyamoto ke keizu* (Miyamoto family genealogical table- 1848) that comes directly from Iori. The popularly held belief that Musashi was the son of Mimasaka province's Hirata Muni was advocated through *Tōsakushi* (1815) by the *Musashi iseki kenshōkai* edited book, *Miyamoto Musashi* (1909). While this theory became famous through the novel *Miyamoto Musashi* by Yoshikawa Eiji, the historical material it is based on is problematic.

[3] By way of an award for distinguishing himself in battle with the cross-shaped spear (*jūmonji yari*), Musashi's adoptive father, Munisai, was awarded a dispensation that allowed him to take the family name of his master Shinmen. (Musashi also takes the family name Shinmen in *Gorin no sho*). It is thought that Munisai was awarded the title "matchless under the sun" after defeating the shogunal family's tactical instructor, Yoshioka Kembō, in a contest performed before the last shogun of the Muromachi period, Ashikaga Yoshiaki (*Kokura hibun*). Some students of the Nitō-ryū style used the name Musō-ryū. Photos and a translation of *Tōri-ryū mokuroku* (Inventory of the Tōri-ryū) appear in the document section of my book, *Miyamoto Musashi—Nihonjin no michi*.

[4] The record of the Kuroda family (*Keichō nenjū samuraichū jisha chigyō kakitsuke*), records the title of vassal (*Kogofudai*) for Munisai before the battle of Sekigahara. Tanji Hōkin, who hailed from the family of the chief retainer of the Kuroda domain, asserted in his book, *Bushū genshinkō denrai* (1727), that he had participated in the battle of Ishikibaru, and the castle sieges of Yasuki and Tomiku. The anecdotal tales from the time of the castle sieges found in this book were probably tailored to seem to be factual, although they are really fictional accounts. However, there is a high probability that his participation in these battles is factual.

[5] *Heidōkyō* has been identified as a work of Musashi completed in his youth. He records that "Enmei-ryū is the greatest of all", and writes in a postscript that he suddenly decided to record the secrets of the art "around early winter of the ninth year of the era Keichō (1604)".

[6] In his later years when asked by the senior retainer of the Kumamoto domain what weapons he had used in his victory over Kojirō, Musashi had fashioned a wooden sword himself, and then presented it to him. There is an extant well-balanced 126-centimetre long sword carved from the evergreen oak (*shirakashi*). In the folkloric tradition of the contest as recorded in the *Ogura hibun* nine years after Musashi's death, "both men came together at the same time", Musashi meeting the attack of Kojirō's "three-foot naked sword" and defeating him with "one blow of his wooden sword." The famous tale of Musashi showing up to an appointed time exceedingly late and then fighting with a wooden sword fashioned from an oar was created from several combined stories that still existed at the time in the

Niten ki appearing 130 years after Musashi's death.

[7] *Heihō kakitsuke* is a fourteen-chapter document on the rationale of technique that has been identified only recently. Please refer to footnote 14. Philological research and translations are given in the document section of my previously mentioned book.

[8] It appears that *Gorin no sho* was handed to one of Musashi's direct pupils, Terao Magonojō, one week before Musashi's death in the form of "the original manuscript, as is" (*Magonojō sōden okusho*, '*Bushū genshinkō denrai*'). Magonojō got five of Musashi's pupils to begin copying the manuscript six years after Musashi's death. Restricting our view to only the completed manuscripts of the Tokugawa period, we see that there are presently ten copies in three different styles, and a comparative examination of these reveals that a revision of the omissions and miscopies in each copy is possible, and shows that there was probably a definitive original version. Refer to *Teihon Gorin no sho*.

[9] The copy of *Heidōkyō* made in 1604 has twenty-eight articles or chapters. The manuscript copies made in 1607, however, are made up of two volumes with a combined total of thirty articles or chapters, with the sentences being slightly rewritten and two articles or chapters added.

[10] These are copies with the endorsement of *Kan'ei 15 nen* (1638) *11 gatsu Shinmen Musashi genshin*, and the transmitted text of the Niten Ichi-ryū, however, the main text of the unsigned copy (*Gyoku senshū*, transcribed in 1759) agrees with their content. While both texts are unsigned, I have called them *Heihō kakitsuke* from the wording found in the endorsement.

[11] Single-page Chinese writing made into preface to the *Gohō tachi no michi*, without title, date, or signature. The characteristics of the paper suggest it is from the early Tokugawa period, and the handwriting agrees with samples of Musashi's writing that have been proven to be his. Handed down by Musashi's direct pupil, Terao Kumenosuke, as *Shiden no sho* (Teachings of the master). Toyoda Masatake, who studied under one of his pupils, wrote the extant annotated text, *Niten Ichi-ryū heihōsho joshō* (1707).

[12] Looking at the first English language translation that also became a best seller, Victor Harris's *A Book of Five Rings* (1974), there appear to be a number of incorrect readings of the Japanese, and a serious example of mistranslation includes the rendering of "*makura no osae*", which well expresses the method of fighting employed by Musashi, as "to hold down the pillow". This phrase refers to stifling one's opponent at the height of their swing when it is thought they will strike and thus render them unable to proceed with the action. The word *makura* (Japanese for pillow) does not refer to the pillow of one's bedding, but has the meaning of "initial, at the beginning", and should be translated as "to stifle (or suppress) the beginning of an attack". This mistranslation has been carried on through into recent translations. In the commentary on this translation that appeared in the mid-1970s amid Japan's striking economic growth, *A Book of Five Rings* was introduced as a business text, due to a Japanese businessman stating that he used the book as a business guide, and the author feels that the book was read with that idea in mind.

[13] *Heihō sanjūgokajō* stated that one "furthermore ought to verbally express points of doubt". While this book used the classification of the mind in the "mind of intent" and the "mind of the heart", in *Gorin no sho* these classifications were removed, and so the chapter on *hōshin* (free mind), *zanshin* (remaining mind) also disappeared. In addition the six chapters on *itokane* and other aspects have also been removed from *Gorin no sho*.

[14] The *heihō* spoken of by Musashi extends to all military aspects, and includes the "single tactics" of warriors and soldiers to the "great tactics" of generals. Accordingly, for methods

of fighting in the Fire scroll, his arguments elaborate upon the use of "single tactics" in battles of "great tactics".

[15] The *Gohō no kamae no shidai* (the order of the five directional stances), found in the expanded edition of *Heihō sanjūgokajō*, was treated with much importance as a folkloric tradition of the techniques of the art by the Niten Ichi-ryū in Kumamoto. For a discussion of this expanded portion as an example of the posthumous writings of Musashi, and for a technical interpretation combined with the description of *Gorin no sho*, refer to the document section of my book; *Niten Ichi-ryū no jutsugi denshō* (Folkloric tradition of techniques in the art of Niten Ichi-ryū) and *Teihon Gorin no sho*.

[16] In most published books of *Gorin no sho*, in the portion referring to confronting numerous enemies simultaneously in the Water scroll, there are forty characters omitted which made the content of the publicly released version difficult to comprehend.

[17] Whilst Yagyū Munenori had not advocated spiritual theories until the *Shinkage-ryū heihō kokoromochi* of six years previous, he quotes the Zen phrase "keep in mind the example of the master of the law (*hō*)" in the *Heihō kadenshō*. While Musashi consistently referred to the world that opens up through thorough training in the Way of military tactics as the "void", Munenori saw the "void" as "an eye into the teachings of Buddhism" and that while hard for one to achieve, a state of "no mind" (*mushin*) would entail one becoming at "one with thorough knowledge" who could freely use all techniques not just those of the sword.

[18] In the *Shijū fujasho* there is emphasis placed on the importance of basic technique with the initial sections of "Ten forbidden practices" and "Ten favourable practices", with cautions given even for the teachings from the founder onwards regarding "inflexibility", "stopping", and "unnecessary fixation". With regard to Munetoshi's comments of "the expelling of disease" and "the rhythm of the void", Munenori introduced aspects of Zen and spoke at length on psychospiritual elements, of which Hyōgonosuke dealt with respectively with short contradictory comments of "victory can also be attained when sick" and "there are certain things which cannot be penetrated".

[19] Yagyū Munenori's eldest son, Jūbei Mitsutoshi wrote *Tsuki no sho* (1643) that details the teachings of his grandfather and father; Hyōgonosuke's third son, Renya Toshikane, wrote *Shinkage-ryū heihō mokuroku* (1637), an oral history of the teachings of his great grand–father and father; and Kotōda Toshisada, who was the grandchildren of one of Itō Ittōsai's pupils, wrote *Ittōsai sensei kenpōsho* (1653). Furthermore, Kamiizumi to the fourth generational Harigaya Sekiun practiced Zen and received enlightenment within the Shinkage-ryū. Negating the *kenjutsu* that had been practiced up until that time as a matter of the "bestial mind", they proposed *kenjutsu* via an uninhibited mind that aimed for awakening to the "inborn nature" (*jishō hon'nen*) of things, and thus it was the middle of the seventeenth century when mental faculties began to be universally emphasized.

[20] After writing his first piece on the performing arts entitled *Fūshikaden* (1400) at the age of thirty-eight, Zeami wrote eighteen artistic treatises by his mid-seventies. It is said that the phrase *geidō* (the "Way" of art) was first coined by Zeami in his work *Kakyō* (1424).

[21] Zen was fully brought to Japan at the beginning of the thirteenth century from Sung dynasty China. From the middle of the fourteenth century, and with the backing of the Muromachi shogunate, Zen took on a remarkably influential role in the field of the arts in the expression of enlightened natural beauty in Chinese verse, ink painting, and *karesansui* (Zen style) Japanese gardens. In noh, Zeami also became a Zen monk at the age of sixty; and in the world of the tea ceremony, after Murata Jukō (1423-1502) became the pupil of

the Zen monk, Ikkyū Sōjun, many tea ceremony experts including Sen no Rikyū (1522-1591) practiced Zen meditation. In *kenjutsu*, furthermore, Yagyū Munenori practiced Zen under Takuan, and Hyōgonosuke practiced meditation at the Myōshinji temple. It appears that Musashi also practiced Zen from his youth, and that in the later years of his life in Kumamoto he was a close acquaintance of the Zen monk Daien Genkō. (The popularly held belief that Musashi had a friendship with Shunzan is mistaken).

[22] Musashi's ink paintings feature a many works depicting birds, the Zen Buddhist patriarch Bodhidharma, and Hotei, done symbolically with a minimum of brush strokes. Three of his works have been designated important national cultural assets and he is renowned in the history of Japanese ink painting as a great warrior-artist. Research into the ink paintings of Musashi is still incomplete, but between ten and twenty works have been mostly confirmed as true examples of his hand. Please refer to the document section of my work *Musashi no sho, ga, saiku* (Musashi's writings, paintings, and craftsmanship).

[23] Japanese warriors placed importance on 'name', and held in high esteem masculinity, courage, purity, and were strongly independent. The warriors of the Kamakura era promoted "favour for service" (*go'on hōkō*) where devotion to one's lord was emphasized, and reciprocal good favour was expected. Whilst there were retainers strongly devoted to their lords who even swore to share the same fate on the battlefield come what may, during the Warring States period when the "oppressed became the oppressors" (*gekokujō*) and wars were frequent, there were many who changed their allegiances in the hope of recognition of their abilities. There was an ambitious undercurrent of hoping to become a "lord of a castle" and a province through one's own ability. Musashi compares warriors to carpenters in the Earth scroll, and states if carpenters continually refined their technique and knew the principles of carpentry well, they could become a master builder, thereby showing if warriors master the way of strategy thoroughly, they could also become generals, or even the lord of a castle.

Bibliography

Miyamoto Musashi's works:
1. *Heidōkyo* (兵道鏡), 1605 cf. Notes 5.
2. *Heihō kakitsuke* (兵法書付), 1638 cf. Notes 8.
3. *Heihō sanjūgokajō* (兵法三十五箇条),1641.
4. *Gohō no kamae no shidai* (五方の構の次第), cf. Notes 15.
5. *Gohō no tachi no michi* (五方之太刀道), 1642-43.
6. *Gorin no sho* (五輪書), 1645.
7. *Dokkodō* (独行道), 1645 cf.

Texts 1 and 2 are published in *Miyamoto Musashi – Nihonjin no michi*.
Texts 3-7 are published in *Teihon Gorin no sho*.

Documents pertaining to Musashi's life:
1. *Kokura hibun* (Musashi's Memorial Monument at Kokura), 1654.
2. *Honchō bugei shoden* (written by Hinatsu Shigetaka), 1716.
3. *Bokoden* (written by Toyoda Masatake).

4. *Nitenki* (written by Toyoda Kagehide), 1776.
5. *Bushu genshin-ko denrai* (written by Tanji Hōkin), 1729.

Books about Musashi:
1. *Miyamoto Musashi Kenshōkai*, (ed.). *Miyamoto Musashi*. Kinkōdō Shuppanbu, 1909.
2. Maruoka Muneo (ed.) *Miyamoto Musashi Meihinshusei*, Kodansha 1977.
3. Takano Sasaburō. *Kendō*. Kendō Hakkōjo, 1915.
4. Uozumi Takashi. *Teihon Gorin no sho* (The standard text of *Gorin no sho*). Shinjinbutsuouraisha, 2005.
5. *Miyamoto Musashi – Nihonjin no michi* (Miyamoto Musashi: The way of the Japanese). Perikansha, 2002.
6. "Research of Miyamoto Musashi's *Gorin no sho*" in *Budo Studies*. International Budo University, 2000.

Chapter 3

Zen and Japanese Swordsmanship Reconsidered

William M. Bodiford
University of California, Los Angeles

Introduction

Today it seems widely accepted by people both in Japan and throughout the world that Zen Buddhism has played a prominent role in the pre-modern ethos of Japanese fencing (*kenjutsu* or *hyōhō*). The precise nature of this relationship, how it might have arisen, or why it should exist, however, rarely have been subjected to careful historical examination. Usually the link between swordsmanship and Zen is simply presented as an obvious fact and portrayed in a favourable light. In October 1978, for example, the Japanese mass-market magazine *Gekkan Kendō Nippon* (*The Kendo-Nippon Monthly*) published a special issue titled "Sword and Zen" (*Ken to Zen*; see figure 1). This issue presented stories of nine famous fencers who were said to have attained Zen awakening (*satori*), excerpts from fifteen pre-modern martial art treatises that were said to illustrate the unity of Zen and swordsmanship, as well as instructions on how to meditate in a lotus posture (*kekka fuza*; the same bodily position employed by Zen priests). The magazine's

Figure 1. Kendo Nippon cover

editors cite these sources as examples of how Zen can improve one's swordsmanship and of how swordsmanship can enhance human life and help its practitioners attain outstanding human virtues.

These purported benefits might very well exist. My purpose here is certainly not to dispute such assertions. Present-day adherents or practitioners of these endeavours can decide for themselves whether or not they find this combination beneficial. It is worth noting, though, that in the modern world incidents of individual athletes crediting this or that religion for their success are not rare. And even more frequently athletes liken the exaltations of physical endeavour to religious uplift. Athleticism and religion have been strongly related in popular culture since the Victorian age when doctrines such as "Muscular Christianity" (i.e., teaching Christian ethics through athletics) contributed to the development of our modern notions of sports and sportsmanship (Guttmann 1992; Mangan 1986 and 1992). One of the most extreme, and yet still representative, examples of the modern tendency to find religious and moral values in sport is Pierre de Coubertin (1863–1937), the founder of the modern Olympic movement, who believed that Olympic sports could function as a secular religion capable of supplanting the theistic creeds of Europe. This kind of thinking influenced the development of the modern Japanese notions of *budō* (martial Ways) and *bushidō* (warrior ethics, or Way of the warrior) that emerged during Pierre de Coubertin's lifetime (Bodiford 2001a). Thus, it is not surprising that many people can see the linkage of swordsmanship and Zen, like the association of any given sport with religious values, in positive terms.[1]

Nonetheless, recently several notable publications have portrayed the link between swordsmanship and Zen in a negative light. Winston L. King, in his 1993 book titled, *Zen and the Way of the Sword: Arming the Samurai Psyche*, unflinchingly and uncritically identifies Zen not just with swordsmanship, but also with the "samurai spirit" of pre-modern Japan, with the continuation of that same samurai ethos after 1868, with the rise of militarism in the 1930s, and with the suicidal methods of the Special Attack Forces (*Tokkōtai*; so-called Kamikaze) in 1945 during the closing days of the Pacific War (*Taiheiyō sensō*; or Second World War). He calls (p. 3) these developments "perversions of noble moral and religious ideals" comparable to the Crusaders of medieval Europe turning the Christian doctrine of love into a policy of killing Muslims.[2] Brian Victoria, in his *Zen at War* (1977), presents a scathing indictment of the entire Japanese Buddhist establishment for their overwhelming support of the militaristic policies of the Japanese government prior to 1945. He reserves his harshest criticism for Zen teachers, Zen priests, and lay Zen apologists who invoked images of Zen's relationship to swordsmanship as a means of justifying their attempts to equate military aggression with Zen teachings. He especially denounces Zen teachers who after 1945 went on to become prominent among Western practitioners of Zen. In this respect, Victoria's goal was not to write an objective historical account but to inoculate a Western audience against an uncritical acceptance of this Zen-sword mythos (Bodiford 1998).

In the face of these recent denunciations of "Zen and the sword" it becomes

Zen and Japanese Swordsmanship Reconsidered

important, I think, for us to try to determine more precisely the historical roots of this supposed relationship between religion and military arts. Before moving on to that subject, I must note that the "Zen" denounced by King and Victoria consists largely of modern intellectual interpretations of Zen that first appeared after 1868, the start of the Meiji period, and that were popularized most prominently by D. T. Suzuki. In this essay I want to focus on Zen as traditionally represented by Zen teachers prior to 1868. That is, I want to explicitly exclude from consideration all post-1868 interpretations of Zen, especially the "Zen and Japanese Culture" (*Zen to Nihon bunka*) types of *Nihonjinron* (examinations of the unique qualities of Japanese-ness) popularized by D. T. Suzuki and his contemporaries.

The kinds of interpretive issues raised by post-1868 models of Zen and their debt to modern Western notions of religion have already been explained and critiqued by many scholars, most notably by Bernard Faure (1993, 52–88) and Robert H. Sharf (1995).[3] Yamada Shōji (1999; translated into English, 2001) and I (Bodiford 2001a) have described, in separate essays, how these modern interpretations of Zen have contributed to an exaggerated estimate of the influence and role of Zen in post-1868 martial arts training. There is no need to repeat or rehearse those arguments here.

Henceforth, when I mention "Zen" I will be referring to certain religious teachings and practices that have been commonly identified as Zen Buddhism (*Zenshū, Zenmon, shūmon*) by members of Japanese Zen schools prior to 1868. The key feature of these teachings and practices is that their religious authority rests on the idea that they have been conveyed through an unbroken blood lineage (*kechimyaku*) from Śākyamuni Buddha (Shakuson) to China (via Bodhidharma, Daruma), and from China to Japan. The members of this lineage constitute the Buddhas and ancestors (*soshi*) who link present-day Zen teachers directly to Śākyamuni. Because of this direct connection to Śākyamuni, no one else but Zen teachers can provide authentic and reliable instruction in proper Buddhist practices, proper Buddhist precepts, proper Buddhist language, and proper Buddhist understanding (i.e., the so-called Buddha-dharma correctly conveyed by the Buddhas and ancestors; *Busso shōden buppō*). Unless one attains proper initiation into this lineage, then even the highest religious awakening or highest *satori* attained without a teacher (i.e., *mushi dokugo*) must be rejected as false. In other words, one must rely on the mediation of Zen priests to attain religious salvation (Bodiford 1991; 1999; 2000; 2001c). The ritual implications of this Zen doctrine can be seen in the medieval-period development of Japanese Zen funeral rituals for ordinary lay people who themselves do not practice Zen. In these early funeral rituals, Zen monks would dress the deceased body in Zen robes, perform a posthumous ordination ritual (*motsugo sasō*, or *motsugo jukai*), and then bestow a Zen lineage chart (*kechimyaku-zu*) on the deceased. As a result of this kind of ritual initiation into the Zen lineage, the deceased lay person, it is said, not only avoids rebirth in hell but also attains Buddhahood (Bodiford 1992; 1994b). This essay will focus on this kind of Zen, the Zen that derives its authority from Zen lineages.

Budo Perspectives

Zen and Japanese Swordsmanship Prior to 1868

The notion that Zen priests, Zen teachings, or Zen practices can benefit one's practice of swordsmanship is not an idea invented during the Meiji Period (1868–1912). Already by the middle of the Tokugawa period (1603–1868) a link between Zen and swordsmanship was widely assumed. We do not have public opinion polls from that period, of course. But we do know that authors of many treatises on martial arts felt it necessary to make comments in which they rejected the importance of Zen training for attaining martial art proficiency. Kubota Seion (1791–1866), one of the directors of military training for the Tokugawa government, for example, in his martial art textbook *Bujutsu kanyōshū* (Anthology of Martial Art Essentials) wrote:

"There are vulgar types who deceive people in regard to their swordsmanship. They say that the founder of our style prayed at such-and-such shrine and received divine initiation, or that he attained a divine dream, or he mastered their art through Zen, or that he was taught by mountain demons (*tengu*). All such stories are falsehoods." (Tominaga 1972, 62)

In the above passage Kubota Seion merely summarizes a similar assertion from the *Bushikun* (Warrior lessons) written in 1715 by Izawa Banryū (1668–1730). Izawa says:

"There are vulgar types who exaggerate and boast of their swordsmanship, saying that the founder of their style prayed at such-and-such shrine and received divine initiation, or that he attained a divine dream, or he mastered his art through Zen, or that he was taught by mountain demons (*tengu*). All of these statements are big lies. A god is merely one aspect of the bright virtue within one's own heart and thus can be grasped only by suddenly opening the spiritual residence within one's heart. It is not something that can manifest itself at a shrine. If it manifests itself, then it is not a god but a fox demon. Moreover, there has never been a case of someone who attained skill in swordsmanship by studying Zen. Even students of Zen must have a sword instructor. Mountain demons are just beasts. On what grounds should human beings, the most spiritually advanced of all living creatures, possibly try to learn from mountain demons or other such creatures?" (Tominaga 1972, 62–63)

Kubota Seion and Izawa Banryū (as well as many other Tokugawa-period writers) would not have felt it necessary to publicly repudiate the connection between Zen and swordsmanship unless the audience of their books believed it to exist.

Where would this notion have come from? Why would people have linked swordsmanship with Zen? No doubt popular warrior tales and stage drama must have played a role. Since I am not a specialist in pre-modern fiction or theatre, though, I will allow other scholars to explore those fields. (Of course, citing popular literature as a source merely begs the question as to its inspiration.) Usually, proponents of a link between Zen and swordsmanship cite three types of texts in support of this association. These three categories are: (1) popular treatises written by Zen monks; (2) treatises that advocate mental cultivation or breathing exercises; and (3) martial art texts that use vocabulary from Zen literature.

As far as I can detect from reading the secondary literature, scholars usually emphasize only the first two categories as authentic expressions of Zen's influence on swordsmanship. They commonly dismiss the third category as mere coincidence or historical accident. The late Tominaga Kengo (1883–1960)- whose posthumously published history of Japanese swordsmanship *Kendō gohyakunenshi* (Five Hundred Years of Japanese Swordsmanship; 1972) remains authoritative even today- suggested that martial art texts used Zen vocabulary only because during the sixteenth and seventeenth centuries when these texts were composed their authors were mostly illiterate warriors. When these illiterate warriors wanted to compose martial art initiation documents to give to their students, they would ask Buddhist priests (the most readily available literate members of society) to write down what they wanted to say. The priests, in turn, would use the only language they knew, which included much Zen terminology. As a result, many martial art techniques or exercises acquired Zen-sounding designations even though they have absolutely no relationship to actual teachings or practices of Zen Buddhist lineages.

Among other sources, Tominaga cites the following two texts in support of this conclusion. First, the *Byōkan chōgo* (Long Conversations While Sick) says:

"The curriculums (*mokuroku*) that function as diplomas for schools of swordsmanship and spear frequently use Zen terminology and teach Zen doctrines such as preventing the mind from wavering. The reason for this is because in former times warriors who were skilled at swords, spears, and other weapons, only knew about military affairs. They knew nothing about literary arts. Therefore, they would ask Zen priests to compose these documents which today have come to be regarded as important scrolls." (Tominaga 1972, 398)

Second, Tominaga cites the *Ittō-ryū mokuroku seikai bengi kyokuhi-ron* (Top secret treatise on the correct understanding of, and resolving doubts about the Ittō-ryū school's curriculum), which explains how the texts used in this school of swordsmanship evolved after the school's founder, Itō Ittōsai Kagehisa, conveyed them to his successor, Ono Tadaaki (1565–1628). It says:

"This curriculum (*mokuroku*) is not the curriculum that the founder, Kagehisa, gave to Ono Tadaaki. The founder's curriculum used rustic language and had a convoluted organization. If it had been conveyed to later generations, the traditions would have become lost, the exercises would have become confused, and ultimately the school's teachings (*ryūgi*) would have been harmed. Tadaaki became concerned, so he emphasized the essential points and eliminated the superfluous elaborations. Hearing that the abbot of the Sōsenji temple in Edo [modern Tokyo] at that time was a virtuous priest, Tadaaki personally met with him and they pondered each phrase one-by-one, reviewed each exercise, and composed the [current] curriculum." (Tominaga 1972, 386)

Tominaga's conclusion that the Zen vocabulary in martial art documents is unrelated to Zen teachings has become the standard interpretation repeated in practically all other scholarly publications on this topic. I wish to challenge this standard view. Below I will argue that literature belonging to the first two genres named above—(1) popular treatises written by Zen monks; and (2) other treatises that advocate mental cultivation or breathing exercises—actually convey very little Zen content. Contrary to popular opinion, they cannot be uncritically accepted as examples of Zen's influence on swordsmanship. Literature in the third category (martial art texts that use Zen vocabulary), on the other hand, can—at least in some cases—help us better understand the relationship between Zen Buddhism and swordsmanship. This argument rests on the simple observation that Confucian doctrines or Daoist exercises are not Zen teachings even when they are repeated by authors who happen to be members of the Zen clergy. When members of the Zen clergy teach Zen vocabulary, however, they are teaching something unique to Zen. No one else teaches Zen language.

Due to limitations of space, I will devote most of my remarks to the third category. Let me just briefly review a few representative texts from each of the first two categories. The texts mentioned in these two categories will, no doubt, be familiar to most readers since, for the most part, they are the same ones that were discussed by D. T. Suzuki in his book on *Zen and Japanese Culture* (1938; 1940; 1959).

Popular Treatises Written by Zen Monks

Without a doubt the martial art treatise most familiar to modern readers, whether in Japan or elsewhere, is the *Fudōchi shinmyō-roku* (Marvellous power of immovable wisdom) attributed to the Zen monk Takuan Sōhō (1573–1643). Written in the form of a personal letter to Yagyū Munenori (1571–1646), who served as fencing instructor to the Tokugawa family, Takuan's essay was first published in 1779, and it has been reprinted countless times ever since. When people write about Zen and swordsmanship, inevitably they cite Takuan's treatise.

The *Fudōchi shinmyō-roku*, however, is not the only treatise written by Takuan that has influenced Japanese martial arts. In 1621 Takuan wrote *Riki sabetsu-ron* (Distinguishing principle and material force), an introduction to the thought of the influential Chinese Neo-Confucian (*rigaku*) scholar Zhu Xi (Shu Ki, 1130–1200; a.k.a.

Zen and Japanese Swordsmanship Reconsidered

Zhuzi, Shushi). Although this second treatise has all but been forgotten today, during the Tokugawa period it was widely cited by practitioners of *jūjutsu* (the ancestor of modern judo), who modelled their teachings on Takuan's explanation of yin and yang (*in'yō*). The existence of this second treatise should serve to remind us that Takuan was not just a Zen monk. He was a highly educated prelate who was equally renowned for his Confucianism (Ishioka 1981, 176).

For a work nominally on swordsmanship, Takuan's *Fudōchi shinmyō-roku* is notable for its almost total lack of any of the technical vocabulary normally associated with Japanese fencing. It also contains little of the technical vocabulary of Zen. Even the words in the title, "immovable wisdom" (*fudōchi*) and "marvellous" (*shinmyō*) are not Zen terms. "Marvellous" is as likely, or more likely to appear in Neo-Confucian texts than in Zen literature.[4] Moreover, Takuan explains immovable wisdom in a manner very reminiscent of the immovable mind (*fudōshin*) that appears in the *Mencius* (*Mōshi*; Book 2A). As one of the Four Books (*Shisho*) endorsed by Zhu Xi's Neo-Confucianism, the *Mencius* was widely studied in Tokugawa times. *Mencius* Book 2A, with its description of the immovable mind and its explanation of how to cultivate flood-like vital energy (*kōzen no ki*), was of particular interest to warriors. Long sections of Takuan's treatise suggest that he was attempting to present a general Buddhist alternative (not a Zen alternative) to Zhu Xi's interpretation of *Mencius*. Takuan also discusses *Mencius*'s flood-like vital energy. Significantly, though, Takuan rejects the Chinese practice of concentrating the mind in the lower abdomen (*tanden*; i.e., lower field of cinnabar) that one normally associates with this kind of energy. Consider the passages below:

"From the viewpoint of the highest techniques of the Buddha-dharma, however, concentrating one's mind below the navel and preventing it from being moved by distractions is an inferior method, not the highest. It corresponds to a beginner's level of training, or to what Confucians refer to as serious-minded diligence (*kei*). It is no more than what *Mencius* [Book 6A] calls finding the lost mind (*hōshin*) [of humanity]. It is not a method that leads to higher progress…" (p. 12)

"[Neo-Confucians] explain the word "seriousness" (*kei*) as concentrating the mind on one task without wavering (*shuitsu muteki*).[5] It means that your mind is devoted to one object without other diversions. The essence of seriousness lies in being able to unsheathe your sword and cut without disturbing your mental composure. When you receive an order from your lord, it is especially important to serve him with this sense of seriousness. The Buddha-dharma also includes this sense of seriousness. For example, Buddhists sound the bell of devotion, when we strike a gong three times, place the palms of our hands together before addressing the Buddha. The sense of seriousness in Buddhist chanting is the same whether explained in Buddhist terms as being single-minded without disturbance (*isshin-furan*) or in Confucian terms as concentrated on one task without wavering. In Buddhism, however, this sense of seriousness is not the highest teaching. Controlling one's own mind and preventing it from becoming disturbed is the practice of a beginner. Buddhists continue in this kind of training only for as many months or years as needed to attain imperturbability so that even when the mind is allowed to wander, it retains full freedom. According to the Confucian teaching of seriousness, the mind must be kept in check. Because mental wandering is seen as a disturbance, the mind must not be given free reign even for an instant. While this practice is useful as a short-term technique for developing unflappability, if one trains in this way constantly, then it results in a loss of mental freedom. For example, it resembles pulling back on a cat's leash to prevent it from pouncing on a baby sparrow. When one's mind lacks freedom like a cat tied to a leash, then it cannot function freely in accordance with its needs. But if a cat is well trained, then it can be released from the leash to go where it may, even right next to the sparrow without pouncing on it. When the free-flowing mind is released and abandoned, like the cat off the leash, then it can wander everywhere without distraction and without becoming harried." (pp. 18–20)

If one adopts the position that anything taught by a Zen monk must be a Zen teaching, then the passages above (assuming that they were in fact written by Takuan) also must be Zen. Any one of the above statements, though, could just as easily have been written by a Japanese Buddhist monk from a Nichiren tradition, from a Pure Land (Jōdo) tradition, or from a Shingon tradition. None of these passages, not their vocabulary, assertions, or interpretations, contain any features that suggest an association with Zen traditions.

There is one more point to note about the passage translated above: a well-trained cat that will not kill a bird is a cat that has internalized a very strict sense of moral limits. In contrast to modern authors like Winston King and Brian Victoria, who have interpreted Takuan's so-called Zen swordsmanship as an immoral endorsement of killing and warfare, for Takuan this kind of immovability clearly implies a firm moral sense that cannot be swayed by fear, intimidation, or temptation. For this reason, we should not be surprised that the *Fudōchi shinmyō-roku* concludes with a series of moral admonitions addressed to Yagyū Munenori and expressed in Confucian terms:

"Because you [Munenori] have mastered swordsmanship to a degree unequalled in the past or present, you now enjoy an attractive rank, stipend, and reputation. You must not be ungrateful for this good fortune even while sleeping, but must always strive to totally requite this benefaction with the finest loyal service to your lord. The finest loyal service requires first that you think correctly, maintain your health, and be single-minded in your devotion to your lord. You must never resent nor criticize others, nor neglect your daily duties. In your own family, you should be exceedingly filial toward your father and mother, avoid even the slightest hint of infidelity in your marriage, observe correct ritual etiquette, and must not love a mistress nor practice pederasty. Do not presume upon your father or mother, but always observe social norms. In employing underlings, do not be guided by personal feelings. Merely promote good men so that they might admonish you for your shortcomings and correctly implement the government's policies, and demote bad men. When the bad men see the good men progress day by day, the bad men will naturally be influenced by your delight in the good, and they will abandon the bad and return to being good. In this way, ruler and minister, superior and inferior, will become good men, their desires will weaken, and they will end their extravagant waste. Then the country's treasury will become full, the people will grow wealthy, children will care for their parents, the strong will be charitable toward the elderly, and the country will rule itself. This is the beginnings of loyalty…" (pp. 23–24)

After Takuan, the Japanese Zen monk who has exerted the most profound influence on Japanese swordsmanship must be Hakuin Ekaku (1685–1768), the author of *Yasen Kanna* (Evening Chat on a Boat, 1757; see Shaw and Schiffer 1956; Takayama 1975; Waddell, 2002). This text explains in detail how to perform the breathing techniques that had been rejected by Takuan. That is, it provides instructions for concentrating the mind in the lower abdomen (*tanden*) to congeal the inner ocean of vital energy (*ki*). Several of Hakuin's disciples who became Zen teachers also taught these techniques. In particular they taught them to swordsmen in the Nakanishi lineage of the Ittō-ryū style of fencing. Swordsmen in this school relied on Hakuin's breathing techniques to enhance their vitality.

Here we have a clear case of teachings that were conveyed within a recognized Zen lineage and that were said to benefit one's swordsmanship. Although Hakuin's explanation of breathing remains well-known even today among practitioners of Japanese fencing, they are rarely mentioned in discussions of Zen and swordsmanship addressed to a wider audience. One reason why Hakuin is relatively ignored while Takuan garners all the attention probably is because Hakuin explicitly identifies his breathing techniques as Daoist methods of inner contemplation (*naikan*; i.e., embryonic breathing, *taisoku*). Hakuin advocates this Daoist breathing as a useful antidote to the debilitating effects of Zen methods of sitting meditation (*zazen*). He states that he learned these techniques in 1710 from a perfected Daoist (*shinjin*) named Hakuyū who was then between 180 and 240 years old.

In short, neither of the two most well-known and widely-read popular treatises written by Zen monks present teachings unique to Zen. Takuan's *Fudōchi shinmyō-roku* consists of a general Buddhist approach to issues of importance primarily to Confucians. Hakuin's *Yasen Kanna* focuses on Daoist teachings. Both of these works remain essential for our understanding of the religious and intellectual climate within which fencing was taught and studied. They cannot, however, inform us of any uniquely Zen approach to swordsmanship.

BUDO PERSPECTIVES

Treatises that Advocate Mental Cultivation or Breathing Exercises

The exact same conclusion can be reached regarding pre-modern treatises that were not written by Zen monks, but which do advocate some form of mental cultivation or breathing exercises.

A member of the Nakanishi lineage of the Ittō-ryū style of fencing named Shirai Tōru Yoshinori (1783–1843), for example, wrote a detailed account of how Hakuin's breathing methods are to be applied to swordsmanship. Shirai's treatise, the *Heihō michi shirube* (Guide to the Way of fencing), stands out as probably the most detailed account available of the esoteric aspects of swordsmanship. Shirai's treatise, however, is written in vocabulary that is even more Daoist and more obscure than Hakuin's writing. It contains no Zen vocabulary-and very little vocabulary that modern readers can understand.

Two more texts should be mentioned in this section. They are the *Tengu geijutsu-ron* (Performance theory of the mountain demons; 1727) by Issai Chozan (1659–1741) and an account of the swordsman Hariya Sekiun written by his student Kodegiri Ichiun (1630–1706). D. T. Suzuki discusses both of them in his *Zen and Japanese Culture* (1938; 1940; 1959), and they both appear in the 1978 issue of the magazine *Gekkan Kendō Nippon* mentioned above. They are perennial favourites in modern discussions of Zen and swordsmanship.

In *Tengu geijutsuron*, Issai Chozan adopts an uncompromising Confucian point of view. He asserts that "Zen monks have never conveyed the ultimate principles of swordsmanship" fasc. 1; p. 320). He argues that Zen teachings are impractical because Zen monks know of nothing worth fighting for. Being unconcerned with society:

"They abandon the proper relations between lords and ministers, are indifferent to punishments and commendations, ignore military readiness, regard the rites, music, punishments, and politics taught by the sages as childlike amusements." (fasc. 1; p. 320)

As a result, Zen monks attain nothing more than what Issai calls an "arrogant vacuity" (*gankū*, i.e., foolishness; fasc. 2; p. 326). To avoid this fate, Issai advocates the practice of Confucian forms of mental cultivation known as quiet sitting (*seiza*) in place of the sitting Zen (*zazen*) meditation taught by Zen monks (fasc. 4; p. 337).

People who are accustomed to defining Zen as a teaching that rejects all rituals might fail to appreciate the distinction between Confucian quiet sitting and the Buddhist techniques of sitting Zen. Both are the same in so far as they require long periods of sitting still while minding one's breathing. Quiet sitting differs from Zen meditation in so far as it eliminates all of the distinctive aspects of Buddhist ritual, such as sitting in the lotus posture, burning incense, observing fixed periods of time, chanting Buddhist scriptures, and so forth. The lack of these ritual features effectively removes quiet sitting from the confines of the Zen lineage and renders it a purely secular activity. As long as

Zen and Japanese Swordsmanship Reconsidered

we define Zen in secular terms, then treatises such as Issai Chozan's *Tengu geijutsu-ron* can be cited as expositions of Zen swordsmanship. As soon as we view Zen within its traditional religious context, though, the *Tengu geijutsu-ron* is revealed as an anti-Zen, Confucian text.

Kodegiri Ichiun's account of his fencing instructor, Harigaya Sekiun, in the treatise known either as the *Sekiun-ryū kenjutsu-sho* (Sekiun's style of swordsmanship) or as the *Kempō Sekiun sensei sōden* (The swordsmanship taught by master Sekiun) suffers from this same problem. It does not discuss Zen teachings as such, but advocates a Japanese form of Confucianism generally known as Heavenly Way (*Tendō*) thought. While the Heavenly Way is not inherently incompatible with Zen Buddhism, it lacks an intrinsic Buddhist (much less Zen Buddhist) content. (For a recent account of Heavenly Way thought, see Ooms 1985; 1990).

In short, the treatises that advocate some form of mental cultivation or breathing exercises generally represent points of view that are unrelated to Zen Buddhism or, sometimes, even critical of Zen. They are extremely useful for gaining an appreciation for traditional methods of self-cultivation. Self-cultivation in and of itself, however, is not Zen Buddhism.

Martial Art Texts that Use Vocabulary from Zen Literature

Above I have discussed treatises that were written for, or at least read by, a wide audience. In this section I want to shift our attention to a radically different type of literature: documents used for secret initiations. Traditionally, the audience for this kind of literature would have been very small. Sometimes the audience consisted only of a single person: the student being initiated.

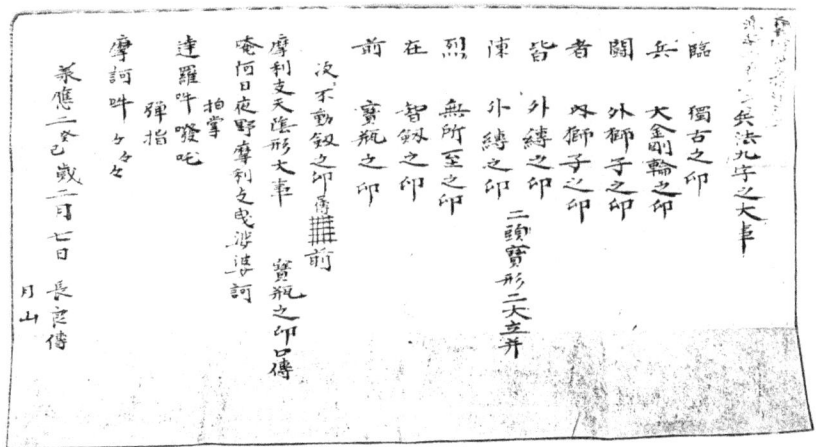

Figure 2. Hyōhō kuji no daiji

Prior to 1868 most forms of traditional culture (from tea ceremony and gardening to swordsmanship) and religious teachings (all forms of Buddhism, etc.) were taught via secret initiations (Nishiyama 1982a; 1982b; 1997). Typically these initiations merely confirmed teachings that had already been conveyed over many years of training. The documents that accompany these initiations, therefore, usually provide very little concrete description of what is being conveyed or confirmed. As likely as not, they consist only of a list or inventory of what already should have been taught. An outsider who sees this list of terms could not possibly know with certainty what they represent. Insiders who, presumably, know what each item represents keep these kinds of documents secret. When a document becomes public, usually it is because the initiation lineage has been broken, the last remaining initiate has died, and the secret knowledge represented by the document has been lost. For this reason, some of the information I present in this section will be speculative.

As mentioned above, it is generally assumed that the Zen terminology found in some initiation documents from traditional schools of swordsmanship probably resulted from borrowed vocabulary. Even though swordsmen might use terminology derived from Zen literature, the terminology actually has different referents and different connotations. Therefore, we should not automatically associate it with Zen Buddhism. This assumption sounds reasonable and in most cases probably is correct. At the same time, however, the documents that I will cite below clearly demonstrate an exception to this rule.

In this regard, it is significant that Zen initiations concerned not just Zen teachings but also all kinds of religious lore, Chinese learning, and folk wisdom. The fact that monks cultivated all forms of knowledge is one of the reasons why the Zen monk Takuan Sōhō could have taught Confucian metaphysics and why the Zen monk Hakuin Ekaku could have taught Daoist breathing techniques. And it helps explain why in some contexts the distinctions between these different religious traditions matter little to teacher or audience.

Some Zen monks also taught magical techniques for military success. Figure 2, for example, is a Sōtō Zen initiation document dated to 1653 and found at Yōkōji Zen monastery (Ishikawa pref.). It is titled: *Hyōhō kuji no daiji* (Important affair of the nine word martial art spell). The nine word martial art spell is a form of Chinese magic for warding off evil spirits and enemy soldiers by drawing a cross four times in the air in front of one's chest while chanting nine words, each one of which corresponds to a protective deity. Although originally associated with Daoism, it also became absorbed into East Asian tantric Buddhism. In Japan its practice was once ubiquitous among specialists in esoteric lore. Although it is not a Zen teaching, it was taught by Zen teachers because prior to 1868 they were frequently specialists in this kind of obscure lore and magic.

When warriors called upon Zen teachers for religious instruction, would Zen teachers ever present Zen teachings to them in a format adapted to their military concerns? Did warriors ever attempt to interpret Zen doctrines in ways that might have been applicable to martial situations? Can these initiation documents provide us with

Zen and Japanese Swordsmanship Reconsidered

evidence of this having occurred? In at least one case I think they can.

The case I have in mind concerns a phrase, "Sword Blades Upward" (*kenjin-jō*) that played a prominent role both in Zen initiations and in the initiations within at least one school of Japanese swordsmanship. To fully appreciate the connotations of this phrase and the roles it seems to have played in these two contexts, we must carefully read through the primary texts.

"Sword Blades Upward" (*kenjin-jō*) originally referred to the suffering inflicted in the sword-tree hell (*kenju jigoku*). Chapter 4, "Hells" (*jigoku*), of the *Cosmology Sūtra* (*Seki-kyō*; part 4, *sūtra* 30, of the *Jō-agon-kyō*, *Dīrghāgama*, T no. 1, fasc. 19), for example, states:

> "Then they [i.e., the beings in the sword-tree hell] are driven to run up trees of swords. When they climb the trees, the sword blades face downward. When they descend the trees, the <u>sword blades face upward</u>. Their hands are sliced away until their hands disappear. Their legs pump away until their legs disappear. The sword blades then pierce their bodies, penetrating all the way in and out. Their skin and flesh falls away. Their viscera and blood flow out. Finally, there exists only white bones held together by sinew." (T 1.123a)

Subsequently "sword blades upward" first appeared as a Zen topic (*Zen mondō*) in the *Record of Linji* (*Linji lu*, *Rinzairoku*; T no. 1985) attributed to the renowned Chinese Zen patriarch Linji Yixuan (Rinzai Gigen; d. 866):

> "[The teacher (i.e., Linji Yixuan)] ascended the hall [to deliver a sermon]. A monk asked: "What is this '<u>Sword Blades Upward</u>' affair?" The teacher replied: "Disastrous affairs! Disastrous affairs!" The monk hesitated to retort, whereupon the teacher struck [him]." (T 47.497a)

"Sword Blades Upward" became a standard topic in the Zen *kōan* curriculum after it appeared in the *Blue Cliff Record* (*Biyan lu*, *Hekiganroku*; T no. 2003) attributed to the extremely influential Zen teacher and poet Yuanwu Keqin (Engo Kokugon, 1063–1135). As is well known, the *Blue Cliff Record* has served as the number one textbook (*Shūmon Daiichi-sho*) for Zen *kōan* training ever since it was first published in the twelfth century. It presents each *kōan* via an initial comment (*suiji*), the *kōan* itself (*honsoku*), poetic verses, and prose commentary on the *kōan* and on the verses.

The *Blue Cliff Record* uses the term "Sword Blades Upward" in its initial comment on *kōan* number 41. Significantly, this *kōan* concerns dying and how to survive dying, two topics that were (and still are) of great concern to military men. The fact that "Sword Blades Upward" alludes to the torments of hell (as indicated by the *Cosmology Sūtra* and by Linji's comment, "disastrous") makes it an ideal pivot word for exploring one's fear of death. In the standard edition of the *Blue Cliff Record*, the key passages of *kōan* number 41 appear as follows:

"The initial comment says: The place where right and wrong mix to engender [results] cannot be known even by the holy ones. The moment of opposition or accord, vertical or horizontal, cannot be distinguished even by the Buddhas. Be the gentleman who eliminates the world and transcends moral relationships, thereby revealing the skills of a great one who stands out from the crowds. Walking across on top of thin ice (*hyōryō-jō*) or running on sword blades [turned] upwards (*kenjin-jō*) truly is being just like a unicorn's horn or a lotus blossom surviving flames. When you see an outstanding fellow, know that you tread the same path. Who has this excellent technique? Test yourself by focusing [on this *kōan*].

(41) Focus [on this *kōan*]: Zhaozhou (Jōshū) asked Touzi (Tōsu): "The moment a person who has died the great death regains life is like what?" Touzi replied: "Going by night is not permitted; but you must arrive by [dawn's first] light."

[Commentary:] . . . Truly it resembles sparks from struck flint or the bright flash of a lightening strike. Only someone who surpasses others can do it. A person who has died the great death completely lacks any buddha-dharma, truth, profundities, gain or loss, right or wrong, long or short. Having arrived here, just take it easy like this. An ancient fellow described it by saying: "With countless dead bodies on the level ground, whoever can pass through the forest of thorns has excellent technique." Yet, you must also pass through the other way before you can obtain it. Be that as it may, present-day people already find crossing over ordinary fields to be difficult. If you have any dependencies or any understanding, then you will become lost. Master Zhe (Tetsu) describe this difficulty as "vision not purified." My late teacher Wuzu (Goso) describe it as "life's root not yet severed." You must make the great death [your] number one [concern], and only then will you attain life. (*Biyan lu*, fasc. 5; T 48.178c–179a)"

From the twelfth century down to the present, all students of Zen Buddhism have encountered the phrase "Sword blades upward" in the *Record of Linji* and in the *Blue Cliff Record*. Because of this connection to specifically Zen texts, "sword blades upward" can be identified with Zen traditions in ways that the aforementioned popular treatises written by Zen monks and the treatises that advocate mental cultivation or breathing exercises can not. Any educated person (not just Zen monks like Takuan or Hakuin) can discuss non-Zen topics like Neo-Confucian methods of controlling the mind or Daoist methods of controlling the breath, but only people who have been initiated into the *kōan* curriculum of Zen lineages can discuss Zen terms like "sword blades upward." It is the *kōan* curriculum alone which is truly unique to Zen.

When students of Zen encounter the phrase "sword blades upward" many of them no doubt will have recognized this term from the descriptions of hell found in Buddhist Sutras. This frightening image of hell as well as the *Blue Cliff Record*'s exhortations to die the great death and return to life will have prompted them to ponder how their practice

Zen and Japanese Swordsmanship Reconsidered

of Zen can assuage their fears of the afterlife. Certain warriors might have asked similar questions: How can Zen teachers save me from hell? How can Zen teachings save my life on the battlefield? If such warriors existed, our texts suggest that they might very well have been trained in the Shintō-ryū school of swordsmanship.

Here I am using the designation "Shintō-ryū" as a generic designation for several interrelated martial art lineages that trace their origins to the Kashima Jingū (Ibaraki pref.) and Katori Jingū (Chiba pref.) shrines in Eastern Japan (Kantō) and that look to Iizasa Chōisai Ienao (d. 1488) as the founder, the reviver, or as one of the most prominent figures in their school's history. Today descendants of Iizasa Chōisai Ienao still reside near the Katori Grand Shrine and still exert familial control over one of these Shintō-ryū lineages, which is officially known as the Tenshin Shōden Katori Shintō-ryū.

Judging from the name and from the historical connection to two prominent shrines, one might automatically assume that the religious background of this style of swordsmanship must be Shinto, not Buddhism, and certainly not Zen Buddhism. We must remember, though, that "Shinto" as it is commonly understood today actually is a very recent development. During the medieval period when the Shintō-ryū began to emerge, Japanese religion consisted of what the late historian Kuroda Toshio (1926–1993) has described as exoteric-esoteric systems (*kenmitsu taisei*). In other words, most religious specialists could and did study a variety of religious doctrines as conveyed in various separate, but overlapping, lineages- each one of which would convey its own curriculum of secret initiations. Thus, a textbook on the Tenshin Shōden Katori Shintō-ryū (Ōtake, 1977–1978) contains references not just to traditions of shrine worship (i.e., Shinto), but also to esoteric Buddhism, Confucianism, and Onmyōdō (i.e., Yin-Yang cosmology). It does not, however, mention Zen Buddhism.

Nonetheless, Zen Buddhist vocabulary- specifically the phrase "sword blades upward"- does appear in Shintō-ryū martial art initiation documents. One of these is a scroll titled *Shintō-ryū hyōhō-sho* (Shintō-ryū martial arts texts), which was copied by Iizasa Morishige (d. 1586; a seventh generation descendant of Ienao). This scroll begins with an untitled preface, followed by a list of terms that appear to be titles of other scrolls (*maki*), such as: (1) "*Onmyō maki*", (2) "*Shishi maki*", (3) "*Himitsu kiri no maki*", (4) "*Byōbu no maki*", (5) "*Tora no maki*", (6) "*Tamasudare-shū*", (7) "*Manji no maki*", (8) "*Hōhō furyo*", (9) "*Chichute*", (10) "*Honzon Marishiten*". These titles are not explained. Each one is followed only by a very brief statement or merely a few terms that appear to indicate their contents.

For example, the third item titled "*Himitsu kiri no maki*" (p. 17a) consists of the following entry:

"The critical phrase (*ikku*): Sword Blades Upward
Soldiers do not arouse clouds of disagreement; Caring for illnesses does not extinguish the embers of short lifespans. Certain death means life, and living means certain death." (p. 17a)

Likewise, the sixth item titled "*Tamasudare shū*" (p. 18), lists 11 terms along with the following comment:

"The aforementioned *Tamasudare* techniques are for when you face an enemy without armor. Just one sword stroke, in and of itself, is the critical word (*ikkuji*) "unheld." Attaining self reliance (*jiyū*) is walking on <u>sword blades [facing] upwards</u> and running <u>over thin ice</u>. This is a marvellously subtle, unobtainable method. Whoever makes good progress along this path will arrive at Buddhahood and at the platform of bodhisattvas. In this way one is able to transcend birth and death, to sever the bounds of past and future. Beneath this one sword stroke truly is "erecting the foundations of peace amidst war." Truly this is the way for one's family to flourish and for one's descendants to prosper forever. You must not convey this teaching to anyone else. Keep it secret. Keep it secret." (p. 18)

Is it just a coincidence or historical accident that this kind of Zen terminology appears in this Shintō-ryū scroll? There are two reasons why I suspect otherwise. First, the content of the teaching—with its emphasis on escaping the bounds of birth and death, and on reaching the realm of the Buddhas and bodhisattvas—suggests something more than just a borrowed name used to designate some kind of technical skill. Second, the use of the words that I am translating as "critical phrase" (*ikku*) and as "critical word" (*ikkuji*) recall Zen teaching techniques. These terms frequently appear in Zen initiation documents that explain the spiritual significance of the key pivot words (*tengo*) used in Zen *kōan*. Could members of the Shintō-ryū have received Zen initiations? Ultimately, we cannot know.

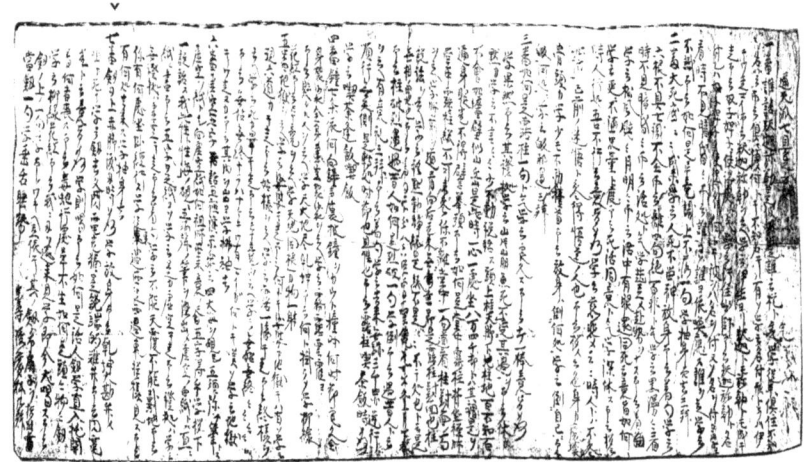

Figure 3. Tsūten-ha shichi gusoku kosoku

Zen and Japanese Swordsmanship Reconsidered

Other evidence, however, does reinforce this possibility. First, the Iizasa family residence, which as I mentioned earlier is located near the Katori Grand Shrine, actually sits right next to a Buddhist temple, the Shinfukuji, that belongs to the Japanese Sōtō Zen school. Shinfukuji owns a land deed and bill of sale signed in 1519 by Iizasa Morinobu (a 4th generation descendant of Ienao), which clearly indicates that the Iizasa family were patrons of this Zen temple (see *Iizasa Morinobu Denchi Baiken*). Second, Sōtō Zen initiation documents concerning the phrase "Sword Blades Upward" use vocabulary that appears to be related to this Shintō-ryū sword technique. It is to those documents that we must now turn our attention.

The Yōkōji Zen monastery mentioned earlier also owns an untitled document dated 1575 that records a series of *kōan* initiations (*sanwa*) received by a Zen monk named Eigen Keishō who subsequently served as the twelfth abbot of Jitokuji temple (modern Toyama City). Keishō represents the Gasan-branch of the Sōtō Zen lineage (i.e., that which originated with Gasan Jōseki, 1276–1366). Ishikawa Rikizan (1943–1997), the first person to attempt a historical study of this kind of literature, gave it the tentative title of "*Sanwa-shū*" (*Kōan* initiation curriculum; see Ishikawa 2001, 777–781; also see Ishikawa 2002). This "*Sanwa-shū*" lists a *kōan* curriculum consisting of twenty-four *kōan*, for which it provides initiations into the questions and answers for eighteen, including the following:

> Item: [The teacher asks:] "What is doing 'Sword Blades Upward'?" The student relaxes his body. The teacher commands: "[State] that very thing." The student replies: "Half the ground is swords and spears." (Ishikawa 2001, 780)

At this point I should explain how this kind of document was used. It presents a predetermined series of questions and answers that the Zen teacher and Zen student would repeat during the course of the student's *kōan* training. Every *kōan* is accompanied by its own special dialog. Students rehearsed these dialogs much in the same way that students of foreign languages might practice language drills. In both cases, the goal of the exercise is to gain fluency in a special kind of otherwise unknown language (Bodiford 1994).

This brief exchange, unfortunately, does not tell us very much. More details can be discovered by consulting

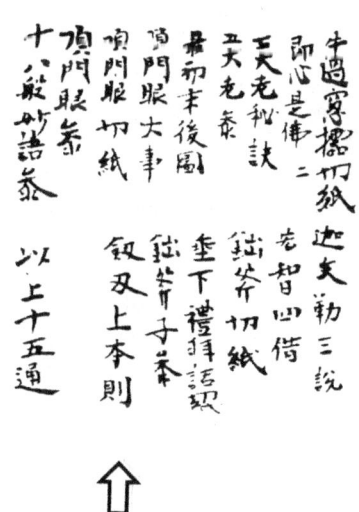

Figure 4. Sample table of contents

similar initiation documents that were used in other branches of the Sōtō Zen lineage. One of the key features of all genre of secret initiations is that whatever one branch omits, another branch of the same lineage will spell out. The culture of secrecy rests on the need for "one-up-manship." Members of one branch always want to assert, "Our teacher knows something your teacher does not know." As a result, each individual lineage branch will emphasize or specialize in an aspect of the esoteric lore that the other branches have ignored. The best way to gain a complete picture, therefore, is to compare initiation documents from several different branches of any given lineage.

Figure 3 shows another *kōan* initiation document, titled the *Tsūten-ha shichi gusoku kosoku* (Seven complete *kōan* of the Tsūten lineage), that also was received by Eigen Keishō and is now owned by Yōkōji monastery. It lists seven initiations, of which the seventh (and highest?) is:

Figure 5. *Kenjin-jō no kirikami*

Number 7: <u>Sword Blades Upward</u>. [The teacher asks:] "The moment when your bare red legs tread over the blades is like what? The student relaxes his body. The teacher asks: "Powerfully inspect the heavens and the earth! Are they living? Are they dying?" The student replies: "Swords long gone: the bright flash of a lightning strike. Still, this dullness is exactly what cannot be figured out." The teacher asks: "What do you mean by saying 'the bright flash of a lightning strike'?" The student shouts. The teacher asks: "What is the living sword (*katsunin-ken*)?" The student says: "Directly enter [the Buddha realm] and release it: who, then, becomes deceased?" The teacher asks: "Grass does not grow in places where poisonous snakes go: What is this sword? What is that sword?" The student replies: "Willows are green; cherry blossoms are pink." The teacher says: "Bring the sword and show it to me." The student immediately shouts loudly. The teacher asks: "[What is] the critical phrase (*ikku*), 'Sword Blades Upward'?" The student walks over and stands next to the teacher. The teacher says: "Use your fan to point out this critical phrase, 'This Sword.'" The student sticks out his tongue as if sleeping. (Ishikawa 2001, 783)

This document repeats some elements also found in the first exchange we reviewed. In both cases the student responds first by relaxing his body. This document, though,

Zen and Japanese Swordsmanship Reconsidered

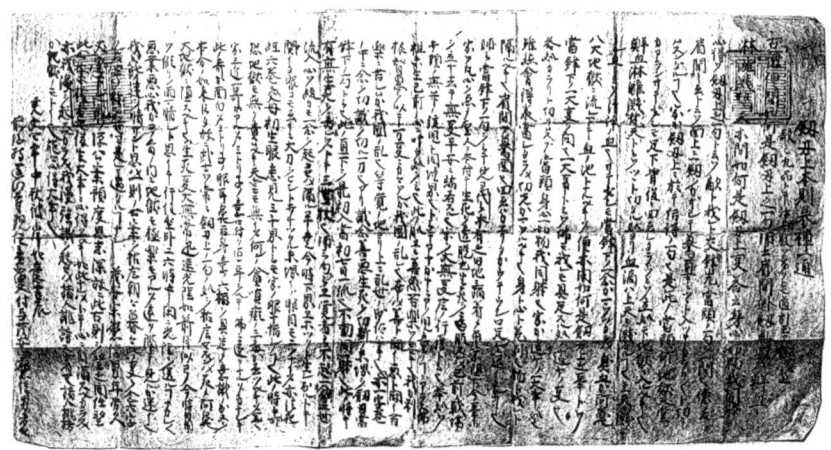

Figure 6. Kenjin-jō honsoku sanzen

provides a much richer sense of the kind of dramatic performance required to properly enact one's mastery of the *kōan*. It is this kind of link between Zen understanding and Zen performance that might have influenced members of the Shintō-ryū to adapt this *kōan* for inclusion in their sword curriculum. For that evidence concerning how "Sword Blades Upwards" was to be performed, we must turn to another kind of initiation document.

In addition to the lengthy *kōan* curriculums seen above, Zen teachers also conveyed individual documents (*kirikami*) to their students.[6] These individual documents could concern not just Zen *kōan*, but any and every kind of topic. Moreover, their contents could be individually tailored to the specific needs of each student who was to receive them (see figure 4 for a sample table of contents for fifteen separate documents, each one concerning a different topic). In other words, different students sometimes received different sets of initiations. Some of the extant individual documents concern "Sword Blades Upward." These documents reveal how the Zen interpretation of "Sword Blades Upward" could have varied from one type of student to the next.

Consider, for example, *Kenjin-jō no kirikami* (Document concerning Sword Blades Upward; figure 5). This document was copied in 1638 by the Sōtō Zen monk Dontaku of Saijōji Zen monastery (Kanagawa pref.) and is now owned by Kōrinji temple. It consists of a central circle, within which there is the word *ryōkyū* (also read as *yaya hisashi*). *Ryōkyū* is a term used in Zen texts to indicate the act of sitting quietly for a while without saying anything. Surrounding this central circle there are various statements written so that they radiate outward like rays of light. They say:

> "Sit with legs crossed in lotus posture: ears lined up with shoulders, nose lined up with navel, tongue pressed up to palate, incisors touching, together, optionally [sit] in a half-lotus posture, hold all ten fingers, and rest them on your lap." (Ishikawa 2001, 786)

Thus, this document describes the proper lotus posture of sitting Zen (*zazen*). Obviously this kind of teaching would be directed at Zen monks living in a monastery where they might actually find time to practice sitting Zen. It has no direct or indirect relationship to Shintō-ryū swordsmanship.

Significantly, however, there also exist Sōtō Zen initiation documents concerning "Sword Blades Upward" that were written specifically for warriors. Zen monks and warriors lived very different lifestyles. Naturally, "Sword Blades Upward" was taught to each of them in very different ways.

In 1664 a warrior named Moan Muneshige received an initiation document titled *Kenjin-jō honsoku sanzen* (Investigating Zen via the main *kōan* of Sword Blades Upward; see figure 6). This initiation document is rather special because in addition to listing the set pattern of questions and answers that teacher and student would exchange, it also provides a lengthy commentary on the meaning and religious significance of the answers. In other words, it attempts to explain not just the *kōan* itself, but also the Zen teaching behind the *kōan*. Moreover, it uses simple language that even a warrior could understand. The document is rather long, but because of its importance I translate it in full below:

[The main *kōan*:] An ancient virtuous monk asked: "What is the critical phrase, 'Sword Blades Upward'?" The teacher replied: "The sword aimed between the eyebrows, there is no turning away; Fresh blood sprays up to Brahmā's Heaven."
[The ancient one] again asked: ""What is this 'Sword Blades Upward' affair?" The teacher replied: "Body and mind unified; Self and other are the same."
[The commentary:] This is how you should understand it. "The critical phrase, 'Sword Blades Upward'" asks about the critical phrase of you and an enemy crossing weapons.
The reply, "The sword aimed between the eyebrows, there is no turning away" refers to raising a sword over your head, instantly entering, and cutting with all your strength. Herein is the critical phrase of attaining life within "Sword Blades Upward." At that very moment there exists neither hells nor heavens. But, if you even slightly start to turn away and retreat, then from right where you are standing you will enter hell.
"Fresh blood sprays up to Brahmā's Heaven" means that drops of blood from the place that you cut will spurt up to the high heavens. Blood spurting up the high heavens is blood that is pure [i.e., not polluting]. But, if in facing the [enemy's] weapon your composure should even slightly waver, then smelly [i.e., polluting] blood will pour down and become the blood in the Avīci Hell (*Abi Jigoku*), the eighth [i.e., lowest and worst] level of the hells.
"The monk again asked: What is this 'sword blades upward' affair?" asks about the single great affair when facing the [enemy's] weapon. "Single great affair" (*ichi daiji*) is this affair that both Buddhas and oneself possess.
The reply refers to cutting with all your strength so that "Body and mind are

Zen and Japanese Swordsmanship Reconsidered

unified; Self and other are the same." Therein lies this single great affair. Be that as it may, if you understand (*etoku*) or consent (*shōtō*), then your weapon will miss, your body and mind will separate, self and other will become dissimilar, between the eyebrows suddenly will become your own face, and you will turn away and retreat backwards.

[The main *kōan*, continued:] The teacher commands: "Try to say a critical phrase concerning "facing the [enemy's] weapon." Answering in place [of the student], the teacher says: "Keep your feet firmly on the originally existing farmland (*hon'u no denchi*); do not fall into past or present affairs."

[The commentary, continued:] This points to the deluded mind to show how the holy ones transcend birth and death. If you transcend birth and death, then you can walk off your former battlefield and abide in peace without incident. This is called touring without major incidents. ["Originally existing farmland"] indicates attaining the same sense realm as that of a newly born baby. It is not necessarily just that of a baby. It is the realm of [your original] mind before the Buddhas and ancestors were born. Therein there is no good or evil, no suffering or bliss. Using our wits and our wisdom to manage all affairs is what causes our kingdom to be disturbed [by wars]. The people of the world fighting over good, fighting over evil, and suffering over pain and pleasure is what disturbs our kingdom. At the level of equivalent awakening (*tōgaku*) and above there is no news of the world being disturbed. Within this single-word scroll there is the single sword stroke that cuts off thoughts and cuts off awareness. The future realm when awareness and thoughts, good and evil, life and death all have been cut off is the critical phrase of "facing the [enemy's] sword blade or weapon." You should face this [situation] at first for seven days non-stop. Without wavering, become one with it. During this period remove yourself from existence and non-existence, birth and death so that the three periods of time [past, present, and future] collapse into one [eternal present].

[The main *kōan*, continued:] The teacher commands: "Say a phrase" [that summarizes the entire *kōan*]. The student replies: "Not arousing a single thought is entering into the passing of the three periods of time."

[The commentary, continued:] This means that as soon as a single thought is aroused, you become separated [from the realm of the Buddhas] and are born into this present world. The eyes that you first open upon being born into the world and the eyes that you use in the future to strike [an enemy] with a great sword are not two different sets of eyes. Likewise in the *Lotus Sūtra* (*Hokekyō*), fascicle 6, when it says "the eyes born of mothers and fathers all can see three thousand realms" it is describing this same set of eyes. At that moment [i.e., when newly born] there are no hells to fear and no heavens to admire. How could the three poisons of greed, anger, and stupidity appear? It indicates drawing close to this. As a newborn baby develops its senses, year by year it grows further away from the Buddhas. Sadly this point is of interest. The six consciousnesses

(visual, aural, olfactory, gustatory, tactile, and waking) possessed by a newborn baby without intellectual faculties is known as the originally existing tathāgata (*nyorai*; i.e., Buddha). Therefore, if warriors fail to concentrate on resolving (*nentei*) the critical phrase of Sword Blades Upward, when they die they will fall into the Avīci Hell.
"Life and death is a grave affair; Impermanence speeds along; Days and nights pass like arrows and months [i.e., moons] resemble their bows." Use these days [as efficiently] as you would a brief clearing from the rains. Whether walking, standing, sitting, or lying down throughout the twenty-six hours of each day and night do not—you must not—idly waste time. If you do evil deeds or think evil thoughts, [then remember that] both hells and Sukhāvatī (Gokuraku) [i.e., Amitābha Buddha's Pure Land of Ultimate Bliss] exist within your own heart. To see them as somewhere distant is delusion. If you want to clear away this delusion, then concentrate on resolving this one *kōan*. Morning after morning and evening after evening think about this one affair, and chant the six-syllable sacred Name [i.e., Namu Amida Butsu, the *nenbutsu* recalling Amitābha Buddha]. Nothing surpasses this practice.
Faithful Layman (*shinnan*) Moan Muneshige, you have laboured for long years in *kōan* training. Because of your deep faith and strong will, I have initiated you into this *kōan*. May it help you to resolve the grave affair of your afterlife (*goshō*). But even if that becomes so, you must not become self-satisfied. You must not become arrogant. Becoming arrogant and strong willed is the same as slandering and belittling other people. Slandering and belittling other people leads to rebirth in hell. Take care that you fully understand this grave affair."
(Ishikawa 2001, 784–785)

In this document we find an explanation of "Sword Blades Upward" in language that warriors can understand. The battlefield metaphors (e.g., "Fresh blood sprays up to Brahmā's Heaven") are very graphic and gruesome. The description of blood spurting out brings home exactly what is at stake. The physical performance of "raising a sword over your head, instantly entering, and cutting with all your strength" consists of a concrete action that would have been familiar to any swordsman. Nonetheless, nowhere in this document can we find a Zen method of swordsmanship. It does not attempt to explain how one might become a better martial technician or a stronger athlete. For all its battlefield descriptions and martial terminology, throughout its primary focus is salvation in one's afterlife (*goshō*). It warns of the dangers of rebirth in hell no less than eight times. Thus, the main purpose of this document is not to improve one's swordsmanship but to offer a method of avoiding hell.

In this regard, we should not overlook the closing exhortation to practice *nenbutsu* (recalling Amitābha Buddha by chanting the words: Namu Amida Butsu). Nowadays the Pure Land practice of *nenbutsu* usually is regarded as being incompatible with or contrary to Zen practice. *Nenbutsu* is said to be the easy practice (*igyō*) while Zen

Zen and Japanese Swordsmanship Reconsidered

consists of the difficult practice (*nangyō*). In reality, though, prior to the modern period, Pure Land style *nenbutsu* was a common practice among Japanese Zen monks (just as in China and Korea) and among lay people of all types.[7] It was especially popular among warriors. They saw the battlefield as a version of hell on earth, and they feared that if their dying view (*rinju*) of this life focused on that vision of hell then they certainly would land in the real hell. For this reason many warrior families, including the ones who sponsored Zen temples and who supported Zen monks, also maintained Amitābha chapels where they could pray for deliverance (*ōjō*) to Pure Land (Kawai 1963; Miyazaki 1992).

In addition to its doctrinal contents, this document's physicality also was religiously meaningful. In medieval times Zen teachers sometimes conveyed these kinds of initiation documents to illiterate people, to corpses about to be buried, and to the ghosts of people who died long ago. In these cases the words written on the page were less important than the fact that there were conveyed by a Zen teacher who represented a direct link to the Buddhas. Even if these recipients of these documents could read, they would not be able to understand their complex Buddhist teachings. For them, these kinds of documents functioned as magical talismans that promised release from the sufferings of hell and deliverance to Pure Land (Bodiford 1994b). Although there is no evidence internal to the document to suggest that it might have functioned in this talismanic way, the possibility cannot be totally dismissed. Afterall, the *Shintōryū hyōhōsho* scroll cited earlier promises benefits—such as "arriving at Buddhahood and at the platform of bodhisattvas" and causing "one's family to flourish and for one's descendants to prosper forever—that can only be described as magical.

Now we have established three key parts of the puzzle: (1) early Shintō-ryū documents use the Zen terminology "Sword Blades Upward," (2) the Iizasa family was associated with a Sōtō Zen temple, Shinfukuji, which is located right next to their family home, and (3) at least some Sōtō Zen teachers provided special initiations into the *kōan* "Sword Blades Upward" that were directed especially toward the concerns of warriors. The next step is to tie these elements together. To do so, we must return to Shintō-ryū initiation documents.

This time we will use documents from a different branch of the Shintō-ryū, one that was conveyed to Fukui Morinao, who recopied his set of four secret scrolls in 1702. These scrolls, the *Shintō-ryū kendō ōgi* (Innermost principles of Shintō-ryū swordsmanship) appear to represent a very early layer of Shintō-ryū swordsmanship.[8] They still record information for types of religious consecrations (*kanjō*), for example, that largely fell out of practice after the start of the Tokugawa period (1603–1868). Therefore, Ōmori Nobumasa, the scholar who first published these scrolls, suggests that their contents probably date from sometime during the late fifteenth or early sixteenth centuries (Ōmori 1991, 225). Based on these scrolls (as well as on other documents that I have not cited), Ōmori also argues that "Sword Blades Upward" constituted one of the most important teachings in early Shintō-ryū swordsmanship. Indeed, it might very well have constituted the innermost principle (*ōgi*) to which the title of the scrolls refer (Ōmori 1991, 231–234).

The first of these four scrolls begins by praising the importance of "Sword Blades Upward" with the exact same language as we saw in the Iizasa family *Shintōryū hyōhōsho* (Shintō-ryū martial arts texts; copied by Iizasa Morishige) cited above. The Fukui version (scroll 1) says:

"Martial arts consists of the critical phrase "Sword Blades Upward." <u>This is a marvellously subtle, unobtainable method. Whoever makes good progress along this path will arrive at Buddhahood and at the platform of bodhisattvas.</u> The initial techniques number thirty-three, which correspond to the thirty-three bodily [forms of Avalokiteśvara (Kannon)]. The attacks number twelve techniques, which represents the twelve links [in the Buddhist doctrine] of causality." (Ōmori 1991, 260)

The Fukui version goes on to quote language that we found in the Sōtō Zen *kōan* initiation document given to the warrior Moan Muneshige in 1664. Unfortunately, at this point the Fukui scrolls are somewhat illegible or damaged. Because of lacuna in the original document, in places my translation is only an educated guess. As far as I can tell, scroll 3 says:

"In regard to this, the words of the Zen teachers say…"What is the critical phrase, '<u>Sword Blades Upward</u>'?" The virtuous one replied: "<u>The sword aimed between the eyebrows, there is no turning away; Fresh blood sprays up to Brahmā's Heaven.</u>" Thus, the use of this single sword stroke cuts away both the dead blade (*setsunin-tō*) and the living sword (*katsujin-ken*), both holding tight (*hajū*) and releasing (*hōgyō*), so that the gap between existence and non-existence will not admit even a hair's [width of difference]. The technique…the statement on the importance of proper eye placement certainly is so. This is the essential essence of the martial path. Throughout the twenty-six hours of the day without gap, cut off all thoughts of anger and greed. Whoever thus strengthens his body will attain the highest reaches of the soldier's path and be able to smash strong enemies. Thus, one is able to cultivate one's body, manage one's household, govern one's kingdom, and bring peace to the realm. Outwardly it promotes wisdom, humanity, and courage. Inwardly it maintains the virtues of the Confucian path and of the Buddhist path. Without…will be renown for ten thousand years." (Ōmori 1991, 274)

Here we might very well have direct evidence not only that Sōtō Zen *kōan* initiations were taught to warriors but also that those warriors thereupon incorporated this Zen lore into their swordsmanship. This phrase, "The sword aimed between the eyebrows, there is no turning away; Fresh blood sprays up to Brahmā's Heaven," is not a common saying. I have not been able to locate any other texts (other than the ones cited above) in which it appears. It is possible that another text exists, and I just have not had time

Zen and Japanese Swordsmanship Reconsidered

to find it. If another text uses this same phrase, then it is possible that the Sōtō Zen initiation documents and the Shintō-ryū sword initiation documents both drew upon that third source, independently and without any connection to one another. If, on the other hand, another source does not exist, then it strongly suggests (to me, at least) that the Shintō-ryū's use of this phrase must be based on Sōtō Zen *kōan* lore. At the present state of our knowledge, there is no other explanation for how the phrase "The sword aimed between the eyebrows, there is no turning away; Fresh blood sprays up to Brahmā's Heaven" can be found both in the Sōtō Zen *kōan* initiation document and in the Shintō-ryū martial art scrolls.

Another problem still remains. Even if, as I have speculated, the special initiations into the *kōan* "Sword Blades Upward" taught by some Sōtō teachers especially for warriors did in fact lie behind Shintō-ryū teachings regarding this concept, it still does not help us understand how that concept might apply to swordsmanship. After all, the two contexts are very different. Zen *kōan* initiations concern soteriology: the grave affair of one's afterlife. How can we avoid falling into hell? Martial art scrolls concern how to master techniques for skilfully encountering and defeating an enemy. How can we survive on the battlefield?

Nonetheless, the Fukui family's Shintō-ryū scrolls strongly suggest that "Sword Blades Upward" must be an actual martial art technique. Scroll 4 says:

"Martial arts that are without equal and without compare are true martial arts. The number of techniques taught in other schools, in this school, and in all schools might seem numerous, but all martial arts simply consist of the critical phrase, "Sword Blades Upward." Look, with this one sword stroke I have used humane thoughts to attain the martial art of cutting through without being cut. Throughout the entire world, knowledgeable people [?]" (Ōmori 1991, 282–283)

What is this one-stroke martial art of cutting through without being cut? Of course, sword strokes, or any artistic technique requiring a high degree of physical dexterity, cannot be learned from secret scrolls. Only years of training under the watchful eye of a good teacher can convey the real meaning of "Sword Blades Upward" as a sword technique. Nonetheless, there exist documents from yet another branch of the Shintō-ryū that address this question.

The Matsuoka family branch (*Matsuoka-ha*) of the Shintō-ryū lineage descends from Matsuoka Hyōgosuke, who was one of the main disciples of the famous swordsman Tsukahara Bokuden (1490–1571). Several scrolls from this branch remain extant today. The *Tenshin Shōden Shintō-ryū hyōhō denmyaku* (Traditions of Shintō-ryū martial arts correctly conveyed from Tenshin), copied in 1861 by Matsuoka Tamaito, begins with the following statement, which it attributes to Tsukahara Bokuden and dates to 1556:

"The aforementioned *Muikken* techniques refer to when you face an enemy without armour. At that moment, just use one sword stroke, which in and of itself is the critical word "inviolate." Attaining self reliance (*jiyū*) is walking on sword blades [facing] upwards and running over thin ice. This is a marvellously subtle, unobtainable method. Whoever makes good progress along this path will arrive at the fundamental significance and marvellous ends correctly conveyed by *Tenshin*. In this way one is able to transcend birth and death, to severe the bounds of past and future. Beneath this one sword stroke truly is "erecting the foundations of peace amidst war." Truly this is the way for one's family to flourish and for one's descendants to prosper forever. You can convey this teaching only to one other person. Keep it secret. Keep it secret." (p. 28)

So far, so good. Here we have a third version of the same kind of praise for "Sword Blades Upward" that we also found in the Iizasa family scrolls and in the Fukui family scrolls cited above. The existence of this kind of language in all three sets of scrolls helps to confirm that we are dealing with three branches of the same Shintō-ryū tradition. The Matsuoka family scrolls, however, do something that the Iizasa and Fukui family scrolls do not. Namely, they go on to list "Sword Blades Upward" (*kenjin-jō*) as the name of a specific sword technique within the set of exercises known as "*Kōjō-nanahon-tachi*" (p. 33). What was this technique?

The *Shintō-ryū hyōhō kanagaki* (Japanese-Language Notes on Shintō-ryū Martial Arts), copied in 1843 by Matsuoka Tokishige, contains the following entry:

"Sword Blades Upward Technique:
This is performed from an upper sword position. As soon as the enemy is about to engage, stick single-mindedly and without disturbance so as to attain victory." (p. 57)

Conclusions

We have traced the genealogy of "Sword Blades Upward" from a Buddhist description of the torments of hell, across its appearances in the classical Zen literature of China, and to its inclusion in many different initiation documents that were handed down both in Zen lineages and in the lineages of sword schools. Perhaps one of the most notable features of the various initiation documents is how little they actually reveal to outsiders. Each document seems addressed to a very specific audience, consisting of someone who is studying a very specific set of practices. The documents address concrete details, not general principles. People who are not familiar with the concrete practices cannot interpret these documents with confidence. Collectively, the documents suggest how "Sword Blades Upward" might have functioned as a teaching device for learning Zen *kōan* language, as a talisman for avoiding hell, and as a specific physical technique for manipulating a sword. They do not, however, suggest a normative Zen

Zen and Japanese Swordsmanship Reconsidered

approach to swordsmanship. They expound no general relationship between Zen and warrior beliefs, behaviour, or martial arts.

It is possible that "Sword Blades Upward" became more of an abstract ideal during the Tokugawa period (1603–1868) after the age of widespread warfare had come to end. This possibility is suggested by a passage in the *Honchō Bugei Shōden* (Brief Biographies of Japanese Martial Art Heroes; 1716) where it tells the well-known story of how the warrior Kamiizumi Hidetsuna (ca. 1508–1577) once saved a small child from a criminal who was holding the child hostage.[9] As the story goes, Kamiizumi first disguised himself as a Buddhist monk by exchanging clothes with a real monk who happened to be nearby, then approached the hungry criminal and offered to give him food. When the criminal relaxed his guard to accept the food, Kamiizumi leaped forward, grabbed the criminal's arm, threw him to the ground, snatched up the child, and carried the child to safety. The story concludes with the following remarks:

"When Kamiizumi returned the Buddhist robes to the monk, the monk praised him profusely, saying: "Truly you are magnificent. I am just a monk, but even I can sense your courage and strength. Here is a person who actually understands the critical phrase, "Sword Blades Upward." With these words, the monk presented Kamiizumi with a miniature vestment (*kara*) and left.[10] (fasc. 6, pp. 60–61)

In the context of this story, understanding the critical phrase "Sword Blades Upward" clearly implies both a willingness to risk one's own life and the skill to succeed. It seems to have become a code word for a high level of martial attainment. But what it actually represents is not spelled out.

Significantly, when Zen monks (Takuan and Hakuin) and other authors (Shirai, Issai, and Kodegiri) did attempt to spell out the relationship between religious forms of self-cultivation and martial arts, they explained it in terms other than Zen (e.g., Neo-Confucianism, Daoism, and Heavenly Way thought). Their treatises demonstrate that Japanese people applied a wide variety of religious teachings to the very practical problems of surviving battles, nurturing health and vitality, and serving a lord. Specific, concrete Zen teachings such as "Sword Blades Upward," however, are conspicuous in these treatises only by their absence. In short, we have shown that at least in some cases specific connections did exist between Zen teachings and swordsmanship. No such connections, however, can be demonstrated for the body of literature that today are most commonly cited as being somehow representative of "Zen and the Sword." Instead of anything related to Zen, what those treatises share in common is simply a concern with self-cultivation. For this reason, it is as meaningless to discuss a generic "Zen and the sword" as it would be to discuss a generic "nationalism and genocide" or a generic "Islam and terrorism." Such broad categories exist more in the popular imagination (in the eyes of the beholder) than in any identifiable, historical reality.

Endnotes

[1] People living in the United States generally hold the concept of "religion" in much higher esteem than is the case in Japan, where *shūkyō* 宗教 (i.e., the modern term created to translate the European notion of religion) can imply many negative connotations.

[2] In this remark King forgets that the Crusades were formally sanctioned by a Christian Church for the purpose of achieving Christian religious goals (namely, access to holy sites in the Middle East for European Christian pilgrims). Japanese military expansion during the first half of the twentieth century, on the other hand, was motivated more by economics and politics, and it lacked any explicit religious goals — except to the extent that the central role afforded to the imperial household (Kokutai 國體) rested on mythological foundations. Regarding Kokutai, see Monbushō 1937 and 1949.

[3] Some critics of the Sharf essay accuse it of attacking Suzuki simply for being a product of his times. Actually, Sharf is attacking modern scholars for failing to locate Suzuki within the broader intellectual currents of his times.

[4] "Marvellous" 神妙 appears three times, for example, in Zhu Xi's sayings (*Zhuzi yulei*, fascs. 5 and 18, pp. 84, 403, and 412). In contrast, it appears only once in any of the well-known Zen texts: see the Preface to the *Blue Cliff Record* (*Biyan lu*; T 48.139a).

[5] For Zhu Xi's discussion of "seriousness" (kei) as "concentrating the mind on one task without wavering" (*shuitsu muteki*), see his sayings (*Zhuzi yulei*, fasc. 17, p. 371).

[6] Kirikami, meaning "documents," should not be confused with the identically written word *kirigami*, "paper crafts".

[7] For an especially well-known assertion of the equivalence of Zen and *nenbutsu*, see Hakuin's *Orategama zokushū* (in Yampolsky 1971, 125–139).

[8] Ōmori (1991, 225) suggests that the use of the modern term kendō (instead of kenjutsu) in the title might date from when the outer covers of the scrolls were replaced during the late Meiji period (1868–1912).

[9] This scene is re-enacted in the award-winning film *Shichinin no Samurai* (Seven Samurai, 1954) directed by Kurosawa Akira (1910–1998) when the character Shimada Kambei (played by Shimura Takashi, 1905–1982) uses the same stratagem to rescue a child hostage.

[10] A *kara* (more commonly known as *rakusu*) is a variation of the monks five-panelled robe that has been reduced in size so that it resembles a small bib. It is often worn in place of the usual monk's robe.

Bibliography

Abbreviations and Primary Texts (by titles)
Biyan Lu (Blue Cliff Record). Attributed to Yuanwu Keqin (1063–1135). 10 fascicles. Reprinted in T, no. 2003, vol. 48, pp. 139–225.
Fudōchi shinmyō roku (Marvelous power of immovable wisdom). Attributed to Takuan Sōhō (1573–1643). Reprinted in *Takuan Oshō zenshū* . In vol. 5 (27 pages, numbered non-consecutively). Takuan Oshō Zenshū Kankōkai, 1928–1930.

Zen and Japanese Swordsmanship Reconsidered

Honchō bugei shōden (Brief biographies of Japanese martial art heroes). 1716. By Hinatsu Shigetaka. 10 fascicles. Reprinted in Hayakawa 1–86. 1915.

Hyōhō kuji no daiji (Important affair of the nine word martial art spell). Copied 1653. Sōtōshū initiation document owned by Yōkōji Zen temple (Ishikawa pref.). Photographed 1980.9.5 by Kaneda Hiroshi. Photo-mechanical reproduction used by permission of Mr. Kaneda.

Iizasa Morinobu denchi baiken (Deed of sell). Signed 1519 by Iizasa Morinobu. Originally owned by Shinfukuji Zen temple (Sawara city, Chiba pref.). Reprinted in *Nihon budō taikei* (Systems of Japanese martial arts). Compiled by Imamura Yoshio et al. Vol. 3, p. 20. Kyoto: Dōhōsha, 1982.

Jō Agon kyō (*Dīrgahāgama*, Long Sermons of the Buddha). 22 fascicles. Reprinted in T, no. 1, vol. 1, pp. 1–149.

Kashū shōjurin daijō gokoku zenji shitsunai mitsuden kirikami (Secret documents on the rites of the inner sanctum Dharma transmission from the Shōjurin Daijōji State-Protecting Zen temple in Kaga province). Copied 1885 by Daikō Kaiun (d.1888). Originally owned by Daijōji Zen temple (Ishikawa pref.). Reprinted as *Nichiiki Sōtō shitsunai tekiteki hiden mippō kirikami* (Documents on the secret rites of Japanese Sōtō Zen inner sanctum Dharma transmission). In *Shūi* (Supplements), pp. 483–565. *Sōtōshū zensho* (Collected texts of the Sōtō Zen school). 1929–1935. Revised and enlarged edition. Edited by Sōtōshū Zensho Kankōkai. Vol. 18. Tokyo: Sōtōshū Shūmuchō, 1970–1973.

Kenjin jō honsoku sanzen (Investigating Zen via the main *kōan* of Sword Blades Upward). Conveyed from Raian to Moan Muneshige in 1664. Sōtōshū initiation document owned by Yōkōji Zen temple (Ishikawa pref.). Photographed 1980.9.5 by Kaneda Hiroshi. Photo-mechanical reproduction used by permission of Mr. Kaneda. Cf. Ishikawa 2001, 2.784–785.

Kenjin jō no kirikami (Document Concerning Sword Blades Upward). Copied by Dontaku in1638. Sōtōshū initiation document owned by Kōrinji Zen temple (Odawara city, Kanagawa pref.). Reprinted in Ishikawa 2001, vol. 2, p. 786.

Linji lu (Record of Linji Yixuan, d. 866). 1 fascicle. Reprinted in T, no. 1985, vol. 47, pp. 495–506.

Riki sabetsu ron (Distinguishing Principle and Material Force). Attributed to Takuan Sōhō (1573–1643). Reprinted in *Takuan Oshō zenshū* . In vol. 2 (29 pages, numbered non-consecutively). Takuan Oshō Zenshū Kankōkai, 1928–1930.

"Sanwa shū" (Kōan initiation curriculum). Untitled document received by Eigen Keishō. Copied 1575. Sōtōshū initiation document owned by Yōkōji Zen temple (Ishikawa pref.). Reprinted in Ishikawa 2001, vol. 2, p. 777–781.

Shintō-ryū hyōhō kanagaki (Japanese language notes on Shintō-ryū martial arts). Copied 1843 by Matsuoka Tokishige. Initiation document of the Tenshin Shōden Shintō-ryū Hyōhō Matsuoka-ryū. Reprinted in *Nihon budō taikei* (Systems of Japanese martial arts). Compiled by Imamura Yoshio et al. Vol. 3, pp. 53–57. Kyoto: Dōhōsha, 1982.

Shintō-ryū hyōhōsho (Shintō-ryū martial arts texts). Copied by Iizasa Morishige (d. 1586). Initiation document of the Tenshin Shōden Katori Shintō-ryū. Reprinted in *Nihon budō taikei* (Systems of Japanese martial arts). Compiled by Imamura Yoshio et al. Vol. 3, pp. 14–20. Kyoto: Dōhōsha, 1982.

Shintō-ryū kendō ōgi (Innermost principles of Shintō-ryū swordsmanship). 4 scrolls. Copied 1702 by Fukui Morinao. Owned by Fukui Morihisa (Kumagai city, Saitama pref.). Reprinted in Ōmori 1991, 260–285.

T. See: *Taishō shinshū daizōkyō* (Taisho period new critical edition of the Buddhist canon). Edited by Takakusu Junjirō and Watanabe Kaikyoku. 100 vols. Daizōkyōkai, 1924–1935.

Table of Contents for 15 Initiation Documents (*kirikami*). No title. Copied ca. 1650. Cover for Sōtōshū initiation documents owned by Yōkōji Zen temple (Ishikawa pref.). Photographed 1980.9.5 by Kaneda Hiroshi. Photo-mechanical reproduction used by permission of Mr. Kaneda.

Tengu geijutsuron (Performance theory of the mountain demons). 1727. By Issai Chozan (1659–1741). 4 fascicles. Reprinted in Hayakawa 1915, 313–342.

Tenshin Shōden Shintō-ryū hyōhō denmyaku (Traditions of Shintō-ryū martial arts correctly conveyed from Tenshin). Copied 1861 by Matsuoka Tamaito. Initiation document of the Tenshin Shōden Shintō-ryū Hyōhō Matsuoka-ryū. Reprinted in *Nihon budō taikei* (Systems of Japanese Martial Art). Compiled by Imamura Yoshio et al. Vol. 3, pp. 28–34. Kyoto: Dōhōsha, 1982.

Tsūten-ha shichi gusoku kosoku (Seven complete *Kōan* of the Tsūten lineage). Copied by Eigen Keishō (fl. 1575). Sōtōshū initiation document owned by Yōkōji Zen temple (Ishikawa pref.). Photographed 1980.9.5 by Kaneda Hiroshi. Photo-mechanical reproduction used by permission of Mr. Kaneda. Cf. Ishikawa 2001, 2.781–783.

Zhuzi yulei (Sayings of Zhu Xi, 1130–1200). Beijing: Zhonghua Shuju, 1986.

Secondary Studies and Translations

Bodiford, William M. "Strategies of Secrecy on Medieval Japanese Religions." Lecture presented at the annual meeting of the European Association for Japanese Studies. University of Warsaw, 2003.

"Kamakura Buddhism as 'The Buddhism of Kamakura.'" Light of Wisdom: Journal of Bukkyo University – Los Angeles Extension 9: 12–21. 2003.

"Religion and Spiritual Development: Japan." In Martial Arts of the World: An Encyclopedia. Edited by Thomas A. Green. Santa Barbara: ABC-CLIO, 2001.

"Written Texts: Japan." In Martial Arts of the World: An Encyclopedia. Edited by Thomas A. Green. Santa Barbara: ABC-CLIO, 2001.

"Zen Buddhism." Chapter 14 of Sources of Japanese Tradition. Second edition. Volume 1: From Earliest Times to 1600. Compiled by Wm. Theodore de Bary, Donald Keene, George Tanabe, and Paul Varley with the collaboration

of William Bodiford, Jurgis Elisonas, and Philip Yampolsky. pp. 306–335. Columbia University Press, 2001.
"Emptiness and Dust: Zen Dharma Transmission Rituals." In *Tantra in Practice*, edited by David Gordon White. pp. 299–307. Princeton University Press, 2000.
"Kokan Shiren's 'Zen Precept Procedures.'" In *Religions of Japan in Practice*, edited by George J. Tanabe, Jr. pp. 98–108. Princeton University Press, 1999.
"Review of Brian (Daizen) A. Victoria, 'Zen at War.'" *Monumenta Nipponica* 53, no. 4: 573–575. 1998.
"Review of Daisetz T. Suzuki, 'Zen and Japanese Culture.'" *Asian Thought and Society: An International Review* 19, no. 55: 91–92. 1994.
Sōtō Zen in Medieval Japan. University of Hawaii Press, 1994.
"Zen in the Art of Funerals: Ritual Salvation in Japanese Buddhism." *History of Religions* 32, no. 2: 146–164. 1992.
"Dharma Transmission in Sōtō Zen: Manzan Dōhaku's Reform Movement." *Monumenta Nipponica* 46, no. 4: 423–451. 1991.
Dornish, Margaret H. "Aspects of D. T. Suzuki's Early Interpretations of Buddhism and Zen." *The Eastern Buddhist*, new series, 3, no. 1: pp. 47–66. 1970.
Faure, Bernard. *Chan Insights and Oversights*. Princeton University Press, 1993.
Guttmann, Allen. *From Ritual to Record: The Nature of Modern Sports*. Columbia University Press, 1978.
The Olympics: A History of the Modern Games. University of Illinois Press, 1992.
Games and Empires: Modern Sports and Cultural Imperialism. Columbia University Press, 1994.
Guttmann, Allen and Lee Thompson. *Japanese Sports: A History* University of Hawaii Press, 2001.
Hayakawa Junzōrō et al., editors. *Bujutsu sōsho* (Martial art treatises). Kokusho Kankōkai, 1915.
Herrigel, Eugen. "Die ritterliche Kunst des Bogenschiessens" (The Chivalrous Art of Archery), *Nippon, Zeitschrift für Japanologie* (Nippon: Journal for Japanese Studies) 2, no. 4. 1936
Zen in der Kunst des Bogenschiessens (Zen in the Art of Archery). Buenchen-Planegg, Germany: Otto Wilhelm Barth-Verlag, 1948.
Zen in the Art of Archery (originally *Zen in der Kunst des Bogenschiessens*, 1948). Translated by Richard F. C. Hull with an introduction by D. T. Suzuki. New York: Pantheon Books, 1953.
Yumi to Zen (The bow and Zen; originally *Zen in der Kunst des Bogenschiessens*, 1948). Translated by Inatomi Eijirō and Ueda Takeshi. Kyōdō, 1956.
Hobsbawm, Eric and Terence O. Ranger, editors. *The Invention of Tradition*. New York: Cambridge University Press, 1983.

ed. *Tsukurareta dentō*. Japanese translation of *The Invention of Tradition*. Translated by Maekawa Keiji, Kajiwara Kageaki, et al. Kinokuniya, 1992.

Hurst, G. Cameron, III. *Armed Martial Arts of Japan: Swordsmanship and Archery*. Yale University Press, 1998.

Hyams, Joe. *Zen in the Martial Arts*. Los Angeles: J. P. Tarcher, 1979.

Imamura Yoshio. *Shūtei Jūkyū seiki ni okeru Nihon taiiku no kenkyū* (Studies in Nineteenth century Japanese physical education). Corrected edition. Daiichi Shobō, 1989 (1967).

———, editor. *Shiryō Yagyū shrinkage-ryū* (Historical Documents of the Yagyū Family's Shinkage-ryū). 2 vols. Revised edition. Shin Jinbutsu Ōraisha, 1995 (1962).

Inoue, Shun. "Budō no hatsumei" (The Invention of Budō). *Soshiorojii* 37, no. 2: 111–125. 1992.

———. "Budō: Invented Tradition in the Martial Arts." In *The Culture of Japan as Seen Through its Leisure*. Edited by Sepp Linhart and Sabine Frühstück. State University of New York Press, 1998.

———. "The Invention of the Martial Arts: Kanō Jigorō and Kōdōkan Judo." In Vlastos 1998.

Irie Kōhei and Sugie Masatoshi, editors. *Nihon budōgaku kenkyū: Watanabe Ichirō kyōju taikan kinen ronshū* (Studies in Japanese Martial Arts: Research Commemorating the Retirement of Professor Watanabe Ichirō). Shimazu Shobō, 1988.

Ishikawa Rikizan "Chūsei Sōtōshū kirikami no bunrui shiron (17): sanwa (shūshi, kōan, kuketsu) kankei wo chūshin to shite (chū)" (A Preliminary classification of the genres of medieval Sōtō initiation documents, part 17: Zen Dialogs [Doctrines, *Kōans*, Secret Sayings], part 2). *Komazawa daigaku Bukkyōgakubu kenkyū kiyō* 49. 1991.

———. "*Chūsei Sōtōshū kirikami no bunrui shiron* (22): *shinbutsu shugō kankei wo chūshin to shite*" (A preliminary classification of the genres of medieval Sōtō initiation documents, part 22: God and Buddha Combinations). *Komazawa daigaku Bukkyōgakubu ronshū* 24. 1993.

———. *Zenshū sōden shiryō no kenkyū* (Studies of Zen Transmission Documents). 2 volumes. Kyoto: Hōzōkan, 2001.

———. "Colloquial Transcriptions as Sources for Understanding Zen in Japan." Translated and Introduced by William Bodiford. The Eastern Buddhist, new series, 36, no. 1. 2002.

Ishioka Hisao. *Heihōsha no seikatsu* (Lifestyles of Swordsmen). Yūsankaku, 1981.

———. "Ken to Zen". *Gekkan kendō Nippon* (English-language title: *The Kendo-Nippon Monthly*). Tokyo, Sukii Jaanaru, October 1978.

King, Winston L. *Zen and the Way of the Sword: Arming the Samurai Psyche*. New York: Oxford University Press, 1993.

Kirita Kiyohide. "D. T. Suzuki on Society and the State." Translated by Richard

Szippl and Thomas Kirchner. In *Rude Awakenings: Zen, the Kyoto School, and the Question of Nationalism*. Edited by James W. Heisig and John C. Maraldo. University of Hawaii Press, 1994.

Kawai Masaharu. "Chūsei bushidan no ujigami ujidera" (Clan gods and clan temples of medieval warrior bands). Reprinted in *Chiiki shakai to shūkyō no shiteki kenkyū*, edited by Ogura Toyofumi. Tokyo: Yanagihara Shoten, 1963 (1958).

Mangan, J. A. *The Games Ethic and Imperialism: Aspects of the Diffusion of an Ideal*. New York: Viking, 1986.

"Britain's Chief Spiritual Export: Imperial Sport as Moral Metaphor, Political Symbol and Cultural Bond." In *The Cultural Bond: Sport, Empire, Society*. Edited by J. A. Mangan. London: F. Cass, 1992.

Matsumae Shigeyoshi. *Toward an Understanding of Budo Thought*. Tokyo: Tōkai University Press, 1987.

Budō shisō no tankyū (Japanese version of *Toward an Understanding of Budo Thought*). Tōkai Daigaku Shuppankai, 1987.

Miyazaki, Fumiko. "Religious Life of the Kamakura Bushi: Kumagai Naozane and His Descendants." *Monumenta Nipponica* 47, no. 4. 1992

Monbushō (Ministry of Education), Japan. *Kokutai no hongi* (Cardinal principles of our national polity). Naikaku Insatsukyoku, 1937.

Kokutai no Hongi: Cardinal Principles of the National Entity of Japan. Translated by John Owen Gauntlett. Edited with an Introduction by Robert King Hall. Harvard University Press, 1949.

Nakabayashi Shinji. "Kendō no ayumi" (The development of Japanese swordsmanship). Reprinted in *Budō no susume*. Shimadzu Shobō, 1994 (1982).

Nakamura Tamio. *Shiryō kindai kendoshi* (Sources for early twentieth-century history of *kendō*). Shimazu Shobō, 1985.

Kendō jiten: gijutsu to bunka no rekishi (Kendo gazetteer: A technical and cultural history). Shimazu Shobō, 1994.

Nishiyama Matsunosuke. *Iemoto monogatari* (Iemoto Stories). Reprinted in *Iemoto sei no tenkai* (Development of the *iemoto* system), vol. 2 of *Nishiyama Matsunosuke chosakushū* (Collected Works). Yoshikawa Kōbunkan, 1982 (1956).

Iemoto no kenkyu (Researches in the *iemoto* system). Reprinted as vol. 1 of *Nishiyama Matsunosuke chosakushū*. Yoshikawa Kōbunkan. 1982 (1960).

Edo Culture: Daily Life and Diversions in Urban Japan, 1600–1868. Translated and edited by Gerald Groemer. University of Hawaii Press, 1997.

Needham, Rodney. *Exemplars*. University of California Press, 1985.

Ōmori Nobumasa. *Bujutsu densho no kenkyū: kinsei budōshi he no apurōchi* (The study of martial arts initiation documents: A new approach to Tokugawa period martial arts history). Seiunsha, 1991.

Ooms, Herman. *Tokugawa Ideology: Early Constructs, 1570–1680*. Princeton

University Press, 1985.
Osano Jun. *Zusetsu Nihon bugei bunka gairon* (Illustrated overview of Japanese martial art culture). Fūyōsha, 1994.
Ōtake Risuke. *Mukei bunkazai Katori shintōyū*. English title: *The Deity and the Sword: Katori Shintoryu*. Partially translated by Donn F. Draeger, Shinotsuka Terue, and Nunokawa Kyōichirō. 3 vols. Minato Risaachi, 1977-1978.
Ōtsuka Tadayoshi. *Nihon kendō no rekishi* (The history of Japanese kendo). Madosha, 1995.
Sasamori Junzō. *Ittō-ryū gokui* (Ultimate secrets of Ittō-ryū swordsmanship). Ittōryū Gokui Kankōkai, 1965.
Sawada, Jaine A. *Confucian Values and Popular Zen: Sekimon Shingaku in Eighteenth Century Japan*. University of Hawaii Press, 1993.
Sharf, Robert H. "The Zen of Nationalism." Reprinted in *Curators of the Buddha: The Study of Buddhism Under Colonialism*. Edited by Donald S. Lopez, Jr. Chicago: University of Chicago Press, 1995 (1993).
"Experience." In Taylor, 1988.
Shaw, R. D. M. and Wilhelm Schiffer. "Yasen Kanna: A Chat on a Boat in the Evening by Hakuin Zenji." *Monumenta Nipponica* 13, no. 1–2. 1956.
Sugie Masatoshi. "The Problems of the Modernization of the Martial Arts of Japan". In Irie and Sugie 1988.
Sugimoto Shunryū. *Zōtei Tōjō shitsunai kirikami narabi sanwa kenkyū* (Corrected edition of studies in Sōtō Zen inner sanctuary documents and *kōan* initiations). Sōtōshū Shūmuchō, 1982 (1938).
Suzuki, Daisetz. *Zen Buddhism and its Influence on Japanese Culture*. Kyoto: Otani Buddhist College, 1938.
Zen to Nihon bunka. (Japanese translation of *Zen Buddhism and its Influence on Japanese Culture*). Translated by Kitagawa Momō. Iwanami Shoten, 1940.
Zen and Japanese Culture (revised edition of *Zen Buddhism and its Influence on Japanese Culture*). Princeton: Princeton University Press, 1959 (1938).
Takayama Takashi. *Hakuin zenji Yasen kanna*. Revised edition. Daihōrinkaku, 1975 (1943).
Taylor, Mark C., ed. *Critical Terms for Religious Studies*. University of Chicago Press, 1998.
Tominaga Kengo. *Kendō gohyakunenshi* (Five hundred years of Japanese swordsmanship). Hyakusen Shobō, 1972.
Vlastos, Stephen, ed. *Mirror of Modernity: Invented Traditions of Modern Japan*. University of California Press, 1998.
Victoria, Brian. *Zen at War*. New York: John Weatherhill, 1997.
Waddell, Norman, trans. "Hakuin's 'Yasenkanna.'" *The Eastern Buddhist*, new series, 34, no. 1. 2002.
Watanabe Ichirō, ed. *Shiryō Meiji budōshi* (Sources of martial art history during the Meiji period). Shin Jinbutsu Ōraisha, 1971.

Zen and Japanese Swordsmanship Reconsidered

ed. *Budō no meicho* (Martial art classics). Tōkyō Kopii Shuppanbu, 1979.

Watanabe Ichirō et al., eds. *Kinsei geidōron* (Tokugawa period performance theory) *Nihon shisō taikei* 61. Iwanami Shoten, 1972

Yamada Shōji. "Shinwa toshite no yumi to zen". *Nihon kenkyū* 19. 1999. "The Myth of Zen in the Art of Archery." Translation of "Shinwa toshite no yumi to zen." Translated by Earl Hartman. Edited by William M. Bodiford. *Japanese Journal of Religious Studies* 28, nos. 1–2: 1–30. 2001. (Available online: http://www.nanzan-u.ac.jp/SHUBUNKEN/publications/jjrs/pdf/586.pdf.)

Yampolsky, Philip B. *The Zen Master Hakuin: Selected Writings*. Columbia University Press, 1971.

Chapter 4

Ken-Zen-Sho: An Analysis of Swordsmanship, Zen, and Calligraphy and their Relevance Today

Terayama Tanchū
Nishōgakusha University

Birth and Maturity

The techniques and philosophies of *kenjutsu* evolved over many centuries. Leaving the historical details aside, I would like to concentrate my discourse on the maturation of *kenjutsu* as a means to escape the 'fear of death' and 'uncertainties of life'.

From the Gempei disturbance (1180 to 1185) through to the turbulent times of the Muromachi *bakufu* (1338–1573), the science of warfare (*heihō* or *hyōhō*) was researched in earnest by warriors. Combat training methodology was fashioned in accordance with defined principles, giving rise to organized *kenjutsu* traditions (*ryūha*) which formally developed techniques and skills ultimately to determine life or death (*shōji-kettei*).

Representative of such traditions were the Kage-ryū of west Japan, and the Tenshin Shoden Katori Shintō-ryū of the east, both formed in the fifteenth century. Interestingly, it is claimed that the founders of these traditions prayed to the deities for secret knowledge, or were bequeathed such wisdom from supernatural beings such as the beasts of the forests and Mother Nature herself.

In due course techniques and philosophies became more sophisticated, and we see the rise of teachings concerned with the essence of 'human existence' such as Kamiizumi Ise no Kami's *"fumetsu no kokoro"* (eternal mind), Miyamoto Musashi's *"iwao no mi"* (the body of a rock- unmoving mind), Yagyū-ryū's *"seikosui"*, Harigaya Sekiun's *"mujushin"* (unfixed mind), Tsuji Gettan's *"ippō mugai"* (only one way), Kamiya Denshinsai's *"jikishin"* (inherent mind), and Yamaoka Tesshū's *"semui"* (fearlessness). All these teachings are expressions denoting a transcendental state or an acceptance of the inevitability of life and death. In this sense, *kenjutsu* evolved from techniques developed for the sole purpose of dealing death in order to stay alive, into deep philosophical Ways (*michi*) utilizing those techniques as a vehicle for understanding the essence of existence.

During the Kamakura period, Hōjō Tokimune (1251–84) the eighth shogunal regent was constantly faced with the threat of Mongol invasions. Being an enthusiast of Zen Buddhism, he invited the priest Wu-hsueh (J: Mugaku) from Song China, and was taught that the greatest utility of Zen was to bring to light the meaning of life, as well as the meaning of death. Dōgen (1200–1253), founder of the Sōtō sect of Zen Buddhism in 1227 had also stated earlier that "the most important task for monks was to accentuate and elucidate the meaning of life and death." (*Shōbō genzō*-1231–53, *Treasury of the true Dharma eye*). Shūhū Myōchō (1282–1337), also known as Daitō Kokushi, monk of the Rinzai sect of Zen Buddhism, stressed that Zen was actually "an investigation of the self." That is to grasp the absolute truth of the self, and to live in accordance with this truth. The "true self" is not simply quantified in years, weight, or height, but is limitless in its expansiveness. Also, Dōgen suggested "the entire world of the ten directions is the true human body. The cycle of birth and death is the true human body itself." (*Shōbō genzō- Shinjin gakudō*). In other words, the body that dwells in all parts of the universe is the true body of the individual.

Humans have long been well aware of their mortality and the limitations of human capacity. After long and arduous training, some notable individuals were able to reach a new level of enlightened understanding where they were able to connect human existence with something that is unlimited in scope and strength. "The 'true man of no rank' (*mui no shin'nin*) who can hear the cosmic laws right here and now (*sokkon mokuzen chōbōtei*) is the epitome of life. To this purpose we engage in Zen to know ourselves. Zen is all-revealing of that which lies within the individual, the 'true self'. 'To study the self is to forget the self.'" (*Shōbō genzō- Genjō kōan*). It is when one is able to "forget the self", and "lose the self" that the world where the self is everything becomes apparent. In order to do this, one has to be able to "set aside body and mind, forget about them, and throw them into the house of the Buddha." (*Shōbō genzō- Shōji*).

In this way, one is able to lose the self through the practise of *zazen*, and hence be awoken to the "primary life", the essence of all existence. Zen matured as a way of living this primary life subjectively.

The pulse of this "primary life" was also applied in the appraisal of the brushworks found in the *Kogahinroku* (*Hua P'in Lu* – Record of classification of painters) by Shakaku (C: Hsieh Ho) (479-?). This treatise deals with paintings, however, it is appropriate to view ink paintings and calligraphy as the same, as the ancient Chinese did (*shoga-ittai*).

Ō Gishi (Wang Xi Zhi 307?-365?) a famous Chinese calligrapher of the Eastern Jin period, in a collection of his letters called *Jironshō* states, "The maturity (*seijuku*) of the writer Chōshi exceeds all others. The whole heart is put into the brushstrokes (*seisaku*)…"

Here, the word *seijuku* (maturity) refers to the technical aspects of the work, and *seisaku* (spiritual make-up) to the spiritual qualities attained through applying the brush with one's whole heart. In other words, classical paintings were valued in accordance with both technical and spiritual attributes, and superior skill in both areas was the utmost aspiration.

Kūkai (774–835), also known as Kōbō Daishi, a Buddhist priest of the early Heian period considered calligraphy and art to be an "extension of what is in the heart" (*Shōryō-shū*). Kōsankoku (Huang Shangu 1045-1105), one of the best-known calligraphers

Ken-Zen-Sho

and poets of the Northern Song dynasty recorded that the works he brushed when he was in his forties actually "did not contain his brush." He explains that calligraphy that did not "contain the brush" is synonymous to the lack of the pivotal character or word (*shigan*) that completes a Zen poem. Without it, it cannot be called complete, and is thus insufficient (*Shan gu ti ba*). In other words, if the brush is not "contained" in the characters, this means the work lacks "spirit resonance" (*ki-in seidō* – circulation of *ki* (breath, spirit, vital force of heaven) that produces movement of life.)

The treatise *Jubokushō* (1352) is an explanation of examples of *shodō* (calligraphy) brushed by Sonen Shinnō (1298-1356) to the Emperor Gokōgon (1338-1374). He states that "a superior work of calligraphy is like a living entity. It must appear to be imbued with spirit and soul". Such a work "shows no sign of weakness whatsoever" and thus that "Buddhist enlightenment is visible through the perfection of the worldly arts".

Therefore, calligraphy (*sho*) was perceived as far more than just a technical pursuit. More importantly, works of calligraphy must contain soul and spiritual resonance, and is thus the manifestation of "primary life". Training in *ken* (sword) and Zen were considered ways of overcoming concerns with life and death. They both require an attitude of self-annihilation to return to the transcendental state of primary life so that the true meaning of life – that which exceeds matters of life and death – can be understood. The pursuit of "primary life" becomes the objective of the artist or warrior's "life path". Similarly, when *sho* is recognised as being in tune with that life pulse, it becomes evident that the "primary life" is all the same. In other words, *ken*, Zen, and *sho* are essentially aspiring to the same understanding of the "primary life" and our very existence.

Musashi and Tesshū

There are a number of historical figures who travelled the paths of *ken-zen-sho*. Great warriors such as Yagyū Munenori (1571-1645) immediately spring to mind. However, in this paper I will limit my analysis to Miyamoto Musashi (1582-1645) and Yamaoka Tesshū (1836-1888).

There are a number of theories concerning the roots of Miyamoto Musashi (see Chapter 2 of this volume), and there are many points about his life and career that are still a matter of great conjecture. One theory states that he was born into the Tahara family of Harima no kuni (modern day Hyōgo prefecture), and became the adopted son and student of Miyamoto Munisai, master of the spear. Being born into a warrior family, Musashi was destined to walk the path of the warrior. His first combat encounter was at age thirteen with Arima Kihei, a swordsman of the Shintō-ryū tradition. It is recorded in his well-known military treatise *Gorin no sho* that by the time he was twenty-eight or nine, he had fought in over sixty duels without being defeated. However, once exceeding the age of thirty, Musashi became acutely aware that despite his undefeated record, he had never actually beaten his foe in accordance with the true principles (*ri*) of the sword. He realised that his success had been due to good fortune more than any other factor.

It also states in the initial pages of *Gorin no sho*, "I continued to train and to seek from morning to night an understanding of the deeper principles. When I reached the age of fifty, I found myself to be naturally on the 'Way' of strategy (*heihō*). Since that day, I have lived without need of searching further into the Way. When I apply the principles of strategy to the various artistic Ways, I am no longer in need of a tutor for any of them."

It took him twenty years of hardship and dedication to reach this level of understanding. His comments are a fair indication that he was able to disengage the self in anything he did. What he was searching for suddenly became very apparent when he understood the importance of "losing the self". This was a significantly more profound level of understanding of strategy than his youthful days of duelling. The embodied principles of strategy which now emanated forth from Musashi's being were completely applicable to any other artistic pursuits to the extent that he was able to master calligraphy, sculpturing, metalwork and so on without the need for tutors. Of course, this would have been impossible without having actually applied himself to learning the basic techniques of these arts. Musashi seemed to have been interested in them since his childhood days, and spent twenty years polishing his artistic skills along with his martial ones, and his enlightenment to the true universal principles of all arts brought his works to life.

These principles are perfectly applicable to Zen. Musashi's thoughts on Zen outlined in his writings, and the profound influence Zen had on him are evident through the repetitive use of Zen terms such as *jikishin* (true mind) and *ginmi* (to know through practice and experience). Also, the Zen influence on Musashi's thought is obvious in his many paintings of Daruma (Bodhidharma) and Hotei (Pu-tai). The scroll entitled *Kū* (Void) in *Gorin no sho* is particularly relevant to Zen.

Many treatises on military strategy organize the contents in accordance with the five elements of earth, water, fire, wind, and void. *Gorin no sho*, often translated into English as *A Book of Five Rings*, is heavily influenced by the Zen teaching of *Go-i* or the "five degrees of enlightenment". These were established by the Chinese Zen master and founder of the Sōtō sect Tung-shan Liang-chieh (J: Tōzan Ryōkai) and Ts'ao-shan Pen-chi (J: Sōzan Honjaku). There are variations but I will limit my explanation to what is called *Shōhen Go-i*.

In order of increasing depths of enlightenment, these degrees are *shō-chū-hen* (正中偏) (*hen* in the midst of *shō*), *hen-chū-shō* (偏中正) (*shō* in the midst of *hen*), *shō-chū-rai* (正中来) ([the one] coming out of the midst of *shō* [and *hen* as polarly related to it], *ken-chū-shi* (兼中至) (entering between the two [polar aspects]), *ken-chū-tō* (兼中到) (having already arrived in the middle of both.) The characters *shō* and *hen* represent polar aspects of reality. *Shō* represents sameness and *hen* difference. *Shō* is fundamental wisdom, and *hen* is wisdom accrued later on. *Shō* is true nature and *hen* represents the attributes. If we apply this to swordsmanship and calligraphy, it would correspond with mind and technique.

Shō-chū-hen (*hen* in the midst of *shō*) is the level of experience where the world of phenomena dominates, but it is experienced as a manifestation of the fundamental, our true nature. Sameness is difference, and could be represented by the "Seeing the cow" and "Catching the cow", two of the stages of "Spiritual Cow Herding" from "The Ten Cow-herding Pictures."[1]

Hen-chū-shō is the second stage of enlightened experience, and here the quality of non-distinction comes to the fore and the quality of manifoldness fades into the background. Differences are the same, so even if "flowers are red and willows are green", "form is none other than emptiness. Emptiness is none other than form."

Shō-chū-rai is an experience in which there is no longer any awareness of body or mind. Both completely "drop away" leaving emptiness or *kū*. This is enlightenment like "Coming Home on the Cow's Back".[2] *Ken-chū-shi* is the stage where each thing is afforded special uniqueness to the greatest degree. Even emptiness has vanished, and it is the gateway to the final stage *ken-chū-tō*. This is the highest level where form and emptiness fully interpenetrate. From here arises action without any movement of brain or heart that instantaneously suits whatever circumstance may occur. In the "Ten Cow-herding Pictures" this would equate with the stage of "To Return to the Origin"[3] to "Entering the City with Bliss-bestowing Hands."[4] The Void scroll in Musashi's *Gorin no sho* is closest to this concept.

In the first section of *Gorin no sho*, Musashi states, "in composing this treatise, I do not borrow from the ancient Buddhist or Confucian writings." I believe that he refrained from including such sources in order to keep his content easily comprehensible. He probably studied Zen not under the priest Shunzan Ōsho who was thirty four years his junior, but under Obuchi Ōsho.

A more recent master of *ken-zen-sho* was Yamaoka Tesshū (Tetsutarō) (1836–88). He commenced studies of calligraphy when he was seven or eight years of age under the auspices of his mother Iso. One of the words he was taught to write was *chūkō* (忠孝). He asked his mother what it meant. She replied that "*chū*" referred to maintaining a correct mind or attitude and loyalty when serving one's lord. "*Kō*" referred to the same attitude in regards to one's parents, or filial piety. Tetsutarō then asked "do you always maintain such an attitude?" His mother remained silent for a while, and then shed a tear. "Oh Tetsu, I always hold such attitudes in my heart, but I am not a great woman, and I find it difficult to fulfil these requirements all of the time. You must become a man who can truly live up to these ideals." (Yamaoka Tesshū, *Fubo no kyōkun to ken to zen ni shiruseshi koto*- Learning parents' teachings, *ken* and Zen).

When he was thirteen, his father Takatomi implored him "if anything at all, a man who enters the martial way should never forget the meaning of filial piety and loyalty." He also told Tesshū to "develop [correct] form through the martial arts (*bugei*), and train the mind through the principles of Zen." When he was twenty-nine he wrote that "this is why I embarked on my study of these two ways." This provided the basis for his future character development, and history clearly demonstrates just how dedicated to the concept of *chūkō* or filial piety and loyalty he was. He wrote about his attitude to the study of *ken-zen-sho* in his youth. Here, I would like to quote some of his writings, firstly in regards to swordsmanship:

"I commenced my study of swordsmanship when I was a young boy, and learned the principles of Zen. I tried to put form to whatever I felt in my mind, and have continued my study as such to this day. When I was nine years old, I entered the tutelage of Kusumi Kantekisai (Shinkage-ryū). Following that, I studied under Inoue Kiyotora (Hokutō Ittō-ryū), Chiba Shūsaku, Saitō, and Momoi. I broadened my practice by engaging in thousands of matches with swordsmen representing many different traditions. For more than twenty years I trained in such a manner without reaching an understanding of the deeper principles that I sought. I searched in vain for a truly enlightened master of swordsmanship to aid me in my quest. Finally I met Asari Matashichirō Yoshiaki, a master of the Ittō-ryū school, and the second son of Nakanishi Chūbei and successor of the Itō Ittōsai style. Knowing of his skill, I sought to engage him in a contest. Indeed, he was a far cry from any of the previous fencers I had engaged. His exterior was flexible, but he was rock-hard on the inside. He had a spiritual concentration so intense that he was able to attain victory over any opponent before they even moved. He was a truly enlightened master of swordsmanship. I engaged him many times after our first encounter, but regardless of how hard I tried, I was never successful in quelling this mighty foe. I would train with many different opponents during the day, and sit and meditate each evening, contemplating the importance of respiration. I would dream of Asari standing before me like a mountain. It was impossible for me to strike at him or drive this vision away."

In regards to Zen, Tesshū received guidance from a number of masters including Gannō, Seijō, and Dokuon, but the most influential master in the course of Tesshū's training was Tekisui, the abbot of the Tenryūji temple.

"Tekisui said to me, 'things are good but please allow an insignificant monk to say one thing. That is, your present state is as if one is looking at things through spectacles. Glasses serve to clarify your vision, and are not meant to impede your eyesight. Yet, one without eye trouble by nature has no need for spectacles. Not only are spectacles unnecessary to a man with good eyesight, but using them makes things appear distorted, and things appear natural without. In your present state you have already reached the periphery. If you can remove this last remaining obstacle, you will instantly reach the stage that you have been searching for so long. You are a man of sword and Zen. Once you are enlightened, you will be able to take charge of death and life, and reach a level in which you possess supernatural powers. The stage you are at now can is one where a riddle will take you beyond the periphery. In the end, all you need is one thing. *Mu*, no-thing'.

I've been giving great consideration to this suggestion by Tekisui, every day and night. It's been ten years since then, yet, there still lingers a sense that I do not fully understand what he meant. I visited Tekisui twice, and told him my thoughts. He presented me with another *kōan*: 'When two flashing swords meet there is no place to escape; move on calmly, like a lotus flower in bloom in the midst of a great fire, and forcefully pierce the heavens!'" (*Kempō to zenri*- April 1880).

Tesshū wrote that he pondered this *kōan* relentlessly for the next three years before awakening to its hidden meaning and became enlightened. In regards to *sho*, he wrote the following words:

"When I was eleven years old, I went to a village by a mountain in Hida, following my father Chōueimon. I learned martial arts everyday, and practiced calligraphy every spare moment I had. At the time, there was a man called Iwasa Ittei who became famous for his skill in calligraphy. My father allowed me to study calligraphy under his tutelage even though I did not know how to write Chinese characters then. Ittei gave me a volume of one thousand words that he had brushed. I practiced copying his work for a month, and finally my characters started to take form.

My father handed me a bundle of *minō* paper suggesting that I write down all that I had learned to date. It was a little after ten o'clock in the evening. Following his suggestion, I wrote one thousand words in sixty-three pages not including the date and signature. Upon completion of this task, I presented it to my father. It was a little before two o'clock in the early hours. My father was astonished and said to me, 'How smoothly the characters are written. I cannot suppress my sense of disbelief, yet, I know that you are the only one who could have written these words. After all, this handwriting is undoubtedly yours. The characters are written so well, and I know you to be an honest person. Do not forget this spirit and strive to master both the sword and the brush' he said affectionately.

My father invited Ittei next day, and put the pages that I brushed before him. Ittei was astounded and said, 'How striking this work is. It is beyond imagination that they were written by a child. Moreover, it is unbelievable that it took him only a short time to do it. I am awed by this child.' He continued his praise, 'this child is dependable and full of potential.' His praise encouraged me greatly....

I happened to hear that a Chinese man called Ō Gishi (Wang Xi Zhi) is excellent at calligraphy. I borrowed books of his calligraphy from my colleague and brother-in-law, or purchased them, and every chance I had I would copy his writings. I did this for over ten years. I also learned by copying the works of other masters. However, my level is far from sufficient. All I can do is copy the works of the masters.

Many years ago, I went to worship at the national temple in Otowa. There, I happened to notice an exquisite work of calligraphy displayed in a corner. The characters were completely free of worldliness, and the brush strokes were pure and unsullied. It was truly the work of an "ascending dragon." When I looked at the work closely, I found that it was in fact that of Kōbō Daishi, the Buddhist patriarch. It is impossible to describe the transcendent beauty present in his writing, and it impressed me such that it has always stayed with me.

Thenceforth, I studied various styles of brushwork done by both priests and laymen. I copied them whenever I had an opportunity, and after a number of years I attained a certain level of mastery. That was in 1872, or 1873.

On March 30, 1880, I realised the true meaning of swordsmanship and Zen. Since such deep attainment enables one to comprehend many things, I simultaneously grasped the essence of calligraphy too. Although I understand the secrets of these pursuits, I am unable to explain them in words."

In 1880, Tesshū was forty-five. The insurmountable image he carried for seventeen years of the Ittō-ryū master, Asari Yoshiaki, dissipated immediately upon this realisation, and he buzzed with energy. One month later on May 14, he told an old acquaintance, Nakajō Kinnosuke, a well-known swordsman in his own right, "If Miyamoto Musashi himself were to come back to challenge me, I would not win, but I would not lose either." (*Yamaoka Tetsutarō nenpu,* edited by Murakami Yasumasa.) When his colleague Nakajō crossed swords with Tesshū to test his seemingly arrogant claim of equality with the legendary Musashi, Nakajō found himself completely unable to move. Nakajō himself was a swordsman of great repute, and this confirmed to him that Tesshū had in fact become an enlightened master of *ken*.

Tesshū owned many copies of works by Miyamoto Musashi, including *Heihō sanjūgokajō,* and reproduced his own version of Musashi's *Dokkōdō* in his later years. He was acutely aware of the importance of Musashi, and concentrated on pursuing the same path to the extent where he was finally able to say he would neither beat nor be beaten by Musashi if he were to come back. By saying this, he is probably referring to the concept of *ainuke,* a term referring to a situation in which both adepts can neither cut nor be cut by the other, indicative of an extremely high degree of skill.

Photo 1. Tesshū's brushwork for the character 'ryū' (龍) or dragon

It is around this time that we witness a change in Tesshū's calligraphy. It became imbued with "spirit resonance" through the attainment of a state of "nothingness". He produced many works in which he recorded his age, so it is a simple matter of comparison to verify his enlightened leap.

As soon as Asari knew that his student had realised "nothingness" in swordsmanship, he officially made Tesshū his successor as the thirteenth Headmaster of the Nakanishi-ha Ittō-ryū. Tesshū then established the Mutō-ryū, (School of the Sword of No Sword.) He was also acknowledged and certified in his mastery of Zen by Abbot Tekisui. Thus, he was a recognised master in swordsmanship, calligraphy and Zen, and collectively he called his style Tesshū-ryū. By this time he had been studying intensively for over thirty years. He had studied swordsmanship under Kusumi Kantekisai of the Jikishinkage-ryū, Inoue Kiyotora of the Hokushin Ittō-ryū, Ittō Shoden-ryū under Asari Yoshiaki, Zen under Gannō of the Chōtokuji temple, Seijō of the Ryūtakuji temple, Dokuon of the Shokokuji temple, Kōsen of the Enkakuji temple, and Sekisui of the Tenryūji temple. He studied calligraphy under Iwasa Ittei, the fifty-first Headmaster of the Jubokudō style, and under many other tutors of various traditions. This period of intensive study was vital to his eventual enlightenment.

Photo 1 shows Tesshū's brushwork for the character '*ryū*' (龍) or dragon. It was written when he was fifty years of age. Considering he achieved "resonant spirit" in his work at age forty-five, this work is even more gentle and warm, and surely attests to the sublime level of brushwork he had reached.

Tesshū wrote "whenever I had a chance to break from my duties each day, without fail I would use the opportunity to pursue my studies of *ken-zen-sho*." His calligraphy rapidly became in great demand, and he mass produced thousands upon thousands of works, often several hundred each day, all of which were eagerly received by people from all walks of life.

The *Hōjō Kata* and 'Losing One's Body'

Kashima Shinden Jikishinkage-ryū was created by Matsumoto Bizen no Kami Naokatsu of Kashima. (There is also a theory that Matsumoto was actually Sugimoto—1478-1534.) In the system, there are a series of four sword forms (*kata*) called *hōjō* which teach the fundamental movements, correct cutting, *ma-ai* (distancing), and *kiai*. Each of the four *kata* are associated with a season (spring, summer, autumn, winter), whose properties are expressed in the movement of each form.

The first *kata*, *hassō happa*, is indicative of spring with its drawn out and large movements. The second *kata*, *ittō ryōdan*, corresponds to summer due to the vigorous and fiery energy that permeates and radiates from the adepts. *Uten saten*, the third form, represents autumn with its pivotal changes, and *chōtan ichimi* represents winter due to its internalised nature. It is the most quiet and subdued of all the forms.

The important thing in the swordsmanship of the Jikishinkage-ryū is not so much in the cutting or thrusting techniques of the sword, but in behaviour and action in everyday life. For example, this could be the act of drinking together, as quoted in a precept taught in the tradition. A good demonstration of this ideal can be found in a well-known story of how Ittokusai Yamada Jirōkichi, the fourteenth successor of the system, was awarded his *menkyo* licence of the Jikishinkage-ryū from his master Sakakibara Kenkichi. The two were walking the slippery snow-covered Kudan slope. The elderly Sakakibara lost his clog, to which Yamada, without thinking, immediately replaced it with his own just as Sakakibara put his foot down. This was a perfect example of *mushin* (acting without thought — state of no-mind), and clearly demonstrated to Sakakibara the level of Jirōkichi's attainment in the tradition, even though it was demonstrated outside the *dōjō*. Furthermore, the teaching "if you remove all the knowledge and trivial skills acquired after birth, the pure brightness of one's life will be revived" is another way of expressing the same ideal. In other words, one objective of training in the tradition is to return to the honesty of spirit of a new-born baby, and responding to society with that same spirit; i.e. a return to one's "primary life."

In the *hōjō* forms, each technique focuses not so much on cutting the opponent but "cutting through one's own centre". The hips are always facing forwards rather than in a side-on stance. This is referred to as the natural and original bodily stance, rather than the result of accrued knowledge, and is a distinctive training method. In other words, the adept is not afraid of being cut, and has no need to assume side-on stances to avoid attack. In fact, winning or losing an encounter is not an issue in the system. Simply cutting through one's own centre is the essence of the Jikishinkage-ryu.

In the *hōjō kata*, if we figuratively place *uchidachi* (adept who performs the role of the aggressor or initiator of the form) with the light to their back, *shidachi* (counter-attacker) will be in their shadow. In all four *kata*, *shidachi* ends up as victor in each encounter. This is in accordance with the philosophy of the Shinkage-ryu, where the '*kage*' refers to shadow. A shadow is created when light is blocked, but the shadow does not move of its own accord. In other words, the shadow moves only when the object blocking the light does. Hence, in order to identify with the shadow, *shidachi* must face death as *uchidachi* initiates all of the attacks and moves first. Accepting death, the adept can reach the state of "absolute self".

In the well-known warrior treatise *Hagakure*, the author states that "the meaning of *bushidō* (the Way of the warrior) is found in death." This should be interpreted only in the literal sense of a warrior's preparedness to forfeit his life in battle, but it also contains the nuances that the warrior should totally dedicate himself to studying the ways of old, and performing his duties selflessly every living moment. This can be confirmed by the subsequent sentence which states that "…this is the substance of the Way of the samurai. If by setting one's heart right every morning and evening, one is able to live as though his body were already dead, he finds freedom in the Way. His whole life will be without blame, and he will succeed in his calling…" The orator of the *Hagakure*, Yamamoto Jōchō commenced his studies of Zen from the age of twenty-one under Tannen, the priest of the Kōdenji temple. It is obvious through his writings that he was heavily influenced by Zen thought.

This kind of attitude is always evident in Zen. Hakuin (1686–1769), the extremely influential Rinzai sect Zen master, painter, and calligrapher, was taught by Dōkyō Etan who was in turn a disciple of Shidō Bunan (1603–1676), a Zen monk of the Rinzai sect. Bunan gained renown as a great spiritual master, residing in a hermitage at Koishikawa in Edo until his death. His calligraphy (photo 2) is exquisite, and his Zen is the product of completely and utterly losing oneself into the task.

Photo 2. "Mu" (nothingness) by Bunan

Bunan was born in a turbulent age in a house in Sekigahara, the site of the decisive battle in the rise of Ieyasu and the Tokugawa shogunate in 1600. Amidst these unsettled times, Bunan was able to see the transient nature of things and was attracted to the tranquillity of Zen, thus deciding to enter the priesthood. For thirty years he studied hard leading a stark and frugal life. When he was finally able to solve the *kōan* "*Shidō bunan yuiken kenjaku*" ("The ultimate path is not difficult to reach. Just do not be particular"), he took the name Shidō Bunan. He was forty-seven years of age at the time.

Thereafter, he left us with a legacy of poems such as "night and day, one must use the sword of the king of Kongō to kill oneself. When you are able to kill yourself thus, you will naturally reach a state of salvation." And, "when the body has been completely killed, the life that is left is called the Buddha", "becoming dead while you are alive, just do what you wish." Thus this piece of calligraphy with its colossal scale and immeasurable warmth was achieved through nothing less than a state of absolute nothingness (*mi wo nakusu*- freeing yourself of your body). That is why it retains an un-relinquishing appeal. It has a transcendental quality and is the product of eternal life. Tesshū also regarded this state of *mi wo nakusu* very highly, and often discussed it with his students.

Japanese Culture and "Following the Way"

One of Japan's most eminent modern philosophers, Nishida Kitarō (1870–1945), wrote in his introduction to "The problem of Japanese culture", (*Nihon bunka no mondai* in *Nishida Kitarō zenshū 12 Vols.*) that the Japanese spirit is something that should radiate naturally like "the wild cherry-flowers glowing in the morning sun." In a similar fashion, Motoori Norinaga (1730–1801) classical scholar of the Edo period stated in *Naobi no mitama* to search for the truth of things means to totally dedicate the self to the cause. Namely, to negate the self, lose the self, to become selfless with no worldly attachments.

One of the recognised characteristics of Japanese culture is the emphasis placed on "following the Way", what ever that cultural pursuit may be. When Dōgen returned from his studies in China, he said he was able to develop a "flexible mind". What he meant by this was he had acquired the ability to "think as a thing, and act as a thing". This means that while one is engaged in studying a way, the adept must surrender body and soul and attain a state of "no mind" or *mushin*. This is precisely what lies behind the deep secrets of swordsmanship, Zen, and calligraphy. In the case of *ken* and *sho*, one utilizes the medium of the sword or brush. However, it is impossible to become fluid in movement if you cannot become one with the implement. As we have seen, in order to become as one with the implement one needs to extinguish the self. Even in Zen, one does not affirm the limitless expansiveness of the born self, but conversely rejects the self first, in order to be awakened to the "true self". Not to do so would leave the individual unable to understand the limitless truth of one's existence. Therefore, judging by the superb examples of work that priests and artists such as Kūkai, Saigyo, Sesshu, and Rikyū left behind, it is clear that they were of this level. That is why their calligraphy takes on lives of their own.

The Void and Universal Mind

In the scroll of the Void (*Ku no maki*) in Musashi's *Gorin no sho* it states, "the warrior must learn the way of strategy by making great efforts to learn the various martial arts. Nothing should be disregarded when studying the way of the warrior. He should study tirelessly from morning to night, making sure his mind doesn't wander. He must strive to polish his mind and will, and hone his skills to learn the two visions; looking and seeing. He should realise that the true void is where the clouds of indecision have completely scattered." In other words, this is referring to being able to distinguish between all things, but at the same time not being one bit taken by anything. This, according to Musashi, is the true "void".

He is not inferring that the void is indicative of "no knowledge" or indifference to the Way of strategy. He is referring to the void which is very much alive. Brushing calligraphy is the same in this sense. The style of character, brushwork, thickness of the ink, and quality of the paper must first be taken into consideration. Then, all of these details must be completely forgotten as one puts brush to paper. This is the only way that the characters will be imbued with life.

In the *Hanya shingyō* (S: *Prajñāpāramitā hrdaya sūtra*) this is called *shikisoku zekū* "form or matter is non-substantial". In such a way, all existence is formless. This is the same as the world one enters when the self is forgotten. If the self is completely gone, the world then becomes the self. A life which is equal with any other life form becomes unique and discernable and truly alive in *kūsoku zeshiki* "emptiness is identical to matter".

In Zen, this state is often referred to as "*mu*" (nothingness). In the first section of the *Hekiganroku*, Emperor Wu of Liang asked Bodhidharma, "What is the first principle of the holy teachings?" The Bodhidharma answered "*Kakunen mushō*, the state of emptiness with clarity". From this world of emptiness, every living being springs forth, as is expressed by the teaching "*muichimotsu chū mujinzō*, (wealth in the midst of nothing to cling to). There are flowers, a moon, and even buildings even though there is really nothing." Here, *samadhi*, the consciousness of the experiencing "subject" becomes one with the experienced "object", the perfect state of spiritual concentration.

Confucius said in the *Analects*, "when I was seventy I could follow what my heart desired without transgressing what was right." One day, Confucius asked his disciples Tsze-lu, Zan Yu, Kung-hsu Hwa and others about their desires. Tsze-lu replied he would like to rule a large state. Zan Yu replied that he would like to make a small state prosperous. Kung-hsi Hwa replied that he would like to act as a small assistant to help the ruler of the state through ritual courtesy and music. Last of all Tsang Hsi, "pausing as he was playing on his lute, while it was yet twanging, laid the instrument aside, "In this, the last month of spring, with the dress of the season all complete, along with five or six young men who have assumed the cap, and six or seven boys, I would bathe in the springs, enjoy the breeze among the rain altars, and return home singing." The Master heaved a sigh and said, "I give my approval to Tsang." If we were to apply this answer to the aforementioned *go-i* surely it would correspond with *ken-chū-tō*, the highest level where form and emptiness fully interpenetrate. A true world of leisure where there are no constraints whatsoever; this is the "true void".

In his younger years when Tesshū engaged in Zen meditation, it was so powerful that scurrying mice reputedly froze when they wandered into the vicinity. However, in his later years when he was transcribing sutras, mice would come and sit on his knees and shoulders. People who were troubled or in pain would visit him until late in the evening, and leave his house totally refreshed and rejuvenated. When people asked

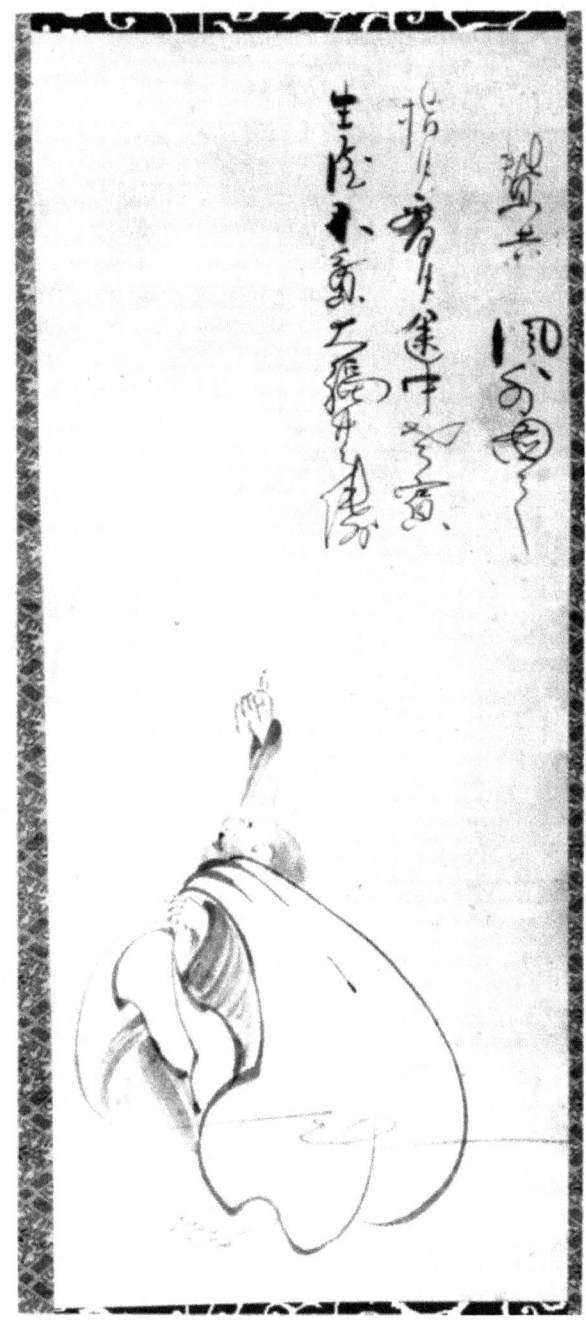

Photo 3. Fūgai Ekun's "Hotei-zu"

him of the secrets of *kenjutsu*, he would always say that the answer can be found at Sensōji temple with the Kannon (Bodhisattva of great compassion) in Asakusa. At the temple, there is a plaque inscribed with the characters "*semui*" (removal of fear and deliverance of salvation). In his later years he was looked up to by his peers as a man who would radiate energy which served to put their minds at ease. He was, to them, a living Buddha, and his fearlessness put their minds at ease.

In regards to his calligraphy, there was a man, Chō Sanshū (1823-1895), who expressed his doubt that Tesshū could possibly write five or six hundred pieces in a single day. In reply to his doubts Tesshū said "you strain your shoulders because you are drawing the characters. I am simply applying ink, so there is no strain at all." In other words, he was insinuating that Chō Sanshū's mind was consciously operating when he brushed calligraphy. However, in his own case, especially in his twilight years, he was impervious to the action of brushing the characters, and what ended up on the paper was an unconscious expression of his soul. Therefore, regardless of how many characters he wrote in a day, there was no physical strain on his body. He drew an analogy to the skills required by a carpenter when shaving wood. "Plane, carpenter, and beam must function together in perfect unison just as mind, body and technique should. Then, mind, body, and technique are ultimately forgotten and one proceeds smoothly until the job is complete."

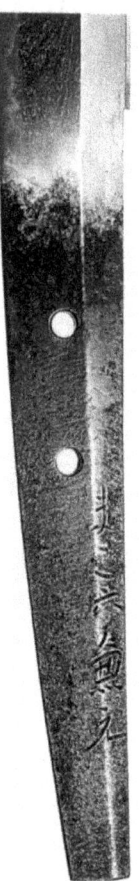

Photo 4. Blade tang from the Muromachi period (1333-1568)

One of Rinzai's (?-867) teachers, Fuke, would explain as he rung his bell, that the essence of Buddhist enlightenment was to act and do what you like, as you like, when you like, and live in a state of absolute freedom. I think that the Japanese monk Fūgai Ekun (1568–1654) of the Sōtō sect and painter also understood this realm. You can discern in photo 3 above the un-worldliness and sublime nature and total freedom of his work. Furthermore, the work resonates with warmth and tenderness rather than detachment. In his later years he became a wandering monk, and lived for a time in caves. His lifestyle was totally free and uninhibited, and this is evident in his paintings. This would correspond to the tenth stage of the "*Cow Herding Pictures*", "*Entering the City with Bliss-bestowing Hands.*"

From a state of absolute nothingness attained by complete and total self-annihilation, the heart that springs forth is one of "compassion, harmony, and honesty." (Bunan's *Sokushin ki*). I think that this corresponds with what modern scientists call "Universal Mind".

Tesshū's sword was a way of *semui* (fearlessness) as it was

Ken-Zen-Sho

able to put people's minds at ease. Musashi's sword was able to pierce the "void", and his enlightenment is evident in the extreme and limitless warmth perceivable in his works of art. The works of the likes of Bunan and Fūgai, although different in form to the others, still all have the very same "primary life" force flowing through them.

The *ken-zen-sho* of Musashi and Tesshū too was imbued with a power attainable only through enlightenment. Even in this day and age of advanced science and technology, we moderns are still attracted to the exploits of our enlightened predecessors. Although these were the exploits of certain individuals, their legacy is an asset for all of humanity.

To digress a little, the Japanese sword is referred to by a number of terms. The straight blades are called *chokutō* (直刀) and *daitō* (大刀), and blades with curvature (*sori*) are called *tachi* (太刀), which stems from the word *tachi* (断ち) meaning "refusal", implying the action of cutting asunder.

The Japanese sword must be able to cut cleanly without bending or snapping. The swordsmith focuses and concentrates on creating the ultimate sword, often reaching a higher state of putting their mind and hearts into the sword as they make it, resulting in the production of many famous swords. For example, from the Heian period are Tomonari and Masatsune swords, from the Kamakura period are the Ichimonji swords, and the Kanesada and Kanemoto swords of the Muromachi period (photo 4) are all examples of workmanship that exceeded making mere implements of destruction, but are elevated into the realm of high art. Within the swords produced by these smiths exists "spiritual resonance", and not only are they exquisite to look at, they glow with the warmth of the enlightened hearts of their makers. That too can be said of the inscriptions in the tangs. These swords can rightly be considered the embodiment of the level of enlightenment that Musashi and Tesshū attained through their study of the martial arts. Thus, one with the knowledge to appraise swords will no doubt recognise these objects too as treasures of the highest artistic attainment humanity has reached.

Endnotes

[1] Representation of the ten stages of the Zen way and different levels of enlightenment shown through ten pictures of an ox and its herder. The following descriptions are quoted from Suzuki Daisetz's *Zen and Japanese Culture*.
Seeing the Cow – Yonder perching on a branch a nightingale sings cheerfully; The sun is warm, the soothing breeze blows through the willows green on the bank; The cow is there all by herself, nowhere is there room to hide herself; The splendid head decorated with stately horns, what painter can reproduce her?
Catching the Cow – With the energy of his whole soul, he has at last taken hold of the cow: But how wild her will, ungovernable her power! At times she struts up a plateau, When lo! She is lost in a misty, impenetrable mountain-pass.

[2] Coming Home on the Cow's Back – Riding the cow he leisurely wends his way home: Enveloped in the evening mist, how tunefully the flute vanishes away! Singing a ditty, beating time, his heart is filled with a joy indescribable! That he is now one of those who know, need it be told?

[3] To Return to the Origin – to be back at the Source– already a false step this! Far better it is to stay home, blind and deaf, straightaway and without much ado. Sitting within the hut he takes no cognizance of things outside, Behold the water flowing on – whither nobody knows; and those flowers red and fresh– for whom are they? (363-388).

[4] Entering the City with Bliss-bestowing Hands – Bare-chested and barefooted, he comes out into the marketplace; Daubed with mud and ashes, how broadly he smiles! There is no need for the miraculous power of the gods, For he touches, and lo! the dead trees come into full bloom.

Bibliography

Nishida Kitarō. *Nishida Kitarō zenshū 19 Vols.* (edited by Abe Yoshishige et al.). Iwanami Shoten, 1978.

Omori Sogen. *Ken to zen* (The sword and Zen). Shunjusha, 1966.

Suzuki Daisetz. *Zen Buddhism and its Influence on Japanese Culture*. Kyoto: Eastern Buddhist Society, Otani Buddhist College, 1938.

Yamada Jirōkichi. *Nihon kendo-shi* (The history of Japanese *kendō*). Hitotsubashi Kenyūkai, 1976.

Kashima Shinden Jikishinkage-ryu. Hitotsubashi Kenyūkai, 1976.

Yamada Ei. *Nihontō* (The Japanese sword). Chūō Tōkenkai, 1965.

Yokoyama Kendō. *Nihon budo-shi* (The history of Japanese martial arts). Shimazu Shobō, 1991.

SECTION 2

BUDO CONCEPTS

Chapter 5

Cultural Friction in *Budō*

Abe Tetsushi
The Gate of Dharma Buddhist College (Hungary)

Introduction

The topic of my presentation is "cultural friction in *budō*", which is relatively rare in conventional *budō* studies. Simply put, it involves the relationship between Japan, which maintains its position as the world's leading *budō* nation, and the non-Japanese countries which have imported *budō* and gone to great efforts to propagate it in their respective regions. The friction I am referring to are the various problems that originate when different cultural values concerning the conceptualization of *budō* clash.

The theme I have been asked to present about is '*budō* concepts', which may seem removed from my title "cultural friction in *budō*". Furthermore, one may wonder whether such a topic is worthy of inclusion in the field of *budō* research at all. The fact is that very little research has been undertaken in the field of the internationalization of *budō*. In addition, it is exceedingly difficult to source and organize the sparse data available to accurately detail the current circumstances surrounding the internationalization of *budō*. Therefore, I will base my presentation on my own individual estimations and observations gleaned from actual experience teaching and researching *budō* in Europe. If we refrain from limiting our research into *budō*'s history, ideals and techniques, but also value consideration of *budō*'s potential in a broader social sense, then I am confident that my observations will in some way make a small contribution to this area of research.

Before entering into my main argument, I would like to outline why I chose this topic in regards to the 'concepts of *budō*'. I have been involved in the international propagation of *budō* – kendo in particular – for approximately twenty years. My initial interest was sparked when I made the acquaintance of a European student who was in Japan primarily to study kendo. Subsequently, in 1986 I was afforded the opportunity to travel to Europe and North America as a member of a kendo friendship delegation. From 1992, I worked as a volunteer kendo instructor in Hungary as part of a larger project made possible by the Japanese government.[1] Since 1995, I have been teaching at a Hungarian university and focusing my attention on the spread of kendo throughout Eastern Europe. In addition to technical instruction, I have also recently been involved in the establishment of a non-profit organization with the objective of strengthening *budō* links between Japan and Europe[2]. It is on the basis of these experiences that the theme of this paper lies.

During my time in Europe, I have had much opportunity for meaningful exchange with practitioners of various *budō*, not just kendo. It is well-known that *budō*, particularly popular in North America and Europe, has gained increasing popularity in recent years. Many enthusiasts participate in their chosen *budō* as a sport with the emphasis placed on competition. However, there is also a large number of enthusiasts who are attracted to *budō* values inherent to Japanese culture. In fact, my observations have led me to believe that *budō* practitioners throughout the world constitute the most significant and dedicated group of 'Japanophiles'.

However, it is also the case that criticism of Japan in the international *budō* world is on the increase. For instance, consider the various activities undertaken by the diverse groups of international *budō* associations – the training of instructors, competition rule amendments, workshops, seminars and the like that are conducted throughout the world. Some disparities exist in the frequency and opportunities available to each country depending on the *budō* art in question. However, for the most part these kinds of activities aimed at promoting *budō* on a broader international scale have been funded and conducted by Japanese organizations, and Japanese nationals have held significant control in areas of management and instruction . This phenomenon is hardly surprising considering the rapid economic growth and development of Japanese society during the latter part of the twentieth century, coupled with the widespread boom in *budō*. Nevertheless, the international *budō* community is heading into a period of upheaval in regards to this traditional system of management.

To offer some concrete examples, the election of a new (non-Japanese) chairman to head the International Judo Federation amidst the contentious issue of [non-traditional] coloured judo-*gi* was indeed a significant event. In the kendo world, we saw ardent opposition from a section of the Korean kendo fraternity towards the – until recently – sole representative of international kendo, the Japan-based International Kendo Federation[3]. In karate, which is arguably the most "international" of all the *budō*, there have been countless controversies, political and cultural. Upon closer investigation of the various problems encountered in the international *budō* arena, it seems obvious that the traditional Japanese style of organizational management and other idiosyncrasies are being rejected by the rest of the world with increasing verve. However, this rejection goes both ways. For example, judo is becoming increasingly competitive due to its Olympic status, a trend that has had a detrimental effect on traditional values. There are various problems with the fragmentation of karate styles and federations on an international scale. These are just a few of the countless complications resulting from the international spread of *budō*, and even though many problems also exist in Japan, *budō* enthusiasts are apt to say in regards to the international situation, "Ah, that is not really Japanese *budō* anyway." My concern is that these problems and resulting negativity will continue to escalate as *budō* becomes even more popular around the world.

Cultural Friction in Budo

This is not only a problem with *budō*. Whenever the traditional culture of one region is "exported" to another, there will inevitably be some form of friction evident in the process of introduction and integration. However, this is not necessarily a negative occurrence. Through such interaction, eventually a form of imported culture will be adapted to suit the needs and characteristics of the people in the region it is being introduced to, and the end result, although possibly different to the original form, will be a new form of culture most suited to the people in its new environment. That is why I am not concerned with the fact that there are problems constantly erupting as *budō* is propagated internationally.

The numerous challenges facing the international *budō* world now can simply be categorized, for the most part, as issues relating to organizational management or disagreement in regards to competition rules. Although true in a broad sense, this limited interpretation is essentially only placing the spotlight on surface problems. Namely, the current problems facing the *budō* world are the result of differences in cultural values between Japan and other countries, and if we are unable to engage in more sophisticated conversations of cultural theory, we will be unable to solve fundamental issues.

The reason for my circuitous introduction is, firstly, that as society becomes ever-increasingly dependent on information technology, cultural factors from an array of sports are influencing attitudes toward *budō*, distorting its appearance before the beginner even starts to understand its cultural significance, creating a distinct possibility that these factors maybe discarded altogether. Secondly, within the numerous issues we have had to face in the international *budō* world, there are many which could be solved if recognized as "cultural friction". However, to our detriment, we tend to overlook this interpretation.

There are numerous systems of *budō*, and each maintains their own peculiar history and philosophy. With regards to advancing a theory that deals with all *budō*, I will restrict my presentation to my specialty, kendo. Furthermore, I will focus solely on Europe, where I have been working, and attempt to discuss concretely the so-called "cultural friction" that I have observed. I will focus my discussion on the meaning of cultural friction in kendo from both a conceptual and practical vantage point.

The Quality of Instructional Theory

In recent years, European *budō* has witnessed the marginalization of Japanese instructors from positions of leadership. With the reduction in coaching positions for Japanese nationals, and decreasing annual invitations for Japanese delegations to come and instruct, the position of Japanese instructors in clubs and federations in Europe are gradually being whittled away. In the case of kendo, an art which is minor compared to karate and judo, the number of enthusiasts is somewhat small, so this trend is not so conspicuous. Nevertheless, such exclusion from traditionally held positions is certainly on the rise overall. To clarify, when I refer to "exclusion", I am not suggesting it is a matter of blatant racial discrimination. Rather, it is occurring at the subconscious level, and being caused by factors other than racial intolerance.

For instance, the technical level of kendo in Europe has reached a sufficient level whereby it is no longer absolutely necessary to rely on Japanese instructors. It is also possible that financial considerations have contributed to a reluctance to import instruction from Japan due to the high costs involved. These factors are undeniable. Yet another primary factor is the fact that Europeans generally find the Japanese instruction methodology and philosophy difficult to comprehend. This may be related to a language barrier – in other words a problem of communication. In kendo, for example, explanations of such things as *shinai* movement, breathing techniques, where to fix one's gaze, opportunities for attack, and so on, are aspects that can be easily misunderstood even for people speaking the same language. Obviously then, to attempt to teach these concepts in a foreign language is potentially very problematic. Nevertheless, there is no direct relationship between the communication and transmission of technique, and the teaching theory and methods *per se*. If the language proficiency of the instructor is high, or if there is access to good translators, this problem can be solved. However, it would be a superficial confrontation of the problem to simply suggest that language and communication are the sole cause of the Europeans' dissatisfaction with Japanese instruction methodology and theory, and difficulty in comprehension. I would like to stress that kendo techniques are firmly connected to Japanese cultural traditions, and Japanese people naturally have an affinity to the traditional methods used to convey technical and conceptual aspects of kendo. However, to those who come from a non-Japanese background without such cultural grounding, comprehension of Japanese kendo instructional theory will inevitably be difficult.

In simple terms, let me outline my experiences in Germany. The first time I did kendo abroad was in 1986, in Hamburg, Germany. The purpose of my visit was to stay about two months to instruct at local *dōjō* and participate in a training camp for the national team. On one particular day, I was asked to oversee instruction of the technique *de-gote* (striking *kote* just as the opponent is about to strike *men*). In order to practice the technique, the receiver must open up their right *kote*, whereby the attacker promptly moves in and makes a cut to the exposed target. While I was watching the instruction, I witnessed something that is rarely seen in Japan. The technique was broken down into very small movements, and the students were practicing each small part of the technique repeatedly. It is true that this method is also utilized in Japan on occasion, but not to the minute extent that it was being done in Germany. For example, in Japan the practitioner might consider the angle of the *kote* when the opponent is launching into a *men* attack, and may consider bending the knee or at the waist to facilitate smoother striking. Still, each technique is not broken down nearly as much as what I witnessed, incredulously, in Germany. Furthermore, even the instructor was unable to execute the technique properly at full speed, so it was not surprising to me that the students were experiencing difficulties.

There are instructors in Japan who are particularly good at explaining techniques,

Cultural Friction in Budo

even though they cannot actually do them, so this is not what grabbed my attention. I became interested in the German instructor's methodology of explaining the failure of execution only from the perspective of the mechanics of the technique. Japanese would generally analyze failure from a different perspective. In my opinion the German instructor's methodology was flawed in that it lacked any attention to the process of creating a striking opportunity (*kikai tsukuri*). For example, at the basic level, by adjusting to the opponent's rhythm then lowering the tip of the *shinai*, the opponent will be enticed into striking *men*, creating an opportunity to strike *kote* first. At a more advanced level, Japanese instructors would use the expression "attack with *ki*" (*ki de semeru*). What this really refers to is the application of pressure through battle for the centre-line and maintaining preferred distance (*ma-ai*), and disruption of the opponent's breathing and movement. Taking the initiative and disturbing the opponent in this way sets up a chance to attack. Striking opportunities will present themselves, and the execution of *de-gote* becomes relatively easy.

"Creating a striking opportunity" is a subtle affair not visibly obvious to a third party. Both external mechanical or physical components, and internal consciousness must be combined for the technique to be successful, making it extremely difficult. An instructor in Japan would concurrently teach the student how to wield the *shinai* with appropriate body movement and footwork, as well as the significance of the relationship between the self and the opponent. Thus, a balance between physical and mental components is emphasized. That kendo can be practiced into one's old age is related to the fact that such emphasis is placed on a balance between these two components. With respect to the German instructor, I suspected that he was unable to recognize the importance of neither "creating striking opportunities" nor how to incorporate this idea into his teaching due to insufficient experience.

Nevertheless, some years have passed since then, and I now wonder if I should have accounted for the differences between the German and Japanese teaching methodology as simply a lack of instructional ability or experience on the part of the Germans. Maybe the Germans conceptualized the *de-gote* technique differently from Japanese? I have given this question a great deal of consideration in the fifteen years that have passed since this incident. During that time I have trained many European students, and I will now outline my understanding of this problem as I currently perceive it.

Eastern and Western Artistic Perceptions

In comparison with European instruction, Japanese kendo instructors have a tendency to use abstract concepts such as *"ki"* (spirit/energy) and *"kokoro"* (mind) frequently. There is insufficient room to discuss this in detail, but perusal of martial arts texts from the Tokugawa period shows that such nebulous terms were used frequently, and have become an integral part of the modern *budō* lexicon. In the classical martial arts (*bugei*), technical aspects such as how to wield a sword and the necessary physical manoeuvring are offset with abstract and subtle psycho-spiritual concepts. Whether such concepts are consciously adhered to or not, modern Japanese practitioners of kendo have inherited such traditions, and are very much influenced and open to them.

I refer to modes of thinking in regards to the characteristics of technique as "*artistic perception*" (*gijutsu-kan*). Restricting my definition to kendo, "artistic perception" is not merely concerned with technical aspects such as rules of competition or technical skill, but is a set of values which take into consideration internal aspects – concepts such as "*ki*" and "*kokoro*". I feel that it may be differing "artistic perception" that has caused the gradual aforementioned "exclusion" of Japanese from the *budō* scene in Europe.

Allow me to explain this "artistic perception" in more concrete terms. In high-level kendo practitioners "*fūkaku*" (dignity) and "*kihin*" (grace) are deemed to be important qualities. Because I too practice kendo, I have an intuitive understanding of what these qualities entail. However, when it comes to answering questions of exactly how it is that these qualities can be expressed though physical movement or otherwise, I find it very difficult to explain convincingly. I am sure I am not alone in this respect. Placing value on such distinct, but at the same time nebulous qualities as *fūkaku* and *kihin*, honed through the act of fencing with bamboo swords, is what makes kendo a unique kind of athletic/aesthetic pursuit.

Of course, this idea of "artistic perception" is not limited to kendo, but is common to the array of traditional Japanese arts which have their own compendium of techniques and underlying views of their significance and meaning. It could be said that kendo has developed its own special "artistic perception". However, I think it is more appropriate to assume that the Japanese "artistic perception" is manifest in kendo. Remembering that my idea of "artistic perception" includes both internal and external factors, if is kendo practiced only with objective of achieving technical proficiency, it will be difficult to acquire the "artistic perception" held in such high regard in kendo circles. Also, I suspect that it would be exceedingly difficult to appreciate "artistic perception" found in kendo without understanding the overall "artistic perception" of Japanese culture. If so, where does that leave European kendo enthusiasts who do not possess a Japanese "artistic perception"? Obviously, Europeans have their own "artistic perception".[4]

What kind of "artistic perception" do Europeans have? Of course, it is impossible to lump all of Europe together in this sense due to the many countries, cultures, and peoples that make up the continent. However, for the sake of argument, by restricting the discourse to include only athletic culture, I think the following assertions can be made.

All aspects of athletic culture, from technical instruction methodology to rules and training methodology, are heavily influenced by modern sports theory. This in turn has evolved from advances in natural sciences attained through the process of social modernization in the West. In other words, modern sports theory has its roots in the development of modern rationalism. In the case of Europeans today, this modern sports theory has infiltrated every possible aspect of life and thought, and is where their "artistic perception" of athletic culture derives from. For this reason, as my experience

Cultural Friction in Budo

Participants at the 2004 Kendo Summer Seminar, sponsored by the AJKF

in Germany illustrated, Europeans possess a different perception of something such as kendo than Japanese. To put it a slightly different way, if they are to have the same kind of appreciation of kendo as Japanese, they would be required to make an in-depth study of Japanese culture as well.

Of course, the opposite is also true. Japanese studying traditional European arts – such as music and dance – often find that they are unable to get past a preoccupation with technique. This is because they are unable to easily grasp the traditional artistic perception of the European arts. Many Japanese musicians and dancers who have an inkling of this concept will live in Europe to study these arts, not only to learn the techniques of the art, but also in an attempt to develop the appropriate artistic perception.

We can see the same kind of phenomenon in the world of baseball. Foreigners playing in the Japanese professional leagues say that "Japanese players are only concerned with techniques required to throw a curve ball, and do not understand the true "manly" essence of a front-on baseball duel." I have also heard comments like "that's not *baseball*, it's *yakyū*!" (*yakyū* being the Japanese word for baseball). The wide varieties of pitches thrown in Japanese baseball are all within the confines of the official rules, and as such are entirely permissible. However, what these attitudes demonstrate is that within the same sport there are distinctly different artistic perceptions, thereby enabling a distinction between baseball *per se*, and *yakyū*.

Furthermore, it has often been pointed out by experts in mind and body theory and comparative athletic culture that the artistic perception of Japanese is based on one-dimensional oriental theories of mind and body.[5] That is why whenever Japanese participate in a given sport, they tend to lump physical and psycho-spiritual aspects into one unified component to be learned concurrently. For example, in *budō*, terms such as *"shinshin ichinyo"* (body and mind united), *"ki-ken-tai-itchi"* (spirit, sword, and body as one) and *"shin-gi-tai"* (spirit, technique, and body) are often employed, demonstrating a typically Japanese artistic perception. The recent popularity of *budō*, yoga, tai chi, and the like amongst Europeans demonstrates a growing attraction to concepts going beyond the bounds of modern sports theory. However, one of the main weaknesses of traditional psycho-spiritual athletic pursuits such as *budō* is that the instruction methodology often becomes abstract and intangible.

On the other hand, based on notions of modern sports theory born of rationalism, the Western approach is generally two-dimensional. When a Westerner learns a given sport, the instructor will often break everything down into pieces so that technical proficiency can be gained in each separate component before being brought together. There is a distinct process of learning in stages, and physical and mental components are often treated as separate entities. In the competitive arena of modern sports, this methodology is evidently superior for elevating technical proficiency and general efficiency. However, there is a downside in that it encourages a clear disparity between body and mind. To clarify this point, although technical mastery may be reached, a similar level of humanistic development or morality is often neglected, and the common problem of performance enhancing drug abuse in many competitive sports attests to this.

I would now like to return to the "exclusion" of Japanese instructors. In Europe, Japanese instructors are frequently invited to teach seminars and training camps. As I explained already, the difference in artistic perception between Japanese and Europeans is evident, particularly during instruction where the theory and teaching methods and philosophies of the Japanese are difficult to understand. In instances where the explanation of a technique is of a high level, the frequency of abstract Japanese terms increases. Although it may be possible for someone with a deep interest or understanding in Japanese culture to comprehend the explanations given, the average European practitioner will generally find it very difficult to follow. Japanese culture can be studied through the technical acquisition of kendo, but when kendo is popularized quickly in foreign countries, supplementing the cultural elements with the technical becomes problematic. In other words, when students are subjected to repeated explanations that they cannot sufficiently understand, they conclude that they "Japanese instruction methodology is too difficult to comprehend". This will inevitably result in the gradual exclusion of Japanese instructors. Besides, it requires significant financial resources to invite Japanese instructors. Therefore, especially in Eastern Europe where most countries are far from economically affluent, there is a distinct and growing tendency to exclude Japanese.

Cultural Friction in Budo

Thus, I assert that the main cause behind the recent trend of Japanese exclusion is the differences in European and Japanese artistic perception. In a broader sense, this is basically the difference between Eastern and Western culture. Furthermore, this is a problem that both instructors and students alike are rarely conscious of.

Incomprehensible *Budō* Concepts

I would now like to consider the problem of "cultural friction in *budō*" from a conceptual basis. In Japanese *budō*, much emphasis is placed upon concepts (*rinen*). Historically speaking, the role of concepts has played an enormous part in the development of *budō*. Without the prominence of ideological concepts in the past, the *budō* of today would be totally different. Actual *budō* practice and the surrounding concepts are deeply interconnected.

However, when we shift our attention to the international *budō* arena, we see small but gradual shifts in conceptual understanding. Specifically, concepts accepted by the Japanese in the social milieu of Japan have not been readily acknowledged when exported abroad. To the Japanese, this poses many problems which have never required consideration before. Until now, Japanese scholars and practitioners of *budō* have focused their attention solely on the status quo in Japan, leaving them unprepared to deal with the current international trends. From here, I will offer some tangible examples of the current situation in the kendo world.

The World Kendo Championships is the most important event on the international kendo calendar. Held every three years, the 12th World Kendo Championships were recently staged in Glasgow in July of 2003. The World Championships have been conducted for more than thirty years, however, in 1999 it was decided that the raising of flags and the singing of national anthems during the awards ceremony would be abolished. The reason for abolishing this practice was to emphasize that kendo was in essence more than just a competitive sport. It was contended that the raising of national flags and the singing of national anthems was contributing to the so-called [undesirable] competitive "sportification" of kendo. Before the championships, each affiliate federation was presented with documents explaining this. It was clearly an exercise [by the IKF] in imposing a concept of how kendo *should* be perceived.

As a Japanese kendo practitioner, this decision was not something that I was particularly concerned with. As long as there are *shiai* (matches) in kendo of course we will be preoccupied with competing and concerns of winning and losing. In spite of this, there is a well-established *tradition* in kendo that promotes downplaying such raw competitiveness as being contrary to the true Way of kendo. I also adhere to this mode of thought, although I and countless other Japanese kendo enthusiasts are well aware through actual experience of the contradictions between the ideal and reality.

However, with respect to this problem, upon asking competitors and officials from the respective European nations, I found there was a surprisingly deep-seated voice of dissent. Their dissatisfaction quite clearly stemmed from the irony that if we accept that the essence of kendo is not competition, then the very existence of the championships could be considered contradictory. Furthermore, it was suggested that considering the remarkable progress the Koreans have made, it is only a matter of time that Japan will be defeated. The implied question was, is it not plausible that the Japanese are preparing an excuse when the inevitable happens along the lines that the true essence of kendo is irrelevant to mere matters of wining and losing in competitions? To many Japanese, such a suggestion may seem preposterous. In any case, there exists no formal written or spoken protest concerning this issue, however, obviously a gap exists between the Japanese and non-Japanese kendo practitioners in their understanding or recognition of kendo concepts, and this is a point of concern.

Although the following is an anecdote, I think it will serve to elucidate my point. Eight years ago, I was involved in preparations to establish a kendo club in a small Hungarian village. At that time I was working as a coach in Hungary while still employed as a JICA volunteer. I participated in a kendo demonstration held at the local elementary school at the request of the Hungarian Kendo Federation. A nun was also in attendance. After the demonstration, she came over to talk to me. At first she began to ask general questions relating to kendo, but gradually her questions became more searching – "What is the *real* value for us doing kendo?" she asked.

When kendo demonstrations are done in Europe, these types of questions are commonplace. I relayed to her that kendo is a traditional Japanese sport. Through training in kendo, I continued, the practitioner cultivates a strong body and develops their character. Furthermore, I explained in a general way, that this kind of human development has wider positive implications for society as a whole. I thought that such an explanation would suffice as it was the standard explanation in Japan. However, upon hearing this "standard explanation", the nun's expression changed from a smile to a more sombre look and the gist of her reply is as follows:

"I don't agree with a thing you say, and I think you are wrong. How can learning to hit somebody with a stick benefit humanity? Rather, wouldn't learning such skills actually have the reverse effect and make that person [more violent and] better at doing bad things? This may be a useful method of education in your country, but of what use could it possibly serve here? Now try and explain this!" the nun demanded. She didn't say it directly, but I got the impression that she was suggesting that I should not attempt to popularize something I could not explain satisfactorily, and that I should not "force Japanese culture" on people. This is a further example of how the Japanese *budō* concepts taken for granted in Japan may not be so easily accepted in other parts of the world.

The Japanese *budō* community is totally insensitive to these issues. I sometimes hear dismissive comments in Japan to the effect that as *budō* becomes internationalized, these problems will solve themselves. Some are so optimistic that they assume, rather arrogantly, that people practicing *budō* around the world will eventually catch on and concur with the Japanese conceptual approach.

Cultural Friction in Budo

The Background and Function of Concepts

Why is it that concepts espoused by Japanese are not readily comprehended by non-Japanese? Also, how exactly are we supposed to interpret these concepts anyway? From here I will offer two perspectives. Firstly, I will look at the importance of having an accurate understanding of the cultural characteristics that provide the backdrop for *budō* concepts. In Europe, there is an unceasing flow of people who take up the study of *budō* because of their interest in Japanese culture.[6] Also, I know of many cases where people have started *budō* because of an appreciation for the perceived "spiritual characteristics". This is a source of great pride for Japanese people when they hear of such motivations. However, precisely what is meant by the so-called spirituality of *budō*? Europeans often make mention of such phrases as *bushidō* and the like, however, I am doubtful as to whether they equate with the same cultural nuances that Japanese would attach to them. This is intrinsically related to the problem of concepts in *budō*.

For example, the All Japan Kendo Federation clearly articulated the official "*Concept of Kendo*" and defined kendo as a means to "*discipline the human character through the application of the principles of the katana*"[7]. In Japan, many kendo practitioners train with these objectives in mind. However, in Europe the meaning behind this concept has not been adequately conveyed. Insufficient information may be one cause. However, it is probably more accurate to surmise that the value of this concept is not understood. Why has this situation come about?

To many Japanese, regardless of whether or not they are *budō* practitioners, kendo or judo invoke notions of education and character development. Of course, there are exceptions, but as most Japanese are exposed to *budō* through the physical education curriculum in schools, or martial arts in novels where the heroes are depicted as the Japanese "ideal", not to mention in various other contexts in daily life, *budō* and education are perceived as being closely linked. The image that "*budō* = education" is prevalent in the minds of many Japanese.

The basis for this image is founded on the common assumption that mastering the techniques of *budō* through hard training and trial and error will result in personal growth of the practitioner, which will in turn benefit society at large. Similar ideas are touted in other cultural spheres also. However, the case of Japan is characterized by typically Eastern ethical and religious attitudes. That is, by focusing one's energies on one pursuit, mastery will result in the acquisition of universal ethics or laws. In the arts world this is referred to by the maxim "*ichigei wa mangei ni tsūzuru*" (one art corresponds to ten-thousand [different] arts). This mentality is evident in many aspects of Japanese society.

However, Europeans generally have a different mode of thinking. For instance, each individual pursuit is just that, a single pursuit. One art is just one art. This is the complete antithesis of the Japanese mode of thinking, and is related to principles of modern rationalism and natural sciences, where physical matters are dealt as physical matters, and spiritual matters are processed separately in the category of spiritual matters. Therefore, it is not easy to accept that *budō* techniques – which are essentially physical movements – are also inextricably linked on the same plane with human development and spirituality.

Europe is made up of numerous co-existing nationalities, races, and religions rich in history and ideas. Originally, education was deemed necessary to nurture individuals who would be able to contribute to the society they lived in. Often I am told by Europeans "I practice kendo because I like it, not because I want to become Japanese". In Europe today, issues of race and nationality feature prominently in the background of educational concepts, more so than most Japanese realize. This is a possible reason as to why the equation "*budō* = education" is not accepted as unconditionally as it is in Japan.

Next, let me turn to the second perspective. Culture is something we can think of in two terms of "protecting" or "utilizing". Culture that requires "protection" means carefully preserving the original cultural appearance of a cultural form as it is transmitted. For example, Japanese people feel that they must preserve and protect kendo in its current form. And *vis-à-vis*, to utilize culture refers to the stance of the recipient of a form of culture that has been transmitted. In other words, to Europeans, kendo is generally viewed as a form of culture that should be utilized.

From this standpoint, we can surmise that while the intentions or motives of both the Europeans and the Japanese for doing kendo maybe similar, there are subtle differences[8]. To rephrase, the Japanese have historically treated *budō* as a "culture which should be protected", and through *budō*, they acquire an identity of what it means to "be Japanese". However, for the Europeans, there is no innate special reason to want to "protect" *budō*. For them, it is always a culture to be "utilized". To make a sweeping generalization, emphasis is placed on *budō* as a form of training which can be used to acquire personal physical, spiritual, and social gains.

I consider an important function of *budō* concepts to be to maintain a balance between protecting culture and utilizing it. That is to say, concepts ensure that the ideals of an organization with a stipulated objective such as a school or company can be referred to when that organization is seen to veer from its original course. For example, the *Concept of Kendo* was established in 1975 by the All Japan Kendo Federation due to concerns in the kendo fraternity that practitioners were forgetting the essence of kendo and the fact that it was based on the principles of a live-bladed sword, the *katana*, rather than a bamboo stick. This was an attempt by the AJKF to uphold the "traditions" of true kendo as opposed to the popular competitive sport which it was becoming. [9] As this example clearly illustrates, concepts are created by "protectors" or guardians of culture and issued to the "users". How this is received, however, depends almost entirely on the users. Nevertheless, as we can see by the aforementioned changes in the format of the World Kendo Championships, concepts can be intrusive. Kendo practitioners are *expected* to embody the *designated* concepts. This actually serves to encourage people to ignore the ideas behind them altogether.

The history of Japanese kendo spans several centuries. Issues relating to such things

Cultural Friction in Budo

as organization, equipment, and rules have been considered from various angles over many generations, and even today, we can say that the development of kendo is still very much in progress. The concepts espoused in kendo have evolved from Japan's long historical context, and some aspects will undoubtedly be difficult to comprehend for people from cultures with different historical environments. Thus, to facilitate understanding of the content it is necessary to sufficiently explain the process of how the concept came to be. Without going to great efforts to achieve this, for the most part the concepts will be restrictive, or remain nebulous and be considered of little or no value. The *budō* world, both in Japan and in other countries, has neglected to tackle this problem with serious intention.

Surpassing Cultural Friction

So far I have discussed the problem of cultural friction in the international world of *budō* with respect to the themes of instruction methodology and concepts. To reiterate, many of the cultural characteristics of *budō* are not necessarily absolute and universal in nature. Comprehension and interpretation varies depending on the specific cultural backgrounds of the nationalities and races of practitioners. If in the future we continue in our attempts to popularize *budō* around the world without being sensitive and conscious of such notions, further problems are sure to arise.

In conclusion, in order to develop the values of *budō* for the twenty first century, how should we approach the issue of cultural friction in *budō*? In other words, how should we direct future research and the practice of *budō*? I would like to conclude with my views on this pressing matter.

Firstly, I would like to stress the necessity for a qualitative change in the *budō* content that is being propagated internationally. A survey of all *budō* shows clearly that they have been popularized laying emphasis on competition and sporting elements. Success of international propagation has been gauged on the number of competitors and international competitions a given *budō* has been able to conduct. The much sought after affiliation with the Olympic movement is a clear example. It is not my intention to criticize the Olympic movement; however, equating admission into the Olympics as the ultimate success in the internationalizing process will do nothing but debase the values of *budō*.

The quality of *budō*'s international propagation in the twenty-first century should also be questioned. I am referring to the need to allow the cultural value of *budō* to come to life rather than stifling it. To elaborate, *budō* should not be disseminated into the world as "Japanese culture". This is too simplistic. Basically, it needs to be asked "how can people from around the world, each with their unique cultural perspectives and viewpoints, incorporate and utilize a cultural phenomenon such as *budō* in their every-day lives?" The implication being that it should not simply be an attempt to force "unique" Japanese culture on the rest of the world. Rather, *budō* should be propagated

Western kendo practitioners performing kendo kata

as a form of culture which sits well with the host culture, and be given room to evolve and show how *budō*'s cultural potential can be of benefit to all people.

Ironically, the first step in achieving this would be to concentrate on reasserting Japanese cultural characteristics found in *budō*. The reason why I make this point is because a look at the international *budō* scene reveals that despite significant progress made in the technical aspects, the cultural aspects are for the most part extremely ambiguous and unfocussed. This is due to the poor quality – if not complete lack – of relevant information. There is an acute shortage of reputable publications pertaining to *budō*. Originally, most of the available *budō* publications outside Japan were sports manuals offering the reader an introduction only to the techniques.

Recently, there have been some good publications abroad touching on the cultural aspects of *budō*, but they are still few and far between. The media (movies and television particularly), have had a widespread influence in distorting the image of *budō*, and this is problematic. However, the real problem lies in the fact that high-quality specialist research conducted in Japan has not been adequately communicated abroad. Furthermore, another problem worthy of consideration is that *budō* specialists in Japan know little of the presence and activities of *budō* researchers abroad. It is precisely the view of Japan from a foreign perspective that is lacking in the research and practice of *budō* in Japan today.

Cultural Friction in Budo

The widespread popularization of Japanese culture through *budō* will eventually, I hope, provide an example for *budō* enthusiasts abroad, who will see how it can be incorporated as a useful addition to their own culture. That is to say, they will be able to observe how *budō* functions in the lives of the Japanese. This will prompt questions of how *budō* can be utilized in a modern-day setting regardless of the culture it has been imported into. Such perspectives will ensure the continued growth of *budō* values in the twenty-first century. In Europe, I am often confronted with simplistic criticisms such as "sumo is for weirdos! Being that fat cannot be healthy!", and "Compared to Western sports, kendo is primitive because there is no distinction made between sex, age or weight, or no defined teaching methodology". Of course, it is vital that we respond appropriately to these opinions. Yet, of greater concern is the fact that the people who hold such opinions have a limited perspective of what *budō* is, and see it only through the tinted lens of rationalistic sport. Thus, the creation of an environment in which these people can become aware of their limited perception of *budō* is of the utmost importance for international propagation. Merely instructing people in the techniques of *budō* is not international propagation.

Secondly, it is critical that we devise a method of instruction which facilitates non-Japanese comprehension of Japanese cultural aspects contained in *budō*. To be more precise, we need to conduct research from an international perspective into the present condition of *budō* dissemination, as well as the history, concepts, and fundamentals of *budō* and ways to teach more effectively outside Japan. In order to do this we need to reconsider the characteristics of *budō* from a comparative cultural perspective.

I predict that *budō* in the international society of the twenty-first century will play an extremely large role for Japanese people and others connected to Japanese culture. This is because *budō* not only found value as an expression of human physical and spiritual potential, but also because in this modern world we live in, where human values are often over-ridden by technology, *budō* has the potential to restore human beings to their original unified state of mind and body. The question of how *budō* concepts should be held in regards to our social condition is an issue which requires ongoing debate.

Endnotes

[1] In 1963, the Japanese government, through the Ministry of Foreign Affairs established JICA (Japan International Cooperation Association- J: *Kokusai Kyōryoku Jigyōdan*). JICA is a special public corporation established to promote international cooperation through the provision of overseas development assistance. It was founded in 1974 in accordance with the International Cooperation Agency Law. As part of their activities, young Japanese volunteers were dispatched to several developing countries in Africa, South America, Oceania, and Asia, with the purpose of providing technical assistance in a variety of fields. With respect to kendo, starting with Hungary in 1992, coaches were subsequently sent to various Eastern European nations such as Bulgaria, Poland and Romania.

[2] In 2001, the NPO 'Budo Culture Forum' was established in Hungary with the aim of

popularizing *budō* culture in Europe, and promoting mutual understanding between Japan and European nations.

[3] The International Kendo Federation was formed in 1970 as the governing body of kendo around the world. In opposition to this, however, the World Kumdo Association was established by a group of Koreans in 2002 with the clear objective of making kendo/kumdo an Olympic sport.

[4] The number of European kendo enthusiasts who reside in Japan has grown over the years. These people are of the belief that to be exposed to the essence of kendo, they must be in Japan. It is thought that after many years of training in Japan, they will be able to acquire Japanese "artistic perception". In fact, watching Europeans who have trained for many years in Japan, one is able to sense their acquisition of *kihin* and *fūkaku* in their movement exactly like Japanese.

[5] Of research conducted in the field of Eastern mind and body theory, Yuasa Yasuo's findings have been particularly influential in the area of *budō* studies. It is clear even in modern Japanese philosophy that Buddhist training has had a profound effect on Japanese attitudes to the relationship between mind and body. For further reference see Yuasa's book *Shintai*.

[6] The most popular Japanese cultural pursuits in foreign countries include noh, the tea ceremony, *ikebana*, pottery, painting, calligraphy, and *haiku*. In Japan, such arts are thought of as somewhat different to the *budō* arts, however, outside Japan it is not unusual to find people who consider them as being the same. Of all Japanese culture aficionados *budō* enthusiasts make up the vast majority. In comparison with the other Japanese cultural pursuits the *budō* practitioner does not have to spend a great deal of money, and as *budō* is a form of athletic culture it is seen as having the added benefits of maintaining health. *Budō* is both accessible, and very practical. This has been one of the reasons for the speedy popularization of karate and judo abroad.

[7] For an in depth analysis of the formulation and objectives of the *Concept of Kendo* refer to Ōtsuka Tadayoshi's *Kendō no rekishi*.

[8] I consider there to be three motivating factors as to why Europeans take up *budō*. Firstly, there is the practical application of *budō* as a means of defence and for use in combative situations. Secondly, people look to *budō* as a challenging competitive sport. Competing for points in matches is enjoyable and is an excellent means for keeping one's mind and body healthy. Furthermore, people also make friends. If the practitioner is able to reach a high level of skill and understanding, there is also the possibility of making a living teaching *budō*. Thirdly, the study of *budō* is seen as an ideal way to study Japanese culture. In Europe, the number of people practicing *budō* for this reason is quite high.

[9] Ōtsuka, op. cit., pp. 184-191.

Bibliography

Ōtsuka Tadayoshi. *Kendō no rekishi* (The history of kendo). Madosha, 1995.
Yuasa Yasuo. *Shintai: Tōyōteki shinshin-ron no kokoromi* (The body: toward an Eastern mind-body theory). Sōbunsha, 1977.

Chapter 6

From "*Jutsu*" to "*Dō*"
The Birth of Kōdōkan Judo

Murata Naoki
Curator of the Kōdōkan Museum

Introduction

What is it about judo that people find so attractive in this day and age? Judo has grown from being exclusively a part of Japanese culture at the time of its inception into an immensely popular sport practiced all around the world. No matter where I travel overseas, most people know what judo is, and I often laugh when I encounter the common preconceived notion that all Japanese must surely be judo practitioners. The fact is that judo is known throughout the world, and its continuing popularity is attested to by its status as an official Olympic event.

Judo was created by Kanō Jigorō in 1882. He was a great admirer of the various traditions of *jūjutsu* which could trace their roots back to the Warring States period of the fifteenth and sixteenth centuries. He adopted and reorganized an array of techniques and ideals from the traditional schools, and formed his own school which he called *Nihon-den Kōdōkan Judō*. Nowadays we often hear calls for people to make some kind of contribution to benefit society. Kanō's contributions were already in full swing at the turn of the nineteenth and twentieth centuries as he dedicated his life to promoting judo both domestically and internationally.

Kanō Shinnosuke, as he was known in his childhood days, was born in what is modern-day Kobe city. He was an extremely competitive child, and hated to lose. Despite being physically diminutive, he made up for his small size with remarkable physical strength. He started studying *jūjutsu* after learning that small practitioners could defeat opponents far bigger in stature. However, during the course of his training, a number of doubts crept into his mind, and his teachers were not always able to give explanations to his satisfaction. Being a student of remarkable intelligence and possessing an extremely analytical mind, he was often dissatisfied with the principles surrounding techniques and general instruction methodology, and so concentrated not only on mastering the techniques, but also thinking of rational explanations to satisfy his own inquisitiveness. His curiosity, and process of finding answers to his own questions was to culminate in his formation of a new form of martial culture, a progression from "*jutsu*" (martial art) to "*dō*" (martial Way). He bolstered his creation with the ideals of *"seiryoku-zenyō"* (maximum efficiency in the use of strength) and *"jita-kyōei"* (mutual welfare and benefit). These ideals were to prove to be universally acceptable to people regardless of nationality. In this dissertation, I will consider the process in which Kanō created judo from *jūjutsu*, and the significance of international judo as a competitive sport.

How was Judo Created?

Everything evolves after a certain amount of struggle, be it a human being, or some form of cultural achievement. It is precisely the struggle and hardship that the gives the newborn entity the ability and attributes to survive and prosper over time. I think that it is pertinent to state that judo was a creation of the founder's diminutive stature, his sharp intellect, and his determination to never lose. As the maxim "strike while the iron is hot" suggests, Kanō stringently tested his judo techniques and ideals as he formulated them. He had to see if judo would be able to stand up to the traditional schools of *jūjutsu*. He found that his judo was able to prevail, and indeed surpass the other schools. Before long, judo started to incorporate new, socially appealing principles—in addition to techniques—which served to enhance the perceived social potential of judo. Various officials, educators, and other people of high social standing from Japan and abroad would pay the Kōdōkan a visit, and listen intently to Kanō's explanations. Eventually, many of them would become ardent supporters of Kanō's ideas. In this way, judo was able to carve out its place in history by keeping in step with the rapidly changing times and receiving continued favour from influential individuals.

Anybody involved with judo in whatever capacity has a duty to know about the course judo's evolution. The origins and history of a given form of culture are its "roots". Above the roots are the trunk, branches, and finally the flowers and fruit. If the roots are forgotten, it is like a kite with a broken string floating aimlessly in the air. Nobody knows where it will land, and there is a chance it might end up in a very precarious situation. It is this vulnerable nature of culture and its constant state

Kanō Jigorō aged eighteen

From "Jutsu" to "Do"

of flux that has surely caused many of our predecessors (such as founders of martial traditions) anguish and worry. With this point in mind, I would like to look at the history of judo, and reaffirm the process of how it was created. I should add that as I have a limited knowledge of the politics, economics, and other aspects of the Meiji period, I am forced to limit the scope of this paper to Kanō, and the various factors which prompted him to develop judo.

Kanō's Self Perception

"Obstinate", "looked down upon for being frail", "never wanted to lose". These are all words that Kanō used to describe himself:

"There is one thing that has not changed in me since I was a child until the present day. I have always been obstinate in everything I do. I think that this aspect of my personality may be of interest to other educators and people in general, so I will take the liberty to offer some comments about my 'obstinate' nature. I believe that I have been able to use this characteristic to good purpose. Comparing personality traits of intellect, morality, and physical bearing, I was considerably inferior to others in the physical sense. I was never ill for extended periods of time, but was rather delicate from childhood. This was obvious from my physique after graduating from university, where despite having participated in a harsh regime of physical exercise, I weighed only fifty kilograms or thereabouts. As far as morality is concerned, I was raised in a strict and stable family environment, and received many good influences as opposed to bad. My intellectual level was also favourable compared to my peers, with whom we would often try to outdo each other at school. I felt confident of my ability in any subject, so long as I applied myself. Nevertheless, my physical presence paled in comparison to my peers.

In my school days, more so than in the physical education of today, anybody who was physically weak was ostracised by the others. This is what prompted me to try and increase my strength. They were violent times with constant fighting, and weaklings were invariably beaten up. I had no problems keeping up with the rest as far as academic pursuits went, but I wasn't so confident with my physique. I then heard of Japanese *jūjutsu*. I surmised that if I too could learn this art, even one as puny as I would become a match for any opponent. I did not possess the high ideals I hold today, but simply wanted to learn the skills needed to defeat others. I started *jūjutsu* to become stronger. I searched for a suitable teacher, but in those days *jūjutsu* was in decline, and so finding a place to study the art was no easy task. At last, in my first year at university I found somebody to teach me *jūjutsu* and was able to commence my studies."

Budo Perspectives

A Born Educator

In Kanō's place of birth there was a so-called *terakoya* (temple school) for the local children to study at. However, it wasn't suitable for studying the Chinese classics. His father, Jirōsaku, worked hard to enhance the children's learning opportunities, and invited a number of well-known Confucian scholars to the school such as Akita Shūsetsu, and Yamamoto Chikuun. At age seven, Kanō learned calligraphy and how to read sutras under the tutelage of Chikuun. One year later, he selected a number of specimens of his own brushwork and made two small booklets, which he distributed among his young relatives, thus demonstrating his early aspirations of becoming an educator. It was evident even in his childhood that he had special qualities, and a bright future was in store. Judo was the ultimate product of his educational aspirations, and Kōdōkan became his podium for lecturing on ethics and imparting his ideals.

The study of *Bujutsu* was centred on hard training and learning from actual experience. Kanō dedicated himself to training and was not inclined to refrain from asking his teacher difficult questions. If a suitable reply was not forthcoming, he would persistently ask again and again. His teacher would reply, "even if I did tell you, you wouldn't understand anyway. Just shut up and train. That's the only way to learn, so get up and let's go."

Kanō would incessantly analyze hand and hip movements, and footwork utilized in *nage-waza* (throws). He was never satisfied with simply doing what he was instructed to do, and felt compelled to understand the mechanics of each technique he executed. Rarely receiving the answers he was after, he began to develop grave doubts about the traditional methods of instruction.

One day, he was able to successfully throw his teacher. This time, it was the teacher who asked a question of Kanō. "Kanō, how did you pull that technique off?" He replied, "I watched how you throw your students, and then I would analyze it with my friends when I got home. I learned that when you are about to throw somebody, they will inevitably stop and become rigid, and try and avoid the flow of the technique. Then you use this against them and execute the throw. I have been watching and analyzing this for a long time, and decided to test it out on you today."

With that, his teacher submitted that he had no more he could teach the young Kanō, and he was awarded a Kitō-ryū teaching licence. This observation that Kanō made is known as *kuzushi* (knocking the opponent off-balance before executing a technique) in the Kōdōkan today. Balance is maintained through a stable centre of gravity. If the centre of gravity is jolted, balance will become unsettled, making it easy to execute a throw. There is also a natural reaction to try and rectify posture when balance is unsettled. This results in the body becoming rigid for a split second, and provides the best opportunity to apply a technique. Kanō deduced that unsettling the centre of gravity was a matter of mechanics, and the subsequent physical reaction is physiological. In other words, Kanō's observation was scientific in nature. There are six to eight directions for *kuzushi* to be applied, and it is one of the first things taught

From "Jutsu" to "Do"

in the Kōdōkan even today. It is not in any way a 'secret teaching' of Kanō's, but was a discovery based on his astute observations, and consequently became one of the leading mechanical and physiological concepts which facilitated his creation of judo from *jūjutsu*.

Old Tradition - New Tradition

Kanō realized that the principles utilized in a *jūjutsu* match could be applied to modern-day living. He learned that the intellectual activity required to become an effective competitor could be employed to deal with an array of different situations in everyday life. He said of *jūjutsu*, "I do not necessarily believe all the traditional training methods are valid, however, with some reformation, *bujustu* training could very well become an effective means for nurturing the individual's intellect, physique, and morality." After all, the concept which lies at the basis of *jūjutsu* is "*michi*" or "*dō*" (Way), with the *jutsu* techniques being the vehicle. His formulation of a new system of safer techniques and moral principles was different to many of the traditional approaches, which is why he thought it inadequate to use the term *jūjutsu*. However, he could not ignore the fact that the techniques he was utilizing and adapting came from *jūjutsu*, and thought it inappropriate to change the name altogether. He decided to utilize the first character of "*jū*" but replace the suffix with "*dō*" to accentuate his emphasis on educational significance. Thus, he named his innovation *jūdō* which signified the birth of something new while still paying respect to traditional culture.

Jūjutsu is a very effective system of unarmed combat, and there are a number of extremely lethal techniques. Training was inevitably a solemn affair, and there was always the potential for serious injury. Kanō was no stranger to perilous training, but was single-minded in his quest to become strong and never be beaten by anyone on the basis of his diminutive size. Due to his dedication to training, he gradually developed a strong physique, and even though he remained obstinate, his remarkable physical growth was also coupled with the development of a controlled, compassionate, calm and collected demeanour. His actions became not controlled by emotion, but by reason.

Kanō repeatedly stated, "Now, judo has become a recognized means of study to nurture physical and mental development. However, this is a recent development. Training in traditional *jūjutsu* was not just for mastering fighting techniques, but has always had great potential for intellectual, physical, and moral education. This forms the basis of judo today." Kanō spoke in regards to the benefits of *jūjutsu* compared to other physical activities:

> "I have had experience participating in a number of different sports. I have done apparatus callisthenics, the horse vault. I have tried rowing. I have even tried sprinting. The sport I spent the most time playing was catch ball and baseball. Granted, rowing was quite good exercise. However, if you don't live near a body

of water, you have to walk a long way to get there, and it is very inefficient use of time. If you desire to take this sport seriously, you require plenty of time, and it is also physically exhausting. If you choose only to go occasionally, it is hardly going to be beneficial as an exercise regime. When I was residing in Kanda, it was most inconvenient as it was a long way away from any stretch of water. I also belonged in those days to a hiking club. As there were only excursions on Sundays and public holidays, I found it to be inadequate as a form of training, despite how physically demanding it was. Playing catch was simply throwing a ball, and really did not constitute an overall effective system for physical development. Baseball requires a large ground to play on, and a large number of other people to play with. The pitcher and catcher get enough action, but the fielders for the most part are idle. The basemen are required to move a little, but this is limited. It is indeed an enjoyable game, but it is far from adequate as a complete exercise system to work out the whole body. When I rowed, I would go from Ryōgoku, up to Mukōjima, and then to the Senjū bridge. This is a full day trip. It is thoroughly agreeable as a form of recreation, but again, the benefits are negligible as an effective way of training the body. That is why I came to believe there really is nothing quite as good as *jūjutsu* for effectual physical development."

Kanō studied the two *jūjutsu* traditions of Tenshin Shin'yō-ryū and Kitō-ryū, and realized that it was not enough to study only one. Through his research into various traditions he was able to see the important overriding concepts of *jūjutsu* and ascertain its usefulness not only for fighting, but also as a way of nurturing intellect, morality, and physique. He wished that those values should be imparted to the populace as widely as possible so that many people could also reap the benefits. In regards to the role of judo in society, Kanō had the following to say:

"The future of the world will see many different societies coming into contact. It is a natural progression for cultures to share with each other. When this happens, we will have opportunities to learn many things from other countries. But, if we have nothing to teach them in return, not only will Japan appear to be insignificant, we will not be able to stem the tide of ridicule. So, what is it that we have to share with the rest of the world? We have judo. There is nothing that compares with judo. Even as I speak it is becoming increasingly popular around the world. Japan has an obligation to share judo with other peoples of the globe. The Kōdōkan must prosper for years to come, and retain an awareness of this great responsibility to the country and its people.

Individual ability, social harmony, rising national power, international accord and cooperation are the things that can be accomplished through tempering the mind and body by training in judo. Taking this into consideration, the role

From "Jutsu" to "Do"

and responsibility of judo for the sake of the future is immense. In days of old, mastery of techniques for combat was the main purpose of *jūjutsu*. Now, it can be utilized to maximize the strength of the individual, promote a peaceful and harmonious society, boost the power and energy of the nation, and intensify international accord. This is a great undertaking, and something which we must all strive to achieve from now on. This is the ultimate mission for judo."

Kanō's visions were consistently high.

The Formation of Judo Ideals

Through training in two different *jūjutsu* traditions, Kanō recognised the importance of researching the ways of other styles. He visited many different *dōjō*, purchased old scrolls and books, and did whatever he could to glean information about the various schools of thought and technique. His teachers did what they could to assist him in his quest for knowledge. He encountered great difficulty in comprehending the "truth" when faced with multitudes of conflicting information written in the countless books he had gathered. Each tradition espoused its own *ri*, or principles on which that school was based. However, most of the literature he read pertaining to the various traditions rarely ventured from the confines of their own principles. There was very little consistency, which troubled Kanō. His intellect would not allow him to be satisfied with segmental principles, as he was searching for theoretical principles that were universal in nature.

Furthermore, an often quoted principle of *jūjutsu* was "soft (*jū*) subduing hard". However, he felt the limitations of this as well. This high principle of *jū-no-ri* contended that the power of an opponent's attack be tamed and then conversely used against them. Kanō considered this principle to be of value, and he incorporated it into his teachings of Kōdōkan judo to explain technique until 1887. Eventually he came to the realization, however, that this principle was limited in its application, and was not able to serve as the underlying principle for all techniques of attack and defence. For example, it would be exceedingly difficult to reverse the flow of power against an opponent who attacks using such techniques as *ryōte-jime* (two-handed choke) or *hadaka-jime* (naked strangle). Moreover, in the execution of *atemi-waza* where the initiative is taken and thrusts, strikes, and kicks are executed, it would be impossible to do these techniques if the adept was required to overcome the opponent's attacks first. These offensive techniques could not exist. Kanō did not want judo to be so restricted. He wanted freedom of movement allowing attack, defence, utilization of the opponent's strength, or not, as deemed necessary. He expected judo to be all encompassing, and while he placed value on *jū no ri*, he also aspired to a more complete basis for his system. He had to create this universal principle. How did he achieve this?

In the spring of 1915 he proclaimed a definition of judo:

"Judo is the way of the highest or most efficient use of both physical and mental energy. Through training in the attack and defence techniques of judo, the practitioner nurtures their physical and mental strength, and gradually embodies the essence of the Way of judo. Thus, the ultimate objective of judo discipline is to be utilized as a means to self-perfection, and thenceforth to make a positive contribution to society."

The formulation of this definition had taken over thirty years since creating Kōdōkan judo. It incorporated all the knowledge he could glean from the old traditional texts, *jū-no-ri*, and all facets of attack and defence. Kanō called physical and mental energy "*seiryoku*". All human action is a result of *seiryoku* regardless of age. Every movement is a manifestation of *seiryoku*. According to Kanō, we use physical energy to move our bodies and mental energy to move our emotions, such as feeling pleasure and displeasure, or brightness or darkness. Kanō advocated that depending on how we use the energy, we could become men of virtue or men of great physical fitness. Or, we could become men of ability or men of wealth, and then start new enterprises. In summary, everything produced by human beings is a result of our making use of physical and mental energy. Kanō asserted that individual development, our place in society, national prosperity and the world's happiness are nothing but the results of having made use of this energy. That is why we should

Seiryoku zenyō brushed by Kanō Jigorō

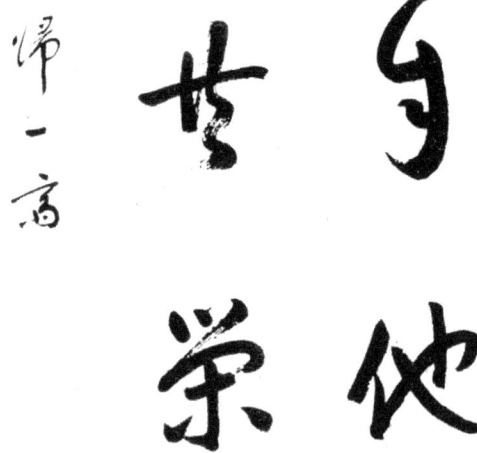

Jita-kyōei brushed by Kanō Jigorō

cultivate that energy as anything and everything can be accomplished by making proper use of it.

He believed that the principle of "*zenyō*" (善用 Maximum Efficiency) could guide a person on the path to self-perfection, enabling that individual to make a "positive contribution to society". Individuals well trained in the principle of Maximum Efficiency would be able to give each other mutual aid and concessions, which in turn would lead to mutual welfare, mutual benefit, and mutual harmony. Any reasonable society needs harmony among its people, and Kanō suggested that we could successfully manage such a society by using this principle of Maximum Efficiency in the use of physical and mental energy. Here, Kanō established his second principle, the principle of "*jita-kyōei*" (自他共栄 Mutual Welfare and Benefit), and he hoped that individuals, groups, societies and even nations would prosper through these combined principles of "Maximum Efficiency" and of "Mutual Welfare and Benefit".

The principle of *jita-kyōei* was first publicised in 1922 at the Kōdōkan. This was the culmination of over forty years of philosophising. The Kōdōkan students learned how to attack and defend, and nurturing their physical and mental strength in the process, use the resulting benefits for the good of society. This, to Kanō, was the way of the ideal judo practitioner.

From here, I would like to draw the reader's attention to Kanō's strongest assertions in regards to judo:

> "The Ultimate Objective of Training in Judo:
> In the days before judo, practitioners of *jūjutsu* were primarily concerned with acquiring techniques that would give them the edge in a violent confrontation. Practitioners may have held faint aspirations of becoming strong for the overall benefit of their domain, but generally speaking the motives for learning *jūjutsu* were quite simplistic. The main concern was to become an effective fighter. Since the formation of Kōdōkan judo, other motivations have been superimposed over the acquisition of fighting techniques. Namely, strengthening the body and nurturing mental strength or spirit, are ultimately for the betterment not only of the self, but for society as well. Although training for physical and mental benefits is often explained, just how this could be put to use for society is an important characteristic often overlooked. From here, I will outline my ideas of the three facets of fighting, physical and mental growth, and social utilization.
>
> Judo must not end with just learning to fight, and training mind and body. The three above-mentioned components of judo are all important in their own right, and it is difficult to place one over the other. However, if one considers the actual process, physical and mental strength are achieved through learning and training in the actual techniques for fighting. Once having attained these benefits from training in the techniques, the practitioner is then in a position to apply them for the better good, if they so wish. Thus, utilizing the strengths

nurtured through training in the techniques of judo for the better good is actually the last part of the process. On the other hand, having the "will" to utilize individual strengths for the good of society is the ultimate objective for people to aspire to in their everyday life. In order to be able to realize this, however, preparation and nurturing of skills is required. In the case of judo, this preparation, so to speak, is achieved through training in fighting techniques, not as the ultimate objective, but as a step in the process.

There are various viewpoints, but in this case, the actual techniques as a form of fighting occupy the lowest level of judo—the base. According to this logic, the final stage of utilizing one's skills and strengths for the benefit of society constitutes the highest level of judo. This leaves the actual training of the body and mind as the middle level.

Categorized in this way, clearly the judo process should not finish with learning how to defeat an opponent. The benefits gained through training should be put to higher use other than just personal satisfaction. Regardless of how wonderful a person the individual practitioner becomes, or however physically strong and dexterous, if they should perish without putting their attributes to greater use, it is somewhat comparable to a rich man dying without opportunity to spend his fortune. He may have perfected himself, but it cannot be said that his wealth benefited society. I implore judo practitioners to consider these three layers, and try to afford each one the attention it deserves rather than concentrating on only one…

When people are able to believe that they are using their energies with ultimate efficiency, they should have no disappointment or anguish. They are in no way wasting their energy. Regret and anguish are mental states which arise from not doing what should have been done, or through indecisiveness and lack of resolve. In the future, if people base their actions on the principles of judo and use it as a reference point, they will not exhaust their spirit and energies through needless distress."[1]

"Don't think about what to do after you become strong—I have repeatedly stressed that the ultimate goal of judo is to perfect the self, and to make a contribution to society. In the old days, *jūjutsu* practitioners focused their efforts on becoming strong, and did not give too much consideration to how they could put that strength to use. Similarly, judo practitioners of today do not make sufficient efforts to understand the ultimate objective of judo. Too much emphasis is placed on the process rather than the objective, and many only desire to become strong and be able to defeat their opponents. Of course, I am not negating the importance of wanting to become strong or skilled. However, it

From "Jutsu" to "Do"

must be remembered that this is just a part of the process for a greater objective. Of the youth today, there are many who participate in sporting activities other than judo, and have strong healthy bodies. It is also common to see many physically strong people suffering from various illnesses, yet some individuals who do no exercise at all and just spend their time reading books remain very healthy. This is not necessarily due to the constitution they happened to be born with. It is because one man maybe careless about his health, whereas the other is careful even though he may not practise sports. So, whether an individual becomes strong through participation in judo or some other physical activity, it will be to no avail unless he uses that strength for the benefit of society. Without such an understanding, if the individual suddenly decides one day that they would like to utilize their strength for the benefit of society, that individual will more than likely break down [through the sudden unplanned exertion] and be of no use at all. Thus and so, it is important to keep in mind from the beginning that you are aspiring to strengthen your body and senses in order to endure the adversities encountered when ultimately making contributions to society. The worth of all people is dependent on how they spend their life making contributions."[2]

The Internationalization of Judo—From "*Michi*" to a Competitive Sport

The following list outlines events of forty years of international judo. Despite opposition by Japan, the following modifications to judo were accepted into the international regulations:

1961- Introduction of weight categories
1973- Introduction of *yūkō* and *kōka* points
1979- Introduction of lost time system
1981- International Judo Federation Dan grade system implemented
1995- Japan loses the presidency of the IJF
1997- Introduction of coloured (blue) judo-*gi*
1997- Shortening of *osae-komi* (hold-down) time
1998- Introduction of smaller match area
1999- Prohibiting of women's black belt with white stripe
2003- Introduction of the 'Golden Score'
      Introduction of *shidō* penalties [for slight offences] and *hansoku-make* penalties [for grave offences]

Kanō made efforts to popularize judo soon after its inception, but an international federation was never formed in his lifetime. It has been over fifty years since the International Judo Federation was created in 1951 mainly due to the influence of the

Kanō Jigorō

From "Jutsu" to "Do"

United States and Europe. The concept of the IJF is to promote judo as a competitive Olympic sport. What is required to ensure that a competitive sport remains popular and successful? In the most basic sense, it must be easily understood, and secondly, it must be interesting. In order to make it easily understood, rules need to be simplified. To be interesting, it must have the attributes of speed, be dynamic, and be colourful. In other words, the sport must be exciting and stimulating for both the spectators and competitors. Judged on these criteria, it is easy to see the motivations behind modifying judo to suit the needs of the international community.

What then, were the problems that stemmed from these modifications? Basically, problems arise as to whether or not Kanō's ideals of *seiryoku-zenyō* and *jita-kyōei* are being upheld. Namely, in regards to actual training, is the practitioner utilizing their physical and mental energies to the utmost efficiency to execute an *ippon* technique? And, once they have accrued the skills to accomplish this technical feat, are they using these skills to make a contribution by helping others and encouraging 'mutual benefit'? Judo, where the perfect point, *ippon*, is substituted for lesser points, and judo in which the competitors merely vie to accumulate essentially imperfect points in order to win matches, is not conducive to the ideals once espoused by Kanō. Such judo cannot benefit both parties. The perfect *ippon* is exhilarating and stimulating. Both the thrower and the thrown are satisfied when an unmistakable *ippon* technique is executed. This is where *jū-no-ri* and *jō-no-ri* (the principle of compassion) combine to form a Way for the practitioner.

Conclusion

Heated competition in championship sports is exciting, and is strongly connected to commercialism. When cash prizes are offered to the victor, revenue is actually circulated endlessly between many different groups, and the sport evolves into what is essentially a "money game". Athletes start choosing which events they will participate in depending on the "size of the carrot" being offered. With the rise of professionalism in sports, traditional ideals of participation for fun and recreation become irrelevant. Such being the case in the sporting world today, it won't be long before gaudy company advertisements are attached to uniforms of judo competitors. The time is approaching where Kōdōkan judo with its ultimate objective of "self-perfection" and "prosperity for the world" will have to tackle the issue of professionalism. The blatant competition oriented form of popular international "JUDO" is already facing this issue, and the question remains: how will Kanō's ideals be accommodated or incorporated into their scheme? Indeed, the question of professionalism and amateurism, and how judo will or should evolve in regards to this international sporting climate is one of the crucial issues facing the judo world in the twenty-first century.

Endnotes

[1] *Judo,* Vol. 4 No. 7, July 1918.
[2] *Judo,* Vol. 4 No. 8, August 1918.

Bibliography

Judōkai Honbu Jimusho, *Judo,* Vol. 1-4. , 1914, 1918.
Murata Naoki, *Kanō Jigorō shihan ni manabu* (Learning from the master Kanō Jigorō). Nippon Budokan, 2001.

Chapter 7

Budō as a Concept: An Analysis of *Budō*'s Characteristics

Irie Kōhei
Professor emeritus - Tsukuba University

Introduction

There is an immense variety of athletic culture found throughout the world. Each example retains its own unique characteristics shaped by the environment and history of its birthplace. Looking at the evolution of sport, we can see how it developed from human experience in everyday life and play. Most sport we are familiar with today was strongly influenced by the Industrial Revolution in Europe (especially in England) and then by the United States in the twentieth century. The popularity of Western sport is such that it occupies an integral part of peoples' lifestyles today, regardless of where they live.

The more influence a form of physical culture retains directly from the lifestyle patterns of a given society, the more obvious and clearly reflected are the modes of thought and actions of the people from whence that culture derived. This is also true of the various martial arts found around the world today. Tracing the history of Japan's *budō*, we can see that, like most of its counterparts in other parts of the world, it originally emerged as a set of practical techniques for combat, and by incorporating influences from other facets of the region's culture, evolved into a multi-faceted cultural form with infinitely more sophisticated objectives than just to kill and maim.

Popular depiction of Miyamoto Musashi duelling Tsukahara Bokuden (1885)

Until now, apart from some notable research in the pre-war period, *budō* research has mostly been centred on theatre, storytelling, and novels. Research into *budō* as an integral form of Japanese athletic culture first became a recognised discipline from about 1965, after the Tokyo Olympics. As far as the actual practice of *budō* is concerned, after the initial hardships Japan experienced in the aftermath of WWII, a continually growing number of people from around the world have been coming to Japan in order to study this aspect of Japanese culture. Their inquisitiveness has not been limited to just learning the techniques, but they have also demonstrated a strong interest in the history and recognized spiritual elements of *budō* as well. However, if *budō* is to be disseminated from Japan to the rest of the world, there needs to be a far more concerted effort to try and understand the various cultural characteristics of *budō* culture. The following paper outlines my understanding of the characteristics of *budō* which need to be considered.

Combative Characteristics (*Bujutsu-sei*)

War is essentially a clash between political or religious groups. Traditionally, a battle will consist of individual members of a given organization engaging in one-on-one combat. It is a contest where the victor enforces their authority over the vanquished. The purpose of studying the martial arts (*bujutsu*) was to hone combat skills to use as a tool to achieve the goals of the group the individual represented.[1]

The most basic form of *bujutsu* is represented by what Odegiri Ichiun termed "*Chikushō heihō*"[2] (beast martial arts). In other words, a method of physically subduing an enemy, just as fighting bulls or cocks try and kill each other, the objective being to use fighting techniques to solve a dispute and place the enemy under your control. Thus, the question of life and death is the central issue in *bujutsu*. In other words, the question of how to survive and thrive in a dangerous combat situation, where loss inevitably meant death. In Japan's case, *bujustu* was influenced by esoteric Buddhist (Shingon) thought in the middle-ages, and gradually incorporated various 'magical' practices to enhance the warrior's confidence in battle. When Japan was ushered into a period of peace and stability with the onset of the Tokugawa period, hitherto all-inclusive *bujutsu* systems divided into schools specializing in particular weapons. A strong Zen influence also became evident as practitioners of the martial arts turned their attention from ultimate combat effectiveness to problems of *ki* and spirit, or the spiritual realm of the self. One of the finest examples of the relationship between Zen and the martial arts was demonstrated by Takuan and his influence upon the Yagyū Shinkage-ryū school of swordsmanship.

Takuan wrote the famous words "kill an enemy without your sword, let people live with the sword…"[3] Furthermore, "kill the evil of one so that ten-thousand may live [in peace]. The sword that kills must become the sword that gives life."[4] This became the basis for the well-known philosophy of the Yagyū Shinkage-ryū, "*setsunin-tō katsunin-ken*" (death dealing blade, life giving sword", and thenceforth the underlying concept for "*bu*" in a period of peace, and was used to justify the position of warriors as the top echelon of society during the peaceful Tokugawa period. As this suggests, Japanese

Budo as a Concept

bujutsu evolved from techniques primarily for attacking and killing an enemy into a way of introspection and living in peace with others. This is a significant characteristic of Japanese *budō*.

Religious Characteristics (*Shūkyō-sei*)

Traditionally an agricultural people, the Japanese have long believed in the presence of the divine in natural processes, appreciated courage and strength as gifts from heaven, and sought and followed divine guidance. They performed martial demonstrations to express their respect and appreciation for the divine forces. As Yanagita Kunio stated, "…the ancients attached much importance to strength and valour. They did not believe that strength came from within the individual, but considered it as something bestowed upon them through good fortune…Sumo was an activity used to ascertain just how much divine assistance was imparted to each wrestler."[5] This suggests a respect of strength and that the outcome of matches was decided by knowing the whereabouts of the deities.

Research has determined that the bow was not only a useful battlefield weapon, but had great religious significance, more so than other weapons.[6] This can be seen clearly in ceremonies conducted in Japanese folk religion, and since ancient times was regarded as the supreme symbol of "*bu*". For example, the ritual shooting of arrows was used as a way to determine the will of the gods, which could be interpreted by where they landed.

In regards to swords, the iron blades imported from the continent were far superior to the stone or bronze weapons traditionally used in Japan in ancient times. Apart from the obvious advantages found in iron over other materials in terms of hardness and sharpness, there was another quality which impressed the Japanese. When iron was polished it became so shiny and reflective that the ancients believed that it must be of divine nature. With the introduction of iron, swords were incorporated into religious ceremonies, and became highly respected religious implements. Japanese reverence of the sword continued through history and *katana* blades of high artistic and practical value were produced, eventually becoming the preferred weapon of the *bushi*. Swords were and still are essential objects in shrine regalia, and again the aforementioned Yagyū Shinkage-ryū which had a profound effect on the development of martial ideals and concepts in the Tokugawa period advocated that "the sword that kills must become the sword that gives life…" (*Heihō kadensho* – chapter entitled *Setsunin-tō*). This became the widely accepted ideal.

Aesthetic Characteristics (*Geidō-sei*)

"*Gei*" (芸) refers to the act of using a part of, or the entire body to create something of cultural worth. The character for *dō* (道) which can also be read as *michi*, means "Way" or "path", and consists of *kubi* "首" (neck) and *shin'nyū* (辶). "首" is supposedly a pictorial representation of the head and hair, and infers the "beginning" or "start" for humanity and all things. "辶" can be further divided into the elements of "彳" and "止" which mean to "go" and to "stop" respectively. Thus, the character for *michi* can be interpreted as meaning an actual way or path where a person stops and starts on their way from one point or destination to another.

However, originally in Japan, "*michi*" had strong nuances of "technique" (術- *jutsu*) or "way of doing something". In ancient China, Confucian and Taoist scholars gave the term philosophical or ideological interpretations such as "correct reason (*dōri*) which humanity must abide by", and "the body of phenomena". Such thought was in turn introduced in Japan, and from the Heian period (794–1185) onwards, it took on an educational tone, and was subsequently associated with scholarly and artistic pursuits.

Konishi Jin'ichi summarized the Japanese *michi* as having the following qualities:
1. Specialist nature
2. Universal nature
3. Hereditary nature
4. Restrictive nature
5. Practical nature[7]

The various religions and arts that preceded the *bujutsu* systems greatly influenced *bujutsu* development. *Bujutsu* was eventually to become a specialist activity and a Way where emphasis was placed on attaining a higher understanding of concepts related to the mind and *ki* through the act of mastering techniques. Eventually, *bujutsu* evolved into a pursuit requiring single-minded devotion where eventual acquisition and comprehension of universal principles would enable the adept to understand the common way of all the arts.

The famous noh actor and playwright, Zeami (1363-1443), wrote "those who desire to understand this way must not be negligent in their study of the other ways."[8] Yoshida Kenkō (1283-1359) also wrote "One who desires to attain mastery in one pursuit must also look to others as well." [9] The legendary warrior, Miyamoto Musashi (1584-1645) also wrote of the importance of being familiar with other arts. "Being familiar and having a broad knowledge of professions [other than just the martial arts] is important for one who wishes to excel in the Way."[10] In other words, this indicates that by mastering one Way, one understands universal principles which are applicable to all Ways. Or, "characteristics [of an art] communicated through universality", and "universality communicated through characteristics".

The Japanese arts can generally be divided into three types; recreational arts that originated in the world of the court nobles; the military arts that evolved in warrior society; and the commoner arts. Of the martial arts, archery and horse riding were included since ancient times in the *rikugei shisō* (philosophies of the six-arts) in China. As such, rather than being viewed as purely practical pursuits, they were categorized with other arts such as verse composition and the popular aristocratic game of *kemari*, each of which developed a number of styles or schools.[11]

Budo as a Concept

As Japan advanced through the tumultuous times of the Warring States period into the relatively tranquil Tokugawa period, the practical application of the martial arts became a less pressing issue. They then transformed into pursuits where adepts pushed themselves to their physical and mental limits, and used their training in martial techniques as a spiritual quest to acquire a deeper understanding of perceived universal truths. This leads into the next characteristic of *budō*, its educational applications.

Educational Characteristics (*Kyōiku-sei*)

The term *bushidō* was coined in regards to the ideal behaviour of the ruling warrior class in the Tokugawa period. There has been considerable research into various aspects pertaining to *bushidō*, and I have no intention to analyse it in great depth here. Suffice it to say, toward the end of the ancient period where landowners were required to maintain armed guards to protect their holdings, feudal relationships based on contractual agreements were entered into where the lord would bestow "favour" on retainers in return for their "service". These relationships dictated the ideal behaviour for both sides, and valour in battle and a strong sense of honour became prerequisites for retainers in their capacity as professional warriors. Naturally, they were expected to excel in the martial arts in order to fulfil their obligations to their overlords.

However, with the onset of social stability in the modern period, the type of relationship between lord and retainer, and the respective expectations were greatly altered compared to what had been the norm in the war-ridden past. In the peaceful times of the Tokugawa period, warriors were elevated in society as "moral leaders" in accordance with Confucian ideals, and were expected to be highly cultured and educated, and worthy of their position at the top echelon of society. The significance of *bujutsu* was also reinterpreted. For example, the Confucian scholar, Kaibara Ekken (1630-1714) stated, "...the martial techniques (*bujutsu*) of the bow and arrow, sword, and lance are no longer pursuits for the sake of war, but are now in fact martial *arts* (*bugei*)..."[12] This was a representative viewpoint of the times, and training in the martial arts was now meant as a way to learn the principles of martial virtue (*butoku*) in accordance with the expectations of Confucian ideals of the warrior-gentleman, referred to as *shidō*.

To be exact, the perceived value of *bujutsu* shifted from being a means to conquer enemies into an educational endeavour where the practitioner trained in the techniques as a way to learn and embody the "greater principles" and thenceforth develop morality and character. In this way, as the perceived practical value of the martial arts started to diminish in the peaceful Tokugawa period, the focus of training was shifted, and they were utilized instead as a valuable educational tool useful for instilling values in the ruling *bushi* class.

In accordance with social needs, the educational application of *bujustu* persisted into modern times. An example demonstrating the continued value placed on *bushi* culture is the book *Bushido: the Soul of Japan*, authored by Nitobe Inazō in 1899. In his exposition of *bushi* ethics, he asserted the importance of such virtues as righteousness, valour, compassion, courtesy, sincerity, and discipline. He claimed that these were all virtues that the Japanese people as a whole had inherited from *bushi* culture, and that the basis of Japanese religious and moral attitudes were based on the "Way of the warrior", or *bushidō*. He also advocated these values be emphasized in the moral education of the Japanese people in an age where Japan was modernizing and forever looking to the West for new ideas.

With the development of a new education system and educational ideals during the Meiji period, many ideas were put forth in an attempt to teach morality to the masses. Apart from reiteration of *bushi* ideals, *bujutsu* was also eventually included as an effective means to train the bodies and minds of Japan's youth. After being banned for a number of years after Japan's defeat in WWII, martial arts were once more reinstated in the school curriculum as a physical education subject, and are widely practiced in schools to this day.

In this age of great technological advances and perplexing flow of information, not to mention the constant examples of strife and war between different states and religions, I believe there is much to be gained from elucidating the universal application and potential of *budō* as an educational tool. One of the important elements of *budō* which makes it such an effective tool is the emphasis placed on *rei* (etiquette/courtesy/decorum/respect).

A term often heard in *budō* circles is that it "begins and ends with *rei*". There many people who believe that the study of *budō* encourages discipline. In countless books outlining *budō*, the importance of *rei* is explained in general terms as being an integral part of *budō* training ensuring that it does not degenerate into an act of senseless violence. *Rei* is viewed as a safeguard which keeps practitioners mindful of their position and the respect which must be shown to others. Of course, this interpretation is very relevant in modern society, but is that all there is to *rei*?

Most people would concur with the idea that good manners and adherence to prescribed forms of etiquette are necessary attributes in society. There are no laws which state that the individual must be polite, however, it is generally accepted that a sense of decorum and respect for others and maintenance of social rules is a prerequisite for personal success and keeping human relationships in order.

The forms of etiquette and manners stressed in various sports were developed in accordance with the historical processes and cultures in which that sport evolved. Generally speaking, the universal idea of courtesy and ideal behaviour promoted in the sporting world is referred to as "sportsmanship". The spirit of sportsmanship signifies an attitude where fairness and even-handedness are expressed through playing and competing as fairly as possible in accordance with the prescribed rules.

As I have already mentioned, archery was considered "one of the six arts, of both practical and moral significance..."[13] in ancient China. The Japanese art of *kyūdō* continues to uphold these ideals as a martial art with a practical purpose, and equally

Budo as a Concept

important, as a way for refining one's deportment. For example, in the text *Raiki* (C: *Li chi*), "The body must move in accordance with the laws of archery. Only when the inner and external self, and the mind and body are conducted properly can one can shoot an arrow rightly. If one can shoot rightly, then the arrow will find its target. The righteousness of the archer can be observed through their shooting." Again, "The Master said, 'Archery is something like the way of the superior man. When the archer misses the target, he turns and seeks the cause for his failure in himself.'" (*Chūyō* chapter 14. C: *Zhongyong*).

In regards to ideal behaviour in other *budō* arts, just before and after a match or training in any given *budō*, the competitors or practitioners will express their feelings of respect to the other by correcting their posture and then bowing. This is the traditional expression of respect and manners in *budō*. At one level, this is similar in meaning to ritualistic actions of shaking hands or hugging at the conclusion of a match in other sports. The ritualistic movements can be divided into two main categories of "expressions of respect", and "expressions of peace". The kinds of *rei* prevalent in the *budō* of the modern period can be categorized in the following manner:

1. *Rei* based upon Confucian principles which make a clear distinction between the self and others, and also demonstrate the will to maintain harmonic relations. It is a socially established pattern of contact. (*Shidō*).[14]
2. *Rei* seen in Buddhist theories of disciplining the mind through tempering the body. (*Shugyō*).
3. Shintoistic ritual used for purification when crossing from the mundane into the sacred realm.

Given such categories, the first *shidō*-type *rei* was developed in the *bushi* society of the Tokugawa period, and corresponds to the role of *rei* in modern *budō* to control the emotions, and stop it degenerating into an act of unbridled violence by maintaining order, and emphasizing the importance of showing respect to one's opponent. This, of course, is a valid interpretation of the role of *rei*. However, the second category of an internal *shugyō*-type *rei*, where the adept performs actions expressing *rei* or adherence to propriety as they throw themselves into hard physical training, pushing their own limitations as they seek a deeper understanding of their very existence. This is a non-superficial type of *rei* which is of the utmost importance in *budō* training. Furthermore, it is this category which needs to be explored, developed to suit the times, and stressed if *budō* education is to continue to be of use to future generations.

Chikara-ishi

Competitive Characteristics (Kyōgi-sei)

To reiterate, all the forms of athletic culture that exist in the world today have developed in accordance with their historical and physical environments. Various historical factors in eighteenth and nineteenth century Europe, in particular England, resulted in modern sporting concepts and forms which survive to this day. Combat sports and hunting, athletics, marine sports and the like have all developed from everyday activities engaged in by humans to ensure survival and prosperity. Other sports such as ball games were primarily created as forms of play. There have been numerous definitions offered by scholars to elucidate what sport actually is. Generally, sports are said to be recreational, competitive, and physical pursuits. The International Council of Sport Science and Physical Education declared that sports were physical activities of a recreational nature that pitted the individual in competition against a human opponent or the elements. Japan has a history of physical culture which falls into this category such as *chikara-ishi* (stone lifting), *kemari* (a kind of ball game), and *suiren* (swimming). The *budō* arts also retain these characteristics.

As we have seen, combat related physical culture, *bujutsu*, like combat systems of other countries, also developed out of techniques designed to physically suppress an enemy. In many cases, the traditional combat arts became outdated and were replaced with the gradual introduction of modern firearm technology. Some forms of martial arts managed to survive by shifting emphasis to new objectives such as maintaining fitness and health, in the same vein as other sports. Other martial arts, unable to adapt to the changing times became totally extinct. *Budō* is a form of physical culture born of combat experience, but was overlaid with philosophical concepts to keep them relevant to the times.

If we consider the historical process in which this evolution took place, we see that the Japanese combat

Illustration of suiren (swimming) from an 1831 text

Budo as a Concept

systems were no different to those developing in other parts of the world in their most basic form where the objective was simply to subjugate an enemy, and training the combatant to be capable of physically and mentally dealing with the stress of being confronted by an enemy in mortal combat. However, in Japan's case, when the practical objectives of the martial arts diminished during the peaceful modern period, they were reinterpreted as ways of educating and instilling moral attitudes and ideals in the ruling *bushi* class. This objective was continued even after the official abolishment of the class system during the Meiji period. Thenceforth, *budō* was used as an educational tool for the masses rather than the elite few. This role continues into the present day where *budō* is included as an integral part of the physical education curriculum in Japanese schools.

For *budō* to successfully make the transition from a purely combat oriented activity into an educational tool in Japanese schools from the Meiji period onwards, and indeed into a popular physical activity internationally, a number of changes had to be made. These modifications were as follows:

1. Safety of participation had to be assured. (Modification of techniques, training facilities, equipment etc.)
2. Impartial evaluation standards [for matches] had to be formulated. (Objective evaluation criteria, quantifiable criteria.)
3. All traditional *ryūha* affiliations had to be discarded.
4. Affiliation to any particular religion had to be abandoned.
5. Needed to break away from class-orientation and become accessible to all echelons of society.
6. Democratization of the governing bodies and open clarity of management practices.
7. Systematization and rationalization of instruction methodology.

Great efforts were made to ensure that these criteria were met, thereby ensuring *budō*'s continuation as opposed to possible extinction. However, a survey of the historical evolutionary processes of the various *budō* arts reveals that this transition was by no means achieved in a uniform manner. From here, I will briefly introduce the examples of judo, kendo, and *kyūdō*.

Judo

Jūjutsu remained a practical and effective means of unarmed combat, and a number of traditional *ryūha* were still operating even when Japan was ushered into an age of rapid modernization. During the early part of the Meiji period, Kanō Jigorō created Kōdōkan judo by incorporating techniques from a number of different *ryūha*, adapting them to make them safe, organizing them in a rational system, and superimposing philosophical concepts with the objective of nurturing individuals imbued with ideals enabling them to make a contribution to society. (See Chapter 6). One of his most significant innovations was the importance he attached to the training method of *randori* (free sparring). Such training was employed to varying degrees in the traditional *jūjutsu* schools, however, the bulk of training usually consisted of *kata* (set forms) repetition. Through this innovation, it was possible to initiate objective criteria for evaluation of techniques, which enabled judo's continued development as a popular competitive sport.

Kendo

In traditional *kenjutsu* training, *kata* was mastered utilizing wooden swords or live blades. From the early to mid-eighteenth century, emulating the practice of many schools of *yari* (spearmanship), protective equipment and bamboo swords were developed to allow safe full-contact training where practitioners could make full strength cuts to their opponents without concern of injuring or killing them, or vice versa. This new kind of training was referred to as *shinai uchikomi-geiko* (striking practice with a bamboo sword). It was revolutionary in that it was not only safe, but gave practitioners freedom in movement, and also facilitated the development of common evaluation criteria for judging valid strikes, thereby enhancing the competitive attributes of *kenjutsu*.

Despite vehement opposition from many "traditionalists" who maintained that *shinai uchikomi-geiko* was nowhere near as effective as the orthodox training method of mastering *kata*, *ryūha* consciousness in *kenjutsu* gradually subsided with the passing of time, and was replaced by a more generic form of popular fencing practiced all over the country. This was a significant turning point in the history of kendo that very much links traditional *kenjutsu* with the modern kendo practiced around the world today. After this, many more innovations were instigated such as the introduction of three referees to judge the outcome of matches, three-point system (*sanbon shōbu*) to decide the winner of a match, time limits, penalties for foul play, and so on.

Kyūdō

Compared to other combat related arts where practitioners test and improve their technical proficiency with a training partner, *kyūdō* is unique in that training was very much an individual affair between the adept and the target. Therefore, safety was never an issue, and it also easily fell into the realm of being an enjoyable recreational pursuit. Furthermore, criteria for assessing the skill of the practitioner were always apparent. With the introduction of the high philosophical ideals attached to archery in China, it played an important recreational and religious role amongst the nobles from ancient times. The medieval *bushi* also conducted numerous religiously significant events based around the bow, which were popular affairs open to spectators. During the transition from the medieval to the modern period, a popular archery contest called *tōshiya* was conducted in Kyoto. Originally participation was an open affair but became restricted to *bushi* during the Tokugawa period. The aim was to shoot as many arrows through the great hall within a given time. It was very easy to ascertain the most skilful archer, so there was little need for umpires and it transcended all *ryūha* affiliation. Apart from these advantages, it was also a popular event with spectators.

Thus, in many ways, the transition over the periods until the present day was not so great for *kyūdō*, especially compared with some of the other *budō* arts. Clearly the process of modernization for each of the *budō* was far from concurrent.

When plotting the historical evolutionary course of, for example, the sportification of *budō*, there were aspects in common with all the respective *budō* arts, such as becoming the exclusive property of the *bushi* class in the modern period. However, there were also many differences in each art's respective evolution brought on by technical characteristics and social relevance attached to the art. There were many complicated factors affecting each individual *budō*, which made each one's evolutionary route a unique affair.

Depiction of a tōshiya archery competition held at the Sanjūsangendō in Kyoto (1831)

Conclusion

To summarize my main points, the world has a rich inventory of athletic culture, evolving continuously with the history and the environment it is situated in. Of all the athletic culture in the world, the sporting forms and conventions developed in eighteenth and nineteenth century England have prevailed, and form the basis for most popular sports enjoyed by millions of people around the world today.

The fundamental elements of a sport are defined as being recreational, competitive, and physical. The competitive nature in particular is what makes sport exciting for many, and to this purpose many innovations have been tried and tested to establish evaluation criteria to enhance competitive characteristics and spectator accessibility. That is why "points", "results", and "records" have become the centre of the appraisal process.

Ideally, mutual agreement and understanding between opposing players is maintained independently by each party as they abide by the stipulated rules of engagement, and ultimate authority is left with a designated impartial referee. These are the confines from whence the spirit of "sportsmanship" materializes. The competitors are expected to play the game with a spirit of "fair play". Generally speaking, clear forms of etiquette or manners are emphasized as an expression of this attitude. However, the forms differ depending on the history and the culture where the sport originated.

There are examples of martial arts around the world that transformed into modern sporting forms. However, martial arts for the most part still retain serious elements stemming from combat oriented roots, and are strongly coloured by actual life experiences of the warriors who developed the arts. The seriousness attached to the Japanese martial arts is demonstrated by the importance attached to concepts and theories behind the techniques. For example, the precept *jiri-itchi* often quoted in *budō* circles, stresses the importance of training in such a way as to unify technique and theory. The aim of this precept is to search for truth by realization of the functions of mind and body through training in techniques.[15] Also, attitudes demonstrated in regards to penalties, criteria for evaluating the quality of techniques, and so on in *budō* are different in many ways to what is standard in other sports.[16]

Furthermore, in regards to the important concept of *rei* in *budō*, in some ways it does correspond to etiquette and manners in the social context (an external ethic), but it also retains a more personal meaning in that it is linked to an internal ethic of self-development. In such ways, it could be said that *budō* preserves many characteristics which are unique, and in many ways sets it apart from other sports.

In this way, violent combat techniques of the past created for the purpose of self-defence or protecting the organization in which the individual was a member, have been remoulded and refined over the course of centuries through the efforts of many generations of practitioners. Furthermore, the stress of mortal combat encouraged warriors of the medieval and early-modern periods to incorporate Shintoistic and Buddhist training methodology to develop spiritual strength and control emotions, thus enabling ultimate combative efficiency. The accentuated spiritual attributes have since become firmly entrenched in *budō* culture and remain an integral component of the martial Ways.

Similarly, the Confucian ideal of the warrior-gentleman as espoused in the popular Tokugawa period warrior ethos known as *shidō*, was the culmination of the refinement of ideal warrior behaviour since the Kamakura period. Commonly referred to as *bushidō*, the system of warrior ethics served to justify the *bushi*'s position at the top of the social pyramid as moral leaders. *Budō* was utilized as an effective educational tool in this period to instil and maintain morality in the ruling warrior caste. Of course, ethics and morals are advocated to maintain social order. They change depending on the era and the location, but are indispensable for the individual to be accepted socially, and in this sense, the study of *budō* facilitated in instilling an understanding of appropriate behaviour, and a sense of decorum. This is one aspect of *rei*. However, through violent confrontation with an enemy, the *bujutsu* adept was exposed to their mortality, and overcoming questions of "life and death", or reaching a level where one was oblivious

Budo as a Concept

to the stress invoked by one's vulnerability was a kind of enlightenment aspired to by warriors. This mentality, although not related in any obvious way to one's role or behaviour in a social ethical sense, was very much an internal ethic which required and facilitated personal development. Such mastery of the mind through mastering techniques was also seen as being applicable to all the traditional arts. The essence of one profession contains a "universal truth" that transcends all professions. I referred to this as "universality communicated through characteristics", and this is a common feature of all the traditional Japanese arts.

In regards to the competitive nature of *budō*, evaluation criteria must be objective, but the artistic assessment which takes into consideration the "quality" and "process" of the technique is different to more clear-cut criteria found in other sports. In the postwar period, *budō* was reinstated as a modern sport, and was made more competitive in nature and active dissemination has been sought on an international scale. In order for a form of culture to be effectively propagated internationally, it must be accessible to people of differing political, religious, ideological experience and creeds. Sportification is the quickest way in this sense. However, it is important to realize that sportification does not equal internationalization. In fact, there are cases where the merits of a cultural form are readily recognized and incorporated into the lives of people from all around the world when the other characteristics are emphasized.

From combat techniques, the importance of spiritual attributes as a way of bolstering effectiveness was realized. This then led to an understanding of martial arts as a way for the learning of universal truths applicable to all arts. Also, through this process it was recognized that training in *budō* was a useful tool for education and self-development, and the warrior class of the Tokugawa period utilized the martial arts for such purposes. The martial arts survived through the rapid modernization of the Meiji period, and are still utilized today as a way of imparting moral education, and the undercurrent of *bushi* ethics can still be seen.

In this paper, I introduced the combat, religious, aesthetic, educational, and competitive characteristics of *budō* and how they overlap. As we have seen, given the number of levels and characteristics contained in *budō*, it is inappropriate to attempt to explain the significance of *budō* from only one perspective. It should also be remembered that the interpretations of the significance of *budō* differ greatly from period to period, and the goals and objectives of each individual practitioner also vary. Each characteristic is linked with the others in a complex mesh of overlapping influences, making it difficult to assert the value of just one feature. This multifaceted nature is what makes *budō* so fascinating.

The future holds many uncertainties, however, earnest consideration of the values our ancestors learned and passed on for future generations—such as the case of *budō* culture—will surely give us in the modern age strength to live in a truly international world. An important theme for research in the future will be to compare the characteristics inherent in martial cultures from around the world with Japanese *budō* arts. This will serve to elucidate the true significance of the martial arts.

Budo Perspectives

Endnotes

[1] Karl von Clausewitz stated, "We therefore conclude that war does not belong in the realm of the arts and sciences; rather it is part of man's social existence. War is a clash between major interests, which is resolved by bloodshed—that is the only way in which it differs from other conflicts." p. 149.

[2] In the *Sekiun-ryū kenjutsu sho*, Odegiri Ichiun (1630-1706) wrote, "many warriors fight no differently to beasts. They defeat those who are weaker than they, are beaten by those who are stronger, and both are killed when their skill level is the same. This situation is hopeless…The warrior must understand that the way to absolute victory is contained within their very being."

[3] See Takuan's *Taiaki* contained in *Shinpen bujutsu sōsho* compiled by the *Budōsho Kankōkai*, p. 245.

[4] *Heihō kadensho*,(1637) – manuscript received by Hosokawa Tadatoshi. Eisei Bunkozō Collection.

[5] Yanagita Kunio, *Yōkai dangi*, p. 93.

[6] According to Suzuki Masaya, in battles from the mid-fourteenth to the mid-fifteenth centuries out of 554 examples, the percentage of casualties caused by arrows was 86%, swords cuts 8.3%, rocks 2.7%, spears and stab wounds 1.1%. From the mid-fifteenth to the mid-sixteenth centuries 1461 examples are analyzed with arrow wounds at 41.3%, guns 19.6%, spears and stab wounds 17.9%, rocks 10.3%, and 3 % for swords.

[7] See Konishi Jin'ichi's *"Michi no keisei to kairitsu no sekai"*.

[8] Nishio Minoru and Nogami Toyoichirō, *Fūshi kaden*, p. 11.

[9] See Yoshida Kenkō's *Tsurezuregusa* (Essays in idleness), entry 181.

[10] Watanabe Ichirō (annotated). *Gorin no sho* (Earth scroll), p. 31, 36.

[11] Ishioka Hisao et al. "Sakanoue no Tamuramaro to sono shūhen no kyūjutsu", *Kokugakuin Daigaku kiyō* Vol. 5, 1962, and "Kishi no bumonteki chii to sono shagei", *Kokugakuin zasshi*, 1966.

[12] Kaibara Ekken. *Bukun*, p. 117.

[13] Refer to Hirase Mitsuo's *Shagaku yōroku* (1788).

[14] In Tokugawa warrior society, there were two main trends of ethical thought pertaining to the ideal warrior. One dictated that the warrior maintain a constant awareness of 'death'. (*Hagakure* type *bushidō*). The other was Confucian based, and emphasized the importance of pursuing the correct Way. (*Shidō*). For more detailed analysis of these modes of thought refer to Sagara Tōru's book *Bushidō*, p. 74.

[15] Many famous early-modern texts about the martial arts make reference to the teaching of *jiri-itchi*. For example see, Yagyū Jūbei's *Tsuki no sho*, and *Ittōsai sensei kempō sho*.

[16] As outlined in detail in Hirase Mitsuo's *Shagaku yōroku*, for example, Japanese artistic perception gives consideration to both the internal aspects as well as the more obvious external physical form of the techniques. In other words, the result (Whether the arrow hits the target or not.) is not always the most important thing. The form and spiritual aspects demonstrated in the process of executing a technique from start to finish (*zanshin*) is evaluated as a whole.

Budo as a Concept

Bibliography

Budōsho Kankōkai. *Shinpen bujutsu sōsho* (New edition of writings pertaining to *bujutsu*). Jinbutsu Ōraisha, 1968.

Hirase Mitsuo. *Shagaku yōroku* (Record of studies in archery). 1788.

Ishioka Hisao, et al. "Sakanoue no Tamuramaro to sono shūhen no kyūjutsu" (Sakanoue no Tamuramaro and *kyūjutsu*). *Kokugakuin Daigaku Kiyō* Vol. 5, 1962.

"Kishi no bumonteki chii to sono shagei" (The military status of the Ki family and their archery). *Kokugakuin zasshi*, 1966.

Kaibara Ekken. *Bukun* (Martial precepts). Contained in Inoue Tetsujirō et al. *Bushidō shū* (*Bushidō* collection). Dai Nihon Bunko Kankōkai, 1934.

von Clausewitz, Karl. *On War* (edited and translated by Michael Howard and Peter Paret). Princeton University Press, 1984.

Konishi Jin'ichi. "Michi no keisei to kairitsu no sekai" (The creation of "Way", and the world of commandments). *Kokugakuin zasshi* Volume 57, Number 5, 1956.

Sagara Tōru. *Bushidō.* Hanawa Shobō, 1968.

Suzuki Masaya. *Katana to kubitori: Sengoku kassen isetsu* (Swords and head taking: Another view of Sengoku period battles). Heibonsha, 2000.

Nishio Minoru and Nogami Toyoichirō (comp.). *Fūshi kaden* (The transmission of the Flower of Acting style (by Zeami)). Iwanami Shoten, 1958.

Watanabe Ichirō, (annotated). *Gorin no sho*, Iwanami Shoten, 1985.

Yanagita Kunio. *Yōkai dangi.* (Discussions of monsters). Kōdansha, 1977.

Chapter 8

Confusion in the Concept of *Budō* in South Korean Society

Na Young-il
Seoul National University

Introduction

There is a tendency towards confusion in South Korea and Japan in regards to the concept of *budō*. *Budō* is usually translated as "martial arts", a term which is applied to all the delineations of *bujutsu* (martial skills), *bugei* (martial arts), and *budō* (martial Ways). In South Korea, however, there is no separate distinction between *bujutsu*, *bugei*, and *budō*. Even in China, whilst there are many terms denoting *bujutsu* and *bugei*, expressions of the concept of *budō* i.e. "martial Way", are rare. Although the term and idea does exist of martial arts being of great spiritual worth to the individual, the concepts are different to those seen in Japan.

While it is standard to describe *bushi* or *samurai* as "warriors" in Japan, this differs to the concept of "warrior" in Korea. In 2002, there was a symposium held by the Japanese History of Physical Education Society on the subject of the "physical culture and warriors' attitudes to the body". I was given the opportunity to outline this issue in regards to the Korean concept of "warrior". However, the interests of South Koreans and Japanese differ greatly from two separate angles. Firstly, the Japanese think of warriors in the traditional sense as individuals who selflessly and willingly sacrificed their lives if so required. Thus, concepts and ideas regarding the physical body, or more precisely the idea of detachment from the body and death, was considered an extremely serious matter. Conversely, in Korea, death is not spoken of in the same terms as it is or was in Japan, and injury is viewed from a Confucian perspective stemming from the belief that the individual is obligated to cherish their body, rather than sacrifice or mutilate it. Secondly, while the characters for *bushi* (武士 - *musa* in Korean) denote "warrior" in both Japan and Korea, there is a difference in nuance. Generally speaking, in Korea the characters used for the word *bushi* are commonly interpreted as simply "*military man*" and refers primarily to soldiers of officer rank. Consequently, the concept of "warrior" in Korea cannot be easily divorced from a distinct military organization or standing army, as opposed to a class or ideal.

Traditional Japanese society was made up of two elite echelons, the *bushi* class, and the nobility (*kuge*), who maintained a strong identification with the *bushi*. The so-called elite in traditional Korean society, on the other hand, consisted of the two hierarchies of the literati and the warrior class, forming a two-sectional aristocratic society. The traditions of the warrior class have not survived (at least visibly) into modern society, and the advent of the Choson (Yi) period (1392-1910) saw a great deal of intermingling of the literati and the warrior class. There were often differences in outlook, but the social structure dictated that the literati maintained a superior level of influence compared to the warrior class.

Thus, from the perspective of a typical South Korean, it is difficult for me to fully comprehend the Japanese concept of the warrior and *budō*, formed under the tense reality of imminent death faced by the samurai in their duties as professional warriors, and its subsequent sportification. That is to say, for South Korean sensibilities, the concept of the warrior and *budō* does not have its foundations in the historical experience of the country in the same way as Japan does. Naturally, in the course of modernizing, old cultural forms and systems have gradually been transformed in South Korea as well as in Japan. Ironically, young Japanese today generally consider compulsory military service for South Korean males to be an anomaly, and see the military culture of Korea as somewhat pre-modern.

Thus far, I asserted that traditional Japanese society was *mu* (J:*bu*, martial) oriented, and Korea's centred on *mun* (J:*bun* literati). Even so, in modern South Korea, after experiencing militarism under the rule of the Japanese emperor, and the Third Republic (government of Park Chung-hee) and Fifth Republic (government of Chun Doo-hwan), martial culture has come to exert great influence in various aspects of society, such as the sudden growth in the number training halls, *dojang* (J: *dōjō*) of the martial arts.

In South Korea the concept of *budō* is understood from a diverse range of delineations, including *budō* as a form of traditional culture, *budō* as a sport, *budō* as forms of physical education or training exercises, and *budō* seen in the purview of ethics and morality. While judo and kendo, both introduced from Japan, have planted firm roots in the soil of South Korea, a large number of differences have arisen in perception between the two countries. Just as there are huge differences between the two Japanese *budō* of judo the popular Olympic event, and kendo, which has taken a completely different route of international dissemination, we can also see equally great disparity in development between *budō* in Korea and Japan.

Taekwondo was developed independently of Japan in South Korea, and in a very short period of time spread to the four corners of the globe, eventually also becoming an official Olympic event. Nevertheless, taekwondo has seen an exceptionally slow rate of development in Japan. This is often put down to the attitude that taekwondo was an offshoot of karate. There exists a strong rivalry between Japan and Korea, and both sides are reluctant to acknowledge the other. The negativity in regards to the difference in environment, concepts, and other aspects of *budō* in South Korea cannot be resolved through egocentric intentions or clear-cut logic. Neither can misunderstandings be settled through a subjective sense of superiority or inferiority. In order to properly understand the essence and philosophy of *budō*, comparison of various perceptions of

Confusion in the Concept of Budo

the same art is a valid means of gleaning some understanding of its inherent universal characteristics. As the attached concepts of *budō* differ between countries, I believe one can draw closer to the essence of the martial Ways through a formula of comparison that seeks to accentuate similarities and differences in a positive way.

In South Korea, there is a tendency to emphasize *budō* as competitive sports. While they may constitute important material for mental, physical, and spiritual training for certain sectors of the population, including students, soldiers, police, and members of the general public, the value of *budō* has mainly found expression by those involved in the field of physical education, i.e. as a purely sporting pursuit. Unlike Japan, the spiritual aspects for the vast majority of practitioners, and furthermore, the educational aspects of *budō*, have not been widely recognized or propagated.

Originally forced upon the Korean population, the concept of *budō* has subsequently evolved through a process of evolution and adaptation to the social, political and cultural climate of the region. The result is what I would call an arbitrary form of *budō*, and in particular, has been heavily influenced by commercialism as it continues to adjust to the realities of the environment in South Korea. The present study will look at how the concept of *budō* in contemporary South Korea has been somewhat confused and utilized in negative ways, and will also investigate how *budō* can be developed as a field of academic study in the future.

Coercion of *Budō* Concepts

It is commonly asserted that "modern" education in Korea was implemented in 1895. From that point onwards, *gekiken* (K: *gukgun*) and judo were introduced from Japan. However, although prominent schools such as Seoul Teachers College included physical education in their curriculum, *budō* was not taught. We can confirm that Japanese style *gukgun* (J:*gekken,* fencing) had been introduced about this time through an 1895 article entitled "319-*won* purchase fees for fencing equipment" in the *Gojong Shirog* chronicle record. Also, with the 1904 military government edict number 17, trainee military officers were subjected to courses in tactics, shooting, physical exercise, and *gekken*. We cannot confirm beyond all doubt whether the course in fencing was Japanese kendo, or a form of fencing unique to Korea. However I suspect that it was most probably Japanese kendo through records of *gukgun* contests between Korea and Japan in 1908.

After the annexation of Korea by Japan in 1910, all matters of governance fell under the control of the Japanese. The government of the time was militaristic. In 1914, the *School Physical Education Curriculum* was established under Korean viceroy order 27, with gymnastics, drills, games, *gukgun*, as well as *jūjutsu* included in the teaching material. Efforts were made to encourage *ssirum* (Korean traditional wrestling), archery, and *naginata* for girls as extracurricular activities.

In 1927, the guidelines were revised under Korean viceroy order number 8. This order saw the addition of kendo and judo as teaching materials in physical education courses in male teachers' colleges, general secondary schools, and technical colleges. The change in name from *gukgun* to kendo (K: *kumdo*), and *jūjutsu* to judo (K: *yudo*) occurred during this period. Specific instruction methodologies and content were not stipulated for kendo or judo, and instructors were left to their own devices. There were, however, "instruction notifications" issued where, particularly in kendo, judo, and some other sports, the instructors were asked to sufficiently emphasize etiquette, and to avoid nurturing exaggerated competitiveness among the students, especially in regards to match training.

Once again, with Korean viceroy order number 36 in 1937, the physical education guidelines were revised. This was around the time of the Manchurian Incident which saw the height of Japanese imperial militarism in colonial Korea. The main point of the revised guidelines was the addition of kendo, judo, and *kyūdō* into male teachers' colleges, middle schools, general secondary schools, and male technical colleges; and *kyūdō* and *naginata* into women's teachers' colleges, girls' secondary schools, and technical colleges for women. The following instructions were also added:

"The instructor shall give astute guidance, mainly through training and competition, in basic and applied movement. The instructor in judo shall give high regard to training in basic technique in particular, and principally teach throwing techniques (*nage-waza*) with immobilizing techniques secondary. Kendo and judo instructors shall give lectures at appropriate opportunities and endeavour to enhance results in combination with actual training. To enhance distributed teaching materials, lectures about kendo and judo shall be conducted appropriately as opportunity arises, and shall be of a plain and simple nature. An outline of the method of refereeing shall also be taught in kendo and judo."

To promote Japanese ideals of *bushidō*, exercise regimes including the *Imperial subject physical exercises* and the *Great Japan national physical exercises* were instigated in October 1937, and kendo was also taught to female students. Furthermore, in 1938, less than one year after the revision of the physical education guidelines, the Korean viceroy government amended the Korean education law as it mobilized for war, and advocated the three educational policies of clarification of the national polity, interior [Japan] and Korea as one body (forced assimilation), and endurance training of a militaristic nature. Physical education classes in middle schools and above consisted of callisthenics, kendo, judo, and games as curricular subjects. *Kyūdō, ssirum*, swimming, skiing, and skating were also recommended subjects. Women were also subjected to changes in physical education, and were made to learn kendo, judo, *kyūdō, naginata*, swimming, skiing, and skating at secondary schools, thus making *budō* education compulsory for female students as well. Training increased from three hours to five hours a week.

The education system was reformed in 1941 with primary schools renamed national

Confusion in the Concept of Budo

schools in accordance with Japan, and "physical education" was renamed "physical training". The physical training curriculum was divided into standard physical exercises and *budō*. Elementary school classes assigned boys basic kendo and judo training, which was continued at a higher level as they entered higher education. Girls in elementary school were subjected to compulsory education in *naginata*. Henceforth, all schools and teachers' colleges implemented *budō* as compulsory subjects. In this way *budō* started to take root in Korea, and as Japanese militarism and imperialism gained momentum, *budō* education became increasingly coercive.

Even so, not all aspects were coercive in the beginning. In his book *History of the development of judo in Seoul*, Abe Fumio states that there were already ten judo training halls in Seoul before 1909. The introduction of judo into Korea occurred before the advent of militarism, and before the formation of the *Kokuryūkai* (Amur River Society; literally Black Dragon Society, an ultranationalist association) and the invasion of the Chinese mainland. The person to first open a *dōjō* in Korea was Kōdōkan fifth-*dan*, Uchida Ryōhei (1874-1937), a Japanese judo instructor to the police who came to Korea as a governmental advisor.

Much effort for voluntary development was made by a number of individuals and groups. In 1908, Military Academy principal Lee Hee-du and the chief of the Academic Affairs Bureau Yun Chi-o, proposed and created the first official military callisthenics organization. They are thought to have practiced such activities as marksmanship, horse riding, *jūjutsu*, and *gukgun*, and as of September 1908 they expanded their activities to include the armed forces. In 1909, the Archery association was formed to promote ethnic archery by Lee Sang-pil, Lee Yong-mun, and others. Furthermore, the Korean Archery Research Society was amalgamated in 1922. The formation of such groups is worthy of attention as these events were before the height of Japan's militaristic aggression. For example, in 1908, the YMCA judo training halls were established by Koreans. At the same time, Lee Sang-jae established a judo club independently to train one-hundred enthusiastic youths in the arts. Ryu Geun-su and Na Su-young were placed in charge of the training regime for the group. A perusal of documents showing physical education activities for central YMCAs between June 1914 and May 1915 shows participants in judo classes at 2,627 over the course of 196 sessions, recording the second highest figures of all available sports classes, and clearly demonstrating the popularity of judo. In 1928, the phrasing and terminology of judo was translated into Korean and circulated. Tournaments such as the All Korean Judo Club Championships were held, among other attempts to develop judo independent of Japanese assistance. On October 30, 1932, the Korean Judo Federation was formed.

Budō Concepts Remade

In 1953, a specialist judo university (now Yongin University) was established for the first time in South Korea. This university has produced a great number of *budō* instructors in judo, taekwondo, kendo, and aikido. In 1982, with Yongin University as the most prominent martial arts university, five other four-year universities including Kyungwon University, Kyunghee University, Keimyung University, Chosun University, and Korea National Sport University, established taekwondo courses in the 1980s and 1990s, and have been extremely active in producing qualified instructors in an array of other martial arts. Furthermore, Yongin University and Sunmoon University offer scholarships to practitioners of judo and Eastern martial arts, and maintain considerably popular physical education courses through having high-level instructors in taekwondo, judo, kendo, and other sports. Two-year universities such as the Incheon Junior College and Chungcheong Junior College also have *budō* majors. This enthusiasm for training martial arts specialists is said to be on a par with, if not superseding the top university *budō* courses in Japan, such as the Nippon Sport Science University (*budō* course established in 1965) and the International Budo University (1984).

The majority of South Korean graduates of *budō* related courses find employment managing training halls, working in sports centres and other facilities, and are active as public employees in the military, police, and fire fighting services, and some are also active as *budō* instructors overseas.

It is difficult to ascertain whether or not these universities focusing on producing *budō* instructors in Korea provide adequate academic study into *budō* culture, or just the physical and technical aspects. However, a look at the curricula being offered at these universities leaves me rather sceptical. I doubt whether the cultural or academic characteristics are covered adequately, which leads me to believe that *budō* 'specialist' education in South Korea is very much incomplete as far as the understanding of concepts and philosophy.

We cannot conclude, even with regard to the taekwondo courses that were started some twenty years ago in South Korea under the guise of academic subjects, that a satisfactory level of research has been achieved at all as far as establishing terminology or distinct fields of research. In essence, common references made to taekwondo courses as 'formal academic study' are unfounded and misleading, and reveal a kind of taekwondo 'identity crisis'. The taekwondo courses differ little from similar sports courses entitled the "study of soccer", the "study of basketball", or "baseball", and so on. The taekwondo courses at universities use phraseology that attach some kind of academic nuance, such as "taekwondo history", "taekwondo philosophy", "taekwondo dynamics", and "taekwondo training methodology" and so on, which is almost empty terminology. As taekwondo and other martial arts become increasingly popular, the issue of the martial arts in an academic context needs to be addressed in South Korea in order to enhance continued growth and development.

Interestingly, in comparison to the situation in Japan, South Korean martial arts seem to be riding a wave of popularity. I have been informed that the popularity of kendo in Japan has waned in recent years. It appears that the number of hours allotted to the study of kendo in physical education classes in Japan has decreased dramatically compared to ten years ago; the complete opposite phenomenon has occurred in South

Confusion in the Concept of Budo

Korea. Furthermore, in South Korea, elementary students form the majority of pupils at private training halls for taekwondo, whereas adults make up the core of *gumdo* (kendo) classes. In South Korea *kumdo* has gradually become an extremely popular pursuit.

Still, there are many aspects of disseminating *budō* in which South Korea could learn much from Japan. Japan gives broadcasts of judo competitions on state-run television. South Korea only does this for special events. While there is not a particularly large audience for such programs in South Korea, by contrast, Japan offers intensive broadcasting to a large viewing audience. Furthermore, sumo appears in the sports pages of the newspaper in a diverse range of articles, and television channels compete to broadcast the latest news as it comes to hand. This contrasts with South Korean *ssirum*, which is only broadcast at a specific time on national holidays. This demonstrates the differences in treatment of *budō* in South Korea and Japan.

As far as concrete data outlining the state of *budō* in the two countries, according to material from the Japanese Ministry of Education that analyzed the state of social physical education facilities in Japan. As of 2000, there were 781 judo *dōjō*, 710 kendo, 955 combined judo and kendo, 23 karate and aikido, and 964 *kyūdō dōjō*.[1] These figures show an overall slight increase over the figures surveyed in 1988 when there were 591 judo, 511 kendo, 729 judo and kendo, 27 karate and aikido, and 739 *kyūdō dōjō*.

There were 5,875 private *dojang* in 1993. Their ranking according to numbers stood at: 3,685 taekwondo, 920 aikido, 248 *wushu*, and 190 judo training halls. Seven years later in 2000, according to the Culture and Physical Education Department in South Korea, 7,979 individuals or groups ran private *dojang* or martial art centres. The total had increased by 2,104 groups which were made up of 324 judo, 252 ssirum, 352 kendo, 318 kyudo, 1,096 taekwondo.[2] Looking at these figures we could state that South Korea has seen a higher growth rate in *budō* in recent years.

The continued growth of *budō* in South Korea from a numbers and commercial perspective is obvious, however, the development and dissemination of accompanying *budō* concepts is not obvious at all. I conducted a survey in 1994 where 438 practitioners and instructors of traditional *budō* in South Korea were questioned to ascertain differences in the understanding of *budō* concepts between the two groups. Compared to the instructors, the trainees generally saw *budō* simply as self-training and self-discipline, or as a means to keep physically fit. In answer to the question of whether a clear distinction should be drawn between *budō* and sport, 54% of instructors stated that they would understand if there was some distinction, although there was no real need to change the *status quo*, and only 25% replied that *budō* and sports need to be developed two-dimensionally, i.e. as separate entities.

In a 2002 survey conducted by the Korean Taekwondo Association over the internet in regards to why respondents wanted to learn taekwondo, 52.11% (2530 respondents) stated that their main motivation was for physical fitness, 9.62% (467) for developing a positive character, 12.75% (619) for weight loss, 10.34% (502) for dispute resolution, and 15.18% (737) for life / etiquette training.[3] The survey showed that the reasons for studying taekwondo were more for physical fitness rather than a conscious effort to study it as *budō*, a cultural and educational pursuit for character development. A similar survey was also carried out in Japan. In 1972, an investigation into the actual state and understanding of *budō* (in this case *Nihon kempō*) was conducted with 328 individuals responding. In answer to the question of whether they considered *budō* (*Nihon kempō*) to be a sport, 66.6% said that they did, and of this 51.9% said that the primary objective of *budō*, like sport, was for improving physical fitness and health. Conversely, of those that said it was not a sport, 17.2% stated that *budō* was different to a sport, and had the aim of fostering the spirit. A further 12.8% stated that *budō* was primarily for self-defence.[4]

Wavering *Budō* Concepts

Who and what is *budō* for? This question is predicated on the issue that *budō* should not be only for the actual practitioners. Difficulties would be posed if *budō* did not have a universal value that is useful to more than just the practitioners. English gentlemanliness is thought to hold a universal meritorious quality, and *budō* is also often touted as possessing universal human values such as courtesy, fairness, and mutual prosperity for the self and others. What kinds of values must *budō* retain in order to fulfil the ideal of being accessible to all people, and not just recognized as a vestige of *bushidō* and Japanese samurai culture, and hence considered primarily the property of Japanese?

In regards to concepts in *budō,* a representative example from Korea would be [General] Choi Hong-hee, the [former] president of the International Taekwondo Federation, who stated in 1975 that the "five great spiritual aspects" of taekwondo included "courtesy, perseverance, honour, self-control, and fortitude in the face of adversity". In an officially authorized taekwondo textbook, emphasis is placed on practical virtues that establish "good human relationships", "peace", "justice", and "responsibility", and making these virtues a part of one's life.

However, the history of conceptualizing *budō* has a much longer and established history in Japan. For centuries, Japanese swordsmanship has been linked to the philosophy of Zen Buddhism, and has utilized expressions that evoke a Zen mental state, such as the sword and Zen as one, freedom from all distracting thoughts, a placid state of mind, and immoveable wisdom. Furthermore, the Dai Nihon Butokukai (Great Japan Martial Virtue Society) which was active as a national organization promoting *budō* in Japan from 1895 until the end of WWII, placed the basis of its teachings in the three martial principles integrity, honour, and courtesy.[5]

Within the philosophical thinking of judo based around the Chinese Lao-Tze's idea of "soft conquering hard", Kanō Jigorō (1860-1939) introduced educative philosophies such as practice "begins with etiquette/respect) and ends with etiquette", maximum efficiency in the use of strength, and mutual benefit. The founder of karate in Japan, Funakoshi Gichin (1868-1957), formulated the following *dōjō-kun* (precepts): "Seek

Confusion in the Concept of Budo

perfection of character; protect the way of the truth; foster the spirit of effort; respect the principles of etiquette and respect others; guard against impetuous courage and refrain from violent behaviour." In 1975, the Japan Kendo Federation advocated the *Concept of Kendo*: "The concept of kendo is to discipline the human character through the application of the principles of the *katana* (sword)." The Japan Budo Association established the *Budō Charter* in 1987 to define what *budō* was. In the introduction it was stated, "*Budō*, the Japanese martial ways, have their origins in the age-old martial spirit of Japan. Through centuries of historical and social change, these forms of traditional culture evolved from combat techniques (*jutsu*) into ways of self-development (*dō*). Seeking the perfect unity of mind and technique, *budō* has been refined and cultivated into ways of physical training and spiritual development. The study of *budō* encourages courteous behaviour, advances technical proficiency, strengthens the body, and perfects the mind. Modern Japanese have inherited traditional values through *budō* which continue to play a significant role in the formation of the Japanese personality, serving as sources of boundless energy and rejuvenation. As such, *budō* has attracted strong interest internationally, and is studied around the world. It appears, however, that in the real world scientific consideration and theorization of the value of *budō* training is rare."

Such definitions and concepts are extremely positive. The perceived values of *budō* lie in developing health and fitness, mental strength, self-defence capabilities, and other attributes that are attained through correct and repeated training of martial techniques. However, despite these efforts to establish *budō* as something more than just a physical activity, the flow of time and changing social conditions have affected *budō* in negative ways. For example, *budō* is becoming increasingly commercial, albeit through necessity. Training halls advertise for members, there are financial links with the organizations and styles a *dōjō* is affiliated to, and great efforts are made to present evidence of superiority of one kind of *budō* over rival organizations. Accordingly, new techniques [or martial arts] are continually developed while retaining traditional forms of etiquette. This process is administered by higher authorities who provide credentials for legitimization (at a price), and much currency is circulated in the form of tax payments, advertising fees, and club fees. Money is now an integral part of *budō* in modern society.

However, in extreme cases this process becomes distorted, and mistakenly becomes the focus of *budō* activity. In contemporary South Korean society, we can see a distinct trend where the value of *budō* is understood mainly through its potential as a commercial product, and the concepts are effectively treated as empty rhetoric.

In the training halls of schools that teach *budō,* and in the private *budō dojang* of South Korea, instruction methodology differs between each school, each instructor, and in each individual's view of the martial arts. However, even if it is not obvious on the surface, the majority of martial arts organizations cannot afford not to advocate commercialism. For example, this is linked to such trends as emphasizing the competitive aspects of *budō* rather than the educational characteristics, and it is the prospect of getting medals and fame that brings students in not so much the notion of becoming a "good person". Gresham's Law states, "*Cheap money drives dear money from circulation*", and as commercialism has made inroads into the *budō* world, there is the imminent danger of an erroneous interpretation of *budō* coloured by commercial packaging coming to the fore, with stimulating but unethical content.

In the past Korea, China, and Japan have all acknowledged *budō* as a way of training the mind and body, and grafted onto the techniques Eastern philosophical ideas from Confucianism, Buddhism, Taoism, and *yin-yang*. Incidentally, recently there has been an upsurge in new varieties of *budō* born in South Korea, that combine sporting elements with religious or ethical ideas. I refer to this as 'fusion' *budō*, and will come back to this idea shortly.

I have observed South Korean and Japanese training halls very closely, especially attitudes to etiquette and ritual. In observing actions such as bowing to the flag as one enters the hall, courtesy shown teachers, senior members, colleagues, and those of less experience, I noticed a greater adherence to etiquette and ritual in South Korea than in Japan. While only some *dōjō* in Japan display a national flag, the majority of South Korean *dojang* do. In Japan, it is common practice to simply bow to the front of the training hall rather than to the flag. While in South Korea, bowing to the flag, instructor, and to each other in unison is strongly emphasized. In Japan, I saw practitioners bowing individually to the front of the training hall upon entry to the *dōjō*, and a mutual bow to the instructor. When I enquired as to the feelings or thoughts that lie behind bowing to the flag and various members of the *dōjō* in Japan, a large number of people replied that this was merely a greeting, and held no special meaning to them. Also, I felt that in both South Korea and Japan, etiquette was slightly more formal in kendo clubs than in judo. Another characteristic I noticed was that Japanese *dōjō* are generally much cleaner than those in South Korea. Although the above observations are quite subjective and generalized, they do indicate some common traits. All said and done, etiquette and ritual, even if it is just going through the motions, is considered an integral part of *budō* training.

As Allen Guttman stated in his argument on the essence of modern sports in *From Ritual to Record* (1979), sports in the modern era emphasize records more than ceremony. *Budō*, however, tends to treat ceremony as more important. Accordingly, there are many who advocate distinguishing between sports and *budō* due to the strong adherence to traditional ceremony in *budō*, represented by the various forms of etiquette. There is an inclination in *budō*, especially in Japan, to emphasize form over content. Nevertheless, we must also, recognize that the paradigm of *budō* philosophy has changed in the twenty-first century. As I have already pointed out, South Korea has a diversity of opinions where *budō* is seen as a sport, as a form of spiritual training, and as a system of combat techniques. There are numerous debates raging concerning what *budō* should be, or which characteristic is the *most* correct. However, in the past century the "Way" of *budō* has been pushed as being the most important aspect. This is mainly due to its connection with mortal combat, and the hard training and solemn discipline expected when undertaking *budō* training. This argument was used

Confusion in the Concept of Budo

to discriminate *budō* from sports. It should be stressed however, that *budō* is far from being the only activity that requires serious consideration to the problems of life and death and spiritual and physical limits. Race car drivers, triathletes, marathon runners, boxers, wrestlers, weightlifters, and rugby players, to name but a few examples, are constantly trying to overcome physical and mental barriers, and the danger of serious injury or even death in their sports is a constant concern.

Still, to return to the resurgence in interest of the "spiritual" aspects of *budō* in South Korea, while different forms of combative sports are gaining rapid popularity in South Korean society recently, I am not the only one who foresees the continued proliferation of "fusion *budō*" i.e. new forms of *budō* which attach considerable importance to religious or spiritual characteristics. The growing popularity of combative sports, although in many ways poles apart from *budō* as a "Way", is actually serving an important purpose in stimulating interest in the so-called spiritual potential and understanding of *budō*.

Either way, as *budō* becomes increasingly popular, other issues are also causing confusion. For example, there is a movement in South Korea, which could be interpreted as being nationalist, or universalist depending on your point of view. In 1977, Li Ho-am submitted a proposal regarding the use of [Japanese] *hakama* to the president of the Korean Gumdo Association. While advocating arguments for the use of *paji* (Korean trousers) rather than the Japanese pleated culottes (*hakama*), during *kumdo* training, he stated "in order to respect the creation of 'beauty', the ultimate objective of physical education, not the traditional and narrow-minded [view of] Japanese beauty, [we should] aspire to pursue a universal beauty for all humankind", and went on to say that present-day kendoists sought a form of "international kendo" not a "Japanese-centric form". Such avocations were not only made by South Koreans, but by Taiwanese as well, and there are also some Japanese who hold the same views. Rather than lightly dismissing such opinions, I feel that Japanese people would be well-advised to seriously consider the implications. Judo uniforms remained white for many decades only because it was considered to be "traditional". However, the fact that they were changed to blue and white due to the "influence of television", in spite of vehement Japanese objections on the grounds of maintaining tradition, suggests that Japanese ideas of tradition and beauty are precariously placed in the international arena, especially if they are unable to justify such practices with any other reason than "tradition".

With overflowing information from the internet, it is easy to see that for *budō* to become truly internationalized, it cannot only be as a totally Japanese form. The same, of course, can be said for the dissemination of Korean forms of *budō*.

My idea of a 'universal' concept of worldwide *budō* in essence differs from the general concept of *budō* held by individuals, or those accepted within the confines of a specific cultural or national setting. In the same way that history differs from country to country, *budō* concepts in each country will also vary, as will each different form of *budō*. Consequently, I see a necessity to find a universal concept of *budō* for the whole world, which would provide universal values and ethical provisions that could be readily tapped into by all peoples.

Presently in Japan, there is a student who is enrolled in a doctoral course in the field of martial arts. Having practiced martial arts in South Korea and completed a Masters degree in the same field in Taiwan, she has come to Japan to add wider breadth to her research, and is now endeavouring to compare martial art literature from South Korea, China, and Japan. It seems, however, that she has encountered serious difficulties. She was unable to find much literature in Japan that provides an all-encompassing definition for all the different *budō*, making comparison with South Korean and Chinese martial arts difficult. Of course there are many clues pertaining to universal attributes in all combative arts in classical Japanese books such as *Heihō kadensho* and *Gorin no sho*, however, it is difficult to source literature outlining a common concept for modern *budō* arts such as kendo, judo, *kyūdō*, and so on. Having said that, there are a considerable number of books relating to *budō* which are popular, but they tend to be based, for the most part, on the same restrictive content. There need to be more books made available to the *budō* public that serve to compare South Korean, Chinese, and Japanese delineations. To go a step further, I believe we need a common treatise available to all people that will serve to promote common development and understanding of the essence of *budō*. Of course this will not be an easy task.

The religions of Christianity, Buddhism, and Confucianism place great importance on classic scriptures. Scriptures can mean specific works of holy people including Holy Scriptures, Buddhist scriptures, and the Four Books and Five Chinese classics; it may also refer to a text that provides precepts for religious instruction. The teachings of Jesus Christ, Buddha, Confucius, and Mencius, are still immeasurably influential and respected, and each character and each sentence of each scripture is pored over, centuries, even millennia after they were first composed. Furthermore, these religions also provide modern interpretations of the classic scriptures to make the wisdom accessible to all. However, in the case of Japanese *budō*, and of course South Korean *budō*, there seem to be only 'interpretations', without any actual 'scriptures'.

Is there no 'scripture' that could be devised and used as a basis for the study of a universal set of *budō* ethics? A UNESCO committee specializing in the fields of humanities, philosophy, and science and technology conducted a symposium in 2001 on ethics for the twenty-first century. Various presentations were given in a number of categories. The theme of the first session was "A common framework for the ethics of the 21st century". The second theme was 'The role of ethics in the 21st century". The third was "A different approach to ethics in the cultural spheres of Christianity, Buddhism, Islam, and Confucianism", and the final session was "The future of ethics".[6] Whilst many different individual opinions were expressed at the gathering, it was difficult to reach a conclusion in which all the participants could agree upon due to there being so many participants representing such a diverse range of cultures, languages, and ethical backgrounds.

Does *budō* need to be the same, or does it retain the potential to override all of these factors? The promulgation of the *Budō Charter* in 1987 by the Japan Budo Association was a valuable exercise, but more efforts need to be made to establish a universal philosophy for *budō*, making the 'martial Way' a truly 'global Way'.

Confusion in the Concept of Budo

Conclusion

We can describe a 'concept' as being an ideal that must be ultimately attained and maintained. The 'concept of *budō*' should be an extraction of common factors from all the different *budō* practiced around the world. A concept formulated in this broad sense would be a valuable exercise in cultural affiliation.

The concept of *budō* in Korea has transmuted into a variety of forms over the last century. At one stage it was forced upon the population, but also developed of its own accord, giving rise to new aspects. While there is still significant opposition and competition in regards to 'Japanese' *budō* in South Korea, there also exists a desire to develop *budō*. Within this composite thinking, there are many people who maintain a perspective of universalism in regard to the concept of the martial Ways.

Recently in South Korea, *budō* federations and groups have attempted integration in a variety of ways. Many tried to create new hybrid groups and integrate each other's methods in a process of fusion and fragmentation. Often these groups inserted the word "international" or "world" in front of their name, and flaunt overseas affiliations as if to give them more credence over rival organizations. Such simplistic politicizing of the martial arts has led to the creation a large number of contentious issues and mistrust that are in need of urgent resolution. Recently, however, the Korean Budō Society was created in 1999, and they were instrumental in forming the World Martial Arts Federation in 2002 in Chungju. This group has served to bring some semblance of order and public trust compared to the mishmash of previous organizations, and provide some hope for the future.

While *budō* has positive functions for individuals such as acquisition of good health and self-confidence, self-restraint, and moderation, from a different angle *budō* could also be used for violent or antisocial purposes. Because *budō* stems from violence and combat, social approval of participation cannot be obtained unless it goes hand in hand with controls that block the potential to misuse violent techniques. Consequently, it is natural that the practitioners of *budō* must develop, and be seen to develop, strong moral principles and ethics.

No one would deny the value of *budō* education that enhances courteous behaviour, encourages self-discipline, and stimulates the individual to strive for a higher understanding of universal and natural principles. In the future, I hope that a 'universal' concept of *budō* will be recognized, and represented in each country by reputable organizations, which will in turn be recognized by such bodies as UNESCO. I also hope that this symposium will in some small way make a contribution to this idea.

Endnotes

[1] Refer to http://www.mext.go.jp/b_menu/toukei/index.htm
[2] http://www.koreataekwondo.org/ (This material has subsequently been removed).
[4] Tsuchitani Hideo, p. 89.
[5] See Inoue Masataka's *Kendō iroha rongo* (Discussions of kendo).
[6] http://unesdoc.unesco.org/images/0012/001246/124626eo.pdf

Bibliography

Guttman, Allen. *From Ritual to Record: The Nature of Modern Sports.* Columbia University Press, 1978.

Tsuchitani Hideo, et al. "Budō no jitai to ishiki ni kansuru chōsa- Nihon Kempō ni kansuru ishiki ni tsuite" (A survey to establish the situation and attitudes to *budō*- A look at the case of *Nihon kempō*). *Budōgaku kenkyū* (Research Journal of Budo) Vol. 9 No. 2, *Nihon Budō Gakkai* (Japanese Academy of Budo), 1976.

Inoue Masataka. *Kendō iroha rongo* (Discussions of kendo). Taiiku to Supōtsu Shuppansha, 1997.

Na Young-il, "A Study on the Present Conditions and the Problems of Traditional Martial Arts". *The Journal of the Korean Alliance for Health, Physical Education, Recreation and Dance (KAHPERD)*, vol. 33 No. 2, pp64-86, 1994.

Chapter 9

The Culture of '*Bu*'

Sakudō Masao
Osaka University of Health and Sport Sciences

Introduction

In the midst of demonstrations demanding the resignation of Russian president Boris Yeltsin in October 1998, the first All Russia Kendo Championship Tournament (Hashimoto Ryūtarō Cup) was held in Moscow. In such a harsh region as Russia and Eastern Europe, delegation members from Japan were forced to ask the question "what is the attraction of kendo to these people?" In response, the late Nikolai Yakovlev, then president of the Russian Kendo Federation replied "unfortunately, no matter where you look in the world, the cultural value of '*bu*' (martial pursuits) has all but disappeared from sight. The world has lost much of the wisdom of our predecessors who constantly lived through peril. Fortunately for the rest of us, Japan has managed to maintain and promote its martial culture, and further develop the wisdom of old warriors. How did the Japanese achieve this? We want to borrow Japanese kendo, learn its inner-secrets, and somehow use it to revive our understanding of our own martial heritage."

The following table depicts the characteristics of Japanese sword and martial culture:

Middle ages: *bujutsu*- combat techniques, practical culture.
Modern age: *bugei*- performance, artistic culture.
Present day: *budō*- win and loss, competitive culture.

In his book *Giving up the Gun*, Noel Perrin questions what prompted Tokugawa Ieyasu to discard firearms in an age where such weapons had proliferated at an incredible rate both in Japan and in other parts of the world. Ieyasu's policy holds worldwide significance, especially now that our very existence and world peace rides on the abolishment of nuclear weapons. Remarkably, with this policy Japan was issued into an era of 250 years of peace, and the martial culture of the sword transformed from combat oriented motivations into an art form. A high level of sophistication resulted from interaction of *bun* (scholarly or artistic pursuits) and *bu* (military pursuits). This developed and solidified into the culture of *budō* which we have inherited today.

In other words, the process began in the middle-ages where combatants used sword techniques in mortal combat. This transformed in the Tokugawa period where the martial arts became an expression of the warrior class, who trained to develop physical and spiritual attributes. The final step in the process resulted in a competitive activity (kendo) where practitioners compete to score valid strikes (*yūkō-datotsu*) on each other to decide the winner of a bout.

This three-step evolution of "practical culture", "artistic culture", and "competitive culture" is not only a product of changing times, but also the result of conscious action to develop and improve, preserve and create. We can sum up the culture of kendo as having developed from the principles of using a two-handed sword and transformed into an athletic activity with its own characteristics of space and time. Cutting was changed to striking, and new inter-relational, athletic, and technical values were developed. Another important aspect of kendo culture is that it can be practiced by everybody as lifelong pursuit, regardless of age or sex. Furthermore, all practitioners are able to participate and learn together. Also, kendo is infused with Eastern ideals of physicality and spirituality which have been continually refined and defined in an ongoing process of improvement. In this paper I will outline the process with which kendo developed into the presently popular competitive sport, and what significance it holds for we moderns.

The First Phase of Modernization— Mid-Tokugawa Period to the Bakumatsu Period

In his book *The Body, Self-cultivation, and Ki-energy*, Yuasa Yasuo claims that from the medieval period onwards, traditional arts (*geijutsu*) adopted the Buddhist approach of ascetic training (*shugyō*), which in turn gave rise to concepts such as *yūgen*[1] and *hana*.[2] These concepts indicate a state of enlightenment attained through dedicated training (*keiko*) and mastery of the arts. This theory of the arts (*geijutsu-ron*) was further applied to the martial arts (*budō-ron*) during the Warring States and modern periods. During this process, *bujutsu* became valued not only as practical systems of combat techniques, but also as artistic pursuits imbued with high aesthetic and spiritual values, where *bu*, *gei* (art), and *bun* (letters) fused, and through the medium of *jutsu* (techniques) formed into spiritual "Ways" (*michi*). The undercurrent for this kind of *shugyō* or *keiko* thought is what Satō Tsūji describes as "reflecting the world of higher principles rationalized by physicality. This is the Japanese concept of *michi* where, through engagement in a given physical pursuit the adept is exposed to a higher understanding of life." This represents the Eastern philosophy of synchronicity of mind and body.

In the transition from practical techniques into artistic Ways (*geidō*), *kata* were developed around the end of the sixteenth century, and were ultimately systemized and refined by the eighteenth century. The *kata* were overlaid with Chinese thought (Zen Buddhism, Confucianism, and Taoism), and amalgamation of technique and

The Culture of 'Bu'

mind (*waza to kokoro*) became a high ideal sought after in each individual *ryūha* or school. Thus, *kata* fulfilled the role of encouraging technical perfection as well as spiritual realization.

By the beginning of the eighteenth century, Japan was in the midst of unprecedented social peace and tranquillity. As a result, the forms of *kenjutsu* became "flowery"—ostentatious and unrealistic—signalling a decline of efficacy and practical application (*kahō kenpō*). The innovation that saved *kenjutsu* from almost inevitable extinction was the development and improvement of training equipment such as the *shinai* (bamboo replica sword) and *bōgu* (protective armour). With this, a revolutionary training method known as *uchikomi-geiko* was developed, where *kenjutsu* practitioners were able to actually make committed full-contact attacks on their opponents without fear of injury or death. This was revolutionary in the sense that it enabled the continuation of *kenjutsu* into the future as a form of athletic culture.

At that time, the already extant *fukuro shinai* (bamboo strips in a leather sheath) of the Yagyū Shinkage-ryū, and the thick cotton *men* (protective mask) and *kote* (gauntlets) of the Maniwa Nen-ryū were combined and improved further by the founder of the Jikishin Kage-ryū, Yamada Heizaemon Mitsunori, and his successor Naganuma Shirōzaemon Kunisato around 1711-1715. Also, Nakanishi Chūzō Tsugutake of the Nakanishi-ha Ittō-ryū continued to make innovations to the equipment and methodology of fencing, and it was largely due to his efforts that *shinai uchikomi-geiko* became widespread.

By the eighteenth century *shinai* and *bōgu* had very much reached the zenith of development and resembled that which is still used today. The *bakufu's* military academy, the Kōbusho, encouraged inter-*ryūha* exchange and matches prompting the formulation of universal criteria for permissible striking targets, and also the logical systemization of techniques. Amidst these developments during the *bakumatsu* period, Chiba Shūsaku of the Hokushin Ittō-ryū was a well-known swordsman who became increasingly prominent. He is often touted as being the father of modern kendo, especially in regards to his innovations to take kendo to a higher level of technical systemization and methodology. In a nutshell, what he accomplished was the bringing together of the practical application of the sword while also greatly enhancing the artistic characteristics of swordsmanship.

Practical →*Embu* (Performance)← Competitive

While retaining various practical attributes of traditional *kenjutsu*, Chiba moved from cutting to striking, thus maintaining a continuous connection with the past while also encouraging completely new concepts where aesthetic form and competition were combined into one new entity. This was at a time when *bushi* and *chōnin* (townsmen) culture overlapped in many respects due to rapid expansion of economic activity. The influence of the merchant class grew considerably which saw increased patronage of the arts. The synthesis of *kata* (for basic techniques) and *shinai uchikomi-geiko* (for practical application) enabled even beginners to participate in the martial arts, and opened doors to those who traditionally would not have had exposure to *kenjutsu* such as wealthy townsmen. What is particularly remarkable with these various innovations in *kenjutsu* was the resulting form was very sports-like and accessible to the masses, and furthermore, it had developed totally independently from any sport in the West. The popular *kenjutsu* boom signified the very beginning of Japan's modernization.

The Second Phase of Modernization— Meiji, Taisho, and Showa Periods

Most explanations of the modernization of *budō* make considerable mention of Kanō Jigorō and his success in turning *jūjutsu* into the modern art of Kōdōkan judo. In 1889, Kanō delivered a speech in which he explained his innovations. Quite simply, he transferred the focus of *jūjutsu* from winning combat to winning a sporting encounter. He also applied the two philosophical pillars of *"seiryoku zenyō"* (most efficient use of power) and *"jita kyōei"* (mutual benefit) to promote judo as a means of physical and spiritual education through the method of competing in *randori* or free-sparring. In the early days of the formation, the Kōdōkan was placed with the various other styles of *jūjutsu* in existence. However, due to Kanō's continually innovative spirit and rationality, and the success of Kōdōkan members in matches against other schools, judo gradually came to lead the *jūjutsu* world in terms of numbers and social recognition.

Kanō divided traditional techniques into groups such as *katame-waza* (holds and chokes) and practitioners would use these techniques to compete for points in *randori*. The dangerous techniques (*atemi-waza* etc.) from the old schools of *jūjutsu* were preserved in *kata* or set moves, which were completely separate from the techniques permissible in *randori*. Thus, *kata* became a means to learn *kihon* basics, and *randori* to engage in mock combat.

Practice on *tatami* mats was necessary due to the importance placed on *ukemi* or receiving the techniques. *Randori* and *ukemi* were not the inventions of Kanō Jigorō as these methodologies already existed in various forms or another in the traditional *jūjutsu* schools. However, he improved the methods employed in traditions such as the Kitō-ryū and Sekiguchi-ryū for *ukemi* and the *randori* used in Jigō Tenshin-ryū. He did this by introducing more throws, and including *katame-waza* in *randori*.

As we have seen, the development and improvement of fencing equipment to enable *uchikomi-geiko* took place towards the middle of the Tokugawa period. Universal targets were designated as well as the systemization of techniques, which in turn led to the development of unified training and teaching methodologies. Another step in the evolution of kendo was the creation of the *Kendō Kata* in 1912.

As Kanō Jigorō's contribution to the modernization of *jūjutsu* was immeasurably large, so too were the innovations introduced into kendo by Takano Sasaburō. Chiba Shūsaku recorded the techniques of Hokushin Ittō-ryū, and Takano Sasaburō revised

The Culture of 'Bu'

and re-organized them into fifty types of techniques for effective use in schools. These were put into use during the Taisho period, but even with Takano's extensive modifications it was found that some of the techniques were irrational and unusable for teaching kendo in schools. Takano's student, Tominaga Kengō, further refined the set of techniques making them more conducive to teaching *en masse* in schools. Techniques that were developed on the premise that they would be executed with a *katana* were changed to be more suitable for the *shinai*, the striking criteria of *ken-tai-itchi* (sword and body striking in unison) was improved and advocated, and techniques were ordered into rational categories for easy progression. Takano Sasaburō's book *Kendō* became the *tour de force* for teaching kendo in schools, and his ideas for teaching large groups of students simultaneously became and had remained the standard.

In this way we see how the concept of "cutting" transformed into "striking" which was more suitable to the times. However, while these developments were taking place, the organization Dai Nihon Butokukai (hereinafter refereed to as Butokukai), had embarked on a path to promote *budō* overall, but in a way that went against the grain of true modernization. They attempted to form old ideas into a new elitist culture and superimpose these ideals through *budō* onto the populace to encourage nationalistic fervour. This trend ran in congruence with Japan's quest to Westernize. The Butokukai acted as the umbrella organization for national kendo dissemination, and through the filter of their ideal of *butoku* (martial virtue) these two notions of Westernization and nationalism were pushed onto the people of Japan.

What were the events leading up to this? Japan embarked on a quest of earnest modernization during the Meiji period as her precarious position on the world stage was recognized. To modernize was in many ways a matter of survival, and this period in Japan's history saw the rise of progressive civil liberty movements. In the early part of the Meiji period, *kenjutsu* went into decline, and there was a distinct blank in activity when the *gekiken kōgyō* martial arts public demonstration matches were banned outright, and the *haitōrei* — a governmental edict banning the wearing of swords in public — was issued in 1876. The Imperial Rescript on Education was issued in the name of Emperor Meiji on October 30, 1890. It articulated the guiding principles of education in Japan. During the 1870s and 1880s there was a struggle at the highest levels of the Meiji government to reconcile the conflicting goals of rapid modernization and the legitimation of a political order centred on the imperial institution. Conservatives called for a revival of Confucian thought and morality. By 1890, when Prime Minister Yamagata Aritomo ordered the drafting of the Rescript, it had been decided that greater efforts would be made to incorporate Confucian ideology into public education, particularly at the primary level. This, followed with the Japanese victory in the Sino-Japanese war of 1894-95 saw a significant upsurge in nationalism. It was amidst this atmosphere that the Butokukai was created in 1895.

In the West, sports clubs usually administered a particular sport. However, the Butokukai was different in that it was formed to serve as an all-encompassing organization to protect and promote traditional martial culture. Furthermore, the patrons of the organization were powerful members of the imperial family, politicians, and wealthy businessmen. The above mentioned Imperial Rescript on Education stated that Japan's unique national polity (*kokutai*) is based on the historical bonds uniting its benevolent rulers and their loyal subjects and that the fundamental principles of education in Japan are based upon this. The Rescript exhorted all Japanese subjects to cultivate a list of virtues, central among them loyalty (*chū*) and filial piety (*kō*), for the greater glory of the imperial house. The Butokukai also promoted its ideal of "*butoku*" in accordance with this concept. These ideals became increasingly influential ten years after the Butokukai's inception with Japan's victory over the Russians in 1905.

There are two incidents in particular concerning the Butokukai that I would like to turn my attention to. The first involves kendo's participation in the Meiji Shrine Sports Tournament, and the other concerns the modification of match rules. During the Taisho period, Japan witnessed an unprecedented upturn in popularity of sports. Schools of all levels encouraged their students to participate in sporting tournaments which were held frequently. The Meiji Shrine Sports Tournament was inaugurated in 1915 and was the predecessor of the currently popular National Sports Meet (*Kokutai*). However, the Butokukai headquarters decided that kendo would not be entered as an event in the second tournament. The reason behind this move was the argument that "*budō* was not a sport". This was an act of defiance in the face of increasing popularity of Western sports in Japan. Nevertheless, the move by the Butokukai to separate kendo from other sports and draw a clear line between them did nothing but bring much scorn and criticism of unbridled elitism and arrogance. In fact, Takano Sasaburō's heir, the much-respected Satō Ukichi was considerably critical of this move by the Butokukai and urged them to reconsider kendo as falling within the realm of sports, albeit while retaining its own unique characteristics. He implored the Butokukai to "take off their old clothes, and wake up". Kendo was subsequently reintroduced from the third tournament.

Secondly, the Butokukai's reluctance to encourage competition was further tested with the introduction of new rules in 1928. Until that time, although there had been a number of proclamations concerning what was expected of match judges and competitors, for the most part matches were conducted more as demonstrations, and the victor eventually decided by mutual agreement. However, 1928 saw an important change in this regard.

During the Taisho period, police and students were enthusiastically engaging in kendo matches, and kendo's participation in the third Meiji Shrine Sports Tournament proved to be the straw that broke the camels back in that it forced the Butokukai to relinquish its negative stance on kendo competition. At this tournament, new rules were implemented to further increase the impartiality and competitiveness of the matches. Targets (*datotsu-bui*) and criteria for valid strikes (*yūkō-datotsu*) were clarified, and penalties were introduced for such actions as insulting comments and *hikiage* (ceasing the fight and walking back to the starting line after deciding that your technique was valid). Thus, with the introduction of new unified rules, subsequent

The Culture of 'Bu'

tournaments such as the Meiji tournament and the *Tenran-jiai* (matches performed in front of the emperor) were conducted in accordance with the same criteria. Matches became competitive rather than demonstrative, and ideal attitudes expected of judges and competitors were now set in reinforced with official rules. This was a significant turning point for kendo, and competition was now clearly defined, with the medium having been found between the dual nature of Westernization and nationalism, an inherent part of the Butokukai's make-up.

The Third Phase of Modernization— Post-war Period

In the late 1930s and during WWII, kendo became firmly under the control of the militarists who sought to utilize kendo (and the other *budō*) arts to nurture nationalism. The period saw the *butoku* ideals of the Butokukai take on a sinister nature, and wartime kendo developed into a harsh form of combat training. It was because of its utilization in the war effort that GHQ banned participation in the immediate post-war period. It had become so Japanese, that it had essentially poisoned itself.

However, the post-war revival of kendo, initially in the form of *shinai kyōgi*, sought to re-instil competition, physical activity, and technical rationality, and provided the inspiration for the development and reintroduction kendo as we know it today. In 1970, the International Kendo Federation was formed to promote kendo throughout the world. Progress continued domestically as well with the formulation of the *Concept of Kendo* in 1975, and many amendments and additions were made to the match and refereeing regulations.

In the post-war period, Japan has been subject to many twists and turns in fortune, and has now become one of the most technologically advanced nations in the world, and boasts a vibrant and powerful economy. However, as the old Japanese saying suggests, "the brighter the light, the darker the shadow", and in the case of Japan, where amongst all the great technological, economic, and social advances that have been made, there is the ongoing problem of moral and cultural decay. *Budō* has found itself providing a moral prop for people amid the woes of a prosperous modern age.

However, we are still faced with the ongoing dilemma of discerning what the "added values" are, and what the "true essence" of kendo is. I was fortunate to have been present at a lecture concerning "spiritual health" delivered by Itō Motoaki at the Nippon Budokan Kenshū Centre at a gathering for junior and senior high school kendo teachers. He made mention of how the individual's spiritual wellbeing affects society as a whole, and in turn the whole world and everything that inhabits it. He talked of "voluntary love", "not being self-serving", "respect for nature", "tolerance of others" and so on. He is an expert in medicine, but what he talked about was precisely what we are expected to aspire to in our lifelong quest to learn kendo. We are expected to train our whole lives while striving to purge ourselves of self-centred actions. Kendo is regarded as a form of athletic culture where the practitioner forever seeks to improve the self both physically and spiritually, not only for the sake of the individual, but for those with whom we coexist. This is ultimately the essence of kendo.

Conclusion

The authorities that govern kendo continue to make amendments to the rules, which in many cases are contradictory and achieve the opposite of the desired results. The point of some of the implemented rule changes, in particular those of 1979, was to encourage more emphasis on correct attitude in matches. However, this served to confuse competitors and referees alike. I believe that there is no need to try and cover up the competitive nature of kendo through rule changes. Competition is a natural part of the evolutionary process of kendo, and should be appreciated as such. That is not to say that other aspects such as the character-building characteristics of kendo should take second place. However, we cannot expect this side of kendo to reach its full potential if we ignore the *status-quo* and kendo's natural progression with the times. In conclusion I hope that kendo will eventually be allowed to complete its course of modernization, and reach its true form of maturity.

Endnotes

[1] Aesthetic ideal cultivated by poets and dramatists from the twelfth through the fifteenth century. The term *yūgen* broadly designated an ambiance of mystery, darkness, depth, elegance, ambiguity, calm, transience, and sadness.

[2] *Hana* or flower was first advocated by the noh playwright Zeami, and refers to the full blossom of one's artistic achievement that is a culmination of one's training.

Bibliography

Ōtsuka Tadayoshi. *Nihon kendō no rekishi* (The history of Japanese kendo). Madosha, 1995.
Satō Tsūji. *Kono michi* (This Way). Gengensha, 1955.
Perrin, Noel. *Giving up the Gun: Japan's Reversion to the Sword 1543-1879*. D.R. Godine, 1979.
Umesao Tadao, Tada Michitarō. *Nihon bunka no kōzō* (The structure of Japanese culture). Kōdansha Gendai Shinsho, 1972.
Watanabe Ichirō Sensei Koki Ki'nen Ronshū Kankōkai. *Budō bunka no kenkyū* (Studies of budō culture). Daiichi Shobō, 1995.
Yuasa Yasuo. *The Body, Self-cultivation, and Ki-energy*. (Translated by Shigenori Nagatomo and Monte S. Hull). SUNY Press, 1993.

SECTION 3

BUDO AND EDUCATION

Chapter 10

What Should be Taught Through *Budō*?

Sogawa Tsuneo
Waseda University

Introduction

What can we teach through *budō*? To put it another way, what are the educational characteristics that *budō* holds? When considering this question it is useful to divide *budō* into pre-Meiji and post-Meiji categories, as it was during the Meiji period (1868-1912) that new possibilities and methodologies for *budō* education were formulated.

The general understanding of *budō* dictates that it originated on the battlefields of ancient and medieval Japan as techniques for killing or subduing enemies. With the onset of the peaceful Tokugawa period (1600-1868), combat systems were redefined as a means of spiritual development. Thus, we see two modes of martial culture for combat effectiveness, and spiritual growth. A third type, as an educational tool in the modern education system, originated in the Meiji period, and an individual who played a significant role to this purpose was Kanō Jigorō.

Kanō Jigorō and Physical Education

In 1882, while Kanō was still at the Tokyo Imperial University, he established the Kōdōkan, and turned his hand to researching the potential of judo as an educational tool. Before creating the Kōdōkan, Kanō had studied a number of traditional schools of *jūjutsu* such as Tenshin Shin'yō-ryū and Kitō-ryū. He was thus able to compare the content and characteristics of each style. His ideas for creating judo were given a significant boost when he was afforded the opportunity to present a lecture about judo and its educational value to the Minister of Education and some foreign emissaries in 1889. Kanō divided his judo into the three main areas of "physical education judo", "combat judo", and "mental education judo". Of course, these three categories form a whole and are difficult to separate; however, each holds its own distinct characteristics.

"Physical education judo" was devised as a system to assist physical development.

According to Kanō, "the objective of judo in this sense is to facilitate healthy development of muscle groups, encourage overall physical wellbeing, nurture strength, and advance freedom and ease of movement of the whole body." On the other hand, "competitive judo" was explained as a direct continuation of Tokugawa period unarmed killing and subduing techniques, or *jūjutsu*. "In the narrow sense, combat judo enables the practitioner to kill, injure, or apprehend a foe if so desired. It also enables defence against an aggressor who would like to do the same to you."

Thus, "physical education judo" aimed for physical strengthening, "combat judo" was for practical application, and the other category of "mental education judo" was designed to aid in intellectual or moral development. Namely, through practicing judo "the practitioner develops their morality and wisdom, and through learning the principles of "combat judo" is able to utilize this knowledge to help overcome any obstacle in life that one may be confronted with." Apart from "combat judo", Kanō's ideas were in accordance with the ideals of three-pillared education system (physical, moral, and intellectual education) popular in the West at the time, and also employed by the Meiji government in the process of modernizing the school system. The reason why Kanō was compelled to design his judo with these goals was due to the social climate and characteristics of the times. The class system had been abolished, and the upholders of martial tradition, the *bushi* class, no longer held their privileged position in society. The martial arts were able to survive through the show-business style *gekiken kōgyō* public demonstrations, and also as self-defence training in the newly-formed police force. However, Kanō's goal was to try and get *budō* recognised as a legitimate addition to the school curriculum.

Depiction of a gekiken kōgyō scene from the Meiji period

In 1872, the Education Order (*gakusei*) was issued to establish Japan's first consolidated, modern school system. Western gymnastics (*taisō*) was incorporated into the system for physical education. The teaching of callisthenics based on the latest in physiological theory commenced in schools thenceforth. The main issue at hand was employing the right system that was beneficial in developing strong young bodies. The

What Should be Taught Through Budo?

newly developed German and Swedish systems of callisthenics were considered the most efficacious for this purpose. At this time, athletics, ball sports, and traditional Japanese *bujutsu* had not been evaluated by medical experts to assess efficacy, and the Meiji government considered callisthenics as the only viable option for physical education.

As callisthenics became the standard menu for physical education, there were a number of vociferous proponents for introducing *bujutsu* into the school curriculum as an officially recognized course of study. In 1883, the Ministry of Education commissioned a survey through the Gymnastics Institute to ascertain the potential of *bujutsu* for physical education. The focus of the survey was *kenjutsu* and *jūjutsu*, and the intention was to analyze these arts from a medical and physiological perspective. The results of this investigation were publicized the following year, and both were ultimately deemed unsuitable for introduction for the following reasons;

Advantages of introducing *bujutsu* into schools:
1. An effective means of enhancing physical development.
2. Develops stamina.
3. Rouses the spirit, and boosts morale.
4. Expurgates spinelessness and replaces it with vigour.
5. Arms the exponent with techniques for self-defence in times of danger.

The dangers were as follows:
1. May cause unbalanced physical development.
2. Always an imminent danger present in training.
3. Difficult to determine the appropriate degree of exercise, as both physically strong students and weaker individuals are apt to be excited too much.
4. Could encourage violent behaviour due to the rousing of the spirit.
5. Exhilarates the will to fight which could manifest into an attitude of winning at all costs.
6. There was a danger of encouraging a warped sense of competitiveness to the extent that the child could even resort to dishonest tactics.
7. Difficult to sustain unified instructional methodology for large numbers of students.
8. Requires a large area to conduct training.
9. Even though *jūjutsu* only requires a *keiko-gi* (training wear) *kenjutsu* requires the use of armour and other special equipment which would be expensive and difficult to keep clean and hygienic.

After *bujutsu* was denied a place in the education system, martial artists sought to develop new ways to make it acceptable. One of the first innovations was the development of *bujutsu* callisthenics. For example, *bokken taisō* (callisthenic exercises with a wooden sword) and *naginata taisō* (callisthenic exercises with a *naginata*) were devised for national dissemination. At this time, Kanō was also energetically formulating his judo. In a lecture in 1889, he delivered his answers to the objections made by the Gymnastics Institute in regards to the unsuitability of *bujutsu* as a form of physical education. He came up with two methods of training for "physical education judo". One involved the participation of two practitioners in free-sparring (*randori*), and the other involved the repetition of techniques in pre-determined sequences, but stopping just before the conclusion of the technique. Both methods were different to orthodox *jūjutsu* training methods, and he devised them to ensure the safety of the practitioners. Moreover, the goal of *jūjutsu* training was put on subduing enemies, so the throwing of the opponent was seen as a mere means to the last objective. But Kanō in his judo *randori* shifted the throwing in the competitive aspect. In this sense, judo shows a clear departure from *jūjutsu*. General impressions of judo today are born from the competitive nature of *randori*. This sportified "physical education judo" holds much in common with, and in fact was significantly influenced by latter nineteenth-century British modern sports ideals. In this sense, Japanese *bujutsu* was adapted "gymnastically" and "educationally" in accordance with European ideals of two-dimensional mind-body thought for the three pillared education system. Judo in its modern sportified form set the way for the evolution of other *budō* arts such as kendo and *kyūdō* which eventually followed suit, and to this day all of them adhere to international standard rule systems.

When considering the educational content of *budō*, three categories come to mind:
1. Pre-Meiji combat techniques.
2. Post-Meiji modern combat sports.
3. Athletic activity to enhance physical development (physical education).

The last two categories in particular have blossomed into internationally popular sports, and are recognised for their physical benefits, and even contributions to promoting world peace. However, the spiritual attributes of *budō* are of particular relevance to people today. We can see a clear split in the attitudes toward the psychospiritual characteristics of *budō* culture in pre-Meiji and post-Meiji periods. Again, it is beneficial to look at the example set by Kanō Jigorō. His "mental education judo" corresponded with the intellectual and moral education of the aforementioned three-pillared system. As far as judo and "intellectual education" are concerned, through training in judo, the practitioner supposedly learns skills of observation, improves memory, learns to hypothesize, develops imagination, learns how to express ideas rationally, develops the ability to listen to new ideas and process them accordingly, and so on. Indeed, these are attributes aspired to by studying standard "intellectual" textbooks. Additionally, in regards to "moral education", the judo practitioner was expected to develop a sense of patriotism. Ideally, the educational and competitive attributes gained from training in judo would help nurture individuals who could be of great service to the nation in fields such as economics, politics, and the military.

Kanō's judo, with its emphasis on mental development retained a very practical character, and he must be lauded for citing the "intellectual educational" benefits

What Should be Taught Through Budo?

to be gleaned from practicing the martial arts. This was an aspect not given much consideration during the Tokugawa period. There were proponents other than Kanō who considered instilling patriotic sentiments through the vehicle of *budō* during the Meiji period, but again, not during the preceding Tokugawa period. During the Tokugawa period, we see terms such as *shidō* which were used to denote the ethical system of the ruling *bushi* class, setting them above the others classes as moral paragons. However, modern concepts such as "nationalism" and "nationhood" were hardly taken into consideration.

Pre-Meiji Martial Arts and Spirituality

The *budō* culture of the Tokugawa period, whether referred to as *shidō* or *bushidō* embodied the spirit of self-control and discipline. Yamamoto Tsunetomo wrote in his classical treatise on *bushidō*, *Hagakure*, "Winning means to defeat your allies. Defeating your ally means to defeat yourself. Defeating yourself means transcending your own physical being. Then the only way you can achieve victory over your foe is by achieving victory over the self." Also, Hayashi Razan (1583–1657) states in his *Santokushō*, "A strong man can defeat other men. But true strength is seen in one who can defeat himself and control his own desires. A man who can defeat himself will have no difficulty in defeating others." Both of these examples demonstrate well the emphasis placed on self-control.

Bushi were expected to sacrifice their lives in the course of duty, if so required. However, compared to the tumultuous Warring States period, *bushi* of the peaceful Tokugawa period had to be more than just fighting professionals. They resided in castle-towns and were expected to carry out administrative duties on behalf of the *bakufu* and their domains. Thus, the importance of *bujutsu* was refocused, and given that there were few opportunities to demonstrate martial prowess in actual battle, *bujutsu* transformed from purely combative techniques into a vehicle for spiritual growth and self-improvement. This is why the emphasis on killing an opponent shifted to "self-control" and "defeating the self". Ideas of "self-control" were brought from Zen Buddhism, such as *fudōchi* (immovable wisdom), *mushin* (no mind), *muga* (no self) and so on.

There was a transformation of martial arts from methods of killing to a form of culture advocating self-perfection. It is this form which came to be known as *budō*, or the martial Ways. In Sekiguchi Ujimune's (1598-1670) *Shinshin-ryū yawara no jo*, he explains how *yawara* was a term extracted from Chinese classics to denote the art's spiritual qualities, as opposed to the terms utilized during the Warring States period such as *koshi no mawari*, and *kogusoku* which referred to the small weapons used in combat. This is a superb example which presents the transition from "*jutsu*" (techniques) to "*dō*" (Way). From this stage, it is clear that spiritual interpretations and applications of the martial Ways were sought after.

The emphasis on spiritual characteristics and development was not limited to the field of martial arts. It also applied to poetry, noh, *kyōgen*, tea, flower arranging and so forth. Furthermore, the transition in *bujutsu* was late in comparison. All the "Way"-ified cultural activities are lumped together as *geidō* (artistic Ways), but it is evident today that *kadō* (Way of poetry) from the end of the Heian period (794–1185) was probably the sounding arrow, so to speak. Fujiwara no Toshinari and his son Sadaie were pioneers in interpreting *waka* poetry as a way of spiritual and cultural development. One of their greatest influences was the sixth century Chinese monk, Chigi, of the Tendai sect of Buddhism and his treatise *Makashikan*. In this book, he talks about *hiza-higyō*, one of the four methods of religious training. "*Za*" refers to the act of sitting and meditating, "*gyō*" to circumambulation, and "*hi*" is a negative prefix. Thus, *hiza-higyō* refers to other actions in everyday life which can serve as a mode of mediation apart from sitting and walking. This could include *waka*, and was most certainly a feature of Zeami's noh. In Zeami's case, aesthetic principles central to his noh works are *hana* (flower), a quality which distinguishes the fine actor, and *yūgen* (subtle beauty), which distinguishes the well-performed play. In this way, cultural pursuits which aspired to spiritual cultivation (*geidō*) were well established by the Tokugawa period, and *bujutsu* was eventually redefined as a "Way" in a similar fashion.

Self-control, *mushin* (no mind), *fudōchi* (immovable wisdom), and other concepts considered ultimate spiritual plains or "enlightenment" in the world of *budō*, were still often referred to by practitioners in the Meiji period. One point in need of clarification here is that the *satori* (enlightenment) sought through mastery of the arts from the Heian period was very much for the benefit of the individual adept. However, in the case of *budō*, as demonstrated by ethical ideals such as *shidō*, it provided clear identity for the social class of warriors who aspired to, or were expected to set a moral example. Even in the Meiji period, after class distinctions had been abolished, the ultimate objective of the practice of *budō* was to acquire virtuous qualities, and Kanō's ideas of nurturing feelings of patriotism (*aikokushin*) through judo is a typical example of this at the time.

However, the spiritual aspects of *budō* culture and the perfection of the self were still considered the ultimate goals of *budō* even after the Meiji period.

The Spirituality of *Budō* in Modern Times

There are many aspects of Japanese *budō* that are difficult for non-Japanese to comprehend. We can see from the writings of Eugen Herrigel (1885-1955)how exotic or unique certain aspects seem to non-Japanese exposed to *budō* culture for the first time. Herrigel was a German philosopher who came to Tohoku Imperial University in 1924 as a teacher of Western philosophy and classics. He resided in Japan for a total of five years. His interest in marksmanship and esoteric Buddhism prompted him to take up archery (*kyūdō*) under the tutelage of Awa Kenzō (see Chapter 1) . In a lecture

What Should be Taught Through Budo?

Herrigel subsequently presented about Japanese archery in Berlin in 1936, he quoted his teacher as saying "you mustn't pull the bow with the strength of your arms. Instead you must pull with your heart. That means that you must learn how to pull the bow while removing all the strength and tension from your muscles." Herrigel was rather bewildered by this advice. It negated all the rational anatomical knowledge he possessed. Also, "Do not breathe with your lungs", "Do not shoot the arrow consciously. Achieve a state of *mushin* and wait until the arrow fires itself", "Hit the target without aiming for it", "Did you watch carefully how I did it? Did you see how my eyes were all but closed just like a picture of the Buddha meditating? I closed my eyes to the extent that I could hardly see the target. By doing this the target seems as if it is coming closer to me instead. That is how I can become one with the target. You have to be able to completely load your heart to be able to achieve this. If the target and I can become as one, that means that the Buddha and I are as one. I can become one with the Buddha, the arrow will exist in the centre of non-movement. Therefore, if we interpret the arrow being in the centre with awakened consciousness, the arrow strays from the centre and re-enters the centre. Thus, you must not aim for the target, but instead, aim for yourself. That way you will be able to hit the self, the Buddha, and the target all at once."

These were the kind of teachings Awa imparted to Herrigel. Three years after returning to Germany, Herrigel relayed his own experience:

Awa Kenzō (1936/7)

"Once I pulled the bow my concentration deepened. The further I pulled it, the more intense my concentration became. After that I became completely unconscious to my surrounds. When my hand let go of the arrow, I was suddenly returned to my self. At that instant, I was able to see my surrounds, the world again. I was catapulted back from another world into normal consciousness."

Herrigel was able to internalize and experience the ethno-scientific world of Japanese *kyūdō*. In this process, he surpassed the technicalities of archery and realized that the awakening to the spiritual realm was the ultimate objective. This was a continuation from Tokugawa period traditions.

In regards to the situation today, many Japanese consider the spiritual aspects of *budō* difficult to grasp. The educational content of *budō* that we teach today contains elements of both a technical and spiritual nature, as outlined in this paper. It is a relatively easy exercise to teach beginners the techniques of *budō*, be it as a practical system of techniques for fighting, or as a sporting endeavour. There is technology available to us to express quite eloquently in words or pictures the biomechanical workings of the techniques. There are also many very technically skilled instructors who are capable of imparting their knowledge. However, this cannot be said for the spiritual aspects of *budō*. Of course, there exists a plethora of literature concerning the spiritual teachings of *budō*, but much of this is nebulous in nature. To fully understand this important aspect requires the student to actually experience it, like Herrigel did. This can only be facilitated if teachers like Awa Kenzō exist. Thus, in conclusion, I would like to say that for the continuation of the spiritual aspects of *budō*, it is vital that we somehow create an environment conducive to maintaining and transmitting such difficult but nevertheless vital aspects of *budō* culture.

Chapter 11

Central Issues in the Instruction of Kendo—With Focus on the Inter-connectedness of *Waza* and Mind

Ōya Minoru
International Budo University

Introduction

Kendo quite simply is "the Way of the sword". Modern kendo involves practitioners striking each other with bamboo swords called *shinai*. However, the roots of kendo can be found on the battlefields of old, where warriors faced each other in mortal combat with live blades. Back then it was a matter of cutting or being cut, living or dying. The warrior had only one chance, and a simple mistake could result in extermination. There was no going back. The question of "life and death" and thus the way one should live one's life is vividly etched in the history and culture of kendo.[1] The character *michi* (道- Way) which is the "*dō*" in kendo, is made up of the components "*kubi*" (首) and the radical "*shin'nyū*" (辶). This basically denotes walking while peering in a certain direction.[2] When writing the character, *kubi*, which means "neck" (indicative of human life)[3], is written first, and corresponds with the expression "to put one's neck on the line". The *shinnyū* radical represents the starting point (at the top) and flows down just like a path. Thus, the character for *michi* can be interpreted as representing the path that one travels or pioneers during their lifetime. In concordance with this interpretation, the All Japan Kendo Federation established the official *Concept of Kendo*:

> "*Kendo is a way to discipline the human character through the application of the principles of the katana*".

However, in recent years, kendo has in many ways deviated from the "principles of the *katana*", and the bamboo *shinai* is manipulated quickly, intricately, and in a very un-sword-like manner in order to score points to win matches. Also, the evaluation criteria for points (*yūkō-datotsu*) have become more lenient, and penalties (*hansoku*) have been continually subdivided. This clearly demonstrates the systematic trend of the "sportification" of kendo, where winning contests is often the focus of participation. To prevent too much deviation from the perceived "Way" of kendo, various measures have been implemented including the standardization of teaching methodology with manuals, creation of new training methodologies such as "*Bokutō ni yoru kendō kihon-waza keiko-hō*" (Training in basic kendo techniques with a *bokutō* (wooden sword)), not to mention many revisions of match and refereeing regulations. These are innovations designed to encourage practitioners to return to the type of kendo advocated in the *Concept*.

However, these are allopathic measures to restore the "ideals" of kendo. Eg. a major problem with the *Concept*, and what it advocates — "a way to discipline the human character through the application of the principles of the *katana*"— is that it doesn't actually clearly define what technical and mental approaches are required, and how the cultural factors of kendo should be advanced.

With these problems in mind, I will use kendo theory based on my experience[4] and from an intellectual perspective to analyse the inter-beingness of *waza* and mind. I will focus my discourse on various issues pertaining to kendo education.[5]

Technical Principles

The execution of technical and psychological applications in kendo occurs within the following process:

On-guard (*kamae*) → Mutual probing of defences/applying pressure (*seme-ai*) → Detection of openings and selection of techniques → Valid strike (*yūkō-datotsu*) → Physical and psychological composure (*zanshin*).

Particular emphasis is placed on valid strikes born of a unity of spirit, sword and body 気剣体一致 (*ki-ken-tai-itchi*). From a technical standpoint, a valid (effective) cut is one in which the adept holds and wields the 'blade' in the correct manner; which in turn is directly related to the way in which the *shinai* is gripped. In addition, good bearing, smooth technique initiation, and correct strike path, all emanating from correct *kamae*, are vital elements. Subsequent to the valid strike, physical focus and composure is also demanded. From a psychological standpoint, "striking with abandon" (*sutemi*), is required when executing the technique. The ability to strike with abandon, with utter conviction, is essentially a product of the unity of mind, spirit and technique 心気力一致 (*shin-ki-ryoku-itchi*) occurring in a kendo engagement. This unity of mind, spirit and technique is a prerequisite to dominating a match and enables an immediate strike in response to an opening produced during the *seme-ai* (probing) stage. Moreover, *zanshin,* or psychological and physical composure following the strike, is concomitant with *sutemi.*

Central Issues in the Instruction of Kendo

I will now isolate and consider a number of the major elements contained in the above process.

a. Fundamental considerations in kamae
Kamae is comprised of an intangible psychological attitude, and a tangible physical attitude, and if the psychological attitude is sufficiently developed, it can preclude the necessity for any outward manifestation. When looking at *kamae* the following considerations are fundamental: Both sides are engaged in a clash of willpower. If this clash is evenly balanced (50:50) then the engagement will end in deadlock. When the balance shifts in favour of one side (60:40 or 70:30) there is an opportunity to utilize techniques. When assuming *kamae*, having a 'steadfast mind' and 'unyielding will' as internal qualities will result in a strong impenetrable *kamae* on the outside. Conversely, if the inside is weak, this will result in the exterior *kamae* being vulnerable and open for attack. Thus, the *kamae* is the cornerstone for kendo, and when two practitioners face-off, it is a clash of wills, or two hard rocks (*ishi* (will) is also the word used for "rock"). This is the most fundamental aspect of kendo.

b. Unity of mind, spirit, and technique (Shin-ki-ryoku-itchi)
The elements of "unity of mind, spirit and technique" was explained by the kendo master Takano Sasaburō in his classic book *Kendō* as follows:

> "*Shin-ki-ryoku-itchi* is the mental action induced from the senses of looking and listening, and the resulting immediate manifestation and application of a technique…When these three elements are in perfect synchronisation, then the opponent's weaknesses or openings can be taken advantage of, and victory obtained… *Victory or defeat is not decided through random manoeuvring, but by promptly taking control of the opportunity as it appears.*"[6]

The *kokoro* (heart/mind) works as cognition, discretion, judgement (water). *Ki* is sparked by the judgement of the mind and provides the energy to put will in motion (wind). This energy fuels the execution of *waza* (wave). Just like the wind blowing over a body of water creating waves. In other words *shin-ki-ryoku-itchi* is "cognition/discretion → mobilisation of will → execution of technique". When this sequence is completed instantaneously and in unison it leads to a valid strike (*yūkō-datotsu*).

The Act of *Seme*

Generally speaking, *seme* is explained with the teaching of *san-sappō* (killing the spirit, killing the sword, and killing the *waza*). Put plainly, *seme* is the process of searching for a way to break the deadlock of *kamae*, putting yourself in an advantageous situation, from where you produce an opportunity to execute a valid strike. In kendo it is often said, "win then strike" – it is at the stage of *seme* that you must win before striking.

"Producing an opportunity to strike", means creatively and dynamically hunting for openings. In other words, searching for movements or shortcomings in your opponent. This is not just passively watching for an opponent's shortcomings or movements, but should be an active, progressive process of creating openings and striking opportunities.

An opening can be one that is manifest, i.e. has form, such as an external physical deterioration of *kamae*, or formless, such as an internal psychological weakness in *kamae*. External form and internal psyche are opposite sides of the same coin: external form will influence the psyche and, conversely, psychological state will be manifest in outward appearance. If the opponent's *kamae* is steadfast and strong with no openings, then executing an attack will be futile. Firstly, the opponent's *kamae* must be broken or unsettled thereby creating an opening for attack. The opponent "must be beaten before being struck".

The main factors in searching for a way to break the deadlock of *kamae* and putting yourself in a situation to execute a valid strike, i.e. the main factors of *seme*, are considered to be: Taking the lead by spirit (*ki*), dominating the centre and adopting an advantageous distance (*ma-ai*). One might define "taking the lead by *ki*" as "a concentration of the will to win" — not winning by striking, but winning the phase prior to striking — "achieving *ki* superiority" or "winning by *kizeme*". "Dominating the centre" involves keeping the tip of your sword pointing at the centre of your opponent, whilst keeping his sword tip away from your own centre. Maintaining control of, or defending your own centre will, of itself, destroy your opponent's centre and open them up for attack.

A kendo exponent executes an attack through the opponent's centre

Central Issues in the Instruction of Kendo

In regards to "advantageous distance", if you divide by two the distance between yourself and your opponent, the space between your hands and sword tip is your "own space", and that between your opponent's hands and his sword tip is your "opponent's space". Your "own space" is like your battle position; your "opponent's space" is their own position. If you break into your "opponent's space", i.e. break down their *kamae*, you will be in an advantageous position. On the other hand, when your opponent breaks into your "own space", you are in danger of being overwhelmed. Thus, exploitation of the physical interval between you and your opponent provides both of you with an opportunity to tip the balance in your own favour.

Thus, the *seme* elements of "taking the lead by spirit" (*ki*), "dominating the centre", "adopting an advantageous distance" (*ma-ai*), are the physical and mental battles that take place before executing a technique. In other words, superiority in the *seme* phase decides the outcome of the encounter. Furthermore, the above mentioned three elements must be conducted inn unison to be effective.

Fuhai-no-kurai and *Suientō-no-kurai* – "Safe Distance" and "Spill Point"

When facing-off in a real combat situation, samurai reputedly drew their swords at a distance of eight or nine paces apart, and then moved forward to the point of engagement.[7] This is why the distance used in modern kendo for the initial bow or in *kata* is stipulated at nine paces. What is the mental disposition experienced as *kamae* are assumed at this distance, and the two opponents progress toward the point of encounter? The adept must expel the so-called "four illnesses of the heart" (surprise, fright, doubt and confusion). Without being able to control these emotive responses to imminent danger, the adept will be unable to react appropriately and execute the ideal technique. When *kenjutsu* came to be practised with *shinai*, it became standard for the *seme* process and execution of *waza* to begin from where the blades touch to where they cross.[8]

In terms of modern kendo, the encounter begins by confronting the opponent "fairly and squarely" from *fuhai-no-kurai* (safe distance) and then detonates at the *suientō-no-kurai* (spill point). Negishi Shingorō explained this state of affairs from the face-off in the following manner:

> "When facing an opponent you first adopt *kamae* at a "safe distance". At this distance your strike will fall short even if you step forward. Then you must consider whether to proceed in a straightforward way or use a surprise attack. Such a surprise attack might be to leap straight ahead with lightning speed and strike *men* or *kote*, or to strike *dō*, by sacrificing your posture and dropping to your knees etc. Alternatively, having regard for the value of winning fairly and squarely, you can act in a straightforward manner and move into the "spill

point". Closing in from a "safe distance" to the "spill point" is the appropriate way to conduct kendo practice. This "spill point" occurs when your two sword tips intersect diagonally, forming a cross. This is the borderline where you can strike or be struck; an extremely risky yet crucial position charged with nervous tension (*ki*). It is like having a cup full of water balanced on top of your sword – one false move and it will spill. "Safe distance" and "spill point" are both *ma-ai* – distances – from which countless other *ma-ai* can be developed".[9]

Fuhai-no-kurai is the distance where even if the adept takes one step forward their attack will not reach the target. Furthermore, an attack executed from this distance will result in an unbalanced posture. *Suientō-no-kurai*, where the tips of the swords cross, corresponds to *uchi-ma* or the distance for engagement. This is an extremely dangerous distance, and if a cup of water were balanced on the sword tips, much concentration would be required to stop the water from spilling. "To spill or not to spill", in other words this corresponds to "being hit or not being hit". Of course, it is impossible to balance a cup full of water on top of a *shinai* – Negishi is simply portraying a state where your spirit does not waver and you maintain the ability to execute techniques even in an extremely tense situation. In order to resolve this problem the practitioner must search for a superior way of being – and this is kendo's ultimate purpose, according to Yuno Masanori.[10]

The ground covered moving in from a distance where the sword tips are apart or barely touching, a "safe distance", into one in which the *shinai* cross, the "spill point", is at most ten to fifteen centimetres. In this highly charged phase the practitioner is apt to hesitate or make a blunder. However, the extent to which you can maintain your presence of mind, discerning movements in your opponent and executing techniques as appropriate, is of great significance.

Responsive Action and *Shinai* Techniques

a. Waza theory

Kendo handbooks usually divide techniques into two categories: "attacking techniques" (*shikake-waza*) and "counter-attacking techniques"(*ōji-waza*). *Shikake-waza* are attacks that you instigate yourself, whereas *ōji-waza* are techniques which occur in response to your opponent's attacks. For example, the following lists the techniques taught at junior[11] and senior high schools[12], and at official AJKF seminars.[13]

Junior High School Kendo-
Shikake-waza
Nidan-waza: kote-men, men-men, kote-dō, men-dō etc.
Harai-waza: harai-men, harai-dō, harai-kote etc.
Debana-waza: debana-kote etc.
Hiki-waza: hiki-men, hiki-dō, hiki-kote etc.

Central Issues in the Instruction of Kendo

Ōji-waza
Nuki-waza: men-nuki-dō, kote-nuki-men etc.
Suriage-waza: men-suriage-men, men-suriage-dō, kote-suriage-men etc.
Kaeshi-waza: men-kaeshi-dō
Uchiotoshi-waza: dō-uchiotoshi-men

High School Kendo-
Shikake-waza
Nidan-waza: kote-men, men-men, kote-dō, men-dō, tsuki-dō, kote-men-dō etc.
Harai-waza: harai-men, harai-dō, harai-kote, harai-tsuki
Debana-waza: debana-men, debana-kote etc.
Hiki-waza: hiki-men, hiki-dō, hiki-kote etc.
Ōji-waza
Nuki-waza: men-nuki-dō, kote-nuki-men, men-nuki-men, men-nuki-kote
Suriage-waza: men-suriage-men, men-suriage-dō, kote-suriage-men, kote-suriage-kote
Kaeshi-waza: men-kaeshi-dō, men-kaeshi-men etc.
Uchiotoshi-waza: dō-uchiotoshi-men etc.

All Japan Kendo Federation Official Seminars-
3rd *dan* and below:
Ippon-uchi-no-waza (straight attack), *harai-waza, ni/sandan-no-waza, debana-waza, hiki-waza, suriage-waza, kaeshi-waza, uchiotoshi-waza*

4th & 5th *dan:*
Ippon-uchi-no-waza, harai-waza, ni/sandan-no-waza, debana-waza, hiki-waza, suriage-waza, kaeshi-waza, uchiotoshi-waza, nuki-waza

6th *dan* and above:
Ippon-uchi-no-waza, harai-waza, ni/sandan-no-waza, debana-waza, hiki-waza, katsugi-waza, maki-waza, katate-waza, suriage-waza, kaeshi-waza, uchiotoshi-waza, nuki-waza, ōji-waza

The above techniques are categorized simply as cause and effect, where one person attacks first, and the other reacts. *Shikake-waza* and *ōji-waza* are further divided into a number of sub-categories such as *"harai-waza"*, and the counter-attacks *"suriage-waza"* and *"kaeshi-waza"*. This is one way to consider kendo techniques – one side attacks *first* and the other side responds *second*: simply conceiving the interaction of technique in terms of before and after. The sub-categories such as *"harai-waza"*, (sweeping the opponent's *shinai* aside and striking) and *"suriage-waza"* (sweeping the opponent's *shinai* up and striking and *"kaeshi-waza"* (striking using the impetus of your opponent's *shinai* to flip your wrists over), are technical applications emphasizing interactive body and sword movement. This sort of kendo technique classification is found in post-war Japanese school physical education.[14]

Psychological Consideration of *Waza*

If techniques are executed in accordance with the opponent's movement and reactions during the course of mutual *seme*, not only are the resulting strikes and manipulation of the *shinai* to execute the attack important, but so too is the significance of the psychological workings of the process. The following is an analysis of the antecedents of *waza*:

> When executing *waza*, use *ki* to take the initiative (*sen*) to cause a jump in the opponent's *kokoro* → change in form → start of the technique → mid-technique → completion of technique.

If the opponent's *kamae* becomes unbalanced due to your *ki* and taking the initiative, move in immediately for the strike. When you take the initiative (*sen*) and probe the opponent using *ki*, and they are prompted into making an attack first, maintain the initiative, and respond by executing *ōji-waza* (counter-technique).

Therefore, *ōji-waza* are actually progressive techniques made while adjusting to, and countering your opponent's *shikake-waza* – and in order to do this you must maintain the psychological initiative throughout the encounter. However, *shikake-waza* and *ōji-waza* are both executed as active techniques. In other words, *ōji-waza* are not techniques where you wait – whenever you utilise any technique you should be actively "taking the lead by *ki*". The only techniques where your *ki* acts after that of your opponent are those in which you strike when your opponent's technique has come to an end, ("*uchiotoshi-waza*").

Striking Opportunities and Selection of *Waza*

The following striking opportunities are listed based on the various stages occurring during engagement with an opponent:

a. Striking when your opponent is immobile
Control your opponent to the point where they cannot strike; cannot retreat; cannot move at all, and then strike. (This is like a snake staring at a frog, mesmerising it, and is complex and extremely difficult).
↓
b. Striking when your opponent shows signs of moving or their kamae starts to change
Discern when your opponent has decided to strike; the moment *ki* is about to take form; sense the movement intuitively and strike. (*Ippon-uchi-no-waza, renzoku-waza, harai-waza* etc.)
↓

Central Issues in the Instruction of Kendo

c. Striking when your opponent is about to attack
   Ki first begins to take physical form in the movement of the sword tip and hands as the opponent contemplates and winds up for the attack. When you discern the beginnings of movement, step in and strike. (*Debana-waza*).

The techniques hitherto are considered superior through virtue of being the result of openings created by applying mental pressure on the opponent. These techniques are described as "striking the heart (*kokoro*) with the heart"[15], "striking essence (*iro*) with essence"[16], or "striking scent (*nioi*) with scent"[17]. The opponent's intentions to attack are revealed in changes in the eyes, facial expression, and also the *kamae*. These techniques are regarded as superior – those that follow are considered passive and are not afforded the same idealistic value.

d. Striking at the start of your opponent's technique
   The opponent's *ki* manifests itself in the form of slight movement. Strike at the unbalanced point just as the opponent begins technique execution. (*Kiriotoshi-waza*). This stage is indicated by the opponent starting to lean forward, or sinking slightly from the knees. These initial movements must be discerned immediately and taken advantage of.

e. Striking in the middle stage of your opponent's technique
   Strike as your opponent's technique is in mid-flight, taking advantage of their unbalanced posture. (*Nuki-waza, suriage-waza*).
   This is where the opponent's initial movements start to take the shape of a technique, and counter-striking at this point is essentially striking the beginning of their technique i.e. before it is able to manifest itself fully.[18]

f. Striking when your opponent's technique is nearing completion
   Strike at the point that your opponent's psychological, physical and technical impetus is just reaching full extension, and they are thinking that their attack was successful. (*Kaeshi-waza*).

g. After your opponent's attack has been completed
   Strike when your opponent has exceeded the point of full extension and their overall posture is ineffective. (*Uchiotoshi-waza*).
   Striking at this stage means to escape a full technique and finish the process with your own counter-attack.[19]

In the stage of mutual probing for openings to attack, if the practitioner is able to capture one of the above stages in the opponent's movements, there is no need to rely on intricate manipulations of the *shinai* to execute attacks. It is effective to attack with a simple strike, so long as the opportunity is appropriate. However, in order to be able to achieve this, you must be stable in spirit and physical posture, and be able to execute any kind of attack in an instant. If, when considering technique you take into account the psychological process inherent in combative interaction, the chain of events comprising a single strike, and the effect of the passage of time, you will arrive at a concept of technique as "striking the opportunity" (striking a point in time), rather than "striking a (tangible) point".

Application of *Waza*

When visiting somebody's house, if the guest decided to enter that house without warning from a side door or from the back without going through the front entrance, this action would be considered extremely unorthodox. In a kendo match, using sneaky techniques to trick your opponent instead of meeting them front-on is also considered unorthodox. What is considered the ideal method is to meet your opponent from the front, and present your *ki* directly against theirs (*aiki*). In other words, techniques are not applied from feinting and pretending weakness to trick the opponent into leaving themselves open. Instead, the perceived ideal for engaging an opponent is to show strength, and pressure the opponent into faltering. Not doing so would make kendo no more than an exercise where victory was decided by nimbleness rather than mental strength, or *shinai* competition.

Valid Strikes (*Yūkō-datotsu*) and *Zanshin*

Detailed descriptions of valid targets, the correct striking area of the *shinai* (*monouchi*), and the components or criteria of a valid strike are stipulated in the regulations governing competition. According to the rules, a valid strike must fulfil the following four criteria: "be full of spirit"; "exhibit proper posture"; "demonstrate a correct blade path"; and "display physical and psychological composure (*zanshin*) following the strike". If these and other conditions are fulfilled in the same instant, they are executed as part of a single technique — the result will be a valid strike. It is unacceptable for these elements to be performed separately at different stages of the one technique. This is an important characteristic of kendo technique. Furthermore, after the target has been struck with the above elements in synchronization, *zanshin* is necessary for it to be completed. *Zanshin* is the psychological state whereby you maintain your guard even after completing a valid strike; you remain alert and able to respond to your opponent's movements. It is the psychological and technical readiness (*ki-gamae* and *mi-gamae*) evinced after a valid strike. *Zanshin*, (literally "remaining mind") is not a question of intentionally *leaving* a psychological reserve when you strike, rather, it is one where such a reserve is *left* as a natural consequence of striking with abandon (*sutemi*).

Central Issues in the Instruction of Kendo

Teachers and students training together

Learning Kendo

a. Student teacher relations

In recent years, education in schools has been conducted by teachers who actively teach a predetermined curriculum of knowledge. The students are taught to "learn for themselves" and "think for themselves" in order to develop the strength and skills to make their way in life.[20] This is the nurturing aspect of education. In another sense, contact with the teacher and their values and lifestyle, although not taught directly, also provides a significant basis for learning, thus adding weight to the idea that "people make people", and "people are made by people".

In the case of kendo, students and teachers are walking the "Way" together. It is through this shared experience that a bond is formed between teacher and student, and it is through this bond that the influence of the teacher extends to the student. The teacher's character has a profound effect on the development of the student's personality, and as such, it is important for the teacher to recognise this responsibility and strive to continually develop their own persona. Education in kendo is a process that involves the teacher's influence permeating the very being of the student to transmit the "Way". This is considered the ideal way of education in kendo.

213

Budo Perspectives

b. Kata

When teaching sporting skills, in order to maintain the student's interest it is often stressed that the content be kept easy at the start and become increasingly more complicated as the level of competency increases. In the case of *budō* this centres on the training of *kata* (predetermined movement). Emphasis has traditionally been placed on *kata* training in order to pass on the knowledge and techniques of each school. Great warriors of old devised systems of *kata* to readily be able to transmit their wisdom accrued through years of actual combat experience. The resulting set forms became the basis for traditional martial schools (*ryūha*). *Kata* are supposed to be choreographed sequences of movements which contain the very essence of the teachings of that school. Extraneous movements are excluded. The adept is only able to access that knowledge through much hard training in the *kata* techniques. They obey the *kata* teachings of the master, following their instructions to the letter. In theory, through constant and arduous repetition of the *kata* the content gradually becomes a part of the student's natural movement, and the essence becomes a part of their being. [21]

c. Defining and learning athletic skills

Defining athletic skills and making their form absolute as with the *kata* outlined above, in many ways goes against the grain of modern coaching science and physical education ideals. This kind of methodology is thought to stymie individuality, creative development, and the initiative and skills to solve problems on your own. However, in *budō*, there is the teaching of *shu-ha-ri* (守破離) . This teaching refers to the process of development where the first stage of *shu* refers to the act of learning the techniques through *kata*, then being proficient enough to apply them or test them in any situation (*ha*), and finally the enlightened stage of breaking away and moving freely in one's own style (*ri*).

Regardless of how important we realise *kata* to be, and the respect we afford it, if we stay bogged down in *kata* technique, we will not be able to evolve. Students will obediently learn *kata* from their teachers, which are then put to use, and finally infused with individual attributes thereby completing the process. In this way, *budō* utilises a predetermined, passive system of repetitive training to form the base, on the understanding that this will evolve into individualistic and unrestricted techniques.

An important aspect of gaining knowledge and technical proficiency is not only the teaching materials or instructors, but how easily the knowledge and skills are able to be absorbed by the student. In other words, the content that the teacher imparts to the students should be in a form that is easily reflected as in a mirror, or easily absorbed like water in sand. The restrictive and repetitive methodology used to teach kendo may seem to be irrational in many ways. Nevertheless, it does function as an extremely effective way to impart the skills and techniques required to do kendo.[22]

Central Issues in the Instruction of Kendo

d. Rei (Courtesy)

Rei (courtesy or etiquette) is the basic moral system which people are expected to abide by in order to ensure the maintenance of social harmony. It is expressed essentially as an attitude of respect, recognition, and gratefulness for other members of the society. *Rei* is something we are taught on a daily basis in our homes and at school, and is by no means something only learned through kendo.

Two kenshi perform zarei (seated bow)

A common scene when competitors in some sporting event win a match are victory poses followed by both sides shaking hands in appreciation for a good game. Kendo takes a different attitude to this, and places emphasis on controlled *rei* and its expression. It is often quoted that kendo begins and ends with *rei*. This is not to say that courtesy is expressed only at the beginning and end of a training session or match, but is continuous from beginning to end.

Why does kendo place so much emphasis on *rei*? By striving to maintain a noble and polite sense of decorum in external appearance and action, this also encourages awareness of correct deportment from the "inside". In theory, through this the practitioner develops dignified demeanour and strength which radiates from within. Depending on how one views it, kendo can appear to be very confrontational and negative, violent and destructive. However, this is merely the exchange of techniques which is of course a necessary stage in learning kendo. However, it is because of the ferocious exchanges necessary to learn kendo that *rei* is so important. Through *rei*, opponents express gratitude and feelings of respect to each other. Also, they affirm that they are not only opponents trying to defeat each other, but are also cooperating fellow enthusiasts of the "Way" of kendo, and their interaction is beneficial to both as they progress.

Another important aspect of *rei* in kendo is that it is not only expressed to the opponent. It should also be directed internally. In the midst of the fury and excitement of kendo exchanges, maintaining the composure to adhere to correct etiquette is extremely important. This also encourages the practitioner to concentrate and focus, remain calm, and control emotions. Thus, the role of *rei* in regards to the opponent and the self plays a significant role in the way a practitioner develops their humanity.[23]

Kendo and Moral Education

In the teaching guidelines for junior and senior high schools in regards to the instruction of kendo, it states that the objectives are "to pay attention to traditional [cultural] movement", and "respect [traditional] propriety and etiquette".[24] In other words, teaching kendo in schools has been linked by the Ministry of Education to moral education.[25] How far can this link between kendo and ideas of moral education and deportment be taken?

In the Meiji period (1868–1912), the government promoted slogans such as *Fukoku-kyōhei* (Enrich the Country and Strengthen the Military) and *Shokusan-kōgyō* (Increase Production and Promote Industry") in their quest to modernise. Western technology and ideals were enthusiastically imported, and used to strengthen cultural policies and the education system. Initially, during this period, Confucianism and Shinto were criticized as being incompatible with the new path Japan was embarking upon, where modern ideals such as liberalism and utilitarianism were what Japan needed most. Japanese society and lifestyle took on many dramatic changes. However, these trends resulted in the Japanese regretting their unquestioned importation of Western ideals to the detriment of traditional values, and sparking a reconsideration of the benefits of Japanese culture and time-honoured standards. With Japan's victories in the Sino-Japanese War (1894-1895) and the Russo-Japanese War (1904-1905), militaristic and nationalistic sentiment grew, and as the general populace was conscripted into military service, suddenly the Japanese people as a whole were deemed to have inherited the *bushidō* spirit.

It was from this period that great efforts were made to introduce kendo into the newly developed school curriculum as an official topic of study. It was stressed by advocates that *budō* contained spiritual values not found in other subjects in schools, and that it should be made a compulsory course of study to impart traditional Japanese values to youth. Thus, through the study of *budō* the younger generations too would understand the "honourable" *bushi* culture that made Japan "unique" in the world. Kendo, it was thought would provide the means for relevant moral education in Japanese schools. Moral education was designed to educate the masses of a suitable system of ethics to enable Japan's continued growth and prosperity. It was thought that through learning the techniques of kendo, the practitioner would be able to develop body and mind, thus making kendo an effective tool for moral education.[26]

Conclusion

Kendo, the "Way" of the sword, originated in a world where the warrior would "cut or be cut", "kill or be killed". The sword was eventually exchanged for a *shinai*, protective armour was developed, and practitioners would face each other in a clash of wills. Through confronting opponents and engaging them in a battle for the centre, and exchanging techniques to try and score a valid point in the process of cognition/

Central Issues in the Instruction of Kendo

discretion → mobilisation of will → execution of technique, the adept embarks on a journey to discover the meaning of techniques, and the spirit that underlies them. Through this journey of mastering techniques, the practitioner is also confronted with questions of the self. They have to keep assessing each moment and consider better ways of doing things which leads onto questions of better ways of being. Through this continual process of polishing technique and self-reflection, the ideal self gradually becomes apparent, thereby confirming the educational value of kendo as a way for character development.

Endnotes

[1] Ogawa Chūtarō, *Kendō no rinen*, pp. 9-5.
[2] *Ibid.*, pp. 35-39.
[3] Nakamura Tamio, *Kendō jiten- gijutsu to bunka no rekishi*, p. 12.
[4] Most of the arguments in this paper are taken from my book *Reidan Jichi—Komorisono Masao kendō kōjutsu roku*.
[5] I consider kendo itself to be a mode of education, so what I am referring to here is not the role of kendo per se in schools or local *dōjō* in nurturing individual attributes, but education in the sense of what should be taught in kendo.
[6] Takano Sasaburō, *Kendō*, pp. 190-92.
[7] Yuno Masanori and Okamura Tadanori, *Kendō kyōshitsu*, p. 240.
[8] *Ibid.*
[9] Nakayama Hakudō (ed.), *Negishi Shingorō sensei ikō kendō kōwa-roku*, pp. 35-36.
[10] Okamura Yuno, op. cit., pp. 197-198.
[11] Ministry of Education, *Chūgakkō shidō yōryō kaisetsu-hoken taiiku-hen*, p. 58.
[12] Ministry of Education, *Kōtō gakkō shidō yōryō kaisetsu- hoken taiiku-hen*, pp. 54-55.
[13] All Japan Kendo Federation Teaching Materials, *Kendō shidō yōkō*, pp. 10-11.
[14] Nakamura Tamio, et al., "Kendō no waza no taikei to gijutsu", pp 1-9.
[15] Kinoshita Hisanori, *Kenpō shigoku shōden*, pp. 154-55.
[16] *Ibid.*
[17] *Ibid.*
[18] *Ibid.*
[19] *Ibid.*
[20] See preface of the Ministry of Education's *Chūgakkō shidō yōryō kaisetsu-hoken taiiku-hen* and *Kōtō gakkō shidō yōryō kaisetsu-hoken taiiku-hen*.
[21] Nakabayashi Shinji, *Budō no susume*, pp. 162-67.
[22] *Ibid.*
[23] Ōya Minoru, "Budō no kokusaika", *Nihonshi shōhyakka budō*, pp. 223-26.
[24] *Ibid.*, p. 52, 55.
[25] For example, refer to Nomura Hideyuki, "Mombushō shitei 'budō shidō ishinkō' no jissen naiyō ni kansuru kenkyū"), *Budōgaku kenkyū* Vol. 34 No. 1, 2001. pp. 11-22. And, "Gakushū shidō yōryōno dōkō kara mita kongo no budō shidō ni kansuru shiron", *Budōgaku kenkyū* Vol. 34, No. 3, 2002. pp. 14-22. Also refer to Fujii Mitsuharu, "Chugakkō kendō bu ni okeru reihō shidō no jissen-teki kenkyū", *Budōgaku kenkyū* Vol. 36, 2003. p. 53. All Japan Kendo Federation "Shidō hō kōshū ni okeru 'jūten jikō', *Kendō kōshūkai*

shiryō shoshū, p. 5. See also Sugie Masatoshi, "Kindai budō no seiritsu katei ni kansuru kenkyū-Meiji ni okeru budō rinen no hensen ni tsuite", *Budōgaku kenkyū* Vol. 6 No. 1, 1973. p. 44.
[26] Ōya Minoru, "Kendō ronkō-ningen renma no 'michi' o saguru", *Kyōshoku kenshū* No. 347, 2001. pp. 98-101. Also "Jutsuri no tenkai to kendō tokuikuron no ginmi". *Kyōshoku kenshū* No. 348, 2001. pp 94-97.

Bibliography

All Japan Kendo Federation Teaching Materials. *Kendō shidō yōkō* (Kendo teaching outline). AJKF, 2003.
"Shidō hō kōshū ni okeru 'jūten jikō'. (Important points when teaching at seminars). *Kendō kōshūkai shiryō* (Collection of kendo lectures and essays). 2003.
Fujii Mitsuharu. "Chugakkō kendō bu ni okeru reihō shidō no jissen-teki kenkyū". *Budōgaku kenkyū* (Research Journal of Budo). Vol. 36, Nihon Budō Gakkai (Japanese Academy of Budo), 2003.
Kinoshita Hisanori. *Kempō shigoku shōden* (The secrets of kendo). Republished by Taiiku to Supōtsu Shuppansha, 1985.
Ministry of Education. *Chūgakkō shidō yōryō kaisetsu-hoken taiiku-hen*, (Explanation of guidelines for course study at junior high schools - Physical education), Higashiyama Shobō, 1999.
Kōtō gakkō shidō yōryō kaisetsu-hoken taiiku-hen, (Explanation of guidelines for course study at high schools- Physical education), Higashiyama Shobō, 1999.
Nakabayashi Shinji. *Budō no susume* (An endorsement of budō). Nakabayashi Shinji Sensei Isakushū Kankōkai, 1987.
Nakamura Tamio. *Kendō jiten- gijutsu to bunka no rekishi* (Kendo Encyclopaedia- the history of kendo techniques and culture). Shimazu Shobō, 1994.
Nakamura Tamio, et al. "Kendō no waza no taikei to gijutsuka ni tsuite" (The systemization of kendo techniques and technical innovations). *Budōgaku kenkyū* (Research Journal of Budo) Vol. 28 No. 3, Nihon Budō Gakkai (Japanese Academy of Budo), 1996.
Nakayama Hakudō (ed.). *Negishi shingorō sensei ikō kendō kōwa-roku* (Collection of teachings by the late Negishi Shingorō sensei). Yūshinkan, 1942.
Nomura Hideyuki "Mombushō shitei 'budō shidō ishinkō' no jissen naiyō ni kansuru kenkyū". *Budōgaku kenkyū* (Research Journal of Budo) Vol. 34 No. 1. Nihon Budō Gakkai (Japanese Academy of Budo), 2001.
"Gakushū shidō yōryōno dōkō kara mita kongo no budō shidō ni kansuru shiron". *Budōgaku kenkyū* (Research Journal of Budo) Vol. 34 No. 3. Nihon Budō Gakkai (Japanese Academy of Budo), 2002.
Ogawa Chūtarō. *Kendō no rinen-Ogawa Chūtarō sensei kōen-roku* (The concept of Kendo-Lecture notes of Ogawa Chūtarō sensei). Tokyo High School Physical

Central Issues in the Instruction of Kendo

Education Federation Kendo Department, 1985.

Ōya Minoru. *Reidan Jichi – Komorisono Masao kendō kōjutsu-roku* (A record of Komorisono Masao's kendo teachings).Taiiku to Supōtsu Shuppansha, 1997.

"Kendō ronkō-ningen renma no 'michi' o saguru". *Kyōshoku kenshū* No.347, 2001.

"Jutsuri no tenkai to kendō tokuikuron no ginmi". *Kyōshoku kenshū* No.48, 2001.

"Budō no kokusaika" (The internationalization of budō). In Irie Kōhei, Futaki Ken'ichi, Katō Hiroshi (editors). *Nihonshi shōhyakka budō*. (Japanese history compendium – budō essays). Tōkyōdō Shuppan, 1994.

Sugie Masatoshi. "Kindai budō no seiritsu katei ni kansuru kenkyū-Meiji ni okeru budō rinen no hensen ni tsuite". *Budōgaku kenkyū* (Research Journal of Budo) Vol. 6 No. 1. Nihon Budō Gakkai (Japanese Academy of Budo), 1973.

Takano Sasaburō. *Kendō*, Heirinkan, 1918.

Yuno Masanori and Okamura Tadanori. *Kendō kyōshitsu* (Kendo class). Taishūkan Shoten, 1979.

Chapter 12

The Promotion of *Budō* for the Disabled

Matsui Kantarō
International Budo University

Introduction

If we assume that *budō* originates as a physical system of attack and defence, where we attempt to attack and physically immobilize or damage our opponent even if we are injured or immobilized ourselves, then it stands to reason that *budō* should be open even to those people with disabilities. Here, I am using the term *"shōgaisha budō"* (disabled *budō*), but in truth, we should not presume a distinction between able-bodied and disabled *budō* practitioners. However, for the sake of discourse I will continue to use the term "disabled *budō*". Furthermore, the notion of "disability" which I will employ is not restricted to physical disabilities. I do not intend to neatly organize everything into a convenient system. Rather, I will attempt to outline some common threads running through a number of individual examples to clarify my stance on disabled *budō* and the potential for positive development.

There are a number of *budō* instructors devoted to instructing disabled students. Firstly, I must stress that I truly respect the efforts of these individuals. The Association of Budo Culture for the Disabled (ABCD) is in its third year, and the national and international workshops on outlining instructional methodology for disabled *budō* practitioners continue to generate much thought and ideas into the potential of *budō* in areas traditionally thought impossible. The effects of *budō* practice by disabled people with the goal of rehabilitation and habilitation are remarkable; the family's burden of nursing is lightened while the individual is at the *dōjō* training; *dōjō* gain new members from the enrolment of disabled students (in a time when the number of children practicing *budō* is falling); and able-bodied students become friends with and learn a great deal from their disabled *budō* classmates.

Despite continued progress and increased understanding being made through the world of *budō*, generally speaking Japan is still far from being a truly barrier-free society. Disabled people withdraw into the family or institutions, and a disabled Swedish friend who often comes to Japan to train in *budō* once remarked, "aren't there any disabled people in Japan?", due to the obvious lack of public facilities catering to disabled people. Also, a Japanese person recently expressed surprised admiration for a Swedish wheelchair-bound boy because he was able to "venture outside by himself and live his life so independently". Yet, in an ideal world where such interaction was "normalized", it would be perfectly natural for those with disabilities to participate in any activity with able-bodied people on an equal footing. The field of *budō* should be no exception. When a *dōjō* accepts disabled students into the ranks, naturally some adjustments have to be made, but generally speaking everybody is in the same situation.

Why Do Disabled People Practice *Budō*?

A large motivating force behind the popularization of *budō* amongst disabled people is not based simply on a philosophy of welfare, but rather in the great rehabilitative potential of techniques that are contained in *budō*. *Budō* is a system of physical exercise, and it can contribute to a disabled person's rehabilitation / habilitation. Also, there is enormous potential for what *budō* can contribute spiritually.

As many disabled people actively partake in rehabilitation programs, some become disillusioned with what they perceive to be the shortcomings of contemporary rehabilitative treatment on offer from the medical profession. Conversely, in *budō* training they gain a new sense of purpose, and many practitioners realize that it is possible for them to become physically stronger just through participating in a typical *budō* training session. Putting on a *gi* and shouting with loud *kiai* can make a big difference to a person's mental disposition and spirit. The same benefits are also gained by mentally handicapped people who are motivated to try *budō* training.

Furthermore, if *budō* is able to spread more widely amongst the disabled, it will contribute to improved overall fitness and health levels, which would in turn reduce medical costs to society, and disabled people will be able to take a more equal place

	Modern medical rehabilitation methods	Judo rehabilitation method
Partners	One: One	One: Any number of people
Amount of Activity	Forty-five minutes per day	Infinite
Independence	Reliant on others	- very independent - self-reliant - creativity - gumption
Psychological condition	Solemn	Bright - mimicry - friendship - competitive - social

Rhythm- Shouting/vocally rich

Figure 1: The potential of judo training for the disabled compared with contemporary medical rehabilitation methodology

The Promotion of Budo for the Disabled

in society. This would have wide-reaching implications in a country like Japan where Japanese schools still insist on separating able-bodied and disabled students.

Dr. Murai Masanao is conducting research on the effects of judo *ukemi* (break falls) on children with severe muscular disabilities. The basis of his study rests on the premise that humans move unconsciously toward a desired objective, such as protecting the neck. Murai found a number of merits in teaching judo to children with cerebral palsy, and this is shown in figure 1.

Swedish Research Regarding Disabled *Budō*

Recently, the Association of Budo Culture for the Disabled (ABCD) was established, and the International Budo University invited Mr. Pontus Johansson to come to Japan to introduce his activities in Sweden regarding the utilization of *budō* for the disabled. Johansson was the bronze medallist in the 400 meter freestyle of the 1990 World Swimming Championships for the Disabled, the silver medallist at the 1991 European Swimming Championships for the Disabled in both the 200 meter freestyle and 100 meter breaststroke, and he also represented Sweden at both the Barcelona and Atlanta Paralympics.

Johansson was born with cerebral palsy, a condition that affects his motor function on the right side of his body from the waist down. At seven months of age he began his rehabilitation, and by the age of eleven, he was able to stand and walk independently. However, the disability took a turn for the worse, and he gradually lost his ability to walk. At the age of sixteen, he began to practice karate to supplement his swimming training. He learned how to regain his balance, and once again became able to stand and walk independently. In Johansson's case, we can find an example of karate contributing to extremely successful rehabilitation. In his capacity as national swim team coach,

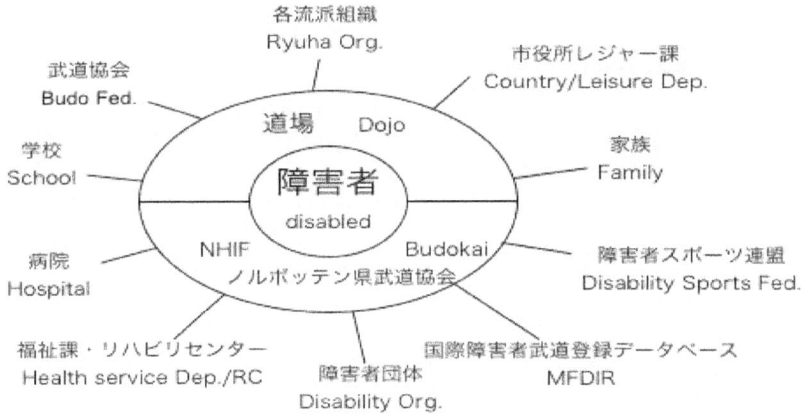

Figure 2: Support structure for disabled budō practitioners in Norrbotten.

he built a weekly karate practice into his swimmers' training program. Currently, Johansson runs his own *dōjō*, but he does not restrict his classes to disabled people. As chief *budō* instructor of the Budo Association of the Norrbotten Provincial Disabled Sports Federation (NPDSF), he has been instrumental in introducing a range of styles and *budō* activities to his students.

In 1998, the activities of Johansson in Norrbotten province began to receive funding from the provincial Welfare Department, and *budō* was officially recognized as a course of the NPDSF. Also, in Luleå University of Technology's nursing course curriculum, *budō* and its use in rehabilitation is studied as an academic subject. In 2003, the Swedish Budo Federation established the Disabled Budo Instruction Course, followed by the formation of a special board in the federation to administer activities.

ABCD *Budō* Workshops

In March of 2001, Johansson came to Japan and conducted work as a researcher at the International Budo University. At the end of his two months of research under his guidance, students of the university undertook a project in instruction methodology and demonstrating the potential for disabled *budō* to members of the public. With support from the media a large response was generated, and ABCD was established to enable continued activities. The organization was purposefully created as a non-formal support group, without the intention of binding disabled people and the group together. Nor did it seek to establish an official membership system (due to possible future complications), and did not actively seek to 'instruct' as such. The ABCD was created primarily as a grass roots organization aiming to provide information services such as introducing *dōjō* to the disabled, and helping *dōjō* to help disabled students. In the future when it becomes accepted as a perfectly natural occurrence (as opposed to a rarity) for disabled people to participate in *budō* training, then the existence of the ABCD would cease to be necessary. The ABCD hopes that this in fact will one day become a reality, and for the last three years, efforts to introduce the activities of the Swedish disabled *budō* by inviting Johansson have continued.

In the workshops conducted by the ABCD, able-bodied participants select a disability at the entrance of the venue, and simulate the disability by tying up a part of their body with judo *obi*. In this way, everyone is participating together with some kind of induced movement hindrance. This is precisely how able-bodied and disabled people practice sports and *budō* together in Sweden. In the workshop, students are required to concentrate in order to discover what

Example of an arm 'disability'

The Promotion of Budo for the Disabled

they *can* do with their 'disability'. Some examples of the body restraints used in the workshop are total/partial leg immobility and total/partial arm immobility. They are encouraged through actual experience to learn about how exhausting even warm-ups can be, and re-learn balance as they experience practicing the techniques of kendo, karate, aikido, and judo. With English interpretations included, the training sessions are usually completed in about two hours.[1]

There are two particularly innovative characteristics of the workshop. The first relates to the form of practice, and the second to the attitude towards practice. With regard to the form or methodology of practice, participants with a variety of disabilities are made

A scene from a workshop warm-up

to practice together. There is a general tendency to assume that people with the same disability are matched as training partners, however, the Swedish system encourages people with different disabilities to train together. The Swedish system also emphasizes training with able-bodied people at community *dōjō*, not just practicing with other disabled people. In this way, disabled people devise ways to overcome obstacles, and this facilitates an attitude of independently searching for one's "own path".

In regards to the attitude emphasized during practice, practitioners are encouraged to concentrate on things they *can* do. Unfortunately, when it comes to sports instruction for disabled people there is an inclination to focus on what such people *can't* do and avoid such areas. Of course, it is not simply a matter of practicing "the things you can do" in the literal sense. If training consists of working on the areas which are mobile, training will be unbalanced. As much of the body as possible should be utilized. Unbalanced training regimes pose dangers of disproportional development, which could actually result in solidifying immobile parts of the body. Comments made by disabled athletes who have attained the highest levels in their respective sports strongly suggest the importance of balanced training. Thus, the objective is not to work on the able parts of the body, but to devise ways to develop the disabled areas. In this sense, even the warm-ups conducted in Swedish *dōjō* are positively exhausting.

Is it Possible to Establish an Overall Instruction Methodology?

Just as with able-bodied people where we take an age-specific approach to training, a number of different approaches are possible. Many studies are being undertaken by researchers with an interest in this field, the results of which are shedding light on several important points. Regarding the instruction of *budō* to disabled people, evidently there are many different possible teaching methods depending on the disability. While it is true that we have seen an increase in the number of disabled *budō* practitioners to date, there has been no specific method of instruction yet devised. Assuming we classify disabilities into certain categories – cerebral palsy for example – the circumstances for each individual would be different. Even though the level of spinal cord damage might be the same, each condition will differ. This makes it nearly impossible to establish a comprehensive instruction system for the disabled. Besides which, we cannot just wait for a system of instruction to be established, but must accept reality and continue to pioneer different methods by trial and error. Rather than devising a pleasing all-encompassing system *per se*, it is more important that we acquaint ourselves with the wide variety of circumstances on a case by case basis. This requires assessing each individual with a positive attitude and establish what is possible for them to do.

In this regard, there is no difference between the way we instruct disabled and able-bodied practitioners. However, this does not mean that the instructor must always directly supervise the disabled student. They should

Karate kata performance at the ABCD workshop conducted at the International Budo University in 2003

The Promotion of Budo for the Disabled

be treated the same as any able-bodied student, and be afforded the space to work things out for themselves. Instructors should teach any student regardless of whether they are able-bodied or disabled, with the attitude that each and every situation is special. In this way, there should be no need to make distinctions in teaching methodology.

Regarding Competition

During the workshops, questions were frequently asked about the role of competition, and whether *budō* will be represented at more events in the Paralympics. Japanese people who witnessed the Nagano Winter Olympic Games were impressed with the subsequent Paralympic events, and many people expressed how watching the Paralympians in their respective events gave them strength. The level of competition is now so high that it truly warrants the level of spectator attention currently received. Of the *budō* arts, judo for the visually impaired is now a Paralympic event.

The development of special rules and categories led to this, and it is indeed a wonderful thing. Also, there are all-Japan and world championships for wheelchair bound karate exponents.[2] Creating appropriate categories may be problematic, but it is not impossible, and can be conducted the same way in which weight classes are utilized in other mainstream competitions. The current level of judo at the Paralympics has increased to the point that "hobbyists" simply have no chance of success.

Another possibility for competition is to encourage disabled *budō* practitioners to participate in regular (able-bodied) tournaments. There are few actual regulations preventing participation of disabled competitors. Even if they are defeated in the first round, the joy derived from having had the opportunity to compete against able-bodied opponents is great. Already we hear of people who have achieved first class results in *kata* competitions. Put simply, competition is an important element, but it is not indispensable. *Budō* is a "Way" with many possibilities, and so there is no need for those who find competition problematic to be excluded.

The Recognition of *Kyū* and *Dan* Grades

One of the differences between sport and *budō* is the existence of the grading systems of *kyū* and *dan*. As a result of individual effort, the colour of one's belt changes and this can prove enormously encouraging to the practitioner who can gage their own progress and also create quantifiable goals. However, under the current grading system for most *budō* arts there are some cases where certain aspects of the grading are difficult to complete depending on the disability, such as the inability to face-off (spar) with an opponent. With this problem in mind, there is a necessity to think about possible alternatives.

One option is to recognize special standards for disabled people. It would not be difficult to develop separate criteria which take into account the disability of the examinee. There are in fact already some individual *dōjō* teaching disabled people that utilize different modes of criteria for this purpose.

Another approach is to adopt an attitude that recognizes the value of honorary "*eternal white-belts*" or othyer honorary titles. This may seem like a paradox, but it does bestow respect upon those who have displayed a determined attitude and continued effort, regardless of grading examinations. This is supposedly the ideal attitude for all *budō* practitioners anyway. Most federations also have honorary grades available for people who have been of service. Making honorary grades available to disabled *budō* practitioners would also be a good way of providing encouragement.

A third option as a compromise between the first two, would be to award grading certification at the discretion of each group's headquarters. It would not be necessary to establish recognized grading criteria in advance, and there is the added merit of gathering the individual information of disabled practitioners in each federation. Currently, information membership is accumulated, but there is virtually no information concerning disabilities. Even in larger organizations, the visible registration of disabled people is practically zero. Disabled people are training at *dōjō* in the community, but collated information about their whereabouts is almost non-existent. Thus, introducing special grading committees in each federation to give disabled members a chance to receive grades for their progress would act as the perfect opportunity to collate this kind of information. The number of people in question is not that great, and the job of the respective organizations would not suddenly become troublesome as a result. The accumulation of this information would be useful in making appropriate decisions regarding grading systems and furthering assistance to individuals and *dōjō* that require it.

How Do We Manage the Dangers?

Regarding the dangers involved in disabled *budō*, the principle of self-responsibility should apply. It is impossible for instructors to know in advance all aspects of every disability, and realistically, for reasons related to safety, there is the possibility that a disabled person would not be accepted into a *dōjō*. However, it is important to try and create circumstances which will create opportunities for disabled people to participate.

Obviously, the disabled person or their guardian best understands the nature of the disability. It is essential that the person receive medical advice before undertaking hard physical activity. Also, the instructor should not rely on reading literature to try and understand the disability of the prospective student. Instead, they should listen to the disabled person, and work together to devise a suitable training regime. The onus rests on the side of the disabled person to inform the instructor of all relevant information, thus lightening the burden on the instructor.

Insurance is also a requirement, although this is the same for able-bodied students as well. Another consideration is the completion of a letter of agreement (not to hold the organization or instructor responsible in case of injury) upon joining the *dōjō*. Generally

The Promotion of Budo for the Disabled

in Europe, with the exception of Britain, the attitude of self-responsibility is high. In America, on the other hand, people are in constant threat of law suits should injury occur, and this is a significant obstacle for the spread of *budō*. In Sweden and Austria, the level of self-responsibility is so high that the necessity of letters of agreement has hardly been considered.

Teaching *Budō* to the Intellectually Disabled

Some people may feel resistance to teaching striking techniques to an intellectually disabled student. I was one such person. However, I had the opportunity to see in Sweden intellectually disabled people actually doing *budō* which served to reverse my opinion. We have to take into account physical problems often associated with intellectual disabilities; such as the vulnerability of cervical vertebrae in people with Downs-syndrome, which certainly does limit the possibilities. Nevertheless, training in an environment together with other people is important for providing opportunities to such individuals to find their own "way" and overcome obstacles with their own strengths.

There are such examples in Japan. I know of one disabled individual who trains very hard. Even when there is a typhoon, or he has sustained an injury, he never fails to appear at the *dōjō*. This serves to stimulate, encourage, and gain the respect of all the other *dōjō* members. Indeed, he is a valued member of the *dōjō* who earns respect, not because of his disability, but by setting an example.

In motion-ability tests, intellectually disabled children amassed a mean score 40% below that of other children. Body size was on average 10% less than non-disabled children. The difference in physique multiplied by four equals the difference in mobility, and also motivation.[3] However, despite the differences in physique, *budō* contains elements such as the rhythmical shouting of *kiai* which is seen to inspire the students and motivate them greatly.[4]

The Advantage of Being Behind

Currently, there are only two *budō* groups registered with the Japan Disabled Sports Association.[5] I think that this lag may actually present some advantages for the various *budō* groups. If normalization becomes a reality, and *budō* practice becomes universal, then it would be ideal for departments to be set up within each organization to administer related activities. Alternatively, it would not be a negative move to initiate separate organizations to administer the special needs of disabled competitors. The current system where able-bodied sports organizations are administered by the Ministry of Education, Culture, Sports, Science and Technology, and disabled sports organizations are overseen by the Ministry of Health, Labour and Welfare is perfectly understandable. However, it would be a significant move for the *budō* organizations authorised by the Ministry of Education to have special committees set up within each organization to assist the many *dōjō* that include disabled students in their membership. It would not be costly either.

Conclusion

A naginata class

Regarding the instruction of able-bodied students together with disabled, just about every case is essentially a world-first. Especially in the pursuit of instructing disabled people, although it may take extra time and resources, the returns and benefits are considerable to all concerned. We cannot wait for *dōjō* to simply become barrier free. Instead, everything should be considered positively. For example, when lifting a disabled student up the *dōjō* stairs to the entrance, this task could be incorporated positively as part of the training regime for the other students. To be sure, the number of disabled

The Promotion of Budo for the Disabled

students is small, but not insignificant. There are about 3,327,000 disabled people in Japan.[6] Simply calculated, the population of a junior high school district is 10,000 people, of which 262 are physically disabled. Intellectually disabled people are not included in these figures, and if we included them the number would be larger still.[7]

Of course, disabilities range from minor to quite severe, so not every disabled person is keen to undertake the practice of *budō*. However, those that wish to learn together with able-bodied students typically are very conscious of their body and potential. The *budō* population in Japan is comparatively small anyway, so even though the numbers of disabled *budō* practitioners may seem small, it is not implausible that there are students with disabilities in many *dōjō* around the country. The possibilities for spreading *budō* amongst the disabled are numerous and great.

Endnotes

[1] Refer to http://www.ne.jp/asahi/news/net/ for further information.
[2] Supported by NPO Nihon Karate Shōtōkai and the Japan Wheelchair Karatedo Federation.
[3] *Shōgaisha supōtsu shido tebiki*, p. 210.
[4] Refer to "Undō kinō shōgaiji/sha ni taisuru shūdan shidō ryōiku-Hangarii no petee hōshiki ni tsuite" in *Gekkan chiiki hoken* Vol. 10, No. 7, 1979.
[5] Japan Judo Federation for the Blind and Japan Wheelchair Karatedo Federation.
[6] Taken from 2001 figures published by the Japanese Ministry of Health, Labour and Welfare.
[7] Based on the 2000 Japanese national census which calculated Japan's population to be 1,29,626,000 people.

Bibliography

Japan Disabled Sports Association (Nihon Shōgaisha Supōtsu Kyōkai). *Shōgaisha supōtsu shido tebiki* (Handbook for instructing sports to disabled practitioners). 2000.

Chiiki Hoken Kenkyūkai, "Undō kinō shōgaiji/sha ni taisuru shūdan shidō ryōiku-Hangarii no petee hōshiki ni tsuite" (Teaching rehabilitative sports for disabled people in groups- A look at the Hungarian Pete method). In *Gekkan chiiki hoken* (Regional physical education monthly). Vol. 10, No. 7, 1979.

Chapter 13

Budō in the Physical Education Curriculum of Japanese Schools

Motomura Kiyoto
Tokyo Women's College of Physical Education

The Historical Circumstances

The Meiji and Taisho periods
Following the establishment in 1872 of Japan's school system, the Ministry of Education, Science, Sports and Culture (now the Ministry of Education, Culture, Sports, Science and Technology) and the Diet (parliament) began receiving various kinds of recommendations and petitions for the possible introduction of *budō*, especially *gekiken* (fencing) and *jūjutsu*, into the school physical education curriculum. In the twenty-fourth session of the Diet, held in 1908, the government passed a resolution on physical education that paved the way for the 1911 revision of the Regulations for the Enforcement of the Middle School Order, which approved *gekiken* and *jūjutsu* as physical education courses. However, these were just as elective courses, not as compulsory subjects.

In the Taisho period (1912-1926), Japan's first Syllabus of School Gymnastics (*Gakkō taisō kyōju yōmoku*) was issued in 1913. This was repeatedly revised, but *budō* was still given the same treatment it received in the Meiji period and was not included as a compulsory subject in the curriculum. However, in 1925 at the fiftieth meeting of the Diet, another proposal was put forward to elevate *gekiken* and *jūjutsu* to compulsory school subjects in middle schools. Furthermore, the names were changed to kendo and judo, to emphasize the "Way", or spiritual characteristics of *budō*.

The Showa period (pre-war)
After this sequence of events, in 1931 the administrative regulations relating to middle schools were amended, and for the first time, *budō* assumed its position as a compulsory subject in the physical education curriculum. In the same year, another revision to the Regulations for the Enforcement of the Middle School Order recognized kendo and judo as "traditional Japanese martial arts beneficial for developing a real and solid sense of patriotism as well as building mental and physical fitness", and made them compulsory. This was followed in 1941 by the National School Order, which replaced *taisō-ka* (gymnastics subjects) — a curriculum category since the Meiji period — with *tairen-ka* (physical discipline subjects), and *budō* practice was enforced even further.

School girls practicing naginata in the 1930s

Post-war

In 1945, the Ministry of Education issued a notice on the post-war treatment of the guidelines for teaching *tairen-ka*, along with another on the treatment of *budō*. These amounted to a ban on *budō* not only in physical education classes but also in extracurricular settings. Then, in 1947, the Ministry established new guidelines for school physical education, replacing *tairen-ka* with *taiiku-ka* (physical education subjects), signalling the beginning of a new era in the history of Japan's physical education program. Three years later, in 1950, a move was made to return judo to the school curriculum: the Ministry of Education officially recognized judo as having developed into a "democratic sport" suitable for teaching to junior high school pupils onwards, and recommended the introduction as a physical education course.

From kakugi to budō

Guidelines for the Course of Study were announced for junior and senior high school curricula in 1958 and 1960 respectively, providing a legal basis for school physical education. The Guidelines also established a new subject category, *kakugi* (combat sports), consisting of sumo, judo and kendo, of which every school was directed to adopt one. In 1989, the Guidelines were amended to replace *kakugi* with *budō*, a move that was in line with the ideal of "promoting international understanding and fostering respect for the culture and traditions of Japan" set forth by the Curriculum Council in a report it submitted in 1987.

Budo in Japanese Schools

The Position of *Budō* in Physical Education as Defined by Official Course Study Guidelines

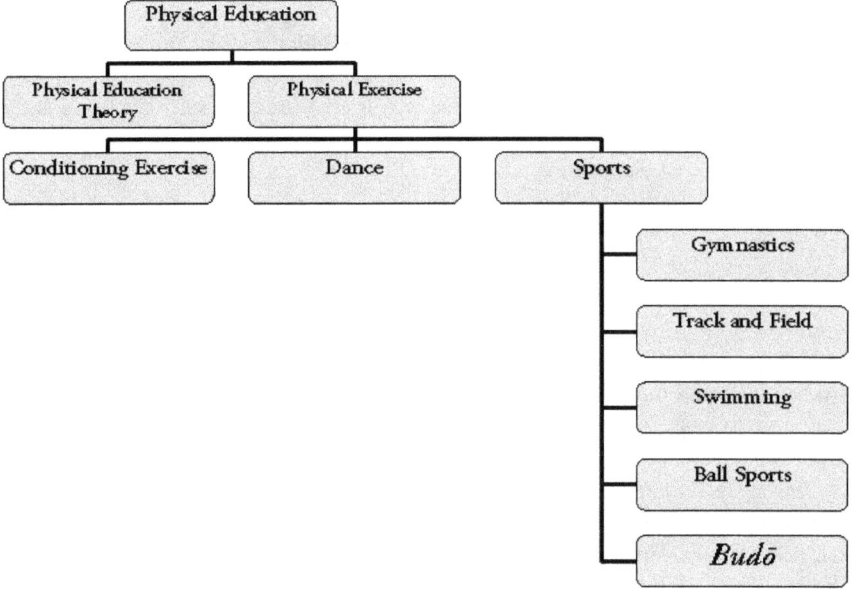

As can be seen from the diagram, the curriculum which was drawn up to realize the aims of physical education, saw that two initial categories were made – that of *Exercise* and *Physical Education Theory*. Within the broad category of the actual techniques of Exercise lie three key points – the aim of achieving direct improvement to ones physical strength (Conditioning Exercise), exercise that gives oneself a sense of achievement, competition and fun (Sports), and a chance to use one's body to express oneself while enjoying a sense of fun and happiness (Dance).

Within the category of Sports, and under the sub-heading of Sports Using Instruments, lie the pursuits of athletics, swimming, baseball, and *budō*. Here we can see that *budō* takes its place in the sphere of sports. Namely, *budō* (*kakugi*) was eventually placed in the category of "sport" in the post-war period to enable students to experience the special characteristics of *budō*.

Budō Instruction from Now

Maintain an international perspective (foster an awareness of oneself as a Japanese person living in a global society)

In order to meet recent social changes, the government has been heavily revising the school curriculum for approximately ten years. The year 1998 saw four basic policies of reform, but the one I would like to introduce concerns "the need to cultivate Japanese people that are sociable and rich in humanity, Japanese that can live in an international society". Also, with regards to *budō* the Ministry of Education, Culture, Sports, Science and Technology issued guidelines that stated "teaching *budō* was to introduce students to unique Japanese culture and must be continued."

Budō derived from traditional Japanese martial techniques (*bugi*) and martial systems (*bujutsu*), and as such are deeply tied to traditional Japanese culture. This is why *budō* is deemed important by the Ministry, and why it is considered beneficial to teach the techniques of *budō* to Japanese youth who are also greatly exposed to international society, as a way of establishing self-identity.

In order to do this, the focus of the activity is not placed on winning and losing, but on the cultivation of an attitude of self-respect. This is based on an understanding of *budō*'s traditional characteristic of being a way of character development through the process of learning the techniques. By teaching *budō* with this way of thinking as the basis, the aim is to cultivate students with an international outlook, as well as an ability to articulate Japanese culture to others through their experience of having studied *budō* and the traditional ideals that underlie it.

Teach the joys of practicing judo or kendo as a sport
Given the limited number of class hours allocated to the instruction of judo (and kendo etc.) in schools, in reality the transmission of *budō* thought and traditional ideals is difficult. Furthermore, the more emphasis given to teaching students about the traditions of *budō*, its way of thinking, and the historical significance behind the movements, the more likely the classes will become rigid and overly strict. It is important to avoid this tendency and make the classes as enjoyable as possible in the limited time available. The classes must be prevented from becoming tedious, lest the original aims become unachievable.

Of course, the original point of physical education classes should be based on imparting the enjoyment and fun of physical exercise. The student learns how enjoyable judo is when they get the opportunity to test the techniques they learned in class in a match, and defeating their opponent with an *ippon*. The student then perfects techniques through free practice (*randori*). In this way, the student's motivation is raised and they continue to seek the answer to the next challenge that confronts them. The student experiences the enjoyment of working things out for themselves as they begin to learn and understand the techniques of attack and defence. It is important for students to be able to sense the enjoyment of meeting challenges and the fun of competition in this way, and derive a sense of personal achievement. Experiencing the positive aspects of judo through such sport-like competition is extremely important.

Teach the joys of practicing judo or kendo as a tradition
If the positive aspects of *budō* are only pursued through a sporting approach, important aspects of self-development and self-control will be difficult to impart. The

Budo in Japanese Schools

difference between judo, for example, and other sports is that in judo the student directly faces their opponent one-on-one, and competes to overwhelm them with various potentially dangerous techniques such as throws, chokes, and holds. This is obviously very different to shooting for goal in ball sports. Because of the inherent danger of directly applying techniques on the training partner or opponent, there must be an attitude of respect maintained by each student. This is where the meaning of *reihō* (etiquette and respect) is a vital element in *budō* education.

Here, the student learns to experience the positive aspects of sports by experiencing the positive aspects of *budō*. For example:

1. The student develops self-discipline, and adopts an attitude of respect towards their opponent.
2. It is taught that etiquette and courtesy are more than simply forms, but in fact are expressions of deep respect for opponents developed through the discipline stressed in *budō* training.
3. With respect to winning and losing and competition, the student learns to adopt an attitude of "fair play".

In this way, through practice and matches and emphasis placed on courtesy and fair-play, the student is able to learn through experience the good aspects of *budō*, which also serve to enhance understanding of the positive attributes that other sports have to offer.

Training students to learn to think independently

To date, judo classes in schools have for the most part been focused on simply teaching and developing the students' technical ability, and on safety. Despite students acquiring a broad range of techniques in practice, the number who use only a limited number in matches is large. Why is this? It is because the students have not been given the opportunity to think about and internalize the techniques by themselves.

With respect to the future of judo instruction, the question of what kind of abilities and strengths should be emphasized is an important issue. In short, it is not just about acquiring technique, but consideration must be given to encourage students to think about what kinds of techniques best suit their physique, how they should practice these techniques effectively, how should these techniques be executed in matches, and so on. Providing an environment where students are able to consider these questions and come up with the answers themselves is extremely important.

The environment should demand active participation from the students in all facets, as opposed to a passive environment which seems to be very commonplace. The student should develop the ability to think and make judgments for themselves, and become an independent-minded individual. Not only should the student analyze the plethora of techniques taught during class, but he/she must be able to also instinctively select and execute these techniques at will. It is vital to allow the students an arena to test their ability and powers of discernment in *randori* or *shiai*. It is here that the student will find meaning behind the activity, and apart from enjoyment, will also reap the benefits of self-reflection and analysis conducted during the course of learning the techniques. In other words, what is needed is conversion from classes revolving around technical guidance to classes that teach students how to think and learn.

Conclusion

Regarding the correct way of teaching *budō* (judo), I have made four mutually related points. The important thing for students is to experience the fun and enjoyment of learning *budō*. Indeed, this is a fundamental element of physical education. It is important to show students the sporting aspects of judo – such as competing and having fun. However, an overemphasis on competition will detract from the other vital characteristics of judo. Educators must also focus on encouraging students to think about the traditional aspects of *budō*. However, if the view of *budō* is limited to solely traditional aspects, the positive potential of sport will be compromised. By balancing the virtues of "sports judo" with "*budō* judo", the goals of the Ministry of Education, Culture, Sports, Science and Technology of utilizing it to cultivate fine people – Japanese prepared to live in the international community, self-conscious, with an ability to think and learn for themselves, and maintaining a zest for life, can be realized. Finally please note that the comments contained in this paper are directed towards physical education classes in schools, and not at extracurricular *budō* clubs.

Bibliography

Motomura Kiyoto, et al. *Jūdō*. Hitotsubashi Shuppan, 1986.
Motomura Kiyoto and Toda Yoshio (editors). *Atarashii kadai ni taiō suru chūgakkō hoken taiikuka no jugyō moderu* (Junior high school class models for new issues). Meiji Shuppan, 2003.
Hoken taiikuka hen: *Kaitei chūgakkō gakushū shidō yōryō no tenkai* (Health and physical education: Revised guidelines for course study at junior high schools- Revised edition). Meiji Shuppan, 1999.
Hoken taiikuka hen: *Kaitei kōtōgakkō gakushū shidō yōryō no tenkai* (Health and physical education: Revised guidelines for course study at high schools- Revised edition). Meiji Shuppan, 2000.

Chapter 14

Budō & Education

Duncan Robert Mark
Zenrin Gakuen
Shorinji Kempo Headquarters

Introduction

This presentation will address the issue of whether *budō* has a role in education. It will first examine the role of education as a whole, then look at the characteristics of *budō* and finally try to define *budō*'s function in education in the twenty-first century from my perspective as an instructor at the Zenrin Gakuen Specialist School (*senmon gakkō*), run by the Shorinij Kempo Federation Foundation at the headquarters in Tadotsu city.

What is Education?

Education is the process through which we all go to some extent or other. It can be academic, vocational, social, humanistic, philosophical, religious, and so on. There isn't a commonly agreed upon definition of education and the dictionary one is tautological and points to the system rather than to its nature. The word education comes from '*educere*' which means to 'draw out'. Education therefore for the sake of this paper is defined as the process of drawing out a person's abilities and skills. This process is illustrated in Natsume Sōseki's *Yume jūya* (trans. *Ten Nights of Dream*) where a wood carver is described as revealing what is within the wood by chipping away the excess. A person is drawn out through all their interactions with their environment. All the actions and thoughts a person sees, hears, reads, and does form the basis of their experience, thus their education. This experience is what draws them out. This experience includes all interaction with the environment, society, people, and of course the education system.

Parents and teachers are the primary interface, but parents often are too busy, and sometimes don't have the experience or knowledge or even the interest to help their children's education. Teachers are often constrained by the system in which they work, and can become disinterested or disillusioned. Additionally, each teacher has a personal definition of education which depends on their outlook on the world, their beliefs, their values and thinking processes. They modify official curricula according to their own preferences, interest, teaching strengths and weaknesses. Teachers are so familiar with these that they are invisible to them, and they are thus unaware of the fact they are doing it.

Through their attitudes to students teachers influence what is brought out in a student, and what is not. Teachers should have the function of opening doors for students, never the function of closing them. Not all people are born with the same abilities, but the vast majority of us never realize but a fraction of our potential. Making the best of what we are and striving hard enough to perhaps even exceed our abilities is what is important.

The current education system is one where a body of knowledge packaged in fixed chunks is fed to students in a predetermined manner. The student is secondary to the system, and they are required to fit into it. It doesn't make allowances for different rates of learning and different personalities. It seems to be a system for holding people back, especially those who do not or cannot conform to the system. However, a discussion of the difficulties in the classroom with mixed abilities, mixed backgrounds, varying parental support and oversized classes is a little beyond the scope of this presentation. Suffice it to say, the education system is intended to re-enforce itself and by extension the social and economic system which depends on it.

Until recently, it was government policy to withhold education from the masses, the common folk, lest they got "ideas in their heads". The argument being that they might question ownership and leadership, and thus destabilize society. For those who were privileged; Latin was a prerequisite for Oxbridge[1], knowledge of Livy[2] and Pliny[3] was the best training for civil servants, and sufficient etymology to complete the Times crossword puzzle quickly was the natural preparation for executive responsibility.

The modern 'official' curricula tend to be Newtonian; they are based on the prevailing view that problems are solved through science. The content is therefore broken down into chunks of information which have to be learned (memorised). The curricula tend to avoid large scale ideas or paradigms as it would be too difficult for curricula and syllabi developers to define what everyone should know. Most textbooks are written within this narrow context and thus avoid alternative, equally valid explanations.

There is another curriculum which is what is learned by the very nature of the place of study. Most schools are sterile environments run to be efficient rather than conducive to learning. Students learn that keeping to the schedule is more important than interest in a subject, that the efficiency of the system is more important than social communication, and that sticking to the rules is more important than for any one student to understand the difference between appropriate and inappropriate behaviour.

The practical purpose of education is to provide a means of assessment and evaluation which has a direct influence on the chances which become available to you, the key to opening the doors of your future. It is vital to the pursuit of lucre, at least for the average person with no exceptional talent. The social point of education is to provide a rounding off of experience, to enable one to meet with others, to enhance a

Budo and Education

sense of community and fellowship. This is what it is at the moment. The 80/20 rule applies, 80% of your education takes place in your home but it is the 20% of your education in formal schooling that decides 80 % of your future.

What Should Education Be?

The education system should be a place where people can explore their abilities and their potential, find out what their interests and aptitudes are, where they can be original and inventive, and where they can push their boundaries, extend their horizons and ultimately to enable people to lead a full and rich life.

People need to acquire the skills to live a constructive life for themselves and for society, but these are largely acquired through early experiences in the home. They need to earn a living, take responsibility for others, live healthily and have sufficient technical skills to understand how to respond to changing needs. Education should be a mix of individual and group oriented work, the level and pace of work tailored to each individual's learning needs, capabilities, and group work to facilitate communication skills and provide a forum for testing their ideas and receiving feedback on their understanding.

There is some idea that there is an order of learning that must be followed so that one can understand more complex ideas, but this is not necessarily the case. It is environment and experience, need or necessity that is important. Ask a six-year old who has been hospitalized for six-months or so because of some illness, and they will be able to tell you almost as much about their illness as their doctor, probably more than most nurses. In Japan, *kanji* are taught in a set order. Children are actively discouraged from learning *kanji* beyond their set curricula. The real difficulty in changing the course of any enterprise lies not in developing new ideas but in escaping from the old ones.

Education is about experiencing life, facing challenges, and finding out about yourself. In *shōrinji kempō* there is the phrase "*kyakka shōko*" which roughly means "examine the area at your feet". Most of the time, it is interpreted as arranging your shoes properly when entering a building. Actually it has a much deeper meaning, which is to start by examining yourself, who you are, why you think the way you do and act the way you do. A thorough examination of your skills and abilities may identify areas of weakness which can be fixed and areas of strength which can be enhanced. If there is anything we wish to change in a child we should first examine it to see if it is not something that could better be changed in ourselves.

This ideal is achieved by encouraging students to have original thought, to explore possibilities, rather than holding them to a defined answer. In terms of examinations it must be to allow originality and creativity, even to encourage it. More important is the attitude and thoughts of the teacher. Openness to individuality, differences in rates of learning and personality, is essential. There is a place for 'rote' learning, that is learning the basics, but this doesn't have to be in the 'Dickensian' sense.

It is best if students are presented with a problem or question and left to investigate it, sometimes individually, sometimes in groups. Then following a presentation of solutions and attempting to obtain a consensus, to present prevailing wisdom and why it is thought to be.

You can lead a horse to water, but you can't make it drink? Sometimes you can't even lead a horse to water. The secret is to make the water appealing, make the horse want to approach the water, make it realize that it is well within its capabilities to approach the water, then to make the horse think it is thirsty and make it think that water is the solution to that thirst. No matter how much you try to force a horse to drink or tell it that it needs water, the horse will not listen. If anything, it may well resist even harder. 'Horse sense' is a double edged term; it can have both a positive and a negative meaning.

There is still a place for the "this is the way it is" approach, the authoritative approach, or is there? Facts tend to be facts only in the context of their time and place. Actually, most of them are just the prevailing theories or myths. With time they are modified or dismissed. This process in the past may have taken centuries and was thus largely irrelevant, but in recent times the rate of progress is such that what we learn as fact today may very well be disproved in ten years time. On the other hand we can't precede every statement with "at this time" or "at the current state of knowledge".

Learning is achieved through the environment, that is your own state of mind or 'motivation', the thoughts and actions, the motivation and enthusiasm of the teacher, and the physical environment, the comfort, quiet and 'air' of the classroom. "Enthusiasm is infectious" is a common saying, for good reason. It is also the case that the best learning takes place when students experience directly, when they are active participants, and when they seek out information for themselves. It is best not to tell students that "this is the way it is", rather let them infer it through their experience. The most pervasive of lessons, those about respect, values, the nature of knowledge, thought processes, self-worth and expectations, are learnt from the environment, atmosphere, and interactions between teachers and students. Often we forget the things we say to students, but the students are profoundly affected by our words and they remain with them for life.

Recent Changes in Education

There have been a lot of changes in the education system (in Japan) in the last few years. In the home and in classrooms there is an increasing use of the computer and internet, so students have access to a much wider range of information much faster. In business and the professions there is an increase in the use of CPD (Continued Professional Development) schemes. There is clearly a need to continue your education to keep up with changes in the profession and therefore in the industry as a whole. There is also an element of learning a new skill outside your immediate working needs, something you might be able to use should a career change become either required or desired.

Life-long learning is a key phrase, which increasingly is taking place through new technology and media, and e-learning. The future of education probably lies in a base

Budo and Education

education in schools concentrating on developing learning skills, black box processes, information filtering skills, and social skills. Post-school education will likely be an on-demand system. You learn what you need when you need it for your job or your life.

What is *Budō*?

A definition of *budō* is problematic as it encompasses a whole range of activities. An etymological analysis of the characters for *budō* is not of much help. It suggests that the word '*bu*' means "walking to war", perhaps foot soldiers carrying a spear and that the word '*dō*' means 'path' or 'Way', but in a Taoist or Zen sense of the word. The arts themselves went through a transition from practical battlefield skills, to arts for display or entertainment, to a means of spiritual development, then to a sporting competitive activity. The terms used to describe these forms are respectively '*bujutsu*', '*bugei*', '*budō*' and '*bu-teki* sports'.

The term *budō* is often *interpreted* to mean to "stop a spear", in other words to "stop violence directed towards oneself". Sometimes an even wider interpretation is assumed in which it is given the meaning to "stop two spears", in other words to "stop conflict between other people". Actually, it doesn't really matter what the etymology of these words are. Rather it is important what meaning we give these words through our actions and activities.

Budō includes the nine *budō* recognized by the Nippon Budokan; kendo, judo, sumo, *kyūdō*, *jūkendō*, *naginata*, aikido, *shōrinji kempō*, and karate. It also includes the forerunners to these *budō*, the *koryū* or classical styles of *bujutsu*, and the offspring that is all the modern interpretations and splinter groups. This discussion is limited to Japanese *budō* but doesn't necessarily exclude other arts.

Most of the nine modern *budō* mentioned above are struggling to maintain their *budō* identity and finding a modern sporting form of their *budō*. Some, judo for example, have gone almost entirely over to sport. However, the founder of judo Kanō Jigorō defined judo (*budō*) as "*seiryoku zenyō*" and "*jita kyōei*". These are "maximum efficiency" and "mutual welfare and benefit". Similarly, the founder of *shōrinji kempō*, Sō Dōshin defined *shōrinji kempō* (*budō*) as "*jiko kakuritsu*" and "*jita kyōraku*". These are "self establishment" and "mutual happiness". Some practitioners of *shōrinji kempō* have suggested making it an Olympic sport, along the lines of ice-dance rather than boxing, but it would present an interesting problem if it were to come about. Can the religious practices of a sect (as is the case with *shōrinji kempō* become an Olympic sport?

In practice the range of benefits under the *budō* banner are said to include:

- Health, physical fitness
- Physical coordination, motor skill development
- Self defence
- Spirituality, religion
- Sport, recreation

Budo Perspectives

It is not the name of the activity or its classification but the actual nature of your actions and activities that make a difference. All of these benefits may be derived from doing *budō* but it depends entirely on the nature of the *dōjō*, which means the thoughts and actions of the instructor. This means there is also no difference from other activities and sports.

There is some convergence in the *budō* world which suggests that *budō* is an exercise which promotes self development and by implication improves society. Also as a side effect, *budō* happens to be, or at least is claimed to be, a practical means of self defence. Whether this is the case or not, again, depends on the nature of practice in the *dōjō*. Claims that it improves the health are dubious when you consider the number of middle-aged *budōka* with bad backs, knees, elbows and wrists.

What is it that makes *budō* different from sports or other activities such as rugby, aerobics, boxing, tennis, the tea ceremony, flower arranging and Nintendo? Practically there probably is no difference, but as I am a *budōka* I like to think there is. I believe the difference lies in a number of areas. Firstly, the philosophical (religious) aspect of *budō* is fundamental to daily practice. This is expressed in the rituals that one goes through in the *dōjō*, and in the ideas which lie behind the conduct expected from practitioners. Secondly, the techniques practiced are intended to cause injury to your opponent (practice partner). In what other world would you invite your opponent to kick you in the groin as hard as they can (with the express intention to avoid/block and counter)? Or take turns in strangling each other, or to apply locks to the joints which might cause serious injury or be permanently disabling? In 'normal' society one would think you would have to be deranged to practice *budō*. However, it is this high level of contact and trust inherent in *budō* that inspires deep friendships and allows one to realize your dependence on other people.

Thirdly, the intensity and concentration required in practice, brought about by its danger, is training in concentration and follow-through in your actions. Intensity and sincerity of practice is vital. Fourthly, every day, every opponent, every time you practice techniques it is different. Learning to adjust and adapt to these differences in the *dōjō* is learning to be flexible and adaptive in society and with people. Reading your opponent and finding the right or at least an effective response automatically is an important skill. Often the effectiveness of a technique depends less on your opponents' movement than on your own attitude and response. The more relaxed you are the more effective your technique regardless of your opponent's efforts.

A *dōjō* should be a place where, when you walk in you 'feel' the air is different, where you naturally become quiet and feel relaxed. This is something like the feeling one gets walking into some temples or chapels. The instructor should ideally be a person who you feel you can trust, someone to whom responsibility comes, one who is sought out for advice and help, and who is competent in one or more fields of endeavour. The roles of the instructor are warrior, priest, healer, and teacher. These roles were traditionally prescribed for a *budō* teacher and are still a valid prescription for today. *Budō* is concerned with living, the process of daily life, not with the end result as such, so in that sense it is not a religion. Or perhaps one can say that as it deals with "how you live", it is in

Budo and Education

fact a true religion, and that all the other groups claiming to be religions are merely mysticism and superstition. Judo has stayed away from religion in order to maintain its status and viability in schools. *Shōrinji kempō* adopted religious trappings to enable it to achieve legal "religious" status, and has since acquired more religious baggage to try to enhance its status with other religious groups.

The Benefits of *Budō* as a Means of Education

It is the combination of the philosophical (religious) base and the nature and intensity of practice that makes *budō* unique. It is this environment which provides an experience outside what you can normally find in society. It functions as a testing ground for 'real' life.

Certainly, Kanō considered judo (*budō*) to be a "rehearsal for life", a means of learning things of value for living your life. He recommended that we study for ourselves, and thus find the benefits of doing judo. That is the reason why it is of benefit to both ourselves and others. He stated that through sports many benefits can be gained, but he also criticised sports as being specific movements with a specific purpose, whereas judo was for all round development of the mind and body. Another comment was that the object of sport was very simplistic, but that the object of *budō* is complex and wide.

If he were to look at modern judo, what would he think? Modern judo encourages the development of one or two techniques with which to win contests but doesn't encourage overall development of the body. Kanō also stated that judo can make us more decisive, that it can help us to overcome indecision, poor judgement and lack of faith. The Kōdōkan has tried to adjust its stance recently with the "Renaissance" campaign, but the message is rather thin and disappointing:

First, let's greet each other in a loud and clear voice with "*konnichiwa*"; second, throwing cigarette butts (garbage) on the street is doing the same to your mind; third, making a friend is a lifelong treasure, always value your friends; fourth, if you see someone who is in need, gather your courage and give a helping hand; and fifth, 'Viva Judo' Let's spread Judo around the world!

I don't think there is any need to comment on this campaign. The point of *budō* is not what is "common sense" but gaining the benefits of experience in a controlled environment, creating an environment conducive to physical and mental (spiritual) growth. Encouraging us to do the right things more often, and thus to help to improve our society and lives. The things we do are like leaves on a branch. They may be different and may even deny each others existence, but they are on the same branch and trunk of human history and evolution. So perhaps *budō* is education and education is *budō*. There is a tendency in Japanese culture and certainly in *budō* to put everything into *kata* (型). Even now the Japanese often excel at activities which require this *kata* mentality, but do less well in activities which need flexibility, adaptability, and originality. This can be seen in their success in synchronised swimming and ice dance and in their failure in rugby. It is true to say that kata, whether of this fixed type or the more fluid type (形)

have a place, but too many people become stuck in the *kata* and fail to realize that it is a tool to finding something more fluid and creative. It is not the end in itself.

Budō means to strive for an ideal, your own ideal perhaps within the context of a societal ideal. One can learn to become physically and mentally tough. You can become tough enough to know when to hold on and when to let go, and tough enough to persevere when you are faced by a seemingly immovable wall. *Budō*, by the very nature of its practice, makes failure a daily experience, and so it teaches us to overcome failure and to seek out success. In fact, we often need to meet failure or be rejected in order to find the spirit to fight and overcome.

Conclusion

The education system is far from perfect, and the education we receive from our family and society is also lacking in many ways. *Budō* can serve to redress the balance to some extent by providing experience outside the normal parameters of daily life. Particularly the emphasis of reliance on other people to make progress, the trust gained by giving yourself to another person, and the atmosphere of formality and sincerity are the keys to the educational value of *budō*.

There is a large overlap with other activities, noticeably in sports, but *budō* retains its uniqueness in two ways; first, the philosophical/religious base – presenting *budō* as a "Way of life" with a code of conduct and thought, and second, the intensity of practice brought about by danger which leads to a development of trust and understanding of the importance of other people. There is also the element of communication both verbal and non-verbal. The experience of sharing pleasure and pain, of accepting responsibility for the pleasure and pain of other people both in the *dōjō* and in society at large is important. Students often get more personal instruction and advice from their *budō* instructors than they get in schools or from their parents. This is a very important consideration as instructors of *budō* are often closer to their students than the students' own parents.

It is also true to say that *budō* is not for everyone, and not everyone should be made to do it. There is a *budō* tale that says that the "best teachers are unknown, that they have to be sought out". That those who are ready for instruction will find the teacher they need. Perhaps we should avoid advertisement, avoid promoting the art, and avoid the trap of earning a living through the art.

Finally, a dilemma we all experience. We spend many hours in the *dōjō* "perfecting" ourselves, achieving "enlightenment", becoming "masters" of self-control and physical discipline. What if we spent all that time in the pursuit of lucre? We could obtain material independence, enhance the quality of our lives, afford the best schooling for our children, and contribute materially to the world. We could perhaps even remain well balanced nice people. Following this materialistic course doesn't necessarily mean we would become megalomaniacs, tycoons or tyrants. Which course is better? Or is one dependent on the other? In the past certainly, and perhaps even now to a certain extent, it is only those with time on their hands who can afford to spend time doing *budō*. Or, is it that to achieve success in the material world we need the self discipline of *budō*. Is it conceivable that we can do both? How one answers this is up to the individual, not through what they say but through what they do.

Endnotes

[1] Oxford and Cambridge Universities.
[2] Roman historian and author of Ab Urbe Condita Libri (Books from the Foundation of the City), a 142-volume history of Rome from its beginnings to 9 B.C.
[3] Roman scholar and naturalist. He wrote the 37-volume Historia Naturalis. His nephew Pliny (originally Gaius Plinius Caecilius Secundus, A.D. 62?-113?), known as "the Younger," was a consul and writer whose letters provide valuable information about Roman life.

Bibliography

Internet Resources:
"A modern term of education", www.derby.ac.uk
"Inquiry into the Purposes of Education". Scottish School Board Association, www.schoolboard-scotland.com, 10 June 2002.
"Jean-Jacques Rousseau on Education". www.infed.org
Lawn, Martin. "Arriving at the Learning Bourse: The struggle over governance, meaning and the European Education Space", 2001. http://www.keele.ac.uk/depts/ed/events/conf-pdf/cPaperLawn.pdf
Szybek, Piotr. "Meaning Constitution in Education". www.leeds.ac.uk
Yero, Judith Lloyd. "Beliefs". Teacher's Mind Resources. www.TeachersMind.com

General Publications:
Dewey, John. *Experience and Education*. Free Press, 1997.
Leggett, Trevor. P. *The Spirit of Budo: Old Traditions for Present-day Life*. London: Kegan Paul International, 1988.
Natsume Sōseki. *Ten Nights of Dream*. (Translated by Aiko Itō and Graeme Wilson). Tokyo: Charles. E. Tuttle, c1974.

Chapter 15

Off the Warpath: Military Science & *Budō* in the Evolution of *Ryūha Bugei*

Karl Friday
University of Georgia

Introduction

The conventional wisdom among scholars and exponents of Japanese martial arts (*ryūha bugei*) ties its evolution closely to the history of warfare, asserting—or rather, assuming—that systems and schools of martial arts originally developed as tools for passing on workaday battlefield skills:

Martial art schools and systems took shape in response to intensified demand for skilled fighting men spawned by the onset of the Sengoku period (1467-1568). Warriors hoping to survive and prosper in the *jakuniku-kyōshoku* (literally, "the weak are meat; the strong eat") world of late medieval battlefields began to seek instruction from talented veterans, who in turn began to codify their knowledge and methodize its study. Thus *bugei ryūha* emerged more-or-less directly from the exigencies of medieval warfare. But the two-and-a-half-century Pax Tokugawa that began in 1600 brought fundamental changes to the practice of martial arts. Instruction became professionalized, and in some cases, commercialized; training periods became longer, curricula were formalized; and elaborate systems of student ranks developed. Most significantly, however, the motives and goals underlying *bugei* practice were recast. *Bushi*, who no longer expected to spend time on the battlefield, sought and found a more relevant rationale for studying martial arts, approaching it not simply as a means to proficiency in combat, as their ancestors had, but as a means to spiritual cultivation of the self.[1]

This account begins from the logical assumption that *ryūha bugei* originated as an instrument for ordinary military training, and evolved from there into *budō*, a means to broader self-development and self-realization. That premise, reified in works like the late Donn Draeger's classic *Martial Arts and Ways of Japan* trilogy, is central to popular conceptions—including those of advanced practitioners—of the *bugei*, particularly in the West. It shapes not just ideas on martial art history, but notions of what *bugei ryūha* are, and how they should be studied, as well. It is also fundamentally misleading.

For, the conventional wisdom notwithstanding, *bugei ryūha* did not evolve in linear fashion from schools of combative arts (*bujutsu*) to systems of personal development (*budō*). *Budō* has, in fact, been a definitive element of *ryūha bugei* from its inception.

BUDO PERSPECTIVES

Ryūha Bugei & Military History

Early modern texts on swordsmanship and other martial arts describe extraordinarily complex phenomena in which various physical, technical, psychological, and philosophical factors intertwine and interact; and in which expertise in combat and spiritual illumination are not contending, or even sequential, achievements, but interdependent developments—inseparable aspects of the whole—to be experienced simultaneously. Issai Chozan's eighteenth century martial art parable, *Neko no myōjutsu* ("The cat's eerie skill"), for example, portrayed a vision of ultimate martial prowess that entailed being in such perfect harmony with the natural order that one transcended any need or desire to fight.[2]

But Issai and his mid-Tokugawa period contemporaries were scarcely the first to contend that martial training can and should reach beyond physical skills and technical expertise. Sixteenth-century instructional writings, as well as early seventeenth-century texts like Miyamoto Musashi's famous *Gorin no sho* or Yagyū Munenori's *Heihō kadensho*, suggest that this notion was already well-established during the late Sengoku era.[3] Careful consideration of the circumstances under which *ryūha bugei* first appeared, moreover, strongly suggests that these arts were *never* meant to be straightforward tools of war—that, rather, visions of martial art as a vehicle to broad personal education shaped and characterized this phenomenon from its nascence.

It is clear, first of all, that *ryūha bugei* could not have accounted for more than a tiny portion of sixteenth-century military training. Estimates based on surviving documentation from the period suggest that there were at most a few dozen *ryūha* around during the sixteenth century.[4] Armies of that era, however, regularly mobilized tens of thousands of men. The fourth battle of Kawanakajima, in 1561, for example, involved 33,000 troops on both sides; Mikatagahara, in 1572, involved 45,000; Sekigahara, in 1600, involved more than 154,000; and Hideyoshi's invasion force in his first Korean campaign numbered some 158,700 men, with a reserve force of more than 100,000.[5] Thus, in order for even a fraction of the troops who made up these forces to have learned their craft through one or more *ryūha*, each and every *ryūha* of the age would need to have trained at least several hundred students a year. *Ryūha bugei* must, therefore, have been a specialized activity, pursued by only a minute percentage of Sengoku warriors.

Nor did the skills that late medieval *bugeisha* concentrated on developing have a great deal of direct applicability to sixteenth-century warfare. In fact, even the earliest *bugei ryūha* were, at best, anachronistic in this regard.

From the eighth through the late fourteenth centuries, Japanese tactical thinking was shaped by the arts of bow and horse, which, by mid-Heian times, became the exclusive preserve of an order of professional warriors, defined by skills they cultivated on their own, using personal (and family) resources.[6]

Early medieval armies were patchwork conglomerations, assembled for specific

Off the Warpath

campaigns and demobilized immediately thereafter. Commanders, therefore, had few, if any, opportunities to drill with their troops in large-scale group tactics, and could not field integrated, well-articulated armies. Accordingly, such forces carried on with little or no direction from their commanders, once the enemy had been engaged. Even senior officers usually fought in the ranks themselves, and were seldom able to exercise much control over the contest beyond orchestrating the initial attack or defensive position. Tactical cooperation, therefore, devolved to smaller units and components. These factors, in combination with the technological limitations of their horses, bows and armour, led the early *bushi* to develop a distinctive, somewhat peculiar form of light cavalry tactics that involved individuals and small groups circling and manoeuvring around one another like dog-fighting aviators.[7]

During the fifteenth century, power continued to devolve steadily and decisively from the capital to the countryside until, in the aftermath of the Ōnin War (1467-77) only the thinnest pretext of local rule drawing its legitimacy from a central governing authority remained. The province-wide jurisdictions of the *shugo-daimyō* (military governors ruling under the authority of the Muromachi Shogunate) broke apart into smaller territories controlled by a new class of local hegemon. These *daimyō* ruled all-but autonomous satrapies whose borders coincided with the area that they—and the lesser warriors whose loyalties they commanded—could dominate by force.

One effect of this new political reality was a shift in the purpose of war. For the first time in the history of the *bushi* the primary strategic objective of warfare became the capture or defence of territory. At the same time, the armies fielded by the emerging hegemonies were increasingly composed of contingents of fighting men bound to their commanders by standing obligations to service, rather than by short-term contractual promises of rewards. These developments transformed *bushi* from mercenaries to soldiers and refocused their attention on contributing to the success of the group rather than on distinguishing themselves as individuals.

The changing makeup and goals of late medieval armies in turn concomitantly made possible and demanded increasingly disciplined group tactical manoeuvre, and an enhanced role for infantry. Faced with a new strategic imperative to capture or defend specific geographic areas, and armed with a growing ability to drill and discipline troops and therefore to field versatile, articulated armies, Japanese commanders now shaped their tactics around companies of archers—and later gunners—utilized to break enemy formations, which could then be chased from the field by pike-men.[8]

Thus *ryūha bugei*, which focused on developing prowess in personal combat, emerged and flourished in almost inverse proportion to the value of skilled individual fighters on the battlefield. Moreover, the weapon that played the most prominent role in this new phenomenon—the sword—played a decidedly minor role in medieval warfare.

Swords never became a key battlefield armament in Japan. They were, rather, supplementary weapons, analogous to the side-arms worn by modern soldiers. While they were also employed in combat, they were used far more often in street fights, robberies, assassinations and other (off-battlefield) civil disturbances. Missile weapons—arrows, rocks, and later bullets—dominated battles, throughout the medieval period.

Scholars and popular audiences alike have shown a remarkable reluctance to accept this reality, and have tended instead, to confound the *symbolic* importance of the sword to early modern *bushi* identity with prominence in medieval battles. Historians, while acknowledging that the early *bushi* were created and defined by the skills of bow and horse, have been both dedicated and creative in their efforts to identify a point at which swords displaced bows as the *bushi*'s weapon of choice. Three hypotheses dominate this discussion. None, however, stands up well to scrutiny.

In the early 1960s, Ishii Susumu and others contended that the Gempei War, in the 1180s, marked a turning point in battlefield tactics. Basing his analysis primarily on the battle accounts in *Heike monogatari* and related literary works, Ishii argued that while late twelfth-century warriors continued to fight as individuals and on horseback, they no longer engaged in the galloping archery duels favoured by their forebears. Instead, they confronted one another at more intimate range, using swords or even grappling techniques to unseat opponents, whom they would then finish off on the ground, with daggers.[9]

More reliable sources however, make it clear that while tactics such as swordplay and grappling from horseback might have *augmented* traditional ones in some large battles, they did not supplant them. Even in the literary war tales, all such incidents occur during the final stages of large battles, at points when the warriors involved had exhausted their arrow supplies and one side or the other was in retreat.[10]

This is scarcely surprising, when one considers how ill suited early medieval swords and armour were to mounted swordplay. It would, to begin with, have been no easy task to close to sword range on horseback, against a mounted adversary armed with bow and arrows. Cutting or stabbing through the heavy *ōyoroi* favoured by Heian and Kamakura warriors, with the slender, short-hilted *tachi* of the era—or even walloping an antagonist with sufficient force to unhorse him— presented a still more formidable challenge, particularly for a warrior whose balance, striking power and freedom of movement were impeded by the rigid, boxy cuirass and loose-hanging shoulder plates of his own armour. Simply knocking the opponent to the ground would not, moreover, have concluded the contest; the warrior himself would have had to dismount, to finish off the opponent with sword or dagger. But repetition of that sort of tactic—which Ishii envisioned as the prevailing form of combat in Gempei battles—would have rapidly exhausted even the hardiest warrior, for his armour added nearly half again to his own body weight. It would also have given the warrior's horse ample opportunity to scamper off, converting him to a foot soldier for the duration of the fray.

Swords were, in fact, rarely employed except under circumstances in which warriors could not use their bows. One searches in vain for a single battlefield example of Heian or Kamakura warriors voluntarily forsaking bow and arrow to fight one another hand-to-hand. All *bushi* carried long swords (*tachi*), as well as shorter, companion blades

Off the Warpath

(*katana*), and trained at grappling; but they viewed these weapons as supplements to their bows and arrows, never as replacements for them. Kamakura warriors were still, by preference and for good reason, first and foremost bowmen on horseback. *Azuma kagami* makes this point explicitly in an entry from 1180:

> "While [Matano] Kagehisa and his retainers camped in the hills north of Mt. Fuji, rats gnawed and ruined over a hundred of their heavy-duty bowstrings. At this inopportune time, Yasuda Saburō Yoshihisa; Kudō Kagemitsu; his son, Kojirō Yukimitsu; and the Ichikawa Intendent, Yukifusa, having heard of the battle at Ishibashi, had set forth from Kai to join it, when they met up with Kagehisa and his men at Mt. Hashida. Wheeling their mounts and letting fly arrows, they attacked Kagehisa. The hour of the fray had come! Their bowstrings severed, Kagehisa and his men unsheathed their swords and brandished them, but they could not thus contend against arrows and stones. . . . Kagehisa cast away his pride and fled like lightning."[11]

Mounted archers continued to take the forefront in Gempei War battles. They also featured prominently in later Kamakura conflicts, including the Ōshū Campaign, the Wada Rebellion, the Jōkyū War, and the Mongol Invasions.[12]

Nevertheless, several prominent historians, including Satō Shin'ichi and Amino Yoshihiko, have argued that exposure to Mongol tactics and military organization led to a change in the mode of combat in subsequent Japanese warfare. The mounted professional warriors, fighting as individuals with bow and arrow that had dominated Heian and Kamakura era battlefields were, they maintain, superseded from this point onward by massed infantries armed with bladed weapons.[13] Popular literature, moreover, sometimes equates the Mongol experience even more directly with the development of swords and swordsmanship on the battlefield.[14]

While it is true that literary accounts, such as *Taiheiki*, do feature swords rather prominently, recent studies have persuasively undermined many of our long-cherished presumptions about fourteenth-century warfare. The most compelling evidence on this point comes from analyses of statistics on wounds, compiled from battle reports. Thomas Conlan looked at 1302 such documents, cataloguing 721 identifiable wounds. Of these, arrows caused some 73%, while only 25% were the result of sword strokes, and fewer than 2% involved spears. Suzuki Masaya examined 175 such documents, and found that nearly 87% of the 554 identifiable casualties reported therein came from arrows, 8% were caused by swords or *naginata*, just under 3% were the result of troops having been struck by rocks, and 1% were caused by spears. Shakadō Mitsuhiro's less extensive survey of some thirty battle reports indicates that 82% of the wounds were caused by arrows.[15]

It would seem, then, that there was no fourteenth-century military revolution comparable to the upheavals sweeping through the political, social and economic structures during the period. Significant innovations in weaponry and military organization notwithstanding, strategic and tactical thinking continued along predominantly the same lines they had followed since the eighth century.

Perhaps the most intriguing attempt to reconcile the prominence of swordsmanship in sixteenth-century *ryūha bugei* with the conduct of battle links an enhanced role for the sword to the introduction of the gun. This thesis, advanced by Tominaga Kengō, Imamura Yoshio, Nakabayashi Shinji, and others, argues that firearms rendered even the heaviest of armours superfluous, leading to a switch to light-weight armours, which increased both the wearer's speed and agility, as well as his vulnerability to sword strikes. Guns are further said to have induced opposing hosts to close with one another as rapidly as possible, which, in combination with the enormous armies of the period, made late sixteenth-century battlefields more crowded, and thereby forced combatants to engage at closer quarters more than ever before. This, goes the argument, boosted the appeal of swords over larger weapons like spears and *naginata*, which required more space to wield effectively.[16]

There is a tantalizing irony—and hence, a powerful natural attraction for scholars and aficionados of martial arts—to the notion that diffusion of a modern, foreign weapon like firearms led to greater use of an ancient, Japanese weapon like the sword. New scholarship on military history, however, refutes both its premises. A revised view, formulated by Fujimoto Masayuki, Nawa Yumio, Suzuki Masaya, Udagawa Takehisa, and others, asserts that guns did *not* revolutionize sixteenth-century warfare; that hand-to-hand combat with bladed weapons (*hakuhei-sen*) did *not* play a pivotal role in late Sengoku battles; and that swords were rarely the first weapon of choice when troops *did* engage at close quarters.[17]

Once again, some of the most compelling evidence supporting these conclusions comes from analyses of casualty reports. Suzuki found that of the 620 battle wounds recorded in the documents he examined for the period of 1501 to 1560, arrows inflicted 380, spears 133, stones (thrown by hand or by sling) caused 100, and only 21 were caused by swords. For the period of 1563 to 1600—after the introduction of the gun—584 reported casualties break down to 263 gunshot victims, 126 men wounded by arrows, 99 wounded by spears, 40 victims of sword wounds or "cutting injuries" (*kiri kizu*), 30 men struck by rocks, and 26 troops injured by combinations of the foregoing weapons—including one unfortunate who was shot by both bullets and arrows *and* stabbed with a spear! Similarly, Thomas Conlan's analysis of 1291 casualty reports from the fifteenth and sixteenth centuries reveals 179 deaths—for which no cause was reported—439 arrow wounds, 343 gunshot wounds, 192 spear wounds, 79 injuries caused by stones, and 50 sword cuts.[18]

In other words, both studies roughly agree that missile weapons (bullets, arrows and rocks) accounted for 75% of the casualties reported during the pre-firearm era and 73% of the casualties occurring after the popularization of guns. Sword wounds, by contrast, amounted to just 5% of the casualties for both periods.

Off the Warpath

Ryūha Bugei & Budō

It would seem, then, that current scholarship on late medieval military history raises several thorny questions about the goals and purposes of sixteenth-century *ryūha*: Why did *bugei ryūha* emerge when they did—at a time when generalship, the ability to organize and direct large forces, was rapidly coming to overshadow personal martial skills as the decisive element in battle, and the key to a successful military career? Why were there so few *ryūha* around during the Sengoku period, and why did they proliferate so rapidly during the early Tokugawa period, *after* the age of wars had passed? And why was swordsmanship— an art that was, at best, of tertiary value to warriors in battle—play so prominent a role in even the earliest *bugei ryūha*?

All these questions become much easier to answer if one sets aside the premise that *bugei ryūha* originated as instruments for teaching the workaday techniques of the battlefield. And indeed, there is little basis for that hoary assumption, beyond the fact that war was endemic in Japan when the first martial art schools appeared. The received wisdom rests, in other words, on what amounts to a *post hoc ergo prompter hoc* fallacy.

A growing body of evidence, on the other hand, points to the conclusion that *ryūha bugei* and the pedagogical devices associated with it aimed from the start at conveying more abstract ideals of self-development and enlightenment. That is, there was no fundamental shift of purpose in martial art education between the late sixteenth and mid-seventeenth centuries. Tokugawa period *budō* represented not a metamorphosis of late medieval martial art, but the maturation of it. *Ryūha bugei* itself constituted a new phenomenon—a derivative, not a linear improvement, of earlier, more prosaic military training.

Military training and the profession of arms in Japan stretches back to the dawn of recorded history and beyond. Until well into the Muromachi period, however, warrior training and military technique centred on individual families. Some house traditions, like that of the Hidesato-ryū Fujiwara, had become famous and well-respected by late Heian times; and one finds scattered references in Kamakura period sources to teachers of mounted archery. In the early fifteenth century, moreover, Ogasawara Mochinaga and at least two generations of his descendents served as hereditary archery instructors to the Ashikaga shoguns.[19]

Nevertheless, the first true *bugei ryūha* appeared around the turn of the sixteenth century. This timing is significant, for it marks the emergence of martial art schools as part of a broader trend toward systemization of knowledge and instruction in various artistic pursuits. During the Muromachi period, virtuosos of calligraphy, flower arranging, music, drama, painting, and the like began to think of their approaches to their arts as packages of information that could be transmitted to students in organized patterns, and to certify students' mastery of the teachings with licenses and diplomas.[20]

The nascent *bugei ryūha* appropriated the forms, teaching methods, and vocabulary of these other applied arts. More importantly, however, the martial and other arts also shared a sense of ultimate—true—purpose, defined in the medieval Japanese concept of *"michi,"* or "path." This construct, born of implications drawn from a worldview common to Buddhism, Taoism and Confucianism, saw expertise in activities of all sorts—from games and sports to fine arts, from practical endeavours to religious practice—as possessing a universality deriving from its relationship to a common, ultimate goal. It held concentrated specialization in any activity to be an equally valid route to attainment of "universal Truth", asserting that all true paths must lead eventually to the same place, and that therefore complete mastery of even the most trivial of pursuits must yield the same rewards as can be found through the most profound. *Ryūha bugei*, emerging within this cultural and philosophical milieu, took its place alongside poetry composition, incense judging, noh drama, the tea ceremony, and numerous other medieval *michi*.[21]

Considered in this context, it becomes apparent that Iizasa Chōisai, Sōma Sadakuni, Aisu Ikōsai, Tsukahara Bokuden, Kamiizumi Ise-no-kami, and other pioneers of *ryūha bugei* were seeking and developing something related to, but *not* synonymous with, military training *per se*. That this new form of martial education was never meant to become boot camp, or even advanced schooling, for the rank and file of medieval armies is clear from the relative numbers involved. And the involvement of men of low social status, like Miyamoto Musashi, demonstrates that it could not simply have been instruction for officers or other elites, either.

In their quest for perfection of skill in the arts of individual combat, Chōisai, Sadakuni, Bokuden, Musashi and their fellow *bugeisha* were military anachronisms, out of step with the changing face of warfare in their times. And in their pursuit of this quest through *musha shūgyō* and other ascetic regimens—their devotion to their arts over conventional military careers and service—they were self-indulgent and quixotic.

None of this, however, detracted from the value or the appeal of what they were doing, for *ryūha bugei* was an abstraction of military science, not merely an application of it. It fostered character traits and tactical acumen that made those who practiced it better warriors, but its goals and ideals were more akin to those of liberal education than vocational training. That is, *bugeisha*, even during the Sengoku period, had more in common with Olympic marksmanship competitors—training with specialized weapons to develop esoteric levels of skill under particularized conditions—than with Marine riflemen. They also had as much—perhaps more—in common with Tokugawa period and modern martial artists than with the ordinary warriors of their own day.[22]

Viewed in this light, the prominent role of the sword in medieval *ryūha bugei* is much easier to understand. For, their secondary role in battlefield combat notwithstanding, swords achieved a singular status as heirlooms and symbols of power, war, military skill and warrior identity. The elegantly curved, two-handed *Nihontō* was born about the same time as the *bushi* order itself, and came, during the early modern era, to be identified as "the soul of the *bushi*." Swords, as emblems of power, appear in the earliest Japanese mythology, and were regularly presented by medieval warrior leaders as gifts

Off the Warpath

or rewards to their followers. By the Muromachi period, expressions like "clash of swords" (*tachi uchi*, *katana uchi*, or *uchi tachi*), or "wield a sword" (*tachi tsukamatsurare*) were recognized as generic appellations for combat, irrespective of the actual weapons employed.[23]

Thus swordsmanship represented a symbolic *sine qua non* of personal combat: the favoured weapon for off-battlefield duelling, and a kind of *michi* within a *michi* for *bugeisha*, then as now. This representational function is reflected in the popularization of the term "*hyōhō*" (or "*heihō*")—which, until late medieval times, designated military science or martial arts in the broad sense—as a synonym for *kenjutsu*.[24]

The special place and nature of *ryūha bugei* as abstract personal education, rather than workaday military drill, was precisely the reason it was able to evolve so rapidly during the early decades of the Tokugawa period.

The most conspicuous developments—the specialization in weaponry, the formalization of training, the lengthening of apprenticeships, the expansion of the *budō* ideal, the exponential proliferation of new *ryūha*, the increasingly cabalistic dedication to principles (*ryūgi*) that uniquely defined each school, and the like—did not involve abandonment or betrayal of earlier warrior legacies. They merely represented logical evolutions within one particular legacy. Specialization, formalization, and idealization of *ryūha bugei* were not inherently deleterious to military preparedness, because this form of martial training had never been about readying troops for war. Military science writ large continued in the guise of *gungaku*, while *hyōhō* continued to focus on personal development.

Nevertheless, the cumulative effect of decade after decade of peace took an inevitable—and well-studied—toll on *bushi* battle worth. By the eighteenth century, it was having a concomitant effect on contemporary perceptions of the *bugei* as well. *Bushi*, who had not made or even trained seriously for war in generations, had lost sight of any separation between martial art and military training. Indeed, *ryūha bugei* had long since overshadowed and supplanted other kinds of soldierly drill. For the *bushi* of the mid-Tokugawa period and later, there was but one form of sophisticated combative training: the individual-centred, self-development-oriented arts of the various *ryūha*.

This evolution in perspective was, no doubt, exacerbated by government exhortations and policies that encouraged *bushi* to believe that only minor differences of circumstance distinguished them from their medieval forebears. One important result was the conviction that the swordsmanship and other martial arts of the day descended directly from instruments of war, and that *bugei ryūha* originated as vehicles to train warriors for battle.

Pundits and scholars ever since have evaluated Tokugawa (and later) martial arts in this light. In consequence, they have directed a great deal of what is ultimately unreasonable—even irrelevant—criticism at late Tokugawa period *bugei*, lamenting their inapplicability to the conditions of medieval battlefields, without realizing that the arts from which they grew were *never* directly appropriate to battle.

Appraising *ryūha bugei* in terms of its utility to warfare and military science is, however, not merely unfair, it is counter-productive to understanding what really happened during the Tokugawa period, and what these arts and schools really were—and are today. By recognizing that *ryūha bugei* began as an activity that was both more and less than mundane military training, it becomes apparent that the modifications and innovations of the early modern era represented progress and sophistication, rather than deviation from or degeneration of the original goals and purpose. The proliferation of these arts, and the extent to which Tokugawa *bushi* substituted them for other forms of military training, were little more than ancillary phenomena to the broader, underlying changes sweeping through warrior society. The evolution of what scholars today term *budō* was a consequence or a symptom—not a cause—of declining war-readiness among the *bushi*.

Ironically, the martial arts today are closer in role and character—particular in their *perceived* role and character—to their remote medieval progenitors than to their late Tokugawa period parents. By rendering the weaponry of the traditional *bugei* all but worthless on the battlefield, the modern transformation of warfare has restored—and dramatically magnified—the boundaries that originally separated martial art from military drill. Because they can no longer harbor any illusions that they are training for war, modern *budōka* need no longer be troubled by many of the doubts and criticisms that plagued their Tokugawa period counterparts. They can freely and unapologetically embrace the objectives that drove their medieval forebears: the quest for perfection of skill in personal combat, and through this, the physical and spiritual cultivation of the self.

Conclusion: History & *Budō* in the West

I have been arguing that prevailing conceptions of *budō* history—which ascribe the origins of *bugei ryūha* to the demands of medieval battlefields, and portray early modern developments as a fundamental transformation of the *bugei* from arts of war to arts of self-perfection—are in error; and that the evolution of *ryūha bugei* was considerably more linear than the received wisdom recognizes. I have tried to establish this by showing how ill suited *ryūha bugei* was to Sengoku era warfare, as military historians now envision it.

In place of the standard narrative, I have suggested that *ryūha bugei* represented a distinct phenomenon from workaday military training—that it was, from its very inception, something closely akin to what we now call *budō*. This, I contend, renders inapposite much contemporaneous and modern criticism of Tokugawa period martial arts, and implies a closer commonality of purpose between medieval, early modern, and modern *bugeisha* than is generally realized or acknowledged.

In closing, I would like to offer some brief thoughts concerning the implications of this position for *budō* education today.

Among the most interesting of recent developments in this field is the attempt to

Off the Warpath

export traditional—*koryū*—arts to places and cultures outside Japan. This endeavour is fraught with challenges, ranging from the logistical to the philosophical. Many of the most formidable ones, however, derive from fundamental misunderstandings, on the part of foreign audience, of what *ryūha* and *koryū bugei* are. Of these, two in particular are closely germane to the points I have been discussing in this paper, inasmuch as both are fostered—rationalized and reinforced, if not necessarily caused—by faulty conceptions and analyses of *budō* history.

Despite repeated explanations, clarifications, and arguments from scholars and exponents of *koryū bugei* traditions—including some of the participants in this conference—European and American martial arts aficionados have been stubbornly resistant to grasping two fundamental precepts that seem to be intuitively accepted by Japanese audiences. The first is that *ryūha* are *systems* of martial arts, not merely teaching organizations, or collections of techniques. The second is that they are tightly controlled, *proprietary* packages of teachings.

In both cases, the resistance to comprehension seems to stem largely from a reluctance to accept certain practical implications of these precepts, particularly with regard to the accessibility of instruction. Mustering an otherwise admirable sense of democratic ideals, Western *budō* enthusiasts decry the rarity, outside Japan, of authorized teachers of *koryū* arts, and turn for resolution to eclectic patterns of study.

Often, this entails a kind of serial monogamy in which the student trains, for periods ranging from a few weeks to a few years, in multiple arts and schools, one after the other. While this pattern is usually a response to changing logistical circumstances—relocations of instructors or of the students themselves—it is nevertheless counter-productive to the deep, cabalistic mastery of *ryūgi* that defines traditional *budō* education. A more troubling phenomenon involves the zeal with which some prospective students embrace problematic sources of instruction, including unauthorized or unqualified teachers, and even self-study using books or videotapes![25]

The most intriguing aspect of these trends is not the practices themselves—for variations on both have also occurred in Japan for almost as long as there have been *bugei ryūha*—but the arguments formulated to rationalize and legitimate them. Curiously, such argumentation is advanced not just by people engaged in these practices, but by individuals affiliated with authentic *budō* organizations, as well. Some lines of reasoning are simply facetious: that the *ryūha* has no legal authority through which to control the use of its name or its teaching; or that Japanese customs and practices do not apply overseas, because instruction there can never fully approximate instruction in Japan anyway.[26]

Others, however, appeal to conceptions of *ryūha* and *bugei* history that relate directly to the questions I have taken up in this paper. At the core of these lies an anachronistic vision of turning back the proverbial clock—of not just embracing the goals of late medieval martial art, but of reviving its pedagogical forms and methods as well. Tokugawa period developments, this line of reasoning begins, represent a degeneration of *ryūha bugei*. *Ryūha* became formalized and cabalistic; their arts, long

259

untested on the battlefield, became artificial and unrealistic; and their exponents became fixated on preservation and imitation, rather than innovation and re-creation. Therefore, the argument contends, martial art enthusiasts today who hop from *ryūha* to *ryūha*, collecting and mixing techniques as they see fit, are simply reaching back past the clutter of Tokugawa period decadence, to study *budō* as the best of their medieval and early modern forebears did.[27]

The conclusions that I have argued demonstrate that this argument has both feet firmly planted on false analogies. First, it mischaracterizes the process by which Sengoku and Tokugawa period *bushi* created new *ryūha*. Such men did not simply wander from teacher to teacher, collecting and combining bits and pieces of technique. They amalgamated them into unique—and coherent—*systems*, combining instruction received, with real experience acquired from duelling or participation in battle. The absence of this latter sort of experience and testing in and of itself marks a critical difference between modern *bugei* enthusiasts and the warriors they claim to be emulating.

Second, and perhaps more importantly, the formalization of *ryūgi* and other Tokugawa period developments are more properly viewed as refinements of medieval *ryūha bugei* than as corruptions of it. The wisdom of abandoning them is, therefore, all the more questionable.

For if there was no fundamental shift of purpose in martial art education during the Tokugawa period—if Sengoku period martial artists were already in quest of the same goals as their early modern descendents—resurrecting medieval pedagogical practices would merely restore the arts to a more primitive form, not a more pristine one. That is, in addition to being problematically and conveniently *selective*—inasmuch as it lacks corroborative experience with actual combat—any such reconstruction would be less akin to forsaking Hip Hop music in favour of Beethoven, than to removing central heating and electric lighting from concert halls. Clearly, then, invocations of lofty sentiments like *fukko* ("Restore the Past!") can yield little value as justifications for ignoring inconvenient features of *ryūha* traditions.

Recognizing that *ryūha bugei* has *always* centred on martial *arts* rather than military technique calls, in the final analysis, for a renewed emphasis on historical-mindedness among teachers and students, as well as scholars, of Japanese martial arts. And it imposes an additional layer of caution on efforts to evaluate the features that came to characterize *budō* practice during the Tokugawa period—including the cabalism, the exclusivity, and the obligations attendant to *ryūha* membership.

Endnotes

[1] See for example, the treatments of *bugei* history in Tominaga Kengo, *Kendō gohyakunen-shi*; Imamura Yoshio, "Budōshi gaisetsu," in *Nihon budō taikei*, ed. Imamura Yoshio, et al., pp. 5-28; Nakabayashi Shinji, "Kendō shi," in Nihon kobudō taikei <vol. 10>, ed. Imada Yoshio et al., pp. 29-132; Donn F Draeger, *The Martial Arts and Ways of Japan*, vol. 1,

Off the Warpath

Classical Bujutsu; The Martial Arts and Ways of Japan, vol. 2, *Classical Budō*; G. Cameron Hurst, III, *Armed Martial Arts of Japan: Swordsmanship & Archery*; Karl Friday and Seki Humitake, *Legacies of the Sword: the Kashima-Shinryū & Bushi Martial Culture*.

[2] Issai Chozan, "Neko no myōjutsu" in *Budō no meicho*, ed. Watanabe Ichirō, pp. 10-16. For more on this text in English, see Karl Friday, "The Cat's Eerie Skill: a Translation of Issai Chozan's Neko no Myōjustu," in *Keiko Shokon*, ed. Diane Skoss, pp. 17-34; Karl Friday, "Beyond Valor & Bloodshed: the Arts of War as a Path to Serenity" in *Knight and Samurai: Actions and Images of Elite Warriors in Europe and East Asia*, ed. Rose Marie Diest in collaboration with Harald Kleinschmidt (Kümmerle Verlag, Germany: Göppingen, 2003), pp. 1-13.

[3] For examples of sixteenth century *bugei* instructional texts, see Tsukahara Bokuden's *Ikunsho* (also called *Bokuden hyakushu*), reproduced in *Nihon budō taikei* vol. 3, pp. 58-66. Fuller discussions of martial art texts can be found in Friday, *Legacies*, pp. 137-51; Ishioka Hisao, *Heihōsha no seikatsu*, pp. 77-92; Imamura Yoshio, *Budōka senshū*; and Ōmori Nobumasa, *Bujutsu densho no kenkyū*. For examples of other early texts, see Watanabe Ichirō's *Budō no meicho*, and *Nihon budō taikei*.

[4] Imamura Yoshio, "Budōshi gaisetsu", pp. 12-15, identifies 39 core *hyōgaku, kyūjutsu, bujutsu, kenjutsu, sōjutsu, hōjutsu, and jūjutsu ryūha* which evolved, by late Tokugawa times, into some 1189 distinct schools.

[5] Suzuki Susumu, *Nihon kassenshi hyakubanashi*, p. 150, 166; Takayanagi Mitsutoshi and Suzuki Tōru, *Nihon kassenshi*, p. 260; Mary Elizabeth Berry, *Hideyoshi*, p. 209.

[6] For more on the origins and early development of the warrior class, see Karl Friday, *Hired Swords: The Rise of Private Warrior Power in Early Japan*.

[7] For details, see Karl Friday, *Samurai, Warfare and the State in Early Medieval Japan*, pp. 102-5.

[8] Karl Friday, "Kisha no ayumi no ikkōsatsu: chūsei Nihon ni okeru kokka to bunka to gijutsu", pp. 21-35.

[9] Ishii Susumu, *Kamakura bakufu*, pp. 117-25. Ishii's conclusions rapidly became the received wisdom on this issue, and remained so until very recently. See, for example, Nishimata Fusō, "Kassen no rūru to manaa", pp. 146-47; or Abe Takeshi, *Kamakura bushi no sekai*, pp. 190-96.

[10] Kondō Yoshikazu appears to have been the first scholar to make this observation; see Kondō Yoshikazu, *Yumiya to tōken: chūsei kassen no jitsuzō*, pp. 187-97. It is also worth recalling that the anecdotes in the various war tales concerning the behaviour of individual warriors, during the closing stages of battles, are the portions of the texts most heavily shaped by later raconteurs—and therefore the least reliable sections of the tales.

[11] *Azuma kagami* 1180 8/25.

[12] *Azuma kagami* 1180 8/26, 1180 12/1, 1184 2/5, 1184 2/7, 1189 8/8, 1189 8/10, 1189 9/9, 1213 5/2, 1213 5/3, 1221 6/12, 1221 6/14; *Mōko shūrai ekotoba*, Nihon no emaki, ed. Komatsu Shigemi, vol. 13. See also Thomas Conlan, *In Little Need of Divine Intervention: Scrolls of the Mongol Invasions of Japan*, which features English translations of many of the main sources for information of the Mongol Invasions.

[13] Satō Shin'ichi, *Nambokuchō no dōran*, pp. 194-95; Amino Yoshihiko, *Mōko shūrai*, pp. 372-73. Satō's and Amino's positions have been restated repeatedly by subsequent scholars; see, for example, Seki Yukihiko, "'Bu' no kōgen: kōchū to yumiya" in Fukuda Toyohiko's *Ikusa*, pp. 1-38.

[14] See, for example, I. Bottomly and A.P. Hopson, *Arms and Armour of the Bushi: the History*

of Weaponry in Ancient Japan p. 49; Gregory Irvine, *The Japanese Sword: the Soul of the Bushi*, pp. 36-38; Clive Sinclaire, *Bushi: the Weapons & Spirit of the Japanese Warrior*, p. 45.

[15] Thomas Conlan, "State of War: the Violent Order of Fourteenth Century Japan" p. 65; Suzuki Masaya, *Katana to kubi-tori: Sengoku kassen isetsu*, pp. 78-80; Shakadō Mitsuhiro, "Nambokuchō ki kassen ni okeru senshō", pp. 27-39, pp. 37-38.

[16] Tominaga Kengo, *Kendō gohyakunen-shi*, pp. 47-53; Imamura Yoshio, "Budōshi gaisetsu", pp. 8-10; Nakabayashi Shinji, "Kendō shi" pp. 38-39; Kiyota Minoru, *Kendō Its Philosophy, History and Means to Personal Growth*, pp. 40-43; Hurst, *Armed Martial Arts of Japan*, 38-41.

[17] Fujimoto Masayuki, *Sengoku kassen no jōshiki ga wakaru hon*; Nawa Yumio, *Nagashino Shitaragahara kassen no shinjitsu*; Udagawa Takehisa, *Teppō to sengoku kassen*; Suzuki Masaya, *Teppō to Nihonjin: "teppō shinwa" ga kakushite kita koto*; also, *Teppōtai to kiba gundan*; Suzuki Masaya, *Sengoku kassen no kyojitsu*.

[18] Suzuki Masaya, *Teppō to Nihonjin: "teppō shinwa" ga kakushite kita koto*, pp. 163-83; Thomas Conlan, "Innovation or Application? The Role of Technology in War".

[19] *Azuma kagami* 1187 8/15, 1190 4/7, 1237 7/19. Futaki Ken'ichi, *Chūsei buke no sakuhō*, pp. 16-18. Futaki maintains that Mochinaga's was not the same Ogasawara house or the same archery tradition as the Ogasawara-ryū of the Edo period, in spite of claims by the latter to this effect. The Muromachi era Ogasawara house, he notes, was from the Kyoto area, while the Edo period house was from Shinano. For background on the Hidesato-ryū Fujiwara, see Noguchi Minoru, *Bandō bushidan no seiritsu to hatten*, pp. 16-46; Friday, *Hired Swords*, pp. 88-91.

[20] Nakabayashi Shinji, "Kendō shi," pp. 42-44; Friday, *Legacies*, pp. 14-15.

[21] Konishi Jin'ichi, *Nihon koten*, vol. 3, *Michi: chūsei no rinen*; Ueda Makoto, *Literary and Art Theories in Japan*; Robert Eno, *The Confucian Creation of Heaven: Philosophy and the Defense of Ritual Mastery*, pp. 64-66; Friday, *Legacies*, pp. 16-17.

[22] This was not the first time that *bushi* had embraced ritualized or symbolic forms of military exercises. The *yabusame* mounted archery demonstrations and competitions of the early medieval period also followed formats that put a premium on skills only abstractly related to the demands of Kamakura era battlefields. See Noguchi Minoru, "Ikusa to girei" in *Ikusa*, editor, Fukuda Toyohiko, pp. 130-53; Nakazawa Katsuaki, *Chūsei no buryoku to jōkaku*; Futaki Ken'ichi, *Chūsei buke no sakuhō*; Takahashi Masaaki, "Nihon chūsei no sentō: yasen no kijōsha o chūshin ni" in *Tatakai no shisutemu to taigai senryaku (Jinrui ni totte tatakai to ha #2)*, ed. Matsugi Takehiko and Udakawa Takehisa, pp. 193-224; Kondō Yoshikazu, *Chūsei-teki bugu no seiritsu to bushi*.

[23] See, for example, *Kojiki* v. 19 or 35; *Azuma kagami* 1203 10/10. Suzuki, *Katana to kubitori*, pp. 35-36.

[24] Tominaga Kengo, *Kendō gohyakunen-shi*, pp. 20-23; Ishioka Hisao, *Heihōsha no seikatsu*, pp. 10-23.

[25] The Katori Shintō-ryū and the Kashima-Shinryū, for example, have experienced multiple incidents in which unauthorized individuals have claimed to be teaching their arts overseas. Some of these mountebanks have, in fact, become quite famous.

[26] Fuller discussions of this sort of argument, as well as examples of similar views, can be found in Karl Friday, *The Whole Legitimacy Thing*. 2000 <http://koryu.com/library/kfriday1.html>; Dave Lowry, Bicycles and Budo, a Look at Koryu "Snobbery" 2003 <http://www.e-budo.com/html/snobb.htm>; and in the discussions surrounding them on E-budo.com and the Japanese Sword Art Mailing List (http://www.e-budo.

com/vbulletin/showthread.php?s=&threadid=6146&; http://www.e-budo.com/vbulletin/showthread.php?s=&threadid=312&; http://www.e-budo.com/vbulletin/showthread.php?s=&threadid=307&; or http://www.e-budo.com/vbulletin/showthread.php?s=&threadid=21592; http://listserv.uoguelph.ca/cgi-bin/wa?a1=ind0006&L=iaido-l#75).
See also the discussion on the Japanese Sword Art Mailing List archived at: http://listserv.uoguelph.ca/cgi-bin/wa?A2=ind0306&L=iaido-l&F=&S=&P=7474.
[27] For recent examples of this line of argument, see Michael Castellani, Re: Kenjutsu dojo in UK, 6/25 2003, on Japanese Sword Art Mailing List (archived at http://listserv.uoguelph.ca/cgi-bin/wa?A2=ind0306&L=iaido-l&F=&S=&P=8009) or Jack Bieler, Re: Kenjutsu dojo in UK, 6/26 2003, on the Japanese Sword Art Mailing List (archived at http://listserv.uoguelph.ca/cgi-bin/wa?A2=ind0306&L=iaido-l&F=&S=&P=9291).

Bibliography

Abe Takeshi. *Kamakura bushi no sekai* (The world of the Kamakura *bushi*). Tōkyōdō Shuppan, 1994.
Amino Yoshihiko. *Mōko shūrai* (The Mongol invasions). (*Nihon no rekishi*, vol. 10). Shogakukan, 1974.
Bottomly, I. and Hopson, A.P. *Arms and Armour of the Bushi: the History of Weaponry in Ancient Japan*. New York: Crescent Books, 1988.
Conlan, Thomas. *In Little Need of Divine Intervention: Scrolls of the Mongol Invasions of Japan*. Cornell University, 2001.
"Innovation or Application? The Role of Technology in War," paper presented at the Association for Asian Studies Annual Meeting, 13 March Boston, MA, 1999.
"State of War: the Violent Order of Fourteenth Century Japan" (Ph. D. diss., Stanford, CA, Stanford University, 1998.
Berry, Mary. *Hideyoshi*. Harvard University Press, 1982.
Draeger, Donn F. *The Martial Arts and Ways of Japan*, vol. 1, *Classical Bujutsu*. New York: Weatherhill, 1973.
The Martial Arts and Ways of Japan, vol. 2, *Classical Budo*, New York: Weatherhill, 1973.
Eno, Robert. *The Confucian Creation of Heaven: Philosophy and the Defense of Ritual Mastery*. State University of New York Press, 1990.
Friday, Karl. *Samurai, Warfare and the State in Early Medieval Japan*. London: Routledge, 2004.
"Kisha no ayumi no ikkōsatsu: chūsei Nihon ni okeru kokka to bunka to gijutsu" (Thoughts on the evolution of mounted archery: The state, culture, and technology in medieval Japan). *Tōkyō Daigaku shiryō hensanjo kenkyū kiyō*. March 2000.
Hired Swords: The Rise of Private Warrior Power in Early Japan. Stanford University Press, 1992.

"Beyond Valor & Bloodshed: the Arts of War as a Path to Serenity," in *Knight and Samurai: Actions and Images of Elite Warriors in Europe and East Asia*, ed. Rose MarieDiest in collaboration with Harald Kleinschmidt (Kümmerle Verlag, Germany: Göppingen, 2003.
Friday, Karl and Seki Humitake, *Legacies of the Sword: the Kashima-Shinryū & Bushi Martial Culture*. University of Hawaii Press, 1997.
Fukuda Toyohiko, ed. *Ikusa* (War). Yoshikawa Kōbunkan, 1993.
Fujimoto Masayuki. *Sengoku kassen no jōshiki ga wakaru hon* (Understanding the common sense of Sengoku battles). Yōsensha, 1999.
Futaki Ken'ichi. *Chūsei buke no sakuhō* (Etiquette of medieval *bushi*). Yoshikawa Kōbunkan, 1999.
Hurst, G. Cameron, III. *Armed Martial Arts of Japan: Swordsmanship & Archery*. Yale University Press, 1998.
Imada Yoshio et al., ed. *Nihon kobudō taikei* <vol. 10> (Compendium of Japanese classical martial arts). Dōshōsha, 1982.
Imamura Yoshio. *Budōka senshū* (Collection of *budō* verse). Daiichi shobō, 1989.
Imamura Yoshio et al., eds. *Nihon budō taikei* (Compendium of Japanese *budō*). Dōshōsha, 1982.
Irvine, Gregory. *The Japanese Sword: the Soul of the Bushi*. New York: Weatherhill, 2000.
Ishioka Hisao. *Heihōsha no seikatsu* (Lifestyles of martial artists). Yūsankakaku, 1981.
Ishii Susumu. *Kamakura bakufu*. Chūō Kōronsha, 1965.
Komatsu Shigemi, ed. *Mōko shūrai ekotoba* (Scrolls of the Mongol invasion vol. 13). Chūō Kōronsha, 1988.
Kondō Yoshikazu. *Chūsei-teki bugu no seiritsu to bushi* (Medieval *bushi* and the evolution of their weapons). Yoshikawa Kōbunkan, 2000.
Yumiya to tōken: chūsei kassen no jitsuzō (Bows and arrows, and swords: A depiction of medieval warfare). Yoshikawa Kōbunkan, 1997.
Konishi Jin'ichi. *Nihon koten*, vol. 3, *Michi: chūsei no rinen* (Japanese classics vol.3, *Michi*: the medieval concept). Kōdansha Gendai Shinsho, 1975.
Kiyota Minoru. *Kendō Its Philosophy, History and Means to Personal Growth*. London: Kegan Paul, 1995.
Matsugi Takehiko and Udakawa Takehisa., eds. *Tatakai no shisutemu to taigai senryaku* (Combat systems and grand strategy). (*Jinrui ni totte tatakai to wa #2*). Tōyō Shorin, 1999.
Nakazawa Katsuaki. *Chūsei no buryoku to jōkaku* (Medieval military power and fortifications). Yoshikawa Kōbunkan, 1999.
Nawa Yumio. *Nagashino Shitaragahara kassen no shinjitsu* (The reality of the Nagashino and Shitaragahara battles). Yūsankaku, 1999.
Noguchi Minoru. *Bandō bushidan no seiritsu to hatten* (The formation and development of Bandō *bushidan*). Kōseisho Rinseishūsha, 1982.

Off the Warpath

Ōmori Nobumasa. *Bujutsu densho no kenkyū* (Studies of *bujutsu* manuscripts). Chijinkan, 1991.
Satō Shin'ichi. *Nambokuchō no dōran* (The upheaval of Northern and Southern Courts). Chūō Kōronsha, 1972.
Shakadō Mitsuhiro. "Nambokuchō ki kassen ni okeru senshō" (Battle wounds of the Nanbokuchō period). *Nairanshi kenkyū* 13. 1992.
Sinclaire, Clive. *Bushi: the Weapons & Spirit of the Japanese Warrior.* Guilford, CT: Lyons Press, 2001.
Skoss, Diane, ed. *Keiko Shokon*, Berkeley Heights, NJ.: Koryu Books, 2002.
Suzuki Masaya, *Teppōtai to kiba gundan* (Firearms units and mounted warriors). Yōsensha, 2003.
 Katana to kubi-tori: Sengoku kassen isetsu (Swords and head-taking: Another view of Sengoku period battles). Heibonsha Shinsho, 2000.
 Sengoku kassen no kyojitsu (Fact and fiction of the Sengoku period). Kodansha, 1998.
 Teppō to Nihonjin: "teppō shinwa" ga kakushite kita koto (Guns and Japanese: What the "gun myth" has concealed). Yōsuisha, 1997.
Suzuki Susumu. *Nihon kassenshi hyakubanashi* (Stories of Japanese battles). Tatsukaze Shobō, 1982.
Takayanagi Mitsutoshi and Suzuki Tōru. *Nihon kassenshi* (An history of Japanese battles). Gakugei Shorin, 1968.
Tominaga Kengo. *Kendō gohyakunen-shi* (Five hundred years of Japanese swordsmanship). Hyakusen Shobō, 1971.
Udagawa Takehisa. *Teppō to sengoku kassen* (Firearms and the Sengoku period battles). Yoshikawa Kōbunkan, 2002.
Ueda Makoto. *Literary and Art Theories in Japan.* Western Reserve University Press, 1967.
Watanabe Ichirō, ed. *Budō no meicho* (Martial art classics). Tōkyō Kopii Shuppanbu, 1979.
Yasuda Motohisa, ed. *Gempei no sōran* (The Gempei disturbance). Daiichi Hōgen, 1988.

Budo Perspectives

SECTION 4

INTERNATIONALIZATION OF BUDO

Chapter 16

The Influence of the Japanese Martial Disciplines on the Development of the United States Marine Corps Martial Arts Program

Richard Schmidt
University of Nebraska
&
George H. Bristol
Commanding Officer
3rd Reconnaissance Battalion,
Okinawa, Japan

Introduction

In the June 19, 2001, issue of "USA Today", Andrea Stone, in her article entitled "Martial Arts to Create a New Breed of Marines" wrote as follows;

"Eastern spiritualism meets Western macho. It's a novel idea, at least for the Marine Corps, which this spring will be requiring every American leatherneck to learn Asian martial arts – a first for the U.S. military. The objective is to meld the physical and mental discipline of the martial arts with the hand-to-hand combat skills the Corps has long emphasized. The Corps, recognizing that Marines are more likely to be deployed on peacekeeping missions than traditional warfare, expects the martial arts to develop skills needed to restrain civilians and to build confidence in Marines, so that they don't overreact in hostile situations."[1]

Stone continued further stating that;

"...The introduction of martial arts is also fitting given the Marines' image of themselves as America's samurai warriors – as in the ads that show a sword-wielding young man slay a dragon and then turn into a Marine....[Recruits] will earn beginner-level tan belts, the Corps' version of the traditional martial arts belt, or *obi*...Bristol, Urso and a platoon of consultants have developed a system for the Marines that borrow from more than a dozen martial arts. They include karate, judo, *jūjutsu*, aikido and arts that use swords, spears and other weapons."[2]

Stone quotes Lt. Col. George Bristol, USMC, the first director of the new program as saying that "he is molding 'ethical warriors."[3] Lastly, she quotes Hunter Armstrong, director of the International Hoplology Society, who studies combative behaviour: "From an untrained observer's eye, it is people fighting. What is not readily seen is the strong character aspect. We are instructing them in the responsibilities of the modern warrior."[4]

The Japanese martial disciplines have demonstrated a remarkable ability to adapt to changing social, cultural, and political contexts throughout their history, both within and outside of Japan. In many instances, as in the case of the internationalization of several of the modern *budō* arts, the adoption of entire systems (philosophy, techniques, ranking systems, etc.) has been virtually complete; in others, partial. In all cases, however, the degree of adoption and/or adaptation has been the result of the interpretations of what the adopting culture deems useful and of value. To understand these interpretations is to understand better the role these disciplines continue to serve in our world today.

One unique example of this phenomenon is how selected aspects of the Japanese martial disciplines have been incorporated into the Marine Corps newest close-in fighting and hand-to-hand combat system that has recently been re-titled the Marine Corps Martial Arts Program (MCMAP). The purpose of this paper, therefore, is to describe this influence.

In an attempt to elucidate this influence the following questions were addressed; "what is the influence of the Japanese martial disciplines on the development of the Marine Corps Martial Arts Program," "what has been the history of the Marine Corps' close-in fighting and hand-to-hand combat systems," "what is the current structure of the new Marine Corps martial Arts Program," "who were the key individuals responsible for the development of the new program and what were their contributions," and "what evidence exists in official Marine Corps documents and related writings that provide evidence for the influence of the Japanese martial disciplines on MCMAP program development."

Throughout history, almost all militaries have trained their professional warriors in some form of close-in fighting and hand-to-hand combat system. Combative theories and techniques were developed and refined, and in many cases, discarded, as they met their ultimate test of effectiveness in the battlefield environment. From the Greek hoplite to the twenty-first century professional soldier, the purpose of close combat was, and is, to dominate the opponent employing one or more armed/unarmed weapons-based systems coupled with the tactic of approach, close, and engagement to effect lethal and/or non-lethal results. From prehistoric times to the present day, regardless of the weapons systems employed, from stone axe, to spear, to sword, to assault rifle, to hand-to-hand combat, this fundamental tactic has never changed. Warriors have sought always to develop methods that integrated mind, body, tactics, and weapons systems that were efficient and lethal. While some methods developed were more successful than others, among most professional warriors, these martial skills were almost always employed within a strict code of martial ethics.

Development of the USMC Martial Arts Program

Historical Overview of the Marine Corps Close Combat Systems

The evolution of the Marine Corps' close combat systems began with the establishment of the Continental Marines in 1775. Marines of this period excelled in the use of the sword and bayonet in close combat fighting when conducting ship boarding assaults on the high seas.[5]

World War I saw the formal implementation of unarmed martial skills that enhanced Marines close combat capabilities in trench warfare. A. J. Drexel Biddle, a Marine officer with a background in boxing and European fencing, developed and taught skills in the use of the bayonet and close combat techniques[6].

During the interwar years between WWI and WWII, upon their return from deployment to the Far East, Marines brought back the martial arts they learned and the Corps close combat systems took on a decidedly more Asian flavour. Techniques from judo, *jūjutsu*, and karate were subsequently included into the Corps' close combat system.

Although the Marine Corps developed several close combat systems from the post-World War II era to the onset of the Vietnam Conflict, the training was not systematized nor was it practiced on a Corps-wide basis. Perhaps most telling was the fact that the close-in fighting and hand-to-hand combat systems were not fully integrated into the combat training continuum in terms of theory or practice.

The U. S. military experienced several dramatic changes following the end of the Vietnam Conflict. Many parts of the military experienced a significant decrease in troop strength, morale, and quality of training. In a move to inaugurate a more professional military, efforts were made to establish courses and activities, known as Professional Military Education (PME), for officers and enlisted personnel, and to improve overall leadership structure of the Corps. The Corps, as it has always had, continued to evolve with the changing times and followed suit in an attempt to improve its close combat system.

In the 1980s, through the leadership of Master Sergeant Ron Donvito, a standardized close combat system known as the Linear In-Line Neural Override Engagement (LINE) hand-to-hand combat system was developed.[7] Previously, close-in fighting and hand-to-hand combat systems still had not been integrated or standardized throughout the Corps. While not an integrated close combat system, the standardization of the LINE method on a Corps-wide basis for the majority of Marines was considered an important evolutionary change.

In 1996 the Marine Corps Combat Development Command in Quantico, with the input of several subject matter experts (SMEs) from numerous martial arts disciplines, conducted an extensive evaluation of its close and hand-to-hand combat systems, to include the techniques from the LINE method, pugil stick fighting, and close combat hitting skills. The outcome of this evaluation resulted in the development of the Marine Corps Close Combat Program. This change was significant as it combined all components of close combat into a single program.[8]

Following the establishment and implementation of this program, in June of 1999, as 32nd Commandant of the Marine Corps, General James L. Jones, put forth his view on how a modern Marine Corps Martial Arts Program should be structured. Understanding that the twenty-first century would see even greater numbers of peacekeeping and humanitarian operations that required a military presence, he believed it necessary for Marines to be trained in not only lethal techniques, but non-lethal techniques as well[9].

In an effort to meet the Commandant's goals, the Corps Close Combat Program, along with selected programs outside the Marines Corps, underwent a period of evaluation at Camp Pendleton during May of 2000. Two specific programs were tested. One was an enhanced version of the Marine Corps Close Combat system that focused on physical techniques to determine its ability to blend with the Corps leadership and core value training programs. A commercial firm, SportsMind, introduced the second program entitled "Marine Warrior".[10] This program emphasized the use of psycho-physiological techniques in an attempt to produce a more complete war fighter. While neither program was selected, aspects of both helped to shape the new Marine Corps Martial Arts Program. The most significant change in the new program was the Commandant's instruction that all Marines would train from entry level and throughout their tenure in Corps. Additionally, while previous Marine Corps close combat programs emphasized primarily physical skills and empty-hand fighting, the new MCMAP program addresses the full use-of-force continuum[11], from battlefield to peacekeeping operations, the training for which is buttressed with a primary emphasis on the development of character and mental discipline. It is of note that General Jones was impressed originally with Asian martial arts when, as a platoon commander in Vietnam, he had the opportunity to view South Korean marines training in taekwondo. So strong was his impression that, in 1986, he introduced martial arts training to his battalion at Camp Pendleton, California.[12] In July of 2000, General Jones directed the development of the Marine Corps Martial Arts Program. The program was officially established and implemented in the fall of 2001.[13] The individual General Jones appointed as the first director of the new program headquartered at Marine Corps Combat Development Command in Quantico, Virginia, was Lieutenant Colonel George H. Bristol.

Description of the Marine Corps Martial Arts Program (MCMAP)

The Marine Corps Martial Arts Program goals are to improve the war-fighting capabilities of individual Marines and units, enhance Marines' self-confidence and *esprit de corps*, and further instil the warrior ethos into the Corps by using a standardized, trainable, and sustainable close combat system.[14] The end-state or outcome goals are Marines highly skilled in the martial arts who possess a high degree of character and mental discipline, both as members of the Corps and of society as well.[15]

Marine Corps Martial Arts (MCMAP) is primarily a comprehensive weapons-based

Development of the USMC Martial Arts Program

system that fluidly integrates the full spectrum of armed and unarmed techniques and tactics commonly found in the combat environment. By design, the program is closely tied to the Marine Corps core values.

Conceptually, the MCMAP is designed on a continuum where a Marine, in the process of closing with and engaging the enemy, may use assault fire, edged weapons, weapons of opportunity, and, possibly, unarmed combat, to defeat an opponent.[16] It is into this continuum that the essence of combative theory from the *koryū bujutsu* is interwoven. It must be emphasized that the MCMAP was designed to be "Marine Corps-specific", meaning that while the program borrowed and adapted some techniques from Japanese, Asian, and other martial disciplines, it also kept battlefield-proven techniques from the past.[17] According to Armstrong, the Marine Corps Martial Arts close combat and bayonet training program was developed on universal principles that were extrapolated from hoplological work"..."the Japanese [martial arts] influence is there, but distilled and adapted to fit the modern Marine".[18]

Organizationally, MCMAP is designed around three primary integrated warrior disciplines: mental discipline, character discipline, and physical discipline (Table 1). Subsumed under mental discipline are warrior case studies, martial culture studies, and combative behaviour. Subsumed under character discipline are character discipline are Marine Corps Core Values (honour, courage, & commitment) and Leadership training. Subsumed under physical discipline are actual fighting techniques and combative fitness, with a third area presently being developed entitled combat (martial arts) sports.[19]

Table 1. Marine Corps Martial Arts Program Disciplines

MENTAL DISCIPLINE
-Warrior Case Studies.
-Martial Culture Studies.
-Combative Behaviour.

CHARACTER DISCIPLINE
-Marine Corps Core Values (honour, courage, & commitment).
-Leadership training.

PHYSICAL DISCIPLINE
-Actual fighting techniques (applicable across the use-of-force continuum from battlefield to military operations other than war [MOOTW].
-Combative fitness (standard physical training (PT) programs, "Semper Fit," water survival, martial arts, rough terrain skills, & adventure training: includes fighting while fatigued, operating in full combat gear, single and multiple opponents.
-Martial Arts (Combat) Sports (currently in development).

Mental Discipline focuses on the development of the combative mindset and the academic study of the art of war. Areas of study include Warrior Case Studies, Martial Culture Studies, and Combative Behaviour. Warrior Case Studies involve guided discussions of battlefield citations of U.S. military personnel who experienced close combat. These studies inform Marines as to the types of behaviour expected of them when placed in a combat environment. Similarly, Martial Culture Studies are used during guided discussions to further develop a Marine's martial ethos through examination of warrior cultures such as the Apache Indian, the Zulus, Spartans, and the Marine Raiders of World War II. Combative Behaviour focuses on the psycho-physiological aspects of battlefield combat. Subject matter encompasses pseudo-predatory versus affective behaviour, the origins of violence, and the human dimensions of combat.[20]

Character discipline uses guided discussions to relate the interconnectedness among ethics, morals, integrity, and leadership. In the program, the Marine Corps Core Values of "Honour", "Courage", and "Commitment" serve as the cornerstone of character discipline. Topics include conflict resolution, seeking and accepting responsibility, and teamwork-based approaches to all aspects of Marine Corps life. Character discipline, identified as the most important component of the program, underscores the importance of the Marine as an ethical warrior and citizen. The Marine Corps Martial Arts Program goal is to integrate character discipline with the Marine's behaviour both on and off the battlefield.[21]

Physical discipline is comprised of the components of physical skills and combative fitness and the fusion that exists between them in order to manoeuvre and fight efficiently on the battlefield.[22] Instruction in fighting techniques includes battle skill orientation, stance, posture, movement techniques, weapons handling skills, striking, cutting, grappling, throwing, restraints and manipulations, and integration of weapons. There are four concentration areas to include rifle and bayonet, bladed weapons, weapons of opportunity, and unarmed combat, both standing and on the ground. The techniques are direct, functionally efficient, and taken from several proven Asian and non-Asian martial disciplines. Similarly, many battlefield-proven techniques, such as those used by the Marine Raiders, comprise an essential component of MCMAP's martial arts skills curriculum. The instructor level courses employ the use of hand grenades and assault fire to complete the gamut of close-range combat. These perishable skills are maintained through a process known as "Sustainment and Integration" training. Sustainment refers to repetition of physical techniques from previously held belt levels, to include executing techniques from both dominant and non-dominant sides of the body. Sustainment hours begin to accrue after the Marine has attained a belt level, and refers to the combining of techniques from the current and previous belt levels or the combination of martial arts techniques with Military Occupational Specialty (MOS) skills.[23]

The second aspect is combative fitness, which is defined as "the ability to fight

Development of the USMC Martial Arts Program

while fatigued in a combat-related environment."[24] It involves battlefield-oriented conditioning in a simulated combat environment. Techniques involve moving on rugged terrain using the techniques of approach, close, and entry to engage an opponent. With Marines wearing full combat equipment, extensive use is made of Obstacle, Confidence, Endurance, Assault, and Combat Battle Courses, as well as Combat Conditioning Drills. Rugged terrain movement and combat swimming often precede fighting drills. Additional combat conditioning exercises consisting of rope climbing, bodyweight squats, "buddy carries", and wind sprints are used in the program to further toughen Marines.[25]

A third aspect, Combat (Martial Arts) Sports, is currently under development. Historically, the Marine Corps has possessed a superlative athletic program, especially in wrestling and boxing teams. The proposed MCMAP combat sports program will most likely consist of a combination of striking, grappling, and wooden bayonet trainer fighting. The purpose of the program will be to give the Marines the opportunity to increase their proficiency in their martial skills and further develop their aggressive fighting spirit in a competitive environment.

The Combat (Martial Arts) Sports program will encompass three areas.[26] The first component will be the development of a competitive combative sports program based on ground fighting, grappling, striking, and bayonet fighting. Competition would begin at the unit level and have the potential to expand to Division/Wing/Fleet Service Support Group/Base/Regional and All-Marine championships. A second facet will be to develop a close combat test that can be added to the Marine Corps' Super Squad competition. This competition is an annual event that takes place throughout the Marine Corps and is based on the skills of the squad's performance as a team and its ability to attain mission accomplishment. The intent of the competition is to provide a Marine Corps-wide medium to stimulate operational proficiency of the rifle squad and to determine, under simulated combat conditions, which Marine rifle squads are most effective in demonstrating their capability for employment in combat. The third and final facet would be to develop All-Marine teams in specific internationally recognized Martial Arts such as judo and taekwondo (both Olympic Sports), as well as others such as *sambo*, karate, etc. This would be in addition to the current and already well known All-Marine Boxing and Wrestling programs.

Regarding the MCMAP program, Bristol summarizes stating that:

"...These disciplines are inter-related and integrated to form a true martial art – principles and techniques to be used in the profession of arms. The range of physical techniques spans the spectrum of conflict, from non-lethal restraints and manipulations to live-blade bayonet fighting. The mental and character discipline – the major emphases of the MCMAP – ties the physical to the ethical and makes a Marine what he is advertised to be."[27]

Belt Ranking Achievement System

The MCMAP operates with a belt ranking achievement system (Table 2) designed to track a Marine's progress and award proficiency throughout a career. The levels are Tan, Grey, Green, Brown, and Black, Black Belt from 1st Degree through 6th Degree. In addition to displaying proficiency in the mental, physical, and character disciplines, promotion to each belt level has military rank, time-in-grade, and Professional Military Education requirements, as well as the Marine's Reporting Senior's recommendation. Marines wear USMC officially approved "coloured" and "Black Belts", known as "Rigger's belts", with their USMC camouflage utility uniforms. Martial Arts Instructors (MAIs) are designated by a tan stripe worn on the buckle side of the belt. Martial Arts Instructor-Trainers (MAITs) and 2nd degree Black Belt and higher are designated by a series of red stripes worn on the buckle side of the belt.[28]

In each belt level, all four major concentration areas – rifle and bayonet, bladed weapons, weapons of opportunity, and unarmed combat – are taught. Techniques are added as proficiency increases. Topics such as Human Dimensions of Combat, Combative Behaviour, Anatomy and Physiology, and Operational Risk Management and Assessment[29] are covered with regard to Marine Corps Martial Arts Program as well as for a Marine's overall development.

Table 2. Marine Corps Martial Arts Program (MCMAP) Belt Rank Structure

NOVICE
Tan Belt
Gray Belt
Green Belt
Brown Belt

APPRENTICE
Green Belt Instructor
Brown Belt Instructor
1st Degree Black belt Instructor
1st Degree Black Belt Instructor Trainer

JOURNEYMAN
2nd Degree Black Belt
3rd Degree Black belt
4th Degree Black Belt
(must possess a Black Belt 1st Degree in MCMAP-approved civilian martial art)

Development of the USMC Martial Arts Program

MASTER
5th Degree Black Belt
(must possess a teaching certificate in a MCMAP-approved civilian martial art)
6th Degree Black Belt

The levels of proficiency take into account not only the specific disciplines of the MCMAP but the level of training in everything a Marine does from marksmanship and swim qualification, to Military Occupational Specialty (MOS) and leadership ability.

Description of Individual Belt Levels

The MCMAP belt levels use a skills progression approach in the teaching of its martial skills. Marines' transition through fundamental, intermediate and advanced levels as their proficiency improves. Marines are required to develop further their leadership skills at the same time. Tan Belt through Green Belt emphasize individual combat techniques, both armed and unarmed, and concentrate on building character and developing leadership skills. Brown Belt and Black Belt emphasize combat techniques against multiple opponents, both armed and unarmed, strengthens character, and expands and reinforces leadership skills.[30]

Each belt grade earned by the individual Marine incorporates aspects of the three disciplines (mental, character, and physical), as well as elements of Professional Military Education. Testing for belt advancement consists of a combined proficiency and performance test. The proficiency test measures fighting techniques developed in the Marine's previously held rank(s). The performance test measures skills and knowledge attained in the Physical Discipline of the new belt. The proficiency and performance tests have a minimum passing score of 90% and 70%, respectively.[31]

Tan Belt training consists of introduction to the fundamentals of the mental, physical, and character disciplines and is conducted during entry-level training into the Marine Corps. Along with the teaching of martial arts skills, this level focuses on the character and knowledge required of the basically trained Marine. Tan Belt is considered the minimum requirement for all Marines. Gray Belt consists of introduction to the intermediate fundamentals of each discipline and is the minimum training goal for all Aviation Combat and Combat Service Support Marines. Green Belt consists of introduction to the intermediate fundamentals of each discipline and is the minimum training goal of all non-infantry ground combat arms Marines. Brown Belt consists of introduction to the advanced fundamentals of each discipline and is the minimum training goal (military rank-appropriate) for all infantrymen.[32]

Black Belt 1st Degree consists of instruction in advanced fundamentals. A current MAI (1st Degree Black belt) may teach Tan Belt through Brown Belt techniques, and award the appropriate belts. Any certified Black Belt 1st Degree may teach Tan Belt through Brown Belts techniques. Current MAITs are authorized to teach and to certify Tan Belt through Black Belt 1st Degree.[33]

Promotion to the grades of Black Belt 2nd through 6th Degree is conducted using a different methodology than that applied through Black Belt 1st Degree. Promotion past Black Belt 1st Degree emphasizes maturity, involvement in unit training, advanced skills, Martial Arts studies, and participation in civilian martial arts. A Black Belt 1st Degree applying for Black Belt 2nd Degree must complete Black Belt 1st Degree Sustainment Training. Additionally, the candidate must submit to the Director, MCMAP an "Elements of Martial Culture Analysis" (EMCA) for review and approval. A 2nd to 6th Degree Black Belt may teach Tan Belt through Black Belt techniques (degree dependent).[34]

For promotion to the rank of 3rd Degree Black Belt, the candidate must submit to the Director, MCMAP a "Unit Training Integration Plan" for review and approval while promotion to the rank of 4th Degree Black Belt requires the Marine to obtain a Black Belt 1st degree in a MCMAP-approved civilian martial art. The categories for MCMAP-approved civilian martial arts are: grappling or throwing arts; striking arts; and weapon arts. The grappling or throwing arts are, but not limited to, judo *jūjitsu*, *sambo*, *hapkido*, and aikido. Striking arts are, but not limited to, karate, taekwondo, kickboxing, *muay Thai*, kung fu, and capoeira. Weapon arts are, but not limited to, Okinawan *kobudō*, *escrima*, *kali*, kendo, and *iaidō*.[35]

The Director of MCMAP convenes a board annually to consider Marines for promotion to 5th and 6th Degree Black Belt. Candidates for Black Belt 5th degree must have the recommendation of their Reporting Senior; attained the rank of Master Sergeant, First Sergeant, Chief Warrant Officer-3 (CWO-3) to CWO-5, Major or above; possess a teaching certificate in a MCMAP-approved civilian martial art; appropriate level PME completed; and five years experience at Black Belt 4th Degree. Candidates for Black Belt 6th degree must have the recommendation of Reporting Senior; attained the rank of Master Gunnery Sergeant, Sergeant Major, CWO-4 to CWO-5, Lieutenant Colonel or above; a teaching certificate in a MCMAP-approved civilian martial art; appropriate level PME completed; and five years experience at Black Belt 5th Degree.[36]

MCMAP Billet Description

The Chief Trainer advises the Director, MCMAP on overall development of MCMAP. The Chief trainer is Resident at the Marine Corps Centre of Excellence (MACE) which is based at Headquarter Marine Corps, Quantico, Virginia; a MCMAP Subject Matter Expert (SME); and is responsible for the research, development, and performance of the techniques and procedures taught in MCMAP. The Chief Trainer's responsibility is to train and certify Martial Arts Instructor Trainers (MAITs).[37]

The responsibility of the MAITs is to train and certify Martial Arts Instructors

Development of the USMC Martial Arts Program

(MAIs) and conduct martial arts training. There is no limit to the number of MAIs each MAIT can certify; however, the MAIT-to-student ratio must not exceed twelve to one. To be designated a MAIT, a Marine must meet the prerequisites for Black Belt 1st Degree and successfully complete the MAIT course. MAIT certification is valid for three years.[38]

The Martial Arts Instructor (MAI) conducts martial arts training and is authorized to promote to one belt level below the level individually held. MAI certification or re-certification is valid for three years. To maintain certification a MAI must provide a minimum of forty hours of instruction annually.[39]

Subject Matter Experts (SMEs) serve as advisors to MCMP due to their unique knowledge and training in the field of martial arts. SMEs are designated by the Commanding General, Training & Education command and are authorized to assist in course development, course revision, supplementary training materials, or other aspects of MCMAP, as required. SMEs may be paid or volunteers. SMEs work directly with the Director, MCMAP on a case-by-case basis.[40]

Some of those who have been designated as SMEs, such as Hunter Armstrong, and Meik Skoss, have trained extensively in the classical and modern Japanese martial disciplines. Armstrong has trained in karate, judo, Chinese combative arts, classical European weapons and fighting systems, as well as classical Japanese martial arts. He is an exponent of Shinkage-ryū *heihō* and Owari Kan-ryū *sōjutsu*. Shinkage-ryū *heihō* involves *kenjutsu* and *battō, naginata, nagamaki, kogusoku*, grappling, *bō*, etc. Owari Kan-ryū includes use of the *kuda-yari* and sword. Armstrong currently contracts with the Federal Government to provide combative training to selected units within the Marine Corps.

Meik Skoss has trained in several classical *koryū* and *budō* for more than twenty-five years. These classical and modern disciplines have included aikido, Shinto Muso-ryū *jōjutsu*, Toda-ha Buko-ryū *naginata-jutsu*, Tendo-ryu *naginata-jutsu*, Yagyū Shinkage-ryū *heihō/kenjutsu*, Yagyū Seigo-ryū *battōjutsu*, judo, tai-chi, Goju-ryū karatedo, *jōdō*, *jūkendō, tankendō*, and *atarashii naginata*.

Key Marine Corps personnel intimately tied to the conceptualization, development, and implementation of the MCMAP program include General James L. Jones, USMC, 32nd Commandant of the Marine Corps, and Lt. Col. George H. Bristol, MCMAP's first director. General Jones is credited with the initial conceptualization of the program. He envisioned the need for the inclusion of non-lethal, unarmed techniques to be included in the new program to meet the needs of the military in humanitarian and peacekeeping operations. He also wanted to improve the warrior ethos of Marines through mandated training and progression in the martial arts, to include growth in the character and mental disciplines.

Lt. Col. George H. Bristol, USMC, is credited with being the primary architect, author, and first director of the MCMAP. He is accomplished in wrestling and *jūjutsu* and a forty-plus year practitioner of judo. Bristol is also an exponent of Shinkage-ryū *heihō* under the tutelage of Hunter Armstrong. As the First Director of MCMAP, Bristol was the sole individual responsible for developing the philosophy and pedagogy, selecting the techniques and drills, and determining other requirements for the program.

It is important to note that Bristol, Armstrong, and Skoss were early colleagues of Donn Draeger, himself a former combat Marine officer and accomplished exponent of several classical and modern *bujutsu* and *budō* and one of the most noted hoplologists specializing in the Japanese martial disciplines. Some of the martial characteristics seen in the new MCMAP program may be reflective of Draeger's influence on these key individuals. As the first director of the program, Bristol had the liberty to select Subject-Matter-Experts whose martial arts training background and philosophy would contribute to the successful development of a "Marine Corps-specific" martial arts program. Bristol believed that SMEs who had experience in training in the *koryū bugei* would best meet this needs.

Official Marine Corps Publications and Related Writings

An examination of official Marine Corps publications[41] related to the design and implementation of the program provides the following documentation of the influence of the Japanese martial disciplines on its development.

The official title of the program is the "Marine Corps Martial Arts Program."[42] Most Westerners, as well as many others, commonly associate the term "martial arts" with martial arts of Japanese, Korean, or Chinese origin. Likewise, the program uses a skill and knowledge-based coloured belt ranking achievement system which appears to be based on the "*kyū-dan*" model similar to that used in modern Japanese *budō*.

The program requires those Marines applying for the rank of Black Belt 4th Degree to hold current ranking in a civilian martial art and to the rank of Black Belt 5th Degree to hold a teaching certificate from and MCMAP-approved civilian martial art. (Several of the Japanese martial disciplines listed in the documents include, but are not limited to judo, *jūjutsu*, aikido, karate, Okinawan *kobudō*, kendo, and *iaidō*.

Bristol[43] has stated that he uses a video clip of the late Donn Draeger, a *koryū* exponent, counterattacking with *kusarigama* to demonstrate to Martial Arts Instructor-Trainers the essence of the *koryū bujutsu*, that is, combative intent or combat mind-set, as being the most critical element in combat.

The program is in the process of developing a competitive Martial (Combative) Arts Sports program that will be comprised of ground fighting, grappling, striking, and bayonet fighting. While not yet definitively determined, the Martial Sports program may be similar in ways to the competitive sports model used in Japanese *budō*. Following this evolution, the program plans to develop All-Marine teams in specific internationally recognized Martial Arts such as Judo and taekwondo (both Olympic Sports), as well as others such as *sambo*, karate, etc.

The program has incorporated the use of the *mokujū* in solo, and partner combative engagement training as well as in the Combative Martial Arts Sports Program. This mock training weapon is used in the Japanese martial art of *jūkendō* (bayonet). It is also

Development of the USMC Martial Arts Program

of note that the MCMAP "Training Logbook," contains a quote from the Emperor Meiji: "Death is as light as a feather; duty, heavier than a mountain" that can be found below the Black Belt 1st Degree issue date.

Prior to the implementation of the MCMAP, the Marine Corps close-in fighting and hand-to-hand combat programs focused on skill development only. The MCMAP is designed around three primary warrior disciplines: mental discipline, character discipline, and physical discipline. Citing Draeger's classification[44] of the Japanese martial disciplines we see that the *kobujutsu* emphasized the hierarchical integration of combat, discipline, and morals in the training of its warriors. The integration of the mental, character, and physical disciplines in the MCMAP can be considered somewhat reflective of this model. We see this emphasis on the development of the "ethical warrior" again in Bristol's writing entitled "Director's Intent" when he states that MCMAP's third goal is "to develop a true martial artist – a Marine highly skilled in lethal technique who can function appropriately in any environment (with a high sense of ethical behaviour)."[45]

In addition to investigating official Marine Corps documents to elucidate the influence of the Japanese martial disciplines on the development of the Marine Corps Martial Arts Program, several articles about the program written by the first director and primary architect of the program were also examined.

In his article entitled "Director's Intent: Marine Corps Martial Arts Program," Bristol states:

"The Japanese have a very good "word-concept" for the realization of martial arts capability. It is their word for shadow – "*kage*". The word can be defined on several levels."

In the arena of military combat he states:

"[This] concept has the shadow being, in effect, a combative mirror – that is, the mimicking quality of the shadow. Opponents approach, close, and enter to do the same thing we endeavour to do to them: finish the engagement. What we see as they close is probably only a slight variation of what they are seeing. In this concept, our own strengths and limitations are played out against a mirror – the shadow that is the opponent. This concept is particularly true for instructors."[46]

In "Keiko Shokon Revisited: Introduction", Diane Skoss writes:

"...Lt. Col. George Bristol discusses how the *koryū* curricula can actually apply in modern warfare...in the direct man-to-man combat of the Marine. Lt. Col Bristol's observations illuminate yet one more side of the *koryū*'s modern relevance, exhibiting innovation in its best sense by incorporating both pedagogy and philosophy into the newly developed Marine Corps Martial Art."[47]

Bristol has written several articles about the MCMAP, many of which have indicated how his experiences have influenced program development. In his foreword to Skoss' *Koryu Bujutsu: Classical Warrior Traditions of Japan*, Bristol writes:

"I have been a United States Marine for my entire adult life, both as an enlisted man and now as an officer of Marines, my primary goal has been to be ready to go into harms way. The physical and mental mindset that galvanizes this calling lies within the tenets of the *koryū bujutsu*...Conflicts will occur, and warriors will engage. Mind-set — and the training that fosters it — will prevail. And mind-set – the combat mind-set – is the heart of the *koryū*. I remain true to that statement, as I believe does the *koryū*."[48]

Bristol also states his basic thesis that the structure of modern military combative training should follow the structure of that of the *koryū bujutsu*. He writes that:

"Training and preparing for combat is rigorous. It must be realistic and tough. However, it should be a professional environment with all goals focusing on a positive end. I would like to emphasize that I said positive – not easy. Once again, *koryū* has the structure and the function to create this setting. The key lies in both the teacher and the student. Major General John A. Lejeune, one of the Corps fabled leaders, termed the ideal between senior and junior Marines a "teacher-scholar" relationship. I believe that if this relationship can exist in the *koryū* training environment, then it can – and must – exist in the military combat training environment;...The *koryū bujutsu* were designed for the battlefield...The system of combat with all applicable weapons was designed so that basic function/proficiency could be gained relatively quickly in a two- to three-year period. Basic function, in realistic terms for that era, meant the ability to survive intact. Refinement came during periods of relative peace where training in battlefield-proven technique could be conducted. Those who trained, fought, survived, and refined became the teachers of the tradition. However, basic function was far more important than refinement, given the nature of battlefield engagement and the relative chances of survival.

At the heart of that basic function is intent. Nothing matters more in *koryū* training than the intent that drives an exponent to close with his opponent. Whether the *naginata* is manipulated smoothly or not, if the cut is made, it is a good cut. In *sōjutsu*, the *maki*, disruption of the opponent's weapon, is important. It is not nearly as important as the *tsuki* – the thrust. I am continually amazed when I watch the fluidity of long-time exponents of *koryū*. But perfection of skill does not take the place of intent, it never will."[49]

Development of the USMC Martial Arts Program

Bristol further describes the usefulness of using the *koryū* pedagogical method as a comparable instructional model for the new MCMAP program when he writes:

"...Three aspects of training that I have encountered solidify the concept of what is just and right. First, training in *koryū* is conducted in a natural training environment, outside and on rough ground. Obstacles, footing, terrain, and weather are a factor. Second, repetition of patterns and technique is never perfect, and as a result, no one ever "gets it." Rather, one keeps at "it" for his lifetime. And finally, rather than excuses or opinions, one wins by winning, that is, maximum effort."[50]

As an example, the Marine Corps Martial Arts Program conducts much of its training out of doors on all types of terrain and in all types of weather and lighting conditions. Standardized motor skill patterns are repeated to the point where the combative techniques become virtually second nature. The goal of this integrated type of training is to physically and mentally imbed the combative skills and combat mind set so that Marines will be able to close with and defeat the enemy.

These statements demonstrate the degree of profound influence the Japanese martial disciplines, especially the *koryū bujutsu*, have had on Bristol's thinking, and how this thinking has, in turn, subtly influenced the development of the Marine Corps Martial Arts Program. It is in these ways that the *koryū* have served as a pedagogical model in the new MCMAP program.

Although the MCMAP has been influenced by selected aspects of the Japanese martial disciplines, again it must be stated that it was the intention of the program developers to create a martial art that was "Marine Corps-specific," that is, a multipurpose martial art developed "of, by, and for Marines".[51] It was not their intention to adopt any already established classical or modern martial art by the Marine Corps, many of which are functionally ineffective in a battlefield environment.[52]

As stated in the introduction, the degree of adoption and/or adaptation of the Japanese martial disciplines throughout history has been a function of the interpretations of what the adopting culture or social unit deems useful and of value. The MCMAP serves as an example of how selected, valued aspects of the Japanese martial disciplines have been successfully adopted and/or adapted to meet the needs of the Marine Corps of the twenty-first century.

Endnotes

[1] Andrea Stone, "Martial arts to create a new breed of Marines", *USA Today*, 19 June 2001.
[2] *Ibid.*
[3] *Ibid.*
[4] *Ibid.*

[5] "A Brief History". http://www.mcu.usmc.mil/TbsNew/Pages/Martial_Arts/Program_Philosophy/History/history.htm
[6] Refer to Chuck Meldon's *Combat Conditioning: The Classic U.S. Marine Corps Physical Training and Hand-to-hand Combat Course.*
[7] U. S. Marine Close-Quarters Combat Manual.
[8] G. H. Bristol, "Director's Intent". See. http://www.mcu.usmc.mil/TbsNew/Pages/Martial_Arts/staff/Director's_Notes/frdir.htm
[9] *Ibid.*
[10] *Ibid.*
[11] Marine Corps Order 1500/54A (16 December 2002).
[12] Bristol, "Director's Intent".
[13] Marine Corps Order 1500/54A (16 December 2002); Marine Corps Order 1510.122A: (03 December 2002); All Marine Message (ALMAR) 042/01 (20 September 2001); Marine Administrative Message (MARADMIN) 537/01 (26 October 2001).
[14] Marine Corps Order 1500/54A (16 December 2002); All Marine Message (ALMAR) 042/01 (20 September 2001).
[15] Bristol, "Synergy", see http://www.tbs.usmc.mil/Pages/Martial_Arts/Program_Philosophy/Synergy.htm
[16] Bristol, "Physical Discipline", http://www.mcu.usmc.mil/TbsNew/Pages/Martial_Arts/Program_Philosophy/Discupline/physical.htm
[17] Meik Skoss, (personal communication), 06 November 2003; Michael Burke, (personal communication), 14 Nov 2003, Okinawa, Japan.
[18] Hunter Armstrong, (personal communication), 03 November 2003.
[19] Marine Corps Order 1500/54A (16 December 2002).
[20] *Ibid.*
[21] *Ibid.*
[22] 18. Bristol, "Physical Discipline".
[23] Sustainment and integration training, Martial Arts Instructor Course (MA-I.26).
[24] Bristol, "Director's Intent".
[25] Sustainment and integration training, Martial Arts Instructor Course (MA-I.26); How to conduct drills and training, Martial Arts Instructor Trainer (MAIT-I.54); Conduct of drills practical application I, Martial Arts Instructor Trainer (MAIT-I.54a); Conduct of drills practical application II, Martial Arts Instructor Trainer (MAIT-I.54b).
[26] Bristol, "Director's Intent".
[27] *Ibid.*
[28] Marine Corps Order 1500/54A (16 December 2002).
[29] Marine Corps Order 1500/54A (16 December 2002); Marine Administrative Message (MARADMIN) 275/02: MCMAP Safety Advisory (16 May 2002), from Commandant of the Marine Corps, Washington, DC, Marine Corps Combat Development Command.
[30] Marine Corps Order 1500/54A (16 December 2002).
[31] *Ibid.*
[32] *Ibid.*
[33] *Ibid.*
[34] *Ibid.*
[35] *Ibid.*

Development of the USMC Martial Arts Program

36 *Ibid.*
37 *Ibid.*
38 *Ibid.*
39 *Ibid.*
40 *Ibid.*
41 Marine Corps Martial Arts Program Logbook. http://www.usmc.mil/directiv.nsf/0/ 78345e1f0c52fd2185256dcd0046b042/$FILE/NAVMC%202933.pdf.; Marine Corps Order 1500/54A (16 December 2002); Marine Corps Order 1510.122A: (03 December 2002); Sustainment and integration training, Martial Arts Instructor Course (MA-I.26); How to conduct drills and training, Martial Arts Instructor Trainer (MAIT-I.54); Conduct of drills practical application I, Martial Arts Instructor Trainer (MAIT-I.54a); Conduct of drills practical application II, Martial Arts Instructor Trainer (MAIT-I.54b); All Marine Message (ALMAR) 042/01 (20 September 2001); Marine Administrative Message (MARADMIN) 275/02: MCMAP Safety Advisory (16 May 2002).
42 2. Marine Corps Order 1500/54A (16 December 2002); All Marine Message (ALMAR) 042/01 (20 September 2001); Marine Administrative Message (MARADMIN) 537/01 (26 October 2001).
43 Bristol, "The Professional Perspective: Thoughts on the Koryu Bujutsu from a United States Marine," in Keiko Shokon: Classical Warrior Traditions of Japan (volume 3).
44 Bristol, "A brief history", http://www.mcu.usmc.mil/TbsNew/Pages/Martial_Arts/ Program_Philosophy/History/history.htm
45 Bristol, "Director's Intent".
46 *Ibid.*
47 Diane Skoss, "Keiko Shokon Revisited: An Introduction" in *Keiko Shokon: Classical Warrior Traditions of Japan*, (volume 3).
48 Diane Skoss, *Koryu Bujutsu: Classical Warrior Traditions of Japan* (volume 1), Foreword by George H. Bristol (pages vi & vii).
49 Bristol, "The Professional Perspective: Thoughts on the Koryu Bujutsu from a United States Marine".
50 *Ibid.*
51 Meik Skoss, (personal communication), 06 November 2003; Hunter Armstrong (personal communication), 03 November 2003; Michael Burke (personal communication), 14 Nov 2003, Okinawa, Japan; G.H. Bristol, "Director's Intent".
52 Hunter Armstrong, (personal communication), 03 November 2003.

Bibliography

Marine Corps Related:
Marine Corps Martial Arts Program Logbook. http://www.usmc.mil/directiv.nsf/ 0/78345e1f0c52fd2185256dcd0046b042/$FILE/NAVMC%202933.pdf.
Marine Corps Order 1500/54A (16 December 2002). Marine Corps Martial Arts Program. Commandant of the Marine Corps, Washington, DC, Marine Corps Combat Development Command.
Marine Corps Order 1510.122A: (03 December 2002). Individual Training Standards for the Marine Corps Martial Arts Program. Commandant of the Marine Corps, Washington, DC, Marine Corps Combat Development

Command.

Sustainment and integration training, Martial Arts Instructor Course (MA-I.26), Detailed Instructor Guide, United States Marine Corps, Martial Arts Center of Excellence, The Basic School, Marine Corps Combat Development Command, Quantico, VA. 07 August 2001.

How to conduct drills and training, Martial Arts Instructor Trainer (MAIT-I.54), Detailed Instructor Guide, United States Marine Corps, Martial Arts Center of Excellence, The Basic School, Marine Corps Combat Development Command, Quantico, VA. 30 November 2000.

Conduct of drills practical application I, Martial Arts Instructor Trainer (MAIT-I.54a), Detailed Instructor Guide, United States Marine Corps, Martial Arts Center of Excellence, The Basic School, Marine Corps Combat Development Command, Quantico, VA. 05 May 2001.

Conduct of drills practical application II, Martial Arts Instructor Trainer (MAIT-I.54b), Detailed Instructor Guide, United States Marine Corps, Martial Arts Center of Excellence, The Basic School, Marine Corps Combat Development Command, Quantico, VA. 05 May 2001.

All Marine Message (ALMAR) 042/01 (20 September 2001). Establishment of the Marine Corps Martial Arts Program, from Commandant of the Marine Corps, Washington, DC, Marine Corps Combat Development Command.

Marine Administrative Message (MARADMIN) 275/02: MCMAP Safety Advisory (16 May 2002), from Commandant of the Marine Corps, Washington, DC, Marine Corps Combat Development Command.

Marine Administrative Message (MARADMIN) 537/01 (26 October 2001). Marine Corps Martial Arts Program, from Commandant of the Marine Corps, Washington, DC, Marine Corps Combat Development Command.

Close Combat – U. S. Marine Corps: MCRP 3-02B: 18 February 1999.

General Publications:

Draeger, Donn, F. *Classical Bujutsu (Martial Arts and Ways of Japan,* Volume 1*).* New York. John Weatherhill, Publishers, 1973.

Meldon, Chuck. *Combat Conditioning: The Classic U.S. Marine Corps Physical Training and Hand-to-hand Combat Course.* Boulder, CO.: Paladin Press, 2001.

Skoss, Diane, ed. *Keiko Shokon: Classical Warrior Traditions of Japan* (volume 3). Berkeley Heights, NJ.: Koryu Books. 2002.

Koryu Bujutsu: Classical Warrior Traditions of Japan (volume 1). Berkeley Heights, NJ.: Koryu Books. 1997.

Stone, Andrea. "Martial arts to create a new breed of Marines". *USA Today,* 19 June 2001.

USMC. *U. S. Marine Close-Quarters Combat Manual.* Boulder, CO.: Paladin Press. 1996.

Chapter 17

Thinking Differently about the Teaching of Judo in Japan[1]

David Matsumoto
San Francisco State University

Introduction

Japan today faces many social issues brought about by a gap between the psychological reality of the Japanese people and the stereotypic conceptualizations of culture and its associated social structures and systems within which they must live. What is the role of judo in addressing these social issues? While Japan is clearly the strongest country in the world in competitive sport judo, it may be the case that much of the educational aspects of judo, especially with regard to intellectual, moral, and physical development, are lacking. Numerous indices, including the declining numbers of people doing judo, and its popularity and image among the general public suggest that we need to re-examine the underlying philosophy and goals of judo practice and search for new teaching methodologies if we are to deliver the educational benefits of judo to a wider portion of the population. The goal of this chapter is to stimulate thinking about these issues.

Below I will first discuss the creation and development of judo and the social and cultural context within which it occurred. I will then discuss contemporary Japanese culture and psychology, contrasting it with stereotypic conceptualizations of a consensual Japanese culture. Using this as a platform we will identify a gap that exists between individual psychological realities and the social and cultural systems within which people live, and use this gap to explain a number of social problems that Japan faces today. We will then entertain new ways of thinking about judo practice and teaching methodologies that will allow us to close that gap, and hopefully address those social problems.

Martial Arts Across Japanese History

The fighting arts of the bushi through the sixteenth century
To know how judo came to be in Japan is to understand the history of Japan and the role of the martial arts in that history. From its earliest recorded history in the *Nihon shoki*, or the Chronicle of Japan (720 AD), and for hundreds of years before, Japan was ruled by emperors thought to have descended from the gods. Imperial rule lasted

for centuries until the end of the Fujiwara period and the beginning of the Kamakura period (1185), when military leaders gained control and the country was ruled by a supreme commander known as the shogun, and his administration the *bakufu*, or "tent government".

The sixteenth century was known as the Warring States period (*Sengoku jidai*) in Japan because no identified *daimyō* ruled supreme, and the various *han* (domains) continuously fought each other for approximately one century to wrestle for the seat of ultimate power. Toward the end of the sixteenth century, three great leaders began a process of unification through military power and conquests – Oda Nobunaga, Toyotomi Hideyoshi, and finally Tokugawa Ieyasu. Ieyasu was the one who finally gained control of the country over all other *han*. He subsequently moved the capital from Kyoto to Edo and ushered Japan into a period of two-and-a-half centuries of continued peace.

Until Ieyasu, fighting was a way of life for the *bushi*, and consequently the fighting arts held great importance. Warriors used bows and arrows for long distance attacks, and used swords and spears in close combat. When they lost their weapons they had to use their bare hands. The fighting arts using bare hands were developed into systems of attack and defence and were known by a number of names such as *yawara*, *taijutsu*, *torite*, or *kumiuchi*. Ultimately they came to be known as *jūjutsu*, or literally, the techniques of *yawara* or "gentleness".

Different clans and *jūjutsu* masters developed different styles of *jūjutsu*. One of the earliest and most prominent styles of *jūjutsu* was known as the Takenouchi-ryū, founded in 1532. Other schools developed, including the Kito-ryū, Tenshin Shin'yō-ryū, Sekiguchi-ryū, and the Kyushin-ryū. The main differences among the various schools of *jūjutsu* were based on the particular styles and specialization of specific techniques by their founders.

The *jūjutsu* that was practiced during the centuries of military rule in Japan until Ieyasu was a combination of techniques that, when actually applied, resulted in death or maiming. They were actually used in battle, and one's prowess in the fighting arts meant life or death for oneself, and survival or destruction of one's *han* or *ie*. The philosophy or way of the warrior during this period of Japanese history was one that centred on the importance of honourable death, as espoused in the *Hagakure* by Yamamoto Tsunetomo.

The evolution of martial arts during the Tokugawa period

Among the many rules established by the Tokugawa shogunate was that the leaders from each of the *han* were required to travel to and spend a substantial portion of their time (and money) in Edo. The *daimyō*, their retainers, and family members essentially served as political hostages, depriving them of the means to attack Ieyasu or his allies, thereby ensuring shogunate control and continued peace. Ieyasu also closed the country off from outside influence, banning foreigners and foreign products from coming into the country, and Japanese from leaving. Thus, Japan was sealed off from the rest of the

The Teaching of Judo in Japan

world for over 250 years.

The practice and meaning of martial arts and *jūjutsu* evolved during the two-and-a-half centuries of Tokugawa rule. For the first few generations after the Tokugawa took control, warriors continued their practice of *jūjutsu* with the full intent and understanding that their techniques might possibly be used in the battlefields once again. Indeed, during that time there were a number of battles and rebellions that had to be dealt with, such as the siege of Osaka Castle in 1614-1615 and the Shimabara Rebellion in 1637-1638. So the martial arts in general, and *jūjutsu* in particular continued to be practiced with much the same intent and fervour as during the previous century.

As peace flourished, over time the practice and meaning of the fighting arts changed. People came to question the validity of the arts and their purpose in society. If there were no wars, what was the point of learning how to fight? Many of the techniques and practice methods of *jūjutsu* came to be stylized rather than to maintain combat readiness and effectiveness.

During this transformation, warriors struggled to find meaning in their practice of the arts. Thus, over time they came to add the study of literature, calligraphy, poetry, and other cultural arts to their repertoire. Of special importance were activities such as the practice of the tea ceremony, which actually had its first elevation in status by Toyotomi Hideyoshi's favoured treatment of noted tea ceremonial master Sen no Rikyū. The year 1804, in fact, saw the beginning of the *Bunka jidai* (Culture era). Warriors, therefore, were supposed to become not only accomplished in the military arts, but also be learned scholars and cultural artisans in many respects.

The Meiji Restoration and the overthrow of the shogunate

In the nineteenth century, the Japanese public came to increasingly question the ways of the military leadership. After over two-hundred years of lasting peace, people saw little benefit in the continued practice of the fighting arts. Over time, the practice of *jūjutsu* and other martial arts even came to be looked upon with disfavour. Martial artists and warriors in general, who were the only people allowed to wear their swords in public, contributed to these images as they engaged in challenge matches so as to seemingly protect their honour.

The Japanese public came to question many of the rules and laws that had been passed down by the warrior government. In particular, the rights and privileges afforded to the warrior class as the top echelon of society were questioned, especially in times of continued peace when the need for such class distinctions was no longer apparent.

Pressure was also applied from the outside as well, from countries who wanted Japan to open its ports for trade and exchange. These social and political movements came to a head in 1853 when Commodore Perry brought his gunships into Tokyo bay and demanded that he be able to dock his ships and open the country to others. While this was not what started the demise of the Tokugawa shogunate, it acted as a catalyst, as once the country was opened to the outside world, it led to the realization that Japan was vulnerable, and the status quo was no longer acceptable. These developments, along with the contributions of extraordinary individuals such as Saigō Takamori of Satsuma, Sakamoto Ryōma of Tosa, Ito Hirobumi of Chōshū, and Katsu Kaishū from the *bakufu*, brought about a change in the leadership of Japan restoring power to the emperor (hence, the Meiji Restoration).

Among the many laws that were instituted during the Meiji period (1868-1912) were those that eliminated the distinctions, rights, and privileges of the warrior class. For example, in 1871 a decree abolishing the wearing of swords (*haitōrei*) was instituted, and warriors were no longer able to adorn themselves with their weapons. Even though the weapon had probably never been used, it was still considered a symbol of a higher, privileged warrior class, but the warriors were unceremoniously stripped of their status, symbolically, and in reality.

Thus, the Meiji period was a tumultuous time for martial artists, who essentially saw their entire way of life slip away from them. Martial arts, and the ways of the warrior that had been held in such high esteem for centuries, became associated with an archaic relic of the past. Traditional warrior culture gave way to modern diplomacy, politics, internationalization, and education.

Kanō Jigoro and the Birth of Judo

The early years

It was during this tumultuous period of Japanese history that Kanō Jigorō began his career. The history of judo is the history of the shift from a classical martial art to a modern sport and can be understood within the social, historical, and political context of Japan. It is as much the story of Kanō, who devoted himself to the education of the youth of his country, blending traditions and modernity, using individual prowess for collective benefits.

The beginnings of judo are closely related to Kanō's life and personality. He was born on 28 October 1860, in what was then the little village of Mikage (more precisely, Settsukoku, Ubaragun, Mikagemura, Hamahigashi, which is currently Kobe city, Nada East district, Mikage-cho). Kanō's birthplace was well known for *sake* brewing and some members of the Kanō family were wealthy sake brewers. Today the brand name of the company *Kiku Masamune* is very widely known.

Very early in Kanō's rigorous education, Western influences were added to Eastern traditions and teachings. One of his grandfathers was a well-known poet and scholar of Chinese classics. During the 1860s, Kanō's father was a high-ranking official working for the government. A born organizer with a strong sense of social responsibility, he contributed to the modernization of Japan along western lines, opening Hyogo harbour to foreign trade and inviting Western ships with open arms. Young Kanō, in whom the same progressive qualities were to be found later in life, was obviously influenced by his father's spirit of enterprise.

The Teaching of Judo in Japan

In 1870, soon after the death of his mother, his father decided to move to Tokyo. It was a time of great cultural and social ferment in Japan from which Kanō obviously benefited. In Tokyo he was sent to another Confucian school to continue his education. At the same time he was sent for English lessons to Mitsukuri Shūhei, a renowned scholar who belonged to a group of influential thinkers dedicated to educational reforms. In his early teens, Kanō developed a strong taste for math and showed a particular affinity for languages. Actually, throughout his life he demonstrated exceptional language ability. While studying *jūjutsu* he would write his notes in English, probably to secure the confidentiality of his research at a time of intense rivalry among *jūjutsu* schools. In his old age, he also kept his diaries in English.

As a boy, Kanō was frail but quick-tempered. Being extremely gifted, he studied with boys who were older and bigger, and he soon understood the need to find a way to defend himself. At the age of fourteen he entered the Foreign Languages School, which was part of the Kaisei Gakkō. There, Kanō was one of the first Japanese to play baseball, introduced one year before by two American teachers. He loved the spirit of the sport, a new concept in Meiji Japan, and certainly found some inspiration in it later on. In 1877, he entered Tokyo Teikoku (Imperial) University, currently Tokyo University. Many among the teachers and students he met there were to become leading figures in Meiji society. Because he paled in physical size compared to his peers, he decided to learn more about the art which enabled the weak to overcome the strong. However, it was very difficult to find anyone who knew how to teach *jūjutsu*. The Kōbusho, the *bakufu* military academy where *bushi* had been taught *jūjutsu* was already defunct as a result of the Restoration. Besides, as *jūjutsu* was a composite of different systems, this fragmentation had proved somewhat detrimental to its continued existence.

After months of patient research, he finally managed to find a former Kōbusho *jūjutsu* instructor, Fukuda Hachinosuke (the grandfather of Fukuda Keiko, who has lived in the U.S. since 1966 teaching and promulgating the techniques and way of judo- her first visit to the U.S. was in 1953). Hachinosuke became his first *jūjutsu* teacher, reluctantly accepted by his father who saw no future in this old tradition. Two years later, when General Ulysses Grant came to Japan, Kanō knew enough to take part in a *jūjutsu* demonstration, and he eventually took over Fukuda's school when he died in 1877. He kept on studying with Fukuda's teacher, Iso Masamoto, but his interest for academic subjects (philosophy, political science, economics) never flagged.

In 1881, he began to study the *jūjutsu* of the Kitō school with another Kōbusho teacher, Iikubo Tsunetoshi, who replaced Iso after his death, paying particular attention to the perceived spiritual side of *jūjutsu*. This time, the stress was put on the spiritual side of the art. Iikubo was an expert at throws, and he gave less importance to *kata* training. However the tradition's main *kata* (originally performed with armour), the *koshiki no kata* was maintained, and proved to be one of Kanō's favourites; he performed it before the Emperor in 1929. The Kitō school is also where the name "judo" was coined by Kanō, who deliberately chose it to underline the "moral" side of his system.

The birth of Kōdōkan judo
1882 was a landmark year for Kanō. He was appointed lecturer in politics and economics at Gakushūin (then a private school for the nobility) where he was to teach for some years and then serve as a director. He also started a private school, the Kanō Juku, and an English language school. Kanō Juku was a preparatory school whose main goal was to nurture the character of the students who studied there. However, this year is said to be when he formally opened his judo academy, the Kōdōkan, in a space rented from a small Buddhist monastery in Tokyo. The number of his students swelled rapidly, coming from all over Japan. Many left old *jūjutsu* masters to train with Kanō. Kanō's method was adopted by the police and the navy, introduced to schools and universities and even spread overseas. What came to be known as Kōdōkan judo was a synthesis of several schools of *jūjutsu* to which he added ideas taken from interviews, readings, and forgotten techniques. In 1889, after his first trip overseas, during which he inspected educational facilities in Europe, he got married eventually having eight children.

Kanō was an exceptional and brilliant educator. He occupied several positions as headmaster of various schools including the Tokyo Teachers Training college. He was considered a most articulate spokesman in educational matters. Kanō's genius essentially lies in the fact that he saw judo as closely linked with education and adapted it accordingly. He saw and developed the guiding principle behind *jūjutsu* where others had just seen a collection of techniques. The ultimate goal was to make the most efficient use of mental and physical energy. Each combination of movements represented a set of ideas. He rejected techniques that clashed with his conception of life. He paid attention to every single aspect of judo and to its potentialities. Judo etiquette and the aesthetic side of judo, was as much part of this mental and physical discipline as the methods of defence and attack. Judo was, from the start, a sport because of its competitive nature, and a way of life in the founder's mind. The teaching of judo became a means of fighting lethargy, negative frames of mind, and anger. Contests in judo and the lessons derived from them had to be used as mirrors of the social scene.

The principles of judo worked inside and outside the dojo, in the workplace, the school, the political world, everywhere. The forces that were to cause the international success of this discipline were already at work in the early days of his teachings. In 1919 in Tokyo, Kanō met John Dewey, the founder of the American educational system who was then a guest lecturer at the Tokyo Imperial University. They exchanged views on education and various parallels could be drawn from their philosophical concepts. One Sunday morning, Kanō took Dewey to the Kōdōkan to show him how his ideas could be illustrated on the mat. Dewey was fascinated. He admired the way the laws of mechanics were blended with old practices, and added to Zen teachings. He immediately saw the importance of Kanō's teachings : "It is much better than most of our inside formal gymnastics. The mental element is much stronger...A study ought to be made here".

The Teaching of Judo in Japan

The Kanō method

Kanō's method derived from old-style *jūjutsu* techniques, but differed greatly from the methods of the past. Excluding all dangerous *jūjutsu waza* (techniques), Kanō encouraged practitioners to grapple with one another. Through learning techniques to subdue the opponent with safe but effective techniques and break falls, striving for victory now became a means of character building. But this method differed to anything in the past mainly because it referred to modern science and rationalistic theories. Turning his back to the traditional ways of teaching, Kanō preferred to explain judo techniques scientifically, always studying attitudes, analyzing forces at play such as problems of equilibrium and centre of gravity, and so on. In 1895, in order to facilitate the learning process, throwing techniques were classified into five sets (*go kyō no waza*).

Kanō borrowed heavily from a long tradition of thought in which mostly Confucian and Buddhist elements merged with Taoism and Shinto. A neo-Confucian philosopher of the sixteenth century already claimed that "knowing" implied "doing". This heritage was common to Kanō and his contemporaries who equally drew from contemporary national and Western studies on education. Kanō's strategy in the field of education was three-pronged: the acquisition of knowledge, the teaching of morality, and the training of one's body by physical education. The *san iku shugi*, or "principle of the three educations" was a popular theory at the time, certainly adapted from Herbert Spencer,

Kanō Jigorō at approximately seventy years of age

one of the most discussed Victorian thinkers, and others.

As an educator, Kanō advocated the "three culture principle". He made this point clear when he wrote: "a healthy body is a condition not only necessary for existence but as a foundation for mental and spiritual activities." He insisted on the purpose of physical exercises: "no matter how healthy a person may be if he does not profit society his existence is vain". *Taiiku*, physical education, was an important factor of Kōdōkan judo. In the Kōdōkan magazines, *Kokushi* (1888-1903) and *Jūdō* (1915 to the present), articles about physical education were numerous. Kanō saw the training of physical education instructors as essential. When he was in charge of the Teachers Training College, he established a physical education department with a wide range of sports.

Kanō designed judo as a way to develop harmoniously the intellectual, moral and physical aspects of the education of young people. He repeatedly showed how the efficient use of one's mind and body was the key to self-fulfilment. But he added to this the Confucian concept of social obligation and consequently helping others to learn or teach was part of the process. Kanō's principles were summed up in the two mottoes launched by the Kōdōkan Cultural society founded in 1922: *Seiryoku zenyō* and *jita kyōei*, one must make good use of spirit and physical strength for the common good and to reach self-realization.

The spread of judo in Japan and around the world

After Kanō created judo in 1882, the story of its spread in Japan and around the world is well known. Part of the reason was Kanō's brilliant transformation of *jūjutsu* into judo as a response to social and cultural changes in Meiji Japan. As discussed above Kanō was not satisfied with the status quo. He was a learned scholar in a number of fields and heavily influenced by thinkers in the West. The accumulation of his experiences led him to change the techniques of *jūjutsu* into judo and modify the goals of judo practice.

One particular aspect of his method that led to the widespread acceptance and practice of judo was undoubtedly his teaching methodologies. Of course Kanō spent much time thinking about the rational basis for judo techniques, and used these bases to explain judo techniques in ways that had never been explained before. But beyond the teaching of *waza*, Kanō's teaching methodology included extended discussions with his students of daily, social, cultural, and worldly affairs. He gave advice and guidance on lifestyle and living. He exposed his students to other martial arts, especially though his connections with masters in karate and aikido, and also to other cultural activities and world affairs. Kanō's methods were not just simply about practicing judo and training to get strong to win in competition; they were varied because they were centred on the three educational principles of judo: intellectual, moral, and physical education.

These methodologies were at the cutting edge of revitalizing and utilizing martial arts in education during the Meiji period. Kanō's unique approach was not only one of the reasons for the spread of judo in Japan; it was undoubtedly one of the major reasons for judo's spread around the world. The timing was also perfect, as the world became

The Teaching of Judo in Japan

increasingly interested in the culture of Japan because of its victory in the Russo-Japanese War at the beginning of the twentieth century. After that war Japanese cultural exports became well known around the world, and one of those exports was judo.

Japan Today – A New Japan

Cultural and psychological suppositions

The culture and especially the psychological composition of the Japanese people have long been objects of study by scholars and laypersons alike, both Japanese and non-Japanese. For instance in the book by the English-educated, Irish-Greek writer Lafcadio Hearn, *Glimpses of Unfamiliar Japan*, Hearn saw the Japanese as a humble, persevering people who, in the face of danger, threat, grief, and other disheartening emotions, manage to maintain a sense of dignity about themselves as they smile. He also saw the Japanese as people who had instituted politeness as a social rule – who brought mannerisms and etiquette in social interaction to its highest standard. (A little known fact is that in 1891, on his return from Europe, Kanō was appointed principal of the college at Kumamoto, where he asked Hearn to join the faculty as a lecturer in English literature. While there, Hearn began a study of judo.)

These images of the Japanese people and culture were promulgated by the Japanese themselves. Nitobe Inazo's 1900 book *Bushido: The Soul of Japan*, gained notoriety after the Russo-Japanese war as people all around the world struggled to find ways to explain why the Japanese were victorious over Russia. In his book, Nitobe tried to demystify the Japanese character using the concepts of the feudal warrior or *bushi*. According to Nitobe, a sense of chivalry, which he referred to as *bushidō*, permeates the Japanese character:

"Chivalry is a flower no less indigenous to the soil of Japan than its emblem, the cherry blossom; nor is it a dried up specimen of an antique virtue preserved in the herbarium of our history. It is still a loving object of power and beauty among us; and if it assumes no tangible shape or form, it not the less scents the moral atmosphere, and makes us aware that we are still under its potent smell. The conditions of society which brought it forth and nourished it have long disappeared; but as those far-off stars which once were and are not, still continue to shed their rays upon us, so the light of chivalry, which was a child of feudalism, still illuminates our moral path, surviving its mother institution."

The *bushidō* that permeated the Japanese character was composed of a set of core values that included rectitude or justice, courage, benevolence, politeness, veracity and sincerity, honour, loyalty, and self-control. Stoicism was a major part of *bushidō*, as were the concepts of *giri* and *on* (two different types of obligations). Training and education in the *bushidō* way was based on the three major principles of wisdom, benevolence, and courage.

Over the years, the writings of many other scholars from other fields reinforced these images of Japanese culture. Ruth Benedict's *Chrysanthemum and the Sword*, in which she cast the Japanese culture as a group-oriented "shame culture" became one of the most widely read books in cultural anthropology. Nakane Chie's work characterizing Japanese culture as a vertical society did the same. Reprints of works by Nakane and Hearn even in the 1990s repeated these characterizations.

Thus the concepts of perseverance, chivalry, self-sacrifice, honour, and loyalty came to be considered as some of the core concepts of the Japanese personality. These concepts of Japanese culture are reinforced today by media, television, movies, and by Japanese laypersons as well. For all intents and purposes they have become stereotypes of Japanese culture and psychology.

Japanese culture and psychology today

While there is a great consensus among Japanese and non-Japanese about the psychological composition of Japanese culture, recent studies in cross-cultural psychology, as well as studies conducted by the Japanese government and news agencies in Japan, raise questions about their validity now. In my recent book, *The New Japan*, I discussed how seven cultural stereotypes are simply not supported by the available scientific evidence. These seven stereotypes include concepts about Japanese group-orientation (collectivism), self-concepts, interpersonal awareness and consciousness, emotionality, work ethics, organizational human resource practices, and marriage. The studies were conducted by Japanese and non-Japanese researchers, have involved a variety of research methodologies, and have included samples from diverse areas of Japan. Collectively they paint a picture that suggests that the culture and psychology of contemporary Japan do not conform to the stereotypes described above.

A number of new studies that have appeared since also support this conclusion. For example Oyserman and her colleagues recently conducted a meta-analysis of fifty studies comparing European Americans with people from other nations, including Japan and other ethnic groups in the U.S. [2] Their comparisons with the Japanese indicated that, contrary to the stereotype about Japanese culture, Americans were significantly higher on collectivism (group-orientation) than were the Japanese. Most recently Shuper and his colleagues administered Hofstede's Individualism-collectivism scale[3] to samples of Canadian and Japanese university students and found no cultural differences in their levels on this variable.[4] This study is significant because it utilized the exact same scale that Hofstede had used over thirty years prior on which differences did exist.[5]

The study of personality traits across cultures also offers some perspective on this issue. McCrae and his colleagues have developed a way to measure the five personality traits that have been empirically shown to be universal in all cultures and languages tested.[6] Most recently they have aggregated their data across thirty six countries, including Japan, and placed the countries on a two-dimensional space that statistically represent the five personality dimensions.[7] In doing so he obtained a visual map of the

The Teaching of Judo in Japan

countries in terms of their personality characteristics. What was surprising was that the Japanese personality was closer to Spain, Russia, Portugal, and Belgium than it was to other countries of East Asia.

The study of values also offers data on contemporary Japanese psychology. Schwartz and his colleagues have measured values in samples of school teachers and college students in sixty seven nations around the world.[8] Like McCrae and colleagues, Schwartz has transformed his data to create visual maps of the countries in terms of their similarities and differences in values. On this map Japan is most similar to Israel; other countries such as the U.S., Brazil, Australia, and Croatia are also relatively close in space to Japan.

Why should the psychological reality of the Japanese be so different than its consensual, stereotypic culture? There are probably many contributing factors. Japan has seen major social and cultural changes since the beginning of judo at the end of the nineteenth century. Arguably the biggest event to occur from then until now was World War II. The changes instituted by the American occupation forces, including changes in the educational system and the removal of the spiritual powers of the emperor may be factors that have brought about the changes we witness today. Moreover, American occupation forces and a cultural elite of Japan may have worked to promulgate the consensual, stereotypic view of Japanese culture. This may not be entirely unheard of. For instance, despite the stereotypic notion of the concept of *iemoto* being centuries old, it itself is a relatively new one, created in the late nineteenth century by the government in order to stimulate land ownership.

Whatever the causes and contributing factors to a changing or different Japanese culture, what is true is that the psychology of the Japanese people is quite different today than in the past. It may be different than when Kanō created judo, but it is most definitely different than the culture and psychology that characterized post-war Japan.

A New Japan and Old Teaching Methodologies

Differences between the consensual, stereotypic characterizations of Japanese culture and the reality of the psychology of Japanese people today bring with them a host of implications and consequences. Research from my laboratory as well as those of others has shown that gaps between individual perceptions of self from ideals leads to negative consequences. This gap exists because despite real changes in the individual psychologies of the Japanese people as whole, they must still live and contend with a consensual concept of culture and social systems and structures (in the educational system, in business organizations, etc.) that do not match their reality. For example cultural discrepancies between individual psychology and ecological level culture have been predictive of both higher levels of anxiety and depression. Depression, in turn, leads to decreased levels of mental health while anxiety leads to increased levels of physical health problems.[9]

This gap analysis can be conducted on the socio-cultural level and applied to Japan today. The gap between consensual culture and psychological reality in Japan is probably at least one of the reasons for the repeated findings of pessimistic attitudes and pervasive anxiety that are typically found in surveys of the Japanese.[10] This gap probably also contributes to changes in physical and mental health in Japan, increases in certain types of crime, problems in the educational system including dropout and bullying, and the proliferation of a pervasive underground culture. These differences also bring about changes in various strata of society, including businesses, the educational system, and home life. For example, a recent Japanese Institute of Labour Administration survey indicated that in 1995, 34% of companies with more than 3,000 employees instituted policies to stop calling each other by title and position, and instead by name + *san*. In 2001, that number reached 59%.

This gap analysis can be applied to the case of judo as well. I believe that there is a gap today between how judo practices are conducted and the psychology of the judo students who participate. Judo practices today are essentially unchanged over the last fifty years since the end of World War II. After the war, judo was first banned but then reinstated by the American occupation forces as a sport, especially within the educational system. The internationalization of judo, with the founding of the International Judo Federation and the creation of the World Championships in 1956, and then the Olympic Games in 1964, helped to foster the view of judo as a sport. Interestingly, however, this almost exclusive view of judo as a sport may be peculiar to Japan. In one comparison of the values of judo teachers in the U.S., Poland, and Japan, for example, to our surprise the Japanese coaches valued individuality and achievement more than did the American or Polish coaches;[11] the Americans and Poles, on the other hand, valued patriotism, honour, justice, and spiritual balance more than did the Japanese, despite the fact that these are more associated with the educational values of judo.

Because of the pervasive view of judo as a sport in Japan, especially among its coaches and instructors, it is no wonder that judo practices focus on competition training rather than educational, moral, or spiritual development. While competition training in and of itself is not bad, the ways in which it is often conducted, under severe conditions of mental anguish and physical exhaustion and pain for extremely long periods of time, is clearly not commensurate with the psychology of the Japanese public today. Thus there is a gap between the philosophy underlying practices of judo as a whole and the individual psychologies of the masses of people to which it could appeal. As a result judo loses its ability to influence intellectual or moral development. These notions have recently been confirmed by a series of studies by my colleagues and me using the Intercultural Adjustment Potential Scale (ICAPS), which show that judo students have extremely low levels of scores related to self-control and self-discipline compared to other Japanese university student samples.[12] This gap analysis can also be used to explain the continuing decline in the numbers of people enrolling in judo classes in Japan, the drop in the number of juniors doing judo, the decline of the numbers of privately owned

The Teaching of Judo in Japan

machi dōjō, and a host of other changing demographics in the judo world.

It seems that judo in Japan, while continuing to demonstrate that it is the strongest in terms of world level competition, has lost some of its appeal among the Japanese public to deliver the educational, intellectual, and moral benefits that it originally espoused. Further I believe that this loss is the result of the ever increasing gap between the philosophy and nature of contemporary judo practices, with its emphasis on harsh brutality, and the dynamic, fluid, and ever changing realities of the psychology of the Japanese people, which is increasingly focusing on immediate gratification. For judo to deliver the benefits it espouses to the public, we need to consider ways of closing this gap. These ways will inevitably lead to considerations of new teaching methodologies.

A New Japan - The Need for New Teaching Methodologies

A new or at least different culture and psychology in Japan suggests that we consider new teaching methodologies for judo. We have been witness to the consequences of a discrepancy between old teaching methodologies and philosophies and the changing psychologies of the people for years now. For judo to be able to deliver the intellectual, moral, and physical educational benefits to a greater proportion of the people than in the immediate past, it needs to revamp its outlook in terms of underlying philosophies in order to be more appealing and more importantly more commensurate with the psychology of the greater population it wishes to serve.

In fact this is exactly what Kanō did when he created judo in the first place. As we discussed above Kanō was not content with just adopting the techniques and teaching methods of the various *jūjutsu* schools in which he was knowledgeable. He adapted those techniques and more importantly modified the teaching methodologies to make them more contemporary, modern, and progressive. In doing so he addressed a great social need at a time of great social and cultural change and upheaval in people's lives in Japan, and his adaptations were the major reason why judo gained so much popularity. If his teachings and teaching methods did not appeal to the public, and if they did not address great personal, social, and cultural concerns of the time, why would it have become so popular among so many people in so short a time? There is little other explanation.

If we can agree that we need to consider the need for new teaching methodologies of judo in order to be able to deliver the wonderful package of benefits to a larger audience of individuals, then the next question becomes how. To answer this one of the first places we need to re-examine is the teaching methods of Kanō himself. One of the issues that the Japanese people and society face today is one of identity. Clearly the new generations of the past decade or two have rejected the ways of their parents and grandparents. Many have questioned the reason they need to sacrifice so much of their time and life for their companies. Today there is much more of a focus on "me" and immediate, not delayed, gratification, and on issues of quality of life. Today the popular image of a worker is not a "salaryman" but a *"furiitaa"* who jumps from job to job making just enough to get by. Today there is much more affluence in the economy, personally, familial, and nationally. Yet the rejection of the old is not accompanied by an adoption of a new identity. While people are fairly sure they don't want to follow in their parents' footsteps, they are not as sure about what it therefore means to be Japanese, or how they wish to live their lives. These are major identity issues, and I believe that it can explain a number of social problems that Japan faces today.

And in many ways this is exactly the same social problem that Kanō faced at the turn of the nineteenth century. For that reason Kanō's original teaching methods may be very appropriate to address the personal and social concerns that face Japan today. Judo instructors may give consideration to focusing less on judo practice to win competition and more emphasis on having regular, meaningful discussions with their students about life, social issues, national and economic concerns, and world affairs. Judo instructors may give consideration to exposing their students not only to the techniques of judo, but to the underlying history and philosophy of judo. We may expose our students to other martial arts so they can gain an appreciation of those. We may bring lecturers on topics related to sports, such as exercise physiology, sport nutrition, and the like. We may expose our students to other spiritual practices such as yoga or meditation. We can schedule regular field trips to other sporting or cultural events so that students can learn to be excellent citizens and gentlepersons of the world. All of these methods are the very same ones that Kanō himself used in the original development and promulgation of judo 120 years ago.

But we can also go beyond those original ways of Kanō. As judo is part of the educational system in Japan, we need to reconsider its role in that system. Does judo exist in that system for itself or for the sake of education? I believe that judo (and all other physical education activities for that matter) exists in the educational system primarily for the sake of enhancing the educational experiences of the students. So we need to ensure that judo student not only mature and develop their basic physical fitness; we also need to pay attention to their academic performance and social skills. Yet are we doing an adequate job? We may be doing an excellent job in developing basic physical fitness skills, but how are we doing in helping judo students develop good skills for life, especially with regard to their eating and drinking habits, or their rest and recovery? Are we ensuring that judo students are among the best academic students? I think not. Are we ensuring that our judo students have the social skills of exemplary citizens in order to transform society? Data from our studies described above and those of others suggest we have a long way to go.

So perhaps we need to place a greater emphasis on academic learning on our judo students. This can be accomplished in many ways. We can require a certain academic performance standard in order to do judo or even compete. We can have students bring instructors their grades. We can make sure they study by arranging for study halls before or after practice. We can read their papers that they write for classes and give them comments. We can put them on a pedestal and recognize their achievements, just

The Teaching of Judo in Japan

as we recognize the achievements of judo players who win competition. There are so many ways in which these can be accomplished. Surely if we work in high schools or universities as teachers or professors, we should be able to comment on our student's academic work in an intellectual manner so that they grow in their cognitive skills and develop intellectually as well.

Research in education and educational psychology has repeatedly shown that one of the most important things students learn from their teachers is not the content of what they are taught, but the way of being of the teacher. That is, teachers are important role models for their students. If we want to improve the academic performance of our students, then we need to model that performance, motivation, and behaviour to them. We ourselves need to be the best students, continuing our own study, and we need to show our students that that is the case. The same is true for our social skills or personal habits. If we want our students to develop in their social or interpersonal skills, then we need to model for them what those skills are like in our interactions with others. If we want our students to develop good habits, like not smoking, drinking and eating in moderation, taking care of ourselves, staying physically fit, and such, then we need to do it ourselves. If we don't model the behaviour that is desired in our students, then it is highly unlikely that students will adopt those behaviours.

There are so many ways in which new teaching methodologies can be created. In my opinion it all starts with redefining what the underlying philosophy and goal of judo practice should be, the population we want to influence, and understanding the powerful influence of our own behaviours and selves as role models. The hunt for new curricula, pedagogy, and teaching methods are all secondary, albeit an important secondary, to these realizations. The cultural shifts and social issues that Japan faces today seem to me to be important reasons why we give serious thought to these potentialities.

Conclusion

Most people I talk with agree that Japanese culture and psychology are different today than they were in the recent past, and quite different than the stereotypic notions of culture and psychology to which we are accustomed. In fact, I have questions as to whether the Japanese people have ever been like the degree to which cultural stereotypes attempt to pigeonhole them. But whether the consensual, stereotypical culture of Japan matched individual reality in the past is an open and hopefully empirical question that can be addressed by social historians.

Regardless of whether or not it was true in the past, however, we know today that the gap between individual reality and stereotypic culture exists today. And we know that contemporary judo practices for the most part are not delivering the intellectual, moral, and even physical benefits to a wide segment of the population that it could. While competitive judo in Japan surely is doing a great job, judo in the larger sense of the word may not be doing as well. For this reason we need to engage in objective discussion about why that might be and creatively and constructively develop ways of improving the situation if judo is to deliver those benefits.

In my opinion, it is exactly those educational benefits, not winning in competition, that is the light of Kōdōkan judo. It is this light that shined brightly when Kanō first lit it, and it is that light that was passed on to millions of people worldwide. This light, however, seems to have dimmed in contemporary Japan, and we need to think about lighting it again and fanning the flame.

While we all say that the ultimate goal of judo practice is the development of one's character and the improvement of society, we need to come to the realization that despite what people believe there is little inherent in the techniques of judo that produces good people. Good people are produced by teachers who are themselves good people, and who cultivate *people* skills, not judo competition skills. It is the cultivation of these people skills that we need to reconsider and refocus our energies.

I have a dream that one day judo teachers and students are society's most intelligent and knowledgeable individuals, who are the best students and professors academically in the educational system, who exemplify the Japanese cultural essence of kindness and consideration in all aspects of life, and who are the leaders of Japan, both socially, morally, educationally, politically, and economically. Judo is the most wonderful cultural art, sport, and activity that exists in the world. Won't you share my dream and help make it a reality?

Endnotes

[1] A portion of this chapter was taken from a previous work (Brousse & Matsumoto, 1999).
[2] See Oyserman, Coon, & Kemmelmeier, 2002.
[3] See Hofstede, 2001.
[4] Shuper, Sorrentino, Otsubo, Hodson, & Walker, in press.
[5] Hofstede, 1980, 1984.
[6] McCrae, 2001; McCrae & Costa, 1989; McCrae & Costa, 1997; McCrae, Costa, del Pilar, Rolland, & Parker, 1998.
[7] McCrae, 2002.
[8] Shalom H. Schwartz, 1994; S. H. Schwartz, 1994; Schwartz, 1999.
[9] Matsumoto et al., 1999.
[10] Matsumoto, 2002.
[11] Matsumoto, Takeuchi, & Horiyama, 2001.
[12] Takeuchi, Okada, & Matsumoto, in preparation.

Bibliography

Benedict, R. *The Chrysanthemum and the Sword: Patterns of Japanese Culture.* New

The Teaching of Judo in Japan

York: Houghton Mifflin and Company,1946.
Brousse, M., & Matsumoto, D. *Judo: A Sport and a Way of Life*. Seoul, Korea: International Judo Federation, 1999.
Hearn, L. *Glimpses of Unfamiliar Japan*. Tokyo: Charles E. Tuttle, 1894 (1976).
Hofstede, G. *Culture's Consequences: Comparing Values, Behaviors, Institutions and Organizations across Nations* (2nd ed.). Thousand Oaks, CA: Sage Publications, 2001.
Culture's Consequences: International Differences in Work-related Values. Beverly Hills: Sage Publications, 1980.
Culture's Consequences: International Differences in Work- related Values (Abridged ed.). Beverly Hills: Sage Publications, 1984.
Matsumoto, D. *The New Japan*. Yarmouth, ME: Intercultural Press, 2002.
Matsumoto, D., Kouznetsova, N., Ray, R., Ratzlaff, C., Biehl, M., & Raroque, J. "Psychological Culture, Physical Health, and Subjective Well-being". *Journal of Gender, Culture, and Health*, 4(1), 1999. pp. 1-18.
Matsumoto, D., Takeuchi, H., & Horiyama, K. "Cultural Differences in the Values of Judo Instructors". *Budōgaku kenkyu*, 34(1), 2001. pp. 1-10.
McCrae, R. R. "Trait psychology and culture: Exploring intercultural comparisons". *Journal of Personality*, 69(6). 2001, pp. 819-846.
McCrae, R. R. "NEO-PI-R data from 36 cultures: Further intercultural comparisons" In R. R. McCrae & J. Allik, eds. *The Five-Factor Model of Personality Across Cultures* (pp. 105-125). New York: Kluwer Academic/Plenum Publishers, 2002.
McCrae, R. R., & Costa, P. T. "The Structure of Interpersonal Traits: Wiggin's Circumplex and the Five Factor Model". *Journal of Personality and Social Psychology*, 56, 1989. pp. 559-586.
"Personality Trait Structure as a Human Universal. *American Psychologist*, 52, 1997. pp. 509-516.
McCrae, R. R., Costa, P. T., del Pilar, G. H., Rolland, J. P., & Parker, W. D. "Cross-cultural Assessment of the Five-factor Model: The Revised NEO Personality Inventory". *Journal of Cross-Cultural Psychology*, 29(1), 1989. pp. 171-188.
Nakane, C. *Tate-shakai no ningen-kankei: Tanitsu-shakai no riron*. Kodansha, 1967.
Japanese Society. Berkeley, CA: University of California Press, 1970.
Nitobe, I. *Bushido: The Soul of Japan*. Tokyo: Charles E. Tuttle, 1905 (1969).
Oyserman, D., Coon, H. M., & Kemmelmeier, M. "Rethinking Individualism and Collectivism: Evaluation of Theoretical Assumptions and Meta-analyses". *Psychological Bulletin*, 128(1), 2002. pp. 3-72.
Schwartz, S. H. "A Theory of Cultural Values and Some Implications for Work. *Applied Psychology: An International Review*, 48(1), 1999. pp. 23-47.
"Are There Universals in the Content and Structure of Values?" *Journal of Social Issues*, 50, 1994. pp. 19-45.

"Beyond Individualism/Collectivism: New Cultural Dimensions of Values". In U. E. Kim, Triandis, Harry C. et al., ed. *Individualism and Collectivism: Theory, Method, and Applications.* (Vol. 18, pp. 85-119). Newbury Park, CA: Sage, 1994.

Shuper, P. A., Sorrentino, R. M., Otsubo, Y., Hodson, G., & Walker, A. M. (in press). "A Theory of Uncertainty Orientation: Implications for the Study of Individual Differences Within and Across Cultures". *Journal of Cross-Cultural Psychology.*

Takeuchi, M., Okada, R., & Matsumoto, D. (in preparation). "Intercultural Adjustment Potential in Japanese Judo Players".

Chapter 18

Folk Martial Arts and Ritual: Continuity through Economic Change[1]

Raymond P. Ambrosi
University of Alberta

Introduction

Martial arts in China have a very long history. Archaeological records reveal that martial arts played an important role among the elite and peasant classes from a very early age.[2] In the modern age, Chinese martial arts have been greatly popularized through *wuxia* "swordsman" novels, movies and media while Chinese pop culture television dramas endlessly recount the exploits of martial experts, generals and swordsmen. Because martial arts are woven into China's society, permeating all social classes, it may be regarded as a type of popular cultural identity.

Modernized acrobatic renditions of "martial arts" promoted by the Chinese government and proclaimed the national sport, have become increasingly popular internationally. But these modern 'sanitized' sport-oriented martial arts have their roots in traditional folk martial arts which were and are practiced primarily by rural people. People in rural areas normally engaged in martial training for defence, health, or spiritual development, and when social conditions deteriorated, they played a central role in many peasant uprisings in Chinese history.[3] The western world's first significant encounter with Chinese martial arts was during the Boxer Uprising of 1900. Upon the defeat of the Uprising, the Qing government brutally suppressed the participants.

These historical events give rise to several questions: Why was the study of military arts popular among farmers in rural areas? What were the central tenets of these groups? What function did these organizations serve in rural areas? What social function do such groups serve in modern society? In order to address these questions, this paper provides a brief overview of the past and present socio-cultural milieu and function of one such martial arts group, the Meihuaquan sect or Plum Flower Boxers as it is found in Guangzong County, Hebei province.

Lu's research[4] shows that since at least the late 1500s, a type of martial art known as Meihuaquan has been popular in the border regions of Shandong, Hebei and Henan provinces. The group's teachings are comprised of a 'military' (*wu*) aspect, consisting of training in armed and unarmed combat skills, and a 'civil' (*wen*) aspect which includes meditation and breathing exercises[5], as well as divination. Both the *wen* and *wu* aspects exist within an encompassing philosophical-religious belief system synthesized from

Daoism, Buddhism and Confucianism folk religious traditions.

Throughout the year, performance of Meihuaquan's martial arts occupies a very important role as a form of recreation and as an organizing force in public celebration of festive occasions. Each year in the late fall, after the crops have been harvested and the agricultural duties finished, rural people occupy their spare time with the practice of the martial and civil training; especially popular is the practice of martial arts. Organized at the grassroots level at various occasions throughout the year, martial arts performances can attract hundreds and sometimes even thousands of villagers from surrounding areas. Fieldwork clearly shows that the festivals and cultural events related to martial arts occupy a prominent role in the lives of villagers in many of the borderland counties.

Surprisingly however, a review of popular and academic literature revealed very little textural information regarding rural folk martial organizations, a glaring oversight by historians and social scientists. Embedded in the rural society for centuries, martial arts are obviously one of the primary leisure and cultural activities. They have a prominent role in local history and in social organization and festivals, and play an important role in funeral ceremonies and local folk-religious systems. Yet this manifestation of folk culture has been either completely ignored or given only very cursory attention by researchers of rural society in China.

This paper aims to address the questions raised above while focusing on the past and present-day sociological significance of folk martial arts associations in the rural areas of north China. In particular, this work aims to show how social organization in the Meihuaquan sect and its use of ritual allow it to function as a network providing mutual aid to its members. The paper also intends to illustrate how performance and ritual play critical roles in maintaining group cohesion and popular appeal. It is the element of ritual and ceremony that ensures such folk organizations continue to play a vital cultural, political and economic role in rural areas in spite of changing circumstances which threaten their survival. To conclude, I will offer some preliminary comparisons of this case-study in China with the folk martial art *bō-no-te* found in Aichi prefecture, Japan.

Borderlands: Past and present

Meihuaquan is but one of many martial arts and folk associations that are concentrated especially along the border areas (See Figure 1) of Shandong, Hebei and Henan. Other folk associations include Daoist associations, Buddhist associations (*pusahui*), Christians, rain appeal societies, and numerous folk religions.[6] Many, like the *Yizhuxiang* and *Shenxiandao*, are highly secretive and exist despite being banned by the state as heterodox religions. Little is known about their current status.[7] A variety of martial arts sects (*quanpai*), including *Daqingquan, Hongquan, Dahongquan, Meihuaquan, Sanhuangpaochui, Shaolinquan,* and *Taijiquan* have been an integral part of the rural culture for many centuries.

Folk Martial Arts and Ritual

Figure 1. Relative location of the study area on a map of China

This border region has been a 'hotbed' of such voluntary organizations owing to the area's historical, geopolitical and economic situation. For centuries, this area has been prone to natural disasters, especially flooding which periodically displaced great numbers of people who were already living on the brink of starvation.[8] When disaster struck, the social order was disrupted and relief from the government was always very slow to arrive. Far from political and economic centres, these ambiguous areas have always been difficult for various provincial governments to manage. They were a convenient haven for criminals, robbers and bandits who could easily flee from the legal jurisdictions of one province into another.

Living within this lawless and impoverished societal context, and having few means of social mobility, many displaced people sought subsistence in outlawry and secret societies.[9] These groups emphasized solidarity and cohesion through mutual aid, offered safety, brotherhood, food, lodging, and provided money or interest-free loans to their members. In addition, they offered the possibility for social advancement, attainment of prestige and political power within the organization. This was undoubtedly an attractive alternative to the 'outside' society where the only means of social advancement was through the imperial examination system.[10] The folk associations and secret societies provided a type of informal social safety net. They were able to provide for the material and psychological needs of people living a very precarious existence.[11]

Owing to the lawlessness which prevailed, only the martial societies which banded together to form village militias were capable of providing any protection for the common people.[12] In this borderland region which had a longstanding reputation for its martial art virtues, people studied boxing and swordsmanship not only as a means of defence, but for recreation and to teach moral education (*wude* – or martial virtue). Marketplace exhibitions of martial skills by wandering teachers were common.[13] For peasants, martial fighting skills were simply a necessity of life and the centre of much of their social activity.

The folk organizations had broad popular support and exerted considerable influence over a large population by administering affairs through a leadership composed of a hierarchical network of masters and students. Some groups, like Meihuaquan, also controlled militias and engaged in religious ritual practices. For these reasons, these groups were considered insidious threats and were banned throughout the Ming and Qing dynasties.[14]

In the late Qing dynasty, poor governance, high taxes, military corruption, banditry, drought and flooding exacerbated widespread poverty, led to the breakdown of socioeconomic systems and displaced large numbers of people. Political corruption, when combined with injustices carried out by the Catholic and Protestant churches, became intolerable. In 1900, rural martial arts associations, led by the Meihuaquan school, combined the popular appeal of their folk religious ritual together with practical fighting skills and rose in rebellion in the Boxer Uprising.[15] The defeat of the rebellion that year which resulted in widespread persecution and execution of its participants, however, did not improve living conditions. Socio-economic decline continued until the 1920s when "brigandage assumed truly endemic proportions".[16]

The Present

The historical underdevelopment and peripheral nature of these regions continues to this day in Guangzong and surrounding counties. The map in Figure 2 clearly shows that the counties of Guangzong, Julu, Pingxiang, and Wei lie within an area largely bypassed by major transportation routes to other parts of the country. Rail lines skirt the perimeter of this underdeveloped region. In 1997, Guangzong county had one of the lowest per capita net incomes of the 138 counties in Hebei province at 1636 *yuan* with real cash in-hand incomes of 400-500 *yuan*[17] per year. Until the early 1990s, per capita grain and protein availability in Guangzong was at a bare subsistence level, a situation which has improved significantly since that time.[18] Poor transportation and relative inaccessibility remain contributing factors to underdevelopment in Guangzong which is designated as a national "impoverished region" and receives financial assistance from the state.[19]

Folk Martial Arts and Ritual

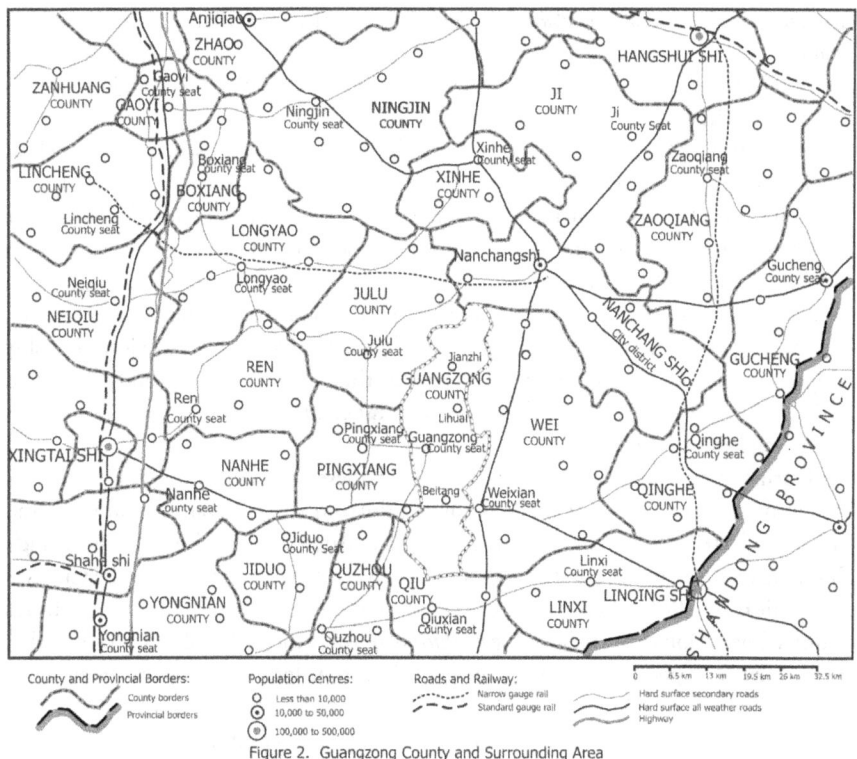

Figure 2. Guangzong County and Surrounding Area

Meihuaquan as a Folk Organization: Recent History

While a variety of martial arts groups are active in the border regions of Shandong, Hebei and Henan provinces, this study examines the Meihuaquan sect in Guangzong country, Hebei for the following reasons. Firstly, Meihuaquan has by far the largest number of practitioners, is well-organized, and it has been an important component of the socio-cultural milieu of the region since the sixteenth century.[20] Meihuaquan folk organizations maintain a wide network of practitioners especially in the border regions. Owing to the group's secrecy, estimating its current membership is very difficult. A conservative guess places the number of people directly involved at 200,000 to 500,000.[21] In Guangzong country, the Meihuaquan school is predominant, having as adherents an estimated 26 to 58 percent of the county's population of 261,000.[22] Regardless of the actual number, Meihuaquan is pervasive and involves a large percentage of the county's population.

Secondly, and most importantly, its organizational structure, which incorporates a well-developed folk religious belief system together with martial arts training, distinguishes it apart from all other folk associations, secret societies and martial arts groups in the region.[23] It is comprised of two sections – a 'Wuchang' engaged in physical martial training, and a *'Wenchang'* engaged in secret ritual, mediation, divination and healing.

Because of this religious/ritual element, the investigation of folk religious groups is a very sensitive issue in modern China. Chinese national law forbids the existence of superstition, sects and secret societies including folk religious practices[24] such as magical healing, exorcism, divination and geomancy. Such groups are considered an insidious threat because of their characteristic trait – fluid belief systems and charismatic leadership which are resistant to state control.[25] The modern suspicion and outlawing of folk religions is simply a continuation of the policy of the late Qing and Republican period. Because Meihuaquan's *Wenchang* involves secret ritual, divination and healing, the group has been labelled a heterodox folk religion and secret society. Harshly suppressed by the Qing dynasty for its role in the Boxer Rebellion, and persecuted periodically[26] until the 1990s, the group's membership is extremely cautious about discussing internal affairs with outsiders.[27]

During the Republican period until the Japanese invasion in 1937, the sect was able to practice freely. During the following thirteen years of warfare and upheaval, practice of Meihuaquan was nearly impossible. After the founding of the People's Republic in 1949, martial arts groups were relatively free to practice until the Cultural Revolution in 1966 when they were again prohibited as heterodox, superstitious counter-revolutionary sects (*fandong daohuimen*). After the Cultural Revolution, other martial arts were permitted to practice openly but some local governments maintained prohibitions against Meihuaquan.[28]

In the late 1980s, Meihuaquan teachers and historians from cosmopolitan areas of China lobbied the rural governments and police organizations to lift their prohibitions. Seeing the value of martial arts as a type of 'patriotic physical education' local government cooperated, relaxed restrictions and began to carefully promote martial arts training. Their efforts succeeded and by the late 1980s, local governments began to promote the *Wuchang*, the martial arts aspect, as a traditional sport for health.

Decades of social strife and prohibition saw many accomplished masters die unable to train a new generation of followers. The longstanding tradition of the *Wuchang* martial training had died out in many villages. Many people, however, continued to secretly teach martial arts and its related *wen* scriptures and ritual practices late at night or inside their homes, out of the sight of prying neighbours. Ironically, the primary targets of political prohibition – the 'feudal superstitions' of *wen* – geomantic rituals, divination, scriptures, and ancestor worship widely regarded as the core of Meihuaquan– were much easier to hide and practice secretly. As a result, ritual and meditation practices survived in many of the same villages where martial art combative training was extinguished.

Recovery

After prohibitions were lifted in the 1990s, rural people, enthused and encouraged, extended considerable effort and the martial arts aspect of Meihuaquan recovered

Folk Martial Arts and Ritual

significantly while the meditation/ritual aspect remained largely underground. Elderly masters organized to teach the new generation and prevent the extinction of their art. Students often travelled widely to seek out masters with special knowledge. Villages which lamented the loss of their martial tradition invited teachers to their village to instruct the youth and so re-establish their martial training tradition. In Guangzong, one village team was responsible for the recovery of Meihuaquan in many of the surrounding villages.

For many village youth, newly "legalized" martial training took on a new vigour and male practitioners of all ages remarked "the practice of boxing (*quanshu*) is something our village has always done, and so we too study it". Women in one village commented that it was common for women in their village to be versed in martial arts (Guangzong informants 2003). Young people are encouraged to learn Meihuaquan for their "health" and "moral education", "for tradition", and to "keep them out of trouble". While the martial arts training of the *Wuchang* became public and widespread, the *Wenchang* arts of meditation, divination and ancestor worship continued to be practiced secretly.

By 1992, visits by small tourist groups led the Guangzong county government to realize that Meihuaquan's colourful performances could be used to promote tourism and economic development. The county government has made efforts to legalize, revitalize and encourage folk martial arts traditions, especially large scale public performance of interest to tourists. The government provided help to organize teams, provide training camps for village youth, and provide demonstration teams with funds for weaponry, uniforms, transportation and meals for on special occasions. The lifting of prohibitions and rural people's enthusiasm caused a significant increase in the numbers of practitioners involved in Meihuaquan martial arts practice between 1990 until at least 1997.

Without exception, small tourist groups have been impressed and have found that the martial arts exhibitions to emanate a genuine quality which makes the performances of the region visually and artistically distinct and more attractive than the performances of commercialized and standardized national sport martial arts. My research indicates that revenues earned from tourism may provide a significant source of income in this region which has limited opportunities for economic diversification. Preliminary observations from fieldwork in 2003 indicate that tourism has significantly boosted local pride and contributed to the revival of folk arts, including martial arts like Meihuaquan.

Current Challenges

The martial arts sects have weathered significant challenges in the past, but will face perhaps their greatest threat in future fundamental changes in the economic and cultural systems in which they exist. Tourism may play a role in exacerbating the rate of decay of martial arts associations, or it may also perhaps contribute to their survival.

The region's isolation and inaccessibility have been largely responsible for both the formation and preservation of localized customs, dialects and martial associations. Even in the 1930s, the county was considered to be quite unique in having rigidly preserved many ancient customs of past dynasties because of the region's isolation and lack influence from contemporary culture (*Guangzong Xianzhi* 1933). While many old customs and practices have largely died out in rural areas with thriving economies, Guangzong's folk customs are still actively practiced.

However, as transportation and communications improve, and the area becomes economically tied with more developed areas, tourism is also likely to increase. Facing an accelerated rate of economic and social change, the region is undergoing significant change. This will present considerable challenges for folk organizations like Meihuquan.

In the 1980s, as China's economy improved, and job opportunities opened to cash-strapped rural areas, younger men began travelling to cities in search of paid labour during the agricultural slack season. Absent from the village during the season when martial training is generally undertaken, they cannot study, teach or take part in public performances. Additionally, prior to the 1990s, most families could not afford formal education for their children beyond elementary school. Children thus had plenty of free time for the study of martial arts. As real cash incomes increased, children were sent to school for longer periods with the result that they cannot devote much time to martial studies. Rural people lament that this is causing a deterioration of martial arts in the region. They hope that regional economic development, perhaps aided through small scale cultural tourism, will keep young men in the region and allow communities to establish schools which feature martial arts in the curriculum as a means to check these trends.

As tourists are increasingly attracted to the region's "authentic" colourful martial arts performances organized by the grassroots Meihuaquan sect, revenues from tourism are seen as a means through which rural people, many of whom live below provincial poverty levels, can supplement their income. Economic conditions of this isolated area give rise to a high economic multiplier effect and as a result, even low tourism earnings can bring significant benefits to the local economy.[29] Fieldwork suggests that tourist interest in the region helped Guangzong county attain provincial recognition as a "homeland of folk culture and Meihuaquan". But tourism is often a "double edged sword" which can bring economic benefits, but which also can also destroy the resource upon which it is based.[30]

Forms of Ritual: Structural Organization

The next section will briefly examine how the division of the sect into *wen* or Civil and *wu* or Martial enables it to function as a mutual aid and communication network. More importantly, the *wen* and *wu* aspects contain many forms of ritual which serves to ensure the group's longevity and endow it with a highly flexible structure.

Lu's research indicates that, since from the late 1500s, the Meihuaquan sect consisted of two components: a *Wenchang* (civil/arts field) and a *Wuchang* (martial field).[31] These two subdivisions are not separate or independent bodies but rather are hierarchical layers which complement each other.[32] It is this unusual organizational system which distinguishes the Meihuaquan school from other regional folk religions and martial sects.[33]

In a typical village, most of the practitioners only study *wu* martial arts training, and are not well acquainted with specific rituals and beliefs of the *wen*. But they regularly participate in *wen* activities during in-home rituals and during public performances during which feature conspicuous and lively *wu* martial arts exhibitions to commemorate ancestral masters. In each village, only a few individuals are accepted into the *Wenchang* to study divination and other *wen* methods.

Wuchang (Martial field)

The *Wuchang* (martial field) is concerned with the practice of armed and unarmed combat for reasons of health, defence, and personal improvement. Physical exercises of the martial field are intended to cultivate and manipulate *qi* energy in the body, to improve the flow and circulation of this energy, to protect the body from illness, and from physical attack. The basic training method, known as the *jiazi* or "Frame", is the foundation for many other unarmed and armed training methods.

During the agricultural slack period from November until early spring, the practice of martial arts is a major recreational activity for anyone who wishes to study. Practitioners young and old gather and practice either at flat open areas where grains are dried or in a local teacher's yard. Generally, students will learn the basic training Frame first, followed by weapons training, and various two person fighting routines. The practice area is often in a prominent location, and anybody may come and watch at any time.

Many of the physical training methods are heavily ritualized including the Frame, which contains many techniques which, at first glance, appear to have little practical application in combat. This is significant because practitioners consider their art to be much more than a system for fighting. Rather, they refer to it as "the wordless book of truth" (*wuzi zhenjing*) and perceive it as a method of spiritual cultivation, a lifestyle and a vocational education to improve their life, enhance their intellect and nurture their health.

Ritual and symbolism is inherent in the practice of Frame which is practiced with the intention of harmonizing the *jing* (body), *qi* (primordial energy) and *shen* (mental vitality) to arrive at a state of *hunyan* or wholism where the mind and body are tightly integrated. The Frame is constructed of postures and movements which symbolize

Chinese cosmological understanding based on *yin-yang, bagua* and Five Element theory. In one regional variation of the Frame, the opening techniques symbolize a fundamental Chinese understanding of nature in which all things progress from the *wuji* or void to the *bagua* and the Ten-Thousand-Things. Upon this symbolic recreation of existence from non-existence, the routine continues with five basic postures which correlate to Daoist philosophical concept of the interconnected Five Elements (metal, water, wood, fire, and earth) and their relationship to the flow of energy in the microcosmic human realm and the macrocosmic natural world. Because the structure of the Frame itself represents the progression from simplicity to complexity and the goal of "returning to the original condition" – the purification and simplification of the spirit and intellect – physical practice of the Frame is in itself a ritual that practitioners perform daily.

While the basic training methods of martial arts in the region are generally practiced individually, Meihuaquan's Frame is unusual in that it is regularly practiced by groups of individuals in a circle. Training in a circular formation is not only symbolic of unity, but creates unity and camaraderie through mutual hard physical training. The fundamental training methods reflect on the connection and continuity of people and nature – they imbue the practitioner with the belief that he can connect with the cosmos.

Other practice and training routines are also symbolically choreographed to reflect the sect's emphasis on justice, equality and righteousness. Many of the weaponry training routines pit multiple attackers with long spears against a single defender armed with special defensive weapons. The spearman, representing bandits or government soldiers, is invariably defeated at the hands of the single defender representing the villager – outnumbered but victorious. Regular performances of these routines deliver the message that the belief in Meihuaquan and its righteous cause will bring victory regardless of the apparent hardship.

Wenchang

The *Wenchang* (civil/arts field) is concerned with meditation practices, healing arts, numerology, *fengshui* (geomancy) and divination. People[34] wishing to study these practices are accepted into the *Wenchang* after a divination ritual which supernaturally confirms their worthiness and dedication. Through a secret ceremony, these select few are conveyed with special status, and may study theory and scripture texts, meditation, genealogies, divination, healing, and how to conduct ceremonies and rituals[35]. People who become adept in *wen* skills command respect and provide leadership for the entire sect.[36]

Ritual experts of the *Wenchang* function as intermediaries between the supernatural Founding Ancestors and believers. The *Wenchang* experts pay homage daily to the Founders by burning incense at a simple shrine in a private room. Through the strict observance of this practice, they obtain mental clarity which enables them to confer with the Founders. In addition to their private ceremonial duties, they may hold many

Folk Martial Arts and Ritual

other divination or healing rituals throughout the day if requested by other Meihuaquan practitioners. The intermediary services of *Wenchang* ritual experts are sought by villagers who wish to appeal to the Founding Ancestors for a wide variety of issues including protection, safe travel, good fortune in business, advice on the treatment of illness and where to find doctors, which direction to seek lost pigs or to pursue business opportunities. *Wenchang* experts are often called upon to mediate problems among villagers, or to heal children who are suffering from 'fright' or 'supernatural' injuries.

Healing non-believers is an important mechanism through which new members are recruited. After being healed, the former patients, and often their entire family, come to believe in the healing efficacy of the Ancestors and wish to join the sect to enjoy the benefits provided by membership. Many of the *Wenchang* experts are well-known healers whose services are in demand not only throughout the local area but in neighbouring provinces. With regard to other ritual services, in some villages, divination and appeals to the Ancestors are provided only to Meihuaquan people, while in other villages, *Wenchang* specialists will provide these services for non-practitioners.

In all cases, sect traditions prohibit them from charging money for treatments or accepting material benefits in exchange for treatment. Because of their skills and virtuous behaviour, they are looked up to as community leaders, embodying and promoting the sect's code of moral conduct.

Playing a central role in the activities of the group, the concept of the Founding Ancestors[37] in Meihuaquan is significantly different from other folk religions or martial sects of the region. In particular, Meihuaquan does not worship any one identifiable patriarch, nor can any particular family lineage claim the patriarch as their ancestor.[38] Rather, adherents assert that the sect has "existed since the beginning of time" by a mythic figure who is usually referred to as *zushi* 'the Founder'.[39] This mythical founder, for which there is no depiction, is a figurehead or a representative of past masters who made life-long contributions to the sect's evolution.[40] The Founder, whose name appears on the modest shrine used in everyday ceremonies, is seen as capable of protecting the sect's adherents, curing illness and providing guidance on not only sect activities but also on the day-to-day affairs of members. As a belief system or folk religion, Meihuaquan adherents are linked together through common belief in the *'lingqi'* or supernatural efficacious powers of the 'Founder'.

For rural people living a marginal existence, the martial skills of the *Wuchang* offer self-protection and promote good health. Divination, healing and meditation skills of the *Wenchang* offer adherents a way to comprehend and cope with the unpredictable forces, such as illness and economic hardship that threaten their very survival. In all, their system of practices and beliefs is a philosophical stance which rural people can readily accept. Both *wu* physical practice methods and *wen* divination, healing and meditation methods emphasize the development of personal intellect and spirit. By participating in the daily ritual of training, which is has as its core the worship of the sect's founding ancestors, practitioners are deeply aware that the tradition is imbedded in local history. They firmly believe that the teaching of Meihuaquan and propagation of the group's beliefs, which emphasize equality and mutual aid, are meritorious, righteous deeds for the betterment of society. The very ritual of practice embodies their belief and bonds them as 'martial brothers'[41].

Social Organization and Ceremony

The above discussion shows how the sect's organization into *wen* and *wu* establishes the trend to ritualize many aspects of the group's activities. From training in combat skills to healing to divination, ritual elevates the activity and imbues it with special meaning for all believers. The next section examines how social organization and participation in public ceremony continues this process and ensures longevity for the group.

The sect's social organization and ritual create strong student-teacher and student-student relationships which link members in a pseudo-kinship system. Social organization within the group follows a Chinese familial model that utilizes generation numbers to identify rank, and terminology suggesting blood relationships. These linkages are further strengthened through what I have called 'ritual bonds' created through ceremonies and performances which commemorate the dead and the sect's patriarchs.

Social Organization Based on the Model of Family

Students are accepted into the sect through a divination ceremony in which the Founding Ancestors must give their consent. Having "entered the door (入門)" of the sect, members are given generational names and numbers. All disciples of a master will be of the same generation and are identified by the same Chinese character and generation number. Because only members possess this special knowledge, it is commonly used as a means of identifying oneself to other practitioners when meeting for the first time. After determining each other's rank, followers will address each other using pseudo-kinship terminology. For example, anyone with the same generation number as their master is addressed as "uncle",[42] while students of the same generation will address each other as "brother"[43] or "sister".

The use of generational numbers for social organization has the interesting effect of creating networks of practitioners over wide areas. Students may study martial arts from experts in their own village. But they generally will not become the sworn disciple of that expert. Rather, they will be introduced to a master in another village who has a high generational number. Though they may meet this master only once or twice a year (or less), this custom has the effect of linking villages and students together in a wide network which allows for a constant exchange of practice methods, as well as knowledge and news among widely separated villages. Such exchanges also help avoid extreme regional variations in practice methods and the separation of groups into independent factions.

Folk Martial Arts and Ritual

Ritual Bonds through Ceremony

Central themes are unity and the upholding of righteous justice – themes which are constantly replayed and reinforced through legend and language, social structure and ritual events. Folk legends in the region recount the exploits of powerful masters who helped disadvantaged people, healed the sick, and punished unjust people and oppressors. These stories emphasize central themes of humility, the importance of dignity over monetary gain, and the dominance and solidarity of the Meihuaquan sect over threatening outside forces. The use of public performance as ritual is very important to commemorate past masters and to reaffirm solidarity among members.

This theme of solidarity is constantly reinforced in everyday language and interaction. The phrase 'Meihuaquan is one family' is commonly heard whenever members gather. Most importantly, solidarity is manifested each time small or large groups gather together to perform. The group performances are not competitions to determine champions, but rather are opportunities to observe other's skills, improve one's own abilities, meet with old friends, and make new acquaintances. Judged competition usually does not take place because winning and losing is considered a crass individual pursuit and thus detrimental to the sect as a whole. Performing together reaffirms the divergent group's common interests and beliefs and maintains long term bonds between villages. Performances and gatherings are important social events for rural people who, prior to television, had limited options for recreation. For public performance, people of all ages travel in tractors piled high with a colourful spears, broadswords, and assorted wooden weapons.

Generally there are three types of public performances: The first variety, *assorted performances,* may occur at any time for a variety of reasons including the establishment of new practice grounds, to celebrate village festivals for local gods, and more recently, to attend regional folk art celebrations or to perform for tourist groups. Attendance ranges from as few as several hundred people to as many as several thousand.

Secondly, performances are held at *funeral ceremonies* and, on occasion, to commemorate prestigious deceased masters. During funerals, a brief performance is held in the yard of the deceased person's home. Following this, the martial arts practitioners will join the procession which carries the coffin to the field for burial. Another brief performance is held at the outskirts of the village before the deceased is carried outside village boundaries to the gravesite. Informants explained that "performance of martial arts was a fitting and auspicious way to send deceased off on their journey to the underworld". Funerals of famous masters are especially important and may attract many hundreds of performers and attendees and spectators from surrounding villages.

Thirdly, *commemorative trans-regional festivals* are those which attract practitioners from surrounding counties and provinces. The largest and most important of these are the exhibitions are held in neighbouring villages in Pingxiang county, Hebei. On the sixth and fifteenth day of the first lunar month, thousands of believers and practitioners from nearby counties and provinces gather at the grave sites of former illustrious patriarchs of the sect. Martial arts performances continue from early morning until late afternoon, while believers burn spirit paper, set off firecrackers at the graves of the patriarchs and make appeals for the sect's propagation, for improving one's martial arts skills, for bountiful crops, good health and the recovery from sickness, and for peace and protection of villages from disaster. Meihuaquan's annual cycle of ceremonies and performances culminate in these two large festivals.

Conclusion

It has been shown that historical social and economic conditions necessitated the existence of secret societies and martial sects. Because these sects offered a governing system separate from the state and exerted strong influence over large segments of the population, they experienced periodic persecution. Meihuaquan was able to survive these purges owing to its internal social organization and the role of ritual. The group's social organization and use of generational names created a flexible system of leadership and allegiance to the sect as a whole rather than to any one particular master or family. To prevent overly strong allegiances to one's own village or master, the generational number system and the custom of becoming disciples of masters in other villages cut across the vertical affiliations of family lineages and create horizontal linkages within and among villages. This cross-lineage function is strengthened through the sect's belief in the Founder, an enigmatic figure who cannot be traced to any particular family lineage. Folklore functions to establish and root Meihuaquan in prehistory, and it promotes egalitarianism, solidarity and righteous behaviour.

Celebrations commemorating both life and death are carried out through the medium of martial arts. This draws together distant villages, provide opportunities for students to meet their formal masters and "brothers", strengthen friendships and forge new relationships. Practitioners are not simply practicing boxing – or fighting techniques – they see themselves as engaged in the lofty goal of propagating a 'sacred' art, in connecting heaven, earth and man, in communion with the Dao. While they are very much aware of the practical day-to-day benefits of membership in this network of social relations, they consider teaching the art to be a magnanimous act for the benefit of society. Their regular participation in ritual elevates the ordinary act of training in fighting techniques to the realm of "sacred". Within this realm of supernatural efficacy, the ability to heal, attracts new members and ensures propagation.

As a result of collective belief constantly reinforced through everyday speech, legend, daily training, mutual aid, and group participation in festive rituals and public performance, the *Wenchang*'s (civil/arts field) belief system serves as a unifying force and authority which has transcended lineages and village affiliations for several hundred years.[44]

Today, the region remains economically underdeveloped and limited government social welfare programs necessitate the existence of such mutual aid organizations.

Folk Martial Arts and Ritual

Fieldwork investigation indicates that Meihuaquan networks provide labour and funds for collective projects and small business, and assistance for building of homes or martial arts high schools. The networks also help adherents find paid employment or marriage partners, and can help them obtain better prices on agricultural commodities. By performing such functions, the associations provide social security and financial assistance which has been, and will continue to be, very important in community stability and integration and in the region's economic development.

What the future holds for folk organizations such as Meihuaquan is difficult to predict. Guangzong's overall standard of living has improved significantly since the early 1990s and its isolation is rapidly fading. As the area becomes increasingly modernized and tied to the market economy of China, folk customs are in danger of being seen as valueless anachronisms and fading away. In addition, as tourism increases, the danger exists that martial arts and folk art performances will become commodified for the tourist trade. Folk performance and the folk organizations themselves could lose their inherent value to locals leading to the erosion their role in integrating rural society. However, preliminary findings suggest that interest in folk art may be growing partly owing to the positive attention they receive from tourism groups and the county government since the early 1990s. The tourists' admiration is contributing to local pride and may play a role in the preservation and revitalization of traditional heritage in Guangzong.

As the economic and social conditions of the border regions change, and tourism and contact with the outside world increases, Meihuaquan and similar folk organizations will change to adapt to new circumstances. It remains to be seen how Meihuaquan will change and whether it will continue to its egalitarian focus as income gaps become more apparent. But it is unlikely that this rural martial association will become extinct; it is tightly wrapped into the socio-cultural and historical backdrop of the region. As long as public participation in Meihuaquan ritual life continues, the sect is likely adapt and survive. These public ceremonies are "affirmation of faith" which not only link members of the sect together in belief, but they also physically bring members together for ritual and physical performance. Thus, ritual plays a crucial role in the maintenance and survival of these groups even in the modern day where out-migration and the changing economy may threaten aspects of traditional culture.

Owing to the difficulties in investigating these issues, there is much that remains to be investigated about Meihuaquan's social organization, the ritual and function of the *Wenchang*, the role of women practitioners, and the degree to which the sect functions as an information and economic network. Future research in this direction and on folk societies in general, will address the dearth of information on this topic and may reveal much about the economic and political role of similar organizations in rural societies.

As part of the concluding thoughts the role of ritual in martial arts, this work will briefly turn its attention to examine a folk martial art association in rural Japan which, like Meihuaquan in China, is highly ritualized and dependent upon ritual public performance for the group's propagation.

In Aichi-prefecture, a folk martial art known as *bō-no-te* is practiced by approximately 3000 people in thirty-five groups in approximately twenty communities. Their art has been handed down since the 1500s. Compared to more well-known Japanese martial arts, the performance of *bō-no-te* appears to be more like a performing art or dance rather than a martial art. In fact, it is often classified by Japanese social scientists as a performing art. This classification is quite misleading because *bō-no-te* is, undoubtedly, a form of martial art which has become highly ritualized but still embodies practical fighting techniques and principles. *Bō-no-te* performances consist of dance-like choreographed fighting sequences in which practitioners primarily use a wooden staff (*bō*). More advanced practitioners also use wooden and steel swords, spears and sickles. *Bō-no-te* choreographed performances generally pit a staff-wielding practitioner, representing the virtuous rural *bō-no-te* expert, against a swordsman who represents a professional warrior and the oppressive ruling class. In these routines, the peasant *bō-no-te* practitioner is always victorious against his oppressor.

Literature and interviews with practitioners and researchers suggest two primary reasons why *bō-no-te* became highly ritualized, and dance-like in its structure and performance. One reason is that the Tokugawa period government banned the practice of martial arts by peasants. In order to avoid the attention of the government, *bō-no-te* practice methods and performance style underwent a process of ritualization in order to disguise its combat effectiveness. Secondly, as the performance of *bō-no-te* became increasingly important as a way to pay homage to the *kami* (gods) during *matsuri* (festivals), *bō-no-te* became increasingly ritualized as its religious significance grew more important.

In the past, it was likely taught in rural areas as a practical method for personal and village defence. By rallying members in solidarity around common goals – the propagation of their art as a system of defence, as recreation, and as an important part of harvest festivals at local Shinto shrines– *bō-no-te* almost certainly functioned as a network of communication and as a social safety network for its members. While four different branches of *bō-no-te* exist in the region, they maintain good relations and cooperate for the propagation of their art. During the harvest festivals which were held several times during the year, the groups congregated at Shrines and performed martial arts as an offering to the *kami*. During this collective participation in public performance, people from scattered villages had the chance to perform together and socialize. Festivals which appeal to the gods for a bountiful harvest are very important in rural societies and are especially common in Japan.

Bō-no-te also faced threats to its survival. During WWII, with most young men away from the villages and unable to study their traditional art, *bō-no-te* nearly died out. After the war, because so many young men never returned, an entire generation was missing and teachers of *bō-no-te* were forced to pass the art to their grandchildren. During this time, *bō-no-te* was designated a cultural heritage property of Aichi prefecture and began to receive government support which encouraged its revival. It has recovered

Folk Martial Arts and Ritual

a base of practitioners spread throughout the rural area in a network of masters and their students. Each year before autumn harvest festivals at local shrines, organizers teach *bō-no-te* for several months at local schools to prepare for the festivals.

The efforts of the preservation societies have ensured the survival and popularity of *bō-no-te*. Over the last twenty years, new threats to the survival of *bō-no-te* have surfaced. Falling birth rates since the middle of the 1970s, have resulted in far fewer children to learn the art. Of the children who could learn the art, more and more are increasingly attracted by other forms of entertainment and few continue *bō-no-te* training into adulthood. In addition, economic growth has changed the nature of rural life. Because rural people generally have employment and work on their farm, recreation time has been severely eroded. Informants noted sadly that the large scale collective performances of the 1980s are no longer possible; there are not enough practitioners and many cannot attend because of time restraints owing to work commitments.

Bō-no-te, like Meihuaquan, existed in scattered villages linked in master-student relationships. Both folk associations served a defensive role for individuals and for villages and provided their members with recreational activity. The choreography of their practice routines, which pit the skilled peasant folk martial artist against oppressive outsiders, reflect their values of solidarity and belief that 'right beats might' – that as workers of the land, their righteousness and skill would defeat oppression. This theme – victory of the peasant martial artist, of righteousness over power – is a theme present in both Meihuaquan and *bō-no-te*. Both groups survived organized persecution which appears to have led to the disappearance of other similar folk organizations which were structurally unable to weather the outlawing of their groups.

This paper postulates that the survival of both groups is largely because of the association of martial arts with public festivals at religious events. The religious event transforms the physical training drills in combat skills to the realm of the "sacred" and so instils special meaning to the practitioners. They no longer believe they are practicing only fighting skills, but are living a part of the heritage which has endured persecution and suppression. Owing to their common belief in their sacred practice, and collective participation in festivals of religious significance, bonds between practitioners and between family lineages became stronger than those in folk associations or martial arts groups which lacked this element of ritual.

Today, festivals and martial arts serve as forms of entertainment, but they are also networks for social activity and crucial mechanisms through which societies are integrated and stabilized. Although these are but preliminary observations, more detailed examination of the social organization of folk martial arts groups in Japan and China may shed considerable light on the function of martial arts folk organizations in rural societies.

Endnotes

[1] This paper is based on field research in China conducted in 1992, 1997-1998, 2001, and 2003. The 1997-98 fieldwork was supported by the Canadian International Development Agency (CIDA), The Canada China Scholars Exchange Program and the China Scholarship Council. The 2003-2004 fieldwork was supported by the International Traditional Martial Art Research and Exchange Association, Hong Kong and the Canadian Meihuazhuang Association. 2003 fieldwork in Japan was possible thanks to the Japan Foundation and the Kansai International Language Centre.
[2] See Ma, Chuangtong wushu wenhua xintan.
[3] Lu, 2003 personal communication.
[4] Lu, Yihetuan yundong quiyuan tansu (Exploring the origin of the boxer movement).
[5] Often referred to by the term qigong
[6] Lu, Shandong minjian mimi jiaomen (Shandong folk secret societies).
[7] Lu, 1998; 2003 personal communication.
[8] Esherick, The Origins of the Boxer Uprising. p.18,19.
[9] See Eshrick, op. cit.; Tiedeman "The Persistence of Banditry: Incidents in Border Districts of the North China Plain"; Topley, "Chinese Religion and Rural Cohesion in the Nineteenth Century", p. 27; Lattimore The Desert Road to Turkestan, p. 152; Kuhn, Rebellion and its Enemies in Late Imperial China: Militarization and Social Structure, 1796--1864, p. 57; Harrell and Perry "Syncretic Sects in Chinese Society: An Introduction".
[10] Yan and Lu, personal communication, 1998.
[11] Ambrosi, "Special Interest Tourism: a Method for Economic Diversification and Cultural Preservation in Rural Hebei Province, China", p. 54.
[12] Tiedemann 1982, p. 414.
[13] Esherick, op. cit., pp. 19, 44-46, 60-61.
[14] Esherick, op. cit., p. 42; Lu, 1989 (personal communication).
[15] *Ibid.*
[16] See Tiedemann, op. cit., p. 416; also Billingsley "Bandits, Bosses, and Bare Sticks: Beneath the Surface of Local Control in Early Republican China".
[17] Approximately $55 USD calculated at 1997 one year average Interbank exchange rate of 0.12063.
[18] China Rural Statistical Yearbook 1993-1998; China County Level Rural Economic Statistics 1980-1987, 1989, 1990, 1991.
[19] Ambrosi, op. cit., pp. 50, 59-72.
[20] Lu, Yihetuan yundong quiyuan tansu.
[21] Yan, personal communication; Lu, 2003.
[22] Li Yunhao, personal interview, 1997, 1998; Liu Baohua, personal interview, 1997-1998.
[23] Lu, 1998, 2003, personal communication.
[24] State-sanctioned religions of Buddhism, Daoism, Catholic, Protestant, Islam are permitted,
[25] Anagnost, "Politics and Magic in Contemporary China", p. 45, 61.
[26] In some areas, practitioners continue to be occasionally harassed, imprisoned and fined by local authorities.
[27] Lu 2003; Ambrosi, op. cit.

[28] Fieldwork 1992, 1998-99, 2003-04; Yan, personal communication 1990, 1998.
[29] Ambrosi, op. cit.
[30] *Ibid.*
[31] Lu, 2003 personal communication.
[32] Yan, "The Martial and Theoretical Fields of Meihuazhuang".
[33] Lu, 1998 personal communication.
[34] Most of the Wenchang practitioners are men, though it appears there are small numbers of women involved in certain villages. People of both sexes emphasized that women have the same skills as the men and thus hold the same respected positions in the community. However, in actuality, even esteemed women Wenchang teachers, in accordance with rural tradition, wouldn't sit at the same table as the men, but sat off to the side with other women. Clearly, their overall social position is inferior.
[35] See Harrell and Perry's 1982; p. 288 regarding the process of acquiring secret knowledge and imparting of special status through ritual.
[36] Yan, 1992-2003 personal communication; Lu 2003, 1998 personal communication.
[37] In this paper, the terms 'Founder' and 'Founding Ancestors' have been used interchangeably in the same way that informants use the term 'zushi' (founding ancestor or teacher) which refers sometimes to one specific deity in Meihuaquan, but also ambiguously also refers to several other lesser deities.
[38] Lu, 1998 personal communication.
[39] Yan, op. cit., 1990.
[40] Lu, 1998 personal communication.
[41] Women also practice Meihuaquan though in far fewer numbers than men. Women tend to stop training in Wu martial arts after marriage and focus primarily upon Wen divination, meditation and healing. This topic is beyond the scope of this paper and will be discussed elsewhere.
[42] Uncle– *Shibo* or *Shishu* respectively if he began studying earlier or later than one's teacher.
[43] Brother– *Shixiong* or *Shidi* respectively if he began studying earlier or later than one's teacher.
[44] See Topely, op. cit., p. 21, 33; Harrell and Perry, op. cit., p.286 on the role of sectarian groups in connecting lineages.

Bibliography

Ambrosi, Raymond. "Special Interest Tourism: a Method for Economic Diversification and Cultural Preservation in Rural Hebei Province, China". Unpublished MA thesis, University of Regina, 1999.

Anagnost, Ann S. "Politics and Magic in Contemporary China". *Modern China*, January, 13 (1), 1987. pp. 40-61.

Billingsley, Phil. "Bandits, Bosses, and Bare Sticks: Beneath the Surface of Local Control in Early Republican China". *Modern China*, Vol. 7, No. 3. Jul., 1981. pp. 235-288.

China County Level Rural Economic Statistics. (*Zhongguo fenxian nongcun jingji tongji gaiyao*). China Statistical Publishing House (*Zhongguo tongji chubanshe*),

1989, 1990, 1991.
China County Level Rural Economic Statistics 1991. (*Zhongguo fenxian nongcun jingji tongji gaiyao*). China Statistical Publishing House (*Zhongguo tongji chubanshe*), 1992.
China Rural Statistical Yearbook 1993. (*Zhongguo nongcun tongji nianjian*). China Statistical Publishing House (*Zhongguo tongji chubanshe*), 1994.
China Rural Statistical Yearbook 1994. (*Zhongguo nongcun tongji nianjian*). China Statistical Publishing House (*Zhongguo tongji chubanshe*), 1995.
China Rural Statistical Yearbook 1995. (*Zhongguo nongcun tongji nianjian*). China Statistical Publishing House (*Zhongguo tongji chubanshe*), 1996.
China Rural Statistical Yearbook 1996. (*Zhongguo nongcun tongji nianjian*). China Statistical Publishing House (*Zhongguo tongji chubanshe*), 1997.
China Rural Statistical Yearbook 1997. (*Zhongguo nongcun tongji nianjian*). China Statistical Publishing House (*Zhongguo tongji chubanshe*), 1998.
China Rural Statistical Yearbook 1998. (*Zhongguo nongcun tongji nianjian*). China Statistical Publishing House (*Zhongguo tongji chubanshe*), 1999.
China Population Statistics Yearbook 1988. (*Zhongguo nianji tongji nianjian*). China Statistical Publishing House, National Statistical Population Statistics Department Publication (*Zhongguo tongji chubanshe, Guojia tongjiju renkou tongji cibian*), 1988. p.556.
China Population Statistics Yearbook 1992. (*Zhongguo nianji tongji nianjian*). China Statistical Publishing House (*Zhongguo tongji chubanshe*), 1991. p.300-302
China Population Statistics Yearbook 1997. (*Zhongguo renkou tongji nianjian*) China Statistical Publishing House (*Zhongguo tongji chubanshe*) 1997. p.252
China Population Statistics Yearbook 1998. (*Zhongguo renkou tongji nianjian*) China Statistical Publishing House (*Zhongguo tongji chubanshe*) 1998.
Ch'en, Jerome. "Rebels Between Rebellions--Secret Societies in the Novel, P'eng Kung Au". *Journal of Asian Studies*, Vol. 29, No. 4. 1970. pp. 807-822.
Dean, Kenneth. *Taoist Ritual and Popular Cults of South-East China*. Princeton University Press, 1993.
Esherick, Joseph. *The Origins of the Boxer Uprising*. University of California Press, 1987.
Guangzong Xianzhi. *Minguo ershier nian ban; Juan si: fengsu lue*. (Guangzong County History. Nationalist period twenty-second year edition (1933): Volume Four: Folk Customs).
Guangzong County Government. *Guanyu shenqing mingming- Meihuaquan zhi xiang de baogao* (Report Concerning the Application for the Title- Homeland of *Meihuaquan*) Guangzong County Government Party Committee, Guangzong County People's Government, 1997.
Harrell, Stevan, Elizabeth J. Perry. "Syncretic Sects in Chinese Society: An Introduction". *Modern China*, Vol. 8, No. 3, 1982. pp. 283-303.
Henning, Stanley E. "The Chinese Martial Arts in Historical Perspective". *Military*

Folk Martial Arts and Ritual

Affairs, Vol. 45, No. 4. (Dec., 1981). pp. 173-179.
Kertzer, David I. *Ritual, Politics and Power*. Yale University Press, 1988.
Kuhn, Philip A. *Rebellion and its Enemies in Late Imperial China: Militarization and Social Structure, 1796--1864*. Harvard University Press, 1970.
Lattimore, OWen. *The Desert Road to Turkestan*. Boston: Little, Brown, and Co, 1929.
Lu, Yao. *Shandong minjian mimi jiaomen* (Shandong folk secret societies). Beijing: Contemporary China Publishing House, 2000.
Yihetuan yundong quiyuan tansu (Exploring the origin of the Boxer movement). Jinan: Shandong University Press, 1990.
Ma, Aimin. *Chuangtong wushu wenhua xintan* (A new exploration about the culture of traditional martial arts). Beijing: People's Physical Education Publishing House. 2003.
Tiedemann, R.G. "The Persistence of Banditry: Incidents in Border Districts of the North China Plain". *Modern China*. 8(4), 1982. pp. 395-433.
Topley, Marjorie. "Chinese Religion and Rural Cohesion in the Nineteenth Century". *Journal of the Hong Kong Branch of the Royal Asiatic Society* (Hong Kong) 8, 1969, pp. 9-43.
Yan Zijie. "The Martial and Theoretical Fields of Meihuazhuang". (Social Science Research, 1991 Issue 3, No. 74. Paper presented to the International Symposium on the Yihetuan Movement and Modern Chinese Society, Shandong University, May 1990.
"Discussing the Origin of Meihuazhuang and the Unity between its Theory and Martial Arts". Unpublished paper presented to the University of Regina Department of Religious Studies. September 1995.

Fieldwork Informants:

China:
Rural Informants of Guangzong county, Hebei Province. 1992, 1997-98, 2001, 2003.
Rural Informants of Pingxiang county, Hebei Province. 1992, 1997-98, 2003.
Rural Informants of Dongming county, Shandong Province. 2003.
Li Yunhao. Minister of Propaganda. Guangzong County, Hebei province, China. Personal communication 1997-1998; 2001; 2003.
Liu Baohua. County Historian. Guangzong County, Hebei province, China. Personal communication 1997-1998; 2001; 2003.
Lu Yao. Professor of History, Shandong University. Advisor to the China Boxer Rebellion Research Association. 1997-1998; 2003.
Yan Zijie. Professor of Mathematics, Shandong University. Seventeenth generation teacher of *Meihuaquan*. Personal interviews 1990, 1991, 1992, 1995, 1996, 1997, 1998, 2001, 2002, 2003.

Japan:
Enomoto, Shōji. Professor in Psychology and Human Relations Dept. Nanzan University, Nagoya. Personal interview 2003, May 10.

Chapter 19

Kendo or Kumdo: The Internationalization of Kendo and the Olympic Problem

Alexander Bennett
International Research Centre for Japanese Studies

Introduction

As I mentioned in the introduction of this volume, I believe *budō* to be Japan's greatest cultural export. However, recently a new phenomenon has started to become apparent. One of the most significant contributors to the popularization of *budō* in recent years is not only the Japanese, but also the Koreans. There has been a noticeable trend in the increasing appearance of *dojang* around the world, rather than *dōjō*. Particularly in regions where Korean immigrants are numerous, *yudo dojang* are springing up in place of judo *dōjō*, taekwondo provides an attractive alternative to karate for self-defence and has the added bonus of being a competitive Olympic sport, *hapkido* is Koreanized aikido, and more recently, kumdo is making inroads into the kendo world, attracting mainly Korean immigrant children at this stage, but has the potential to change the face of kendo internationally, which will eventually have far reaching consequences even in Japan.

This interesting phenomenon of the gradual 'Koreanization' of *budō* overseas is perceived by the Koreans as the Internationalisation of their own Korean martial arts heritage. The Koreans are aggressive in their dissemination, sometimes nationalistic, and often very commercial in their approach, providing attractive packages for their students and instructors alike, not to mention propositions of business partnerships with already existing *dōjō*.

What effect could this possibly have on Japanese *budō*? In this paper I will consider the case example of kendo. The situation concerning the spread of kumdo as opposed to kendo has become particularly conspicuous in Japan recently due to the World Kumdo Association (WKA) inauguration in Korea, and their overtly opposing policies to the current chief international governing body of kendo, the Japan based International Kendo Federation (IFK). In particular, the WKA's mission to turn kendo/kumdo into an Olympic event is something vehemently opposed in traditional Japanese kendo circles. Nevertheless, my findings actually show that although the specialist kendo journals are touting this development as a major concern, the reality is that the situation is not as critical as they advocate, at least at this stage. Still, the formation of the WKA has rekindled an old debate concerning the question of "strong kendo" (sports oriented) and "correct kendo" ('traditional' and culturally oriented).

The Olympics are the apex of the sporting world, but is considered unattractive by many Japan-centric *kendōka*. However, judging by the status quo of kendo in Japan there are significant contradictions and inconsistency in ideals and reality that must be addressed. In this sense, I consider the kumdo tremors coming from Korea as a 'Black Ship'—a catalyst to look at state of the rest world—which will provide the impetus for earnest self-reflection of what kendo is or should be to people in the twenty-first century.

The Korean national kumdo team after their narrow defeat by Japan at the Kendo World Championships in Glasgow, 2003

Kendo or Kumdo?

Many Koreans still remember the brutal Japanese occupation lasting from 1910 until the end of World War II. During this period, Koreans were in many ways forced to disregard their own culture in a process of 'Japanization'. The ensuing brutality represented an across-the-board attempt to root out all vestiges of Korean culture, and to forge the nation into the role of a Japanese satellite state. In Japan, kendo and other *budō* arts were eventually elevated to compulsory subjects in schools[1] and utilised by the fascist government to encourage fighting spirit, instill nationalistic fervour, and

The Internationalization of Kendo

nurture pride in Japan's noble warrior past and the consequential moralistic values based on a Showa reinvention of 'bushidō', which was perceived as making Japan unique in the world.[2]

As colonies of Japan, the Taiwanese and Korean populace were also 'encouraged' to participate in these activities.[3] Koreans took to budō with unexpected enthusiasm, and even when the war ended and the Republic of Korea was established, they maintained a commitment to kendo that persists to this day, evident in the comparatively high level and large population of enthusiasts.[4] However, in many ways the old wounds of the occupation have still not healed, and in a nationwide revisionist stance, a number of Koreans refuse to entertain the notion that the sport's origins lie in Japan, and instead call it "kumdo", insisting that it originated in Korea.[5]

To demonstrate this revisionist mentality, I have quoted the historical information placed on the official homepage of the Korea Kumdo Association.[6]

"Our nation boasts a long history and tradition of swordsmanship. In the Koguryo dynasty (?-688) mountain ascetics perfected their technique in sword and other weapons. Similarly, the Paekche kingdom held specialist departments for the manufacture of swords, and there are records suggesting that sword masters were sent to Japan to teach swordsmanship. However, kenjutsu developed greatly during the Silla dynasty (668–935). Where a military academy was established in the capital city of Kyongju and was open to young men of aristocratic birth. Upon completion of their training, these young men were given the title *hwarang*, meaning "Flower Knight". This period was indeed the time when the military arts flourished. One of the most significant contributions to future swordsmen to come form this period was the book *Bon gook gum bup* (本国剣法). This treatise forms the basis for two-handed sword techniques and modern kumdo... The Koryo dynasty (935-1392 AD) inherited the Silla *kenjutsu* legacy and continued to develop it further. However, during the Chosun dynasty (1392-1910), military arts became disfavoured compared with civil arts, and fell into disarray. On the other hand, during this period, the recipients of our culture in Japan continued to develop the culture of the sword and it began to flourish over there."

The official explanation continues to inform readers that in the middle of the Chosun dynasty, the importance of the military arts was once more recognized through the experience of a number of wars and rebellions. During the Chungjo era (1776-1800) the text *Sok pyungjang tosul* (武芸図譜通志) (Revised illustrated manual of military training and tactics) included sword techniques among the twenty-four martial arts recorded, and was adopted in the instruction of military training.

From there, the official history proceeds to explain how *kenjutsu* (*gekiken* or *gekken* 撃剣) was taught at the Korean police academies from 1896, and then from 1904 in the military academies. Also, there is mention of a tournament held between the

Korean police and their Japanese counterparts in 1908. In September of the same year, *gekiken* was also included in the first official national physical education program for the general public. According to the text, the term *gekiken* was changed to kumdo in 1910, although Japanese records state this as happening in Japan on August 1, 1919.[7] Nevertheless, it is stated that this change in nomenclature helped promote kumdo as a sport with a popular civil following. Similar to trends in Japan, kumdo was also introduced into schools from 1906 (although Japan was in 1911), and was recognized as an official curricular subject in junior high schools in 1927 (again, Japan was 1931.)[8] I have placed the rest of the information found on the official KKA website in a table for easy reference. It is interesting to note that for the most part, development of kumdo in Korea was fairly much in parallel with Japan, although in some cases Korea's advancements seem to predate Japan.

1935	Kumdo included in the 16th National Chōsen Sports Festival
1938	National Chōsen Sports Festival prohibited by Japanese
1945	Kendo began to flourish again after Korea was liberated from Japanese colonialism
1947	Korean kumdo began to restructure itself with the holding of the Seoul Police Kumdo Tournament
1948	Approximately 100 highly ranked kumdo instructors gathered in Changdeokgung Palace and formed the predecessor to the Korean Kumdo Association
1950	The 1st National Police Kumdo Tournament was held
1952	A committee was created to oversee the formation of the KKA
1953	The KKA was inaugurated and became affiliated with the Korean Amateur Sports Association The 1st National Individual Kumdo Championships were held (*Same year that the All Japan Kendo Federation was formed)
1956	Kumdo was once more included as an official event of the National Sports Festival after a break of 20 years

The Internationalization of Kendo

1959	Kumdo became increasingly popular with the President's Cup Grade Category Tournament, and the National Student Championships
1964	The Student Kumdo Federation became affiliated with the KKA
1970	The Student Federation separated into the Collegiate Federation and the Secondary Schools Federation The International Kendo Federation was formed, and a Korean became the Vice President
1972	Kumdo was included in the National Youth Sports Meet
1979	The news agency Dong a Ilbo joined forces with the KKA in sponsoring the President's Cup National Championships
1988	The Korean Social Kumdo Federation was formed and followed by the 1st National Social Championships
1993	Inauguration of the SBS Royal National Championships

Korea obviously has a long history of kumdo although some of the top KKA officials readily acknowledge that the modern form of kendo/kumdo widely practiced today was in fact systemized by the Japanese. "However, the further development of kumdo from now on rests in our hands, and we must strive to overtake the Japanese in matters of theory and technique. This is what we must do to reinstate Korea as the true suzerain nation of kumdo."[9] This may seem like a preposterous claim to Japanese kendoka, but is it?

Despite wrangling of suzerainty, kumdo and kendo are essentially the same, save for a few cosmetic differences. Koreans use their native language in the sport, have changed the colour of the scoring flags (blue and white as opposed to red and white), and have abandoned the squatting bow (*sonkyo*) and certain other forms of Japanese etiquette considered important aspects by Japanese fencers. Also, there was a successful move to change certain parts of the attire used in kendo. Many Korean now use *hakama* that have no *koshi-ita*, and are secured with Velcro belts. This was argued as being more practical, and indeed it probably is, however it is also a clear form of protest against the overt Japanese dictation of what is acceptable in kendo and what is not.[10]

Apart from these superficial differences, a casual observer would be hard pressed to tell the difference between a kendo and a kumdo practitioner. Both arts seek to score points on one another by striking designated targets: *men* (*mori*), *dō* (gap), *kote* (*ho-wan*), *tsuki* (*mok*) with a bamboo or carbon-graphite *shinai* (*jukdo*). Both use the same kinds of *bōgu* (*hogoo*) and a stomping lunge (*fumikomi-ashi*) is usually employed to strike, often leading to the combatants' bodies colliding sharply as they cry out or "*kiai*" (*kheup*). Both maintain a sporting character, with many regional and national tournaments hotly contested at all levels. Both also maintain a strong metaphysical character, including meditation before and after practice, ritualised bowing, and Zen conceptions of achieving victory by emptying the mind of distracting thought of any kind. Both also purport to be "Ways" for developing character, body, and mind.

In fact, in many countries around the world kumdo and kendo coexist side-by-side, and apart from a few differences in terminology, most people accept that they are doing essentially the same thing, and train and compete in the same environment. Recently with the ban on Japanese culture lifted and the ensuing popularity of things Japanese among Korea's youth, even a number of young Korean fencers are starting to admit in whispered tones that they are essentially practicing a "Japanese sport", and are starting to question the cultural insistence by their seniors that Korea is the suzerain nation of the art. Although, to some of the older generation who still practice kumdo actively, any hint of Japanese influence or suzerainty of the modern form of kendo/kumdo is abhorrent.

Plethora of Federations

Recent articles in the leading kendo journals in the world outline kumdo federation developments in Korea, especially the formation of the World Kumdo Association (WKA) and the prospect of kendo becoming an Olympic sport.[11] In the 2000 Kendo World Championships in Santa Clara, and more recently in Glasgow (2003) this prospect was debated to a certain extent by the IKF especially in light of the ceremony in Korea in October 2001 to celebrate the inauguration of the World Kumdo Association, a self-acclaimed rival to the IKF. There were reputedly representatives from thirty countries in attendance. This newly formed entity is currently moving to amass as many affiliates as possible, and openly states inclusion in the 'Olympic Family' as one of its main objectives.

The mother organization behind the formation was the Korean Kumdo Federation (KKF), which combined forces with a number of other groups to create the WKA. Before delving into the details surrounding this new federation, it is necessary to clarify the state of Korea's hordes of kumdo organizations.

The International Kendo Federation (IKF—国際剣道連盟) was formed in 1970 at a meeting in Tokyo attended by seventeen countries and regions with the aim of cultivating goodwill through the international propagation of kendo (*iaidō*, *jōdō*). The IKF is responsible for holding the World Kendo Championships every three years, international seminars, assistance in developing federation infrastructure in kendo developing countries, and information exchange.

The Internationalization of Kendo

The Korean affiliate to the IKF is the Korean Kumdo Association (KKA－大韓剣道会), not the Korean Kumdo Federation (KKF－韓国剣道連盟). They are entirely different rival organizations. In addition to these two groups there is also the World Haedong Kumdo Federation （WHKF－世界海東剣道連盟), which although propagates an art it calls kumdo but is in fact very similar in nature to *iaidō*, and utilizes a two-handed sword to conduct *kata*. Furthermore, the WHKF reportedly has approximately 100,000 members, which makes it a significant force not taken lightly by the KKA. As far as the Korean government is concerned, they are unable to interfere in any way to help reconcile differences, as kumdo is considered no more than a recreational activity.[12]

The KKA relies heavily in its publicity through publications to maintain its prominent position, and are going to great efforts to promote kumdo as an art that utilises *bōgu* and *shinai*, completely different to what the World Haedong Kumdo Federation is engaged in. There are many offshoots and variations of these federations to be found in Korea itself, and various places around the world. The large number of kumdo associations is a cause of great confusion.

Of course, Japan also has its share of organizational rivalry and confusion, although to a much smaller scale. For example, the Dai Nihon Butokukai (Great Japan Society for Martial Virtue- my trans.), Nihon Kendo Kyōkai (Japan Kendo Society- my trans.) and a variant form of kendo at the Nippon Budokan is the Ikkenkai Haga *dōjō*. They engage in a very physical pre-war style of kendo, which is noticeably different to the style of kendo encouraged by the All Japan Kendo Federation. There are also a number of separate *iaidō* federations.

Nevertheless, all rival organizations to the AJKF in Japan are very small and hardly visible. The AJKF prohibits anyone from simultaneously belonging to and holding grades from the AJKF and other rival organizations. This had the immediate effect of strangle-holding the activities of other groups.[13]

The AJKF is the only kendo organization recognized by the government sanctioned Japan Amateur Sports Association (日本体育協会). They are also affiliated with the Japan Olympic Committee, although are not rated highly by the JOC.[14] In other words, the AJKF is publicly recognized as being the representative of kendo in Japan. In order to be able to participate in the All Japan Kendo Championships and the prestigious National Sports Festival (Kokutai), and the World Championships, the Japanese competitor must be a registered member of the AJKF.

The AJKF equivalent in Korea is the government acknowledged Korean Kumdo Association. They are also afforded the same rights as their Japanese counterparts to participate in the South Korean National Sports Meet. Members of this federation are afforded other benefits through being governmentally recognized, such as opportunities to progress through to high school or university on the basis of good competition results, and also some of the top-ranked kumdo practitioners are employed by local governments to teach full time as professionals. They also oversee kumdo which is taught as a compulsory subject at the police academies. Any members of the many other non-recognized organizations are not afforded these same opportunities. However, it seems that many kumdo practitioners in Korea are unaware of the reasons for such disparity, and the KKA reportedly receives many protests at this unequal treatment.[15]

The Olympic Proposal

The Korean kumdo specialist magazine Kumdo World published a special eight-page feature covering the World Kumdo Association formation ceremony and festivities, including interviews with all the leading figures in the WKA hierarchy. The following is a portion of what was written about the event:

"The Korean Kumdo Federation (KKF) conducted a ceremony to mark the foundation of the World Kumdo Association on October 27th (2001). With the extensive internationalisation of kumdo, the second most popular Korean martial art, learning from the taekwondo experience, thirteen of the existing eighty or so feuding domestic kumdo organizations decided to join forces to create the WKA. The government sanctioned KKA has received much criticism for following the lead of the Japanese, and being affiliated with the International Kendo Federation (IKF), which is an organization made by Japanese for Japanese kendo. Until now, kumdo has failed to find a place in the Asian Games and the Olympic Games. To these ends, the KKF, propagator of Korean style kumdo announced that they were aspiring to be accepted as an Olympic event, and to spread kumdo internationally."[16]

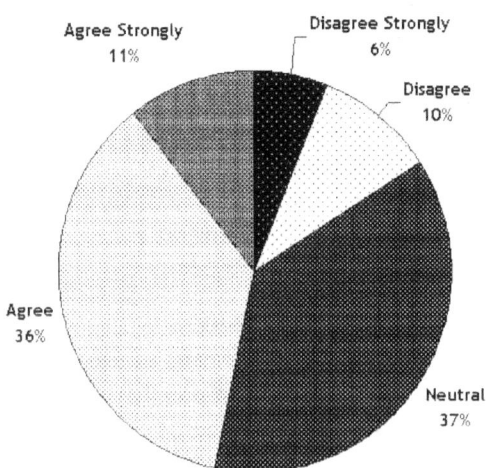

What does this have to do with the status quo of kendo in Japan? At present, the

The Internationalization of Kendo

Japan-based International Kendo Federation is the 'recognized' international body for overseeing the development and maintenance of kendo throughout the world, being recognized by itself as such. So far, the IKF has showed little interest in becoming affiliated with the Olympic movement. However, there have been voices from within the hierarchy of the federation who state otherwise. I clearly recall a speech given at the closing ceremony of the 2000 Kendo World Championships at Santa Clara in which a Taiwanese official of the IKF expressed his opinion that kendo should strive to become an Olympic sport "to spread the goodness as far and as wide as possible." However, the general opinion of the IKF officials, and most Japan-centric kendo enthusiasts around the world is to keep kendo out of the Olympics.

To test this theory, a total of 264 people from 36 countries answered a *Kendo World* questionnaire, which was conducted over the Internet. The majority of respondents indicated that they were opposed to kendo becoming an Olympic sport, however, almost 30 percent were in favour.[17]

In Korea, the KKA is concerned with what the WKA is advocating in their views to internationalise kumdo, but at the same time the KKA also agrees that kumdo/kendo should become an Olympic event. In fact, the Managing Director of the KKA was quoted as saying the following:

"Kumdo/kendo in countries outside of Japan will never achieve a big following unless it becomes an Olympic sport. It should be developed and made accessible to all people by making appeals to the wonderful attributes to be gained from kendo. Kendo should be for all people all around the world. In Korea and Taiwan, even though there is a certain amount of understanding of the art, it is still difficult to popularise. Representative organizations from other countries, in actuality are no bigger than 'clubs'."[18]

In this sense, even though becoming an official Olympic event is generally opposed by kendo enthusiasts, becoming affiliated with the IOC through belonging to a recognized organization such as General Association of Sports Federations (GAISF) evidently seems attractive to many small kendo federations around the world. This is because of the greatly increased possibilities for receiving financial finding. In regards to the Olympic issue we also investigated the financial possibilities of becoming affiliated to the IOC. The following chart shows the extent of opinion regarding whether becoming affiliated to the IOC would be financially beneficial for kendo in their country.[19]

Here, the majority of respondents clearly see the financial advantages of Olympic affiliation. This very point was raised at the recent Glasgow World Kendo Championships where a number of European federations expressed their desire to become affiliated with GAISF in order to increase the standing and status of kendo in that country, and also make them eligible for governmentally funded financial aid. Without such financial assistance, the propagation of kendo in each country is very difficult.[20] Naturally, kendo has a cultural base in Japan, and is recognized widely throughout the country as traditional Japanese culture even by people who do not participate. Comparatively speaking, raising the profile of kendo and raising funds for propagation and mere survival is not as big an issue in Japan as it is for the rest of the world's kendo federations.

The Process of Induction into the 'Olympic Family'

This Olympic ripple, which has appeared on the otherwise calm and Japan-centric kendo pond has the potential to develop into a wave of far-reaching consequences to the international kendo community, and Japan. It will more than likely be exasperated by issues of nationalism highlighted by a turbulent history of less than amicable relations between Japan and Korea. As I have already shown, it is true that many Koreans consider kumdo as traditional Korean culture. Naturally, the Japanese also claim kendo as their 'unique' culture, and a gift to the many kendo aficionados around the world. Other nationalities are not so concerned with issues of suzerainty, but will probably eventually be coerced into taking sides one way or another as the situation gets out of hand. In fact this is already evident to a certain extent now.

Having said that let me review the facts of this recent development in the kendo world that is starting to cause concern. The WKA was formed in October 2001 as a rival organization to the IKF. The WKA is seen to be recruiting individual clubs and federations on an international scale. The WKA is politically ambitious, and is open about its ambitions of Olympic inclusion. The WKA states clearly that it has no qualms about changing the style and content of kendo to gain the much-coveted status of becoming an Olympic event, like its predecessor taekwondo.

Its first aim is to become affiliated as an IF (International Federation) with an IOC recognized association such as the aforementioned General Association of Sports Federations (GAISF). GAISF, founded in 1967, groups together the international sports federations and various associations with the aim of defending worldwide sport, keeping the representative bodies informed, and cooperating and coordinating their activities. GAISF, along with other IOC affiliated groups such as the Association of Summer Olympic International Federations (ASOIF), the Association of International Winter Sports Federations (AIWF), and the Association of IOC Recognized International Sports Federations (ARISF) look after the interests of the affiliated sports federations. Belonging to one of these IOC recognized groups doesn't mean that the sport in question automatically becomes an Olympic sport, but it does mean inclusion in the Olympic movement. They are considered the 'official' international representatives (IF) of whatever sport they act for, and are allowed to vie for admission as an official Olympic sport. There are a number of martial arts organizations already affiliated with GAISF such as judo, aikido, karate, *jūjutsu*, taekwondo, wrestling, fencing, *sambo*, and more recently *wushu*, which is scheduled as a demonstration sport in the Beijing Olympics of 2008.

How feasible are the WKA's aspirations? Interestingly, from my research I have found that even though the WKA does have very powerful officials, it does not have

The Internationalization of Kendo

the membership to pose as a serious contender to become a member of GAISF. Yet. To become a GIASF recognized International Federation (IF) requires exposure to intense scrutiny, and needs to be approved at numerous board meetings. Korea has had a successful history of using political weight and know-how to influence sporting decisions in the past. We see examples of Korean success in the Chairman elections of the International Judo Federation, and co-hosting the FIFA 2002 World Cup with Japan. A significant strength that the WKA possesses is its ties with officials connected with taekwondo's successful entry into the Olympics. Of particular importance in this development was the nine-times elected President of GAISF, Korean Dr. Un Yong Kim, who is also President of the World Taekwondo Federation, and has recently been re-elected as Vice President of the IOC.[21] Incidentally, the president of the WKA is Jung Hak Seo who was the first Vice President of the International Kendo Federation when it was formed in 1970.[22] Thus, with such a network at their disposal, the WKA certainly has a number of political advantages to advance their objectives.

Nevertheless, to become a sport contested at the Olympics, certain criteria must be met as outlined in the *Olympic Charter*:

"To be included in the programme of the Olympic Games, an Olympic sport must conform to the following criteria:
1.1.1 Only sports widely practised by men in at least seventy-five counties and on four continents, and by women in at least forty countries and three continents, may be included in the programme of the Games of the Olympiad."[23]

From what I can ascertain, the WKA does not come anywhere near reaching these figures. The WKA as of November 2003 claims to have approximately thirty international affiliates. Of those, I have only been able to confirm branches in Korea, USA, Taiwan, Canada, Russia, and the UK. Furthermore, information on actual registered members is impossible to ascertain. However, it is fair to assume that the WKA is absolutely no match for the forty-four IKF affiliates (420,404 members not including Japan), and the thirty-eight countries that are seeking affiliation (817 registered members.)[24]

For the WKA in its current state to become affiliated with GAISF would require large-scale fabrication of figures, and some remarkable political manoeuvring, or both. Nonetheless, if through some means the WKA were to become affiliated with GAISF, even if membership is significantly less than that of the IKF, they will be recognized by the IOC as the world's representative kendo/kumdo organization. If they then decide to adapt the current form of kendo to fit the requirements of the Olympics, they would be well within their rights, and the IKF would be virtually powerless to stop them promoting a hybrid version as "kendo", or "kumdo" as the case may be.

Judging from the aforementioned political situation in the Korean kumdo world, it is difficult to imagine that the thirteen organizations that make up the WKA are doing the same style of "kumdo". Furthermore, it seems that some of the WKA officials are not kumdo practitioners, but taekwondo.²⁵ This begs the question, exactly what kind of kumdo/kendo do they intend to popularise around the world? One of the officials of the WKA also mentioned the possibility of introducing electronic scoring equipment along the lines of that utilised in Western fencing matches.

"We intend to introduce electronic armour to assist in umpiring. We also intend to make kicks valid for scoring points, and also an accumulative point system to encourage positive and successive attacking. We are looking at ways to make it more interesting."²⁶

For kendo traditionalists, the act of adapting kendo to suit the requirements of the IOC is the most worrying factor. Indeed, the WKA proposition to use electricity to "accurately" score points, as is done in fencing is almost unthinkable in a conventional sense. Kendo points are based on the technique having been executed with *ki-ken-tai-itchi* (気剣体一致) and meeting a number of other stringent (often nebulous) requirements that are not obvious to the untrained eye.

According to the official IKF *Kendo Shiai and Shinpan Regulations* a valid strike (*yūkō-datotsu*) must consist of the following elements:

"SECTION 2- Article 17. *Yūkō-datotsu* is defined as the accurate striking or thrusting made onto *datotsu-bui* of the opponent's kendo-*gu* with *shinai* at its *datotsu-bu* in high spirits and correct posture, being followed by *zanshin*."²⁷

The rules for scoring a point in fencing are as follows:

"At epee the target includes the whole of the fencer's body including his clothing and equipment. Thus any point which arrives counts as touch whatever part of the body (trunk, limbs, or head), the clothing or the equipment it touches… Only the indications of the electrical recording apparatus can be taken in to consideration for judging the materiality of touches. In no circumstances can the Referee declare a competitor to be touched unless the touch has been properly registered by the apparatus."²⁸

Obviously, a mere touch with the blade on the target in kendo is not sufficient according to the current rules. Even though it looks to be connecting, often the attack is not deemed valid in kendo because some of the aforementioned criteria are not met. This aspect of kendo makes it very difficult to follow for people who are not versed in the ways of *ki-ken-tai-itchi*, and all the elements that have to be present in a strike to make it valid. (Actually, this is a constant point of confusion even for seasoned kendo exponents.) One important aspect of any Olympic sport is its accessibility to spectators who do not actually participate in the sport. If kendo were to become an Olympic sport, issues

The Internationalization of Kendo

such as the difficulty in judging or understanding *ippon* would have to be overcome with rule changes. One of the foreseeable changes would be the simplification of what constitutes or is judged as a point. Hence, it the WKA's idea to use electrical devices such as those used in fencing, which would undoubtedly aid in its "followability", at least on a superficial level. This, to most kendoists, would be totally inappropriate as such things as striking correct target areas with *ki-ken-tai-itchi* from correct *ma-ai* (間合) with the correct part of the *shinai* maintaining correct *hasuji* (刃筋) with *sae* (冴) on impact, followed with *zanshin* (残心) and so on, contain the essence of what kendo is, and should be retained even if this means casual observers have absolutely no idea of what is going on. Thus, it would be close to impossible for kendo in its current form to become an official Olympic sport.

However, if enough changes were made to its current form, what would be the consequences? Although one can only speculate, it is probable that under such circumstances many newcomers would be attracted to the Olympic version. For good or for bad, the Olympics are the most prestigious sporting event in the world, and many athletes in a number of sports have been financially set up for life through Olympic success. Many lament the apparent loss of *budō* virtues such as respect, modesty, and general courtesy in judo since it became washed away in the tide of 'Olympism', and the fervour to win at all costs to get the gold.[29] Even the Olympics itself is not what it used to be. It states in the first section of the Olympic Charter:

> "Modern Olympism was conceived by Pierre le Coubertin, on whose initiative the International Athletic Congress of Paris was held in June 1894....Olympism is a philosophy of life , exalting and combining in a balanced whole, the qualities of body, will and mind. Blending sport with culture and education, Olympism seeks to create a way of life based on the joy found in effort, the educational value of good example and respect for universal fundamental ethical principles."[30]

It is widely recognized that the so-called Olympic Family is really the Olympic industry using sports as a vehicle to create billions of dollars of revenue. This is not necessarily a bad thing, as people want drama in their lives, and the spectacular sporting stage of "do or die" antics offered us by the Olympics fulfils these needs. Why shouldn't the athletes who dedicate their lives to their sport profit, and sponsors who make it possible reap the benefits? In many ways, although being the target of much criticism in the last decade, the Olympic movement must be commended for their amazing ability to keep with the times, and to a great extent influencing the times.

However, regardless of the controversy surrounding the ethical fortitude of the Olympic movement, what would kendo gain from becoming an Olympic sport? Again, we must rely on pure speculation to answer this question, and it would seem that the perceived benefits I have outlined such as more exposure, more revenue, and more prestige could very well be offset with negative factors such as diminished importance of kendo's own perceived "traditional" ideals as winning became not everything, but the only thing. Who cares about how nice a person you are when you have an Olympic medal draped around your neck, and a massive endorsement check in the mail from a corporate sponsor? It is difficult to know what the far-reaching implications would be. But, it seems apparent that the time has come for the kendo world to reassess its motives and what it holds dearest in its kendo ideals.

The IKF claims to be "a non-political and friendly organization and its purpose is to propagate and develop kendo (including *iaidō* and *jōdō*) internationally and to foster the mutual trust and friendship among the affiliates." If it wants to do this successfully, it might even want to consider becoming a member of GAISF, so that at least then it has the power to decide its own fate, and the fate of kendo as we know it now, before a hybrid version is able to usurp that privilege.

If kendo were to become an Olympic sport as desired by the WKA, many things would have to be changed, which it is thought would detract from kendo's perceived essence. Much of this paranoia stems from the example of judo's inclusion into the Olympics. The ideals of Kanō Jigorō, the founder of Kōdōkan judo have for the most part taken the back seat in recent years where winning the gold medal rather than developing body, character, and sociability has earned the scorn of many traditionalists.

We see incidents of doping, money for winning, cheating (suspicious *dōgi*), point system instead of clean *ippon* which is seen to advantage brute strength over technique, unbridled emotional outbursts in victory or defeat when the essence of *budō* is said to be to control emotion and show respect, death threats (by Japanese) to international referees who are perceived to have made flawed judgments, raucous crowds of the kind seen at football matches, and so on. Also, the recent introduction of blue judo-*gi* was seen as spitting in the face of Japanese tradition, although very few Japanese exponents could offer much more of a persuasive argument than "white traditionally signifies purity in Japan."

What resulted from this furore was a clear demonstration that, although the suzerain country for judo, the Japanese authorities were completely unable to express convincing opinions on the international stage when it counted[31], be it through linguistic deficiency, lack of political clout, or perhaps even confusion about their own so-called traditional values. What compounds matters for many is the fact that not only Japan is unable live up to the Kanō legacy and demonstrate political *savoir-faire*, the same could also be said out on the mat where it is no longer surprising for Japan's top judo practitioners to be defeated with relative ease. All of this has prompted judo authorities to instigate the "Judo Renaissance" in Japan in an attempt to go back to basics and reconsider Kanō Jigorō's humanistic and educational ideals.

With judo looked upon as an example of the overwhelming negative power of internationalisation, kendo practitioners appear to be very wary of too much international propagation, and especially want to avoid any contact with Olympism. There is a stigma attached which is deep-rooted, and in my opinion has certain legitimate grounding. Having said that, the current form of kendo is not really that old anyway, and a very similar debate was raging a few centuries ago about the introduction of such

The Internationalization of Kendo

ghastly apparatus as *shinai* and *bōgu*. This, it was argued would completely corrupt the real *kenjutsu* into some ridiculous form of senseless stick fighting. Cultural evolution is not necessarily a bad thing. It can be stopped if necessary, as long as the main motives are not sentimental longings for "the way it was in the good old days." When faced with issues like this, it offers an important opportunity to reassess the whole point of doing kendo in the first place.

The Great Kendo Contradiction

What is it that Japan can and should do from now? Barely a century has passed since the Butokukai was formed in 1895 and *budō* was systematically propagated in Japan. In fact, it wasn't until 1918 thanks in large part to the efforts of Nishikubo Hiromichi that the term *budō* was denoted as the official term for the martial arts instead of *bujutsu*, thereby stressing the character building attributes as opposed to the combative or competitive aspects.[32]

Since the Bakumatsu era, many aspects of the martial arts were in a state of constant flux, and adaptations were made to fine-tune it in order to suit the needs of the day. It is no exaggeration to say, using Hobsbawm's term, that a "new tradition" was being persistently developed in Japan before *budō* was ever exported.[33] There were numerous reinterpretations and refining of the rules for competition, ranks, reviews of techniques, and motivations for training and teaching. Kendo has often found itself torn between conflicting definitions. The cause of this is what Ōtsuka Tadayoshi calls the "dual structure" (二重構造) of kendo, or the inconsistency between ideals of the *katana* versus *shinai*.[34]

In short, the principle of *butoku* (武徳) or martial virtue espoused by the Butokukai encouraged the adept to use the *shinai* as a sword in order to attain a state of transcendence over issues of life and death, and also to instil a sense of affinity with the *bushi* and their ethos known as *bushidō*. Given such considerations, it was deemed preposterous to celebrate the scoring of a point on an opponent, and do flashy unnatural moves with the *shinai* that could never be successfully accomplished with a real sword. In effect, the seriousness of the endeavour based on the principles of that most Japanese of weapons, the *katana*, was precisely what was needed to encourage the perceived ideal character qualities of people of the time.

To encourage these qualities, matches were conducted at the Butokukai where competitors were given scores based on their attacking, posture, attitude, and spirit i.e. those who were deemed to be upholding the principles of the katana scored highly. This system of scoring continued for eight years until 1927 when a unified definition for criteria to judge a valid point was devised by the Butokukai. "A valid strike (*yūkō-datotsu*) will be when the attack is conducted in full spirit, and the technique is executed with the proper blade angle (*hasuji*), while maintaining correct posture."[35]

In 1929, against the wishes of numerous kendo leaders, the first of three Emperor tournaments (*Tenran-jiai*) were held in Kyoto to decide the number-one fencer in Japan. To many, this would spell the demise of kendo, regardless of the honour involved in performing before the Emperor himself. This event saw for the first time a time limit on each bout of five minutes, which encouraged the "cowardly behaviour" of some exponents who after scoring first, would sit on that one point until time was up without putting up much of a fight. Nevertheless this provided the catalyst for many more similar tournaments in other sectors of the kendo world up until war loomed.

Wartime kendo called for realism. The *shinai* was shortened to that of a real sword, as was the *tsuka* (handle) of the *shinai* to encourage true cutting action rather than relying on leverage. Also, terminology was changed to "cut" (*kiru*) and "jab" (*tsuku*) rather than "strike", and matches were decided by *ippon-shōbu* (first valid cut i.e. representing true mortal combat). Practitioners fought to kill.

A valid cut was redefined then as being one made "with emphasis placed on vigorous attacking, the cut or thrust must be accurate and conducted with the spirit of true combat. Particular importance is to be placed on posture and attitude."[36]

After the initial prohibition of *budō* enforced by GHQ in the aftermath of Japan's defeat for several years, kendo was eventually reinstated for educational purposes.

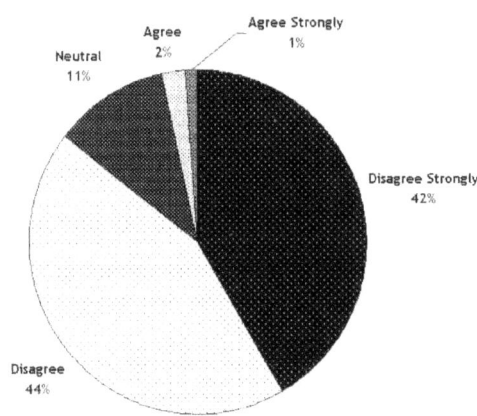

Question 5: Shiai is more important than any other aspect of kendo
- Agree Strongly 1%
- Agree 2%
- Neutral 11%
- Disagree 44%
- Disagree Strongly 42%

Various changes were made, but the definition of a valid strike (*yūkō-datotsu*) remained almost the same as the pre-war explanation, and even now is relatively unchanged and abstract in nature.

Having said that, it is the relative romanticism in successfully completing the process of scoring the elusive perfect strike that is so attractive to kendo enthusiasts around the world. But it is also the cause for much confusion. As Ōtsuka Tadayoshi points out, the emphasis still placed on "ideals of the *katana*" has stymied the development of the "ideals of the *shinai*." In other words, there are many aspects of kendo that are nebulous to say the least, and there are calls for complete revision of the current kendo rules and regulations. Although a number of amendments have been made

The Internationalization of Kendo

to the rules of kendo in the post-war period, some commentators call for debate on what constitutes a valid strike to make it more rational and easier to understand, and conducive to the actual implement being used, a *shinai*, and the natural progression of the art as a logical modern sport.

Regardless of whether one agrees with this logic, there is much uncertainty in what is expected of the kendo practitioner. That is to say, there exist contradictions in what is considered "strong kendo", and what constitutes "correct kendo".[37] Put simply, strong kendo wins matches, but is often sneaky, relies on trickery, can be cowardly, and often pushes the rules to the limit. So-called "correct kendo" conducted in the true spirit of fair-play is honest, straight, usually executed with big textbook cuts, and stringently adheres to the rules. It may not win, but it is aesthetically pleasing, and shows the admirable trait that the adept is more concerned with developing the self rather than being preoccupied with matters of winning or losing, or being hit. Ideally being strong by being correct is what many kendo practitioners aspire to, but reality dictates that the majority are caught somewhere between the two poles.

This tendency is also very evident in countries outside Japan. From my experience with international kendo, I have trained in *dōjō* which concentrate entirely on "correct kendo". Every strike is big, straight and powerful. These exponents are, for the most part, completely oblivious to finer techniques such as well-timed *de-gote* as they roll through like bulldozers. They also very rarely participate in kendo competitions, or if they do it is without much success.

On the other hand there are also *dōjō* which concentrate purely on techniques to win at *shiai*. I would class this type as a minority at this stage, but certainly growing in recent years. This is obvious by the increasing competitiveness seen at the World Kendo Championships every three years. Nevertheless the general attitude toward *shiai* by non-Japanese practitioners is expressed in the graph below.[38]

I attribute negation of the supremacy of competition to the missionary efforts of Japanese instructors who have conscientiously propagated "correct kendo" as an historical and important Japanese cultural tradition, emphasizing the value of executing large, powerful (but not too forceful), straight techniques with total conviction. In other words, the remnants of pre-war *katana* kendo. Nevertheless, as kendo matures outside Japan, these attitudes are starting to change. I perceive three main reasons for this.

Firstly, as I have already mentioned, kendo is considered a minority sport in most countries. Each local federation requires financial assistance from government sport trusts and foundations to enable them to publicise the activity to attract more members. Kendo also has to compete with hoards of other minority sports for limited funds. Therefore, the most reliable way to gage the merit of funding is through favourable competition results. The prospect of funding is also another motivation for wishing to belong to an organization recognized by GAISF, and is an issue that I believe the IKF should prioritise without delay.[39]

Secondly, the rapidly increasing presence of Korean kumdo *dojang* are providing many countries with a different style which is characteristically more dynamic than

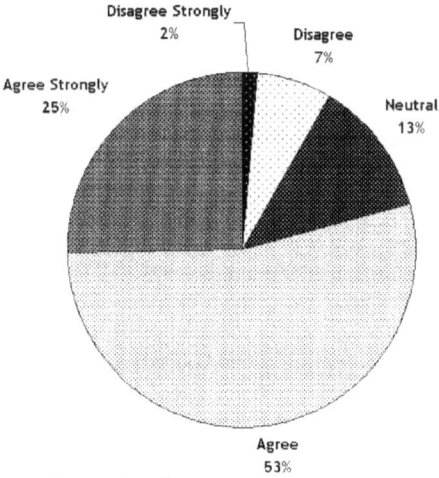

Question 4: Shiai is an important aspect of kendo

- Disagree Strongly 2%
- Disagree 7%
- Neutral 13%
- Agree 53%
- Agree Strongly 25%

Japanese kendo, and openly advocates a competition oriented form. That is not to say that aspects of etiquette, character building, and metaphysical aspects are not an important part of kumdo. However, kumdo tends to openly place more value competition and commercialization. Kumdo will undoubtedly gain more international momentum in the event their national team defeats the Japanese at the World Championships. Many predict this is not far away.

Thirdly, non-Japanese kendo practitioners are becoming acutely aware and frustrated with the blatant contradictions in what they are being taught as "correct kendo" by Japanese instructors, and the actual status quo in Japan. Japanese kendo, despite all romantic ideals to the contrary is now very much an activity where winning, often at any cost, is the most important thing. An individual's entire career can be decided by one point that they scored in one match at junior high school. Regardless of an awareness of what is "correct", like most things in modern society, performance and innovation is a matter of survival, not only for the competitor, but also the coach, and in some cases the entire institution. The persuasiveness of argument for "correct kendo" is greatly diminished, as is trust, when the very advocators of this ideal resort to other means in order to gain victory in competition. However, this is the reality of kendo in Japan. The issue that must be addressed is how to come to grips with these seemingly opposing ideals.

Very few people outside of Japan would deny that *shiai* (competition) is not an important aspect of one's overall kendo training. Again, this is evident in the replies to survey results in the pie chart.[40] However, there are many in Japan and around the world who advocate that although *shiai* is important, it must not become the sole objective. Therein lays the greatest fear of kendo becoming an Olympic sport, the ultimate achievement for any athletic activity.

The Internationalization of Kendo

Some kendo authorities suggest that to solve this dilemma of sport kendo and correct kendo, two types of kendo should be popularised. One would be traditional 剣道 which upheld the "true way" based on the principles of the sword. The other would be KENDO, a mixture of Japanese and Western ideals in which sporting aspects would be encouraged.[41] The ultimate destination for KENDO would be Olympic participation. These are the terms in which judo (JUDO) is often referred to.[42] However, to most non-Japanese kendo practitioners, this would seem an extremely condescending and hypocritical stance. Before labelling a new kind of kendo with Roman letters to solve the dilemma of sports versus tradition, there are many issues which have to be properly debated and brought to a consensus first. At this crucial stage of kendo's development, such an initiative would be a superficial and be neglecting the wider issues. What then are those wider issues? For example:

- Is kendo in Japan in its current state satisfactory to kendo practitioners? (i.e. competition rules, *yūkō-datotsu* criteria, grading criteria etc.)
- Has kendo evolved to suit the modern era for people with modern needs? (For example, why are fewer people taking up kendo in Japan? What are the main social problems facing youth today, and how could kendo possible help contribute to rectifying these?)
- Is kendo truly helping people develop body and spirit as the relatively recent *Concept of Kendo* promises?
- If not, what changes can be made to help achieve these goals?
- Are there any outdated traditions, rituals, or modes of thought that should be reviewed or even scrapped entirely in order to make way for new traditions?
- What are the essential elements (traditional, cultural, metaphysical and physical) that must be maintained at all costs?
- Are these elements being maintained now anyway?

Considering the cultural differences, these are precisely the issues that kendo practitioners outside Japan have had to ask themselves for it to work in their respective countries. In this respect, Japan could very well learn from the kendo minnows of the world.

The ever-increasing popularity of kumdo in Korea and the push of kumdo overseas as a traditional form of Korean culture in recent years, and the formation of the WKA has been a most timely development for Japanese kendo and *budō*. It has opened the way for much needed self-reflection in the Japanese kendo world by providing the potential spectre of Olympism.

As the extent of Japanese *budō*'s international propagation has exceeded the wildest expectations of Japanese nationalists and humanists alike, now is not the time to try and force-feed Japan-centric values on the rest of the world. The "missionary" phase *budō*'s international propagation has served its purpose. It is true that many countries still lack highly ranked leaders are barely breaking in to a second generational structure as opposed to the luxury of three generations in Japan where younger practitioners have the luxury of many highly experienced sensei and *sempai* to look up to.[43] Indeed, there is still a distinct lack of human resources and literature to aid in the deeper understanding of kendo/*budō* ideals outside Japan. In this respect the value of contact with highly ranked Japanese instructors who are dispatched to teach by the IKF cannot be understated, even though they can be financially debilitating for small federations. Nevertheless, now there are growing numbers of experienced non-Japanese *budō* practitioners who, through much trial and error, and a certain amount of confusion have managed to adapt what was originally Japanese into something workable in their own communities. It goes without saying that when Japanese *budō* is transplanted in another country or society, with another language, and another set of cultural values, it has to adapt to suit that particular cultural climate. Not to do so would have the same results as planting a cactus in a rain forest, or putting a fresh-water fish in the ocean.

Common sense dictates that each country is different, and the needs of each society's people differ greatly. Thus, even though many aspects of Japanese culture will remain obvious and clearly visible in say a kendo club in the Middle East, there will undoubtedly be many aspects that will be changed out of necessity for it to be of use to the locals and survive into the future. A very simple example would be *zarei* (kneeling bow). It would be unlikely to see *zarei* to another person in say an Islamic country, where this ritual already exists as the ultimate expression of deference to Allah. There must be a change made, but the essence of showing respect to one's opponent or the like does not necessarily have to be omitted. In fact, such *budō* ideals as respect, cooperation, and so on are considered to be absolutely essential even if the form it takes is different.

Conclusion

In effect, Japan's international contribution to the world through the spread of *budō* was to provide a blueprint, which although retaining essential elements, has evolved sometimes successfully, and sometimes not. The evolution is subtle in some cases, such as the aforementioned Korean adaptations in kumdo, and more explicit in others with the creation of hybrid arts hardly recognisable as having its roots in Japanese *budō*. Still, the extensive popularity and recognition of Japanese *budō* proves beyond any doubt that it has core elements of universal value to mankind, even if that form differs from region to region, and indeed time to time.

In short, kendo and *budō* in general has carved out a very significant niche in many different cultures. It has matured into something more than just "traditional" Japanese culture, but has had to make some changes in the process in order to survive. *Budō* in Japan also has a history of change to fit the ideals and needs of the era in question.

Even though Japan has been instrumental in introducing the ideals of kendo to the rest of the world, with the ever-increasing competitive level of Korean kumdo coupled with initiatives for propagation, and the fringe elements that seek Olympic inclusion, the

The Internationalization of Kendo

Japanese kendo world is starting to see the actual extent of kendo's internationalization, and the possible routes it could take in the future.

This is a cause of unease for many, especially the lack of reliable information indicating the true state of affairs. Is the internationalisation of *budō*/kendo Japan's equivalent to Dr. Frankenstein and his creation, who came back to haunt him until both were destroyed? That may be too much of a dramatic analogy. Nevertheless, the objective of Japanese kendo at this stage should not be to seek to tame or control the "monster". Instead, Japan would be prudent to return to drastically pioneering kendo at home again, in the manner it was in the Meiji, Taisho, and early Showa periods. Japan has blessed the world with a wonderful blueprint. What the world needs now is a reliable role model to look up to and aspire to, which does not promote contradictions and double standards. Who will fill that role?

Endnotes

[1] Imamura Yoshio, *Nihon budō taikei*, vol.1, pp. 100-111.
[2] For a detailed account of the use of sports by Japan's fascist pre-war government see Irie Katsumi's *Nihon fashizumu-ka no taiiku shisō*.
[3] Thomas A. Green (ed.), *Martial Arts of the World*, pp.295, 597.
[4] The KKA boasts 400,000 members compared to Japan with 1,288,000 members.
[5] Although the pronunciation is different, both use the same characters "剣道".
[6] See http://members.at.infoseek.co.jp/koreawatcher/docs/kkahistory.htm
[7] *Dai Nihon Butokukai enkaku-gen, Kaihō* Vol. 2 No. 4, August 1919, pp. 101-103.
[8] See the All Japan Kendo Federation's publication *Kendō no rekishi*, pp. 605-607.
[9] Seo Byung- Yoon, (Managing Director of the Korea Kumdo Association), "*The Many Questions Regarding Kumdo and Kendo*", http://members.at.infoseek.co.jp/koreawatcher/docs/kumdowakendo.htm
[10] See Sin Seung-Ho (Director of Collegiate Kumdo Federation) article "*The Responsibilities of the New Generations of Kumdo Practitioners to Develop Kumdo*", http://members.at.infoseek.co.jp/koreawatcher/docs/community35.htm
[11] For example, "*Kankoku de sekai kendō renmei setsuritsu*" (The Formation of The World Kumdo Association in Korea), *Kendō Nippon Monthly* (April 2002), Ski Journal, pp. 86-95, and more recently "*Tokushū- Nihon kara sekai e*" (Special Report- From Japan to the World), Kendō Nippon (November 2003), pp. 46-58.
[12] See "*Kankoku de sekai kendo renmei setsuritsu*", in Kendō Nippon (April 2002), p. 86.
[13] The All Japan Kendo Federation has 1,288,000 registered kendo members and 72,000 iaidō members (IKF document-March 2002) making it by far the largest kendo organization in Japan and the world.
[14] See "*Tokushū- Nihon kara sekai e*", *Kendō Nippon* (November 2003), pp. 46-47.
[15] Seo Byung- Yoon, op. cit.
[16] Quoted from "*Kankoku de sekai kendō renmei setsuritsu*", p. 88.
[17] See Alexander Bennett and Hamish Robison, "Survey: Kendo and the Olympics",

Kendo World (Vol. 1 No.1), KW Publications, 2001- We conducted a survey through the internet to ascertain the attitudes of international kendo practitioners towards the introduction of kendo into the world's most prestigious sports tournament. In summary, our survey presents the opinions of 264 English speaking practitioners of either kendo or kumdo from 36 countries, of all experience levels, and of all rankings. We can justly assume that the results of the survey provide a reasonable and fair assessment of their opinions and experiences as related to kendo and the Olympics. We can also assume that this un-weighted self-selected sample provides a fair approximation of a random un-weighted sample survey of 264 respondents providing a precision level of 6% 95 times out of 100.

[18] *"Kankoku de sekai kendō renmei setsuritsu"*, p. 89
[19] Bennett, Robison, op. cit.
[20] Abe Tetsushi, *"Ōshū kara mita kendō no kokusaika"*, p. 53.
[21] See http://www.olympic.org/uk/organization/ioc/members/bio_uk.asp?id=33
[22] 徐廷學
[23] See http://www.joc.or.jp/olympic/charter/pdf/olympiccharter2002.pdf
[24] IKF statistics valid as of March 20, 2002.
[25] Seo Byung- Yoon, op. cit.
[26] *"Kankoku de sekai kendō renmei setsuritsu"*, *Kendō Nippon* (April 2002), p. 88.
[27] *The Regulations of Kendo Shiai- The Subsidiary Rules of Kendo Shiai and Shinpan*, (Revised March 23, 2003), International Kendo Federation.
[28] *Fencing Rules 2000 Edition*, United States Fencing Association, http://www.usfencing.org/Forms/Rules99.pdf, p. 27.
[29] For example, see D. Matsumoto, "Jūdō ni okeru riidaashippu to kagaku no juyosei—karaa jūdō-gi no mondai", pp. 44-63.
[30] See Olympic Charter, (July 2003) http://multimedia.olympic.org/pdf/en_report_122.pdf p. 9
[31] T. Ōtsuka, *Nihon kendo no rekishi*, pp. 195-243.
[32] Y. Sakagami, *"Kendō no kindaika to sono teiryū – sanbon-shōbu wo chushin ni"*, p. 178.
[33] See Eric Hobsbawm and Terence Ranger's *The Invention of Tradition*.
[34] T. Ōtsuka, Nihon kendo no shisō, p. 144.
[35] *Ibid.*, p. 143.
[36] *Ibid.*. p. 146.
[37] *Ibid.*, p. 211.
[38] Bennett, Robison, op. cit.
[39] Since writing this paper, I have it on good authority that the AJKF/IKF has made contact with GAISF for this purpose. However, even though I have no material proof yet, it is conceivable that the IKF will become affiliated with the GAISF in the near future.
[40] *Ibid.*
[41] F. Murakami, M. Sakudō, "A Study on the Internationalization of Kendo", p. 35.
[42] S. Sekine, Zen Nihon Jūdō Renmei 50 nen shi 1949-1999, p. 258.
[43] F. Murakami, M. Sakudō, op. cit., pp. 34-35.

The Internationalization of Kendo

Bibliography

Abe Tetsushi. "*Ōshū kara mita kendo no kokusaika*" (The internationalisation of kendo from the perspective of Europe). *Kendō Nippon*. Ski Journal, November 2003.

All Japan Kendo Federation. *Kendō no rekishi* (The history of kendo). 2003.

Bennett, A., Robison, H. "Survey: Kendo and the Olympics". *Kendo World* (Vol. 1 No.1). Auckland: KW Publications, 2001.

Green, Thomas A. ed. *Martial Arts of the World*, ABC Clio, 2001.

Hobsbawm, Eric and Ranger, Terence. *The Invention of Tradition*, Cambridge University Press, 1983.

Imamura Yoshio et al. *Nihon budō taikei* (Systems of Japanese martial arts). Dōhōsha Shuppan, 1982.

Irie Katsumi. *Nihon fashizumu-ka no taiiku shisō* (Physical education ideals under Japanese fascism). Fumaidō Shuppan, 1986.

Matsumoto, D. "Jūdō ni okeru riidaashippu to kagaku no juysei- karaa jūdō-gi no mondai" (The need for leadership and science in Judo- The problem of colour judō-*gi*). *Budōgaku kenkyū* Vol. 29, (Research Journal of Budo). Nihon Budō Gakkai (Japanese Academy of Budo), 1997.

Murakami, F. and Sakudō, M. "A Study on the internationalization of kendo", *Osaka Budogaku Kenkyū* Vol. 11. No. 1, March 2002.

Ōtsuka Tadayoshi. *Nihon kendō no rekishi* (The history of Japanese kendo). Madosha, 1995.

Nihon kendō no shisō (The ideals of Japanese kendo). Madosha, 1995.

Sakagami, Y. "*Kendō no kindaika to sono teiryū – sanbon-shōbu wo chūshin ni*" (The modernization of kendo and the undercurrents- A look at the significance of *sanbon shōbu*). Sports Bunkaron Series 9, in T. Nakamura (ed.) *Nihon bunka no dokujisei* (The identity of Japanese culture). Sōbun Kikaku, 1998.

Sekine, S. *Zen Nihon Jūdō Renmei 50 nen shi 1949-1999* (Fifty year history of the All Japan Judo Federation 1949-1999). All Japan Judo Federation, 1999.

Chapter 20

Tilting at Windmills: Observations on the Complexities in Transmission of the *Koryū Bujutsu* in Japan and the United States

Meik Skoss
Associate editor- Koryu Books

Introduction

Cultural transmission is a very complex process, with unforeseen issues and problems. Different groups throughout the world have developed their own types of music, dance, sports, and fighting arts, but it is not an easy thing to introduce any of these traditional forms of human expression into a wholly new social or cultural context. The Japanese martial arts – both the modern systems widely known and practiced throughout the world and the more exotic classical disciplines that are only now coming to be introduced to other countries outside Japan – are an excellent case in point. My essay will focus on the situation in the United States of America.

A Brief Comparison of *Koryū Bujutsu* and *Gendai Budō*

It is helpful to compare and contrast the distinctive elements of the *koryū bujutsu* (classical martial arts) and *gendai budō* (modern cognate combative systems), though this sort of dichotomy is, in itself, not something that most Japanese recognize when thinking about their country's martial arts. Briefly, then, the classical Japanese martial arts (*koryū bujutsu*) are usually:

1. Creations of the feudal period (prior to the *haitōrei* [Sword Abolishment Act] of 1876/Meiji 8), especially by the *bushi* (warrior class).
2. Of an exclusive nature, frequently open only to *bushi* or to men, with arcane knowledge and codes of behaviour peculiar to a society at least nominally under military rule.
3. Primarily concerned with developing effective skills for battlefield combat and/or personal self-defense, always within the overall context of the mores of the *bushi* class.
4. Not amenable to sportive competition, by virtue of the skills and methods

used to train warriors for combat; training mainly through the use of *kata* (pre-arranged training forms).
5. Practiced by modern-day people as a form of cultural preservation, as an "art" to be studied in depth, as a way of training body and mind in a way similar to that of their ancestors.

Modern cognate combative systems (*gendai budō*), on the other hand, share the following characteristics. They are typically:

1. Disciplines created since the abolishment of the feudal political and social system based on Confucian ideals, and new social classes not based upon hereditary positions.
2. Of an inclusive nature, open to all members of society, men and women, old and young alike.
3. Primarily concerned (in the present day) with *ningen keisei* (personal cultivation), combining physical and mental training to develop "whole" individuals, as productive members of society.
4. Organized around a centrally developed curriculum, with techniques and training methods created to ensure the safety of participants, enabling exponents to engage in competitive matches with relative safety.
5. Conducive to sportive competition. This characteristic has become increasingly important as the primary reason or motivation for training, in some cases completely overriding the elements of wholesome physical and mental development.

Donn F. Draeger, a pioneer Western researcher and writer on Japanese *budō*, in his book *Classical Bujutsu*, expressed the differences in the hierarchy of values between *koryū bujutsu* and *gendai budō* in the following manner:

> *Bujutsu*: 1) combat; 2) discipline; 3) morals.
> *Budō*: 1) morals; 2) discipline; 3) aesthetic form.

This is probably a little more black-and-white than how the Japanese usually look at the differences between the classical and modern systems, but they are a useful way of approaching the similarities and differences between them. Mr. Phil Relnick, the first non-Japanese person to receive a *menkyo kaiden* (license of complete transmission, a recognition of both technical skill and personal suitability as someone responsible for continuing the transmission of the *ryū*) in Shinto Muso-ryū *jōjutsu* cautions his students that the only color in Japanese culture and society is gray, i.e., that ambiguity is very common in the way people think and act. Another way of saying this is that *context* is all-important.

Tilting at Windmills

A Comparison of Characteristics: *Koryū Bujutsu* and *Gendai Budō*

A major difference between the classical martial arts and their modern forms is that the classical arts are particular, discrete systems, each with its own curriculum and training methods, even philosophy, as developed over time more or less without outside influence or interference. Instruction is personal and emphasizes correct performance of skills through repetitive practice; the training itself is the end purpose.

Because *koryū* practice has, up to the present time, always been practiced in small groups centered on a particular *dōjō* or area, people know where each stands in the hierarchy, thus ranking or grading people in the same way as *gendai budō* is notably absent. While there are several *ryū* that now award the modern style *dan-i* (grades, or "belts"), most do not. Technical and teaching licenses exist, but these types of certification are awarded solely at the discretion of the instructor and/or the headmaster. Formal examinations for licenses are generally non-existent because the close contact developed by daily training is in itself enough to determine the individual's fitness for recognition.

The *gendai budō* are mostly comprised of large, and very highly centralized, organizations, with standardized curricula, training and pedagogical methods and objective grading standards. These are partly a development of the close connection of many *budō* to formal education in the schools, but also in part because coherency of this sort is the simplest way to administer large groups of people. Often, instruction is conducted in large groups, everyone doing an identical thing, more or less in cadence. Performance in competition, with its attendant emphasis on "star" individuals, may supplant the erstwhile aim of personal development. In the worst instances, personal relationships between teacher and student or student and student become strained. Though they are still important to an extent, they may be subsumed by the goal of winning, of rising to the top at the expense of other people. Examples of this include the "guts pose" after matches have been decided, advertising around the venue and on the training uniforms themselves, and the occurrence of competitors arguing with the referees and judges – what was once a dignified form of austere training has become an example of crass personal exhibitionism and commercialism.

Introduction of *Koryū Bujutsu* and *Gendai Budō* Outside Japan and the Preservation of Classical Arts in Modern Japanese and U.S. Society

The martial arts were first introduced to Westerners outside Japan during the Meiji period, when Japanese began to travel to Europe and North America on business and government service. Many of these first travellers were once members of the *bushi* class, so were skilled to one degree or another in the classical arts. Probably the first systems seen in the West were *jūjutsu*: Tenjin Shin'yo-ryū, Ryōi Shintō-ryū, and

Tsutsumi Hozan-ryū. The modern art of Kōdōkan judo (or *jiudo* as it was then called) followed soon after. In fact, no less a person than U.S. President Theodore Roosevelt, and members of his family, studied with directly with Yamashita Yoshitsugu, the first man in judo to be awarded the grade of *jūdan* (tenth-degree, the highest grade awarded in the Japanese martial arts). Other early pioneers in spreading *budō* overseas included Tomita Tsunejirō (U.S.A.), Maeda Mitsuyo (Central and South America), Koizumi Gunji and Tani Yukio (England), Ishiguro Keishichi (France), and Takagaki Nobusaku (India). Although I do not have precise dates, some information indicates that kendo and sumo were also introduced to the U.S. and South America sometime in the middle of the Meiji period, probably around 1890.

The creation of the Dai Nihon Butokukai during the 1890s and subsequent efforts to create a national standard for the arts of judo, kendo, sumo, *kyūdō*, and, later, *naginata*, led to the adoption of these disciplines by the Ministry of Education as physical education classes. One reason was the desire of the national government to train its citizens (especially the males) in physical skills that would be useful in military service. Martial arts, especially *gendai budō*, were seen as a very effective means of developing a national polity centred upon the Emperor, using him as the symbol by which Japan could industrialize and militarize. The high level of government support during the early Showa period led to an increase in the number of people training in *budō* and *bujutsu*, but the defeat of Japan in World War II and the view by the Allied Occupation that martial arts contributed to Japanese militarism and their subsequent ban for several years had consequences that were not necessarily beneficial in the long run.

A positive development for the *koryū* during this period of increased martial fervour in the 1930s was the Nihon Kobudō Shinkōkai's (Japanese Classical Martial Arts Promotion Association) founding, an attempt to revitalize the *kobudō* community. The natural curiosity of Japanese people for things that were seen as "new" and "progressive" during the modernization of Japan in the late nineteenth century, along with the government's support of judo and kendo in public schools for reasons of national polity, had led to a gradual eclipse of *koryū* ("old style") culture. The classical martial arts, along with other aspects of traditional Japanese culture, were seen as outmoded and not of any use and the headmasters and senior exponents of the surviving *koryū* were not disposed to let their schools die from neglect. They believed that there were important values and insights to be gained from these older arts that would prove invaluable, regardless of the times, and they sought to establish a larger presence in the *budō* community, and society at large. The Kobudō Shinkokai remains a very active organization and sponsors demonstrations and other events throughout the country during the year. It also encourages the member *ryū* to seek recognition as *mukei bunkazai* (Intangible Cultural Assets) in their local communities as a way of preserving and making people in their areas more aware and appreciative of their martial heritage.

Tilting at Windmills

What Attracts Americans (or Japanese) to the *Koryū*?

Given that classical martial arts are archaic methods of fighting, with little or no practical use in modern society, why would anyone, especially people of another country and cultural background, want to study them?

People who are interested in studying martial arts have, of course, a number of different reasons for doing so, but there are some common factors. They are interested in complex, demanding physical and mental training. They are not afraid of striving to improve, even when there is no discernible progress or immediate reward. They are strong-willed, motivated to succeed in what they do.

Most exponents of classical martial arts probably start out in one or another of the modern disciplines. At some point, however, they have an opportunity to observe the classical martial arts. They may not be immediately attracted to this kind of practice, but gradually they begin to understand that there is a profound technical and philosophical depth to classical systems that offers a very rewarding challenge to people who study them.

In other instances, there is a desire for exclusivity or originality, fed by the sense of special cachet that some people attach to training in "real samurai arts". Movies, books, Japanese anime (films and derivative media) are some common starting points. Or it may be that *koryū* is the "flavour of the month" in some of the popular media. These are not, perhaps, the most mature source of interest, but does it really matter, so long as the individuals training come to value the arts in, of, and for themselves?

Finally there is a perception that the *koryū bujutsu* offer a type of rigor and connection to history that is not approached by the *gendai budō*. It isn't any better, or truer, than a modern art, but there may be a sense that these "old ways" have lessons to offer their exponents that newer systems do not. This view can be and, of course, is disputed by those on either side of the divide, but again, it is perhaps not so important – if there is a sincere interest in beginning study, why not do so?

Differences in American and Japanese Cultural Context

So, what are some of the roots of confusion when Americans study the martial arts? The primary causes for misunderstanding are differences in the cultural context. These are not impenetrable or insurmountable, but they must be understood if people are to derive the full benefit that arises from studying this aspect of traditional Japanese culture.

One example is the difference in social hierarchy. Although this is clearly an oversimplification, American society believes in a more-or-less level playing field. People are considered intrinsically equal, equal rights are assured with equal opportunities and equal expectations of reward for effort. Differences of age, education, class and wealth do exist, but they are not thought to be of primary importance. Basically, society is horizontally structured and these "minor" differences can be overcome with application and hard work. Or, as the saying goes, the sky is the limit.

Japan is not like this. There is a strict vertical hierarchy. Age matters, as it is assumed that people with more experience have more wisdom, or at the least, better understanding. The person who has entered a school, company, or martial art before another will always be in a superior position of seniority. The junior may have better skills, more ability, a superior record of accomplishment, but the authority of seniority will always reside in the person who began first. This counts for a great deal. For much of its history, Japan placed a primary importance on hereditary position, based on family and historical precedent. Though this hierarchy was not absolute, and vertical movement in the social structure was possible, it was vastly more difficult than in the West, and was by no means assured or considered a "right" of the individual.

This is reflected in teaching methodologies, both in education and martial arts training. Students in Japanese schools and *dōjō* are more passive compared to those in the United States, where relationships between teacher and student tend to be more egalitarian. At higher levels in the United States, there is a sort of easy collegiality, with students often challenging instructors in a dialectic process.

In Japan, however, teachers lecture or demonstrate while students listen or observe, repeat the lesson, and do not try to display originality or individual expression until considerable time has passed in study. It is best described in an old expression: *shu-ha-ri*, where *shu* (J: *mamoru*) means "to protect, obey, abide by", ha (J: *yaburu*) is "to tear, rip, break," and *ri* (J: *hanareru*) connotes "to separate, leave". In classical martial arts the concept means that students, in the beginning, follow the instructor without questioning or doubting what the teacher shows them, whether or not they are able to apply the techniques "well" or "successfully". This is "*shu*". With practice, they begin to master these skills and concepts to an increasing extent, beginning to develop their own interpretations and a certain personal style; this is "*ha*". Finally, after amassing considerable experience, the students find that the principles and techniques of the art have become internalized; it is now an integral part of them. They no longer need to follow the codified methods of the system without deviation, but instead are able to "re-create" it anew at each moment. This separation from the art is known as "*ri*". At this point it is difficult to determine whether the exponents are doing the art or the art is "doing" them.

The problem for American students of martial or other traditional Japanese arts is that this process goes directly against the way they have been raised and taught to approach learning. Teachers, while more knowledgeable than students, are not accorded the same sense of respect, even awe. Students are taught to "think for themselves" and examine what they are learning in an analytical, critical, manner. The Socratic dialogue, a dialectic process where teacher and student confront one another in an attempt to arrive at "objective truth" is held to be the ideal.

Giving oneself over, or up, to the instructor is therefore very difficult for the

Tilting at Windmills

American student. Trusting that the "truth" of the system and integrity of the instructor will lead the individual to the goal to which he aspires is not at all easy and requires a leap of faith that many, perhaps most, Americans find all but impossible to do. They listen and accept the necessity for trusting their teacher, but only on an intellectual level and find it hard to develop the sense of *junansei*, pliancy and receptivity, which is expected and required of them. There is more to this difference in position than merely technical matters. An instructor brought up in the Japanese manner also learns that organizational and personal matters are part of the mix. In return for the teacher's guidance, students are expected to show a certain degree of deference and willingness to help their teachers, even if it is inconvenient or difficult for them to do so.

A further example of this difference in perspective is how Japanese people and Americans view themselves in relationship to other individuals, to the groups to which they belong, and to society as a whole. It may be simplistic to say Japanese are more group-oriented, Americans more individualistic, but it is easy to discern that Japanese view themselves primarily in relation to their group at the same time that Americans do not.

If a Japanese tenders a name card, the order of information in Japanese is *always* the name of the company, then the department of the company, the section within the department, the sub-section, then the individual's position in the section, and finally the individual's name, family (the larger group, of course) name, personal name last. Postal addresses work the same way, from the country to the prefecture, to the city or district, to the ward or town, and lastly to the neighbourhood area. If a residence is in an apartment building, the building name and apartment number come after that. Finally, the name of the person – and yes, the family name comes first, the personal name last. For an American, business cards, postal addresses and one's place are in the reverse order.

In broad cultural terms, then, in the United States, the individual is placed before the group and it is relatively rare that a sense of responsibility to the larger group will come before that of an individual or his or her family. In the martial arts, Americans tend to focus on themselves, what they have learned or achieved, where Japanese will, at least superficially, give primacy to the art, *dōjō*, or *ryū*.

This can lead to *dōjō* or style-hopping, or an even more distasteful occurrence not uncommon in the U.S., where individuals who believe they have not been judged or treated correctly will argue with instructors, referees, or officials of the organization. If Japanese are dissatisfied with the state of affairs, they will not openly confront his teacher or seniors with demands to correct the situation. Americans will, and do, act to "throw out the wrongdoers" to bring in a more amenable set of people or policies.

That is not to say that changes are never warranted or advisable. No system is perfect, no individual is infallible, but how misunderstandings and other disagreements are handled is a critical factor. When differences in viewpoint and approach conflict in these ways, though, it becomes difficult for the instructors and students alike to work together productively.

Budo Perspectives

Cultural context is an enormous issue for those practicing the *koryū* outside of Japan, but the future transmission of *koryū* is also threatened by a lack of interest in their native land. Martial arts are seen in Japan as "3-K" (*kiken, kitanai,* and *kusai*: dangerous, dirty, and smelly) and their popularity, especially that of *koryū bujutsu*, has decreased significantly – skiing and tennis are much more widely done as pastimes, while, for the average sports fan, the sports of baseball and soccer are by far the most popular. Finally, the importation of American "mass culture," insistent on "new", "hot", and "trendy", coupled with the demanding, incessant, almost frantic nature of modern life conflicts with the long-term, slower pace required in traditional martial arts. They have come to be seen by many younger people in Japan as having no place or value in modern circumstances.

By contrast, the United States has seen a surge of interest in *koryū bujutsu*. Part of this is due to marketing and popularization through mass media. The martial arts have gone through a series of "booms" since judo was first popularized after World War II. This was followed by karate in the 60s, kung-fu in the 70s, *ninjutsu* in the 80s, and Gracie "*jiu-jitsu*" and various spin-offs of this latter system in the 90s. Along the way, there have been booms of taekwondo, something called "*kyūshojitsu*" (which resembles *atemi-waza* found in classical *jūjutsu* or *kumiuchi*), military-style close combat and, finally, *kobudō*. One must be cautious, however, about the last term, since that word has come to mean in the United States Okinawan weapons arts (usually), as well as the *koryū bujutsu* of Japan.

The popular conception of the classical Japanese martial arts, however, is not one that would be recognized by most experienced *budō* exponents. One of the major problems is the dearth of accurate information. A second is that, what little accurate information exists is often wildly romanticized, distorted and exaggerated to sell magazines, movie tie-in products, or aggrandize the unscrupulous individuals who do anything to earn money or garner fame.

Occasionally, a confused individual who has trouble separating fantasy from reality comes to watch a practice. Most do not return, some even leave in the middle of that first exposure: what they see is not what they seek. Since the *koryū* are, by their very nature, serious business and require incredible effort and attention to detail, those who merely wish to play at martial arts go on to try other things. Interestingly, "sports *chambara*" – which can only be defined as "playing samurai" – is becoming increasingly popular. As the pace of life becomes more rapid, and people become busier and increasingly unsettled, those who could benefit from the firmness and gravity of serious training are seeking the sorts of diversions that merely compound their un-ease. It is not a loss, however, as this saves the old arts from people who would disrupt the subtle atmosphere of the *dōjō*.

The "Martial Arts Industry" is another factor. A loosely organized group of businesspeople who operate commercial martial arts 'studios' for profit, they may, or may not, have a degree of technical skill. However, the real abilities they have are too often swept aside in order to attract and "process" large numbers of clients (it's probably

Tilting at Windmills

inaccurate to call them students). As large numbers equal large profits, the owner of such an establishment feels compelled to structure training so that it appeals to the masses. Since novelty, what's "hot" (and what's not), "quick 'n easy" advancement in "rank" and other awards such as trophies are what sell, there is a move away from – being absolutely honest here, an almost complete absence of – the old-style careful, painstaking instruction that characterizes the martial arts. There is no time, nor is there any incentive, for anything else.

This problem is exacerbated when the cachet of "classical" arts is considered. The *bushi*, or samurai as he is commonly known in the United States, is a figure of mystery and awe. Take a couple of judo throws, add in some kicks, strikes and punches from karate, plus a little bit of fancy sword movement from *kembu* or movie-style swordsmanship and – presto! – a completely new old art has been created. Sometimes they have reasonable names; most often, though, they do not. Samurai-ryū? Clouds of Iga-ryū? Dragon Warrior-ryū? These and others are to be found in advertisements and telephone directories in most cities in the United States. In fact, one can all too often observe the putative art of a *dōjō* as it morphs into the "Next Best Thing" with the "Flavour of the Month".

Conclusion

In the end, the problem of transmitting the *koryū bujutsu* correctly appears to be one of cultural context, Japanese as well as American. The changes in the societies of both countries in the years since World War II have been rapid and profound. Mass production and a culture of obsolescence, coupled with a thirst for novelty and the latest fashion threaten the continued transmission of *koryū* in Japan. The problem is even more acute in the United States and other places because of the sheer depth and breadth of the traditional martial arts. Given their complex technical nature, and their inseparability from the culture that gave rise to them in the first place, it is doubtful that a complete transmission can occur without the careful nurturing and training of people who will care for them. The *koryū* are both adaptable and fragile; balancing the needs of the *koryū*'s cultural context with the present-day context in which they are practiced, regardless or where, will probably prove their greatest challenge.

Bibliography

Draeger, Donn F. *Classical Budo*. New York: Weatherhill, 1973.
Classical Bujutsu. New York: Weatherhill, 1973.
Draeger, Donn F. and Smith, Robert W. *Comprehensive Asian Fighting Arts*. Kodansha International, 1989.
Skoss, Diane (editor). *Keiko Shokon*. Berkeley Heights, N.J.: Koryu Books, 2002.

Sword & Spirit. Berkeley Heights, N.J. : Koryu Books, 1999.
Koryu Bujutsu. Berkeley Heights, N.J.: Koryu Books, 1997.

Chapter 21

Budō's Potential for Peace: Breaking Down Barriers in the Israeli/Palestinian Conflict

Danny Hakim
Wingate Institute (Israel)

Introduction

"We are already two years into a new century after bidding farewell to the war-stricken twentieth century. Have we progressed at all toward peace? The fact that we can't proudly and confidently say yes indicates the great uncertainty, which still engulfs the world. With all the mistrust arising from cultural and religious differences, how are we supposed to offer hope for future generations? One answer to this question can be found in promoting *budō*. An inquiry into the process of *budō*, originally a form of combat, has developed into a spiritual pursuit which places emphasis on mutual respect and is a means of education, and spreading it to the people of the world will go a long way in contributing to world peace." (Matsunaga Hikaru, Nippon Budokan Chairman, March 2002).

This paper considers the effect that *budō* can have in contributing to world peace. More specifically, it posits how *budō education* can be used to break down barriers between peoples in regions of severe conflict in general, and offers practical suggestions for achieving this goal in one of the longest and most violent disputes in modern history, the Israeli-Palestinian conflict.

The centrist position on resolution of this conflict acknowledges the need for co-existence. The Israeli and the Palestinian peoples – Jews, Muslims and Christians – share only a very small tract of territory, which will ultimately, most likely, serve as two states. Finding a *modus vivendi* is vital as their economies, cultures and infrastructures are sure to be linked. With the "Al-Aqsa *intifada"* now in its fourth year and no end in sight, the road to coexistence seems interminably long. But it is my conviction that it *is* possible to alleviate the pain and shatter the barriers of hatred.

Budō- "The Way of Stopping Conflict"

Most frequently, *budō* is taught in the *dōjō*, within the framework of "martial arts". The study of *budō* encourages practitioners, including youths, to:

1. Learn to respect themselves and others.
2. Maintain emotional well-being.
3. Increase their self-confidence.
4. Find peace within themselves and with others.

Ideally, and in concert, these elements could break down barriers of fear between people. The process has been considered successful for individuals for centuries. I am suggesting extending it to the macro-level, to advance coexistence to a wider scale. This paper recommends drawing on *budō* education to sow harmony in troubled places.

What is *Budō*, and How is it Taught in the *Dōjō*?

Budō is unique in the modern world of physical activities. It includes elements of sport, exercise, game, play and recreation – though it is linked to a more profound set of values than all of these. As fighting systems of self-defence, *budō* is rooted in East Asian traditions. Despite the influences of today's world, *budō* continues to reflect its roots, even as they develop in many instances into modern sports.

The Japanese word *budō*, loosely translated as "martial arts," is often interpreted as "the Way of stopping conflict". The word is made up of two Chinese characters – "*bu*," (武) which encompasses both "stop" (止) and "halberd" (戈) and "*dō*" meaning "the Way," as in karatedo, aikido, judo, kendo. Students of the martial arts learn to deal with and control conflict, both within themselves and between themselves and others. Indeed, this is a major aspect of their training. The ideological focus of martial arts training, combined with unique discipline and ritual, qualitatively differentiates these activities from other forms of exercise.[1]

The Japanese word *dōjō*, is loosely translated as a training hall, with "*dō*" meaning "the Way" and "*jō*" meaning "place". Hence, a *dōjō* is a place where "the Way" is taught.

Budō includes the nine martial arts officially recognized by the Nippon Budokan: judo, karate, kendo, aikido, *kyūdō*, *naginata*, *jūkendō*, *shōrinji kempō* and sumo. Internationally, *budō* also refers to other East Asian martial arts that have philosophical and spiritual elements, such as taekwondo, kung fu and tai chi.

Official estimates of the number of people around the globe learning karate are 9.1 million, judo 6.7 million and taekwondo 4.6 million.[2] It is estimated that there are another 1.5 million practitioners of *shōrinji kempō*. Unofficially, there are over 200 million practitioners of *budō* in the world.

Although different *budō* may vary in physical technique, they all share a general concept that training enhances the connection between the mind, body and spirit. The mind develops concentration, focus and self-discipline. The body becomes fit

Budo's Potential for Peace

while one learns to defend oneself. The spiritual training offers emotional stability and a way to live in harmony and balance with the world.

Budō is considered a way of life. All *budō* share the general philosophy that by training the mind and body one develops *ki* (inner power) and with this energy one can create *wa* (harmony) with oneself and with others in the world.

Here follows a list of the martial arts that comprise *budō* and a brief explanation of them:

Judo

Kanō Jigorō founded Kōdōkan judo in 1882. It was derived from *jūjutsu*. Kanō believed that the ultimate purpose of judo practice was to perfect the self also for the benefit of others. He devised the concepts of *"seiryoku zenyō"* and *"jita kyōei"* (maximum efficiency and mutual prosperity), which are the idealistic foundation stones of judo training. (It is a paradoxical distraction unfortunate that in Olympic judo the focus on moral development has received less attention than its role as a competitive sport).[3]

Karate

The actual, precise origin of karate is unknown. Some believe that karate originated in China with the Buddhist monk Daruma, in the sixth century B.C.E. Others believe it started in Greece much earlier. Modern karate however was developed in Okinawa around the sixteenth century and was officially exported to mainland Japan in 1922 by Funakoshi Gichin. Funakoshi is known as the father of modern karate. When karate was no longer needed for self-protection against oppressors, it was turned into an art of self-perfection for the public. Funakoshi stressed, "the ultimate aim of the art of Karate lies not in victory or defeat, but in the perfection of the character of its participants". The five karate principles of the *dōjō* are all considered equally important:

> *One! To strive for the perfection of character!*
> *One! To defend the paths of truth!*
> *One! To foster the spirit of effort!*
> *One! To honour the principles of etiquette!*
> *One! To guard against impetuous courage!*

In most *dōjō* in the world these principles are recited and application is encouraged beyond the *dōjō* walls as well. They transcend cultural barriers and create a format for respect and cooperation between individuals and groups. Needless to say, were they to be applied to peoples in conflict, the world would be a very different place.

Kendo

The Ogasawara-ryū traditional school of etiquette created in the Muromachi period (1333-1568), related specifically to the practice of archery and horsemanship, and other *bugei* (military arts). Its code of manners became prescribed behaviour in warrior society, and many of these traditions are continued today in kendo clubs around the world.[4]

Makita Minoru, of the International Budō University kendo club, notes how kendo develops character through technique, training, and competition: "The strict forms of etiquette and ceremony before and after *tachiai* (facing an opponent in combat) in kendo incorporates a discipline that is an essential part of kendo's attempt to create respect and develop character."[5]

Kyūdō

Before firearms the most effective military weapon was the bow and arrow. Over centuries of training in archery, the traditional form of *kyūdō* evolved. It preserves the essence of *budō* - it is never the purpose to strive to beat an opponent; rather, the main objective of the endeavour is to defeat the self through constant practice and refinement.

Shōrinji Kempō

The founder of *shōrinji kempō*, Sō Dōshin created his art based on a desire to improve the nation by cultivating qualities – such as courage and the ability to act – in young people. When training in pairs, for example, the point is not to compete against one another, but rather to teach one another. One of the principles of *shōrinji kempō* is "happiness for self and others". This means to recognize the existence of both the self and others, and living in a way that consistently seeks improvement and development.

Aikido

Aikido makes the most explicit claim to being an art of peace. Its founder, Ueshiba Morihei (1883-1969), had a vision of the "Great Spirit of Peace", which could lead to the elimination of all strife and the reconciliation of humankind. He said, "The Way of the warrior has been misunderstood as a means to kill and destroy others. Those who seek competition are making a grave mistake. To smash, injure, or destroy is the worst sin a human being can commit. The real Way of the warrior is to prevent slaughter – it is the Art of Peace, the power of love."

Unlike the authors of old-time warrior classics such as *The Art of War* and *The Book of Five Rings*, which accept the inevitability of war and emphasize cunning strategy as a means to victory, Ueshiba understood that prolonged fighting – with others, with ourselves, and with the environment – would lead to ruin.

"The world will continue to change dramatically, but fighting and war can destroy us utterly. What we need now are techniques of harmony, not those of contention. The art of Peace is required, not the art of War."

Budo's Potential for Peace

He thus taught the "art of Peace" as a creative mind-body discipline, as a practical means of handling aggression, and as a way of life that fosters fearlessness, wisdom, love, and friendship. He interpreted the art of Peace in the broadest possible sense and believed that its principles of reconciliation, harmony, cooperation, and empathy could be applied to all the challenges we face in life – to personal and work relationships, interactions with society, and to interactions with nature. Everyone can be a warrior for peace.

"Foster peace in your own life and then apply the art to all that you encounter. A warrior is always engaged in a life-and-death struggle for peace", he said.

Promoting Respect and Harmony Through the Practice of *Budō*

Dōjō

A *dōjō* is a miniature cosmos where we make contact with ourselves – our fears, anxieties, reactions, and habits. It is an arena of confined conflict where we confront an opponent who is not really an opponent but rather a partner engaged in helping us understand ourselves more fully. It is a place where we can learn a great deal in a short time about who we are and how we react in the world. The conflicts that take place inside the *dōjō* help prepare us to handle conflicts that take place outside. Thus, the total concentration and discipline required to study *budō* carries over to daily life.[6]

Japanese *machi-dōjō* (community *dōjō*) tends to resemble a kind of family structure in the relationships of the kinds of people training in them. Often the teacher will take the role of parent, and exercise disciplinary measures. The more senior *budō* practitioners and students serve as older brothers and sisters to the junior ones.[7]

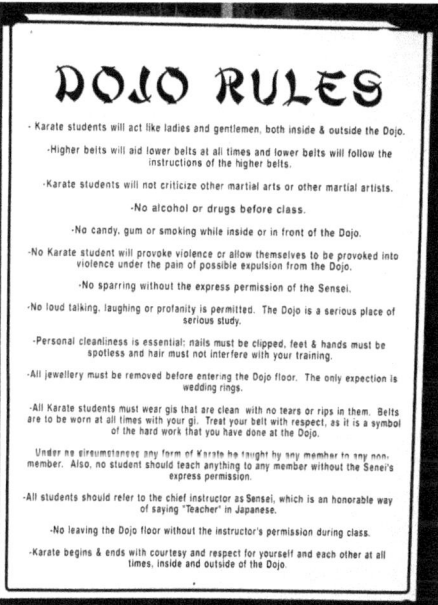

A typical list of dōjō rules from a martial arts studio in Canada

This type of family-style system found in Japan is replicated in many *dōjō* around the world. The environment nurtures personal development in children, giving them confidence and a safe place to express themselves.

If such *machi-dōjō* can maintain this family-like atmosphere, and if teachers believe that *budō* can be a means of cultivating personality, then we can see how respect and harmony can be achieved not only within *dōjō* but between *dōjō* and beyond. The environment that *budō* engenders in the *dōjō* can play an important role in creating peace and co-existence beyond those walls.

Rei (Etiquette/courtesy)
The concept of showing respect is an integral part of *budō*. The first lesson begins with the practice of bowing, and this is reinforced at every training session. Only those who grasp the depth of its meaning reach a high level of proficiency. *Rei* may be defined as the will to establish a relationship based on mutual trust, goodwill, understanding, and respect of individual feelings by showing respect. In society, it is a means of maintaining harmony between people for a better society. Bowing to express this attitude to the *dōjō*, to one's senior, to one's sensei and to one's opponent engenders a relationship of honour. Proper behaviour can help achieve what *budō* endeavours to develop in individuals, but only when one really understands and accepts what the behaviour means. When you bow, for example, you have to actually feel gratitude and respect toward the person you are bowing to. If you don't, it is all just empty formality with little substance. It is the content, and not necessarily the form, that is most important.

Of course, the custom of bowing as a form of respect is not unique to Japan. Different manifestations of bowing have in the past been adopted, and adapted, in line with religious sensitivity while maintaining the significance of showing respect to others. For example, Kanazawa Hirokazu, chairman of Shotokan Karate International who teaches extensively throughout the world, reputedly has over one million Muslim students. He has adapted two styles of bowing that suit the religious values of his students. Kneeling and placing one's forehead near the ground, as in traditional Japanese custom (*zarei*); and kneeling while holding one's hands together upright and bowing the head to the hands. The latter of these two types of bowing has been integrated into the local *dōjō* training of many Muslim cities and towns and has become socially acceptable in those *dōjō*. The practice has fostered harmony and respect between religious and less religious members of those *dōjō*.

The dō-gi (uniform)
The *dō-gi* is the traditional outfit for practicing *budō*. In most types of *budō*, the *gi* is plain white with no added colours or designs. It symbolizes equality, regardless of colour, creed, religious or social background. It creates an instant equalizing effect for new and old members of a *dōjō*. Although the colour of the belt shows a difference in basic levels of skills, after achieving the level of black-belt there is no distinction between levels.

The language of the dōjō
All *Budō* practitioners speak a common language in the *dōjō*. They understand common words and concepts in Japanese, as it is an integral part of learning in the

Budo's Potential for Peace

dōjō. In karate, terms such as *tsuki* (punch), *mae-geri* (front kick), *kiba-dachi* (horse riding stance), *kata* (form), *kumite* (fight) etc. and concepts such as *wa* (harmony), *ma-ai* (distance), *zanshin* (continued mental and physical awareness) and *ki* (vital energy) are regularly used in the *dōjō* regardless of the country or which *budō* is being taught. This form of communication offers a common language, which breaks down the barriers of stereotyping and bridges the cultural divide between peoples in conflict.

The spirit of "Oss"
"*Oss*" has become an important word in the vernacular of karate, understood and exchanged among practitioners throughout the world both as an everyday greeting and also to mean "thank you", "glad to meet you", goodbye", and "I understand". It must be uttered with a bow, showing respect, sympathy and trust to the other party. *Oss* (押忍) is in fact written with these two Chinese characters. The first literally means "pushing", (symbolizing the fighting spirit, the importance of effort, and facing all obstacles, pushing them away, with a positive and unchanging attitude. The second means "suffering" but expresses courage and perseverance, keeping spirits high even in the face of hardship.

In his book, *Karate – My Life*,[8] Kanazawa states "*Budō* is an activity where one develops the mind and spirit during the process of tempering the spirit. Winning matches is not the final goal of *budō*. Knowing your limitations and disciplining yourself is the ultimate objective. That is the true meaning of *oss*…*Oss* means to never retreat from problems or hardships, but to stick with them, never giving up and achieving what you set out to achieve….Perseverance (*nintai*), effort (*doryoku*), and achievement (*tassei*) are the underlying concepts of *oss*."

Its spirit can be tapped to forge strong relationships at the grassroots level between people in conflict.

The Psychological Benefits

Cultivating a child's development in Japan
Kanno Jun, a professor of psychology at Waseda University and a youth counselor, has been involved in developmental and clinical psychology particularly helping children who face development problems such as dropping out of school, school violence, domestic violence, delinquency and developmental disorders.

In his article, "*Budō* – Cultivating Young Minds," he talks about his experiences interviewing many *budō* instructors and children. He notes the developmental attributes of *budō* and the role of instructors. His experience and observations over thirty years touched on many issues relevant to all children in the world,[9] including:

- Spiritual problems facing modern children.
- Mistrust of other people and developing a "victim mentality".

- Hunger for love.
- Underdevelopment or ignorance of social skills.
- Mental strength and resilience.
- Nurturing a healthy self-image to act as a basis for physical development.
- *Budō*'s contribution to the development of social skills, such as courtesy, generosity, consideration and so on.
- *Budō*'s contribution to the development of discipline and strength to endure hardships.
- Drawing on *budō* to enhance the ability to understand yourself, which leads to self-development.
- The nurturing of trust through the process of receiving instruction and working hard with one's peers.

He concludes that "*budō* offers a vehicle to educate children in areas in which schools and homes are failing".

Emotional well-being and therapy in the U.S.

The psychologists Wingate and Sachs have studied the effects of martial arts on emotional development in the U.S. They found that martial arts training contributes to psychological well-being in children and adults. Martial artists display lower levels of anxiety and depression than do non-martial artists. Maintenance of emotional well-being and stress reduction were important reasons for training among traditional *karateka*. They concluded that martial arts enhance the development of character and improvement of the individual more than other sports. In the traditional view of these arts, perfection of character and perfection of technique are inseparable because of the Eastern approach to mind and body in general.

The specific aspects of martial arts training that lead to improvements in psychological well-being result from the three ideological claims most often made about martial arts: that practicing these arts a) promotes the formation of moral character; b) promotes non-violent attitudes and behaviour; and c) promotes spiritual development.

Further literature describes the therapeutic relevance of *budō*.[10, 11, 12] Other studies explicitly note the parallels between the goals and methods of *budō* and verbal psychotherapy, in that both are disciplines for gaining understanding into one's character with the aim of growth toward a new and stronger way of being with oneself in the world. Both *budōka* and psychotherapy patients learn to understand and deal with resistance, in themselves and others, to manage both evasion and confrontation, and to cope with aggression and vulnerability.[13]

Trauma therapy in Israeli and Palestinian communities

Many Palestinian and Israeli children have experienced degrees of behavioural changes due to trauma developed from the reality of living in a state of war and occupation. A nationwide survey of schools found that six percent of Israel's two million children suffer from Post-Traumatic Stress Disorder (PTSD) with another twelve percent displaying partial symptoms. Fifty-five percent of Palestinian children have started developing PTSD.

The United Nations children's agency UNICEF says that parents report behavioural changes among eighty percent of children living in Palestinian areas. Even though Israeli and Palestinian children differ culturally from those in, say, Japan and America, one should consider the extreme circumstances in which they live. In this context, the effect of *budō* education in the local *dōjō* may have a greater therapeutic impact.

In 2002, dance therapist Yael Perpignan researched the therapeutic benefits of Shotokan karate in a *dōjō* in Israel.[14] Perpignan interviewed karate practitioners from beginner to advanced levels. She examined the theories of Feldenkreis, Laban Movement Analysis and Jung and the therapeutic elements of karate using these psychological models of behaviour. Her research showed positive results in self-confidence, learning to cope and not giving up, concentration, calm instinct, self-control, and intuition. She also explored interpersonal relationships: relationships with peers in the *dōjō* and outside and the opposite sex. Further studies on the benefits of *budō* on trauma victims, mentally challenged, and the physically disabled are underway and are being documented.

Respect, Harmony and Breaking Down Barriers in the Israeli-Palestinian Conflict

This section is based on my own research, experience and the discussions with my Palestinian counterpart, Dughan Khalil. Khalil is the chief instructor and coach of Shotokan Karate International in the Palestinian Authority. I am presently the senior instructor and coach of Shotokan Karate International in Israel. Both Khalil and I have been training in Shotokan karate for over thirty years. We first met in 1997 when we did our 5th *dan* black belt test together under Kanazawa Hirokazu. This experience was the first of many that forged a mutual respect and friendship. In September 2003, we both passed the 6th *dan* black belt test and were awarded the title of *renshi*. We both also follow the philosophy of Kanazawa of respect and harmony, and maintain that this belief has enabled us to break down barriers in our personal lives. We now accept responsibility to channel our skills and understanding to the younger generation through the education we provide in our *dōjō*.

Victims verses aggressors

Both Israelis and Palestinians believe that they are the victims of terror or occupation and that the other side is the aggressor. Media and education reinforce this belief. The victim/aggressor belief is a fundamental obstacle, preventing Palestinians and Israelis from thinking in terms of coexistence. The mistrust, suspicion and negative stereotyping run so deep in both societies that many people believe that it is not possible to coexist with the other.

In a joint Israeli-Palestinian survey in 1999 conducted by the Van Leer Jerusalem Foundation, 71 % of Jews said Palestinians in general were violent, and only 15.4 % called them non-violent as a group. Among Palestinians, 91.5 % labelled Jews as violent and 8.4 % said they were non-violent.[15]

Israeli parents train their children to watch out for suspicious objects and suspicious-looking people; years of random suicide bombers extinguishing innocent lives have impacted on daily life. Similarly, Palestinian parents tell their children not to play outside in fear of them being in the line of fire of the Israeli defence forces. Children growing up in this environment, needless to say, are exposed to fear and anxiety. Not all Israeli Jews subscribe to the whole list of prejudices against Arabs, of course, and not all Arabs hold negative stereotypes of Jews. Even so, the constant imagery in the media coupled with politically-influenced education creates a convincing pattern of stereotypes and beliefs, which makes it difficult for either side to trust each other and work towards a peaceful solution.

Respect and harmony versus stereotyping and fear

Respect teaches tolerance, which is the first tool necessary to break down barriers of hatred. Respecting others immediately puts one on an equal playing field. Having respect for oneself and for others discards the notion that one is a victim and others are the aggressors. Respect helps break down stereotypic images and hatred developed from years of indoctrination. These stereotypes have worked their way thoroughly into literature, education, history, language, and social mores on both sides.

Khalil makes the case that:

"Respect is the foundation of our relationships with parents, teachers, fellow students and all that we interact and communicate with in this universe. Respect cannot be requested. You can earn [respect] by how you treat others and carry yourself. Respecting others is beyond race, religious belief and culture. You have to respect yourself first in order to make harmonious relationships with others. This can be achieved by training in traditional karate. In this way we can build global education and global relationships between nations.

Harmony means respect, treating others the way we want to be treated. We will not always agree, we should not, as we should be allowed to think for ourselves, to make our own choices, what is right for us. We respect the right to disagree and still live in harmony. We each have a heart, we each have a soul and though we are different in many respects, inside, we are the same. No matter what the colour of our skin, religion, culture or beliefs, we can still live in peace, respect and harmony.

Then more people will join us in spreading the seeds of peace among young

Budo's Potential for Peace

generations, building together a future of authentic peace. I truly believe in the power of respect, harmony and love. Harmony is the secret to inner peace. Harmony is the state of being humble, neither proud nor haughty, neither arrogant nor assertive, it is humility. People have to know each other better to spread the messages of peace, respect and harmony in their surroundings. This will lead to the harmony of spirit, body and mind so that the feeling of hate and violence will disappear and everywhere truth and love will triumph. It will be great [when] the seeds of peace blossom in our countries..."

The famous warrior Miyamoto Musashi said that "becoming the opponent means you should put yourself in the opponent's place and think from the opponent's point of view."[16] Understanding one's opponent is the first stage of respecting them and forging a partnership in harmony.

Applying *Budō* to the Middle East Context

The popularity of budō in the Middle East
For those living in the Middle East, Asian culture – Japan's in particular – is seen as exotic and interesting. It is significantly different to any Western culture and therefore has an appeal without prejudice or ulterior motives. While American culture is seen as "conquering" the Middle East, Japanese culture is not seen as politically or socially "threatening". Nor do the Japanese have any historical imperial influence in the area.

Tradition and history are sources of pride and identity amongst Muslims and Jews and it is natural for them to respect and honour the traditional forms of etiquette propagated in all Japanese cultural activities like *budō*. Indeed, to provide just one example, karate is one of the most popular sports in Iran today, and the Iranian National Junior Karate team is among the most successful teams in the world. In the World Junior Karate Championships in October 2003, Iran won more medals than any other country, including Japan.

Japanese initiatives for bringing peace to the Middle East
In April 2003, the Japanese Minister for Foreign Affairs, Kawaguchi Yoriko, announced a new Japanese initiative for "Peace in the Middle East, towards the peaceful coexistence of the two states."[17] The initiative is aimed at confidence building between Israelis and Palestinians. It is designed to help uproot the distrust and hatred between the two sides. In launching the initiative, Kawaguchi stated, "In order to achieve 'two-state vision', which aims at realizing the peaceful coexistence of the two states of Israel and Palestine, it is necessary to promote confidence building through various levels of dialogues and cooperation. This project will support grassroots groups, NGOs and local governments to carry out activities such as raising public awareness, cooperation and peace activities between Israelis and Palestinians."

There are many ways to promote further exchanges between Palestinian and Israelis and other peoples in conflict through the avenues of *budō* culture. It is with this aim that the Budo Movement for Peace was established.

The Budo Movement for Peace (BMP)

The Budo Movement for Peace was established in November 2003 in order to actively implement the ideals of *budō* to stop conflict. It is the responsibility of all people practicing *budō* to make the world a more peaceful and safer place for future generations.

Mission Statement:
To bridge the gap between peoples in conflict through the Japanese *budō* concept of respect and harmony.
Goals:
-To spread the *budō* concept of respect and harmony in the world through *budō* organizations, government and non-governmental organizations, educational institutions and the media.
-To organize international events and exchanges relevant to fulfilling the mission.
The Budo Movement for Peace will:
-Address *budōka* from areas in conflict to bring them together and exchange ideas on how *budō* education can assist them in stopping conflict at the grassroots level.
-Share knowledge and strategies to implement activities between *budōka* in the region.
-Obtain support from the Japanese and other governments to realize these initiatives.
-Obtain support from all *budō* institutions in the world.
-Obtain support from international peace organizations and the network of *dōjō* to organize exchanges, events and distribute *budō* educational material such as films.

Examples of confidence building exchange events include bringing together Palestinian and Israeli *budōka* to organize regional events or exchanges where one or a number of Japanese masters come to officiate. Such events would include conducting training clinics, demonstrations and perhaps friendly competitions. Alos, using leading personalities in *budō* to promote the cause for world peace.

With the active participation and support of international peace organizations such as the Institute of World Affairs (IWA) and the International Labour organization (ILO), and with support from governments and sports organizations such as the

Budo's Potential for Peace

Nippon Budokan, the Wingate Institute for Sport and Physical Education, coupled with educational institutions such as Neve Shalom and the International Budo University, these events can make a significant impact on both peoples.
"Fight for Peace", a documentary

An Israeli and Palestinian girl practicing karate together in Delphi

The BMP plans to produce a series of documentaries and TV programs that promote the theme that Japanese budō culture can transcend barriers of conflict and help promote the peace process. In June 2003, Budoco Ltd. was established to produce the first film of this kind. The films will be used as educational tools in building confidence between Palestinian and Israeli children and other peoples in conflict. The initial intention is to make a large impact upon the youth community in Israel and the Palestinian Authority. An educational road show media kit will be presented in schools. This kit includes screening the film and encouraging discussions with the students immediately afterwards, drawing on the characters from the film to talk of their experiences. The characters of the film may serve as role models: their *budō* values could become relevant and a significant part of the children's lives in Israel and the Palestinian Authority.

Peace TV

Budoco Ltd. plans to make a TV series based on the *budō* philosophy and the values and characters presented in the documentary above. The series will be used as an educational tool for peoples in conflict around the globe. Funding is currently being sought for this project, which will include cooperation with other peace-building groups and individuals, televising their activities in order to show determined, even Sisyphean, efforts toward peacemaking to the widest audience possible.

Assistance from other organizations

A number of non-governmental organizations (NGOs) and other groups are assisting in the Budo Movement's coordination of activities and dissemination of information. At the forefront of these groups is the Wingate Institute for Physical Education and Sport, which is actively using sport and *budō* to promote coexistence between Israel and its Arab neighbours. To date, it has conducted a number of courses along these lines – for swimming coaches, football coaches, and special Olympics training camps for retarded children from the Palestinian Authority and Jordan. In 1998, Kanazawa Hirokazu was invited to lecture on the spirit of *budō* at Wingate's Martial Arts instructors' course. In addition, a number of the Palestinian karate team members have passed the *budō* instructors course at Wingate.

Also, the Washington, DC-based Institute of World Affairs (www.iwa.org) is an active partner in teaching conflict resolution techniques with the BMPeace. The IWA and the ILO (International Labour Organization) is planning to hold their first major

Palestinians, Israelis, and Cypriots practicing karate kata together in one of the original stadiums for the Olympic Games in Delphi, Greece

Budo's Potential for Peace

international event with the BMP in Kosovo in July 2006. A similar event has already been held in Delphi, Greece in 2005, which brought spirited young *budō* practitioners from countries in conflict (Israel, Palestine, and Cypress) to train with *budō* masters, and actively learn about conflict resolution.

Conclusion

For the past three years I have been working with victims of terror as a volunteer martial arts therapist. Some of these victims were seriously disabled when a suicide bomber boarded the bus they were on; others lost a limb, or their sight, or both, when a bomb exploded inches from them. Some lost their entire families in these circumstances. I have witnessed them regain self-confidence, self-esteem and inner peace. The results have far exceeded my initial expectations considering these individuals' lives were changed so drastically and dramatically – in just a flash. It has taught me that *budō* education works, even in the most dire and extreme circumstances.

Having been trained for years in the principles of *budō*, I was unexpectedly called upon to apply them all to real life. Through this experience I learned that *budō* education can empower victims of terror and also serve as a source of power to create a bridge of peace.

My deeper conclusion is that *Budō* can help stop conflict. Knowing this has inspired us (BMP) to take *budō* beyond the *dōjō*, into corners of the world touched by strife. By instilling children, in particular, with its principles and values, we can nurture a new generation to grow up with confidence and strength, and with the tools to help dissipate the fear and anxiety that remain the foundation of their daily lives. I fully understand that it is an ambitious goal. And I believe that with support it can be achieved.

Endnotes

[1] Wingate, *Exploring the Karate Way of Life.*
[2] Refer to www.wkf.com World Karate Federation web page .
[3] Takeuchi Masayuki, "How Can *Budō* be Used as a Way to Develop Character in Modern Society", p.72.
[4] Inoue Yoshihiko, *Kendo Kata: Essence and Application*, p.157.
[5] 14th International Seminar of Budo Culture discussion, March 2002.
[6] Hyams, *Zen in the Martial Arts*, p. 12.
[7] Kashiwazaki Katsuhiko, "Budō for Character Building", p. 103.
[8] Kanazawa Hirokazu, *Karate My Life*, p. 283.
[9] Kanno Jun. *"Budo – Cultivating Young Minds".*
[10] Tart, "Aikido and the Concept of Ki", pp. 18, 332-348.
[11] Seitz, F.C., Olsen, G.D., Locke, B., Quam, R., "The Martial Arts and Mental Health: The Challenge of Managing Energy", pp. 70, 459-464.
[12] Parsons, "Psychoanalysis as Vocation and Martial Arts", pp. 11,453-462.

[13] Weiser, Kutz, Kutz, Weisler, "Psychotherapeutic Aspects of the Martial Arts".
[14] Perpignan, *The Therapeutic Elements of Traditional Shotokan Karate*.
[15] Shipler, *Arab and Jew: Wounded Spirits in a Promised Land*, p. 174.
[16] Miyamoto Musashi, *A Book of Five Rings*, p. 40.
[17] Kawaguchi Yoriko, "Peace in the Middle East: Towards the Peaceful Coexistence of the Two States".

Bibliography

Hyams, Joe. *Zen in the Martial Arts*. Penguin Putnam Inc., 1979.
Inoue Yoshihiko. *Kendo Kata: Essence and Application*. (Translated by Alex Bennett). Auckland: KW Publications, 2003.
Kanazawa Hirokazu. *Karate My Life*. (Translated by Alex Bennett) Auckland: KW Publications, 2003, p. 283.
Kanno Jun. "*Budō* – Cultivating Young Minds". Contained in the 14th International Seminar of Budo Culture Seminar Proceedings, Nippon Budokan, March 2002.
Kashiwazaki Katsuhiko. "*Budō* for Character Building". Contained in the 14th International Seminar of Budo Culture Seminar Proceedings, Nippon Budokan, March 2002.
Kawaguchi Yoriko. "Peace in the Middle East: Towards the Peaceful Coexistence of the Two States". Japan Ministry of Foreign Affairs web page, April 2003.
Shipler, David. *Arab and Jew: Wounded Spirits in a Promised Land*. Penguin Books, 2002.
Miyamoto Musashi. *A Book of Five Rings*. (Translated by Thomas Cleary). Shambhala Publications, 1993.
Seitz, F.C., Olsen, G.D., Locke, B., Quam, R. "The Martial Arts and Mental Health: The Challenge of Managing Energy". *Perceptual and Motor Skills*. 1990.
Takeuchi Masayuki. "How can *Budō* be Used as a Way to Develop Character in Modern Society". Contained in the 14th International Seminar of Budo Culture Seminar Proceedings, Nippon Budokan, March 2002.
Tart, C.T. "Aikido and the Concept of *Ki*". *Psychological Perspectives*, 1987.
Parsons, M. "Psychoanalysis as Vocation and Martial Arts". *International Review of Psychoanalysis*. 1984.
Perpignan Yael, *The Therapeutic Elements of Traditional Shotokan Karate*, (Unpublished MA Thesis Paper in Expressive Therapies). Lesley University Graduate School, 2002.
Weiser, M., Kutz, I.,Kutz, S., Weisler, D. "Psychotherapeutic Aspects of the Martial Arts". *American Journal of Psychotherapy*, vol 49, no1., 1995.
Wingate, C. *Exploring the Karate Way of Life*. (Unpublished doctoral thesis). Temple University, 1993.

SECTION 5

PUBLIC LECTURES

Chapter 22

The Paradox of "Judo as an Olympic Sport" and "Judo as Tradition"

Anton J. Geesink
10th dan, IOC member

Born on the 6th of April 1934 in Utrecht, Anton Geesink is a teacher at the Royal Military Academy in Breda; Professor at the Academy of Physical Education in Amsterdam and at the Central Institute for the Education of Sports Teachers in Overveen; national and international judo instructor and coach. He took the Olympic Gold medal (judo) in Tokyo in 1964; world judo champion (1961, 1964, 1965); 21 European Judo Championship titles; Dutch judo champion (several times) and national champion in Greco-Roman wrestling (3 times). He also holds the highest grade of 10th Dan judo. His awards are numerous including four times national sportsman of the year; Prix de l'Académie Française (1962); Queen's Order of Knight of Oranje Nassau (1962); the City of Utrecht honoured him with a statue in the centre of the city (1995); Order of Merit in Gold of the Republic of Austria; Order of the Sacred Treasure, Gold Rays by His Majesty the Emperor of Japan (1997). He holds an honorary Doctorate in letters from Kokushikan University in Tokyo (2000), and was unanimously elected to the IJF Hall of Fame (2003). He also holds numerous positions in sports administration including lifelong honorary membership in the IJF, and is an IOC member. The following is a transcription of his public speech given as the second to last presentation at the Budō Symposium held at the International Research Centre for Japanese Studies, Kyoto, Japan.

Introduction

With the evolution of judo to the modern age, judo as both traditional *budō* culture and modern Olympic sport has been practiced simultaneously as an undivided whole. This forced unity of traditional and sporting aspects has resulted in a conflict in the manner and content of judo education. The dichotomy poses not only a nuisance to young judo practitioners struggling with too many disparate elements in their judo education, but ultimately serves to impede the overall promotion of judo itself.

Children begin judo study for a variety of reasons. For one, it may be because of some fighter they idolize, for another, it may be due to seeing dynamic competition on the television. Parents may encourage their child to take up judo on the advice of a teacher, doctor, or physical education teacher. Whatever the reason for stepping foot into the *dōjō*, Western children are normally forced to learn a great number of techniques very early in their training, in order to pass grading examinations.

Budo Perspectives

In my opinion, ninety-five percent of the techniques taught in the early stages of the training of judo outside Japan are unnecessary. Furthermore, the requirement for the young student to learn *kata* is also counter-productive. A curriculum requiring the young student to master excessive or impractical skills is not conducive to beginner development. Teaching superfluous techniques is time consuming, tedious, and as a result is frustrating for both teacher and student alike. This situation does not contribute to judo as a tradition or philosophy, nor as an Olympic sport. Therefore, it is essential that a clear division be made between judo as a culture, and the Olympic sport. I will explain these topics separately.

Judo as an Olympic Sport

The Olympic sport of judo is most commonly engaged in by young people. Their aim is to become a champion competitor. The young have little appreciation for "tradition," and often regard such matters as a burden. However, eventually, the youthful desire to be "young, strong, and handsome" will come to an end, for some sooner, for

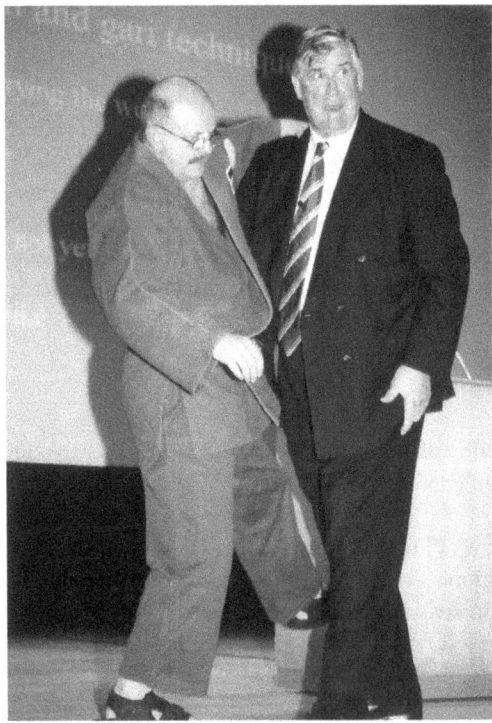

Anton Geesink (right) demonstrating techniques from his judo curriculum with Mr. Martin Franken on stage at the IRCJS, November 2003

Judo as an Olympic Sport or as Tradition

some later in life. Much depends on the age at which a person starts practicing sports at the highest level: If one starts at age ten, it is possible by age twenty-two to become a top-level competitor or champion (i.e. practicing judo as an Olympic sport). If one starts at the age of twenty, growing motivation and interest in judo as a mental and physical activity rooted in tradition may arise around the age of thirty to thirty-two.

The characteristics of judo as an Olympic sport can be summarized in the following way:

> Goals: Competition; winning (several levels).
> Target group: Youth.
> Period: Limited number of years.

Judo as a Tradition

Judo as a mental and physical pursuit rooted in tradition is a lifetime commitment. It is broad encompassing part of judo that never ends. In the study of the culture of judo, exponents study the *kata*, judo's history and traditions, and the development of judo to our present day. Going beyond judo as a competitive sport, we find the traditional culture of judo, that of being the mental and physical activity. This entails the lifetime commitment of mature judo study.

The characteristics of judo as a tradition can be summarized the following way:

> Goals: Study, preservation and transmission of the rich history of judo (the timeless culture of judo without end).
> Target group: Usually adults.
> Period: Lifetime commitment, following a career of judo as a sport of physical activity.

Judo as Physical Activity

Judo actually has a third dimension: judo as a physical activity. This can be summarized thus:

> Goals: Varied and personal aims (beauty, health, finding out about Judo, and recently in the Netherlands for weight control).
> Target group: All ages.
> Period: Lifetime with different aims.

Failure to identify and separate these disparate aspects of judo, and attempting to include them all in a single program, results in conflicting goals, and ultimately the failure to achieve any of them successfully. Frustration at expending great efforts with poor results diminishes personal motivation, individual development, and the development of judo in the greater picture. The single program approach fails to address the specific needs of the different target groups because too many responsibilities are presented to the instructor. "If you try to please everyone with the same approach, you will end up pleasing no one." However, if judo can be experienced and practiced according to the specific needs of exponent according to their stage of judo maturity, as I describe above, we can do full justice to the totality that judo offers, not at once, but as a natural progression.

Consequences of Approaching Judo as an Olympic Sport with a Specific Program

Based on my description of the different dimensions of judo, I would like to examine the consequences of using the specific approach, as opposed to the all-inclusive single program. I would like to address only the case of judo as an Olympic sport. This is not because I feel that judo tradition is less worthy, but because I am an Olympian and a member of the IOC. Also, most young people practice judo as an Olympic sport; therefore, this is the area of the greatest impact, and for the promotion of judo in the future. Young people aim to become the best, to become a champion through training long and hard, and for the most part have little interest in the traditional or historical aspects of judo. Most regard these aspects as tedious and an inconvenience. This lack of appreciation for history or culture is not unique to young judo people, but youth in general, and we should acknowledge it honestly as we consider judo education.

My career in the sporting world has progressed steadily, in stages, over a number of decades. Leading up to my current positions in sports administration, I passed through the many stages required to become technically and managerially informed about elite sports as well as sports in general. I started as a young sportsman and became a World and Olympic champion. From there, I became a club trainer, teacher, national federation coach, and then member of numerous committees. After demonstrating social and community commitment in these positions, various managerial positions followed. In 1985, I was elected Member of the Executive Board of the International Judo Federation. I also served as Director of Education and Coaching of the federation. In 1987, I was elected as an International Olympic Committee member. I regularly visit the All Japan, European, World Championships, Olympic Games, and most other major Judo events. In the course of these activities, I meet with thousands of judo exponents from many countries. In addition, I respond to invitations from around the world to demonstrate and teach judo. Not only has this career been a source of inspiration and pleasure for me, it has provided invaluable insights about the nature of judo education. I base my conclusions on these experiences.

Judo training curricula and examinations should correlate to personal skill levels and experience. The individual judo-*ka* needs an examination "made to measure" in order

Judo as an Olympic Sport or as Tradition

to do justice to the many different levels of students. Through careful consideration, the instructor should teach techniques suitable for each student. The teaching method should start at an easy level, and gradually progress to more difficult content. Grading examinations should be a logical follow-up to this training and experience. During an examination, the student should demonstrate progress relating to the standards prescribed by the teacher. For the judo-*ka* that desires to compete, only those techniques and skills required for winning matches are necessary. Anything else at this stage of their career is superfluous.

The practice of teaching an excessive number of techniques, and spending a great deal of valuable time and energies practicing techniques that do not suit the student are inefficient and wasteful. The result is retarded development and therefore poor performance in competition. This only serves to diminish the appeal of judo.

With this realization, I felt the need to develop a basic teaching method based on rational pedagogical, didactic, and biomechanical principles. In my teaching method, I avoid giving pupils the impression that any technique is unique and different from the other techniques. Rather, I emphasize the principles that are common to the broad range of techniques.

Included in the rational approach of my system, I would like to point out that there is no place for mysticism in Olympic judo. Outside of Japan, judo is in some places invested with figurative mystical elements. This conclusion is in no way a condemnation of other dimensions, or the manner in which judo has been approached in the past. My position is based on the fact that judo was not made an Olympic sport until 1964, and even then, society has changed from ten, twenty, thirty years hence. Judo should be kept rational, and free from unrelated elements. Just as societies and times change, we should adjust accordingly.

Requirements of the Capable Competitor

In order to become competent, the competitive judo practitioner needs to master to types of techniques: *tokui*, or specialty techniques, and non-specialty techniques.

1. *Tokui-waza*: These are "techniques of personal preference," or techniques that the practitioner is particularly skilled at executing. They agree well with the physique and character of the judo-*ka*, and can be considered natural to him or her. Practicing, studying, or using these techniques in contests gives the practitioner a great deal of pleasure. Pleasure is also had during the exercise of *uchikomi* (repetitive training) and *randori* (free sparring). I refer to this as "eating what is tasty and good for you." These techniques can be utilized to great effect during contests.

2. Non-specialty *waza:* Complete training also entails learning things that do not go well with the nature of a specific judo-*ka*. Even though they may not be incorporated into the repertoire, they are required knowledge without which the judo-*ka* cannot be

competitive. I call this "eating that which is not tasty, but is still good for you." The best way to measure and understand the strength of one's opponent is to familiarize one's self with the techniques they may use. This is the only way to learn the precise moment to take action should the opponent attack with any particular technique. In other words, these techniques are not studied for use *per se*, but to discover the danger of the given technique, and how best to deal with it.

To give an example of this principle, let's compare two judo-*ka* both 100 kilograms, but of different builds. One judo-*ka* is 2 meters in height and uses one leg to pivot on, and the other leg to sweep with (e.g. *harai-goshi* (hip sweep) or *uchimata* (inner thigh reaping throw)). Another judo-*ka* measures 1.8 meters, and uses techniques in which both feet are kept on the ground, with throwing accomplished by bending the knees (e.g. *seoi-nage* (shoulder throw)). The taller judo-*ka* has to learn *seoi-nage*, and the shorter *harai-goshi*, and so forth. Each must learn the effective technique of his potential adversary, not for attacking, but for defending. This is what I mean by "eating things that are not tasty, but nevertheless good for you."

The Anton Geesink Basic Teaching Method

The Anton Geesink Basic Teaching Method is a combination of elements drawn from *budō* practice in the twenty-first century, with particular regards to judo as an Olympic sport. The lack of attention to rational biomechanical and pedagogical didactical principles in arbitrary curriculums can result in equally arbitrary results, poor development of the individual student, and failure to promote judo's potential merits. It is with these issues in mind that I created the following curriculum based on the following components.

Biomechanics

A judo-*ka* that stands in a stable position cannot be toppled by throwing technique alone. It is of extreme importance that before attacking, the opponent is put off balance.

Neuro-physiology

Each action causes a reaction. Judo, therefore, is a game of action-reaction, and because of that it is dynamic. Our muscles are operated by nerve impulses. For a judo-*ka*, it is important to know that different kinds of nerve impulses exist.

Reflexes

Reflexes are the increasing of muscle-tension when that muscle is being triggered from outside stimuli. For example, when a doctor strikes just under the kneecap with a hammer the lower leg moves up in the classic quadriceps reflex.

Judo as an Olympic Sport or as Tradition

Automatism

This refers to the condition where one has experienced a certain situation so many times that reactions become automatic. One has at their disposal an "auto-pilot", which can handle a number of routine actions in a standard manner. For example, when pushed a person will shift their foot automatically in order to remain balanced. Another example, upon practicing a certain technique so many times that one can actually "dream" it, that is, they can execute the movements without having to think about them during execution.

Conscious reaction

When a number of signals enter the brain, a person is able to put them together, make sense of what is happening, and react in a conscious and deliberate manner. Conversely, sometimes a human reacts without thinking (reflex; automatism). In other cases, they react after having consciously thought about the reaction, often described as "seeing something coming."

Pedagogical and Didactical Principles

Before introducing the elements of my pedagogical and didactic approach, I would like to introduce concepts that I have developed myself. Upon first learning any new skill, some experimentation must be conducted, whether intended or not. Usually we regard this as "trial and error" as we struggle to find the correct method. I view this not only as a practical process in the pursuit of acquiring a new skill but believe it to be in itself both an individual-specific learning tool, and a means to experience the joy of experimentation and discovery.

With regards to the judo engagement, I use the terms: playing-, working-, assisting-arm, and standing-, playing-, working-, and assisting-leg," These terms relate to the function of the arms and legs of the *tori*, (the person executing the throw), during the preparation and execution phases of a technique. During the playing-arm/leg phase, the arm or leg probes and adjust to find the position where applied force will be most effective to the technique. Upon finding the spot, the role and term changes to the working-arm/leg.

Exercises that encourage curiosity

Experimentation and varied implementation of the "playing-arm or leg is useful for revealing the broad number of possibilities in the judo engagement. With this understanding, I have developed a battery of these "playing arm and leg" exercises. This group of techniques is not only an aim in itself, but is also a means to prepare the judo-*ka* for *ukemi-waza* (the technique for falling properly in a given situation, commonly referred to as "break falls").

The beginner must always be prepared to be thrown. By learning and training in playing-arm or leg techniques, initially without *ukemi-waza*, the *tori* will use a great deal of effort and will improve their general condition, especially strength and coordination. In the process, both *tori*, and *uke* (the person being thrown) faced with the circumstances will also become curious about the how and why of *ukemi-waza*. Upon arriving to this stage of development, meaningful inquiry and study of *ukemi-waza* can begin. This is just one example of the utility of the playing-arm and leg techniques to encourage curiosity about other techniques.

Staged progress from easy to difficult
Techniques in which the *tori* stands on both legs during execution (included in the playing-arm group) are easier than techniques using only one supporting leg, (such as in *ashi-waza*, or foot sweeping techniques). Learning the group of playing-arm techniques has the advantage that they can be practiced from the most natural body position with both feet on the ground, shoulder-width apart. As the *tori* becomes proficient at the given technique, he can progress on to more difficult variations of the same technique or similar techniques with only slight adjustments.

Staged progress from the known to the unknown
That which is known to a person adds stability to their life. It is the basis of natural learning, the opposite of controlled external learning. In daily life, that which is learned in a natural way often becomes a great source of joy. In judo, it results in the joy of practicing, and encourages continuation. Japanese judo has an advantage over European judo in that the former allows room for natural learning: the Japanese judo-*ka* learn by "just doing it" (through *randori*). The European judo-*ka* by contrast is trained by considerably greater amount of externally controlled instruction. However, both cases have the shortcomings of either failing to provide a structured approach to the knowledge/ability base, or failing to allow for the natural learning.

In my method, the techniques are grouped together based on the movements involved. If a pupil masters the fundamental technique in each group, all the derived techniques of the family-group can be learned easily, because they can be discovered by a natural learning process and out of curiosity. I employ ninety-five percent of the known, but allow for five percent of the unknown to take advantage of a student's curiosity and joy of natural learning, and thereby encourage the student's progress. This is my didactic system of progressing "from known to unknown."

Address the specific needs of the individual student
The teacher must master the full spectrum of techniques and principles; however, the competitive judo-*ka* needs to know only those things useful to win matches. In judo, the characteristics, qualities, and needs of the individual pupil must be treated according to the principle of "much talent – minimal methodological training, less talent – maximal methodological training." Techniques that agree with the body-type of the individual practitioner should be the central focus of their training. The methodological training goes from known to unknown, from easy to difficult, and takes into account the ability

Judo as an Olympic Sport or as Tradition

that Mother Nature has given us: to stand on the ground with both feet (literally and figuratively). In other words, if there is nothing new to learn from standing with both feet on the ground, it is time to start learning the techniques done with only one foot on the ground while using the other leg as a sweeping leg.

Judo's high educational value
Judo has high educational value; such being the case, great significance must be given to responsibility for one's partner. I have made it a habit of never using the word "opponent" but rather, "partner". I stress the concept that the *tori* is responsible for the successful *ukemi-waza* of the *uke*.

Manner and Timing of the Instruction of Falling Technique

I have observed programs in which beginning students engage in exercises where they are thrown before adequately learning to break-fall correctly. This is unnatural and detrimental to the student. If we fall awkwardly, we consider it and accident. The natural fear of falling needs to be transformed into a curiosity about break-falling. Only then is student ready to begin *ukemi-waza* training. My curriculum starts with *ne-waza* (hold-down techniques on the mat done without rising to standing position), as this type of grappling does not require falling. Such "ground work" does however involve constant and vigorous pulling, pushing, and turning about, and in the process, develops physical fitness and agility required in the switch to playing-arm and leg exercises to which *ukemi-waza* are eventually introduced.

I also have developed a group of playing-arm exercises designed for implementation before students have had sufficient time to develop physical fitness from engaging *ne-waza* practice. In this case, *ōgoshi* and its related family-group of playing-arm techniques take on the roll of preparing the student for real *ukemi-waza*. *Tori* are not allowed to complete the throw, but are required to stop at the point where the *uke* has been lifted off the ground. At this point, the *tori* allows the *uke* to study the situation and consider the mechanics of the eventual fall and *ukemi-waza*. For the sake of completeness, I would like to point out that although a beginner, a student may have acquired a high degree of physical fitness prior to starting judo, for example in gymnastics or other rough and tumble athletic sports. In this case, it may be acceptable to start with the group of playing-arm exercises concurrent with the introduction of *ne-waza*.

In other approaches, I have often observed *ukemi-waza* being taught as an independent technique. The practicing of *ukemi-waza* in this way can have an adverse effect on the success of a judo-*ka*: the more elegantly they learn to fall down, the more easily they become ready to accept defeat in a contest. If during the course of training, you practice *ukemi-waza* a dozen times or more, and automatic acceptance of being thrown down is conditioned, with the adverse result of easy defeat in competition. I personally do not pay much attention to falling technique, but in saying this, I do not suggest that *ukemi-*

waza is not an important part of judo, I simply believe that such training needs to be functional.

One criterion I set for exercises in which falling are conducted is that the *tori* is well versed in the given technique(s). The reason for this is the *tori* plays an essential role in guiding and protecting the *uke* during the throw. Only after I am reasonably satisfied that *tori* is capable of assuming this responsibility, do I allow throwing exercises to be conducted to completion. Given this set of circumstances, even when the *uke* is inexperienced with *ukemi-waza*, they need not fear falling, as the *tori* ensures the fall will lead to a correctly executed *ukemi-waza*. For me, it is impossible to train in *ukemi-waza* alone. If I am in charge of a training session, falling is only practiced as the logical conclusion of a throw.

Fundamental Concepts of My Curriculum

Fundamental starting points of my curriculum are addressing human characteristics such as the fear of falling, creativity, dynamics of postural and movement, and practical educational demands. I classify these central aspects as follows:

1. The natural fear of falling in humans cannot be denied.
2. The instruction of techniques needs to be natural and logical.
3. The learning process and its graduation can be expedited.
4. Terminology must be correct.
5. The responsibility of judo-*ka* for each other should be utilized to heighten the joy of participation.
6. Mysticism has no place in Olympic judo.
7. Contrasting coloured uniforms leads to greater clarity.

This approach is very simple. The more logical the teaching process is, the greater the improvement in ability and understanding. This assurance and success lead to the joy of playing, and perpetuate motivation.

Kumikata (engagement positioning)

The location on the judo-*gi* where the partner is grabbed, the *kumikata*, determines to a great degree how effectively the partner can be imbalanced. It should be a location that allows for minimal effort, but where the partner is unable to pull free. In actual practice, this means grabbing the shoulder at the very top of the sleeve. Apart from biomechanical reasons, grabbing that spot has a practical advantage in that the judo-*gi* has the least amount of slack there. That means the force applied here will be transmitted to the partner most efficiently. This manner of *kumikata* also plays a vital role in reading the body language of the partner, so important in judo. Changes in muscle tension indicating the initiation of technique can be sensed though the grasp, and in this way, the grip serves

Judo as an Olympic Sport or as Tradition

as a warning device.

The function of the left and right arms
When throwing is conducted on the right, *tsukuri* (positioning) is performed with the right arm. Using the right arm is the only correct way to force the partner into an unstable position (his left leg in front) so a throw on the right side can be executed successfully. Any force applied with the left arm actually impedes the attempt to get the partner in the ideal left-in-front-position, the position necessary for throwing. In the case the *tori* pulls with the left hand the reaction of the *uke* is to move their right foot to the front again, thus regaining a stable position. The left hand, if used at all, only functions in the very last phase of the throw near its completion. If the *tori* fears that *uke* will not fall on their back as they attempt to extend and post their right hand on the mat, *tori* should pull the *uke's* right arm at the level of the elbow, causing the *uke* to roll over on their back.

Kuzushi
Theoretically, nobody can be thrown by technique alone, without employing *kuzushi* (breaking of balance) first. However, in reality, there are some judo-*ka* so strong that they can throw without *kuzushi*. In competitive judo however, judo-*ka* are trained to such a high degree of physical and technical capability that the deciding factor is most often only a small difference (including strength), therefore throwing without *kuzushi* does not occur at this level.

The original form of *kuzushi* as found in *jūjutsu* is indirect. *Uke* initiates an attack and subsequently loses balance as the *tori* reacts and utilizes the reaction. *Uke* is then stopped by a counter-throw or clasping technique, such as *seoi-nage* (shoulder throw) or *nage-no-kata* (throwing forms). In Olympic judo, this type of indirect *kuzushi* is rarely, if ever found. The *kuzushi* we must often encounter is the direct form, in which the *tori* manoeuvres the *uke* from a stable position to an unstable one.

The second form of *kuzushi* appears when the partner attacks at an inopportune moment and with the wrong technique. In this case, the *tori* loses their balance by their own action, resulting in being thrown down themselves. In some cases, indirect *kuzushi* can be seen. For example, during an attack using *uchi-mata*, the partner steps aside, causing the attacker to "float in mid-air," thereby leaving them vulnerable to counter-attack.

The relationship between break-falling and opportunities to win
I approach break-falling from its functional nature, and approach differing from the norm. In the first standing technique (*ōgoshi*- large hip throw) I briefly describe in what way the *uke* can break their fall and what the responsibility of the *tori* is in this case. A second aspect of break-falling is the fact that *uke* can, by the use of their *ukemi-waza*, prevent *ippon* (winning point) from being scored against them. Thirdly, and no less important, the *uke* should be able to make use of the break-fall to transform their role of

uke in to that of *tori* (*go-no-sen*, or executing one's technique at the moment of weakness in the opponent's attempted attack).

Technical Aspects of Judo in My Curriculum

Terminology:
The terms below play an important role in my curriculum. Some of these terms, as well as the principles behind them, are employed during judo training.

Tori and uke
Tori is the judo-*ka* in the stable position, while *uke* is in the unstable position. In the stable position bodyweight rests on both legs, with feet shoulder-width apart. A judo-*ka* is unstable, obviously, when they have lost their balance.

Preparation and execution
Uke will never actively assume and unstable position. They are forced into such a position by:
   a. A wrong action putting them off-balance.
   b. By an action from *tori*.

Both judo-*ka* are situated opposite each other in stable positions. The feet are positioned shoulder-width apart. Judo-*ka* A pulls judo-*ka* B forwards with the right hand via the left lapel. To restore balance, judo-*ka* B steps their left foot forward. From that moment, both judo-*ka* have a name, judo-*ka* A (stable) is *tori*, and judo-*ka* B (unstable) becomes *uke*.

Action and reaction
Reflexes, automatisms, and conscious movements all play and important role in judo. Judo is a game of action and reaction. During a contest, the judo-*ka* seldom has enough time to consciously consider all the situations that confront them simultaneously. Therefore, it is important for the judo-*ka* to be confronted often during training with situations in which preferred techniques (*tokui-waza*) can be applied. This way conscious thinking eventually becomes an automatic response to known situations. This results in most parts of the match to become clear-cut, or conducted by conditioned reactions, allowing the judo-*ka* to concentrate on the few really new situations that arise during the engagement.

Playing-, working-, assisting-arm and leg
These terms relate to the function of the arms and legs of the *tori*, (the person executing the throw), during the preparation and execution phases of a technique. During the playing-arm/leg phase, the arm or leg probes and adjusts to find the position where applied force will be most effective to the technique. Upon finding the spot, the role and

Judo as an Olympic Sport or as Tradition

term changes to the working-arm/leg.

Strength and technique
During contests, the use of technique and force varies. In cases where the match is conducted on the basis of technique, the *uke* determines the outcome to a great extent by what techniques they can be conquered. If strength is the determining role, *tori*, with the use of a lot of physical force, determines how to overcome their opponent. In this case, *kuzushi*, directly or indirectly plays a deciding role.

The strength required in judo can be found in, and extracted from judo itself. I trained and practiced many types of physical games besides judo, not as an aim in itself, but as an alternative, and to do things that give me joy. However, during practice, we need to understand that muscle-strengthening exercises in all forms are also found within judo itself. Training sessions are, as I have noted, focused on technical aspects that are always the starting point for me; however, in the process of conducting these exercises, physical training is actually achieved simultaneously.

Distance, speed, and strength
There is a relationship between distance, speed, and strength. In order to explain the relationship I would like to use the example of a boxing punch: Standing in front of a partner at a near-distance of just a couple of centimetres, but not touching, with my fist at chest level, I can attempt to punch at the chest of the partner with all my might to no avail. The reason is because there is not sufficient distance, therefore speed is not developed, and ultimately no force is issued to the target of the strike. Now, increasing the distance from the partner to just under arm's length, with my fist again at chest level, I can execute the punch with a great deal of force. Later, I will return to this example as it applies to *ōsoto-gari* (large outer reap), *harai-goshi* (hip sweep), and *uchimata* (inner thigh reap).

Important Practice Forms (Contest Judo)

The learning and studying of techniques has three steps:

1. Learning the mechanics of the technique
2. *Uchikomi*
3. *Randori*

Step 1: Learning the techniques
I will cover this further on.

Step 2: *Uchikomi*
Uchikomi, repetitive practice, is a very important practice form that enables polishing

techniques in the most extensive manner. Only those throws mastered by the judo-*ka* are practiced in *uchikomi*. All basic mechanical properties (speed, strength, balance, agility, and coordination) are employed during *uchikomi* practice. Because of the repetitive nature of this form of exercise, incorrect execution of the movements can be very detrimental in that they condition the faulted execution to become habit. Accordingly, it is very difficult to recondition the judo-*ka* to perform the technique correctly once again.

Uchikomi practice must include the entire technique up to the point just before the throw is completed. *Uchikomi* training is fruitless if not done to this point. If for example, only the set-in, or the approach to the technique is done, and the actual lifting of the opponent off the ground is not, even long hours of practice in this way will be of no consequence.

In order to lift *uke*, the legs are utilized by bending at the knees. When achieved, many thousands of kilograms can be lifted in a mere thirty minutes of training. It is not only strength, but coordination as well that makes this possible. Combined with correct technique, this repetitive training hones the judo-*ka*'s ability. Another similar example is weightlifting. As with judo where lifting the *uke* from the floor is essential, a weight lifter does not only approach the bar and touch it and then retire. In order for his training to be effective he must actually lift the weight.

Ability to execute a technique without the need to precipitate the opportunity by manoeuvring or *kuzushi* etc., indicates an enormous surplus of physical advantage over the opponent. In present-day, contest judo, this imbalance is not allowed to occur. Competition judo-*ka* are all well trained, and the implementation of weight categories has made large disparities impossible.

Step 3: *Randori*

Randori, or free sparing, is a contest without a referee, without tactics, and without score-keeping. The objective of *randori* practice is to try out newly acquired techniques in actual practice, to improve on mastered techniques in free form, and to improve stamina and fitness. A good judo-*ka* never tries out something new in a match. It may be acceptable to try something new in a match if the opponent is winning, and the dire situation calls for "all or nothing"; however, this is the least desirable situation to find oneself in. Instead, skills are honed with *uchikomi* and *randori* practice to prepare.

I would also like to mention, due to its random nature, the judo-*ka* should only be allowed to engage *randori* practice when they are in very good physical shape, they are not fatigued or injured. If the judo-*ka* were at less that full capability, they will be unable to make any positive gains regardless of effort. In the worst case, they might be re-injured or precipitate a new injury. In such cases it is recommended that the judo-*ka* rest or engage in lighter exercise such as walking, cycling and swimming. Also, this is a good opportunity to study techniques (without necessarily having to do them) and also the philosophical side of judo.

Judo as an Olympic Sport or as Tradition

Please be warned that the following detailed explanations will be difficult to follow for those not versed in judo techniques.

Classification and Explanation of Judo Techniques in my Curriculum

1. *Ne-waza* (Ground work)
   Phase 1: *Kesa-gatame* (scarf hold)
   Phase 2: *Ne-waza* with playing arm
   Phase 3: Combinations of *gatame*
   - From *kesa-gatame* to *yoko-shihō-gatame* (side-locking four-corner hold).
   - from *yoko-shihō* to *kuzure-yoko-shihō-gatame* (modified side-locking four-corner hold).
   - from *kuzure-yoko-shihō gatame* I to *kuzure-yoko-shiho-gatame* II.
   - from *kuzure-yoko-shihō gatame* II to *kuzure-kesa-gatame* (modified scarf hold).

Uke lies on their back with one or both of his knees pulled up for two reasons:
   - Safety: When one or both knees are pulled up, *uke* clearly demonstrates that they are alert and conscious. If the knees are stretched out this is a sign that they could be unconscious.
   - Technique: When both knees are outstretched, *uke's* possibilities for movement are limited. With the legs stretched out, all *uke* is able to do is roll. The legs are the longest and strongest part of the body. That force can only be utilized if one or both knees are pulled up.

Phase 1: *Kesa-gatame*
Uke lies on their back with knees pulled up. *Tori* sits on the ground along the right side of *uke*. *Tori* has their right arm around *uke's* head, and grabs the right sleeve just above the elbow with their left hand. With the left hand, *tori* pulls *uke's* sleeve, and with the left-upper arm tightens the *uke's* underarm against their body, causing the elbow to point outwards. *Tori* is on *uke* with full weight.

Phase 2: Group *ne-waza* with playing arm
- From *kesa-gatame* I to *yoko-shihō-gatame*
Tori holds *uke* in a *kuzure-kesa-gatame,* and *uke* attempts to break free by pushing against the throat of *tori*. *Uke* attempts to free their right arm in order to turn onto their stomach, thereby breaking the hold. *Tori* waits until *uke* tries to place the left hand on their back and catches it while their left arm is placed over the left shoulder. *Tori* is now in control of *uke* with a *yoko-shihō-gatame*.
- From *yoko-shihō-gatame* to *yoko-shihō-gatame* I

Uke tries to free themselves by turning to the left or right, or by trying to bridge. At the moment that *uke* bridges, *tori*'s tight arm becomes the playing arm. *Tori* pushes this arm under the bridge and takes *uke*'s belt keeping him under control in *kuzure-yoko-shihō-gatame* I.

- From *yoko-shihō-gatame* I to *yoko-shihō-gatame* II

The only possible means to escape for *uke* from this position is to turn onto the left side. *Tori* anticipates this movement by turning their left arm into the playing arm, and pushing it through under the head and over the right arm of *uke*, *kuzure-yoko-shihō-gatame* II.

- From *yoko-shihō-gatame* II to *kesa-gatame* I

Because the left arm (working arm) is now doing the work, *tori* can use their right arm as the playing arm. Turning to the left is impossible for *uke*, so they will want to turn to the right. For *tori* this is the moment to return to the first position of the series.

By making good use of the playing arm and the working arm, and by anticipating *uke*'s movements, *tori* is able to keep *uke* under control for the prescribed thirty seconds. With this series, the possibilities of *ne-waza* are certainly not exhausted. It does however clearly show that the principles of "action-reaction" and "from known to unknown" do in fact feature in the *ne-waza*. At the end of the playing arm techniques in *tachi-waza*, the relationship with *ne-waza* will become obvious.

    2. Group *Tachi-waza* Performed Standing on Two Legs
        Phase 1: *Ōgoshi*
        Phase 2: Group of playing arm techniques
        Phase 3: Group of special "playing arm" techniques:
          - *Sukui-nage* (scooping throw).
          - *Te-uchimata* (hand inner-thigh reaping throw).
          - *Ushiro-goshi* (back hip throw).
          - *Utsuri-goshi* (hip transfer)

Phase 1: *Ōgoshi*:
Tori performs the *kuzushi* by pulling at *uke* with the right hand, after which *uke* is forced to step forwards to regain balance. *Tori* steps forward to the right, follows with his left leg and ends up standing exactly in front, with their back to *uke*. *Tori*'s feet are shoulder-width apart, with space between the bodies of *tori* and *uke*. *Tori* bends his knees, and by simultaneously placing the right arm around *uke* and stretching the knees is able throw *uke*.

Ōgoshi is used as the basic technique for the whole playing arm group, in which terms like "stable-unstable", "working arm", "playing arm" and "assisting arm" are introduced to the practitioner. Once this basic technique has been mastered the judo-*ka* enters the realm

Judo as an Olympic Sport or as Tradition

of "knowing", not one of "learning", and the technique can be pulled off unconsciously.
Phase 2: Group of "playing arm" techniques:
When the basic techniques of what I call the "Group of playing arm techniques" have been mastered, the practitioner is in a position to master a number of related techniques quite easily.

Ōgoshi II: *Tori* is unable to grab *uke* around their waist with the right arm, as is the case with *ōgoshi*, so puts their right hand on *uke*'s left shoulder instead of on their back.

Ōgoshi III: In grabbing the body of *uke*, *tori* also encloses their left arm.
Koshi-guruma: *Tori* grabs *uke*'s *obi* across the left shoulder, or their judo-*gi* at the top of the back section.

Seoi-nage: *Tori* does not grab *uke*'s *obi* as in the previous throw across the shoulder, but puts their right arm across the front of *uke*'s body, and goes under the right armpit to execute *seoi-nage*.

Coming from the known, one meets the unknown. In addition to that principle, the judo-*ka* quite naturally chooses the playing arm technique that feels most comfortable to them. When up against a smaller judo-*ka*, the bigger judo-*ka* will quite often put his arm across the other's shoulder. When up against a taller judo-*ka*, the smaller judo-*ka* will prefer to put their right arm underneath *tori'*s arm (*seoi-nage*). Alternatively they will choose one of the special playing arm techniques which will be discussed in the next section.

The left arm is only an *assisting* arm, coming into action when the partner wants to put their right arm to the ground in the last phase of the execution.

Phase 3: Special "playing arm" techniques
The following are several "playing arm" techniques that are placed apart because of their extra high muscle-strengthening value, and are known mainly as take-over techniques.

Sukui-nage
Tori steps in right-left, and ends up standing on the right side of *uke*. From there, *uke*'s right arm (playing arm) will go from the front through *tori*'s legs and grabs the *obi*. Meanwhile, *tori* bends deeply at the knees with back held straight. *Tori* then straightens his knees causing *uke* to hang in the pit of the elbow. *Tori* brings *uke* into a vertical position and controls his fall with the assisting arm (left).

Te-uchimata
Tori steps in left-right (right-left is also possible). This time *tori* ends up standing across the left side of *uke*. *Tori'*s left arm stays in place. Coming from behind, the right arm now

clasps the left upper leg of *uke*. Also in this case *tori* bends deeply at the knees. Then, by straightening the knees, *tori* is able to lift *uke* off the ground and bring them into a horizontal position, then throwing *uke* down in a controlled fashion with the left arm.

Utsuri-goshi
Tori steps in right-left (left-right is also possible), ending up to the left side of *uke*. Then, putting their right arm around the waist of *uke* and simultaneously sagging at the knees then straightening up again, *uke* is lifted off the ground. In defence, *uke* will move their legs from left-front to left-behind in a scissor-like fashion. *Tori* then turns the hips across the front of *uke* and catches them with the left hip, throwing them with *ōgoshi*.

3. Group *Tachi-waza* With Playing Leg
Tsurikomi-goshi (lift-pull hip throw).
Tai-otoshi (body drop).
Harai-goshi (hip sweep).
Uchimata (inner thigh reaping throw).

Tsurikomi-goshi
This technique forms the ideal transition from "playing arm" to "playing leg" techniques. It is almost identical to *ōgoshi*, but in *tsurikomi-goshi*, the right hand is not displaced; the consequence of that is the elbow bends and is placed under the right armpit. *Ōgoshi* executed in this fashion is called *tsurikomi-goshi*. The "playing leg" functions as the challenger, the provocateur, and will eventually initiate the decisive action. The playing leg is constantly moving, looking for a suitable point of departure for execution of a technique. In the playing leg techniques that follow, that right arm remains in the same position as it is in *tsurikomi-goshi*, and the technique executed is determined by *tori*'s right leg. In comparison with the "playing arm" techniques it is the placement of the right arm that determines the kind of technique being used.

Tai-otoshi
Tori steps in the same manner as *tsurikomi-goshi*. The knees remain outstretched as *tori* pulls *uke* towards him with the right hand, and thrusts his right leg backwards along the right side of *uke*, pushing his right thigh against *uke*'s right thigh in such a way that the right leg of *uke* is pushed backwards. The action with the right leg is such that it moves from the outside to the inside.

Harai-goshi
The playing leg goes up across the side of the partner. The initial phase is identical to *tai-otoshi*. Instead of pushing backwards, the right leg in *harai-goshi* is whipped up in an upwards direction, with the emphasis on the thigh. An initial move forward of the playing leg is necessary as without creating some distance, adequate speed and force will

be difficult to create.

Uchimata

The right leg goes upward in a short cut. In *uchimata* the right leg of *tori* has more of a leverage function than a throwing function. It rises so that *tori* can bend his body forward more easily. Stepping in can be done in different ways as was pointed out in *ōgoshi*. Three ways of stepping in can be applied in the execution of theses techniques.

4. Group *Harai* (Sweep) Techniques
Deashi-harai (forward foot sweep).
Kouchi-harai (small inner sweep).
Ōuchi-harai (larger inner sweep).

Uke steps forwards in three possible ways:
a. To the inside of *tori*'s right foot with the left foot.
b. In the direction of *tori*'s left side with the right foot.
c. In the direction of *tori*'s right side with the left foot.

Ashi-harai

Tori steps backwards to the right and aside in the direction of the left foot. *Tori* ends up standing to the right of *uke*. *Tori* makes a sweeping movement with the sole of his left foot against the right heel of *uke* thus enlarging *uke*'s step, causing him to fall.

Kouchi-harai

Uke steps forwards to the right. *Tori* steps backwards to the left and to the side in the direction of the right foot. *Tori* ends up standing with the right side facing to the front of *uke*. *Tori* places the sole of his right foot against the right heel of *uke* and sweeps, thus enlarging *uke*'s step and causing him to fall.

Ōuchi-harai

Uke steps forwards to the left in the direction of *tori*'s outer right leg. *Tori* steps backward to the left and at the same moment hooks his right leg behind the left lower leg of *uke*, making a rotating movement, thus enlarging *uke*'s step in the same way as the previous *harai*.

The characteristics of *harai* are as follows:
1. *Uke* undertakes the action.
2. *Tori* prevents *uke*'s moving leg – I call it the "burdened leg" – from reaching the ground, and sweeps it away in a forward direction.
3. Execution of *harai*: *Tori* steps away from *uke*, thereby creating the space necessary to enlarge *uke*'s step.
4. The *harai* can also be executed in a static way when *uke*'s burdened leg hits the ground, causing *uke*'s weight to rest on both feet in some kind of spread stance.

5. Group *Gari* (Reap) Techniques
Ōsoto-gari (large outer reap)
Ōuchi-gari (large inner reap)
Ōuchimata (large inner thigh reaping throw)

The differences between *harai* and *gari*:
Gari-
a. The burdened leg, that is the standing leg, is moved away powerfully.
b. *Tori* steps towards *uke*.
Harai-
a. The burdened leg is swept away before reaching the floor.
b. *Tori* steps away from *uke*.

Tori tightly pulls to the right. This forces *uke* to step forward to the left and respond forcefully. *Tori* goes along with that movement by stepping forwards to the left, causing *uke*'s left leg to become the standing leg. *Tori*'s left foot is standing next to *uke*'s right foot. With the right arm *tori* keeps contact with the upper body of *uke* and with the right thighbone sweeps away *uke*'s standing leg.

Ōsoto-gari
Tori pulls with the right hand. *Uke* steps left forward, exactly as in *ōsoto-gari* but less fiercely. *Uke* gets the chance to follow with the right leg. This causes a situation in which the left leg is the standing leg and the right leg of *uke* is almost touching the ground. That is the moment in which *tori* can attack with *ōsoto-gari*, but because the attack takes place between the legs it is called *ōuchi-gari*.

Ōuchimata
The position of *uke* in the preparation to *ōuchimata* is 95% the same as *ōuchi-gari*. The 5% difference is the due to the fact that *uke*'s right leg stays behind. *Uke* stands on the left leg, with the right leg off the ground. *Tori* steps to the right with the left foot forward, and places it near *uke*'s left foot maintaining enough space between them. In one twisting movement to the left on the left leg, the right leg moves in an upward direction and then continues downwards, then behind and up, with the thigh moving *uke*'s left thigh forcefully upwards.

The principles "distance-speed-force" holds true for all three techniques.

6. Group *Hiza-guruma* (Knee wheel)
Harai-tsurikomi-ashi (Lift-pull foot sweep)
Sasae-tsurikomi-ashi (Supporting-foot lift-pull throw)
These three techniques are closely interrelated, though of a very different nature. They are techniques in which timing is decisive for successful execution. If the right moment is

not seized, these throws cannot be done. In other words, technical knowledge and timing are essential. Also, during their execution the function of *tori*'s right arm becomes clear.

Hiza-guruma
The *judo-ka* are in *shizentai*.
Uke steps backwards to the right. *Tori* follows closely by stepping forward to the right and places his foot near *uke*'s left foot, while also placing the sole of his left foot on the outside of *uke*'s right knee. It is *tori*'s intention to prevent *uke* putting his right foot on the ground. *Tori* pushes with his foot and enlarges *uke*'s step by thrusting that leg sidelong behind *uke*. Because *tori* pulls *uke* towards him with his right hand, *uke*'s right foot cannot find the ground. *Tori*'s left hand (assisting arm) comes into action by pulling *uke*'s right sleeve, who consequently falls on his back. It causes *uke* to spin around on a longitudinal axis.

Sasae-tsurikomi-ashi
Uke steps backwards to the right. *Tori* follows right forwards, exactly as in *hiza-guruma*. The moment in which *uke*'s right foot reaches the ground, *uke* realizes they are in an unstable position and will immediately step forwards again. *Tori* now makes a sweeping movement with his left leg forwards and places the sole of his foot above the instep of *uke* before he is able to place his foot on the mat. In reaction, *uke* stretches his knee causing him to stumble over and will be supported as it were by three points of support – the right and left arm, and *tori*'s left foot.

Harai-tsurikomi-ashi
Now *uke* steps backwards with the left leg. *Tori* follows closely with the right foot. When *uke* wants to step backwards with the right foot, *tori* is one step ahead and by makes a sweeping movement forwards with the left foot, placing it above *uke*'s right instep. To this forward sweeping movement, *uke* reacts by keeping their knee rigid, resulting in the same situation as in *sasae-tsurikomi-ashi*. *Uke* steps back to the right once more, *tori* follows right forwards. The same takes place in *hiza-guruma* and *sasae-tsurikomi-ashi*. *Tori*'s left leg follows synchronically with a sweeping forward movement and contacts *uke*'s instep at the moment during which *uke*'s right foot has not yet passed the left leg. *Uke* responds by rigidly stretching their leg. *Tori*'s left leg continues to move in a forward direction. Here also, the situation develops in which *tori* "carries" *uke* on three points of support: the right and left arm, and *tori*'s left foot. In all three techniques, the synchronic functioning of the left and right arm, and left leg plays a very important role.

(Footnote to *sasae-tsurikomi-ashi* and *harai-tsurikomi-ashi*: pay attention to the stretching of *uke*'s attacking leg.)

7. Group *Renraku-waza* (Combination techniques)
The principle of *renraku-waza* is used in regards to incorrect reactions by *uke* to a feint movement made by *tori*. *Uke* ends up standing in an unstable position, to which *tori* is able to take advantage. For example, *tori* pretends to attack *uke*'s right leg with his right

leg using *kouchi-gari*. *Uke* manoeuvres from a stable position into an unstable one. It is unnatural if *uke* does not respond to a feint. Human beings respond to an attack (feint) with defensive movement usually without thinking. The correct way of avoiding an *ashi-waza* (foot technique) attack is to never step away with the leg under attack.

8. Different Forms of *Kata*
a. *Randori-no-kata*
Nage-no-kata (Throwing forms) and *Katame-no-kata* (Grappling forms) are *Randori-no-kata* (Free practice forms). As I pointed out, they reflect present-day judo, and therefore need to be periodically adjusted, and if necessary renewed and/or improved analogous to contest-judo. These *kata* need to reflect the development of present-day judo. For example, *uki-otoshi* (floating drop) does not exist anymore in contest-judo. It would be logical, and based on IJF-statistics, that this technique in *Randori-no-kata* should be replaced by *tai-otoshi*.

b. Classical *kata*.
Traditional *kata* have historical value. They are the treasury of the past, of the origins of judo. Whoever goes deeply into the history of judo will find a great amount of meaning in them.

Anton Geesink takes gold at the 1964 Tokyo Olympic Games

Conclusion

This lecture, conducted here in Japan, my second home, has allowed me to share with all my judo family the background and motivating factors that have led to my developing this curriculum, one so different from other respected or conventional models. I think that it is necessary that my motives be known, so that anyone who sees my curriculum in action can understand its rationale. This will allow anyone that uses (elements) of the curriculum to do so with meaning, with understanding and conviction. I sincerely hope that these principles that I introduced in this lecture, will contribute to the broader development of judo in the twenty-first century, and add to its progress into the future.

Budo Perspectives

Chapter 23

The Role of Judo in an Age of Internationalization

Yamashita Yasuhiro
Professor- Tokai University

Winner of the All Japan Judo Championships for nine consecutive years beginning in 1977. Four-time winner of the World Judo Championships. 1984 Los Angeles Olympics gold-medal winner in men's open weight division of judo, and recipient of Japan's National Medal of Honour in the same year. Since ceasing active judo competition in 1985 with 203 consecutive victories, Yamashita Yasuhiro has devoted himself to teaching judo. He holds a seventh-dan judo black belt and a variety of posts, including director of the All Japan Judo Federation, manager of the men's national team, trustee at the International Budo University, board member of the National Commission on Educational Reform, and member of the education ministry's Central Council on Education. As of September 2003, Yamashita Yasuhiro was appointed Education & Coaching Director of the International Judo Federation. The following is a transcription of his public speech given as the last presentation at the Budō Symposium held at the International Research Centre for Japanese Studies, Kyoto, Japan.

I am very embarrassed after having received some kind words of encouragement from the esteemed Mr. Anton Geesink. Today, I would like to talk about the role judo can play in this international age, and also what contributions I can make in my capacity of Education & Coaching Director of the International Judo Federation.

For the last few days, a symposium dedicated to *budō* culture has been conducted here at the International Research Centre for Japanese Studies. I must profess that I am no scholar of *budō*, but I am a practitioner. I think that it is my responsibility to take the many wonderful ideas presented at this symposium to heart, and try to implement them using my position as a practitioner and as a federation officer. Using my past experience as a top-level competitor, instructor, and administrator, I would like to share some of my ideas of how I intend to work for judo.

Firstly, I would like to make reference to the educational potential of judo. When talking about the value of judo in education, I am compelled to reminisce on my childhood experiences learning judo, and the wonderful teachers I came into contact with. This forms the basis for my activities in the judo world today.

I began my study of judo when I was ten years of age. When I first entered elementary school at age six, I already had the physique of a twelve year old. Not only was I physically big, I was also extremely energetic. I tended to direct my energies to mischief, and caused my school a lot of trouble with my delinquent tendencies.

When I turned ten years of age, one of my classmates refused to come to school any more because, apparently, he was scared of me. My mother and father ran a food store, and they were busy from early in the morning until late at night. They didn't have time to always keep an eye on me, but were becoming greatly concerned about how I was turning out, and couldn't bare to think that I would grow up being hated by other people. That is why they decided I should do judo. The judo teacher was renowned for his strictness and emphasis on etiquette. My parents thought that if I did judo, it might calm me down a little. They took me to the *dōjō* and instructed the teacher to "straighten me out".

That is how I started judo, but I just thought of it as play while I was at elementary school, and it didn't encourage me to improve my behaviour in any way. Actually, after the Los Angeles Olympics, I went back to my hometown in Kumamoto prefecture where my old classmates held a party in my honour. They presented me with a certificate which had the following inscription;

> "*Presented to Yamashita Yasuhiro. At elementary school, you terrorized the school with your size, and made our lives miserable. Nonetheless, your wonderful performance and fighting spirit demonstrated at the Olympic Games, even though you were injured, resulted in a gold medal which made all of us overflow with joy. This not only absolves you from your rotten behaviour at school, but has made your classmates proud to know you. We hereby express our respect, and pledge our friendship forever, Yatchan!*"

I really was a problem child! But I was also a full of life. I also liked to fight. That is understandable considering my size. Nobody could match me. Anyway, I began training in judo. By putting on the judo-*gi* and doing what I was told in the *dōjō*, nobody could condemn me for throwing my weight around. Judo served to boost my fighting spirit and satisfy it at the same time. It wasn't long before I became totally hooked. I just loved every minute.

When I entered junior high school, I was fortunate to come under the tutelage of a great judo teacher who was to become my mentor. His name was Shiraishi Reisuke, and due to his superb coaching I was able to take the All Japan title for junior high school students three years running. One of the amazing things about him was that he didn't only concentrate on making his students strong at judo. He taught us judo as a "way of life". He would use every opportunity to teach us about the meaning of '*dō*' (Way) in judo. After listening to him so many times, I actually started to change. *Sensei* would always say to us:

> "If you train as hard as you can, you will become physically and mentally stronger, more appreciative of others, learn to cooperate, develop the fortitude necessary to achieve your goals, and will be able to make good friends. You are

The Role of Judo in an Age of Internationalization

all training for the moment to become champions. But, the most important thing is to become human beings who can go out into the big wide world and make your way, not only for your own sake, but for the benefit of others in society. Of course, it is important for you to strive to become a judo champion. But it is just as important for you to utilize what you learn in judo to be come a champion of society as well. You can learn so many things through judo. But just doing judo is not enough. Even if you become a judo champion, but don't apply yourself to study, you will not be able to become a champion of life. *Bunbu-ryōdō*! That means to balance your training in the martial arts with scholarly study as well. Study hard!"

This is the basic philosophy behind what he taught us. To be honest, I didn't really enjoy studying very much, but I did at least learn that it was very important. He would also tell us:

"If you want to become strong, you must be respectful. Listen to what people tell you. That is the secret to becoming strong at judo. You should show your strength on the *tatami* mats. I often see it at competitions, be they high school students, university students, or even police; pompous idiots who think they are special because they win tournaments. They walk across the floor like they own the world. Whatever you do, don't turn out like that. Truly strong individuals never flaunt their strength, just like a clever hawk never shows its talons. One other thing, the stronger a person gets, the more important it becomes to couple that strength with kindness."

As a competitor, I was able to eventually become number one in the world. Now my strength completely pales in comparison to what it was when I was at my peak. It has been eighteen years since I retired from competition. My skill in judo has declined for sure, but I feel certain that my strength as a human being far exceeds that of my competitive days. I am aspiring to become a person far kinder than I ever was strong. As Shiraishi *sensei* taught me, "Don't just become a judo champion. Aim to be a champion of life. Use what you learn in the *dōjō* for the benefit of society. Otherwise there is no point…" I think that these tenets of wisdom lie at the base of what I want to do for judo now.

One of my favourite maxims is, "tradition is not just a matter of preserving form. It is to preserve the soul, the spirit." Shiraishi-*sensei* taught me such things, and I thought about them throughout my competitive career. Now, as an instructor, I can't suppress my feelings of doubt. I fear that maybe we have been too concerned with the form of judo, and perhaps lost the most important aspect, the heart. In judo nowadays, many people focus only on wining matches to the detriment of the educational values around which judo was originally created. We seem to have lost sight of the ideals set forth by the founder of judo, Kanō Jigorō. I feel this very strongly. When it comes to the Olympic Games or the world championships, all we seem to care about are the match results.

I was in the Japanese national team for ten years as a competitor, and was national coach for a further eight. I have been to, and competed in the Olympics and world champs. I too wanted to win and take my place on the podium. Now, however, I question whether this is really judo. Is it judo *just* to want to win? Is it judo *just* to excel in techniques? We must now try to reassess Kanō Jigorō's vision and ideals. With these issues in mind, the Japanese judo world is starting to move, and a wonderful thing is happening.

In 2001, the All Japan Judo Federation and the Kōdōkan collaborated to instigate what is known as the "Judo Renaissance". Each year, a poster is produced which promotes judo's role of helping youth follow their dreams, make friends, learn respect, and challenge themselves. We are also trying to encourage judo practitioners to reconsider Kanō Jigorō's ideas and motives for creating judo. I am referring to his ideals of utilizing judo as a means for self-development. We instigated this project in the autumn of 2001.

Unfortunately, possibly due to insufficient promotion, some people are under the mistaken impression that the purpose of the "Judo Renaissance" is merely to encourage people to "pick up their rubbish". This couldn't be further from the truth. I would like to take this opportunity to restate the objectives of this undertaking.

There are four committees charged with running the "Judo Renaissance". I am the chairman of the first committee, where we are working hard to promote the renaissance and the value of judo for character development. We engage in such activities as making promotional posters and the like to get the word out. There are some individuals who are keen to appeal to the public, and let them know that the judo world is actively conducting a campaign to tidy up the state of judo. I am totally against this plan, as I think it is imperative that we, the judo fraternity, concentrate our efforts first and foremost in appealing to judo practitioners before trying to show the general public what a 'great bunch' of people we are. We need to spread the message among judo people, starting with young children right through to elderly teachers. The higher up the teacher is, the more important it is that they perceive judo as being a part of *budō*, where character development is the ultimate objective. They have to be able to demonstrate this important characteristic of judo by setting an example to their students. This has been lacking to date. Having said that, any problems inherent in the younger generation of judo practitioners and coaches is a result of my generation's negligence. That's why our campaign must be focused internally rather than externally.

The second committee is in charge of promoting judo education. Their central responsibility is to ensure that children and teachers are doing judo the way it is meant to be done. The third committee is in charge of volunteer activities, and is made up primarily of national team members and coaches who are involved mainly with volunteer clean-ups. The fourth committee was set up to facilitate interaction with disabled people.

The Role of Judo in an Age of Internationalization

Actually, during the World Championships held in Osaka in September 2003, various problems came to the fore such as the [gaudy] "hairstyles" of national team members, not to mention vehement criticism against the way traditional etiquette was not adhered to. Some remarked sullenly that if this is the result of the so-called "Judo Renaissance", then it would be better to stop it altogether. To be honest, this irked me considerably. I replied to these critics by asking them how they expected something that took ten, twenty, even thirty years to degenerate into its current state to be fixed instantly. That is precisely why we must join hands and spend five, or even ten years trying to rectify the situation step by step.

I have a dream. It is my greatest hope that through efforts made in the "Judo Renaissance" campaign we will in some way be able to help children through the educational quagmire that exists today. As I have already mentioned, when I was young, I was not exactly a good child. However, I discovered through talking with successful judo competitors that there were others who were even worse than I when they were young. I want to get hold of kids who are in trouble, or who take delight in causing trouble or hurting other people, and somehow set them back on the right path through judo. I am sure that it is possible to take these kids off the streets, and use that pent up energy for good things instead of mischief. It's just a matter of channelling it in the right direction.

On the other hand, there are also many kids in schools who have shut themselves off. They have no belief in themselves, have no friends, have even forgotten how to laugh. By kindly taking them by the hand and introducing them to the world of judo, I know they can regain their confidence, open up, make friends, and bring smiles back to their faces.

It is important to make strong and successful competitors, however, I am of the firm belief that it is extremely important to collaborate with the teachers in the schools and bring these troubled children into judo, reaching them to focus their energies on positive things. This will surely bring light into their lives. If judo can do this, I would love to see other *budō* arts do the same. If judo can bring the desired positive results, of course other *budō* can be successful as well.

Furthermore, this positive action not just limited to *budō*. All sports should be able to achieve the same goals in this respect. Sports organizations in Japan need to join forces, and instead of just concentrating on competition results, use the attributes of sport to bring hope to all troubled children. This is the direction Judo Renaissance should head, and where I intend to take it.

Having had the opportunity to travel around the world through judo, I have seen that Japan is far from being the only country with troubled children. Many other regions are faced with the same complicated issues. We tend to pay attention only to what is before our eyes, and anything out of sight is put out of mind as well. When the Judo Renaissance starts making headway in Japan, then is the time to start making efforts to help people of the world. We need to work together and help children lead healthy and prosperous lives through practicing judo.

To tell the truth, this kind of movement is more advanced in Europe than it is in Japan. In fact, the posters I mentioned before were actually modelled off French and German posters featuring top players from their respective countries. Our first poster was basically a plagiarized version of theirs. To demonstrate the level of understanding of judo's potential in Europe, in May of 2003, I received the following message from a Dutch judo instructor.

"A young man came to learn judo from me. I asked him why he wanted to learn judo. He told me that until a few days previously, he had been living in a boys' home. When he was discharged from the home, his teacher advised him that he should take up judo. He was told that judo would be of great benefit to him from now on. And that is why he visited my *dōjō*."

This shows how the educational characteristics of judo are recognized in Europe, sometimes even more so than in Japan.

About twelve or thirteen years ago, there was a one-hour television program entitled "The day Japanese judo was defeated". The hero of the program was none other than Anton Geesink-*sensei*. I remember what he said vividly: "Before expressing your own happiness, you have to show proper respect to your opponent." In the same program, the head-coach of the Japanese judo team at the fateful Tokyo Olympics where Japan was defeated, the late Matsumoto *sensei* said, "I really think it was a good thing that we lost to Geesink." Still, I doubt whether he really thought that at the time. However, I do believe that his intentions for saying "it was good that Japan lost" later on is something we should take note of. If we are going to do judo, instead of just putting up appearances, we need to be genuine about our approach, and take the true spirit of judo seriously.

With this point in mind, next I would like to talk about the social meaning of judo from an international standpoint. Judo is now firmly entrenched as an Olympic sport. The fact that judo is able to maintain this status is in no small part due to the efforts of Anton Geesink. In Japan, people remember Geesink-*sensei* as the man who defeated Japan's hero Kaminaga, and thus ultimately defeated Japan at the Tokyo Olympic Games. His presence in judo and the Olympics was absolutely massive.

Presently, there are 187 affiliate nations of the International Judo Federation. I understand that this makes judo third or fourth in the rankings of Olympic sports as far as international membership is concerned. There are also a comparatively large number of competition divisions in the judo event as well. The IOC instigated a campaign called Olympic Solidarity Courses where the objective is to support the activities of Olympic event sports organizations. They achieve this by offering financial support to countries that are disadvantaged. They award scholarships to individual athletes, fund international coaching courses, and so on. I have it on good authority that of all the sports receiving such financial assistance, judo ranks at number three.

The Role of Judo in an Age of Internationalization

The number of nations taking medals at international judo competitions has increased markedly since the days where Anton Geesink was the exception. For example, in the 2001 World Championships, an African champion was born. There are also champions from Iran. In the 2003 World Championships held in Osaka, an Argentinian took a world number one spot. There are medallists hailing from an increasingly diverse range of continents and countries. This can only be thought of as a huge plus for judo. I should add that few judo competitors become entangled in doping scandals as well.

There is a notable individual I would like to introduce who studied judo, the Japanese *budō* and popular Olympic sport, and is utilizing what he has learned through his training to benefit society. In May 2003, a Japan-Russia summit meeting between Japanese Prime Minister Junichirō Koizumi, who was visiting Russia to attend the international events dedicated to the 300th anniversary of St. Petersburg, and Russian President Vladimir Putin was conducted in Russia. Prime Minister Koizumi asked me to accompany him to Russia as he knew of President Putin's love of judo.

The morning of the summit meeting, Japan's national broadcaster, NHK, aired a television mini-documentary about President Putin in the show "Good Morning Japan". Some of you may have seen it. President Putin talked about his love of judo, and how he had been a street urchin looking for a way to be tougher when he started judo, after trying his hand at wrestling and boxing. There was footage of Putin in his judo *dōjō* at his home in Russia. He talked about how judo taught him "the way", and helped make him what he is today. President Putin also mentioned how the skill of using the strength of the opponent against themselves was an important method even in politics. I suspect there was a certain amount of lip service for the sake of the Japanese audience, but I'm sure that most of the interview portrayed his true feelings.

I am roughly the same age as President Putin. When he was at university he was skilled enough to take third place in a national student tournament. Still, regardless of how strong he was, I would have undoubtedly beaten him. So what! That is not the point. The issue I would like to bring your attention to is which of us has been able to utilize our knowledge of judo and the ideals learned through training for the better good of society. In this sense, President Putin far exceeds my level. Putting *dōjō* experience into actual practice in society is what lies at the heart of judo.

President Putin's ideas about judo and sports seem to have had an effect on other world leaders. At the G-8 summit in Genova in July 2001, Prime Minister Silvio Berlusconi of host country Italy gave the leaders of each nation a book titled *Judo: The History, Theory, and Practice*. President Putin is one of the three authors of the Russian original. Why did Prime Minister Berlusconi give this book to the leaders of the world? According to the media at the time, among the teachings of Kanō Jigorō, founder of judo and the Kōdōkan, was: "*Seiryoku- zenyō*", which means to employing your energy with maximum efficiency. This is done for the sake of "*jita-kyōei*" or mutual benefit and prosperity.

This was the spirit Berlusconi expected of the leaders of the developed nations who gathered in Genova. Maximum efficiency in the use of one's strength for the purpose of good, respecting others, and working together to build an international society where all members prosper was first articulated in Japan, and as this example demonstrates, has already moved beyond the realm of judo and transcended national boundaries. The sad thing is that most Japanese are not aware of this fact. I didn't even know that such a thing had taken place until I read the newspaper article. It is something that Japanese people could be proud of, if only they knew about it. People like President Putin and Prime Minister Berlusconi seem to understand this aspect of judo better than many Japanese.

To give one more example, in October of 2003, there was a soccer match in Tunisia between Japan and the host. A sports writer by the name of Masujima Midori went to cover the match. She made mention of judo in one of her articles. Her translator, a person by the name of Sikib, was one of only a handful of Japanese speaking guides in the country. Considering over ten thousand Japanese tourists travel to that country each year, Sikib must be a very busy person indeed.

She started her article by saying "IJF director Yamashita Yasuhiro would surely shed tears of joy…" Apparently, Sikib was a black-belt judo practitioner, who started learning Japanese after becoming interested through judo. President Putin also became interested in Japanese culture after being exposed to the Japanese language during judo training. So too did Sikib, and because of that, he was now able to work as an interpreter. When Masujima-san boarded the chartered flight to go to Bucharest for the next match, she turned around and saw Sikib bowing to her deeply in the Japanese way. Of course, Tunisia is predominantly a Muslim country, and such protocol of bowing deeply is usually only done to Allah. Sikib obviously had a deep respect and understanding for Japanese culture through his study of judo.

I have heard from non-Japanese that the act of merely putting on a judo-*gi* and standing barefooted on *tatami* mats is a Japanese cultural experience for many. Donning a judo-*gi*, tying up the *obi*, standing barefooted on *tatami* mats, sitting in the formal kneeling position of *seiza*, abiding to Japanese forms of etiquette, and, on top of all that, being told what to do in Japanese… This is the exposure that people get to Japanese culture just by doing judo.

I wouldn't be so bold as to say everybody, but surely a large majority of non-Japanese judo and *budō* practitioners have developed an interest and understanding of Japanese culture through their exposure to these pursuits. Considering this possibility, I believe that judo has played a significant role in promoting Japan, and is an extremely valuable cultural contribution. If judo became even more popular around the world, then this would surely facilitate deeper understanding and favourable relations between Japan and other countries.

I hear that many people in Africa and Latin America still think that Japan is a part of China. Even though Japan is the second largest economy in the world, there are people who still think this. If you look at a map, Japan is a tiny country right at the eastern edge. Still, Japan boasts a unique culture. For Japanese people, the way we are

The Role of Judo in an Age of Internationalization

perceived by the rest of the world is an issue of great importance. I wonder if Japan is understood properly. In the twenty-first century, Japan must continue to play an active role in the international community, and needs to be understood and trusted by the rest of the world. Otherwise, Japan's future outlook is very bleak indeed. Furthermore, it is in this area that judo can play an important role.

Each year, the All Japan Judo Federation, Kōdōkan, Nippon Budokan, Japan Foundation, JICA and other organizations fund trips for judo instructors to go overseas and teach at the bequest of various judo federations. When Japan funds such endeavours, the recipient nations are always grateful to receive assistance, and very good relations are maintained by the many excellent teaching staff that go. However, as long as the money is being fronted by Japan, there are some Japanese individuals who go forth to teach in foreign countries with an incredibly arrogant attitude. In such cases, the recipient nations are still happy to receive assistance, but it is difficult to suppress bad feelings resulting from the condescending attitude of the instructor. It is sad that this happens, but true. On the other hand, there are some countries that only want assistance to raise the technical level of judo in that country, and that is the extent of interaction. This is a shame as well.

This autumn (2003), the Judo Federation published an article entitled "The Purpose of Sending Instructors Overseas". The gist of the article was to stress that instructors dispatched from Japan were expected to go to their various destinations to 'help', not to 'take control'. The purpose for sending instructors overseas, I think, is not only to assist with technical instruction, but to impart the 'heart' of judo, and show the wonderful educational characteristics and value that it has. Through this, not only will the technical level of the practitioners from the respective countries be enhanced, but so too will the relationships based on trust between our countries.

In many cases, Japan gleans much respect from overseas simply by paying money to send instructors. This serves as a platform to augment stronger relations from an array of angles. It also promotes overseas understanding of the Japanese people and culture. However, before trying to encourage a deeper understanding of Japan, it is vital that the instructor have a firm comprehension of the culture, history, and customs of the host nation. This is the only way to engage in positive inter-cultural interaction. And, it is through such interaction that the instructor can become a valuable link between the two countries. This is the main objective for sending instructors from Japan to teach overseas.

I feel that it is immensely significant that the All Japan Judo Federation took up this issue. The reason being, that it will make selection of 'suitable' instructors possible, and will also provide a focus for the next step of deciding the calibre of instructors we want, or need, to nurture in Japan.

Of course, I am not belittling the fact that top-level judo competitors from Japan also fulfil an important role with inspirational performances, which serve to provide other competitors with goals to aim for, and dreams to chase. These athletes provide us all with hope and enjoyment. However, I think this is only one dimension of judo's function. The other, as I have already stated, is to provide a means to link other countries, thereby building bridges of friendship, and from a Japanese perspective, demonstrate to the world what makes Japan tick and to promote Japanese culture.

In November of 2002, it was decided that my name would be forwarded as a candidate for the position of IJF Education & Coaching Director. The All Japan Judo Federation was very supportive of this appointment. As the AJJF was in favour, I, and many of my colleagues thought that successful election was a foregone conclusion. In fact, it wasn't even considered necessary to campaign. Then, I received a correspondence from a colleague overseas. He informed me that since a year ago, there had been a movement to prevent any Japanese from occupying this post. Apparently, the presidents of the European Zone, African Zone, and Pan-American Zone were collaborating to this effect. This works out to be 120 votes out a possible 187. Of course, Japan has a number of supporters within these zones, but the bottom line was that in retrospect, we had no right to be as optimistic as we were at first. Absolutely nobody in the AJJF was aware of this situation.

As it turned out, the opposition relinquished, and I was successfully elected to the position of Education & Coaching Director at the World Congress in September 2003, unopposed. Still, it was a precarious situation, and it made me realize the weight of my responsibilities, and served to strengthen my resolve. After election, I had to deliver a five-minute speech with my terribly inadequate English. I relayed the following three points to those present at the IJF Congress.

Firstly, I wanted judo to continue to be popular as a dynamic, attractive, and easily understandable Olympic sport. To this purpose, I pledged to do the best I possibly can in this area. Now that judo is an Olympic sport, it belongs to the whole world, but is still an effective means through which international understanding of Japan can be facilitated. But, if judo is to continue to prosper, it has to remain judo of the world, not only Japan.

One of the reasons why there was a concerted movement to prevent a Japanese from the taking the Education & Coaching Directorship was because each time any nation put forth ideas to make judo easier to understand and enjoyable to watch, even for people who have never done it before, inevitably Japan would say "no", and stop the ideas from being implemented. There are many Japanese officials who are adamant that 'Japanese' judo contains traditions which should never be changed. Not knowing why the Japanese were always anti-change, it was thought prudent, for the sake of judo, to remove Japanese directors from the IJF, as this would be the only way to apply change if deemed necessary.

Recently, I was honoured to have an opportunity to have a meal with Anton Geesink, and was able to talk with him for three hours about the responsibilities of my new position in the IJF. He told me that, "if judo is to survive as an Olympic event, it is imperative that people who don't actually do judo are able to understand it. If somebody turns on the television, and it just happens to be judo, of course they

The Role of Judo in an Age of Internationalization

are going to change the channel if they don't understand what is going on." Even in Japan, judo is said to be difficult to follow for people who have never done it before, let alone people in non-Japanese countries.

Thus, it was obvious to me that we really have to make efforts to make judo simple to follow. The biggest sponsor of the Olympics is the television. Geesink-*sensei* also added that "sports that aren't followed on television are in peril, even if the venues are packed to capacity." Of course, I have a job to look after the interests of Japan, but at the same time, my responsibilities as the Education & Coaching Director of the IJF are to ensure that every effort is made to promote judo internationally, and make it interesting for spectators who may not have ever even stepped foot in a *dōjō* before.

I made a pledge at the Congress that I would cooperate with everybody and work together to achieve these goals. There are certain elements of judo which must not and cannot be changed, as judo would stop being judo. These elements must be protected. Having said that, there are other aspects of judo which need to be reviewed and changed to ensure its continued international dissemination. I recognize this fact, and fully intend to act upon it.

The second pledge I made was to give total support in encouraging the development of technical levels and other areas of judo in the various countries and continents, and continue to try and increase the number of practitioners.

Actually, Geesink-*sensei* was the Education & Coaching Director three generations before me. When he held office, he took the initiative to invite judo instructors from around the world to a seminar in the Netherlands. He also managed to collect most of the funds necessary from sponsors in the Netherlands and Europe to run the event. I am a university professor, and only have limited staff and funds. But, I feel confident I can do the same. The AJJF and Tokai University, where I work, will surely support any such endeavours that I decide to undertake.

There is still a limit to what I can do. However, by stressing how judo is contributing to international exchange and understanding, I am confident that there is room in the budget of the Ministry of Foreign Affairs to provide financial assistance. The Japan Foundation also allots funds for such activities. This is also in accord with the goals of the Japan International Cooperation Agency (JICA). There are huge financial resources to be found in the plethora of organizations in Japan, which have been set up to promote international understanding.

I actually went to the office of the Japan Foundation recently and talked about this very topic. I was told that "the Japan Foundation has never provided funds for sporting endeavours, but as judo can be used as an effective way to promote Japanese culture and international accord, there is a certain amount of overlap. Please come up with a concrete plan and we will gladly investigate the possibilities."

Being a soccer supporter, or a supporter of basketball, volleyball, track and field, or whatever sport is great. However, being a judo supporter may mean that the practitioner has to overcome some difficult problems in order to participate. There are people in certain countries around the world that practice judo without *tatami* mats. In some countries, just to buy a judo-*gi* costs the equivalent of two to three months wages. We want the people of those countries to also be able to enjoy judo and learn about Japanese culture on equal footing. Thinking twenty or thirty years into the future, now is the time for all of us to cooperate and plant the seeds. Won't you also join me in getting the Ministry of Foreign Affairs, the Japan Foundation, JICA, other organizations and companies behind judo to facilitate greater international exchange and goodwill, and better understanding of our country, Japan? If we truly believe that judo and other *budō* really have this potential, then we should start moving immediately.

The third pledge that I made was in regards to the ideals of judo's founder, Kanō Jigorō, for using judo as a means of self-perfection or character development. His underlying philosophy for judo was to utilize it as an effective educational tool for personal development. This is an important aspect of judo that I intend to push as much as possible. I know many instructors overseas who consider judo to be an "educational sport", nay "more than just a sport", in fact "a way of life". If judo does have educational value, then in theory, judo practitioners should be wonderful individuals, and hence also become wonderful teachers. We want judo practitioners to understand that judo is not just a matter of beating your opponent, but is a way were both can feed off each other and grow as people. An 'opponent' in a match is also a 'partner' who deserves the utmost respect. Everybody has heard of this concept, but the conflict lies with our retaining a strong desire to win.

I have been very fortunate to have been the Japanese national coach for the past eight years. I also had four years coaching experience before being promoted to head-coach. During these twelve years, I forged numerous friendships with coaches from all around the world. I have asked these people their opinions on how to make judo more attractive, and promote it on a wider scale. At the same time, I also urged top-level competitors and national coaches to take particular care to improve their manner or decorum. It doesn't matter what wonderful words of wisdom you impart to others about the virtues of judo, if the top players act rudely or in a contradictory manner, nobody is going to take it seriously. If the educational value of judo is ignored, judo will lose its soul.

After introducing these three points explaining my stance on judo, and what I wanted to achieve as the IJF Education and Coaching Director, I added that regardless of hair colour, the colour of your eyes, skin, race, or religion, I am sure that Kanō Jigorō considers all people who are training hard in judo to be his children or grandchildren. If he was still alive, I know that is how he would feel. Judo was created in Japan, but is now an asset to the people of the world. That is why I promised to carry out my duties as Director to the best of my ability. Of course I am not Prime Minister Berlusconi of Italy, but I too want to stress the importance of Kanō Jigorō's ideals of *seiryoku-zenyō* and *jita-kyōei*. This was what I promised at the IJF World Congress upon election.

The naughty young urchin that I was, judo changed me. I learned much from my teacher at junior high school about judo as a way of life. What I learned from him provides the basis of the goals of the Judo Renaissance, to promote judo as an effective

The Role of Judo in an Age of Internationalization

educational tool that encourages personal development. To reiterate what Shirai-*sensei* said:

> "Becoming a judo champion is indeed a wonderful feat. However, the most important thing is to try and become a champion of society. A social champion has much more value. There is only one champion in each category at the Olympics. There is only one all-Japan champion. And, there is only one national student champion. But 'anybody' can use what they learn through judo to become a champion of life."

I treasure this advice. Finally, I would like to say that there are two great men who exert great influence on me, from above. One is Kanō Jigorō. The other is the founder of Tokai University, Matsumae Shigeyoshi. Matsumae-*sensei* worked hard for eight years as the President of the IJF. He loved judo, and came from the same part of Japan, Kumamoto prefecture, as me. When he was alive, he treated me like a grandson, and while I was actively competing he told me the following:

> "Yamashita, do you know why I am supporting you so much? It's not only because I want you to win your matches. That really has nothing to do with it at all. I want you to make friends with athletes all over the world through Japanese judo. But that's not all. I want you to become a man who can make a contribution to world peace through sports. That's why I am supporting you."

I deeply regret that while he was still alive, although I knew in theory what he meant, I was not able to put it to practice. Now that he's gone, I think I have come some way in understanding the true meaning of his words.

I have a very vivid dream of what I would like to achieve at the end of my life. Of course, I don't know how much longer I'll be here, or which way I'll be sent when I die. But, when I do finally reach the end of my mortal coil, I hope that Kanō Jigorō will be there to greet me with the words, "So, you're Yamashita? Thank you for your hard work to promote judo…" Then, I hope to see Matsumae Shigeyoshi once more. "Well done Yamashita, I knew I could count on you…" I will work hard while I'm still here to earn these words.

The first stage of my judo career was as a competitor. The second stage was as a coach. I believe that the third stage will be as an official working for the promotion of judo. I am still very inexperienced, and will undoubtedly make many mistakes along the way. Whatever the case, you can be sure I will spare no effort in cooperating with people in Japan and overseas to promote the values of judo, and encourage as many people as possible to try and reap the benefits of doing judo. I want judo to help create strong links between Japan with the rest of the world. This is the third stage, and it is for these goals that I will dedicate the rest of my life.

www.ingramcontent.com/pod-product-compliance
Lightning Source LLC
Chambersburg PA
CBHW071234160426
43196CB00009B/1053